Applied Clinical Neuropsychology

An Introduction

Jan Leslie Holtz, PhD, is Professor of Psychology at the College of Saint Benedict and Saint John's University where she has been teaching since 1986. She graduated with a BA, Phi Beta Kappa from Hamline University in Saint Paul, Minnesota and received her PhD in Clinical Psychology in 1984 from the University of South Dakota. She completed her Clinical Internship at the Veterans' Administration Medical Center in St. Louis, Missouri. Dr. Holtz has served as the chair of the psychology department at the College of Saint Benedict and Saint John's University and has extensive experience teaching a diverse range of courses in psychology there and at the College of Saint Scholastica. Her research interests include neuropsychology as well as sexual harassment and violence. Her most recent research interest is bullying, particularly at the elementary and secondary levels. She frequently presents her research at national conferences. She is a Licensed Psychologist in the state of Minnesota. In addition to her teaching and research activities she maintains a private practice in clinical psychology and is a board member of the Brain Injury Association of Minnesota and the Minnesota Stroke Association. She is also on the editorial board of *The Educator's Guide to Controlling Sexual Harrassment.*

Applied Clinical Neuropsychology

An Introduction

Jan Leslie Holtz, PhD

SPRINGER PUBLISHING COMPANY
NEW YORK

Instructors Resources (Learning Objectives, PowerPoints, Image Bank, and Test Bank) for this book are available from textbook@springerpub.com

Copyright © 2011 Springer Publishing Company

Springer Publishing Company, LLC
11 West 42nd Street
New York, NY 10036
www.springerpub.com

Acquisitions Editor: Nancy Hale
Cover Design: David Levy
Composition: Absolute Service, Inc.

ISBN: 978-0-8261-0474-8
E-book ISBN: 978-0-8261-0475-5

10 11 12 13/ 5 4 3 2 1

The author and the publisher of this work have made every effort to use sources believed to be reliable to provide information that is accurate and compatible with the standards generally accepted at the time of publication. Because medical science is continually advancing, our knowledge base continues to expand. Therefore, as new information becomes available, changes in procedures become necessary. We recommend that the reader always consult current research and specific institutional policies before performing any clinical procedure. The author and publisher shall not be liable for any special, consequential, or exemplary damages resulting, in whole or in part, from the readers' use of, or reliance on, the information contained in this book. The publisher has no responsibility for the persistence or accuracy of URLs for external or third-party Internet Web sites referred to in this publication and does not guarantee that any content on such Web sites is, or will remain, accurate or appropriate.

CIP data is available from the Library of Congress.

Special discounts on bulk quantities of our books are available to corporations, professional associations, pharmaceutical companies, health care organizations, and other qualifying groups. If you are interested in a custom book, including chapters from more than one of our titles, we can provide that service as well.

For details, please contact:
Special Sales Department, Springer Publishing Company, LLC
11 West 42nd Street, 15th Floor, New York, NY 10036-8002
Phone: 877-687-7476 or 212-431-4370; Fax: 212-941-7842
Email: sales@springerpub.com

Printed in the United States of America by Bang Printing Company.

This book is dedicated to my late parents,
H. Arnold Holtz, PhD, and Martha J. (Bjur) Holtz,
extraordinary teachers and very special parents.

Brief Contents

Contents

Preface

As with many individuals who write textbooks, the inspiration for this text was need. I developed a course approximately 15 years ago to fill the void in our curriculum for an applied course in clinical neuropsychology. To my surprise and distress there was no text available to fit my needs. The majority of texts were excellent biopsychology or physiological psychology texts with little or no applied information. Particularly lacking were the diagnosis, assessment, and rehabilitation of various central nervous system difficulties. Graduate texts were very specific and did not cover all of the areas needed in one course. Hence, this text was developed to meet my needs as an academic and for use with upper-division undergraduate students, beginning graduate students, and as a reference for professionals. The text contains information from my practice in clinical neuropsychology for illustrative purposes.

The text is designed to fit within the average academic semester. In my course I divide the subject matter into four sections: (1) central nervous system structure and function including diseases and disabilities, (2) test theory and evaluation of assessment tools, (3) various forms of rehabilitation, and (4) issues related specifically to the older adult (geriatrics) and children (pediatrics).

I would like to thank all of my students, colleagues, and friends who have assisted in the preparation of this text. I would also like to thank my family for their assistance and patience in a very long process.

Instructors Resources (Learning Objectives, PowerPoints, Image Bank, and Test Bank) for this book are available from textbook@springerpub.com

Applied Clinical Neuropsychology

An Introduction

Introduction to Clinical Neuropsychology

1

Key Terms

clinical neuropsychology
experimental neuropsychology
trephination
Edwin Smith Surgical Papyrus
brain–behavior relationship
ventricular localization hypothesis
cell doctrine
brain hypothesis
Hippocratic Oath
contralateral control
holistic medicine
mind–body problem
cardiac hypothesis
humors
dualism
monism
localization of brain functioning

phrenology
neuroplasticity
scientific method
asylum
mental hygiene movement
moral therapy
diagnostic classification system
aphasia
lateralization
equipotentiality
principle of mass action
split-brain studies
corpus callosum
Veterans Administration (VA)
posttraumatic stress disorder (PTSD)
clinical psychology
scientist–practitioner model

case study
double dissociation technique
lesion approach
electroencephalography (EEG)
evoked potential
X-ray
angiography
computed tomography (CT) scan
single photon emission tomography (SPECT)
positron emission tomography (PET)
magnetic resonance imaging (MRI)
intracranial brain stimulation
transcranial magnetic stimulation

Learning Objectives

After reading this chapter, the student should be able to understand:

- Important events and key figures in the evolution of brain science from its origins to the present
- The various hypotheses and explanations for brain functions and brain-behavior relations throughout history
- The origins of localization theory and the reasons it continues to be an important area of study
- Factors that led to the formalization and definition of clinical neuropsychology as a field of study and an applied science
- Definitions, methodology, and common imaging techniques used in the study of brain science

Case Vignette

Marvin Martindale is a 36-year-old Caucasian male who was involved in a moving vehicle accident which was not his fault. He was hit head on by another driver who claimed he did not notice that Marvin was directly in front of him. This of course implies that the other driver was in the wrong lane. The other driver's vehicle was traveling at approximately 40 mph and was much larger. Marvin was fortunate in that he was wearing a seat belt which prevented serious injury to his torso. However, he was abruptly propelled forward, slamming his head violently into the steering wheel with his brain ricocheting back and forth several times in his skull.

The police arrived at the scene and had to remove him from his car. The paramedics took Marvin to the hospital. He managed to maintain consciousness during the traumatic event, but the EMTs' protocol still directed them to put Marvin on a backboard to avoid complications. At the hospital he was given various medical tests including the standard MRI and CT. Marvin spent a week in intensive care. After that period of time he was transferred to a rehabilitation unit at the hospital. While in the rehabilitation unit he had intensive physical, occupational, speech, and recreational therapy in addition to rehabilitative nursing, dietetics, and social work services. He did very well with each of these programs. After 1 month a discharge plan was developed by the staff. Due to his closed head injury, which left him with residual cognitive, memory, and emotional difficulties, it was suggested that he should not be left unsupervised when he first returned home.

When it was time to be released, his wife picked him up from the hospital and took him home. Marvin and his wife had three children, two of whom were 18 months old, the eldest being 3. Marvin worked as a manager in a grocery store prior to the accident. In this position he hired and fired employees, oversaw the work of the employees, and completed accounts payable and accounts receivable. Marvin eventually tried to return to his employment but had trouble concentrating and his temper was difficult to manage at work. After a few weeks of struggling Marvin applied for disability payments.

A few months after the accident Marvin's wife stated her husband exhibited a much more prominent temper and was more sexual. Marvin's wife also stated that his judgment was poor and his child care skills had deteriorated. After several months of these adverse behaviors, she decided to file for a divorce.

Marvin was devastated by the loss of his wife, children, and job and looked to his church for answers. Finally, someone there provided him direction and suggested he return to his physician. The physician quickly recognized that Marvin's continuing difficulties were likely caused by his accident. The physician then referred Marvin to a clinical neuropsychologist to help determine the nature and extent of his difficulties.

The clinical neuropsychologist interviewed Marvin and completed a series of neuropsychological tests with him. Interview questions included background information about his school, work, and family life, both before his accident and subsequent to it. The information from before and after the accident helped the clinical neuropsychologist determine which deficits were likely caused by the accident. Examples of topical areas covered on tests include memory abilities, concentration abilities, frustration tolerance, and recognition of other emotions. The results of the tests indicated that Marvin was suffering from attention, concentration, and memory deficits which could be explained because the accident injured the parts of his brain (frontal and left temporal areas) where these abilities are localized. Marvin also had difficulty inhibiting aggressive and sexual urges which are difficulties sometimes noted in individuals with brain damage. The clinical neuropsychologist was able to explain these impairments to Marvin in a manner that he understood. The clinical neuropsychologist was also able to help Marvin understand the reason that his wife divorced him and questioned his child care abilities with reference to his difficulties. The explanation helped Marvin but did not completely alleviate his sadness over his losses.

In order to assist Marvin, the clinical neurophysiologist formulated a treatment plan to address each of his issues. The plan included individual therapy for emotional difficulties, cognitive rehabilitation for attention, concentration, and memory difficulties, and vocational rehabilitation to help Marvin return to a steady form of employment which he was able to do with his disability. Through the aid of the various individuals involved with his case Marvin was able to obtain maximum recovery from his injuries. Individual therapy helped Marvin to label and express his feelings in a manner appropriate to the situation. A series of cognitive rehabilitation tasks were developed to help Marvin cope with cognitive losses. Memory deficits were addressed by the use of notes and various other memory aids such as simplifying and reducing the information to be remembered and linking the information to existing information to form associations. Vocational rehabilitation services matched Marvin's current physical and mental functioning with job skill requirements and helped him to obtain employment.

The outcome for Marvin was positive. He learned to understand and cope with his emotions and also compensate for his cognitive and memory losses. It was very important to him to be able to go back to work in an environment that was suitable to his level of functioning. Finally, with the aforementioned skills acquired, he was able to convince his wife that he could manage short unsupervised visits with his children. The skills that he learned allowed him to pay attention to all three children and also be aware regarding appropriate activities for them and protect them from potentially dangerous situations.

Marvin's case is an example of a scenario frequently faced by a clinical neuropsychologist. Moving vehicle accidents are the most common reason for traumatic brain injuries which occur more frequently in males than females. The treatment plan prepared for Marvin is an example of the type of program a clinical neuropsychologist would develop which includes assessment, diagnosis, and treatment.

Throughout this text, we will look at the aforementioned areas: assessment, diagnosis, and treatment as we explore the field of clinical neuropsychology. All of the case examples contained in this text are from the author's neuropsychological practice and are included as illustrative examples of the work of the clinical neuropsychologist. In all of the cases identifying information has been removed to preserve the anonymity of the individuals involved. Additional ethical issues will be discussed as they pertain to each particular case.

What Is Clinical Neuropsychology?

clinical neuropsychology
a division of psychology that specializes in the clinical assessment and treatment of patients with brain injury or neurocognitive deficits

Clinical neuropsychology is a specialty area in the field of psychology that focuses on how the brain functions within the normal individual and what happens to an individual with brain illness or brain injury. A clinical neuropsychologist looks at patients like Marvin and asks the question "Why does he behave and think as he does?" The field of clinical neuropsychology is considered applied because it deals with the assessment, diagnosis, and treatment of those individuals with brain illness or injury as opposed to looking at only brain structures and functions. The clinical neuropsychologist will use the knowledge available about the brain to work with people who have brain impairment. In our introductory case study the clinical neuropsychologist administered numerous tests to Marvin to assess the performance of various parts of the brain. In addition, the clinical neuropsychologist interviewed the patient and others who knew the patient to determine a diagnosis and formulate a treatment plan. The clinical neuropsychologist in this case study interviewed Marvin and his ex-spouse for specific information regarding his difficulties.

experimental neuropsychology
the field of psychology that focuses on brain–behavior relationships usually using animals as subjects

There are other areas within neuropsychology that also study the brain. The field of **experimental neuropsychology** focuses on brain–behavior relationships within humans and other animals. Experimental neuropsychology does this by describing structures and functions, as opposed to focusing on assessment, diagnosis, and treatment. However, before we can explore the assessment process and the development of a treatment plan for Marvin there is much to learn. This introductory chapter will trace the origins of brain science to the modern era. By looking at the history of brain functioning, we will review the various ways people throughout history thought the brain functioned and how they treated individuals with behavioral difficulties. We will begin by focusing on less scientifically proven techniques used by very early people such as trephining, and we will end with very advanced medical imaging techniques, such as **positron-emission tomography (PET)**, **computed tomography (CT)**, and **functional magnetic resonance imaging (fMRI)**. This chapter will also cover the development of the field of clinical neuropsychology. The reason a historical perspective is necessary is that many of the early questions regarding the structures and functions of the brain remain to this day.

Historical Background

Clinical neuropsychology is a relatively new field of study with a history dating back to the beginning of the 20th century. The term *neuropsychology* was first used by Sir William Osler on April 16, 1913, in an address entitled "Specialism in the General Hospital" given at the opening ceremony for the Phipps Psychiatric Clinic at Johns Hopkins Hospital (Osler, 1913). Hans-Leukas Teuber (1916–1977) first used the term in a national meeting during a speech at the **American Psychological Association (APA)** meeting in 1948 (Teuber, 1955). Donald Hebb (1949) used the term as the subtitle of his 1949 book *The Organization of Behavior: A Neuropsychological Theory*. During that time period neuropsychology represented the combined interests of many disciplines including psychologists, neurologists, psychiatrists, speech pathologists, and others interested in the relationship between the brain and behavior. As time passed the term became widely used and appeared in the title of Lashley's writings, *The Neuropsychology of Lashley* published in 1960 after his death in 1958 (Beach, 1961). The major use of the term neuropsychology was ultimately related to the study of the relationship between the brain and behavior. Most of the subjects for the early studies were animals.

Even though the field of clinical neuropsychology is relatively recent, the study of the brain, the core of clinical neuropsychology, goes as far back as the start of civilization. We will begin by tracing the study of the brain by the ancients and work through various historical explanations of brain functioning. Throughout history philosophers and scientists have tried to understand the reasons people behaved as they did, specifically after brain illness or injury. As stated previously, the reason for the historical study of the brain is to understand how scholars and researchers at different times in history understood the same difficulties facing the clinical neuropsychologist today. The clinical neuropsychologist does this in the modern era with modern tools. After a thorough discussion of the various conceptualizations of brain functioning, a chronological description of the field of clinical neuropsychology is presented.

Ancient Hypotheses to Modern Theories of Brain Functioning

The early study of the brain is explored through archival data and relics from early people. Ancient civilizations provide us some indications of what they viewed as the role of the brain and how individuals with brain difficulties should be or were treated.

NEOLITHIC PERIOD OR STONE AGE

Trephination was an early procedure that involved boring, cutting, scraping, or chiseling a piece of bone from the afflicted individual's skull (see Figure 1.1). The procedure is believed to have developed as a way to relieve the pressure caused by brain swelling. Trephining is estimated to have first occurred approximately 7,000 years ago during the Neolithic period or Stone Age. It is assumed that some of the subjects who received the procedure exhibited behaviors which were not accepted by their culture (Lisowski, 1967). Examples of the types of behaviors not usually accepted by society at the time could include behaviors that resemble the delusions and hallucinations of schizophrenia or, possibly, behaviors similar to our case study that were secondary to traumatic

trephination
the oldest known surgical technique in which a small piece of bone is removed from the skull leaving a hole in the skull; the procedure has been done for medical and religious reasons

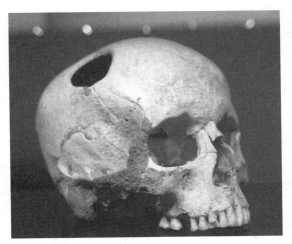

FIGURE 1.1 Adult skull from 3500 BCE showing trephination. *Source:* Natural History Museum, Lausanne.

brain injury (TBI). Many accounts of trephining relate the procedure to the release of evil spirits which were thought to reside within the individual's head (brain). Early people often attributed behaviors to supernatural causes. The boring of a hole allowed the spirits to escape with the hope of returning the individual to his or her original condition.

Archeologists have been able to recover thousands of trephined skulls from various parts of the world. Bereczki and Marcsik (2005) discuss surgical and symbolic trephinations found in ancient populations. Surgical trephination completed for medical purposes involved removal of a bony portion of the cranial vault. Successful trephinations showing evidence of healing were found in Bronze Age sediments in present-day Hungary and frequently occurred until modern times. Symbolic trephination involved only the external cortical layer and was regarded as a special pagan custom in the Carpathian Basin. Its use disappeared at the beginning of the 12th century with the spread of Christianity. Verona (2003) systematically studied trephined skulls to see if there was a pattern to the use of trephining. He looked at 750 skulls collected from Peru and concluded that the ancient Peruvians did trephine some children and adult women but focused mainly on adult men. He found no preference for the side of the brain trephined and that most trephining occurred in areas we now know as the frontal and upper parietal regions. He also discussed that most trephinations occurred after the individual had received a skull fracture from events such as blows from a club or a projectile from a slingshot. In these instances the procedure would clearly appear to be for medical reasons, not religious rituals.

Clearly, trephining would appear to be a very crude way to treat the brain because it involves exposure of brain tissue to the elements and to various forms of disease and infection. Some individuals who experienced the trephining procedure and survived probably had residual damage caused by the lack of precision in the procedure which may have affected multiple areas of the brain. However, there are other accounts which state that individuals who had undergone the trephination procedure were able to function "normally" after. In fact, many historical references state that the surgeons who practiced trephination were more skilled than originally thought and were aware of the possibilities of infections. There are also accounts of individuals having had multiple trephinations, as well as accounts of individuals who died from the procedure (O'Connor & Walker, 1967).

THE EGYPTIANS

The next indication of how early people conceptualized the brain came from the Egyptians as early as the Third Dynasty (2650–2575 BC). They were thought to have been advanced in many and diverse areas but, surprisingly, were not as advanced in their understanding of the brain. The Egyptians' lack of brain knowledge is shown through examining early Egyptian burial practices. The process of mummification could take as long as 70 days to complete. The reason for the lengthy process was due to the fact that many internal organs, such as the lungs, liver, stomach, and intestines were kept and preserved in various types of containers related to religious practices. The important point in the study of brain science, in the process of mummification, was that the brain was discarded even though all the other organs were felt to be important. The heart was never removed when the body was prepared for burial because it was considered the seat of the mind and soul (Leca, 1981).

Even though the Egyptians appeared to discard the brain and not understand its function, a contradictory finding arose with the discovery of the Edwin Smith Surgical

Papyrus written approximately in the 17th-century BC (Wilkins, 1964). Imhotep is thought to be the founder of Egyptian medicine and the original author of the papyrus. However, there also may be at least three other authors who wrote and/or edited the document. The **Edwin Smith Surgical Papyrus** (see Figure 1.2) is one of the first accounts of **brain–behavior relationships** (Breasted, 1930). A brain–behavior relationship exists when a function of the brain is thought to cause or influence a particular behavior.

The papyrus was purchased by Smith in 1862 and contained two sections. According to Finger (2000), an eminent historian of brain science, one section of the papyrus is believed to be authentic and the other possibly not. Smith made an attempt to translate the papyrus but never published it. In 1920, after Smith's death, his daughter gave the document to the New York Historical Society. The Society then asked James Breasted to translate the document, which he completed in 1930. Included in the document are references to head or brain injuries and their treatment. Although the document is called a *surgical papyrus*, there were no indications that actual surgery was performed. The document gave reference to what are currently the meninges (the layers of tissue covering the brain) and the cerebrospinal fluid. The papyrus also discussed early ways to determine which patients could be successfully treated, which patients' status was questionable, and which patients were too severely impaired for treatment. As stated by Finger (2000), this manner of determining the severity of injuries foreshadows our current system of triage, particularly within the military.

Within the Edwin Smith Surgical Papyrus are accounts of 48 individuals with physical injuries and 27 with trauma to the head. As stated earlier, there were no suggestions of operating procedures being involved. Included, however, were ways to reduce intracranial

Edwin Smith Surgical Papyrus
early Egyptian manuscript which described the techniques used to treat various forms of difficulties including brain trauma

brain–behavior relationship
a relationship that exists between certain functions of the brain and overt behaviors

FIGURE 1.2 A section of the Edwin Smith Surgical Papyrus showing the hieratic script. Light and dark text are the result of the use of two different types of ink. *Source:* Courtesy of The New York Academy of Medicine.

hemorrhaging and the removal of fragments of bone from the ear canal and blood clots from the sinuses. The papyrus also included prescriptions for head wounds, including the mixing of fat from lions, hippopotamuses, crocodiles, snakes, and ibexes. The fats were then applied to the patient's head as soon as possible to make the body uninhabitable to evil spirits. There are also accounts of other supernatural treatments of patients' difficulties, as we recall the Egyptians still believed that illness and other maladies were caused by various deities.

Another papyrus bought by Smith, named the Eber Papyrus (1555 BC) after Smith sold it to Georg Eber in 1873, contains many early prescriptions. The Eber Papyrus is a massive work, 65 feet long, and contains at least 900 prescriptions for ailments in various parts of the body. According to Finger (2000), some of these prescriptions contain ingredients that are used at present, whereas other prescriptions included the use of urine and feces. The use of ingredients similar to those of the present suggests some understanding of the workings of the central nervous system, whereas the use of urine and feces again refers back to the supernatural tradition. The *Ebers Papyrus* is often thought to contain more magical or superstitious forms of healing than the Edwin Smith Surgical Papyrus (Sarton, 1927).

After conquering Egypt, Alexander the Great founded the city of Alexandria about 334 BC. It was intended to be the link between Greece and the Nile Valley. Although supposedly controlled by the Greeks, the city retained its own government. Alexandria was a city associated with learning and philosophy. There were a number of historically important individuals including Herophilus (335–280 BC) and Erasistratus (304–250 BC) working within the city. These individuals were the first to propose the brain as the center of reason. They provided the first accurate and detailed description of the human brain including the ventricles (Tascioglu & Tascioglu, 2005). During this period arose a climate of scientific inquiry free from the prohibitions of Athens which forbade the use of dissection in the study of anatomy and physiology. Finger (2000) suggests that Herophilus and Erasistratus completed most of their work on cadavers and that they also used condemned criminals for **vivisection**, hoping that physicians could learn new facts about the human body. Vivisection is the dissection of the body, animal or human, while it is still living.

During the same period there arose a theory of brain functioning which continued into the Middle Ages. The theory stated that the fluid-filled compartments of the brain were responsible for higher mental, as well as spiritual processes. The cavities were thought of as cells, the lateral ventricles forming the first cell, the third ventricle the second cell, while the fourth ventricle comprised the third cell. Within the ventricles were believed to reside animal spirits. This theory became known as the **ventricular localization hypothesis**. Later the theory was termed the **cell doctrine** because of the aforementioned divisions of the ventricles into cells (Tascioglu & Tascioglu, 2005). As we now are aware, the ventricles are the sites that produce and transport cerebrospinal fluid and have no role in higher order brain functioning. **Cerebrospinal fluid**, which cushions the brain within the skull, is made in the choroid plexuses and flows through the ventricles and the subarachnoid space, the space between the layers of the brain.

ANCIENT GREEKS

The classical Greeks, like the Egyptians, were interested in accounts of brain–behavior relationships. Heraclitus (540–480 BC), a philosopher of the 6th-century BC, called the mind an enormous space whose boundaries we could never reach (Kirk, Raven, & Schofield, 1995). Heraclitus stood primarily for the radical idea that the universe is in constant

ventricular localization hypothesis
the hypothesis that mental and spiritual processes reside within the ventricular canals

cell doctrine
a term synonymous with the ventricular localization hypothesis, i.e., that the ventricles were the location of higher order mental and spatial processes

change and that there is an underlying order or reason to the change. He is considered to be, along with Parmenides, the most significant philosopher of ancient Greece until Socrates and Plato.

Pythagoras (582–507 BC), a mathematician, was the first to suggest that the brain was the organ responsible for human thought. With the assistance of other writers these ideas are described in what is now called the **brain hypothesis**, the idea that the brain is the source of all behavior (Edelstein, 1967). It is difficult to determine which of the Pythagoreans was responsible for the brain hypothesis because few of the original writings exist. The Pythagoreans, followers of Pythagoras, believed in natural science and philosophy. The Pythagoreans lived together in a communal group and followed a strict ethical code of conduct. They also had a code of silence believing man often spoke to his own detriment. It is often suggested that this is the turning point in time between treatments for ailments being strictly related to religious ideas and the beginning of scientific healing.

brain hypothesis
the hypothesis that the brain is the source of human thought and behavior

Years later Hippocrates (460–379 BC), considered to be the founder of modern medicine, further expanded the understanding of the brain. Hippocrates is probably best known for the oath he demanded from physicians working with him, which is now referred to as the **Hippocratic Oath**. However, history tells us that it may not have been Hippocrates himself but a group of writers who wrote the Hippocratic Collection and who also composed the Hippocratic Oath. It is a sacred oath that at least some physicians at the time swore they would follow. The Hippocratic Oath stated that as physicians they would respect and practice medicine to the best of their abilities and that they would not aid in suicide, perform abortions, or make personal information public (Jones, 2003). The statement has changed somewhat in modern times but most physicians agree to the principles involved.

Hippocratic Oath
an agreement that Hippocrates demanded of physicians ensuring that they would do no harm in their quest to appropriately treat their patients

Hippocrates believed, as a central tenet, that the brain controlled all sensing and movements. Hippocrates was the first to indicate that damage to one side of the brain affected the other side of the body. The modern way of expressing this principle is **contralateral control**. Many of Hippocrates' ideas were clearly contradictory with other conceptualizations of his time, which suggested that behavior was controlled by divine causes. Hippocrates and his followers, as described by Finger (2000), believed that a physician should be an astute student of nature and an expert craftsman, rather than a god-inspired priest. By this statement, Hippocrates not only removed himself from the religious description of the brain and heart but also began the use of observation as a tool of science. In terms of treatment of the brain and body, Hippocrates and his followers stressed the benefits of a sound body, a healthy environment, and exercise. Above all, according to Hippocrates, the patient was to be treated as a whole, not an assemblage of parts. Hence, Hippocrates was a physician who practiced **holistic medicine**, a belief that the body, mind, and soul must be addressed for successful treatment of the patient. Hippocrates foreshadowed the changes in treatment of mental patients in the 1700s–1800s in which the main goal was to treat mental illness with a combination of therapy and healthy living habits, such as adequate diet, sleep, and exercise. In addition to the change from supernatural to a more naturalistic approach to dysfunction and treatment came a new way of conceptualizing disorder. Borrowing somewhat from the Pythagoreans came the idea of balance between the humors: blood, yellow bile, phlegm, and black bile. Each of these was associated with a specific element: air with blood, fire with yellow bile, water with phlegm, and earth with black bile. In addition, each substance was associated with a particular organ: blood with the heart, yellow bile with the liver, phlegm with the brain, and black bile with the spleen. In the Hippocratic Collection there are many references to the imbalance of humors as the cause of various ailments. The treatments for difficulties caused by imbalances of humors were procedures to restore the balance of the humors such as bloodletting.

contralateral control
the premise that one side of the brain controls the motor and sensory functions of the opposite side of the body

holistic medicine
a type of medical practice that treats the entire patient; it involves physical, psychological, and spiritual aspects of healing

Plato (420–347 BC), a student of Socrates and philosopher of human behavior, thought that the soul was divided into three functions: appetite, reason, and temper, which resided within the brain. Plato chose the brain because the brain was closest to the heavens. Plato also discussed the **mind–body question**, which has continued to this day to be a major philosophical issue. The mind–body question discusses the essence of the mind. The mind–body question also addresses the connection between what was thought of as immaterial (soul) with something thought to be material (body). Plato took this concept further by describing physical health as the harmony between the mind and body. This is somewhat similar to the Hippocratic physicians' view of holistic medicine. In addition, historians credit Plato with some of the earliest references to mental health (Finger, 2000). The concept introduced by Plato suggested that a balance between all parts of life would lead to good mental health, a concept with strikingly modern qualities.

Aristotle (384–322 BC), a student of Plato, disagreed with him and believed the heart rather than the brain to be the main organ of rational thought. The heart was the organ that was warm, active, and the center of the soul. According to Aristotle, the brain was without blood and functioned to cool hot blood as it came from the heart. Aristotle was the designer of the **cardiac hypothesis**, which stated that the heart was the originator of numerous emotions (Karenberg & Hort, 1998). An equally important idea emphasized by Aristotle was that direct observation of the subject was critical.

Unfortunately, the Greeks were hampered in their ability to investigate the central nervous system, and to prove or disprove their various theories because dissection was considered to be sacrilegious. However, questions arise regarding the extent of dissections completed in secret, such as with newly buried corpses or those too poor to afford a proper funeral. In the case of secret dissections, more information may have been gathered regarding the nervous system but not openly disseminated.

THE ROMANS

Continuing the work of those who came before them, the Romans also involved themselves in the study of the brain. The Romans believed in the importance of the brain, but they disagreed regarding the particular part of the brain that was responsible for each attribute.

Galen (131–201 AD), a giant in the history of the understanding of physiology and anatomy, had an influence for approximately 1,300 years after his death (Finger, 2000). He is considered the first experimental physiologist and physician. He also described many of the major brain structures. Galen was a believer, similar to Aristotle, that the only valid sources of data were direct observations.

Galen was hampered by his period during which the Roman authorities forbade human dissection. He tried to gain knowledge by dissecting as many and as varied animals as possible starting with those he saw as most closely resembling humans. He completed not only dissections but also vivisections on these animals. He was also a physician for the gladiators and used their wounds as a means to study the human body. Occasionally, he was able to view a human cadaver even though he did not complete autopsies. Galen wrote an extraordinary amount concerning anatomy and physiology based on his dissections. Much of his work, however, was destroyed by fire.

In his writing, Galen accurately described many organs of the body. He also took the bold step to challenge Aristotle's belief in the heart as the center of functioning and stated that the brain was the center of reason and emotion. Through his dissections he was able to view the system of ventricles within the brain. Galen, however, misunderstood their functioning and believed in the ventricular localization theory. He felt that the ventricles housed animal spirits, which were produced within what we now refer to as the *choroid plexus*.

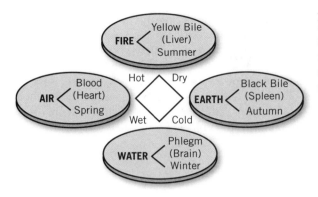

FIGURE 1.3 The theory of four elements expanded to include dual qualities and single associated humors, body organs, and even seasons of the year.

Galen also believed in the earlier theory that the functions of the body and brain were based on a balance of bodily fluids or **humors** (blood, yellow bile, phlegm, black bile). Galen's belief in the four humors (see Figure 1.3) led to many of the treatments suggested for various disorders. During this time period, Galen was very interested in the study of stroke or what was then termed *apoplexy*. He believed that stroke resulted either from an accumulation of a thick cold humor (such as phlegm or black bile) in the ventricles or from obstructions of the flow of animal spirits.

humors
the belief that a balance of bodily fluids including blood, mucus, and yellow and black bile were responsible for the functioning of the body and the brain

THE MIDDLE AGES (500–1400)

The early Egyptians, Greeks, and Romans were followed in their study of the brain by many theorists spanning the subsequent centuries, which collectively fall into the historical period in the Western world termed the Middle Ages or Dark Ages.

The time period began with a rudimentary understanding of the brain as the organ of thought and emotion. However, the proposed structures and functions of the brain were inaccurate as many of the earlier writings were unavailable and not based on scientific knowledge of the workings of anatomy and physiology. Not being able to study the human body through dissection during this period also led to many of these anatomical misunderstandings. During the Middle Ages, there was a return to superstitious beliefs regarding the causes of many of the difficulties people exhibited. Salient among these were the torturous practices leveled against those believed to be possessed by demons, which we now know may have been afflicted by brain impairments. Examples of symptoms often mistaken for possession by the devil include visual and auditory hallucinations and delusions of grandeur or persecution, commonly noted in schizophrenia.

During the later part of the Middle Ages, the works of Aristotle were rediscovered and translated (between 1200 and 1225), and made available to an expanded audience. His views were accepted as sacred and any questioning was unacceptable. His views were particularly in agreement with the time due to his heavy emphasis on the heart and his nonreliance on any scientific methodology because during this period the church was considered the ultimate authority on all matters.

The initial move away from the ventricular localization theory started in the 13th century. Albertus Magnus (1206–1280) theorized that behavior resulted from a combination of brain structures including the cortex, the midbrain, and the cerebellum. It is very interesting, historically, to note that Magnus was a Dominican monk because at that time clergy were not thought to stray from recognized doctrine.

In general, there was a stagnation of new learning during the Middle Ages. Natural philosophers, such as Avicenna, had access to the Greek and Roman books of science. The Arabs and Nestorian Christians venerated, collected, and translated the works of Hippocrates, Aristotle, and Galen (Finger, 1994). They based their own medical practices on these classics. The works of Middle Eastern scientists and healers only became familiar to Europeans at the end of the Middle Ages. Most of the information became available when Europeans went south to conquer Moorish Spain. The material then spread to France and Italy and began a revival of interest in anatomy, physiology, and medicine.

RENAISSANCE EUROPE (1400–1600)

The Renaissance is generally considered to have begun in Italy in the mid-14th century and ended during the 16th century. The Renaissance marked the end of medieval Europe and allowed intellectual freedom to flourish. This ushered in a period of significant change scientifically, artistically, and socially. Included was a rapid expansion of knowledge of anatomy and physiology supported by reacquisition of earlier texts, which remained active in Arabic thought when Europe was in the Dark Ages. Surprisingly, one of the major factors in the start of the Renaissance was the plague of the 1300s, the Black Death. This pandemic led to a questioning of the existing religious, political, and social structures and subsequently led to freer inquiry and thought. Labor had become scarce, which loosened the ties that had kept workers shackled to their land or their employers. The net result was a society in which the pursuit of knowledge became acceptable. The results were dramatic as evidenced by the rapid expansion of science and the arts.

In the late 15th century, Leonardo da Vinci (1452–1519) conducted several hundred human dissections on cadavers in secret due to religious prohibition against autopsies. He drew detailed diagrams of the human body from these dissections. da Vinci conducted experiments on cattle to determine the true structure of the ventricles. The information da Vinci learned from his cattle experiments demonstrated that the actual function of the ventricles did not correspond to the thinking at the time. However, after completing all of his dissections and work with cerebrospinal fluid, he continued to believe in the ventricular localization hypothesis of brain functioning. It is a striking historical question as to why he held to a theory that he was able to disprove.

In 1543, Andreas Vesalius (1514–1564) published the first accurate book on human anatomy entitled *On the Workings of the Human Body*. It was one of the most important medical science books ever written (Idowu, Malomo, & Osuagwu, 2006). He completed his work through dissections and careful observations and ultimately proved that Galen's views on ventricular flow were incorrect. Vesalius began the history of public dissection allowing medical students and doctors to view the procedure in a manner foreshadowing current medical practices. Even though the church retained authority over the soul, he took the risk to expose the rest of the body to scrutiny. Through his work, he found fault with the ventricular localization hypothesis and the movement of animal spirits. He also claimed to find at least 200 errors in the anatomical works of Galen (Finger, 2000). He was able to show that to truly understand the workings of the human body one must study humans, not other animals. Vesalius' ideas were not well received by the public or the scientific community at that time.

During the 17th century, scientists were looking for a single site for the functioning of the mind. The philosopher Rene Descartes (1596–1630) disagreed with the tripartite soul introduced by Plato. He believed in a complete separation of the mind and body. He felt that the mind was immaterial and without substance, whereas, the body functioned similar to a machine. Descartes also dealt with the mind–body problem or the question of the relationship between the two entities. The complete separation of mind and body is referred to as **dualism**. **Monism** states that there are no fundamental differences and a unified set of laws underlie nature. Descartes was a dualist who erroneously speculated that mental processes resided within the **pineal gland**. His idea was that the pineal gland is the only structure not composed of bilaterally symmetrical halves. Presently, the pineal gland is not fully understood, but most researchers believe that it is involved with sleep regulation and melatonin production. However, it lies near the ventricular system and in Descartes' thinking, he may have attempted to relate this to the earlier ventricular localization hypothesis. He also viewed the cortex as a covering of the pineal body.

Thomas Willis (1621–1675), known for his study of blood circulation and for whom the Circle of Willis is named, also studied brain function. In 1664, he published *Cerebri Anatome*, a work without equal at the time, which was mainly devoted to the study of the brain (O'Connor, 2003). Willis used clinical evidence from living patients with movement disorders and observed degeneration in the various structures at autopsy to back his claims. He also described sensations residing within the corpus striatum (Meyer & Hierons, 1964). He stated that the cerebral gyri controlled memory and will. According to Willis, imagination was also a cerebral function located in the corpus callosum. The **corpus striatum** was thought to be related to sensation and movement. The cerebellum was thought to control the voluntary and involuntary systems. At that point in history, the pons and medulla were considered to be part of the cerebellum.

Willis was the first person in the post-Renaissance period to divide the brain into functional parts based on comparative anatomy, theory, and clinical practice. Although he did not accurately localize various abilities, his writings became a strong impetus for others to look at the functional working of individual brain areas.

Following the ideas of Willis, Emanuel Swedenborg (1688–1772) concluded that the cerebral cortex was the source of understanding, thinking, judging, and willing. He also went further than Willis and stated that certain functions were represented at different anatomical sites on the cortex. Swedenborg saw the localization of function as the way to understand the difficulties which arose with patients with various types of pathologies. He took his ideas further to include other structures. However, most of his ideas were not accepted or published during his lifetime. One reason he was not accepted was that Swedenborg began to have visions and eventually felt his calling to be in theology. Leaving science for theology was not accepted by many in the scientific community at that time (Akert & Hammond, 1962).

18TH CENTURY: LOCALIZATION THEORY

Localization of brain functioning is one of the most interesting questions that began to be studied by Swedenborg and others during this period and continues to the modern era. The localization of function refers to the idea that the brain has certain functions which are localized or located within specific areas. Franz Joseph Gall (1758–1828) began to write about this idea in 1810. He stated that certain physiological characteristics of individuals appeared to reflect their intellectual or cognitive capabilities.

Gall correlated 27 faculties of the mind with skull features and located these abilities on maps of both hemispheres. He became an early advocate of the idea of cortical localization of function. The theory of **phrenology** was developed from Gall's ideas. The theory of phrenology suggested that abilities were so localized that they would appear as protuberances on the skull. A person could exercise a particular ability by rubbing or massaging that area and develop more of the particular ability or trait. The ideas Gall proposed appealed to the average person and phrenology began to be practiced in the salons of

---

dualism
the view that within each person resides two entities, a mind with mental properties and a body with physical properties

monism
the view that there is only one basic and fundamental reality, that all existence is this one reality; hence, the mind and body operate according to the same principles

localization of brain functioning
the theory that certain abilities are localized to certain areas of the brain

phrenology
inaccurate theory developed by Gall which stated that bumps on the head related to certain abilities residing within the brain; the theory led to belief in reading the bumps and increasing abilities by rubbing the corresponding bumps

Europe. The influence of phrenology lasted many years and regrettably had a widespread impact leading the study of the brain in a nonproductive direction.

In addition to the theory of phrenology, which has been considered to be highly inaccurate, Gall was responsible for several significant discoveries in neuroanatomy and neurophysiology. In essence, his work was recognized for some of the earliest views on the idea of localization of functions. Gall, through his dissections, proposed that the cortex and its sulci and gyri were functioning parts of the brain and not just coverings of the pineal body. He also stated that a large pathway, the pyramidal tract, leads from the cortex to the spinal cord, implying that the cortex sends information to the spinal cord to command movement of the muscles. Gall and his colleagues also discovered the role of the corpus callosum in the communication between the hemispheres.

Gall's student Johann Spurzheim (1776–1832) worked with him studying phrenology for 9 years. The two parted company because Spurzheim felt there were no bad or evil functions as described by Gall (Carlson, 1958). He contended that bad traits were caused by underdevelopment of the specific functions.

Pierre Flourens (1794–1867) disputed Gall stating there was no localization of function within the cortex. Flourens supported his opinion through studying animals usually with very small brains, which if ablated would destroy more than one function. **Ablation** was a type of surgery in which removing part of the brain led to generalized, not localized, disorders of behavior. He proclaimed there was no specific localization of ability, but rather the amount or extent of tissue damage is what mattered. In other words, the greater the mass of impaired tissue, the more dysfunctional the individual will appear. Flourens also stated that the brain operated in an integrated fashion, not with discrete functions. Without knowing it, Flourens was describing the modern term **neuroplasticity**, which states that various brain areas are able to take over functions for one another when an area is injured or destroyed. The reason that neuroplasticity is possible is that the brain functions as a whole, similar to the way Flourens described. Flourens also believed that the cerebellum was responsible for coordinated movement and that the medulla was required for basic life functioning.

19TH-CENTURY ADVANCES

The 19th century was a time of great advances in many areas of psychology, which would ultimately make an impact on the study of the brain. The **scientific method** became a reality in psychology with the development of the first laboratories. Wilhelm Wundt (1832–1920) is credited with the first psychology laboratory in Germany in 1879. Soon thereafter, others developed in various parts of Europe and the United States. The scientific method refers to the reliance on the procedures of science as a means of understanding, as opposed to theorizing without any practical data to validate the theory. The advantages of the scientific method are the ability to manage or control all parts of the experiment, which leaves nothing to chance. Through the use of the scientific method researchers began to be able to make cause and effect statements for the first time. The researcher could say that A caused B because no other variable could have done so in a controlled situation. The scientific method allowed the researcher to look at the structure and function of the workings of the brains of lower animals. Through the process of scientifically looking at lower animals, the scientist was able to relate findings to humans. However, many scientists felt it was a large leap to go from the functioning of animal brains to the functioning of the human brain.

Along with the scientific method, another movement occurred beginning in France and Great Britain, which fought for better treatment of individuals who were mentally ill (or suffered from brain impairment). Phillipe Pinel (1745–1826), a French physician, was shocked by what he saw as brutality toward the mentally ill. Objectionable practices

neuroplasticity
the brain's natural ability to form new connections to compensate for injury or changes in one's environment

scientific method
a method of research in which a problem is identified, a hypothesis is formulated, and relevant data are gathered; from these data, cause–effect relationships can be stated

included not only incarcerating patients with prisoners, but also punishment such as chaining individuals to walls for behaviors over which they clearly had no control, such as delusions and hallucinations. Pinel became head of two **asylums** or mental hospitals, Bicêtre and Salpêtrierè. Pinel's ideas for change included the use of kindness and humanity in the treatment of the patients. These principles of treatment led to better lives for the patients.

At the same time as Pinel, William Tuke (1732–1822) began to improve the care of patients in England. Simultaneously, in America, other individuals such as Eli Todd (1769–1833) began to pursue better treatment for the mentally ill. Dorothea Dix (1802–1887) traveled all over the United States campaigning for reform. Clifford Beers (1900–1979) authored a text in 1908 entitled *A Mind That Found Itself: An Autobiography* (Beers, 1908). This book chronicles Beers' experience with bipolar disorder and his treatment. The movement that these individuals initiated was termed the **mental hygiene movement**. Along with this movement came the development of **moral therapy**, which referred to the humane care and treatment of patients.

At the same time as changes were occurring in the treatment of the mentally ill, attempts were begun to formulate **diagnostic classification systems**. Emil Kraepelin (1856–1926), writing in 1913, was one of the first individuals to describe mental illness and categorized it based on what was termed **endogenous** (curable) versus **exogenous** (incurable). The terms have since been defined as biochemical versus stress induced, respectively. His work foreshadowed our current diagnostic classification system. The diagnostic system which is currently in use is the ***Diagnostic and Statistical Manual of Mental Disorders, Fourth Edition, Text Revision* (DSM-IV-TR)** published by the American Psychiatric Association; it will be discussed in greater detail in a subsequent chapter (American Psychiatric Association, 2000). At this point, suffice it to say that it is a way to classify mental disorders similar to the manner in which physicians classify physical difficulties using the ***International Classification of Diseases* (ICD-10)**. The advantages of a diagnostic classification system are multifold and include appropriate treatment, research, communication among professionals, and payment for services.

While all of these events were unfolding, Charles Darwin (1809–1882) was conceptualizing the origin of the species. Darwin's ideas radically changed the way people understood our relationship with other animals. His theory of evolution and the belief that all living things have a common ancestry was an impetus for the study of lower animals with relation to understanding human functioning. Darwin stressed the survival value of outward expression of emotions by animals and humans. He also believed that the human mind contained primitive inclinations that were held in check by higher mental functions. Many of Darwin's supporters gave credence to the ideas promoted by therapists. Darwin stated that the expression of feelings had survival value, while therapists state that the expression of feelings leads to better mental health and functioning of the individual.

asylum
an early institution specializing in the care of the mentally ill

mental hygiene movement
the movement to treat psychiatric patients with kindness and dignity; it instigated the release of mental patients from prison and the building of mental hospitals

moral therapy
therapy created for mental patients based on the ideas of the mental hygiene movement; kindness and respect were the main components

diagnostic classification system
a system for classifying medical and psychiatric disorders; it lists symptoms of a particular disorder and various other important facts for diagnosis; in psychology, it usually refers to the *DSM-IV-TR* published by the American Psychiatric Association

Localization of Brain Functioning Areas: Higher Cortical Areas

Localization of functioning, as stated previously, began to be a topic of interest in the early 1800s. Gall and, subsequently, Swedenborg investigated various types of localization; however, it took a longer time to look into the localization of higher cortical functioning. Much of the impetus for looking at higher cortical functioning came from the aforementioned world events, which included the growing concern for the treatment of individuals with various difficulties. These difficulties had begun to be seen as residing within the cerebral cortex.

Paul Broca (1824–1880) is often given credit for the discovery of localization of language within the left hemisphere. His work will be discussed later in this section.

However, his work clearly was based on those who came before him, Jean-Baptiste Bouillaud (1796–1881), Simon Alexandre Ernest Aubertin (1825–1893), as well as Marc Dax (1771–1837) and his son Gustave Dax (1815–1874).

Jean-Baptiste Bouillaud was a well-respected French scientist who made all of his assertions based on clinical data and/or autopsies. In 1825, after examining data from a large number of cases, he asserted that the brain had several special organs. One of the special organs was related to speech and difficulties with speech were evident when the specific area was damaged (Stookey, 1963). The difficulties described and the impaired brain areas clearly foreshadow Broca's discoveries.

Simon Alexandre Ernest Aubertin (1825–1881), Bouillard's son-in-law, was also a French physician. He also argued from clinical cases that there were specific higher order cognitive functions localized within certain areas.

Marc Dax (1771–1837), was another French neurologist who discovered through clinical practice the link between the damage to the left cerebral hemisphere and the loss of the ability to produce speech. Dax wrote two papers in 1836, one entitled *Observations Tending to Prove the Constant Coincidence of Disturbances of Speech With a Lesion of the Left Hemisphere of the Brain* and *Lesions of the Left Half of the Encephalon Coincident With the Forgetting of Signs of Thinking* (Roe & Finger, 1997). He died the following year without publishing his findings.

Gustave Dax (1815–1874), while studying medicine in the 1860s, published his father's works along with his own findings (Buckingham, 2006). The Dax work was published 6 weeks before Broca's paper was published with both stating similar conclusions.

The localization of brain function was further expanded by the work of Paul Broca (1824–1880). Broca examined two clinical cases in detail of individuals who were unable to speak coherently, but were able to understand the spoken word. After their deaths, he examined their brains and found defects or destruction of tissue in exactly the place he had theorized. The area in the posterior, lower region of the left frontal lobe became known as Broca's area. Broca is also credited with articulating the concept of **aphasia**, which literally means the inability to use or comprehend language. Broca was one of the first localizationist psychologists, meaning that he believed that certain abilities were located in specific brain areas. Broca also helped perpetuate the idea that verbal abilities were confined to the left hemisphere. In essence, Broca discovered through clinical cases that language production was localized to the left hemisphere. This principle became known as **lateralization**. In contrast, speech is a motor function not specifically localized in a similar manner.

As can be seen, there were many researchers who, through clinical case studies, noticed that verbal abilities resided within the left hemisphere. It remains a historical question who discovered them first and who should receive credit for their discoveries.

Several years after Broca wrote, another researcher, Carl Wernicke (1848–1904), described a second language area of the brain. He was able to discover the new area through the study of dysfunctions in his patients' abilities. This second area was located in the temporal lobe somewhat to the posterior and inferior to Broca's area. Damage here led to a particular dysfunction, the inability to make sense with language even though the utterances were grammatically correct whether spoken or written. Wernicke's discovery led to the belief that the strict localizationists were not correct, that is, expressive language is located in the frontal lobes whereas, receptive language is located in the temporal lobes. Language, in general, does not totally reside in one locale.

Following the discoveries of Broca's and Wernicke's areas (see Figure 1.4), another area between the two was discovered. The difficulty was caused by damage to the nerve fibers connecting Wernicke's and Broca's areas in the arcuate fasciculus. Damage to this area resulted in what we now term **conduction aphasia** or the inability in both reception of

aphasia
an impairment of the ability to use or comprehend language, usually acquired as a result of a stroke or other brain injury; it may involve difficulties with spoken, written, or gestured language

lateralization
the idea that certain abilities reside in one side of the brain or the other; for the majority of individuals, verbal abilities reside in the left hemisphere and spatial abilities reside in the right hemisphere

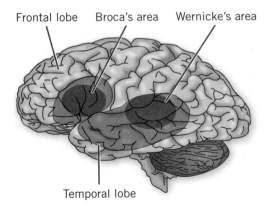

Frontal lobe   Broca's area   Wernicke's area

Temporal lobe

FIGURE 1.4 Broca's and Wernicke's areas.

language and the production of language. Many patients with conduction aphasia become very frustrated and even suicidal because of their inabilities with the understanding and expression of language. To clarify the three types of aphasia, a person with expressive (Broca's) aphasia can understand what is spoken to him or her but has difficulty responding in a grammatically correct manner. A person with receptive (Wernicke's) aphasia can grammatically produce speech with content inappropriate to the question. A person with conduction aphasia neither understands the question nor responds grammatically. To further illustrate the distinctions in aphasic communication, a model question presented to each aphasic could be "How was your day?" The expressive aphasic patient may say "ok," "good," "fine," and "hi." The receptive aphasic patient may respond, "Thank you very much for the rutabagas" and the conductive aphasic patient may respond, "I live under a tarp, per se, tomorrow." Clearly, the individuals exhibit different disabilities, which could lead to different types of functioning and frustrations.

Another researcher, John Hughlings Jackson (1835–1911), wrote in the 1800s in Great Britain, but was not published in the United States until the 1950s. He disagreed with Broca, Wernicke, and others and believed in holistic brain functioning. Hughlings Jackson saw the brain as functioning in a hierarchical manner. Each level higher would control more complex functioning. The three levels he often described were the spinal cord, the brain stem, and the forebrain. He stated that the location of function was not the issue but the amount of tissue damage was the important variable to study. His studies, completed on lower animals, suggested that larger amounts of tissue damage caused more traumas. Hughlings Jackson was somewhat ahead of his time in that he discovered not only where ability was localized but also how the entire brain functions in the expression of a particular ability or disability.

Karl Lashley (1890–1958), in his work with animals, was noted as America's most eminent early neuropsychologist because of his way of exploring brain functioning. He believed in a combination of localization and **equipotentiality**, or the belief that higher cortical functions are too complex to be confined to any single area of the brain. Lashley, through his experiments, also proposed the **principle of mass action**, which states that the extent of impairment is directly proportional to the mass of the removed tissue. Lashley also stated that each part of the brain was responsible for more than the one function. Lashley felt more allegiance to the equipotentialists than the localizationalists.

As the century progressed, Alexander Luria (1902–1977), was pursuing the study of the brain in Russia. Luria stated that a viable theory of the brain must encompass both the localization and equipotentiality theories and findings, which did not fit either theory.

equipotentiality
the idea that mental abilities depend upon the entire brain functioning as a whole

principle of mass action
Lashley's idea that the extent of brain impairment is directly proportional to the amount of tissue damage

split-brain studies
studies conducted on humans with severed corpus callosums to determine the extent of communication between the two hemispheres

corpus callosum
a large mass of myelinated axons connecting the right and left hemispheres; it functions to allow communication between the two hemispheres

Luria described each area of the central nervous system as being involved in one or more brain functions. The first area regulated the arousal level of the brain and proper muscle tone. The second area played a role in the reception and analysis of sensory information from the external and internal environments. The third area was involved with planning, executing, and verifying behavior (Luria, 1966).

At approximately the same time that Luria was studying the functions of various areas of the brain, Roger Sperry (1913–1994) began studying **split-brain** subjects, those in whom the **corpus callosum** had been severed. The corpus callosum is the large band of nerves that joins the right and left hemispheres of the brain. Sperry dispelled work stating that the corpus callosum served no function. Sperry studied split-brain subjects and demonstrated important consequences for each hemisphere after separation of the corpus callosum. During independent testing of the hemispheres, the left hemisphere was more verbal, rational, and analytical, while the right was more spatial and emotional. Sperry received a Nobel Prize for his work in 1981.

During the time of Sperry's initial work, Ward Halstead (1908–1968) developed the first neuropsychology laboratory in 1935 at the University of Chicago. While other researchers were studying and theorizing about brain structure and function, Halstead began the arduous task of assessing brain impairment. He not only attempted to develop tests to measure brain impairment, but also he wanted his tests to be reliable and valid measures of the constructs that he was studying (Halstead, 1947). Halstead worked almost exclusively with neurology patients, those individuals who had diseases or damage to their central nervous systems, and developed assessment devices which differentiated between patients with brain damage and those without. Halstead developed, in collaboration with his student Ralph Reitan, the Halstead-Reitan Neuropsychological Test Battery. The Halstead-Reitan Neuropsychological Test Battery has been the most popular and most widely used fixed test battery in the United States and abroad for approximately the past 50 years.

At the same time that Halstead and Reitan were working, Luria as stated previously, also developed his theory in Russia. Luria's works were translated into English and published in the United States by Anne-Lise Christensen (1927–). Charles Golden (1949–), while at the University of Nebraska, developed the Luria-Nebraska Neuropsychological Battery based on Luria's original ideas of brain functioning. There is some disagreement within the field regarding whether the Luria-Nebraska Neuropsychological Battery truly reflects Luria's ideas regarding brain functioning. As will be described in the chapter on test batteries, the Halstead-Reitan Neuropsychological Test Battery and the Luria-Nebraska Neuropsychological Battery have been the most commonly used test batteries. Each battery has its own strengths and weaknesses and each follows a separate way of conceptualizing brain functioning.

The two test batteries were developed in different manners and the directions for administering test items reflects this. The Halstead-Reitan Neuropsychological Test Battery was designed to be administered in a standardized fashion to all subjects and allowed for comparability between subjects, whereas the Luria-Nebraska Neuropsychological Battery was designed to fit the needs of the individual patient and administration of test items could be altered to fit individual needs. There is less comparability of scores across individuals with this approach. Currently, other test batteries are being developed and will be discussed, as well as the issue of the use of a composite of individual tests as opposed to a test battery. After a brief glance at the two major fixed test batteries, you might begin to guess which one, if either, was given to Marvin. Considering Marvin was in a moving vehicle accident, which may often lead to legal issues, he was given the Halstead-Reitan Neuropsychological Test Battery. This battery is more useful in forensic situations due to the manner in which it was constructed. He could also have been administered a more flexible test battery, which would allow the choice of tests to be governed by his presenting symptoms.

The Development of Clinical Neuropsychology as a Profession

At the same time the aforementioned tests were being developed, world events were shaping the need for clinical neuropsychologists and their expertise and services. It is crucial to the understanding of the work of the clinical neuropsychologist to understand the events which led to the development of the field of clinical psychology. Clinical neuropsychology is considered to be a subspecialty of clinical psychology.

World War I (1914–1918) was the first war where many individuals who would have died in earlier wars were saved by advancements in medical practice. However, these individuals often had residual damage from warfare believed to be related to the noise, shaking of the brain, and various other difficulties which occurred dependent on the job of the soldier. Collectively, these individuals were said to suffer from **shell shock**, a term given because of the force exerted by the explosions of large munitions.

Economically, the Great Depression (1929–1941) caused a tremendous number of people to become poor, underfed, or homeless. Many of these individuals we could assume suffered from depression, substance abuse, posttraumatic stress disorder (PTSD), or various central nervous system illnesses or injury.

World War II (1939–1945) provided a strong impetus for the services of clinical neuropsychologists. Advances in wartime medicine allowed even more wounded service people to return home than in World War I. These survivors often returned with physical and mental difficulties causing them impairment in their daily lives. At this point in time, the soldier's psychiatric ailments were often termed **battle fatigue**. The similarities in the symptoms seen in veterans of the Great Wars and victims of the Great Depression were impetuses for the eventual creation of the term *posttraumatic stress disorder*.

The creation of the **Veterans Administration (VA)** in 1930, primarily in response to the needs of World War I veterans, led to increased training for clinical neuropsychologists. The VA was created to service the physical and mental health needs of those who had served in the armed forces. As the study of the brain continued, it became clear that warfare could cause brain damage and that assessment, diagnosis, and rehabilitation services were needed (van der Kolk, 1997).

The Korean War (1950–1953) furthered the involvement of clinical neuropsychology within the VA because, again, many more individuals returned home with obvious impairments. The VA system became one of the primary trainers and employers of clinical neuropsychologists.

The Vietnam Conflict (1960–1973) and its political aftermath paved the way for additional services for veterans, but not until 10 years after the soldiers' reentry. Along with the activism of Vietnam Veterans' groups for the treatment of emotional issues came the naming of soldiers' difficulties as **PTSD** in 1985. Posttraumatic stress disorder means that an individual has experienced a stressor beyond the capacity for most people to endure. The symptoms develop after the stressor and may include flashbacks of trauma, dreams, exaggerated startle response, and hypervigilance. Research on the symptoms of PTSD clearly shows brain impairment is possible particularly in the areas of memory and new learning (van der Kolk, 1997).

After the establishment of PTSD as a diagnostic category, the application of the term to other difficulties including survivors of rape, incest, and natural disasters was begun. All

Veterans Administration (VA)
a U.S. government agency created to service the physical and mental health needs of those who had served in the armed forces

posttraumatic stress disorder (PTSD)
a mental disorder occurring after a traumatic event outside the range of usual human experience and characterized by symptoms such as reliving the event, reduced involvement with others, and exaggerated startle response; earlier terms for PTSD include shell shock and battle fatigue

of these traumatic events also have been shown to have brain sequela. Current examples of individuals who could develop PTSD would include first responders such as police and fire fighters and survivors of hurricanes, tornados, and other types of natural disasters.

These historical examples relate to the development of the field of clinical psychology and its subspecialty clinical neuropsychology. Clinical neuropsychology began within the general medical service of most facilities. It was greatly influenced by the interactions between neurology, neurosurgery, psychiatry, and other medical disciplines. At the present time, clinical neuropsychologists are often assigned their primary responsibilities through the medical service.

Clinical Neuropsychology as a Subspecialty of Clinical Psychology

Ward Halstead began the first clinical neuropsychology laboratory in the 1930s. After the Second World War, the VA was expanded and the need for clinical neuropsychologists was great. However, during this period, the education for clinical neuropsychologists was more experiential than academic. The majority of early individuals who became interested in clinical neuropsychology had their primary training in clinical psychology.

clinical psychology
a branch of psychology devoted to the assessment, diagnosis, and treatment of mental and behavioral disorders

scientist–practitioner model
guidelines that state that to be accredited by the APA, a clinical or counseling doctoral program must contain a prescribed number of classes or credits in the scientific bases of behavior and a certain number of classes or credits in the practice of psychology

Clinical psychology is the branch of psychology dealing with mental illness. Training for professionals was not standardized until the late 1940s as a consequence of a major meeting entitled the Boulder Conference held at the University of Colorado in Boulder, Colorado. This meeting led to the historic **Boulder model** (Raimy, 1950). The Boulder model developed the framework for the training of clinical psychologists. The guidelines were termed the **scientist–practitioner model**. These guidelines stated that to be accredited by the APA, a doctoral program in clinical psychology must contain a prescribed number of classes or credits in the scientific bases of behavior and a certain number of classes or credits in the practice of psychology. This model is still upheld in the accreditation of PhD programs. APA recognizes clinical neuropsychology as a separate and distinct field of study. Division 40 (Clinical Neuropsychology) of APA was created in 1980. The APA defines a clinical neuropsychologist as follows:

> A Clinical Neuropsychologist is a professional psychologist who applies principles of assessment and intervention based upon the scientific study of human behavior as it relates to normal and abnormal functioning of the central nervous system. The Clinical Neuropsychologist is a doctoral-level psychology provider of diagnostic and intervention services who has demonstrated competence in the application of such principles for human welfare following:
>
> A. Successful completion of systematic didactic and experiential training in neuropsychology and neuroscience at a regionally accredited university;
> B. Two or more years of appropriate supervised training applying neuropsychological services in a clinical setting;
> C. Licensing and certification to provide psychological services to the public by laws of the state or province in which he or she practices;
> D. Review by one's peers as a test of these competencies.
> (APA, 1989)

Division 40 of the APA considers the attainment of the American Board of Professional Psychology (ABPP) or the American Board of Clinical Neuropsychology (ABCN) diplomat status in Clinical Neuropsychology as the clearest evidence of competence as a clinical neuropsychologist, assuming that all of the criteria have been met (www.theabcn. org/abpp-diploma/index).

There are three major organizations that exist for the perpetuation of clinical neuropsychology. These three organizations are **Division 40 (Clinical Neuropsychology)**, as already described, of the APA, **The International Neuropsychological Society (INS)** and **The National Academy of Neuropsychology (NAN)**. These organizations function to further the development of the field.

The INS was founded in 1967. It currently has more than 4,500 members throughout the world. It holds two professional meetings per year, one in the United States and the other abroad. The INS is a multidisciplinary organization, which has as its goal the enhancement of communication among the scientific disciplines that contribute to the understanding of the brain–behavior relationship.

The NAN was founded in 1975. Current membership totals more than 3,300 members from 24 countries. The goals of NAN are to advance the scientific study of brain–behavior relationships using neuropsychological techniques, develop standards of practice, develop training guidelines, provide continuing education, and provide an information resource in neuropsychology.

In order to find out more about the actual workings of clinical neuropsychologists, Sweet, Moberg, and Suchy (2000) reviewed a 10-year follow-up survey of clinical neuropsychologists working in private practice and institutions. The sample included 422 respondents, 60.2% ABPP's and 41.4% general Division 40 members of APA. The PhD was by far the most common degree for both groups with 9 out of 10 holding this type of degree in both groups. The field of study where it was granted was primarily clinical psychology. The majority of the respondents did agree with the statement by the APA and felt that clinical neuropsychology is a subspecialty of clinical psychology. Respondents described the need for broad predoctoral training in clinical psychology, as well as specialty training and an internship in clinical neuropsychology.

Sweet et al. (2000) included journals subscribed to by clinical neuropsychologists as examples of interest areas and expertise. The top six most commonly subscribed to journals in 1999 were *Archives of Clinical Neuropsychology*, *Neuropsychology*, *The Clinical Neuropsychologist*, *Journal of the International Neuropsychological Society*, *Journal of Clinical and Experimental Neuropsychology*, and *Neuropsychology Review*. The number of journals specifically related to clinical neuropsychology gives an indication of the depth and breadth of the field according to the authors.

METHODOLOGY SPECIFIC TO CLINICAL NEUROPSYCHOLOGY

Clinical neuropsychology, being an applied field, has methodological issues similar to other applied fields. An applied field means that knowledge taken from research and clinical practice is used in the treatment of patients. Clinical neuropsychology has also shared methodology with other disciplines.

Subjects

One of the main questions for the clinical neuropsychologist is the type of subject from which research findings have been taken. As can be seen from the historical background, many studies of the brain have come from individuals who had sustained traumatic injuries or suffered from various illnesses. They have been excellent subjects to assist the clinical neuropsychologist to understand the effects of damage to particular areas and to assist in developing rehabilitation methods. Investigation of a single individual with central

case study
a detailed analysis of an individual focusing on his or her history and current life situation; it is often a way to study individuals with central nervous system illness or injury

nervous system illness or injury is termed the **case study** method. The case study method has added a wealth of information to the clinical neuropsychological literature.

It is very challenging to compare the difficulties of one individual to others, even with similar injuries because other extraneous variables may confound the research results. Examples of confounding variables which could cause problems with comparability of subjects include age, gender, socioeconomic status, social support network, access to physical medicine, and rehabilitative services. Marvin's case is a good example. He has a brain injury caused by an automobile accident and many things are known about brain injury from motor vehicle accidents. There are other specifics to Marvin's case which may make it difficult to develop a treatment plan based only on case study information. Examples of confounding variables in Marvin's case include being a 36-year-old White male from a lower middle class background, high school educated, lacking support from his ex-wife and having few friends as a social support network. Many researchers try to overcome these difficulties exemplified by Marvins's case by gathering groups of individuals with as similar as possible injuries and matching background factors. By having many individuals with similar difficulties, the clinical neuropsychologist is able to see the pattern of strengths and weaknesses with various difficulties. This information is very important in developing a treatment plan for rehabilitation.

Techniques Dealing With Subject Variables

double dissociation technique
a research technique in which lesions have opposite or dissimilar effects on two distinct cognitive functions; it was developed to help determine when cognitive functions are independent

The **double dissociation technique** was developed to help researchers determine when cognitive factors are independent. As described by Shallice (1988), a double dissociation occurs when lesions have opposite or dissimilar effects on two distinct cognitive functions. For example, lesion 1 causes difficulty with cognitive function 1 but not cognitive function 2, while lesion 2 causes a problem with cognitive function 2 but not cognitive function 1. We make an assumption that the functions are independent because the changes in one do not affect the other. A commonly given example to illustrate the double dissociation technique is the study of individuals with Broca's aphasia and Wernicke's aphasia. It is clear from the studies of these two groups that the abilities, which reside in these areas, do not cause each other, even though they may affect one another greatly. Hans-Lukas Teuber (1955) used the double dissociation technique to demonstrate lateralization of function. Lesions in the left hemisphere of right-handed people produce deficits in language functions not evident with lesions in the right hemisphere. Lesions in the right hemisphere produce deficits in spatial tests not evident with left-hemisphere lesions.

lesion approach
the lesioning of animals and sometimes humans to study the effects of the lesion on various brain functions

Another approach often referred to as the **lesion approach** involves the use of lesions in humans and other animals. Specific lesions may be made in humans and animals who have all of the extraneous variables eradicated by having similar genetic qualities and environments. This is the closest we are able to come to showing the effects on behavior of specific lesions. When the lesion approach is used with humans it is usually in areas where the individual has some form of difficulty for which the lesion should help eradicate the difficulty. Lesion studies in animals are different. Lesions are often used to create deficits in animals and observe functioning afterward. Care and treatment of research animals is always kept foremost in the researcher's mind when completing lesion studies.

IMAGING TECHNIQUES IN THE STUDY OF THE HUMAN BRAIN

In addition to the choice of subjects for research in clinical neuropsychology, there are also issues related to the use of various techniques for studying the human brain. As time has passed, the clinical neuropsychologist's role has changed from one in which diagnosis was made based on results of testing to one in which testing is used to evaluate the strengths and weaknesses of the individual and help develop an effective treatment plan.

The advent of advanced medical imaging techniques has allowed the diagnosis to be made much quicker and then corroborated by neuropsychological testing. However, there are times and circumstances where medical techniques are not able to view difficulties or the deficits are so small and the determination of diagnosis is greatly enhanced by performance on neuropsychological tests.

Electrical Techniques

Electroencephalography (EEG) is the oldest technique which records brain waves and their pattern as a person completes different tasks (see Figure 1.5). The use of the EEG began in 1928 when Hans Berger (1873–1941) used it to measure brain waves. Berger's intention was to find evidence for telepathy, the unscientific manner of communication between individuals. He did not find what he desired but discovered that the brain waves of a sleeping brain were very different from an awake brain. Researchers have since used this technology to record and measure the activity of nerve cells in the brains of individuals who are normal and those suffering from various difficulties and diseases. The EEG measures the firing of nerve cells, which tend to fire in a synchronous pattern leading to alpha, beta, theta, and delta waveforms.

> **electroencephalography (EEG)**
> a record of brain wave patterns as an individual completes a task

The EEG was the first technique to record the electrical activity of the brain. However, it is limited in that it does not reveal the contents of thought but reveals only that the person is thinking. Other techniques building on EEG technology have produced more sophisticated brain wave evaluations. One manner in which to expand on the EEG is to employ a computer to map the activity of the brain's electrical activity as it is occurring in the individual's head. The techniques have been termed **brain electrical activity mapping** (BEAM). It produces a color-coded map of the brain as various areas exhibit activation.

A further advance using EEG technology is to record changes in the EEG signal in response to a sensory stimulus. This procedure has been termed an **evoked potential** (EP) or an **event-related potential** (ERP). The difficulty with this procedure is that multiple

> **evoked potential**
> the ability to record changes in EEG activity in response to sensory stimuli; the response is termed an evoked potential or event-related potential

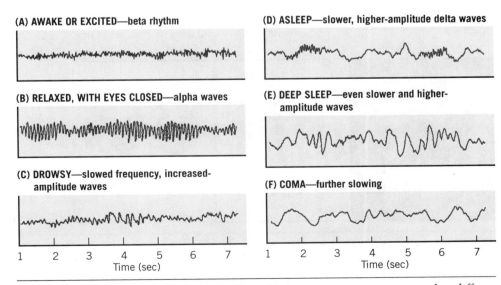

FIGURE 1.5 Characteristic EEG recordings. Brain wave patterns correspond to different states of consciousness in humans. *Source:* Adapted from Kolb, B., & Whishaw, I. Q. (2009). *Fundamentals of Human Neuropsychology*, 6th ed. New York: Worth Publishers.

recordings need to be made and an average computed because of the multitude of signals which are produced by the brain. The EEG is particularly useful in the recording of seizure activity, which registers as a very nonsynchronous pattern. The EEG is also used to detect brain wave patterns in individuals with sleep disorders due to the fact that different sleep states are associated with particular forms of electrical activity. It is the main diagnostic tool used in sleep laboratories. In addition, the EEG is effective in diagnosis of individuals with TBI in which the seizure threshold may have changed.

Radiological Techniques

The first radiological recordings of brain structure and function came from **X-rays**. Early X-ray pictures of the brain were very crude and did not capture the essence of the brain difficulties only external boundaries. The X-rays were absorbed by different structures to different degrees; hence, the images of bone were clearer than soft tissue, which was clearer than the blood vessels and ventricles. A second difficulty was that it produced only a two-dimensional image of the three-dimensioned brain. X-rays also introduced radiation into the brain. At the time they were introduced, the safety range for radiation had not been determined. However, now it is thought that the radiation the brain is exposed to using the X-ray is minimal.

A method of enhancing the X-ray is termed **pneumoencephalography**. In this procedure a small amount of cerebrospinal fluid is removed and replaced by air. The X-rays are taken as the air moves up the spinal cord. Because of the presence of air the ventricles stand out clearly. This procedure is not used very often as it is outdated and painful to the patient. A procedure similar to pneumoencephalography is **angiography** with the exception that a substance that absorbs X-rays is injected into the bloodstream. This procedure reveals the conditions of the blood vessels. It can be a dangerous and painful procedure and has been replaced by newer technologies.

The **CT scan** was developed in the early to mid-1980s and is based on the X-ray principle (see Figure 1.6). An X-ray beam is passed through the same area from many

X-ray
an imaging method in which radiation effects the density of different parts of the brain to various degrees, which then appear on the X-ray film

angiography
the use of radiopaque substances to allow visualization of blood vessels; it is considered a form of X-ray

computed tomography (CT) scan
a computer-assisted imaging process based on multiple X-ray images of the brain; it provides a three-dimensional perspective of the brain with clear differentiation of brain structures

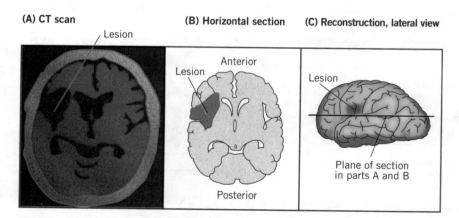

(A) CT scan   **(B) Horizontal section**   **(C) Reconstruction, lateral view**

FIGURE 1.6 Computed tomography. **(A)** Horizontal CT scan of a subject with Broca's aphasia. The region at the left is the location of the lesion. **(B)** A schematic representation of (A) with the area of the lesion shown in blue. **(C)** A reconstruction of the brain, showing a lateral view of the left hemisphere with the lesion shown in black. *Source:* Adapted from Kolb, B., & Whishaw, I. Q. (2009). *Fundamentals of Human Neuropsychology*, 6th ed. New York: Worth Publishers.

different angles thus creating many different images which may be combined using computer technology. The computer is able to produce a three-dimensional view of the three-dimensional brain, which had been lacking with previous technologies. Cerebrospinal fluid, brain tissue, blood, and hard tissue all appear as different shades on a CT scan and allow a much better view of diseased or dysfunctional areas. However, the CT scan does introduce radiation into the individual's system. A more advanced form of CT scan is termed an **enhanced CT** and involves injecting a contrast agent to provide better visualization of brain structures. The difficulties include that this procedure is more invasive and patients have been known to react poorly to the contrast agent.

Single photon emission tomography (SPECT) is similar to CT but is much simpler and inexpensive. Radiolabeled probes are injected into the patient. Tissues will absorb the probes as they circulate in the bloodstream. As the camera rotates around the patient, it picks up photon emissions and relays this information to a computer which converts the information into a film representation. The radiolabeled probes do not have to be synthesized but are commercially available. The pictures using this technique are less clear and it takes longer to get them than with PET. It is important to understand that SPECT does not provide views of brain structures but rather shows metabolic activity of various parts of the brain.

Dynamic Brain Imaging

Positron emission tomography (PET) was the first technique to follow the CT scan using a different form of technology (see Figure 1.7). It allows the researcher to determine the amount of a particular substance being used by a specific brain section. The substance is usually radioactive labeled glucose or oxygen, which is metabolized by the brain and the radioactivity is later recorded by a special detector. The PET scan measures metabolic activity of different brain regions with the idea that the more active regions will use more glucose. Positron emission tomography is the only procedure through which researchers can examine the cerebral glucose use and oxygen metabolism three dimensionally. Positron emission tomography has proven to be effective in the diagnosis of head trauma, brain tumors, and stroke through suppression of metabolic activity even when the brain structures appear normal using MRI or CT.

Magnetic resonance imaging (MRI) does not use radiation and for that reason has become favored over the CT scan. The MRI machine broadcasts a radio frequency (RF) pulse that specifically affects hydrogen atoms. This pulse is directed toward the area of the

single photon emission tomography (SPECT)
a technique that measures the emission of single photons of a given energy from radioactive probes; these emissions are used to construct images of the probes located within the body, thereby detailing the flow of blood in a given area

positron emission tomography (PET)
a technique used to visualize brain activity based on cerebral blood flow; it tracks the metabolism of glucose, oxygen, and/or neurotransmitters

magnetic resonance imaging (MRI)
a brain imaging technique requiring the use of magnetic fields; gives a clearer image than CT scan and is less dangerous because it does not use radiation

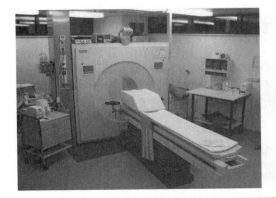
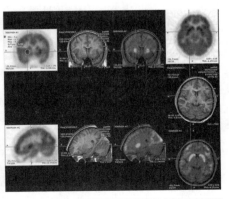

FIGURE 1.7 PET scanner and resultant images.

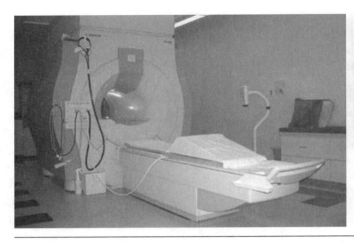
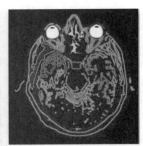

FIGURE 1.8 Magnetic resonance imaging. The subject is placed in a long metal cylinder that has two sets of magnetic coils arranged at right angles and a coil that surrounds the head. This coil perturbs the static magnetic fields to produce an image of a horizontal section through the head (right). *Source:* Courtesy of Intermountain Medical Imaging, Boise, Idaho.

body being examined. Some of the RF pulse's energy is captured by protons and alters their physical characteristics. The magnets of the machine alternate between being on and off and, during the period that the magnets are turned off, the energy absorbed by the protons is slowly released. This release of energy is observed by coils in the machine that send the signals to a computer for processing into a two-dimensional or three-dimensional picture (see Figure 1.8). The images garnered from the MRI are also much clearer than from CT scan. MRIs allow for a three-dimensional view of the brain. Individuals with loose metal imbedded in their bodies cannot have MRIs because the magnetic fields would move the body metal (e.g., heart pacemakers, etc.) However, metal, attached to live tissue, such as in the case of dental fillings, is allowable.

While MRI gives excellent pictures of the brain, it is often of interest to observe how the brain metabolizes or uses certain nutrients such as glucose or how oxygen is distributed. This is very important because the brain functions using these substances. It also is necessary to determine deficits when there is an obstruction of these nutrients. To accomplish this, a substance is injected into the circulation with a **tracer**, which can then be recorded via computer. A tracer is an inert substance used as a transport.

Neuronal activity changes are measured by fMRI, which accompanies changes in cerebral blood flow and blood oxygenation. Based on these, the researcher is able to infer the activity levels of various brain regions. The fMRI is an adaptation of an MRI scanner in such a manner as to allow detection of increased or decreased blood flow in particular areas of the brain. In comparison to SPECT, PET, and CT, fMRI does not involve radiation exposure.

Brain Stimulation

intracranial brain stimulation stimulation of brain tissue used in treatment of various central nervous system diseases, such as Parkinson's disease

Intracranial brain stimulation is the process through which actual brain tissue is stimulated. Early studies indicated that movements may be elicited by stimulating the motor cortex, sensations by stimulating the sensory cortex, and that disruption of cognitive activities such as speech may occur through stimulating the speech centers of the brain. Electrical brain simulation is used less as a diagnostic tool and more as an adjunct to various forms of treatment. Electrical brain stimulation has been very helpful in the treatment of Parkinson's disorder. The difficulty with this procedure is that it is invasive needing the skull to be opened to insert the electrode. This procedure is therefore used rarely and when other options may have failed.

Transcranial magnetic stimulation is a procedure in which the brain is able to be stimulated through the skull. The original use for this procedure was by neurosurgeons to stimulate brain tissues and monitor the condition during brain surgery. It has currently been used in a manner similar to intracranial brain stimulation as a treatment for various disorders. The advantage to this technique is that it is noninvasive.

transcranial magnetic stimulation
procedure in which the brain is stimulated through the skull

As can be seen, there are various techniques that can be used to investigate the structure and functioning of the brain. In Marvin's case, both CT and an MRI were used. The CT scan gave an overall view of the structures of his brain to determine as best and as clearly as possible the structures which were affected by the impact of the motor vehicle accident. The MRI with the use of contrast dye was able to further evaluate the use of oxygen and glucose by his brain and to determine if there were any impediments to its flow to the brain. The use of multiple techniques is often employed to correctly ascertain the difficulties the individual is experiencing.

Summary

The text and the first chapter began with a case study of an individual who sustained a closed head injury from a motor vehicle accident. Unfortunately, this is a fairly common difficulty with which the clinical neuropsychologist works. The case study also highlights many of the roles and functions which the clinical neuropsychologist performs and will be explored in the remainder of the text.

The chapter includes a brief history of the understanding of brain functioning throughout time. The time periods are divided not only by the historical events but also by the types of technology which occurred in various locales during various periods. The study of brain functioning is important because many of the historical issues remain as current concerns. However, in juxtaposition, many of the early themes of structure and function of the brain have been disproved.

The chapter also includes an introduction to the field of applied clinical neuropsychology and its place within the broader umbrella of clinical psychology. Techniques particular to research in clinical neuropsychology are discussed in this chapter. Also included are general research techniques, which are shared with experimental neuropsychology and imaging techniques shared with the multiple disciplines in the area of the neurosciences.

Questions for Further Study

1. Which questions are left unanswered regarding the functions of the brain? Explain the current theories regarding their functions.
2. Explain the changes that may have occurred in the role of the clinical neuropsychologist with the advent of advanced imaging techniques.
3. As best as you are able to speculate, what will be the strengths and weaknesses of the individual in the case study in 5 years and in 10 years? What types of assistance will he need, if any?

References

Akert, K., & Hammond, M. P. (1962). Emmanual Swedenborg (1688–1772) and his contributions to neurology. *Medical History, 6,* 255–266.

American Board of Clinical Neuropsychology. (2010). Retrieved July 11, 2010, from http://www.theabcn.org/abpp_diploma/index.html

American Psychiatric Association. (2000). *Diagnostic and statistical manual of mental disorders* (4th ed., text rev.). Washington, DC: Author.

American Psychological Association. (1989). Definition of a clinical neuropsychologist. *The Clinical Neuropsychologist, 3*(1), 22.

Beach, F. (1961). Karl Spencer Lashley: June 7, 1890–August 7, 1958. *Biographical Memoirs of the National Academy of Science, 36,* 162–204.

Beers, C. W. (1908). *A mind that found itself: An autobiography.* New York: Longmans, Green, and Co.

Bereczki, Z., & Marcsik, A. (2005). Trephined skulls from ancient populations in Hungary. *ACTA Medica Lituanica, 12*(1), 65–69.

Breasted, J. H. (1930). *The Edwin Smith Surgical Papyrus.* Chicago: The University of Chicago Press.

Buckingham, H. W. (2006). The Marc Dax (1770/1877)/Paul Broca (1824–1880) controversy over priority in science: Left hemisphere specificity for seat of articulate language and for lesions that cause aphemia. *Clinical Linguistics and Phonetics, 20*(7–8), 613–619.

Carlson, E. T. (1958). The influence of phrenology on early American psychiatric thoughts. *American Journal of Psychiatry, 115,* 535–538.

Edelstein, L. (1967). *Ancient medicine: Selected papers of Ludwig Edelstein.* Baltimore: Johns Hopkins University Press.

Executive Committee of APA. (1989). Definition of a clinical neuropsychologist: The following statement was adopted by the executive committee of division 40 at the APA meeting on August 12, 1988. *The Clinical Neuropsychologist, 3*(1), 22.

Finger, S. (1994). *Origins of neuroscience: A history of explorations into brain function.* New York: Oxford University Press.

Finger, S. (2000). *Minds behind the brain: A history of the pioneers and their discoveries.* New York: Oxford University Press.

Halstead, W. C. (1947). *Brain and intelligence: A quantitative study of the frontal lobes.* Chicago: University of Chicago Press.

Hebb, D. O. (1949). *The organization of behavior: A neuropsychological theory.* New York: John Wiley & Sons, Inc.

Idowu, O. E., Malomo, A. O., & Osuagwu, F. C. (2006). Lecciones de historia anatomia humana desde el origen hasta el renacimiento [Lessons from history: Human anatomy, from the origins to the Renaissance]. *International Journal of Morphology, 24*(1), 99–104.

Jones, D. A. J. (2003). The Hippocratic oath: Its contents and the limits to its adaptation. *Catholic Medical Quarterly, 54*(3).

Karenberg, A., & Hort, I. (1998). Medieval descriptions and doctrines of stroke: Preliminary analysis of select sources. Part II: Between Galenism and Aristotelism—Islamic theories of apolexy (800–1200). *Journal of the History of the Neurosciences, 7*(3), 174–185.

Kirk, G. S., Raven, J. E., & Schofield, M. (1995). *The presocratic philosophers: A critical history with a selection of texts* (2nd ed.). Cambridge, UK: Cambridge University Press.

Leca, A. P. (1981). *The Egyptian way of death: Mummies and the cult of the immortal.* Garden City, NY: Doubleday.

Lisowski, F. P. (1967). Prehistoric and early historic trepanation. In D. Brothwell & A. T. Sandison (Eds.), *Diseases in antiquity* (pp. 651–672). Springfield, IL: Charles C. Thomas.

Luria, A. R. (1966). *Higher cortical functions in man.* New York: Basic Books.

Meyer, A., & Hierons, R. (1964). A note on Thomas Willis' views on the corpus striatum and the internal capsule. *Journal of the Neurological Sciences, 1,* 547–554.

O'Connor, J. (2003). Thomas Willis and the background to Cerebri Anatome. *Royal Society of Medicine, 96*(3), 139–143.

O'Connor, D. C., & Walker, A. E. (Ed.). (1967). *A history of neurological surgery* (pp. 1–22). New York: Hafner.

Osler, W. (1913). Specialism in the general hospital. *John Hopkins Alumni Magazine.*

Raimy, V. C. (Ed.). (1950). *Training in clinical psychology.* Englewood Cliffs, NJ: Prentice Hall.

Roe, D., & Finger, S. (1997). Gustave Dax and his fight for recognition: An overlooked chapter in the early history of cerebral dominance. *Journal of the History of the Neurosciences, 5,* 228–240.

Sarton, G. (1927). *Introduction to the history of science.* Baltimore: Carnegie Institution of Washington.

Shallice, T. (1988). *From neuropsychology to mental structure.* New York: Cambridge University Press.

Stookey, B. (1963). Jean-Baptiste Bouillaud and Ernest Aubertin: Early studies in cerebral localization and the speech center. *Journal of the American Medical Association, 184,* 1024–1029.

Sweet, J., Moberg, P., & Suchy, Y. (2000). Ten-year follow-up survey of clinical neuropsychologists: Part II. Private practice and economics. *The Clinical Neuropsychologist, 14*(4), 479–495.

Tascioglu, A. O., & Tascioglu, A. B. (2005). Ventricular anatomy: Illustrations and concepts from antiquity to renaissance. *Neuroanatomy, 4,* 57–63.

Teuber, H. L. (1955). Physiological psychology. *Annual Review of Psychology, 6,* 267–296.

van der Kolk, B. A. (1997). The psychobiology of posttraumatic stress disorder. *Journal of Clinical Psychiatry, 58*(9), 16–24.

Verona, J. W. (2003). Trepanation in prehistoric South America: Geographic and temporal trends over 2,000 years. In R. Arnott, S. Finger, & C. U. M. Smith (Eds.), *Trepanation: History, discovery, theory* (pp. 223–236). Lisse, The Netherlands: Swets & Zeitlinger.

Wilkins, R. H. (1964). Edwin Smith surgical papyrus. *Journal of Neurosurgery, 5,* 240–244.

The Nervous System: Structure and Function

2

Key Terms

physical abuse
soma
nucleus
deoxyribonucleic acid (DNA)
chromosomes
cytoplasm
mitochondria
adenosine triphosphate (ATP)
endoplasmic reticulum (ER)
ribosomes
Golgi complex
lysosome
microtubules
lipid bilayer
dendrites
axons
axon hillock
action potential

sodium-potassium pump
myelin sheath
nodes of Ranvier
synapse
synaptic vesicles
neurotransmitters
electrochemical process
reuptake
degradation
central canal
cerebral ventricles
choroid plexus
blood-brain barrier
cerebral cortex
corpus callosum
frontal lobes
occipital lobes
temporal lobes

parietal lobes
hippocampus
limbic system
basal ganglia
thalamus
hypothalamus
pituitary gland
reticular activating system
pons
cerebellum
medulla
somatic nervous system
afferent nerves
efferent nerves
autonomic nervous system
sympathetic nerves
parasympathetic nerves

Learning Objectives

After reading this chapter, the student should be able to understand:

- The structure and function of the components parts of the neuron and how the neuron communicates as a part of the central nervous system
- The organization and functioning of the brain and its component structures and how they operate in conjunction with the spinal cord and peripheral nervous system
- The effects of behavioral, chemical, and other social prenatal and postnatal factors which may affect the central nervous system and the reasons these factors are important for development
- The aforementioned principles in relation to the work of the clinical neuropsychologist

Case Vignette

*S*herry is a 22-year-old disabled White female. She lives on her own, paying for expenses through Social Security disability payments. She is involved in a somewhat chaotic relationship. The difficulties in the relationship are due to the fact that she sometimes wants to be very close to her boyfriend and at other times wants to keep him at a distance. He takes various drugs on a recreational basis and sometimes offers them to Sherry. Dependent on her mood, she may take what is offered to her or she may decline. Recently they discovered that Sherry is pregnant. Sherry is aware that taking drugs and drinking alcohol are not good things to do while pregnant. However, at times when she feels stressed, these substances become her main coping mechanism.

Sherry is a high school graduate. She has recently tried to complete college courses but finds the college atmosphere too stressful for her. She stated that when there is an accumulation of people, such as in large lecture classes, it causes her a great deal of anxiety and often leads her to have flashbacks of her early life.

Sherry is the eldest of two children born to her biological parents. Beginning at the age of 4, she was sexually abused by various family members and others who had contact with her. Court records indicate that those individuals include her father, her uncle, her paternal grandfather and paternal grandmother, and a school bus driver. Her mother left the family when Sherry was 6 years old because of the chaotic atmosphere and the abusive situation. No one knows where Sherry's mother has relocated.

Sherry told her maternal grandmother about the abuse which led to involvement by social services. After an investigation, Sherry was removed from the home of her biological father and placed in foster care. From the time that she was 7 until she was of legal age she has resided in various types of facilities. There were short periods of time in which the county attempted to reunite her with her father and brother. Throughout all of the turmoil she has remained in contact with her brother and they have a relatively good relationship.

The prognosis for Sherry is guarded. She has had a long history of abuse which may have left her with brain impairment. After a thorough evaluation by a clinical neuropsychologist, the diagnosis, which has been applied to her symptoms, is posttraumatic stress disorder. Posttraumatic stress disorder has been shown often to lead to brain impairment. Sherry also exhibits symptoms but does not meet the complete criteria for borderline personality disorder. She has received a myriad of services ranging from residential treatment to individual therapy to work programs, *all geared toward helping her live on her own and function within society. Posttraumatic stress disorder is the diagnosis that allows her to collect Social Security disability payments.*

Sherry's remaining issues, addressed by her clinical neuropsychologist, stem from the chaotic emotional history she has experienced. She craves attention and often lacks the skills to evaluate the appropriateness of relationships. These issues may have led her to her current boyfriend and the circumstances leading to her pregnancy. Sherry is currently working with the clinical neuropsychologist to learn decision-making skills and to evaluate the short-term versus long-term consequences of her actions. These skills are very important while she is pregnant as she learns to manage stress while at the same time avoiding chemical use. These skills will also be advantageous after the birth of her child in learning appropriate parenting skills.

As we explore the nervous system and its development, keep Sherry and her baby in mind. Assuming that Sherry will be able to function at least to some extent in society, what becomes the fate of her child? Look carefully at what factors have already affected the baby's development. Also, consider the choices that were made once the baby's existence was known. The clinical neuropsychologist must take all of these factors into consideration as if the baby needed to be evaluated. The clinical neuropsychologist would consider not only the prenatal environment and behavioral factors but also the genetic backgrounds of both parents. Also postnatal parenting behaviors and the general environment in which the child is reared are crucial in its development.

Central Nervous System

Within the nervous system reside all of the structures and functions that make us truly human. We share many structures with other vertebrates and to some degree comparable functions, but it still remains that the human brain with its superior cortex separates us from the other vertebrates.

Included in this discussion of the nervous system will be a focus on prenatal factors, postnatal factors, and the many and varied neural structures and their functions, which develop into an intact adult. This voyage into the nervous system is essential for the clinical neuropsychologist. It would be very difficult to determine if a client's abilities were impaired unless the clinical neuropsychologist understood where that ability was localized and how it functioned in an intact individual. Sherry's baby is a case in point; if the baby were to need neuropsychological evaluation, the clinical neuropsychologist must understand normal development before he can determine whether an ability has become a disability.

Prenatal Development

EXTERNAL FACTORS

Prenatal development refers to all of the steps involved with the formation of the various structures and functions of the body and, for our purpose, specifically of the central nervous system. These structures and their functions will be discussed later in this chapter, but we will first look at some of the variables which can affect the proper development of this complex system. We begin by saying that it is crucial that many external factors are taken into consideration when looking at how a prenatal brain is developing. To begin, we will explore some of the most common complications involved with development which often occur due to the effects of parental decisions. For example, proper nutrition is critical for the development of an intact central nervous system. Many fetal difficulties such as low birth weight and smaller head circumference may be caused by malnutrition (Ramakrishnan, 2004). Improper nutrition may also lead to other physiological difficulties later in life such as obesity and problems in programming the appetite regulatory system correctly in the developing fetus (McMillen, Adam, & Mühlhäusler, 2005).

Abstaining from alcohol and other drugs, decreasing stress level, and avoiding physical or emotional abuse are also desirable for the proper formation of the central nervous system. Alcohol and various other drugs which cross the placental barrier can directly affect the fetus. **Fetal alcohol syndrome**, which can cause serious cognitive difficulties, is directly related to alcohol consumption. Stade, Stevens, Ungar, Beyene, and Koren (2006) evaluated fetal alcohol disorders in Canada and found that 1 out of every 300 live births was affected and that fetal alcohol disorders were the leading cause of neurologically based developmental disabilities among Canadian children and youth.

Many studies have explored stress levels and the effects that they may have on prenatal development. Some of these studies have shown that increased stress levels raise the amount of cortisol in the body (Dahlgren, Kecklund, Theorell, & Åkerstedt, 2009). **Cortisol** is a steroid hormone released by the adrenal cortex which elevates blood sugar and metabolism and helps the body adapt to prolonged stress. However, excess cortisol for too long a period of time may lead to the depression of the immune system and leave the individual vulnerable to various illnesses. Examples of illnesses that could affect a compromised immune system include pneumonia, bronchitis, or other serious systemic infections.

physical abuse
episodes of abusive behavior which result in physical injury to a person

Another area that could lead to developmental complications is **physical abuse**, both prenatally and postnatally. Severe physical abuse to the mother may lead to brain impairment in the baby especially if she is struck in the stomach. **Shaken baby syndrome** may result from physical abuse and can lead to traumatic brain injury. In cases of shaken baby syndrome, the infant is shaken so hard that his or her brain impacts the skull in a manner similar to the effects of a motor vehicle accident. The characteristic injuries observed in shaken baby syndrome include subdural hemorrhages, retinal hemorrhages, and fractures of the ribs or long bones (Altimier, 2008). **Emotional abuse** is a further form of abuse in which an individual is verbally made to feel bad about him- or herself and abilities. Emotional abuse to the mother may lead her to neglect herself and fail to care for her physical needs. Lack of care of the mother while pregnant could greatly affect the child and also cause neglect of any other children. All of these factors are extremely important as we begin to understand the development of the central nervous system.

Development of the Central Nervous System

As we begin our discussion of prenatal development, we will first explore the development of the structures which eventually become the central nervous system. Next, we will pursue the growth and differentiation of neurons, the smallest building blocks of the central nervous system. Terms that will be used in this section involve location of various structures and include **dorsal** (superior)—toward the back or toward the top of the brain; **ventral** (inferior)—toward the belly or the bottom of the brain; **rostral** (anterior)—toward the head; and **caudal** (posterior)—toward the rear or away from the head (see Figure 2.1).

When the sperm and egg unite, the process of cell division initiates very quickly. The period from the time of conception to approximately 2 weeks later when implantation in the uterine wall occurs is termed the **germinal period**. The developing cells are called a

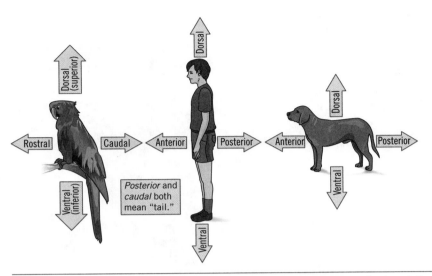

FIGURE 2.1 Spatial orientation terms. *Rostal* (beak), *caudal* (tail), *dorsal* (back), and *ventral* (stomach) parts of the brain are located toward those body parts. *Superior* and *inferior* may be used to refer to structures located dorsally or ventrally.

zygote. By the end of the 1st week, a mass of cells with a fluid center has formed which is called the **blastocyst**. The blastocyst enters the uterus and by the 11th–15th day following conception, the blastocyst implants on the uterine wall. The blastocyst consists of the inner tissue which will become the embryo, and the **trophoblast**, which will provide nutrition.

Once implantation occurs, it is now considered an **embryo**. The **embryonic stage** lasts until the end of the first trimester. The growth of cells is fairly rapid. The embryo then begins to differentiate into three distinct layers (see Figure 2.2). The **ectoderm** is the outermost of the three layers of the embryo which develops into the skin, sense organs, and nervous system. The **mesoderm** is the middle layer and becomes the muscles, blood, and excretory system. The **endoderm** is the innermost layer and becomes the digestive system, lungs, and other internal organs. In addition to the cell layers, the life support system for the embryo develops simultaneously. The **amnion** is a sack of fluid in which the embryo floats for temperature regulation and protection. The **umbilical cord** connects the embryo to the placenta. The **placenta** is a group of tissues in which blood vessels from the embryo and mother mix but do not join. Very small particles cross from the mother's blood to the embryo, such as water, salt, and oxygen, while carbon dioxide and waste from the baby return to the mother (University of Virginia Health System, 2006).

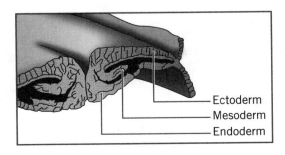

Ectoderm
Mesoderm
Endoderm

FIGURE 2.2 The three cell layers: ectoderm, mesoderm, and endoderm.

FIGURE 2.3 Formation of the neural tube in an embryo. A long depression, the neural groove, forms in the neural plate **(A)**. By Day 21, the neural groove is visible **(B)**. On Day 23, the neural tube forms **(C)** as the neural plate collapses inward.

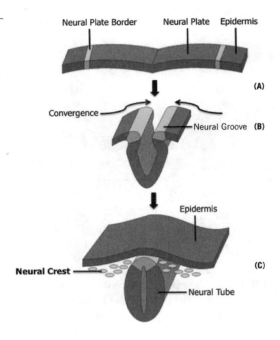

The next development is the beginning of the nervous system (see Figure 2.3). The first recognizable structure during nervous system development is the **neural plate** made up of ectodermal tissue on the dorsal surface of the developing embryo. The neural plate begins to become evident at approximately 3 weeks of age and appears to be induced by signals from the mesoderm layer (Fair & Schlagger, 2008). At the time the neural plate becomes evident the cells are **totipotent** or able to become any cell in the body. As the neural plate develops, the cells begin to lose their ability to form into any type of tissue making them specific to central nervous system development.

As time progresses, the neural plate folds to form the **neural groove**. The lips of the neural groove fuse to form the **neural tube** by approximately the 24th day after conception. The inside of the neural tube becomes the spinal canal and the cerebral ventricles. The swellings at the end of the neural tube develop into the forebrain, **midbrain**, and **hindbrain**.

The central nervous system changes greatly in the first 7 weeks of development. By the end of these 7 weeks, the embryo is referred to as the **fetus** which has begun to resemble a more human shape. Although it appears to be a very short period of time, the brain is almost a complete replica of the adult brain at approximately 100 days from the time of conception, although the structures are not completely developed.

The **neural crest** is dorsal to the neural tube. It is formed from cells that differentiate from the neural tube as it is being formed. Neural crest cells develop into the neurons and glial cells of the peripheral nervous system. Glial cells appear in many parts of the body as development continues. They colonize at specific locations such as the gastrointestinal tract where they help to continue formation of both the central nervous system and the peripheral nervous system (Anderson, Newgreen, & Young, 2006).

Prenatal Neuronal Development

In order to understand how the neuron functions as the basic building block of the central nervous system, we will first need to have an intimate understanding of how the neuron develops. Most researchers divide the process into several stages: induction, proliferation (neurogenesis), migration and aggregation, differentiation, axonal growth and synaptic formation (maturation), programmed cell death (apoptosis), and synaptic rearrangement.

The process of **induction** begins when part of the ectoderm becomes the nervous system. This occurs during the development of the neural plate. As stated previously, cells at this point are described as totipotent. Another name for these cells is multipotent because the embryonic neural crest tissue tends to give rise to many cells that are highly specific later in the adult's life, a unique quality of vertebrates (Teng & Labosky, 2006). In modern neuropsychology these cells are most commonly termed **stem cells**, because they are able to develop into different types of cells and have an almost unlimited capacity for self-renewal. This is very important when discussing the fact that as these stages progress the cells become more specific which leads to more specialized cell function (Trentin, Glavieux-Pardanaud, Le Douarin, & Dupin, 2004). **Proliferation** is a term used to describe a time of immense cellular division, which occurs once the neural tube is formed. It is also termed *neurogenesis* because it is the beginning of the development of neurons and occurs for the first 5 months of gestation. **Cell migration** begins after the first neurons are developed and continues several weeks after neurogenesis is complete. As these cells migrate to their appropriate place, they follow chemical pathways that help to lead them to the correct area or location (Marín & Rubenstein, 2001). Once cells have migrated, they begin to **aggregate**; that is, they move toward other cells that have migrated to a similar area to form nervous system structures. After aggregation comes a time of axonal, dendritic, and synaptic formation also called **maturation**. Some axonal growth takes place while the cell is migrating, with the early cell often looking as though it has a rudimentary tail. These structures then develop along with other features of the neuron when they reach the location where they will take on a specific role.

When the primitive neuron reaches its specific location, the process of maturation will give the neuron all of its distinguishing features. The axon (the sending end of the neuron), if it has not already started to form, will do so upon arrival at the appropriate site. Also, the dendrites (the receiving end of the neuron) will also show signs of growth. Once axons have reached their intended sites, they develop synapses with the appropriate surrounding neurons. A single neuron can grow an axon but it takes two neurons and their coordinated effort to create a synapse (Yuste & Bonhoeffer, 2004). The formation of new synapses is termed **synaptogenesis**. This is a process that is carried out throughout life, although most heavily during the early periods of development. Because these distinct areas develop at different times, some neurons begin to develop axons before they have any other neurons or muscle tissues with which to link. However, not all primitive neurons will go on to form these bonds. Bonding depends very specifically on the levels of nerve growth factor, which has been shown to promote the survival and growth of a neuron. Nerve growth factor has been found to be released by organs with which the neuron has begun to form a synapse. If a neuron does not receive nerve growth factor or does not bond correctly to receive this factor, the neuron will begin the preprogrammed process of nerve cell death (**apoptosis**) and degeneration after a certain time. After death, the space that is left on the postsynaptic membrane is filled by sprouting axons of living neurons. This leads to a massive rearrangement of synaptic connections.

At the 12th week, the brain starts to assume more of a concrete model of the adult brain. Some of the most noticeable characteristics that can be found include the **ventricles**, which have developed their characteristic butterfly shape. Even more evident are all of the major subdivisions of the brain that now appear: **telencephalon, diencephalon, mesencephalon, metencephalon,** and **myelencephalon** (see Figure 2.4). The functions of these structures will be covered later in this chapter.

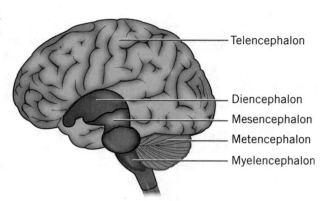

FIGURE 2.4 Early structures of the brain: telencephalon, diencephalon, mesencephalon, metencephalon, and myelencephalon.

Telencephalon

Diencephalon
Mesencephalon
Metencephalon
Myelencephalon

soma
the cell body that contains all of the organelles

nucleus
the center of the neuron containing DNA

deoxyribonucleic acid (DNA)
the genetic code of the human being

chromosomes
the human has 23 pairs of chromosomes; they contain strands of genes that contain DNA

At this point in our discussion of neural development we begin to wonder about the fate of Sherry's baby. When the mother found out she was pregnant, what actions did she take? How did her choices in behaviors affect her baby's development? What other variables affect the baby's development? How does the pregnancy affect the relationship between Sherry and her boyfriend? These questions come to mind specifically as we look at prenatal development. However, they also will concern us as we learn more about the structures and functions of the neuron and eventually the entire central nervous system, and ultimately, the fate of the baby considering the behaviors of the two parents.

The Neuron

The building blocks of the central nervous system are the neurons. As Carl Sagan (1934–1996) was apt to say during his television interviews: "There are billions and billions of stars in the galaxy" (Sagan & Druyan, 1997). The same is true of our brains and the neurons in the central nervous system. The actual number is highly debated, but it is estimated that there is somewhere on the order of 10^{11} to 10^{24} neurons at any given time functioning in our nervous system (Weiss, 2000). At birth, it is estimated that a baby may have as many as 100 billion neurons (Fair & Schlagger, 2008).

Structure of the Neuron
Neurons are special cells that accomplish a task that few other cells are capable of doing in an efficient manner. Neurons are the main cells in the body that specialize in communicating with one another or with muscles, glands, or other tissues.

Neurons may be of many different sizes and shapes, but all contain the same inner structures. These structures are similar to those that reside in most other cells. The cell body or **soma** is the area where neurons assemble proteins, generate energy, and maintain metabolism. Various **organelles** reside in the soma, where they have their own specific tasks and functions, and are also covered in a specific membrane.

Organelles of the cell body are created and given instructions in almost the exact same fashion as any other cell in the body. The **nucleus** of the neuron contains **deoxyribonucleic acid (DNA)**, the genetic code of the human being. If neurons are the building blocks of the central nervous system, DNA would be considered the building blocks of life. Each strand of DNA is composed of **chromosomes**, which are long strands of **nucleotides** that are paired together (see Figure 2.5). When these nucleotides form sequences, they

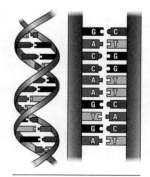

FIGURE 2.5 Graphic of DNA double helix.

make up the components of genes. Each gene carries instructions that can be added to other genes in the DNA segment to synthesize a specific protein necessary to bind with other proteins and finally form organelles. From there, the neuron is given structure and function as defined by the DNA and organelles.

The remainder of the cell is made up of **cytoplasm**, which is the clear, semigelatinous internal fluid of the cell that helps to hold all of the other organelles in place and gives the cell a definite shape. **Mitochondria** reside within the cell body and are the sites of energy production; sometimes they are referred to as the power plant inside of the cell. Within the mitochondria, fats, sugars, and proteins from food react with oxygen to produce **adenosine triphosphate (ATP)**. ATP is the fundamental source of energy for all cells including the neuron. ATP consists of adenosine bound to ribose and three phosphate groups (PO_3). Phosphates form high-energy covalent bonds. A great deal of energy is needed to form the bonds and a great deal of energy is released when they break. ATP can break off one or two of its three phosphates to provide energy. The cycle in which ATP is produced is termed the **Krebs cycle** after its discoverer Hans Krebs (1900–1981; see Figure 2.6).

Now that we have an understanding of where and how the energy to run the cell is produced, we will look at other important organelles (see Figure 2.7). The **endoplasmic reticulum (ER)** on appearance resembles a system of spherically shaped membranous sacs. The ER is composed of two areas, the smooth ER and the rough ER. The smooth ER, which does not contain ribosomes, is important for the synthesis and production of lipids that are used in carbohydrate metabolism. The smooth ER is also involved in the detoxification of the cell from drugs and poisons (Cooper & Hausman, 2009). The rough ER receives its name from the rough or lumpy looking appearance that occurs because of the presence of ribosomes. **Ribosomes** are the structures inside of the rough ER which take in materials and synthesize proteins. From this point, the proteins are carried either to different areas of the cell where they are needed or to the Golgi apparatus for further modification. The **Golgi complex** is a system of membranes that package molecules into vesicles or can also modify the molecules further. These vesicles can then travel anywhere they are needed in a cell or can also be transported out of the cell if need be. Another very important cellular organelle is the **lysosome**. This organelle provides the neuron with an advanced yet fairly simple recycling process. The purpose of this organelle is to take in dangerous bacteria, viruses, and old or damaged organelles and break them down into proteins so that they can be reused by the cell to build new organelles and structures. The roles of the **microtubules** are a means for quick transport of materials within the neuron or cell as well as maintaining cellular structural support. Microtubules aid in both transportation and ensuring the cell or neuron maintains its integrity.

cytoplasm
the internal fluid that holds organelles in place within the cell

mitochondria
the organelle that is the site of energy production for cells

adenosine triphosphate (ATP)
the energy source for neurons and other cells; ATP consists of adenosine bound to ribose and three phosphate groups

endoplasmic reticulum (ER)
a network of tubules within a cell that transports synthesized lipids and membrane proteins to other locales

ribosome
a structure within the rough endoplasmic reticulum that synthesizes proteins

Golgi complex
a system of membranes that package molecules into vesicles

lysosome
a cellular organelle that contains digestive enzymes and provides the neuron help in recycling and reusing materials

microtubules
the tubules that quickly transport materials within the neuron

FIGURE 2.6 The Krebs cycle. Energy in the form of ATP is transported through the cell membrane from one part of the body to another.

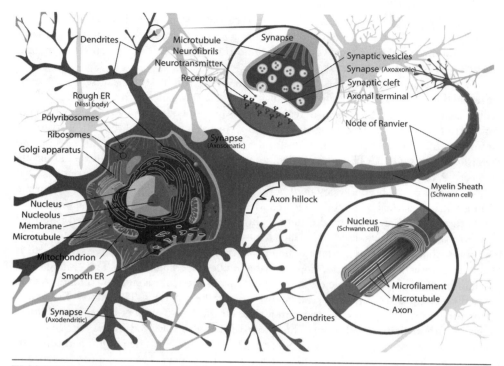

FIGURE 2.7 Typical nerve cell. This view inside a neuron reveals its organelles and other internal components.

As described earlier, DNA is the genetic code for humans and other organisms. Information coded in the DNA is transcribed as **messenger RNA**. **Transcription** is the synthesis of RNA from a DNA template (see Figure 2.8). This is accomplished through RNA polymerase (an enzyme) basically unzipping the DNA helix and reading one half of the DNA strand while concurrently building the same strand to match the strand

FIGURE 2.8 DNA replication. As the two strands of the original DNA molecule unwind, the nucleotide bases on each strand attract loose complementary bases. Once the unwinding is complete, two DNA molecules, each identical to the first, will have been created.

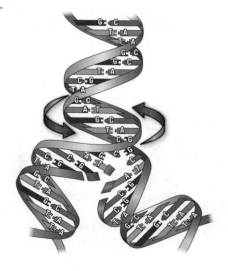

being transcribed. When this process is done, the new RNA strand breaks away from the mother DNA molecule and is carried elsewhere for further use. RNA is similar to DNA except that it contains the nucleotide base uracil instead of thymine and has a phosphate and ribose backbone instead of a phosphate and deoxyribose backbone. The structure of transcribed RNA is called messenger RNA because it carries the genetic code from the nucleus of the cell. Messenger RNA exits through small pores in the nuclear membrane and enters the cytoplasm. At the ribosomes on the rough ER the messenger RNA is transcribed into proteins. These proteins are then transferred to the Golgi complex in transport vesicles where further processing occurs and are packaged into lysosomes, peroxisomes, or secretory vesicles.

With a basic understanding of the organelles within the interior of the neuron and their function, we will now explore the exterior of the neuron in more depth. Neurons are covered by a cell membrane composed of a **lipid bilayer**, essentially two layers of fat (see Figure 2.9). Protein molecules are embedded in this bilayer and form the basis for the cell membrane's functions. This bilayer is made up of a hydrophilic exterior (attracting water) and hydrophobic interior (repelling water). This gives it polarity and allows the cell to be selectively permeable to different substances. Parts of the membrane contain **channel proteins** through which certain molecules may pass, allowing needed nutrients and ions into the cell. Other parts of the membrane contain **signal proteins**, which transfer a signal to the inside of the neuron when particular molecules bind to them on the outside of the membrane. The cell membrane covers the cell body or soma, with the main task of protecting and providing enclosure to the entire cell, somewhat similar to our skin.

lipid bilayer
a membrane that covers the neuron and is made of two layers of fat; it allows selective permeability to certain substances

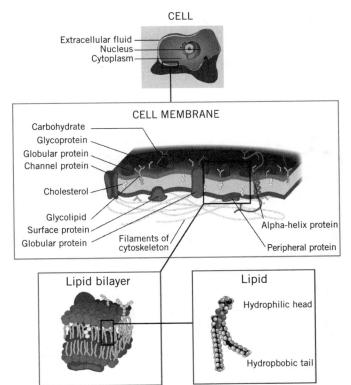

CELL

Extracellular fluid
Nucleus
Cytoplasm

CELL MEMBRANE

Carbohydrate
Glycoprotein
Globular protein
Channel protein

Cholesterol

Glycolipid
Surface protein
Globular protein

Filaments of cytoskeleton

Alpha-helix protein

Peripheral protein

Lipid bilayer

Lipid

Hydrophilic head

Hydropbobic tail

FIGURE 2.9 Structure of the cell membrane.

The next areas to be examined are the particular features of the neuron that are specifically involved with the communication and transmission of signals to other cells (see Figure 2.10). The point at which a neuron first receives a signal from another neuron is where the dendrites are located. **Dendrites** are relatively short, treelike structures, which receive information and bring it to the soma. A neuron may have many dendrites that branch out to other neurons and act as message receivers bringing in multitudes of chemical and electrical information. From there, the primary task is to relay an electrical message to the soma. Dendritic branches are also divided into segments, which are called orders. These orders are named based on their locations in relation to the soma. The locations that are closest to the soma are denoted as first order, those that branch from the first order are known as second order, and so on. On the opposite end of the cell is the axon. Axons send information from the soma to the presynaptic terminal. Signals traveling through the axon generally travel in one direction, starting at the soma. In rare instances, the information may flow in the reverse direction. While a neuron may have many dendrites to receive information, there is almost always only one axon per neuron. However, the axon may have many branches, which, in most cases, leave the axon some distance from the cell body. Axons can also be of various lengths depending on their placement and function, ranging from a few millimeters to a meter.

The **axon hillock** resides at the junction of the soma and the axon. It is at this point where an impulse or signal is determined to be strong enough to be sent down the axon and on to the next cell. If the sum of the **depolarization** and **hyperpolarization** reaching this section of the axon is sufficient to depolarize the membrane to a level called the **threshold of excitation**, then an **action potential** is generated (see Figure 2.11). In a sense, the axon hillock is receiving mixed messages and has to sort out which message is the strongest. The **all-or-nothing principle** applies here: either the signal is strong enough to produce an action potential or it dissipates. While the aforementioned point at the axon hillock has long been thought to be the origin for the action potential, recent research has questioned whether a spot adjacent to the axon hillock might be the actual origination of the impulse (Pinel, 2006, p. 81).

dendrites
the structures that receive information and send it to the body of the neuron

axon
the structure that sends information from the cell body of the neuron to the synapse

axon hillock
the structure on the body of the axon that determines whether an impulse is strong enough to cause an action potential

action potential
the massive momentary reversal of the membrane potential from −70 to +50 mV; it is synonymous with the firing of the neuron

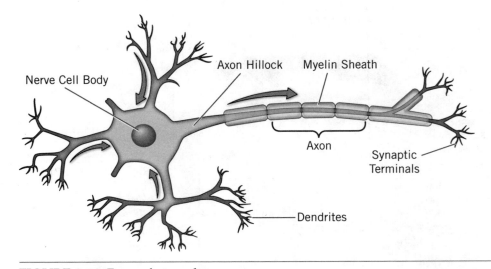

FIGURE 2.10 External view of neuron.

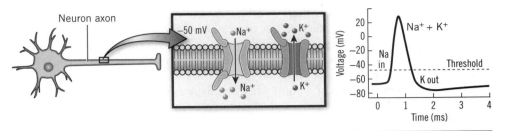

FIGURE 2.11 Triggering an action potential. The combined influx of sodium ions (Na^+) and efflux of potassium ions (K^+) results in an action potential that consists of the summed voltage changes due to Na^+ and K^+.

In the **resting state**, without any stimulation, the electrical charge within the neuron is -70 mV. At this point, the neuron is polarized. During the resting state, the concentration of the sodium ions (Na^+) and chloride ions (Cl^-) are greater outside the neuron than inside, while the potassium (K^+) ions are more concentrated on the inside. The mechanism that transports Na^+ ions out of the neuron and K^+ ions into the neuron is referred to as **sodium–potassium pumps** (see Figure 2.12). The pumps are membrane-embedded protein mechanisms which use the majority of ATP produced by the neuron to propagate the ion flow.

The action potential is a massive momentary reversal of the membrane polarization from -70 to $+50$ mV. The two processes which aid the generation of the action potential are diffusion and the concentration gradient. **Diffusion** is the tendency of molecules to move from areas of high concentration to areas of low concentration. The **concentration gradient** is the attraction of a region of high levels of molecules to an area of low concentration.

sodium–potassium pump functions to maintain the cell potential; it pumps sodium ions out of the cell and potassium ions into the cell by active transport

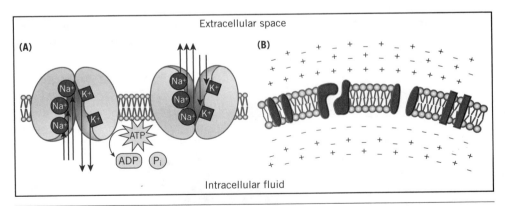

FIGURE 2.12 (A) Sodium–potassium pumps preserve the cell's resting potential by maintaining a larger concentration of potassium (squares) inside the cell and sodium (circles) outside the cell. The pumps use ATP as energy. **(B)** The cell membrane's selective permeability and the concentration gradients formed by active pumping lead to a difference in electrical potential across the membrane called the resting membrane potential.

After this has taken place, there is a brief period of time (1–2 milliseconds) in which it is impossible for another action potential to take place. This brief period is called the **absolute refractory period**. In a sense, the neuron must return to its initial resting potential and reset itself before it can fire again. There is also a **relative refractory period** when the neuron can respond to a series of impulses which have a greater depolarization charge. This is at a point when the neuron has started to repolarize, but has not yet reached its resting potential; therefore, it requires a very large stimulus or series of stimuli.

Looking at the axon more in depth, we find small oval-shaped bands which encircle the axon and appear as if they were made up of a fatty substance. Taken together these fatty ovals are known as the **myelin sheath**. Myelin is produced by **oligodendrocytes** in the central nervous system and by **Schwann cells** in the peripheral nervous system. Schwann cells are the only cells capable of guiding axonal regeneration. Therefore, in the human, axonal regrowth occurs only in the peripheral nervous system. The myelin sheath speeds conduction of impulses and provides insulation to the axon similar to an electrical wire. Along the axon are gaps where myelin does not exist. The gaps are termed the **nodes of Ranvier** (see Figure 2.13). The gaps further aid in transmission and allow the impulse to skip or jump along the length of the axon. The electrical movement of the action potential along the nodes of Ranvier is termed **saltatory conduction**. Jumping between nodes allows for much faster conduction than waiting for an action potential to build up along the axon (Catterall, 1984).

At the end of the axon is a gap between neurons. This gap is referred to by many different names. It can be referred to as a **synapse**, a synaptic cleft, a synaptic gap, or synaptic junction but they all carry the same meaning (see Figure 2.14). At the end of the axon projecting into the synaptic gap are **synaptic vesicles** or boutons. Neurotransmitters are contained inside the boutons. **Neurotransmitters** are proteins which have been packaged and stored by Golgi bodies in a series of vesicles infused by microtubules to gather at the terminal ends of the axon. The vesicles gather together to await an action potential. Often the neurotransmitters are located next to **active zones**, which are areas of protein accumulation in the membrane that allow the vesicles to deposit their contents into the synapse.

At the time of release of neurotransmitters the process goes from an electrical to an **electrochemical process**. Information received from adjacent cells is received by the dendrite. This information is passed through the soma and down the axon to the

---

myelin sheath
the fatty substance that covers the axon and speeds conduction

nodes of Ranvier
the gaps in the myelin sheath that speed axonal conduction

synapse
the junction across which a nerve impulse passes from an axon terminal to a neuron, muscle cell, or gland

synaptic vesicles
structures that store neurotransmitters; the vesicles release the neurotransmitters into the synaptic cleft when a nerve impulse reaches the synaptic cleft

neurotransmitters
a chemical that is released at the terminal ends of the axon; their function is to excite or inhibit the postsynaptic cell

electrochemical process
as the action potential travels down the axon, it is electrical, whereas, the release of neurotransmitters at the synapse is chemical

---

FIGURE 2.13 Myelination. An axon is insulated by **(A)** oligodendroglia in the central nervous system and **(B)** Schwann cells in the peripheral nervous system. Each glial cell is separated by a gap, or node of Ranvier.

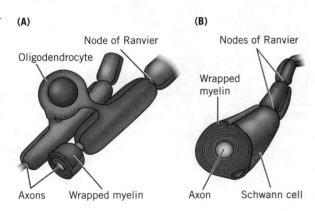

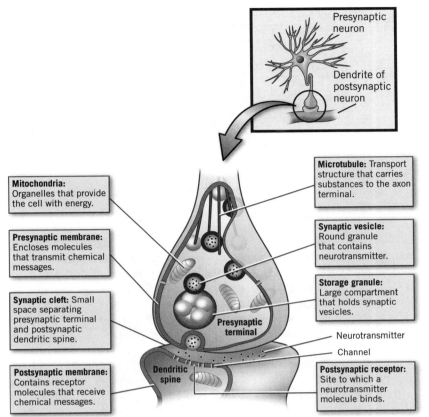

FIGURE 2.14 Characteristic parts of a synapse. Storage granules hold vesicles containing neurotransmitters that, when released, travel to the presynaptic membrane. They are expelled into the synaptic cleft through exocytosis, cross the cleft, and bind to receptor proteins on the postsynaptic membrane.

Presynaptic neuron

Dendrite of postsynaptic neuron

Mitochondria: Organelles that provide the cell with energy.

Presynaptic membrane: Encloses molecules that transmit chemical messages.

Synaptic cleft: Small space separating presynaptic terminal and postsynaptic dendritic spine.

Postsynaptic membrane: Contains receptor molecules that receive chemical messages.

Microtubule: Transport structure that carries substances to the axon terminal.

Synaptic vesicle: Round granule that contains neurotransmitter.

Storage granule: Large compartment that holds synaptic vesicles.

Presynaptic terminal

Neurotransmitter

Channel

Postsynaptic receptor: Site to which a neurotransmitter molecule binds.

Dendritic spine

synaptic vesicles and is electrical. When the neurotransmitter is released, it becomes a chemical process.

Currently, there are approximately 100 or more neurotransmitters which have been discovered (Hyman, 2005). The original discovery of neurotransmitters came through the work of Otto Loewi (1873–1963) and Henry Dale (1875–1968). These two individuals shared a Nobel Prize in 1936 for their discoveries relating to chemical transmission of nerve impulses (Lambert & Kinsley, 2005). Each neurotransmitter can be categorized as either excitatory or inhibitory in relation to its effect on the adjacent neurons. An **excitatory neurotransmitter** increases the likelihood of an action potential in the postsynaptic neuron. An **inhibitory neurotransmitter** decreases the likelihood of an action potential in the postsynaptic neuron. The brain's most frequently occurring excitatory neurotransmitter is glutamate, while the most frequently occurring inhibitory neurotransmitter is gamma-aminobutyric acid (GABA). Other very common neurotransmitters related to mood and cognitive states to be described later include acetylcholine, norepinephrine, epinephrine, dopamine, and serotonin. Each one of these neurotransmitters has a different function and many work together to give a coordinated effect. An example of neurotransmitters working together would be the depletion of norepinephrine and serotonin in depression and the increase of these neurotransmitters by the use of antidepressant medications such as fluoxetine (Prozac), which is a selective serotonin reuptake inhibitor (SSRI).

FIGURE 2.15 Exocytosis.

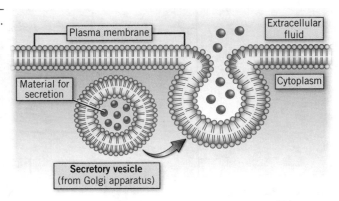

The process of neurotransmitter release is termed **exocytosis** (see Figure 2.15). Small neurotransmitters, when excited by action potentials, open **voltage-gated calcium channels**. These are released as pulses each time an action potential triggers an influx of calcium ions. **Peptide** neurotransmitters (chains of amino acids) are gradually released in response to general increase of intracellular Ca^{2+} ions. After being released, the neurotransmitters send a signal by binding to receptors in the postsynaptic membrane. Each receptor is a protein that has binding sites for certain neurotransmitters. A molecule that binds to another is referred to as its **ligand**.

The different types of receptors to which a particular neurotransmitter can bind are referred to as receptor subtypes (see Figure 2.16). **Ionotropic receptors** are those that are associated with ligand-activated ion channels. When a neurotransmitter binds to one of these channels, the associated channel opens immediately producing a postsynaptic potential. **Metabotropic receptors** are those that are associated with signal proteins and **G proteins**. These receptors are more prevalent than the ionotropic and their effects are slower, longer lasting, more diffuse, and more varied. The metabotropic receptor is attached to a portion of the signal protein outside the neuron. The G protein is attached to a portion of the signal protein inside the neuron.

FIGURE 2.16
Ionotropic and
metabotropic receptors.

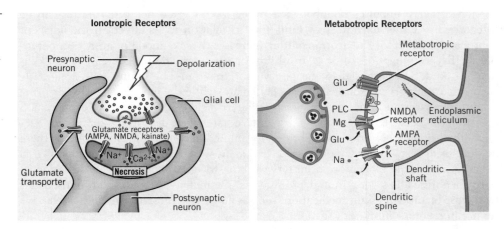

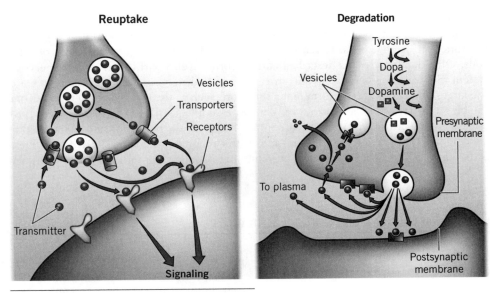

FIGURE 2.17 Reuptake and degradation.

Autoreceptors are neurotransmitter receptors that are located in the presynaptic cell and control the neurotransmitter release by the presynaptic axon. The function of autoreceptors is to regulate and monitor the amount of neurotransmitters in the synapse. This is important in relation to maintaining proper bodily homeostasis and function, both of which will be affected if there are too many or not enough neurotransmitters to signal the need for certain processes to take place.

When the neurotransmitter has been released something needs to happen to prevent the neurotransmitters from remaining active at the synapse. Neurotransmitters accumulating in the synapse could present a dangerous or potentially life-threatening problem depending upon the neurotransmitter involved. For example, theoretically too much dopamine in the synapse could trigger the delusions and hallucinations characteristic of schizophrenia.

There are two processes or events that the human body uses to remove excess neurotransmitters from the synapse. **Reuptake** is the more common process and involves the neurotransmitters being drawn back into the presynaptic bouton (see Figure 2.17). The process is analogous to a vacuum cleaner. **Degradation** is the process in which neurotransmitters are broken apart within the synapse by enzymes. The enzymes are proteins that stimulate or inhibit biochemical reactions without being affected by them.

reuptake
the return of excess neurotransmitter into the presynaptic axon

degradation
the process by which neurotransmitters are chemically broken apart by enzymes within the synapse

Glial Cells

Neurons are not the only cells that play an important role in the nervous system. Glial cells, which we have mentioned earlier, are more abundant than neurons in the central nervous system. Their role has often been thought to be supportive of the neuron's

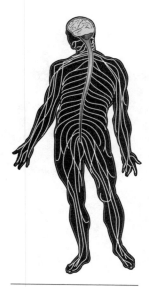

FIGURE 2.18 The human central nervous system and peripheral nervous system.

central canal
traverses the length of the spinal column and contains cerebrospinal fluid

cerebral ventricles
a system of four communicating cavities within the brain that are contiguous with the central canal of the spine; they contain cerebrospinal fluid

functioning, but recently increased research has begun on glial cells to study their role in brain functioning. Current research has already expanded what we know regarding the function of glial cells. Researchers have found that there are four types of glial cells. Oligodendrocytes, as described earlier, form myelin within the central nervous system. Schwann cells form myelin in the peripheral nervous system. **Astrocytes** are the largest glial cells and perform many functions such as the passage of chemicals from the blood into the central nervous system. For example, astrocytes have been shown to release chemical transmitters which contain receptors for neurotransmitters and conduct signals that participate in neurotransmitter reuptake (Haydon, 2001; Oliet, Piet, & Poulain, 2001). **Microglia** work by removing cellular debris in the cases of injury or disease.

Central Nervous System: Cortical Structures

Now that we understand the structures and the function of the organelles of the neuron, we are ready to move on to larger structures. The central nervous system is divided into the brain and the spinal cord (see Figure 2.18). The brain is divided into two hemispheres. The right hemisphere of the brain controls the motor and sensory functions of the left side of the body; the left hemisphere of the brain controls the right. This arrangement was first noted and described by Hippocrates almost 2,400 years ago.

The brain is contained within the skull for protection. Inside of the skull the brain is covered by several layers termed **meninges**, with each layer serving to protect and cushion the brain (see Figure 2.19). The outermost layer is referred to as the **dura mater**. The second layer just under the dura mater is the **arachnoid layer**. Underneath the arachnoid layer is a space called the **subarachnoid space**, which contains **cerebrospinal fluid** (CSF) and large blood vessels. The layer closest to the brain is called the **pia mater**, which essentially clings to the brain. Again, the aforementioned layers function to protect the brain.

Cerebrospinal fluid is a clear waterlike fluid which cushions and supports the brain. Cerebrospinal fluid fills the subarachnoid space, the central canal of the spinal cord, and the cerebral ventricles, and also acts as a protective fluid. The central canal runs the length of the spinal cord and the CSF also serves to cushion the vertebrae. The cerebral ventricles are four large enclosures in the brain which give a characteristic butterfly shape on a brain scan (see Figure 2.20). The cerebral ventricles consist of two lateral ventricles, the third ventricle, and the fourth ventricle all connected to one another. The ventricles are also connected to the central canal and subarachnoid spaces.

FIGURE 2.19 Cerebral security. A triple-layered covering, the meninges, encases the brain and spinal cord, and the cerebrospinal fluid cushions them.

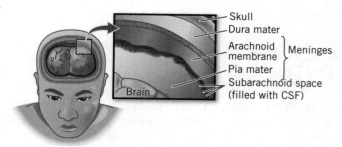

- Skull
- Dura mater
- Arachnoid membrane } Meninges
- Pia mater
- Subarachnoid space (filled with CSF)

Brain

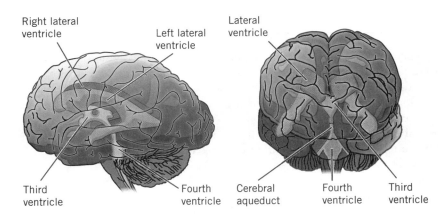

Right lateral ventricle

Left lateral ventricle

Lateral ventricle

Third ventricle

Fourth ventricle

Cerebral aqueduct

Fourth ventricle

Third ventricle

FIGURE 2.20 Cerebral ventricles. The four ventricles are interconnected. The lateral ventricles are symmetrical, one in each hemisphere. The third and fourth cerebral ventricles lie in the brain's midline and drain into the cerebral aqueduct that runs the length of the spinal cord.

Cerebrospinal fluid is produced by a group of capillaries which resemble a meshlike structure called the **choroid plexus** contained within the ventricles. The excess CSF flows through the ventricles and around the superior sagittal crest and eventually drains into blood-filled spaces which run throughout the dura mater and then drain into the large jugular veins of the neck.

While the CSF cradles the brain, another mechanism keeps toxic chemicals from entering the brain. The **blood-brain barrier** is composed of the compacted cells that generally make up the walls of blood vessels (see Figure 2.21). Being so tightly packed, they make up a barrier that is impervious to most compounds except the nutrients that the brain requires. The blood-brain barrier differs from blood cells in other parts of the body which are not as tightly packed and do not form any kind of protective barrier against foreign substances. While the blood-brain barrier does not permit the introduction of proteins and other large molecules into the brain, there are a few exceptions such as glucose which is actively transported across the barrier and oxygen because they are required for normal brain function. Sex hormones are large molecules but are allowed passage into certain areas of the brain.

choroid plexuses
a group of capillaries that produce cerebrospinal fluid

blood-brain barrier
a group of compacted cells that are so tightly bound together they keep toxic substances out of the brain

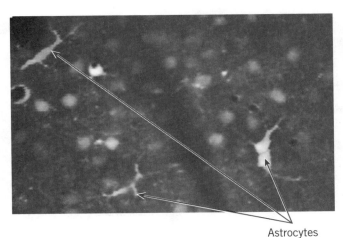

Astrocytes

FIGURE 2.21 Astrocytes attach to neurons and blood vessels to provide support among different structures in the brain; stimulate the cells on blood vessels to form tight junctions forming the blood-brain barrier; and transport chemicals excreted by neurons to blood vessels.

The Brain

The brain is composed of five major divisions (see Figure 2.22). The divisions are evident during prenatal development and continue to develop over time until at birth we have telencephalon, diencephalon, mesencephalon, metencephalon, and myelencephalon. The telencephalon consists of the cerebral hemispheres; the other four divisions may be collectively termed the *brain stem.*

cerebral cortex
the convoluted surface layer of gray matter of the cerebrum that controls the coordination of sensory and motor information

The **cerebral cortex** covers the cerebral hemispheres, right and left, which are contained within the telencephalon. The cortex contains much more surface area than is apparent because of the sulci and gyri (see Figure 2.23). The large furrows are known as **fissures** and the somewhat smaller ones are known as **sulci**. The ridges between the fissures and sulci are the **gyri**. These structures give the cortex the appearance of a topographical map. The central fissure and the lateral fissure on the lateral surface of each hemisphere divide the hemisphere into four lobes: frontal, occipital, temporal, and parietal. The largest gyri include the precentral gyrus which contains the motor cortex, the postcentral gyrus which contains somatosensory center, and the superior temporal gyrus which contains the auditory cortex.

The two hemispheres of the brain are roughly mirror images of one another. The symmetrical appearance is due to the fact that many structures are symmetrical and/or represented within each side of the brain. As stated previously, the left hemisphere controls the right side of the body and the right hemisphere controls the left side of the body. This relationship becomes very apparent in the case of an individual who has had a stroke. The most common scenario is an individual who experiences a left hemisphere stroke and then experiences left hemisphere cognitive difficulties and right hemisphere paresis (paralysis) or hemiparesis (half paralysis).

The aforementioned example of a stroke leads to the next principle of brain function. The left hemisphere, in most individuals, is involved with verbal abilities. As was stated by Paul Broca (1824–1880) and others, we speak with our left hemisphere. The right hemisphere, in most individuals, is concerned with nonverbal functions such as spatial reasoning and music. These abilities are lateralized for most individuals, roughly 75–90% of the population (Fischer, Alexander, Gabriel, Gould, & Milione, 1991). The remaining 5–30% of individuals are termed *not normally lateralized.* These individuals have their verbal abilities in the right hemisphere and their spatial abilities in the left. It is not totally understood why this occurs and does not appear to be related to the handedness of the

FIGURE 2.22 The divisions of the adult human brain.

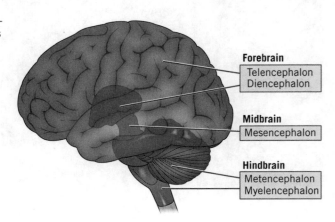

Forebrain
Telencephalon
Diencephalon

Midbrain
Mesencephalon

Hindbrain
Metencephalon
Myelencephalon

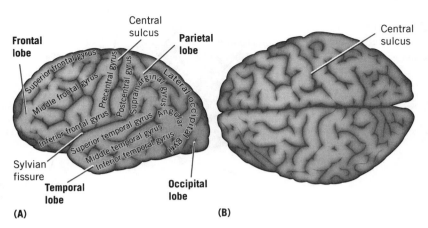

(A)

(B)

FIGURE 2.23 **(A)** Lateral view of the left hemisphere and **(B)** dorsal view of the cerebral cortex in humans. The cortex includes the four cortical lobes and various key gyri. Gyri are separated by sulci and result from the folding of the cerebral cortex occurring during development of the nervous system.

individual. Most individuals do not learn about where their abilities are localized unless they experience an accident or illness and the localization is revealed through neuropsychological testing or brain imaging techniques.

The hemispheres of the brain are connected by a band of fibers termed the **corpus callosum**. The corpus callosum allows the two hemispheres to communicate with one another. An early treatment for epilepsy was to sever the corpus callosum. Separation of the hemispheres did stop the flow of neural activity from one hemisphere to the other, but it also stopped the communication between the sides of the brain. Roger Sperry's (1913–1994) work on split-brain patients further illustrated the role that the corpus callosum has in communication between the two hemispheres. Sperry won the Nobel Prize for his work investigating the functions of right and left hemisphere in patients receiving commissurotomies or severing of the corpus callosum to relieve seizures.

corpus callosum
a band of neural fibers that allows the right and left hemispheres of the brain to communicate

Moving from the corpus callosum, we now look at the cell layers. Within the cortex are six layers labeled I through VI starting at the surface (Northcutt & Kaas, 1995). There are two different kinds of cortical neurons, pyramidal and stellate. **Pyramidal neurons** resemble pyramids just as their name suggests. They are large multipolar neurons, with a large dendrite which extends from the apex of the pyramid toward the cortex surface and a long axon. **Stellate neurons** are star shaped and are short, with either few or no axons present. The six layers differ in terms of the number and density of each of the neurons. Many of the long axons and dendrites travel vertically, which is the basis for the columnar organization. Although the neocortex is six layered, there are some variations in the number of layers in the subcortical areas.

LOBES OF THE BRAIN

The lobes of the cortex have demarcations and each lobe is associated with specific functions (see Figure 2.24). Some of these functions are the same in both sides of the brain whereas other functions may differ.

The **frontal lobes**, sitting predominantly at the front of the brain, are much more developed in humans than in other animals. Many researchers consider the frontal lobes as the area which clearly separates us from other animals. Due to their position the frontal lobes suffer more moving vehicle accident difficulties, more sports injuries, and more gunshot wounds than any of the other lobes. The extent of damage to the frontal lobes is significant because the frontal lobes house our unique abilities to think, reason,

frontal lobes
the lobes in the front of the brain; they are responsible for higher order cognitive abilities such as thinking, reasoning, and planning

FIGURE 2.24 Four lobes of the cerebral cortex, in lateral view of the left hemisphere.

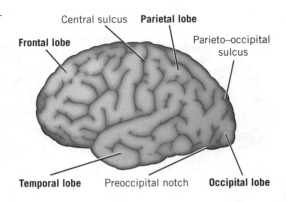

use language, and all of our other higher order cognitive processes. In one study, it was found that six specific clusters of the medial frontal cortex were found to be highly active when tests were administered to simulate attention to one's own actions, empathy, and the valuation of other's behavior (Seitz, Nickel, & Azari, 2006). This study demonstrated positive correlations with regard to reasoning and other unique abilities with frontal lobe activity.

The **occipital lobes** are directly in the back of the brain. A good way to remember their location is that they are opposite of the frontal lobes. The occipital lobes have been found to play an important part in vision. Different parts of the occipital lobes deal with vision in both eyes versus vision in one eye. At the **optic chiasma** some of the axons of the optic nerve cross over to the other side of the brain or **decussate**. The axons on the nasal side are those which cross to the opposite side of the brain. Decussation allows each eye to view part of both the right and left visual fields. This ability is very important because in the case of accident or injury the site of the difficulty may cause loss of vision in one or both eyes or lead to **visual field cuts** in both eyes. Visual field cuts are alterations in the amount that can be seen by each eye because of accident or illness. The occipital lobes are the most specialized in functioning.

The **temporal lobes** reside on the side of the cortex in the area where we consider our temples to be located. The temporal lobes are involved with processing of information through hearing (also known as auditory interpretation). The left temporal lobe processes auditory information for speech and is the site of **Wernicke's area**. The right temporal lobe processes auditory information in the form of tones or music.

The **parietal lobes** are situated at the top of the brain and are considered to be the association cortex. This means that the parietal lobes are responsible for spatial orientation, visual perception, speech, and pain sensation. These abilities then make it a particularly important area of the brain when thinking about how we interact with the people, places, and objects of our environment. To generalize and make this easier to comprehend, we can say that the main role of the parietal lobes is to integrate information from all of the senses. The parietal lobes are the least localized of the four lobes.

OTHER CORTICAL STRUCTURES

In addition to the four lobes of the cortex, various other structures are contained within the telencephalon. The **hippocampus** is located within the cortex, but is not considered to be neocortex and thereby contains only three layers. The hippocampus has been implicated in memory functioning. Looking at this structure more in depth, the hippocampus

occipital lobe
the center for vision, located in the back of the brain

temporal lobe
the lobe responsible for processing information through learning; the left temporal lobe is related to speech and the right to music or tone patterns

parietal lobe
the association cortex that integrates information from the senses

hippocampus
the structure responsible for memory functions

is very important for new memory formation and for the linking between our senses and old memories. For instance, imagine walking into a kitchen in the morning and smelling bacon and eggs cooking. For many this would be a very pleasant sensation that would recall past events where they had eaten this meal and experienced a pleasant emotion. This linking of experiences in our memory with sensory information also happens to many survivors of various types of trauma. Many survivors will remember exactly what it smelled like, the sounds they heard, or certain minute images that they saw, and, therefore, every time they see, hear, or smell something that is similar to what took place, the brain automatically recalls the events to conscious thought.

The hippocampus is often also thought to be part of the **limbic system** (see Figure 2.25). The limbic system includes the mammillary bodies, the amygdala, the fornix, the cingulate cortex, and the septum. The structures form a ring around the thalamus. The **mammillary bodies** act as a relay center for information going to the amygdala and hippocampus. They have also been found to be one of the areas most affected by alcohol use and have recently been connected with autism (Duprez, Serieh, & Raftopoulos, 2005). The **amygdala** is a bundle of axons that carry signals from the hippocampus to the mammillary bodies. The amygdala has also been implicated in control of the rage emotion. The **fornix** is a C-shaped bundle of axons in the brain that carries signals from the hippocampus to the mammillary bodies. The **cingulate cortex** is an area that regulates blood pressure, heart rate, rational cognitive functions, with the anterior part being responsible for making memories permanent. The **septum** is a thin membrane of nervous tissue that forms the medial wall of the lateral ventricles also called the *septum lucidum*. These limbic system structures are involved with motivated behaviors such as fighting, fleeing, feeding, and sexual behavior. In a more general sense, this system is very involved with how we respond to something that takes place in our environment such as a harmful object approaching, or how we react to being alone or with an intimate partner.

The **basal ganglia** are also contained within the telencephalon (see Figure 2.26). The structures within the basal ganglia include the amygdala, caudate nucleus, putamen, and globus pallidus. The basal ganglia play a role in voluntary motor behavior. The reader will notice that the amygdala is included with both the limbic system and the basal ganglia.

limbic system
set of structures related to emotional behavior; the structures are the mammillary bodies, the amygdala, the fornix, the cingulate cortex, and the septum in addition to the hippocampus

basal ganglia
the set of structures involved with voluntary motor behavior; the structures are the amygdala, caudate, putamen, and globus pallidus

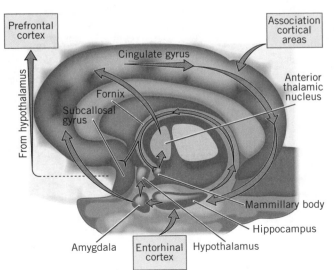

FIGURE 2.25 Major connections of the limbic system (medial view of the right hemisphere).

FIGURE 2.26 Major inputs and outputs of the basal ganglia. The basal ganglia form a cortical–subcortical motor loop that monitors motor behavior.

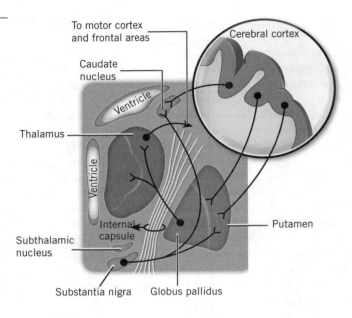

thalamus
the major relay center for the brain; all senses except for smell send information through the thalamus and pass it on to the cortex

The amygdala has been shown to be very active in the moments that our minds need to differentiate an emotional response, such as fear or frustration. The **caudate nucleus** is partly responsible for body movement and coordination. The **putamen** is a structure that is thought to play a role in reinforcement learning. The **globus pallidus** is a pale spherical area of the brain, which is a component of the basal ganglia and relays information from the other nuclei to the thalamus.

The diencephalon is the second layer of the brain. Within the diencephalon reside the thalamus and the hypothalamus (see Figure 2.27). The **thalamus** consists of many

FIGURE 2.27 Midsagittal view of the hypothalamus showing various nuclear groups. The hypothalamus is the floor of the third ventricle and sits below the thalamus. *Source:* Adapted from Pinel, J. P. J. (2010). Biopsychology, 8 ed., Pearson Education.

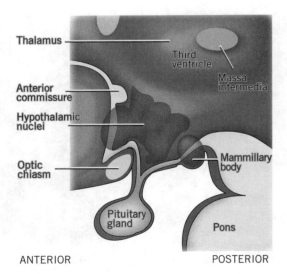

paired nuclei which project onto the cortex. The thalamus is considered a major relay station for sensory information. All of the senses, except the sense of smell, send information through the thalamus. Once the information reaches the thalamus, it is routed to appropriate areas in the cortex. The **hypothalamus** is located just below the thalamus. The hypothalamus regulates the release of hormones by the pituitary gland, which dangles below it. The hypothalamus regulates temperature within the body and the initiation and cessation of fluid intake. It also signals the organism to start or stop eating and one's interest in sexual behavior. Similar to the thalamus, the hypothalamus is composed of many paired nuclei.

hypothalamus
the organ that regulates the release of hormones by the pituitary gland

The **pituitary gland** is often referred to as the master gland. The pituitary gland releases **tropic hormones** or hormones that stimulate or change other functions. The anterior pituitary receives information about hormone release from chemical messages that travel from the hypothalamus through the **hypothalamopituitary portal**. Neurons in the hypothalamus also extend to the posterior pituitary, which when activated, release two neuropeptides. Many of these hormones relate to sexual functioning in females and males. In addition to the pituitary gland, two other structures are connected to the hypothalamus, the optic chiasma and the mammillary bodies. The optic chiasma, as described earlier, is the point where the axons of the optic nerve decussate. The mammillary bodies are a pair of small round bodies in the brain often considered to be part of the hypothalamus located behind the pituitary.

pituitary gland
a gland that releases hormones that stimulate other parts of the body

The mesencephalon, technically the middle brain, has two divisions, the tectum and the tegmentum. The **tectum** on the topmost portion of the mesencephalon contains the **inferior colliculi** which function with auditory information, and the **superior colliculi** which have a visual function. The **tegmentum** contains the **reticular activating system** (RAS). The RAS has an arousal function and keeps the organism alert and on track. The RAS is what helps us to keep our systems operating appropriately to our surroundings. It is the RAS which allows the organism to be alert while walking, swimming, or participating in other physical activity in which the organism needs to pay attention to its environment. Also included in the tegmentum is the **periaqueductal gray** which is involved with the pain-reducing effects of certain drugs, and the substantia nigra and the red nucleus, which are together part of the sensorimotor system. The **substantia nigra** is a layer of large pigmented nerve cells in the mesencephalon that produce dopamine and whose destruction is associated with Parkinson's disease. The **red nucleus** is a large well-defined, somewhat elongated cell mass of reddish gray hue that is located in the mesencephalic tegmentum. It receives a massive projection from the contralateral half of the cerebellum and receives additional projections from the ipsilateral motor cortex.

reticular activating system
a set of structures that are related to arousal and alertness

The metencephalon contains many of ascending and descending tracts and parts of the reticular formation. The pons and cerebellum are also located here. The **pons** forms a bulge in the brain stem. Its function is to relay information from the cerebral cortex to the cerebellum. The pons is also responsible for sleeping and controlling autonomic functions.

pons
the structure that relays information from the cerebellum to the cerebral cortex

The **cerebellum** protrudes from the back of the brain and is often referred to as the little brain (see Figure 2.28). The role of the cerebellum has historically been thought to deal with balance, coordination, posture, and movement. Cerebral palsy is caused by problems with the cerebellum. Individuals who have cerebral palsy have difficulty with movement and functioning in their environment. Recent research also indicates that the cerebellum has a role in various cognitive functions (Gordon, 2007). Hence, it is sometimes the case that individuals with cerebral palsy exhibit cognitive or emotional deficits.

cerebellum
the structure at the back of the brain involved with movement, coordination and posture; it is often referred to as the "little brain"

FIGURE 2.28 Gross anatomy of the cerebellum showing the underlying deep nuclei.

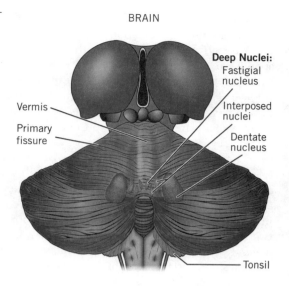

BRAIN

Deep Nuclei:
Fastigial nucleus

Vermis

Interposed nuclei

Primary fissure

Dentate nucleus

Tonsil

SPINAL CORD

medulla
a part of the hindbrain that regulates respiration and cardiovascular functioning

somatic nervous system
consists of peripheral nerves that send sensory information to the central nervous system and motor nerves that project to skeletal muscle

afferent nerves
nerves that carry information to the central nervous system from the senses

efferent nerves
nerves that carry motor signals away from the central nervous system

autonomic nervous system
this division regulates the body's internal environment; it is part of the peripheral nervous system

sympathetic nerves
the part of the autonomic nervous system that arouses the organism in the situation of "fight or flight"; has an effect opposite of the parasympathetic nerves or nervous system

The myencephalon or medulla is a lowest structure of the brain and is connected to the spinal cord. It is composed predominately of tracts ascending and descending from the brain. Nuclei in the **medulla** regulate respiration and cardiovascular functioning. Damage to the medulla is almost always fatal. The reticular formation is also involved here. As described earlier, the RAS has an arousal function and is related to attention, sleep, and various cardiac, circulatory, and respiratory reflexes.

Peripheral Nervous System

In addition to the brain and spinal cord, the clinical neuropsychologist must understand how information is sent to and received from the senses and the brain. These functions involve the peripheral nervous system.

The peripheral nervous system is located outside of the brain and the spinal cord. The peripheral nervous system is composed of two divisions, the somatic and the autonomic nervous systems. The **somatic nervous system** is in contact with the environment outside of the individual. It is composed of **afferent nerves**, which carry signals from the various senses such as the eyes, ears, skin, and the skeletal muscles to the central nervous system. It also contains **efferent nerves** that carry motor signals from the central nervous system to the skeletal muscles.

The **autonomic nervous system** regulates the body's internal environment. It contains afferent nerves that carry sensory signals from the internal organs to the central nervous system. It also contains **efferent neurons** that carry motor signals from the central nervous system to the internal organs. There are two types of efferent nerves in the autonomic nervous system. The **sympathetic nerves** or the sympathetic branch of the autonomic nervous system stimulate, organize, and mobilize energy resources in threatening situations. It is often referred to as initiating the fight-or-flight response.

The **parasympathetic nerves** or the parasympathetic branch of the autonomic nervous system conserves energy and is associated with states of relaxation and sexual arousal. Each organ is innervated by the sympathetic and parasympathetic systems. An example of how the sympathetic and parasympathetic systems work together: In the presence of an angry growling dog, the sympathetic system would energize (increase blood pressure, heart rate, etc.) allowing the individual to flee and afterward the parasympathetic system would help the individual relax (lower blood pressure, reduce heart rate, etc.).

parasympathetic nervous system
one of two systems within the autonomic nervous system; its role is calming and the opposite of the sympathetic nervous system

The Spinal Cord

The spinal cord is connected to the base of the brain where it contains many ascending and descending fibers. In the center of the spinal cord resides the central canal which is filled with CSF.

If one were to look at a cross-section of the spinal cord, it is made up of two areas delineated by the inner H-shaped core of gray matter and a surrounding area of white matter (see Figure 2.29). Gray matter is composed of cell bodies and unmyelinated interneurons. White matter is composed of myelinated areas, which give the white matter its color. The dorsal horns are on the dorsal areas of the spinal gray matter. The ventral horns are on the ventral areas of the spinal gray matter.

Spinal nerves are in pairs and attached to the spinal cord. One is attached on the right and one is attached on the left at 31 different points along the spine. Each of the spinal neurons divides as it nears the spinal cord and its axons are joined to the spinal cord via the dorsal root or the ventral root. Their dorsal root axons are sensory or afferent and their cell bodies group together outside the cord to form the dorsal root ganglia. Their function is to bring sensory information to the spinal cord or brain. The neurons of the ventral root are motor or efferent neurons that extend their axons outside of the central nervous system and directly or indirectly control muscles.

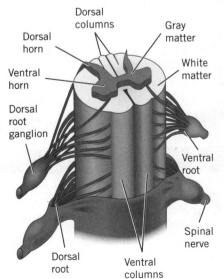

FIGURE 2.29 Gross anatomy of the spinal cord showing the central butterfly-shaped gray matter which contains neurons, and the surrounding white matter tracts which convey information down the spinal cord from the brain and up the spinal cord to the brain from peripheral receptors.

At the beginning of the chapter, the reader was introduced to Sherry who was pregnant. Throughout the chapter, the fate of the child's developing brain should have been considered. As we close the chapter, Sherry has given birth. The baby appeared 3 weeks premature, which is not unusual in a case where the mother occasionally used chemicals. The parents have decided to raise the baby together and have given her the name Rose. Sherry's social worker has become very active in providing support services for the family. They receive, in addition to Sherry's disability money, Women, Infants, and Children (WIC) coupons, which are redeemable for milk, cereal, and other nutritional products for the baby. The social worker has strongly suggested that Sherry and the baby's father attend parenting classes to learn appropriate techniques to manage a newborn. This is particularly important because of Sherry's dysfunctional background. With further discussion, it appears that the baby's father also came from an alcoholic and abusive family.

The attending physician completed the usual tests of the baby after birth and determined that the majority of her reflexes were intact. He is somewhat concerned about her small head circumference and will monitor it carefully. The physician spoke clearly and directly to the parents regarding the need to take appropriate care of the child and to watch for certain behaviors that may be indicative of future difficulties.

The prognosis for Rose is guarded, similar to that of her mother. If she is given appropriate care and nutrition, she may develop normally. If she is neglected or her parents use the skills their parents applied to them, then she may exhibit physical or emotional difficulties.

Summary

The chapter begins with a complicated case study of a young woman who is pregnant. The case study is designed to illustrate the issues which must be considered in the formation of the developing child's cortex. In addition, the case study discusses the choices made by parents and the subsequent effects on the child.

The prenatal and postnatal influences on the central nervous system are reviewed to illustrate the issues which are often faced by clinical neuropsychologists who are working with clients. The neuron is discussed in detail to allow the student to understand how each component works and also anticipate what may happen when there is a central nervous system accident or illness.

The brain is the focus of the remainder of the chapter. The discussion begins with broad structures such as the hemispheres and lobes. The functions of each area are discussed to allow the student to differentiate function from dysfunction. The internal structures such as the limbic system, basal ganglia, and so forth, are all covered to allow the student to understand the functioning of the brain as a whole. The chapter concludes with a discussion of the peripheral nervous system and the spinal cord.

Questions for Further Study

1. Are all drugs or medications considered to be teratogens for a pregnant woman or are there some substances that would be considered safe and/or even helpful?
2. Most individuals are considered to be normally lateralized (language in the left hemisphere, spatial in the right). Are nonnormally lateralized individuals predisposed to any type of difficulty?
3. Are there gender differences in the functioning of the brain or are these socially learned behaviors?

References

Altimier, L. (2008). Shaken baby syndrome. *Journal of Perinatal and Neonatal Nursing, 22*(1), 68–76.

Anderson, R. B., Newgreen, D. F., & Young, H. M. (2006). Neural crest and the development of the enteric nervous system. *Advances in Experimental Medicine and Biology, 589,* 181–196.

Catterall, W. A. (1984). The molecular basis of neuronal excitability. *Science, 223*(4637), 653–661.

Cooper, G. M., & Hausman, R. E. (2009). *The cell: A molecular approach* (5th ed.). Sunderland, MA: ASM Press and Sinauer Associates, Inc.

Dahlgren, A., Kecklund, G., Theorell, T., & Åkerstedt, T. (2009). Day-to-day variation in saliva cortisol—Relations with sleep, stress and self-rated health. *Biological Psychology, 82,* 149–155.

Duprez, T. P., Serieh, B. A., & Raftopoulos, C. (2005). Absence of memory dysfunction after bilateral mammillary body and mammillothalamic tract electrode implantation: Preliminary experience in three patients. *American Journal of Neuroradiology, 26,* 195–198.

Fair, D., & Schlagger, B. L. (2008). Brain development. In M. M. Haith & J. B. Benson (Eds.), *Encyclopedia of infant and early childhood development* (pp. 211–225). Oxford, UK: Elsevier.

Fischer, R. S., Alexander, M. P., Gabriel, C., Gould, E., & Milione, J. (1991). Reversed lateralization of cognitive functions in right handers. Exceptions to classical aphasiology. *Brain, 114,* 245–261.

Gordon, N. (2007). The cerebellum and cognition. *European Journal of Paediatric Neurology, 11*(4), 232–234.

Haydon, P. G. (2001). GLIA: Listening and talking to the synapse. *Nature Reviews Neuroscience, 2,* 185–193.

Hyman, S. E. (2005). Neurotransmitters. *Current Biology, 15*(5), R154–R158.

Lambert, K., & Kinsley, C. H. (2005). *Clinical neuroscience: Neurobiological foundations of mental health.* New York: Worth Publishers.

Marín, O., & Rubenstein, J. L. R. (2001). A long, remarkable journey: Tangential migration in the telencephalon. *Nature Reviews Neuroscience, 2*(11), 780–790.

McMillen, I. C., Adam, C. L., & Mühlhäusler, B. S. (2005). Early origins of obesity: Programming the appetite regulatory system. *The Journal of Physiology, 565*(1), 9–17.

Northcutt, R. G., & Kaas, J. H. (1995). The emergence and evolution of mammalian neocortex. *Trends in Neurosciences, 18*(9), 373–379.

Oliet, S. H., Piet, R., & Poulain, D. A. (2001). Control of glutamate clearance and synaptic efficacy by glial coverage of neurons. *Science, 292*(5518), 923–926.

Pinel, J. P. J. (2006). *Biopsychology* (6th ed.). Boston: Pearson Allyn and Bacon.

Ramakrishnan, U. (2004). Nutrition and low birth weight: From research to practice. *American Journal of Clinical Nutrition, 79*(1), 17–21.

Sagan, C., & Druyan, A. (1997). *Billions and billions: Thoughts on life and death at the brink of the millennium.* New York: Ballantine.

Seitz, R. J., Nickel, J., & Azari, N. P. (2006). Functional modularity of the medial prefrontal cortex: Involvement in human empathy. *Neuropsychology, 20*(6), 743–751.

Stade, B. C., Stevens, B., Ungar, W. J., Beyene, J., & Koren, J. G. (2006). Health-related quality of life of Canadian children and youth prenatally exposed to alcohol. *Health and Quality of Life Outcomes, 4,* 81.

Teng, L., & Labosky, P. A. (2006). Neural crest stem cells. *Advances in Experimental Medicine and Biology, 589,* 206–212.

Trentin, A., Glavieux-Pardanaud, C., Le Douarin, N. M., & Dupin, E. (2004). Self-renewal capacity is a widespread property of various types of neural precursor cells. *The National Academy of Sciences, 101*(13), 4495–4500.

University of Virginia Health System. (2006). *High-risk newborn blood circulation in the fetus and newborn.* Retrieved November 28, 2009, from http://www.healthsystem.virginia.edu/UVAHealth/peds_hrnewborn/fetlcirc.cfm

Weiss, R. P. (2000). Memory and Learning. *Training and Development, 54*(10), 46–50.

Yuste, R., & Bonhoeffer, T. (2004). Genesis of dendritic spines: Insights from ultrastructural and imaging studies. *Nature Reviews Neuroscience, 5*(1), 24–34.

Neuropathology: Neurodegenerative Disorders

3

Learning Objectives

After reading this chapter, the student should be able to understand:

- The underlying causes and symptoms of degenerative disorders
- The similarities and differences in cortical disorders and subcortical disorders that may lead to dementia
- The characteristics, symptoms, and treatment approaches for progressive disorders of the central nervous system
- The causes, risk factors, symptoms, and treatment approaches for cerebrovascular disorders
- The types of tumors which may affect the central nervous system, their severity, and possible treatment
- The causes, symptoms, and treatment approaches for metabolic and endrocrine disorders

Topical Outline

- Degenerative Disorders
- Progressive Disorders of the Central Nervous System
- Cerebrovascular Disorders
- Brain Tumors
- Metabolic and Endocrine Disorders
- Seizures

M r. Alfred was recently referred for a neuropsychological evaluation by his primary care physician. He was seen by his physician at the request of his wife who was concerned about her husband's thinking and behaviors. Mr. Alfred is a 73-year-old White male who resides in the northern part of the United States. He is presently retired. Mr. Alfred was an electrician by profession and also inherited the family farm, which he worked with his sons. He and his wife had four children, three sons and a daughter. Mr. Alfred performed well on his job and also appeared to get along well with the family. However, the children reported that when they were small he had a temper and was not afraid to physically punish them.

Mr. Alfred suffered a head injury 40 years ago while at work when a large metal-covered light fell from the ceiling and rendered him unconscious. He stated that he awoke quickly and went back to work with a headache. No one was present to confirm the amount of time he was unconscious. His wife reports that he had no apparent or serious aftereffects. During this time period, neither his temper nor his treatment of the children appeared to be related to the head injury. Ten years ago, Mr. Alfred suffered from depression and was treated with antidepressant medication and ultimately electroshock therapy (ECT). His wife again reported that he had no apparent aftereffects. Mr. Alfred stated the antidepressants did not help with his depression and caused him to experience dry mouth, constipation and general tiredness. He reported the ECT left him with memory difficulties, which made him not only concerned but angry.

Within the past 18 months, Mrs. Alfred stated that her husband has become verbally abusive, calling her names and demanding her to do things in a manner he had never used before. She also agreed with the children that he never had the most congenial temperament but felt the current abusive behavior is different from the way he treated the children when they were young. Mr. Alfred has also demonstrated memory difficulties, which he denies, and he has gotten lost while driving. Again, this is a new difficulty not related to the ECT-induced memory loss 10 years previously. Mrs. Alfred does not want her husband to drive a vehicle due to the aforementioned issues. Mr. Alfred becomes very upset when the topic of his driving is discussed. In addition, Mrs. Alfred describes symptoms in her husband, which are similar to the depressive symptoms that Mr. Alfred experienced several years ago.

Mr. Alfred has trouble sleeping and often wanders around the house and yard at night and sleeps during the day. Mrs. Alfred is now suffering from sleep deprivation because she feels that she needs to be awake when her husband is, for the safety of both parties. Mrs. Alfred has persuaded her daughter to stay overnight on occasion so she is able to rest. The daughter, however, would rather have her father "sent to a home." Mrs. Alfred feels that Mr. Alfred wants to remain at home and is confused regarding what to do. Her latest problem is that Mr. Alfred set the dog's dish of food on fire and has no explanation for his action.

As is similar to other individuals receiving services from a clinical neuropsychologist, Mr. Alfred participated in a detailed clinical interview that looks at all components of his life. His wife was also interviewed to corroborate his symptoms and life experiences. Neuropsychological testing was completed, which showed a pattern of cognitive decline in addition to difficulties with memory and control of anger and other emotional reactions.

Considering the pattern of test results, there are several different difficulties Mr. Alfred could be experiencing. In addition to a primary difficulty, it needs to be determined whether his depression is a separate difficulty, a symptom of a major difficulty, or a reaction to his difficulties.

The prognosis for Mr. Alfred may not appear to be good. His cognitive deficits and memory difficulties appear to be irreversible. His behaviors, which have become noticeable, do not appear to be controllable. In this case, it may be best for Mr. Alfred and his family that he *reside in a care facility. However, the removal from his home does not imply that death is imminent or that the quality of his life would be poor. At times, circumstances are often too difficult for the family or social system to manage and in those circumstances, outside placement may be extremely helpful.*

After Mr. Alfred and his family discussed the neuropsychological results and the treatment plan prepared, he agreed that he would feel better in a "safe" environment where he did not feel a "burden" to his family. One month later, he moved to an assisted care facility. His wife came to see him on an every-other day basis. With less worrying on both of their parts, their relationship improved. The adult children also began to visit their father twice a month and started to develop a more positive relationship. Even though living outside of his home was not Mr. Alfred's original choice, it appears to have lessened the stress for him and his family. His relationships have also improved, which leads to a better overall quality of life.

Introduction

The discussion of neuropathology has been divided into two chapters due to its breadth and scope, as well as the number of difficulties involved. As a way to logically divide the various difficulties and make them familiar to the reader, they have been separated into neurodegenerative disorders (chapter 3) and acquired disorders (chapter 4).

Neurodegenerative disorders refer to difficulties that involve or cause destruction of neurons or various structures of the brain. Mr. Alfred's difficulty is a classic example of a neurodegenerative disorder, which will be discussed in the next few pages. **Acquired disorders** reflect an accident, insult, or disease process coming from a source outside of the cortex. Knowledge of the various difficulties which an individual may sustain is crucial for a clinical neuropsychologist. The roles of conducting assessment, applying a diagnosis, and undertaking treatment all require the professional to have a working understanding of the various ailments, their etiology or causal factors, if known, course of illness, prognosis, and rehabilitation. In the words of the Proceedings of the National Academy of Neuropsychology's Houston Conference on Specialty Training and Education in Clinical Neuropsychology (Hannay et al., 1998), "in order to make diagnostic sense out of the behavioral patterns that emerge in neuropsychological assessment, the practitioner must be knowledgeable about the neuropsychological presentations of many kinds of neurological disorders and their underlying pathology."

Another reason why it is necessary to understand the clinically presented symptoms and the causes of various disorders is that, very often, dissimilar difficulties present themselves with similar symptomology. A common example is the distinction between dementia, with its multiple causes, and depression. Both dementia and depression may reflect sadness, concentration and attention difficulties, vegetative signs such as sleeping and eating difficulties and other similar symptoms. However, the causal factors are clearly dissimilar and require very different treatment plans and rehabilitation strategies. Another factor to consider is that the majority of central nervous system diseases or difficulties involve depression as a secondary symptom, which suggests that it is a reaction to the primary diagnosis. In the case presented at the beginning of the chapter, there is the suggestion that Mr. Alfred may have dementia, depression, both, or neither. Questions of diagnosis and treatment such as these will become easier to answer as we pursue the understanding of the various central nervous system difficulties.

neurodegenerative disorders
disorders that involve progressive loss of function or destruction of neurons or various structures of the brain

acquired disorders
disorders caused by an accident, insult, or disease process coming from a source outside of the cortex

Degenerative Disorders

By the nature of the term, **degenerative disorders** involve difficulties with destruction of neurons and/or specific areas within the central nervous system. In many of these difficulties, the loss of neurons or neural tissue is not repairable and the loss of abilities is permanent. The etiological factors are unknown for many of the degenerative disorders. These disorders tend to occur more often in the older population and as the population as a whole ages, more and more of these disorders are surfacing. Recent estimates are 3–4 million patients with dementia in the United States who incur medical costs of up to $100 billion annually (DeKosky & Orgogozo, 2001). These figures may be low because of underreporting in rural areas (Camicioli et al., 2000).

CORTICAL DEMENTIAS

cortical dementia
damage within the cerebral cortex, which leads to symptoms of dementia

Cortical dementia refers to damage within the cerebral cortex (refer to chapter 2) and demonstrates a progressive decline in cognitive abilities. Memory and other higher order functions such as reasoning and the ability to do abstract thought are examples of the types of cognitive abilities lost with dementia. Dementia takes a downward course with the result being the death of the individual. During the early stages of degenerative disorders, differences usually appear, which will be discussed later. As the disease process progresses, patients with different etiologies tend to show many similar symptoms, which often makes the diagnosis more difficult. According to Lezak, Howieson, and Loring (2004), many of these difficulties eventually become neuropsychologically indistinguishable. In a sense, some difficulties may progress to the point where neuropsychological test results are very similar and not useful for diagnostic purposes.

Dementia is usually described in reference to behaviors falling within three stages. Stage one involves behaviors that may deviate from the norm for the individual. The individual himself or herself may not be aware of the changes at this time. Examples of stage one symptoms would be small changes in personality or memory lapses noticed by the individual's friends and family. During stage two of dementia, the individual often notices memory problems and tries to conceal them from others. Confabulation may occur, similar to individuals who consume large amounts of alcohol, in which the individual develops a cover story or excuse for the lack of memory. As stage two progresses, the individual may become geographically lost or wander and may engage in activities which are dangerous to self or others. Sundowning, or the worsening of symptoms toward the end of the day, begins during stage two. Families of individuals with dementia usually begin to consider placement in treatment facilities such as nursing homes during stage two. Stage three involves serious cognitive deterioration in addition to problems associated with self-care. Many families find that an individual with stage three dementia requires care outside of the family environment. The decision to place a family member in a care facility is extremely difficult emotionally and financially. During the third stage of dementia, many family members experience significant distress and it is at this point that professionals working with patients with dementia often address these types of problems with the primary caregiver or extended family. Patients with stage three dementia may be unable to toilet, dress, or feed themselves; however, these symptoms are quite variable between individuals. Individuals usually do not die from dementia, but from some other opportunistic agent which invades a nonintact central nervous system (Askin-Edgar, White, & Cummings, 2002; Filley, 1995; Keene, Hope, Fairburn, & Jacoby, 2001). A central nervous system that has significant impairment in neurological tissue is not able to fight off viruses or any other invading process as well as a fully intact central nervous

sundowning
in patients with dementia, the worsening of symptoms as the day progresses

system. The most frequent cause of death for patients with dementia is pneumonia. Dementia is more common in the aged population, but is not synonymous with aging. Dementia affects approximately 5–8% of the population older than the age of 65, and 25–50% of individuals 85 years and older (Monk & Brodaty, 2000).

ALZHEIMER'S TYPE DEMENTIA

The most common form of cortical decline is **Alzheimer's type dementia**. The term *Alzheimer's disease* was first used by Alois Alzheimer in 1906. A clear diagnosis of Alzheimer's disease cannot be made without an autopsy. However, recent refinements in neuroimaging and neurochemical profiling have increased the likelihood of making a diagnosis in living patients (Boller & Duykaerts, 2003). Alzheimer's disease is characterized by neurofibrillary tangles and amyloid plaques. **Neurofibrillary tangles** are made from tau proteins and develop when microtubules, which transport substances from the soma to the end of the axon, become twisted. **Tau** is the protein which maintains the microtubules' structure, but in Alzheimer's disease it is altered, which allows the twisted microtubules to group together into tangles. The volume of these tangles obstructs living tissue and often strangles it. The **amyloid plaques**, which were first described by Alzheimer, were referred to as "cellular trash." We now know that the plaques are made of an amino acid peptide protein core termed *beta-amyloid*, hence the term *amyloid plaques*. These plaques also obstruct living tissue. It is important to note that the plaques and tangles appear in normally aging individuals and individuals with other degenerative diseases. The key to a diagnosis of Alzheimer's disease is the extent of the tangles and plaques and the regions of the brain they gravitate toward.

Loss of neurons is another common feature of Alzheimer's disease, particularly in the temporal area. If neurons are no longer able to communicate with major memory areas within the cortex, significant memory loss may occur. Loss of neurons also leads to changes in anatomical structures, which may point to the enlargement of ventricles with Alzheimer's disease. As was stated earlier, it is difficult to obtain a visible picture of these plaques and tangles on any form of brain scan (Khachaturian, 2000; see Figure 3.1). However, as techniques advance, it is hoped that clearer images may be developed so that it may be easily diagnosed before autopsy.

Alzheimer's disease is widespread with 10% of the population aged 65 and 25% older than the age of 80 exhibiting symptoms. These figures are separate from those individuals who exhibit signs of normal aging (Evans et al., 1989). Alzheimer's disease has an inherited genetic component. If an individual has a first-degree relative

Alzheimer's type dementia
dementia characterized by neurofibrillary tangles and amyloid plaques; a diagnosis cannot be made until autopsy but is termed Alzheimer's type based on behavioral symptoms

neurofibrillary tangles
composed of tau protein; tangles of dead tissue in the brain symptomatic of Alzheimer's disease

tau
proteins that researchers believe result from abnormal phosphorylation

amyloid plaques
deposits of aluminum silicate and amyloid peptides believed to cause loss of neurons and vascular damage

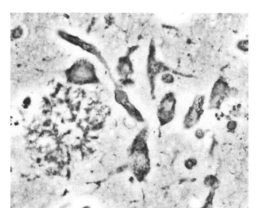

FIGURE 3.1 Alzheimer's disease. Burnt-out neuritic plaque consists of an amyloid core only, lacking dystrophic neuritis.

allele
any one of a number of viable DNA codings that occupy a given position on a chromosome

(parent or sibling) with the disease, it doubles the person's chances of acquiring the disease compared to those without affected first-degree relatives. The other three well-established risk factors for Alzheimer's disease are age, the gene for the protein apolipoprotein E (Apo E) on chromosome 19, and Down syndrome. **Apo E** is a normally occurring protein that helps carry phospholipids and cholesterol within the body. This gene has three types, the E4 **allele** type has been linked by researchers to various disorders including Alzheimer's disease (Corder et al., 1993; Roses & Saunders, 1997). **Down syndrome** is the most frequent cause of mental retardation and is caused by a trisomy on chromosome 21. Almost all individuals with Down syndrome show mental and physical deterioration characteristic of Alzheimer's disease if they live longer than 30–40 years (Skoog & Blennow, 2001). There are other factors which may be related to increased risk including being female, lower levels of education, and exposure to aluminum in drinking water (McDowell, 2001).

Additional causes of Alzheimer's disease have been investigated but are controversial. Traumatic brain injury is one suspected precursor to Alzheimer's disease. Nothing is definitive regarding the association of Alzheimer's disease with traumatic brain injury, but it appears that the more serious the injury, the more likely it is the individual will develop Alzheimer's disease (Plassman et al., 2000).

A low level of estrogen in postmenopausal women is another theory which has been proposed for Alzheimer's disease. Several studies of women on estrogen replacement therapy indicate less risk for Alzheimer's disease; however, these results may be confounded with educational level and socioeconomic status. The greater the education level and the higher the socioeconomic status, the more likely a woman will consult a medical professional for symptoms of menopause (Brinton, 2001; Carr, Goate, & Morris, 1997).

In addition to the dementia described earlier, the most distinguishing cognitive features of Alzheimer's disease are severe verbal memory difficulties. This memory loss begins slowly in the first stages of the disorder and progresses to severe in the end state. The difficulty is in all stages of memory, encoding, storage, and retrieval. There are also other deficits which are usually noted in orientation, psychomotor performance, language, speech fluency, and complex reasoning.

Treatment for Alzheimer's disease may involve preventive measures such as drinking red wine, which contains antioxidants that may have a protective effect (Orgogozo et al., 1997). Medications which stop the development of amyloid plaques have been developed (Janus et al., 2000). Other medications that keep tau in its normal form have also been explored (Cutler & Sramek, 2001).

Treatment for cognitive deficits is usually with anticholinesterase inhibitors that enhance cholinergic function (Cummings et al., 1998). Some patients may improve with the use of these medications and some patients may not respond positively. Other medications are continuously being developed to deal with cognitive and memory deficits.

In addition, patients who suffer from depression may need to take an antidepressant. Others who exhibit psychotic symptoms or have behavior management issues may profit from the use of typical or atypical antipsychotic medications (Askin-Edgar et al., 2002). Individuals, depending on their level of impairment, may profit from individual or group therapy. Memory aids and changing the environment to help with deficits have also been shown to be helpful.

In the case study, Mr. Alfred was exhibiting the aforementioned signs of dementia, which was further investigated using imaging techniques and determined to be most probably of the Alzheimer's type. Medications were employed both for depressive symptoms and to help with his declining cognitive functions. He also profited from the aforementioned changes in his environment.

FRONTOTEMPORAL DEMENTIAS

Frontotemporal dementias (FTDs) are degenerative disorders of the frontal and temporal lobes with the remainder of the cortex maintaining relative integrity (Askin-Edgar et al., 2002). These difficulties have a slow onset and progression. The age of onset is usually between 40 and 65 years of age. There does not appear to be gender differences in incidence. Frontotemporal dementias account for approximately 20% of progressive dementia cases (Grossman, 2001).

The symptoms of FTD and Alzheimer's disease are extremely similar and, in later stages, almost indistinguishable. Changes in social behavior and personality, lack of insight and stereotypic behaviors such as the repeating of a behavioral sequence, and eating a great deal of food, best differentiate frontotemporal dementia patients from those with Alzheimer's disease (Bozeat, Gregory, Ralph, & Hodges, 2000). Other common features of FTD include speech and language changes, extrapyramidal symptoms, and primitive reflexes (Neary et al., 1998).

The etiological factor in FTD is unknown. According to Bird (1998), however, approximately 40–50% of cases are transmitted by autosomal dominate inheritance. This implies that it is a dominant non sex-linked gene. Most individuals have tau pathology and a small percentage have a tau gene on chromosome 17 (Higgins & Mendez, 2000). There is also a greater-than-average incidence of brain trauma 4 years prior to the occurrence of symptoms; however, cause and effect have not been established (Mortimer & Pirozzolo, 1985). The pattern of decline will vary between patients and often is based on whether decline is more extensive in the frontal or the temporal area. The parietal and occipital lobes are often spared any type of deterioration.

In the past, frontotemporal disorders were termed *Pick's disease*. Pick's disease is now thought to be a subtype of FTD (Kaufer & Cummings, 2003). Pick's disease was first described by Arnold Pick in 1892. It was often referred to as early-onset Alzheimer's disease. The type of social and emotional behavior deficits exhibited are similar to those previously described as FTD. The difference, which sets Pick's disease apart from other FTDs, is the presence of **Pick bodies** comprised of tau proteins, which are shaped differently than the neurofibrillary tangles seen in Alzheimer's disease (Armstrong, Cairns, & Lantos, 1999; see Figure 3.2). It is estimated that 20% of patients with FTD have the classic Pick's disease with the presence of Pick bodies (Higgins & Mendez, 2000).

In an article by Grossman (2001), which summarized a meeting regarding FTD, she discussed the relevant treatment options to deal with depression, psychosis, and socially

Pick bodies
composed of tau protein and shaped differently than neurofibrillary tangles; they are symptomatic of Pick's disease

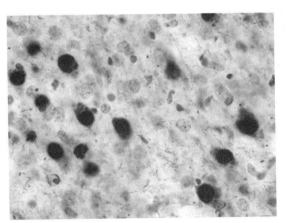

FIGURE 3.2 Pick's disease is a dementia characterized by the presence of distinct spherical inclusions called Pick bodies. Pick bodies (dark structures in this image) are composed of numerous tau fibrils arranged in a disorderly array. *Source:* Courtesy of Northwestern University and Michelle E. King.

FIGURE 3.3 Brain cells containing a Lewy body.

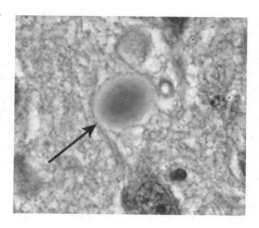

abnormal behaviors using medication. The article also found safety-enhancing interventions helpful to manage patient's behaviors and communication strategies to deal with aggressive behaviors while avoiding restraints.

DEMENTIA WITH LEWY BODIES

Dementia with Lewy bodies (DLB) accounts for approximately 20% of patients with dementia. It was first diagnosed as a separate syndrome in the 1970s. The symptoms of DLB include progressive dementia, **extrapyramidal** signs similar to Parkinson's disease (PD), visual hallucinations, delusions, and possibly severe cognitive fluctuations (McKeith, 2002). In common with patients with Alzheimer's, patients with DLB frequently have an elevated **ApoE4 allele** (Lippa et al., 1995). Patients most often have neuropathological findings similar to both PD and Alzheimer's disease (McKeith). DLB is somewhat more common in men, usually occurring after the age of 50. These patients have a more rapid decline than other patients with dementia.

The distinct pathological finding in this disorder is the presence of Lewy bodies (see Figure 3.3), which are protein deposits found throughout the cortex, paralimbic areas, and in the substantia nigra. In some cases, senile plaques are common although neurofibrillary tangles are few (Weiner, 1999). When Lewy bodies occur with neurofibrillary tangles and amyloid plaques, it is considered a Lewy body variation of Alzheimer's disease.

Individuals who have DLB have shown improvement in cognition and behavior using cholinesterase inhibitors (Barber, Panikkar, & McKeith, 2001).

SUBCORTICAL DEMENTIAS

aphasia
loss of expressive or receptive language

apraxia
inability to perform purposeful movements

agnosia
the loss of the ability to interpret sensory stimuli, such as sounds or images

Subcortical dementias are dementias that affect subcortical brain structures. The distinction between cortical and subcortical dementias is largely behaviorally based (Bondi, Salmon, & Kazniak, 1996). The behavioral changes that differentiate subcortical dementias from cortical dementias include (a) cognitive slowing with problems in attention and concentration, executive disturbances including impaired concept manipulation, visuospatial abnormalities, and memory difficulties that affect retrieval more than new learning; (b) absence of **aphasia** (loss of expressive or receptive language), **apraxia** (inability to perform purposeful movements), and **agnosia** (inability to recognize sensory input); and (c) emotional features including apathy, depression, and personality changes (Cummings, 1986). In summary, the cognitive functions involved include disabilities related to arousal, attention, processing speed, motivation, and emotion, as opposed to the involvement of higher order functioning as in cortical dementias.

Many of the subcortical dementias have movement difficulties as a major symptom of the disease. This usually involves the **extrapyramidal motor system**, which modulates movement and maintains muscle tone and posture. Very often, the movements seen in subcortical dementias appear to be uncontrollable or they are jerky, halting, or rigid. Fatigue, anxiety, and stimulants make the symptoms worse, whereas symptoms may decrease with volition and most are absent during sleep.

PARKINSON'S DISEASE/PARKINSONISM

Parkinson's disease (PD) is a movement disorder with attendant symptoms. It was originally described by Parkinson in 1817 as an involuntary tremulous motion with lessened muscle power. Symptoms in addition to shaking may include the aforementioned lessened muscular power, difficulty moving from resting to walking and vice versa, a tendency to bend forward while walking, and cognitive and emotional sequelae. Not all patients with PD exhibit all of the symptoms; hence, the clinical picture may point toward PD with multiple symptoms or parkinsonism, as a syndrome, with fewer symptoms present. Almost always present is a "resting tremor," which disappears during movement and in sleep, as well as a slowed moving pace. Another classic symptom is the lack of facial expressions often referred to as "masked faces."

Depression is one of the most common symptoms of PD or parkinsonism with estimates ranging from 40–60% of patients. However, the severity of depression appears unrelated to the severity of motor symptoms (Askin-Edgar et al., 2002). Parkinson's disease is associated with the depletion of the neurotransmitter dopamine in the basal ganglia, subthalamic nucleus, substantia nigra, and the interconnections to each other and to thalamic nuclei. The etiology of PD is unknown. It typically affects individuals in their 50s. Some studies indicate that more males are affected than females, whereas other studies indicate no sex differences.

There are studies that indicate a family pattern that may point to the hypothesis of genetic inheritance. There are suppositions related to several causative factors such as viral encephalitis, drugs with dopamine antagonistic properties, toxic substances, and vascular disease. Also possibly related to the appearance of PD is traumatic brain injury such as in the case of former boxer Muhammad Ali who was repeatedly hit in the frontal lobes during his boxing matches.

Many individuals find it offensive to list PD as a form of dementia, but the incidence of dementia in PD ranges from 2–93% with most studies citing 10–30% of patients with PD exhibiting dementia (Mahurin, Feher, Nance, Levy, & Pirozzolo, 1993). Another 20% of patients show some signs of cognitive impairment (Lieberman, 1998). Slowness of thought, difficulties with tasks that require sustained attention, memory retrieval, and executive functions are examples of cognitive difficulties (Basset, 2005).

Treatment for PD has several components. Medical treatment focuses on the alleviation of symptoms or curtailing disease progression. L-Dopa began to be used for the aforementioned issues in 1967 to replace dopamine depletion in the substantia nigra. L-Dopa is also associated with the side effects of nausea and vomiting. Sinemet has been shown not to have the aforementioned side effects. L-Dopa has had equivocal findings in its treatment of cognitive difficulties (Arciniegas & Beresford, 2001). Also L-dopa's effects on motor symptoms tend to wear off after 2–3 years with significant problems after 8–10 years (Askin-Edgar et al., 2002). There is debate regarding when to start treatment if the treatment begins to wear off so suddenly. Other medications have been used either alone or in addition to L-dopa. Most are anticholinergic medications to deal with motor symptoms but have an adverse effect on selective attention and planning (Glatt & Koller, 1992).

Surgical treatments including lesioning or placing a deep brain stimulator in several regions of the globus pallidus, subthalamic nuclei, or ventral intermediate thalamic nuclei have been relatively successful (Eskander, Cosgrove, & Shinobu, 2001).

HUNTINGTON'S DISEASE

Another form of subcortical dementia is Huntington's disease once termed *Huntington's chorea.* The word *chorea* is Greek for dance and refers to the involuntary spasmodic movements seen in patients. George Huntington first described the disease in a paper he wrote in 1872 when he was 22 years old (Huntington, 1872). The spasmodic symptoms are very blatant and involve involuntary movements that become disabling because of their severity. Huntington's disease also has cognitive and personality impairments. In a sense, the dementia strikes at all of the functions of the human being—motor, cognitive, and emotional behaviors. Nancy Wexler (1945–), a researcher on Huntington's disease, described it as "the most diabolical disease known to mankind" during a PBS Brain series video (Public Broadcasting System, 1989).

gamma-aminobutyric acid (GABA)
the most common inhibitory neurotransmitter in the central nervous system

Huntington's disease is anatomically caused by atrophy of the GABAergic neurons of the caudate nucleus and putamen in the corpus striatum (Folstein, 1989; see Figure 3.4). **Gamma-aminobutyric acid (GABA)** is the most common inhibitory neurotransmitter. The atrophy may also affect the cerebellum, thalamic nuclei, and other subcortical tissue. Also reported are effects on the basal ganglia (Harris et al., 1996). Huntington's disease is a steadily progressive disease, which tends to affect an individual anywhere between

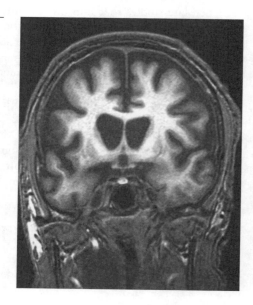

FIGURE 3.4 MRI brain scan of a patient with Huntington's disease showing atrophy of the caudate nuclei, enlargement of the frontal horns of the lateral ventricle, and generalized atrophy. *Source:* Courtesy of F. Gaillard.

10–20 years of age. As is the case with many disorders, the first symptoms may appear to be quite mild and are often ignored, but as more motor symptoms are involved, the disease becomes visible to the individual and others. As the disease runs its full course, pneumonia is the most common cause of death.

Huntington's disease is a hereditary condition. For many years, Huntington's disease was passed from generation to generation because of lack of knowledge regarding its cause. The majority of symptoms arise in one's 30s or 40s and, very often, after one has had children and therefore had already passed on the Huntington's gene.

Huntington's disease is caused by an excess number of trinucleotide CAG repeats (cytosine, adenine, and guanine) on chromosome 4 (Kremer et al., 1994). This is an autosomal dominant disease and has 100% penetrance so that half of all offspring of a carrier parent will acquire the disease if they live long enough (Folstein, 1989). The disease affects men and women equally. Huntington's disease occurs more frequently in Caucasians than in African Americans and is rarely observed in Asians (Lieberman, 1995). Vessie, in 1932, traced the disease to Bures, England, in 1630. There is supposition that some individuals tried at the Salem witch trials may have had this disorder (Okun, 2003).

With the discovery of the Huntington's disease gene in 1993, it has become a serious ethical issue whether individuals should be tested to determine whether they will develop the disorder or pass the disorder on to their offspring. Fear regarding the emotional aftermath of receiving the diagnosis may keep practitioners from suggesting this procedure.

Unfortunately, treatment for patients with Huntington's disease tends to be palliative, in the sense of making the person as comfortable as possible. Neuroleptic medications are most often used to deal with the spasmodic movements (Lerner & Riley, 2002). It tends to be the case that whatever mediation is used alleviates some symptoms but at the same time introduces more side effects or increases other symptoms.

PROGRESSIVE SUPRANUCLEAR PALSY

Progressive supranuclear palsy is a subcortical dementia also known as Steele-Richardson-Olszewski disorder (Steele, Richardson, & Olszewski, 1964). The classic feature of this disorder is an inability to look downward on command. Similar motor, cognitive, and emotional disturbances observed in other subcortical dementias occur with progressive supranuclear palsy. The progression of cognitive decline appears to be greater than in the other disorders already described and is consistent with degeneration of both cortical and subcortical regions (Soliveri et al., 2000). The sites of lesions in progressive supranuclear palsy are in the upper brain stem to the basal ganglia and may include the limbic structures and the basal ganglia (see Figure 3.5). The degenerative process appears to disconnect ascending pathways from these structures to the prefrontal cortex.

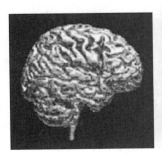 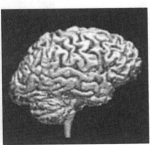

FIGURE 3.5 Progressive supranuclear palsy (left) showing cortical atrophy versus a normal brain (right). *Source:* Adapted from Cordato, N. J., et al. Frontal atrophy correlates with behavioral changes in progressive supranuclear palsy. *Brain* (2002), 15, 796.

Progressive supranuclear palsy is a nonfamilial condition that tends to develop in one's 60s. The risk factors for the conditions are unknown but some researchers suggest a connection to environmental toxins (Golbe, 1996).

Progressive supranuclear palsy has had limited response to dopaminergic or anticholinergic drugs even though symptoms resemble PD (Kompoliti, Goetz, Litvan, Jellinger, & Verny, 1998). The emotional symptoms may be treated with antidepressants.

Progressive Disorders of the Central Nervous System

MULTIPLE SCLEROSIS

Multiple sclerosis (MS) is a disease caused by the destruction of the myelin sheath which covers the axons of neurons (see Figure 3.6). As described earlier, myelin facilitates neural conduction. At the demyelinated sites, multiple discrete plaques are formed by astrocytes. The size of the plaques varies from 1 mm to several centimeters.

The symptoms of MS are many and varied and each individual may have a different combination of symptoms. Classic symptoms include weakness, stiffness, lack of coordination, gait disturbances, bladder and bowel difficulties, sexual dysfunction, sensory changes, heat sensitivity, and fatigue (Miller, 2001).

Cognitive impairment is evident in 40–60% of patients but may be difficult to detect, particularly during the initial stages. Intellectual functioning is significantly affected in about 20% of patients, and memory is one of the most commonly affected areas. The extent of cognitive deficits is related to the location and extent of damage. Emotional sequelae are also evident and many patients will experience denial of their symptoms even when they become wheelchair bound or bedridden. The denial appears to be a defense used by the individual to appear less impaired.

Multiple sclerosis is characterized as a relapsing and remitting disorder. It has all of the hallmarks of a progressive disorder but often exhibits static periods where the progression ceases but the lost functions are never regained. Multiple sclerosis tends to follow one of several courses. These include the following:

- *Relapsing–remitting.* The most common; it is characterized by clearly defined disease relapses. Recovery can be full or with sequelae and residual deficit. No progression of disease between relapses.
- *Secondary–progressive.* The next most common type. First characterized by relapsing–remitting course then progression. Relapses and remissions may or may not occur.

FIGURE 3.6
(A) Demyelination (dark areas) in multiple sclerosis. **(B)** Demyelinization plaques visible in MRI scan. *Source:* Courtesy of John Rose, MD, University of Utah.

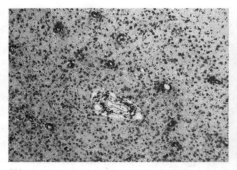

(A)

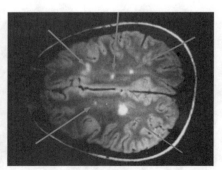

(B)

- *Primary–progressive.* The next most common type. There is unremitting disease progression from onset for most patients, but occasional stabilization and even improvement in functioning in others. No clear relapse.
- *Progressive–relapsing.* The least common type. Disease progression occurs from onset. Acute relapses also occur from which patients may or may not fully recover (Lublin & Reingold, 1996).

Multiple sclerosis generally does not shorten the life span of the individual.

The etiology of MS involves multiple factors. Genetic factors influence susceptibility (Compston & Coles, 2002) and autoimmune diseases are more common in the first-degree relatives of patients with MS (Broadley, Deans, Sawcer, Clayton, & Compston, 2000). Multiple sclerosis is 2–3 times more common in women. The average age of onset is 30. The prevalence of MS varies around the world. Northern sections of many countries show a much higher rate of MS than southern areas. There are also researchers who question the role of infection in the etiology of MS.

There have been studies that have evaluated psychological stress and the occurrence of MS. Warren, Greenhill, and Warren (1982) found that 75% of patients with MS experienced at least one major negative life event prior to onset of symptoms compared to slightly more than 50% with other chronic illnesses. Only one-third of healthy adults exhibited a serious negative event within 1 year (Grant et al., 1989). Grant found patients with MS, compared to healthy adults, to have experienced qualitatively more extreme stressful events. However, this does not prove cause and effect and can be biased by self-report. These types of findings may also explain the relapsing–remitting nature of the disorder.

The treatment for MS has been dramatically changed since the mid-1990s. Injectable medications (B-interferons and glatiramer acetate) suppress immunoactivity (Comi, Filippi, & Wolinsky, 2001). Each medication has a different effect but all impact disease activity, reducing relapse rates and stopping new lesion formation. High-dose corticosteroids are used in acute attacks and are considered to be standard treatment. Neuropsychological effects have been shown with the use of medications in that there has been an increase in cognitive and memory functioning. Cholinesterase inhibitors developed to treat dementia has improved cognitive function in patients with MS.

Counseling for emotional sequelae has proved to be beneficial. Also, cognitive rehabilitation programs for cognitive deficits have been helpful.

NORMAL PRESSURE HYDROCEPHALUS

Normal pressure hydrocephalus results from the accumulation of cerebrospinal fluid caused by lack of reabsorption or obstruction of its flow. Sometimes the obstruction can be identified and other times it cannot. Normal pressure hydrocephalus is a condition which can be corrected; however, if it is left unchecked, it is capable of producing progressive deterioration. Normal pressure hydrocephalus is a disease of old age not similar to the type of hydrocephalus which is sometimes present after birth. The difficulty with the buildup of cerebrospinal fluid is that it greatly enlarges the ventricles, which then causes pressure within the brain. If untreated, normal pressure hydrocephalus becomes a dementia with symptoms including gait disorder, urinary incontinence, and cognitive impairment. Treatment of the disorder is similar to the treatment for children with hydrocephalus and involves the implantation of a shunt, which redirects the cerebrospinal fluid to the heart, which then redirects it into the circulatory system (Hurley, Bradley, Latifi, Katherine, & Taber, 1999; see Figure 3.7).

FIGURE 3.7 Shunt used to recirculate cerebrospinal fluid.

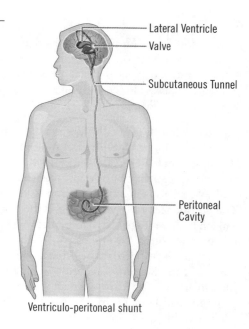

Lateral Ventricle

Valve

Subcutaneous Tunnel

Peritoneal Cavity

Ventriculo-peritoneal shunt

Cerebrovascular Disorders

There are many conditions which could be listed as vascular disorders. They are caused by different etiologies and run different courses. However, all disorders within this section involve difficulty with the circulatory system, which includes the arteries, veins, and capillaries. These vessels are intrinsic to the transport of oxygen and glucose to the brain.

CEREBROVASCULAR ACCIDENT

Cerebrovascular accident (CVA) or stroke is the most common of the cerebrovascular disorders. This was once described as apoplexy and investigated by Galen. The onset of the stroke is most often painless. The symptoms often surprise the individual as they begin to occur. A stroke is a focal or circumscribed neurological disorder of acute development caused by a pathological process in blood vessels (Walton, 1994). The process is a disruption of the flow of oxygen and glucose to the brain. The process of disruption may be sudden or may become progressively worse over a period of years. Many areas of the brain are able to survive with oxygen deprivation for only a few minutes or even less. A CVA results in **cerebral ischemia**, which is defined as loss of blood flow to the brain. If it lasts long enough to destroy neurons the damaged area is termed an **infarct**.

Strokes are generally caused by one of two processes. Thrombic strokes are caused by the occlusion of a cerebral blood vessel by a clump of blood particles and tissue overgrowth, which is termed a **thrombus** (see Figure 3.8). As the thrombus grows, it narrows the opening of the blood vessel and reduces blood flow. The most common cause of a thrombus is atherosclerosis in which fatty deposits build up inside the vessel and narrow it.

cerebral ischemia
the restricted blood flow to the cerebral area of the brain

infarct
localized necrosis resulting from obstruction of a blood vessel

thrombus
fibrinous clot formed in a blood vessel

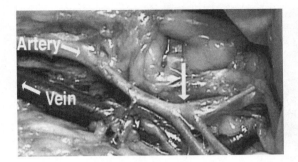

FIGURE 3.8 Thrombus.

Embolic strokes are caused by a clump or plug of thrombic material that has broken away from the blood vessel wall and travels to other areas, usually the brain. Hence, the difference between the two processes is that an **embolus** travels to the brain from another area of the body.

embolus
similar in structure to a thrombus but develops outside of the brain and then travels to the cortex

Sometimes, the interruption in blood supply to the brain is caused by the breaking of a blood vessel, termed a **hemorrhage**. Common causes of a hemorrhage include hypertension or the introduction of a foreign object such as a bullet. Risk factors for stroke include age, cardiac disease, transient ischemic attacks (TIAs), hypertension, and diabetes mellitus (Allen, Sprenkel, Heyman, Schramke, & Heffron, 1998). Smoking is a risk factor for those younger than 65 years old as is gender, with men at a 30% greater risk.

hemorrhage
in neuropsychology, it refers to cerebral hemorrhage which is defined as massive bleeding into a structure of the brain

The symptoms that characterize a stroke tend to be focused on one side of the person's body. The stroke will strike one hemisphere and paralyze (paresis) or partially paralyze (hemiparesis) the opposite side of the body. A left hemisphere stroke will involve verbal and comprehension difficulties with aphasia as a common symptom. Patients who develop aphasia often become very frustrated during the rehabilitation process. In right hemisphere stokes, perceptual and visual–spatial deficits tend to be more prevalent.

Emotional reactions differ between right and left hemisphere strokes. Individuals with left hemisphere strokes tend toward depression and tend to view their symptoms as more serious than they really are. Individuals with right hemisphere strokes tend to exhibit indifference and downplay their symptoms (Heilman, Blonder, Bowers, & Crucian, 2000).

There are few nonsurgical treatment options available. The best option is to give medications to control the patient's blood pressure.

TRANSIENT ISCHEMIC ATTACKS

Transient ischemic attacks are temporary obstructions of a blood vessel for less than 24 hours and many TIAs last only minutes. Many people do not know they have experienced them because they generally do not produce significant or long-lasting effects.

Transient ischemic attacks are characterized as stroke-like phenomena. They tend to occur in one hemisphere with behavioral sequelae on one side of the body. Transient ischemic attacks tend to, but not always, pave the way for a major stroke. The variables that point toward a stroke are similar to those discussed previously. Those who have more than one TIA without a stroke may have a different process evolving. The literature suggests that even a mild TIA will leave some residual cognitive impairment.

Treatment for TIAs involves continual use of antiplatelet therapy, often aspirin. Surgical removal of atherosclerotic plaques may need to be done if there is significant arterial narrowing.

VASCULAR DEMENTIA

This category includes decline in cognitive functioning that results from any number of vascular etiologies. The symptoms necessary to diagnose dementia of the vascular type are not agreed upon by researchers. This causes a great deal of confusion with various patients exhibiting various symptoms and all being diagnosed with vascular dementia. The term *vascular dementia*, previously called multi-infarct dementia or atherosclerotic dementia, covers multiple conditions resulting in widespread cognitive impairment. The cognitive impairment is caused by multiple infarcts at various sites within the brain.

Chui et al. (2000) discuss the categories of vascular dementia. **Cortical atherosclerotic dementia** is caused by multiple infarcts of the large blood vessels, which supply blood to the brain. **Subcortical atherosclerotic dementia** is caused by many infarcts to the smaller blood vessels leading to difficulties in blood supply to subcortical structures. **Lacunar strokes** are caused by small infarcts in the gray nuclei of the basal ganglia, internal capsule, or pons (Cummings & Mahler, 1991). Lacunar strokes give rise to sensory and motor symptoms.

In **Binswanger's disease**, the onset of symptoms is slower than with lacunar strokes. Multiple infarcts in periventricular areas and cerebral white matter are accompanied by demyelization. Cognitive and executive functions are symptoms of Binswanger's disease, in addition to gait disturbances and incontinence. There are specific risk factors for vascular dementia including hypertension, diabetes, high fatty count in the blood, and cigarette smoking (Awad et al., 1987).

There is currently no medication approved for the treatment of vascular dementia. Because some of the same cholinergic deficits that are found in Alzheimer's disease are found in vascular dementia, it is possible that cholinesterase inhibitors may help. Medications such as donepezil have been shown to provide benefits in cognition and activities of daily life (Farlow, 2006).

Currently the treatment for vascular dementia is preventive and supportive. Preventive measures include medication to relieve hypertension and lifestyle changes to help lower the patient's blood pressure. The supportive aspect of treatment includes treatment of psychiatric complications such as depression, measures to help the patient maintain as much independence as possible, and support groups. There are no medications that are recommended specifically for vascular dementia (Sachdev, Brodaty, & Looi, 1999).

HYPERTENSION

Hypertension refers to elevated blood pressure. Blood pressure is read as systolic over diastolic. Systolic pressure is the maximum arterial pressure during the contraction of the left ventricle of the heart. Diastolic pressure is the pressure in the arteries when the heart is at rest. Normal blood pressure is considered to be 120/80 or less. Figures in the range of 121/81 to 139/89 could be considered prehypertensive or borderline hypertensive. The figures fluctuate depending on the source but, generally, 140/90 is considered high blood pressure. Hypertension is the major predictive factor in any form of cardiovascular disorder. High systolic pressure is a major risk factor for stroke. Hypertension has been estimated as the cause of intracranial hemorrhages in 25–94 % of cases (Allen et al., 1998).

---

cortical atherosclerotic dementia
multiple infarcts of the large blood vessels which supply blood to the brain; this leads to symptoms of dementia

subcortical atherosclerotic dementia
multiple infarcts of the smaller blood vessels lead to difficulties in blood supply to subcortical areas; these infarcts then lead to symptoms of dementia

lacunar strokes
small infarcts in the basal ganglia, internal capsule, and pons, which lead to sensory and motor symptoms.

Binswanger's disease
caused by multiple infarcts in the periventricular area and cerebral white matter with demyelization; the disease causes symptoms of dementia

Unfortunately, hypertension often goes undiagnosed. Many people appear symptom free until hypertension is discovered in a routine medical examination. Risk factors for developing hypertension include obesity, excessive use of salt, excessive use of alcohol, lack of exercise, and smoking.

Hypertension alone can cause cognitive deficits. The longer it goes undetected and untreated, the more marked are the cognitive deficits (Dufouil et al., 2001). Individuals who have high blood pressure at age 50 have a correlation with having cognitive deficits at age 70 (Kilander, Nyman, Boberg, & Lithell, 2000). Even without evidence of cerebral changes, such as those evident in MRI, hypertension has been associated with mild cognitive impairment as measured by neuropsychological tests, which may worsen with the duration and severity of the hypertensive condition (Swan, Carmelli, & Larue, 1998; Wilkie, Eisdorfer, & Nowlin, 1976).

Also possibly contributing to cognitive difficulties may be antihypertensive medication which may slow reaction time or cause memory deficits. Research is equivocal on the effects of medications. To treat an individual with hypertension the medications discussed previously may be necessary. Also suggested are changes in lifestyle that decrease the risk factors for hypertension. Changes in lifestyle would include weight loss, if necessary, smoking cessation, decreased use of salt and alcohol, and increased exercise.

MIGRAINE HEADACHES

Migraine headaches are neurological disorders of the brain's vascular structure; hence, they are included with other vascular difficulties. Migraine headaches are the second most common category of neurological disorders. Migraine headaches are considered to be a lateralized headache; however, only 60% of individuals who have migraines report that the headache remains on one side (Derman, 1994). Migraines have often been thought to be signaled by the presence of an **aura**, which may involve lights flashing, unusual body and sensory sensitivity, and sensitivity to sounds (see Figure 3.9). In 1988, the Headache Classification Committee of the International Headache Society began the use of the terms *migraine without aura* to replace common migraine and *migraine with aura* for the classic migraine.

aura
a sensation, as of a cold breeze or a bright light, that precedes the onset of certain disorders, such as an epileptic seizure or migraine headache

The symptoms of migraine vary among individuals. Some individuals have sensations days before the onset of the migraine, whereas others only hours before. Some individuals experience depression, euphoria, irritability, restlessness, fatigue, drowsiness, yawning, mental slowness, and fluid retention (Victor, Ropper, & Adams, 2001).

The migraine aura usually occurs within a half hour before the headache. The headache itself may begin on one side of the brain and then spread to the other. Some individuals have only unilateral (one-sided) headaches. The pain of migraines is associated with nausea and possible vomiting. Other symptoms may occur and usually the person is sensitive to light and sound.

Women tend to experience migraines more often than men. There has been some evidence of a hereditary component to the difficulty. Migraines tend to occur in individuals who experience major stress, too much or too little sleep, and who consume certain foods (especially anything containing nitrates). In general, there are no clear causes or triggers that can be applied to all individuals who have migraines and each person must be evaluated individually. To cope with migraines, many individuals who have migraines retire to a dark quiet room for the duration of the headache. After the headache, they tend to feel fatigue for hours or even days.

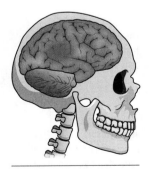

FIGURE 3.9
Migraine aura.

There are basically two theories that attempt to explain the occurrence of migraines. The **vascular theory of migraine** (Graham & Wolff, 1938) states that the aura is associated with intracranial vasoconstriction and the headache with an inflammatory reaction around the walls of dilated cephalic vessels (Lauritzen, 1994). These symptoms are seen as the cause of the pulsating aspects of the headache. The **neurogenic theory of migraine headache** states that the headache is caused by the serotonergic and adrenergic pain-modulating systems. This theory appears to be more related to current research, which indicates a drop in serotonin levels with migraines and a decrease in migraine pain with the administration of antidepressants that work with this neurotransmitter.

A careful diagnosis of migraines differentiating them from cluster and tension headaches needs to be made before medication is administered. Also, it needs to be clear that the headache is not a symptom of a more serious condition such as a vascular disorder or brain tumor. However, although many individuals who have migraines do experience TIAs, very few progress to experience a cerebral vascular accident. In rare instances, an individual may have a migraine stroke. Medications used for migraines include antidepressants such as serotonin agonists and blood pressure medications such as beta-blockers and calcium channel blockers (Ferrari & Haan, 2002).

Brain Tumors

A large variety of tumors are subsumed within the category of brain tumors. A tumor is a mass of new and abnormal tissue that is not physiologically beneficial to its surrounding structure. Many of the tumors are cancerous. However, the presence of a tumor does not indicate a cancerous process. In addition, secondary brain tumors are more common than primary brain tumors in adults, while the reverse is true in children. Secondary brain tumors begin outside of the brain, while primary tumors develop within the brain.

Brain tumors are graded in terms of their level of severity. Grade 1 tumors are the least serious, whereas Grade 4 tumors are considered to be the most serious (Kleihues & Cavenee, 2000; see Figure 3.10). The grading is based on the most malignant area within the tumor.

PRIMARY BRAIN TUMORS

Gliomas

gliomas
tumors that develop from glial cells within the brain

Gliomas are tumors that develop from glial cells within the brain. These are the most common types of primary brain tumors in adults (DeAngelis, 2001). They are slightly more common in men than in women.

Gliomas may be further subdivided into astrocytomas, oligodendroglial tumors, and mixed tumors. Malignant astrocytic tumors, glioblastoma multiform, and anaplastic astrocytomas are the most common glial tumors in adults (DeAngelis, 2001). **Glioblastoma multiform**, which constitute 80% of malignant gliomas, grow quickly and are highly malignant. They tend to appear later in life in the 60s and 70s. Malignant **astrocytomas** appear earlier in life in the 40s and 50s. They tend to infiltrate brain tissue and are difficult to remove surgically. Radiation treatment and chemotherapy are the usual treatments of choice. Treatments tend to be palliative to make the person as comfortable as possible, but

astrocytomas
tumors caused by growth of astrocytes; they tend to not grow very quickly and are rarely malignant

> ### WHO Tumor Grading System
>
> The World Health Organization (WHO) grading system is contained in the volume *Histological Typing of Tumors of the Central Nervous System*, the first edition of which dates back to 1979 and the second (the last) to 1993. The WHO grade has four categories of tumors:
>
> - **Grade I:** Tumors are slow-growing, nonmalignant, and associated with long term survival.
> - **Grade II:** Tumors are relatively slow growing but sometimes recur as higher grade tumors. They can be nonmalignant or malignant.
> - **Grade III:** Tumors are malignant and often recur as higher grade tumors.
> - **Grade IV:** Tumors reproduce rapidly and are very aggressive malignant tumors.

FIGURE 3.10 Brain tumor grading. *Source:* WHO Tumor Grading System, 1993.

are not able to restore the person to earlier levels of functioning. Average survival time for glioblastomas with treatment is 1 year, whereas for anaplastic astrocytomas it is 2–4 years (DeAngelis, 2001).

Lower grade astrocytomas occur in younger adults in their 20s and 30s (DeAngelis, 2001). These tumors are infiltrative but grow much slower. Surgery may be able to remove the entire tumor but there is the chance the tumor is already crowding other brain areas. Radiation is often the treatment of choice.

Oligodendrogliomas constitute up to 20% of all glial neoplasms (Fortin, Cairncross, & Hammond, 1999). They occur more often in men than women and appear at a younger age, usually in the 20s or 30s (Victor et al., 2001). These tumors are usually of lower grade. Very often, the first symptoms are seizures or headaches. Treatment using radiation or chemotherapy works well (Olson, Riedel, & DeAngelis, 2000). Very malignant oligodendrogliomas necessitate more invasive treatment such as surgery followed by chemotherapy and/or radiation.

Meningiomas arise from the cells that cover the meninges. They are the second most common form of brain tumor in adults. Meningiomas grow between the brain and skull. These tumors are more common in women than in men and are usually evident in a person's 60s and 70s. Most meningiomas are benign. They also tend to be fairly well encapsulated. The symptoms that occur with meningiomas are due to pressure on other tissue. The symptoms often include headaches and various forms of paralysis. Very often these tumors do not involve brain tissue and can be completely removed. Chemotherapy tends not to be helpful for inoperable tumors but radiation is helpful; however, many patients will have a recurrence within 10 years.

glioblastomas
tumors of the brain that are a form of gliomas; they grow quickly and are highly malignant

oligodendrogliomas
a glioma which is thought to originate from oligodendrocytes of the brain

meningiomas
the type of tumor that develops from cells that cover the meninges; most meningiomas are benign

Central Nervous System Lymphoma

Central nervous system lymphoma has been on the increase in the past decade, usually thought to be related to the increase in individuals with compromised immune systems (Schabet, 1999). However, this difficulty can also occur in individuals without compromised immune systems but usually later in life.

The lesions that cause central nervous system lymphoma tend to cluster around the ventricles. Patients may exhibit cognitive and/or behavioral changes usually associated with subcortical involvement. Treatment of central nervous system lymphoma consists of cranial irradiation and corticosteroids. This is a short-term treatment and the difficulty usually recurs leaving survival time from diagnosis at 12–18 months.

SECONDARY BRAIN TUMORS

Metastatic Brain Tumors

metastatic intracranial neoplasm
cancerous tumor originating in different parts of the body and then transported to the central nervous system

Metastatic intracranial neoplasms are cancerous tumors originating in various parts of the body and are then transported to the central nervous system. The most common sources of metastatic tumors are the lungs, breasts, skin, gastrointestinal tract, heart, and kidneys (Dropcho, 2002). A metastatic tumor tends to grow faster and show effects sooner than one that developed within the brain. Simple metastatic tumors occur when only one tumor forms at a site. It is more common, however, to have multiple metastatic tumors.

Symptoms that cause the patient to seek medical help are similar to gliomas and include headache, seizures, and cognitive and behavioral changes (Victor et al., 2001). There are several ways brain tumors may cause difficulty with brain functioning. The first is an increase in intracranial pressure, which causes headaches and other difficulties. Seizures are often produced by brain tumors. Brain tumors can cause various types of paralysis and aphasia. Finally, brain tumors may cause certain hormones or endocrine functions to change (DeAngelis, 2001).

Whole brain radiation is the most common treatment for this type of tumor. However, even with treatment, survival time is usually 4–6 months (van den Bent, 2001).

Metabolic and Endocrine Disorders

Metabolic and endocrine disorders of the brain are a secondary effect of a systemic difficulty located elsewhere in the body. Many of the symptoms include cognitive disturbances such as confusion or delirium (Godwin-Austin & Bendall, 1990). Psychological symptoms are more common with endocrine disorders than with metabolic disorders (Boswell, Anifinson, & Nemeroff, 2002).

DIABETES MELLITUS

diabetes mellitus
type 1 diabetes: A severe, chronic form of diabetes caused by insufficient production of insulin and resulting in abnormal metabolism of carbohydrates, fats, and proteins; *type 2 diabetes*: A mild form of diabetes that typically appears first in adulthood and is exacerbated by obesity and inactive lifestyle.

Diabetes mellitus is often referred to as type 1 diabetes. Very often this occurs early in life and, in the past, was referred to as juvenile diabetes. The pathology that causes difficulties is the inability to produce insulin by the pancreas in the cells of the islets of Langerhans. Children and adults with diabetes mellitus have a higher risk than the general population for cognitive impairment. The main difficulty, which relates to cognitive impairment, is the lack of control of glucose levels in the blood (Holmes, 1986).

When the individual with diabetes is hypoglycemic (low blood sugar), they show slowed cognitive abilities (Holmes, Koepke, Thompson, Gyves, & Weydert, 1984). However, when the individual is hyperglycemic (high blood sugar), the symptoms abate. Diabetics are also at greater risk for dementia (Ott et al., 1999). Complicating the picture is the fact that individuals with diabetes often have other difficulties such as hypertension and cerebrovascular disease. This makes it difficult to attribute the cause of any cognitive difficulties to the diabetes unless the individual's entire medical status is known.

The control of diabetes through measuring blood sugar and the use of insulin are the best treatments available. Also encouraged is the increased screenings for all individuals who are at risk for diabetes due to family history or lifestyle factors.

HYPOTHYROIDISM

Cognitive difficulties are fairly common with thyroid insufficiencies in addition to symptoms of fatigue, lethargy, and sluggishness. Concentration and memory difficulties are the most common problems (Abrams & Jay, 2002). Cognitive symptoms tend to arise slowly and can be overlooked at first. Many times, individuals gain weight, become lethargic, and then exhibit memory and concentration difficulties. Serious mental health difficulties such as delirium and hallucinations can occur when hypothyroidism is severe (Abrams & Jay, 2002). The condition can be controlled or even reversed with thyroid replacement medication.

LIVER DISEASE

The liver controls the removal of toxic substances from the body. As one could predict, anything that interferes with the removal could be a cause of liver disease. Etiological factors include infections, excess alcohol usage, and various metabolic disorders. The types of symptoms vary by toxicity and usually include attentional difficulties and response slowing. Treatment for liver disease is mainly preventive. There are vaccines available for hepatitis A and B. Treatment also involves protecting and supporting the remaining liver functions, minimizing further damage, and addressing the cause of the damage.

UREMIA

Kidney failure is the reason for uremia or uremic poisoning. The symptoms include apathy, lethargy, and cognitive dysfunction. Even those individuals who are treated with dialysis tend to exhibit memory and learning problems and reduced mental flexibility (Pliskin, Kiolbasa, Hart, & Umans, 2001). Treatment with dialysis appears to improve cognitive status in comparison to patients who do not receive dialysis. However, even with dialysis, many patients continue to display memory and learning problems and reduced mental flexibility (Pliskin et al., 2001).

Seizures

Seizures can arise for many different reasons. In this chapter we will focus on epilepsy, a neurological disorder. In the following chapter, we will focus on seizures that occur secondary to brain trauma, substance abuse, or any other condition which may lower the seizure threshold of the individual.

EPILEPSY

Epilepsy occurs for many reasons and is exhibited in individuals in many different manners. Epilepsy is an episodic disturbance of behavior and perception caused by hyperexcitability and hyposynchronous discharge of the nerve cells of the brain. In a sense, the brain is short circuited. Epilepsy is the most prevalent of the chronic neurological disorders (Hauser & Hesdorffer, 1990). The lifetime incidence is 2–5% of the population. Epilepsy is usually

epilepsy
any of various neurological disorders characterized by sudden and recurring attacks of motor, sensory, or psychic malfunction with or without loss of consciousness or convulsive seizures

FIGURE 3.11 Seizure categories. *Source:* Pellock, J. M., Bourgeois, B. F. D., Dodson, W. E. (2008). *Pediatric Epilepsy*, 3 ed. NY: Demos Medical Publishing.

Seizure Categories

I. Focal seizures (previously known as partial or local seizures)

A. Simple focal seizures (consciousness not impaired)
   1. With motor symptoms
   2. With somatosensory or special sensory symptoms
   3. With autonomic symptoms
   4. With psychic symptoms
B. Complex focal seizures (with impairment of consciousness)
   1. Beginning as simple focal seizures and progressing to impairment of consciousness
      a. With no other features
      b. With features as in A.1-4
      c. With automatisms
   2. With impairment of consciousness at onset
      a. With no other features
      b. With features as in A.1-4
      c. With automatisms
C. Focal seizures secondarily generalized

II. Generalized seizures (convulsive or nonconvulsive)

   1. Absence seizures
   2. Atypical absence seizures
   3. Myoclonic seizures
   4. Clonic seizures
   5. Tonic seizures
   6. Tonic-clonic seizures
   7. Atonic seizures

III. Unclassified epileptic seizures

classified as focal or generalized and with reference to whether the etiology is known or unknown (Tran, Spencer, & Spencer, 1998; see Figure 3.11). Focal or partial seizures have a localized origin. **Generalized seizures** involve large regions of both hemispheres simultaneously. If the cause of the seizure is known, it is termed **symptomatic**. If the cause of the seizure is unknown it is termed **idiopathic**.

Partial seizures arise from a specific focal area of the brain, may be without loss of consciousness (simple) and may include only one modality of expression (motor, somatosensory, autonomic, and psychic). **Complex partial seizures** include loss of consciousness. Partial seizures may also progress. Many seizures are preceded by an aura similar to a migraine headache. Primary generalized seizures may be nonconvulsive in which consciousness is briefly lost, or convulsive which involves major motor manifestations (grand mal seizures).

Epilepsy tends to present at greater levels in families either as a general lessening of the seizure threshold or an inherited predisposition to seizures (Berkovic, Howell, Hay, & Hopper, 1998). Behavior and cognitive functioning may be altered by seizures, which are often determined by etiology, frequency, duration, and severity. Memory and learning problems are common among many epileptics (Helmstaedter & Kurthen, 2001). Psychiatric symptoms may appear in patients with epilepsy. Personality disorders are more common in this group (Lishman, 1997). There is also a higher rate of comorbidity for psychological disorders.

After the seizure, many individuals exhibit shame or anger along with confusion. In many states an individual who has been diagnosed with epilepsy is prohibited from driving a vehicle. Often the individual must prove they are seizure free for a period of time before they are allowed to drive. Physicians have the authority to take away driving privileges of patients with seizure.

Treatment for most individuals involves antiepileptic medications. Patients may need to try various doses to alleviate the symptoms and may need to change medications to obtain the relief they need. Surgery has been performed to relieve the spread of seizures from one side of the brain to the other. Operations often involve partial disconnection of the two hemispheres of the brain. The most commonly performed operation is an anterior temporal lobectomy, which is complicated when the pathology is hippocampal sclerosis. Two-thirds of cases can be expected to be seizure free (Polkey, 2000). Vagal nerve stimulation is a recent development which delivers intermittent stimulation. It tends to improve seizure control but does not completely eradicate the seizures.

Individual or group counseling can be very helpful for individuals with epilepsy. Education for those with epilepsy is important in order to know the etiology of seizures. Also very important is the social support from a group, so that the individual understands that others also have this ailment.

After reviewing the major central nervous system degenerative disorders, it is clear that Mr. Alfred has dementia, probably of the Alzheimer's type. It also appears that he may be experiencing secondary depression because he reacts to the changes in his abilities and circumstances. In addition, the case study implies that he may have had a concussion or possibly a closed head injury more than 40 years ago. It was crucial for Mr. Alfred to have been evaluated by the clinical neuropsychologist not only to verify behaviorally his dementing process but also to assess his current strengths and weaknesses. Although he eventually moved out of the home into an assisted care facility, his situation improved and his relationships with his family also improved. At the time of this writing, Mr. Alfred is still living and has declined somewhat more in his cognitive abilities. However, with the aid of the multidisciplinary professionals available to him, he is much more physically and mentally healthy than he was when he first came to his visit the clinical neuropsychologist.

Summary

Neuropathology has been divided into two chapters, the present focusing on neurodegenerative disorders, and chapter 4 exploring acquired disorders. This chapter begins with a case study illustrating the symptoms and issues that are salient in neurodegenerative disorders. Degenerative disorders that lead to dementia are explored within the cortical and subcortical structures. Similarities and differences between the processes are illustrated. The progressive disorders of these central nervous system difficulties and the distinguishing characteristics of these difficulties are also reviewed.

Cerebrovascular disorders are another large grouping of disorders which deal with any form of difficulty within the vascular system. Types of occluding processes along with risk factors are evaluated. Brain tumors, primary and secondary, comprise another large category. Types of tumors and sites of origin as well as causes within the central nervous system are explored. Metabolic and endocrine disorders, usually having cognitive difficulties as a secondary problem to the systemic difficulty, are also explored. Each disorder has a primary systemic difficulty and secondary neuropsychological sequelae.

Seizure disorders have been divided into those caused by epilepsy and other systemic problems. Epilepsy and its varieties are discussed within this chapter, whereas seizures, as a reaction to head trauma and other nonsystemic problems, will be covered in the next chapter.

Questions for Further Study

1. Many central nervous system degenerative disorders are diagnosed by medical professionals. What additional information is provided by a neuropsychological evaluation?
2. All of the difficulties in this chapter have the potential for a comorbid diagnosis of depression. Why is that the case?
3. Lifestyle has become an increasingly discussed issue. What types of lifestyle factors could preclude or exacerbate disorders discussed in this chapter?

References

Abrams, G. M., & Jay, C. A. (2002). Neurological manifestations of endocrine disease. In A. K. Ashbury, P. M. McKhann, W. I. McDonald, P. J. Goadsby, & J. C. McArthur (Eds.), *Diseases of the nervous system: Clinical neuroscience and therapeutic principles* (3rd ed., pp. 2033–2043). Cambridge, UK: Cambridge University Press.

Allen, D. N., Sprenkel, D. G., Heyman, R. A., Schramke, C. J., & Heffron, N. E. (1998). Evaluation of demyelinating and degenerative disorders. In G. Goldstein, P. D. Nussbaum, & S. R. Beers (Eds.), *Human brain function assessment and rehabilitation: Neuropsychology* (pp. 187–208). New York: Plenum Press.

Arciniegas, D. B., & Beresford, T. P. (2001). *Neuropsychiatry: An introductory approach*. Cambridge, UK: Cambridge University Press.

Armstrong, Cairns, N., & Lantos, P. (1999). The spatial patterns of Pick bodies, Pick cells and Alzheimer's disease pathology in Pick's disease. *Neuropathology, 19*(1), 64–70.

Askin-Edgar, S., White, K. E., & Cummings, J. L. (2002). Neuropsychiatric aspects of Alzheimer's disease and other dementing illnesses. In S. E. Yudowfsky & R. E. Hales (Eds.), *The American psychiatric publishing textbook of neuropsychiatry and clinical neurosciences* (4th ed., pp. 953–988). Washington, DC: American Psychiatric Publishing, Inc.

Awad, I. A., Spetzler, R. F., Hodak, J. A., Awad, C. A., Williams, F., & Carey, R. (1987). Incidental lesions noted on magnetic resonance imaging of the brain: Prevalence and clinical significance in various age groups. *Neurosurgery, 20*(2), 222–227.

Barber, R., Panikkar, A., & McKeith, I. G. (2001). Dementia with Lewy bodies: Diagnosis and management. *International Journal of Geriatric Psychiatry. 16*, S12–S18.

Basset, S. S. (2005). Cognitive impairment in Parkinson's disease. *Primary Psychiatry. 12*(1), 50–55.

Berkovic, S. F., Howell, R. A., Hay, D. A., & Hopper, J. L. (1998). Epilepsies in twins: Genetics of the major epilepsy syndromes. *Annals of Neurology, 43*(4), 435–445.

Bird, T. D. (1998). Genotypes, phenotypes, and frontotemporal dementia: Take your pick. *Neurology, 50*(6), 1526–1527.

Boller, F., & Duykaerts, C. (2003). Alzheimer's disease: Clinical and anatomic issues. In T. E. Feinberg & M. J. Farah (Eds.), *Behavioral neurology and neuropsychology* (2nd ed., pp. 515–544). New York: McGraw-Hill.

Bondi, M. W., Salmon, D. P., & Kazniak, A. (1996). The neuropsychology of dementia. In I. Grant & K. M. Adams (Eds.), *Neuropsychological assessment of neuropsychiatric disorders* (2nd ed., pp. 164–199). New York: Oxford University Press.

Boswell, E. B., Anifinson, T. J., & Nemeroff, C. B. (2002). Neuropsychiatric aspects of endocrine disorders. In S. C. Yudofsky & R. E. Hales (Eds.), *Textbook of neuropsychiatry and clinical neurosciences* (4th ed., pp. 851–876). Washington, DC: American Psychiatric Publishing, Inc.

Bozeat, S., Gregory, C. A., Ralph, M. A., & Hodges, J. R. (2000). Which neuropsychiatric and behavioral features distinguish frontal and temporal variants of frontotemporal dementia from Alzheimer's disease? *Journal of Neurology, Neurosurgery, and Psychiatry, 69*(2), 178–186.

Brinton, R. D. (2001). Cellular and molecular mechanisms of estrogen regulation of memory function and neuroprotection against Alzheimer's disease: Recent insights and remaining challenges. *Learning and Memory*, 8(3), 121–133.

Broadley, S. A., Deans, J., Sawcer, S. J., Clayton, D., & Compston, D. A. (2000). Autoimmune disease in first-degree relatives of patients with multiple sclerosis: A UK survey. *Brain*, 123(Pt. 6), 1102–1111.

Camicioli, R., Willert, P., Lear, J., Grossmann, S., Kaye, J., & Butterfield, P. (2000). Dementia in rural primary care practices in Lake County, Oregon. *Journal of Geriatric Psychiatry and Neurology*, 13(2), 87–92.

Carr, D. B., Goate, A., Phil, D. and Morris, J. C. (1997). Current concepts in the pathogenesis of Alzheimer's disease. *American Journal of Medicine*. 103(3A), 3S–10S.

Chui, H. C., Mack, W., Jackson, J. E., Mungas, D., Reed, B. R., Tinklenberg, J., et al. (2000). Clinical criteria for the diagnosis of vascular dementia: A multicenter study of comparability and interrater reliability. *Archives of Neurology*, 57(2), 191–196.

Comi, G., Filippi, M., & Wolinsky, J. S. (2001). European/Canadian multicenter, double-blind, randomized, placebo-controlled study of the effects of glatiramer acetate on magnetic resonance imaging-measured disease activity and burden in patients with relapsing multiple sclerosis European/Canadian Glatiramer Acetate Study Group. *Annals of Neurology*, 49, 290–297.

Compston, A., & Coles, A. (2002). Multiple sclerosis. *Lancet*, 359(9313), 1221–1231.

Corder, E. H., Saunders, A. M., Strittmatter, W. J., Schmechel, D. E., Gaskell, P. C., Small, G. W., et al. (1993). Gene dose of apolipoprotein E type 4 allele and risk of Alzheimer's disease in late onset families. *Science*, 261(5123), 921–923.

Cummings, J. L. (1986). Subcortical dementia. Neuropsychology, neuropsychiatry, and pathophysiology. *British Journal of Psychiatry*, 149, 682–697.

Cummings, J. L., Cyrus, P. A., Bieber, F., Mas, J., Orazem, J., & Gulanski, B. (1998). Metrifonate treatment of the cognitive deficits of Alzheimer's disease. Metrifonate Study Group. *Neurology*, 50(5), 1214–1221.

Cummings, J. L. and Mahler, M.E. (1991). Cerebrovascular dementia. In: R.A. Bornstein and GG. Brown (eds.). Neurobehavioral aspects of cerebrovascular disease. Oxford University Press, New York, NY. Pp. 131–149.

Cutler, N. R., & Sramek, J. J. (2001). Review of the next generation of Alzheimer's disease therapeutics: Challenges for drug develpment. *Progress in Neuro-Psychopharmacology and Biological Psychiatry*, 25(1), 27–57.

DeAngelis, L. M. (2001). Brain tumors. *New England Journal of Medicine*, 344(2), 114–123.

DeKosky, S. T., & Orgogozo, J. M. (2001). Alzheimer disease: Diagnosis, costs, and dimensions of treatment. *Alzheimer Disease and Associated Disorders*, 15(Suppl. 1), S3–S7.

Derman, H. S. (1994). Headaches: Diagnosis and treatment. In S. H. Appel (Ed.), *Current Neurology* (Vol. 14). St. Louis, MO: Mosby.

Dropcho, E. J. (2002). Remote neurologic manifestations of cancer. *Neurologic Clinics*, 20(1), 85–122.

Dufouil, C., de Kersaint-Gilly, A., Besacon, V., Levy, C., Auffray, E., Brunnearau, L., Alperovitch, A. and Tzourio, C. (2001). Longitudinal study of blood pressure and white matter hyperintensities. The EVA MRI Cohort. *Neurology* 56, 921–926.

Eskander, E. N., Cosgrove, G. R., & Shinobu, L. A. (2001). Surgical treatment of Parkinson disease. *The Journal of American Medical Association*, 286(24), 3056–3059.

Evans, D. A., Funkenstein, H. H., Albert, M. S., Scherr, P. A., Cook, N. R., Chown, M. J., et al. (1989). Prevalence of Alzheimer's disease in a community population of older persons: Higher than previously reported. *Journal of American Medical Association*, 262(18), 2551–2556.

Farlow, M. (2006). Use of antidementia agents in vascular dementia: Beyond Alzheimer disease. *Mayo Clinic Proceedings*, 81(10), 1350–1358.

Ferrari, M. D., & Haan, J. (2002). Migraine. In A. Asbury, G. M. McKhann. W. I. McDonald, P. Goadsby & J. C. McArthur (Eds.), *Diseases of the nervous system* (3rd ed., pp. 920–926). Cambridge, UK: Cambridge University Press.

Filley, C. M. (1995). *Neurobehavioral anatomy*. Niwot, CO: University Press of Colorado.

Folstein, S. E. (1989). *Huntington's disease: A disorder of families*. Baltimore: Johns Hopkins University Press.

Fortin, D., Cairncross, G. J., & Hammond, R. R. (1999). Oligodendroglioma: An appraisal of recent data pertaining to diagnosis and treatment. *Neurosurgery, 45*(6), 1279–1291.

Glatt, S. L., & Koller, W. C. (1992). Effect of antiparkinsonian drugs on memory. In S. J. Huber & J. L. Cummings (Eds.), *Parkinson's disease: Neurobehavioral aspects.* (pp. 303–312). New York: Oxford University Press.

Godwin-Austin, R. B., & Bendall, J. (1990). *The neurology of the elderly.* Heidelberg, Germany: Springer-Verlag.

Golbe, L. I. (1996). The epidemiology of progressive supranuclear palsy. *Advances in Neurology, 69,* 25–31.

Graham, J. R., & Wolff, H. G. (1938). Mechanism of migraine headache and action of ergotamine tartrate. *Archives of Neurology and Psychiatry, 39*(4), 737–763.

Grant, I., Brown, G. W., Harris, T., McDonald, W. I., Patterson, T., & Trimble, M. R. (1989). Severely threatening events and marked life difficulties preceding onset or exacerbation of multiple sclerosis. *Journal of Neurology, Neurosurgery, and Psychiatry, 52*(1), 8–13.

Grossman, M. (2001). A multidisciplinary approach to Pick's disease and frontotemporal dementia. *Neurology, 56*(4), S2.

Hannay, H. J., Bieliauskas, L. A., Crosson, B. A., Hammeke, T. A., Hamsher, K., & Koffler, S. P. (1998). The Houston Conference on specialty education and training in Clinical Neuropsychology: Policy statement. *Archives of Clinical Neuropsychology, 13*(2), 157–250.

Harris, G. J., Aylward, E. H., Peyser, C. E., Pearlson, G. D., Brand, J., Roberts-Twillie, J. V., Barta, P. E., Folstein, S. E. (1996). Single photon emission computed tomographic blood flow and magnetic resonance volume imaging of basal ganglia in Huntington's disease. *Archives of Neurology, 53,* 316–324.

Hauser, W. A., & Hesdorffer, D. C. (1990). *Epilepsy: Frequency, causes and consequences.* New York: Demos Publishing.

Heilman, K.M., Blonder, L.X., Bowers, D., & Crucian, G. P. (2000). Neurological disorders and emotional dysfunction. In J.C. Borod (Ed.). The Neuropsychology of emotion. New York: Oxford University Press. Pp. 367–412.

Helmstaedter, C., & Kurthen, M. (2001). Memory and epilepsy: Characteristics, courses, and influence of drugs and surgery. *Current Opinion in Neurology, 14*(2), 211–216.

Higgins, J. J., & Mendez, M. F. (2000). Roll over pick and tell Alzheimer the news! *Neurology, 54*(4), 784–785.

Holmes, C. S. (1986). Neuropsychological profiles in men with insulin-dependent diabetes. *Journal of Consulting and Clinical Psychology, 54*(3), 386–389.

Holmes, C. S., Koepke, K. M., Thompson, R. G., Gyves, P. W., & Weydert, J. A. (1984). Verbal fluency and naming performance in type I diabetes at different blood glucose concentrations. *Diabetes Care, 7*(5), 454–459.

Huntington, G. (1872). On chorea. *The Medical and Surgical Reporter, 26*(15), 317–321.

Hurley, R. A., Bradley, W. G., Jr., Latifi, H. T., & Taber, K. H. (1999). Normal pressure hydrocephalus: Significance of MRI in a potentially treatable dementia. *Journal of Neuropsychiatry and Clinical Neurosciences, 11*(3), 297–300.

Janus, C., Pearson, J., McLaurin, J., Mathews, P.M., Jian, Y., Schmidt, SD, Chisht, M.A., Horne, P. et al (2000). AB peptide immunization reduces behavioural impairment and plaques in a model of Alzheimer's disease. *Nature* 408 (6815), 885–1012.

Kaufer, D. I., & Cummings, J. L. (2003). Dementia and delirium: An overview. In T. E. Feinberg & M. J. Farah (Eds.), *Behavioral neurology and neuropsychology* (2nd ed., pp. 495–514). New York: McGraw-Hill.

Keene, J., Hope, T., Fairburn, C. G., & Jacoby, R. (2001). Death and dementia. *International Journal of Geriatric Psychiatry, 16*(10), 969–974.

Khachaturian, Z. (2000). Toward a comprehensive theory of Alzheimer's disease—challenges, caveats, and parameters. New York Academy of Sciences. 924, 184–193.

Kilander, L., Nyman, H., Boberg, M., Lithell, H. (2000). The association between low diastolic blood pressure in middle age and cognitive function in old age. A population-based study. *Age and Ageing* 29(3), 243–248.

Kleihues, P., & Cavenee, W. K. (2000). *World Health Organization classification of tumours: Pathology and genetics of tumours of the nervous system.* Lyon, France: IARC Press.

Kompoliti, K., Goetz, C. G., Litvan, I., Jellinger, K., & Verny, M. (1998). Pharmacological therapy in progressive supranuclear palsy. *Archives of Neurology, 55*(8), 1099–1102.

Kremer, B., Goldberg, P., Andrew, S. E., Theilmann, J., Telenius, H., Zeisler, J., et al. (1994). A worldwide study of the Huntington's disease mutation: The sensitivity and specificity of measuring CAG repeats. *The New England Journal of Medicine, 330*(20), 1401–1406.

Lauritzen, M. (1994). Pathophysiology of the migraine aura: The spreading depression theory. *Brain, 117*(Pt. 1), 199–210.

Lerner, A. J., & Riley, D. (2002). Neuropsychiatric aspects of dementias associated with motor dysfunction. In S. C. Yudofskey & R. E. Hales (Eds.), *Textbook of neuropsychiatry and clinical neurosciences* (5th ed., pp. 907–934). Washington, DC: American Psychiatric Publishing, Inc.

Lezak, M. D., Howieson, D. B., & Loring, D. W. (2004). *Neuropsychological assessment* (4th ed.). New York: Oxford University Press.

Lieberman, A. (1995). Other forms of movement disorders. In J. P. Mohr & J. C. Gautier (Eds.), *Guide to clinical neurology* (pp. 875–882). New York: Churchill Livingstone.

Lieberman, A. (1998). Managing the neuropsychiatric symptoms of Parkinson's disease. *Neurology, 50*(6), S33–S38.

Lippa, C. F., Smith, T. W., Saunders, A. M., Crook, R., Pulaski-Salo, D., Davies, P., et al. (1995). Apolipoprotein E genotype and Lewy body disease. *Neurology, 45*(1), 97–103.

Lishman, W. A. (1997). *Organic psychiatry: The psychological consequences of cerebral disorder* (3rd ed.). Oxford, UK: Blackwell.

Lublin, F. D., & Reingold, S. C. (1996). Defining the clinical course of Multiple Sclerosis: Results of an international survey. National Multiple Sclerosis Society (USA) Advisory Committee on Clinical Trials of New Agents in Multiple Sclerosis. *Neurology, 46*(4), 907–911.

Mahurin, R. K., Feher, E. P., Nance, M. L., Levy, J. K., & Pirozzolo, F. J. (1993). Cognition in Parkinson's disease and related disorders. In R. W. Parks, R. F. Zec, & R. S. Wilson (Eds.), *Neuropsychology of Alzheimer's disease and other dementias.* New York: Oxford University Press.

McDowell, I. (2001). Alzheimer's disease: Insights from epidemiology. *Aging, 13*(3), 143–162.

McKeith, I. G. (2002). Dementia with Lewy bodies. *The British Journal of Psychiatry, 180*(2), 144–147.

Miller, A. E. (2001). Clinical features. In S. D. Cook (Ed.), *Handbook of multiple sclerosis* (pp. 213–232). New York: Marcel Dekker.

Monk, D. and Brodaty, H. (2000). Use of estrogens for the prevention and treatment of Alzheimer's disease dementia and geriatric cognitive disorders. 11(1), 1–10.

Mortimer, J. A., & Pirozzolo, F. J. (1985). Remote effects of head trauma. *Developmental Neuropsychology, 1,* 215–229.

Neary, D., Snowden, J. S., Gustafson, L., Passant, U., Stuss, D., Black, S., et al. (1998). Frontotemporal lobar degeneration: A consensus on clinical diagnostic criteria. *Neurology, 51*(6), 1546–1554.

Okun, M. S. (2003). Huntington's disease: What we learned from the original essay. *Neurologist, 9*(4), 175–179.

Olson, J. D., Riedel, E., & DeAngelis, L. M. (2000). Long-term outcome of low-grade oligodendroglioma and mixed glioma. *Neurology, 54*(7), 1442–1448.

Orgogozo, J. M., Dartigues, J. F., Lafont, S., Letenneur, L., Commenges, D., Salamon, R., et al. (1997). Wine consumption and dementia in the elderly: A prospective community study in the Bordeaux area. *Revue Neurologique, 153*(3), 185–192.

Ott, A., van Rossum, C. T., van Harskamp, F., van de Mheen, H., Hofman, A., & Breteler, M. M. (1999). Education and the incidence of dementia in a large population-based study: The Rotterdam study. *Neurology, 52*(3), 663–666.

Plassman, B. L., Havlik, R. J., Steffens, D. C., Helms, M. J., Newman, T. N., Drosdick, D., et al. (2000). Documented head injury in early adulthood and risk of Alzheimer's disease and other dementias. *Neurology, 55*(8), 1158–1166.

Pliskin, N. H., Kiolbasa, T. A., Hart, R. P., & Umans, J. G. (2001). Neuropsycholocigal dysfunctions due to liver disease. In R. E. Tarter, M. Butters & S. R. Beers (Eds.), *Medical neuropsychology* (2nd ed., pp. 85–106). New York: Kluwer Academic/Plenum Press.

Polkey, C. (Ed.). (2000). Temporal lobe resections. In J. M. Oxbury & M. Duchowny (Ed.), *Intractable focal epilepsy* (pp. 135–150). London: W. B. Saunders.

Public Broadcasting System. (1989). Confronting the killer gene. *Nova.* Boston: Author.

Roses, A. D., & Saunders, A. M. (1997). Apolipoprotein E genotyping as a diagnostic adjunct for Alzheimer's disease. *International Psychogeriatrics, 9,* 277–288.

Sachdev, P. S., Brodaty, H., & Looi, J. C. (1999). Vascular dementia: Diagnosis, management and possible prevention. *Medical Journal of Australia, 170*(2), 81–85.

Schabet, M. (1999). Epidemiology of primary CNS Lymphoma. *Journal of Neuro-Oncology, 43*(3), 199–201.

Skoog, I., & Blennow, K. (2001). Alzheimer's disease. In A. Hofman & R. Mayeux (Eds.), *Investigating neurological disease. Epidemiology for clinical neurology* (pp. 157–173). Cambridge, UK: Cambridge University Press.

Steele, J. C., Richardson, J. C., & Olszewski, J. (1964). Progressive Supranuclear Palsy: A heterogeneous degeneration involving the brain stem, basal ganglia and cerebellum with vertical gaze and pseudobulbar palsy, nuchal dystonia and dementia. *Archives of Neurology, 10*(4), 333–359.

Swan, G. E., Carmelli, D., & Larue, A. (1998). Systolic blood pressure tracking over 25 to 30 years and cognitive performance in older adults. *Stroke, 29*(11), 2334–2340.

Tran, T. A., Spencer, S. S., & Spencer, D. D. (1998). Epilepsy: Medical and surgical outcome. In M. Swash (Ed.), *Outcomes in neurological and neurosurgical disorders* (pp. 407–440). Cambridge, UK: Cambridge University Press.

van den Bent, M. J. (2001). The diagnosis and management of brain metastases. *Current Opinion in Neurology, 14*(6), 717–723.

Victor, M., Ropper, A. H., & Adams, R. D. (2001). *Adams and Victor's principles of neurology* (7th ed.). New York: McGraw-Hill.

Walton, J. N. (1994). *Brain's diseases of the nervous system.* Oxford, UK: Oxford University Press.

Warren, S., Greenhill, S., & Warren, K. G. (1982). Emotional stress and the development of multiple sclerosis: Case-control evidence of a relationship. *Journal of Chronic Disease, 35*(11), 821–831.

Weiner, M. F. (1999). Dementia associated with Lewy Bodies: Dilemmas and directions. *Archives of Neurology, 56*(12), 1441–1442.

Wilkie, F. L., Eisdorfer, C., & Nowlin, J. B. (1976). Memory and blood pressure in age. *Experimental Aging Research, 2,* 3–16.

Neuropathology: Acquired Disorders

4

Learning Objectives

After reading this chapter, the student should be able to understand:

- The definition, symptoms, and treatments of acquired disorders of the central nervous system
- The similarities and differences between open and closed head injuries and their prevalence, pathophysiological effects, and treatment
- The varieties of toxic conditions, including alcohol-related disorders and illegal and legal drugs, and their neurological and neuropsychological effects
- The different types of environmental and industrial neurotoxins and their impact on the central nervous system
- Different conditions of oxygen deprivation and how they affect the body and central nervous system
- The impact and neurological and neuropsychological effects of nutritional deficiencies for humans of various age
- The effects of infectious processes on the central nervous system
- The difference in causes and effects between seizures caused by primary and secondary disorders of the central nervous system

Topical Outline

- Traumatic Brain Injury/Head Injury
- Toxic Conditions
- Environmental and Industrial Neurotoxins

- Oxygen Deprivation
- Nutritional Deficiencies
- Seizures
- Infectious Processes

Case Vignette

Carly is a 32-year-old mother of two who is presently in the process of completing her bachelor's degree in elementary education. She graduated from high school with very good grades and subsequently enrolled in the local state university. She was doing extremely well in school, had been accepted into the Education Department, and was deciding whether she should focus on elementary or secondary education or both when her life changed.

During the fall semester of her junior year, when she was 20 years old, Carly met and fell in love with her current husband. He was exciting and had wonderful plans for their future together. He was not as focused as Carly and had not chosen his major or even narrowed his areas of interest. With Carly's help, he determined that art and music were his strongest areas and that he needed to decide a major from between the two. At the same time that Carly was helping her soon-to-be husband focus, she was losing her own interest in school. During Christmas break, he asked Carly to marry him and she accepted. She agreed to finish the spring semester but then wanted to become a wife and mother.

Soon after they were married Carly found employment as an office manager with the local school district. Even though she had lost interest in finishing her schooling, she still preferred the educational atmosphere. Carly's husband completed his last year of college and graduated with a degree in art history. Two children were born soon after his graduation, first a boy and a year later a girl. Once her husband was able to obtain employment, she decided to stay home with the children. Her husband was not able to find work using his degree but did obtain employment with a distributing company and progressed within the company into a managerial position.

Money was limited with only one person working in the family; therefore, they eventually chose to buy an older building in the country and renovate it instead of buying a house in the city where they lived. After work and on the weekends, Carly's husband worked stripping old wood and fixing and repairing floors, the ceiling, and other parts of the building. They learned that the building had been used as an old schoolhouse, which pleased Carly. Carly even contacted the local historical society to find out more about the history of the building.

When the children became 10 and 11 years old, Carly decided that she wanted to finish her degree and pursue teaching. She enrolled at the same college she had originally attended and found she could continue with her education major after taking a few refresher courses. She began school with enthusiasm. However, she soon found that her concentration was not as good as it used to be and that her memory did not seem to be adequate. She became fearful regarding her abilities as a student.

Carly's husband reassured her and suggested that her school difficulties may be caused by her poor sleeping habits. He reminded her that for unknown reasons, everyone in the household had not been sleeping well during the past summer. Carly also revealed that she had been having severe headaches and an occasional bloody nose. Her husband stated that he too had been experiencing *similar symptoms. Somewhat relieved, Carly completed the fall semester. She seemed to feel a little better at school than when she went home. She attributed her change in symptoms to trying to cram for tests at home. She also felt a struggle between being a student, a wife, and a mother.*

Student teaching began in the spring semester. According to the classroom teacher with whom she was working, Carly performed very well. Carly did not physically feel better and began to think that her symptoms were psychosomatic. Concerned that her symptoms may affect her classroom behavior, she went to the college counseling center. She began therapy to sort out her mixed feelings and to see if her physical complaints were caused by her feelings.

At the same time that she was student teaching, her children began to complain of headaches to their school nurse. Carly and her husband went to the school and met with the nurse. Carly had told herself that her headaches and other symptoms were emotional in nature and that the same was true for her husband, but when it came to the children, Carly felt they needed to consult a physician. Both children were seen by their pediatrician. Blood work showed that both children had elevated levels of heavy metals in their bloodstream. The physician was concerned and questioned the parents in detail. He also requested that both parents have blood work performed. The physician's suspicions were correct that something was awry in the situation. The entire family had elevated levels of heavy metals, which could account for the headaches, bloody noses, and concentration and memory problems. The physician was puzzled as to how the family became exposed to these toxins and what damage the exposure had caused.

Because Carly's symptoms were the most pronounced, the physician referred her to a clinical neuropsychologist. The clinical neuropsychologist completed a battery of tests which revealed that she had concentration, memory, and abstract reasoning deficits. These were evident even though she was a bright and motivated person. Through a thorough history the clinical neuropsychologist was able to determine some of the potential causes of the problems. The family had moved to the country, which meant they had been exposed to fertilizers, pesticides, and herbicides used by local farmers. The main cause, however, appeared to be the restoration of their home. Questioning led to the realization that in the basement of the house were large barrels of cleaning solutions, materials for stripping wood, and chemicals to remove paint and varnish. The family had been living in a toxic environment and had not realized it.

The realization of the toxic environment forced the family into making a decision to sell their property and move into the city. It was difficult to sell the property, which they had worked so hard to restore, but it appeared to be the safest alternative. Six months after they left the old house for their new townhouse, the family members had repeat blood tests. The results, which were not completely back to normal, were dramatically reduced in terms of toxins. Carly also stated that she had been feeling much better and that her headaches were almost nonexistent. Carly was able to complete her teaching degree and, within 1 year, was employed in the local school district teaching third grade. Fortunately, for the entire family, the symptoms that they had experienced never returned once they changed their residence.

This case may seem to be very complex and the clinical neuropsychologist needed to function as a detective to determine the cause of the family's difficulties. There is a question of how long the family could remain in the house if the physician had decided all of the symptoms were caused by emotional factors. How long can a person remain in a toxic situation before their difficulties become permanent? What types of situations might anyone put himself or herself in without realizing the potential consequences? These types of questions will be discussed in this chapter.

Introduction

As was described in the previous chapter, the number and variety of difficulties which can affect the central nervous system are so vast that the disorders have been divided into two chapters. These chapters are based on whether the difficulty or disorder is degenerative or whether it was acquired through some form of interaction with the environment. The latter will be the focus of this chapter. Clearly, the individuals in the case study had interacted with environmental toxins.

Traumatic Brain Injury/Head Injury

One of the most common and severe difficulties for an individual to experience is a traumatic brain injury (TBI). Estimates of individuals who experience TBI vary by study and are difficult to calculate due to the fact that mild TBI may not always be treated. Based on the 2000 U.S. Census, approximately 1,250,000 Americans were treated in hospital emergency rooms (Jager, Weiss, Coben, & Pepe, 2000) following TBI, almost 230,000 were hospitalized, and more than 50,000 died (Thurman, Alverson, Dunn, Guerrero, & Sniezek, 1999). Kraus and Chu (2005) investigated the variability by study and concluded that an average rate of fatal and nonfatal hospitalized brain injuries would be estimated at 150 per 100,000 persons per year. International rates also vary as do the quality of records available. The reported rates in Great Britain are similar to the United States (256–300 per 100,000; King & Tyerman, 2003), and France (281 per 100,000; Cohadon, Castel, Richer, Mazaux, & Loiseau, 2002). China has a rate one fourth of the United States, whereas the Republic of San Marino has an annual rate 16 times greater than China (Naugle, 1990). The United States Congress passed the TBI Act of 1996. It was reauthorized in 2008 to provide appropriations through fiscal year 2012 and is now Public Law S.110–793 (2008). It provides for various services that are administered through the Department of Health and Human Services and will be discussed in the next chapter. Of particular interest at this juncture is a mechanism to track the number of TBI cases within the United States.

The peak ages for TBI are in the 15–24 year range. People older than 64 years and children, younger than the age of 5 are the next groups most at risk for TBI (Jager et al., 2000; Kraus & Chu, 2005; Richardson, 2000). Males sustain TBI at a far greater rate than females except in the older-than-64 age range and children younger the age of 5 (Jager et al., 2000). TBI can result from a myriad of causes and the actual TBI tends to be classified as either an open or a closed head injury. It is not only the nature of the injury but also other pathophysiological processes set in place by the injury which are different in closed versus open head injury. Presently, many more individuals are surviving TBI than ever before because of advanced medical technology, which may present more difficult rehabilitation problems. An example of a more complex case is James Brady, the former press secretary to the late President Ronald Reagan. He was shot in a foiled assassination attempt on then-President Reagan's life. He sustained a wound to the right frontal lobe of his brain leaving him paralyzed on his left side. He was fortunate to have the financial resources and technological support to be able to survive. He and his wife now travel across the United States campaigning for gun safety. They also have been instrumental in the passage of the Brady Handgun Violence Prevention Act of 1993 (Pub. L. No. 103–159). The law went into effect in 1994 and requires a criminal background check to be conducted on individuals before a firearm may be purchased from a federally licensed dealer, manufacturer, or importer unless an exemption applies.

Glasgow Coma Scale

Response	Score
Eye opening subscale (score 1–4)	
Opens eyes on his/her own	4
Opens eyes when asked to do so in a loud voice	3
Opens eyes to pain	2
Does not open eyes	1
Verbal response subscale (score 1–5)	
Carries on a conversation correctly and tells examiner where he is, the year, and month	5
Seems confused or disoriented	4
Talks so the examiner can understand him/her but makes no sense	3
Makes sounds that the examiner cannot understand	2
Makes no noise	1
Motor response subscale (score 1–6)	
Follows simple commands	6
Pulls examiner's hand away on painful stimuli	5
Pulls a part of his body away on painful stimuli	4
Flexes body appropriately to pain	3
Decerebrate posture	2
Has no motor response to pain	1
Total score	3–15

FIGURE 4.1 Classification of TBI severity based on the Glasgow Coma Scale. *Source:* Teasdale & Jennett (1974).

The severity of a TBI, whether caused by an open or closed head injury is usually measured by a combination of the following factors: (a) length of posttraumatic amnesia (PTA), the period between receiving a head injury and regaining continuous day-to-day memory for events; (b) depth of unconsciousness usually measured immediately after resuscitation using the Glasgow Coma Scale (GCS); and (c) length of unconsciousness and/or presence of neurological signs (King & Tyerman, 2003). The GCS (Teasdale & Jennett, 1974) measures depth of coma through determining the individual's responsiveness level in eye opening, motor movement, and verbal communication (see Figure 4.1). Scores on the GCS range from 3–15, with higher scores indicating more intact functioning. Scores of 3–8 are classified as having a *severe TBI* and those with scores of 9–12 having *moderate TBI* (Clifton, Hayes, Levin, Michel, & Choi, 1992). Some researchers subdivide the scores further as 6–8 being *severe* and 3–5 as *very severe* (Zhang, Jiang, Zhong, Yu, & Zhu, 2001). Scores between 13 and 15 are considered to be *mild TBI*. As with use of any particular strategy to classify degree of TBI, there is the chance of misclassification as was evidenced by Sherer, Struchen, Nakase-Thompson, and Yablon (2005) who compared three indices of TBI severity and found discrepancies in classification dependent upon the index used. However, in clinical practice, the GCS is used heavily.

OPEN HEAD INJURY

Open head injury occurs when an impact against the skull is so great that the skull is penetrated and the brain is exposed. The most common cause is a gunshot wound, but any object sharp enough to pierce the skull and expose the cortex may cause an open head injury. In addition, the force behind an object can make many nonlethal objects

open head injury
a brain injury which occurs when an object penetrates the skull and exposes the brain to the elements

potentially lethal (pens, pencils, keys, or any sharp object). A classic example of an open head injury, familiar to many, is the case of the late President John F. Kennedy. He was shot from a distance with a rifle where the bullet penetrated his skull and not only caused his brain to be exposed to the elements but also caused pieces of brain tissue to leave his skull. Unfortunately, he did not survive the injury, which is often the case with these types of difficulties.

As stated previously, open head injuries have been known to occur accidentally or intentionally from various everyday objects. Many of these objects penetrate the skull and remain within the brain, whereas others penetrate the skull and then leave opposite their point of entry. Gunshot wounds, as described earlier, are the leading cause of open head injury. Military gunshot wounds cause more deaths than civilian gun-related wounds because of the types of weapons and the higher velocity of the bullets or fragments. The rate of death is higher for open than for closed head injury.

The amount of damage in an open head injury is related to the amount of energy exerted on the brain. The mortality risk is related to the type of object impinging on the brain. An object that penetrates the brain and fragments causing internal ricochet or debris to be driven further into the brain is likely to cause more brain involvement. Clean wounds cause less damage than those with more brain involvement. A **clean wound** implies that the damage is mainly along the path of the invading object. Secondary effects of open head injuries may include hypotension (low blood pressure), hypovolemia (low blood volume), contusions, and intracranial hematomas.

Neuropsychological difficulties with open head injuries include specific cognitive deficits and behavioral changes related to the site of the lesion (Grafman et al., 1988). In addition, patients tend to show the effects of general diffuse brain impairment, such as difficulties with concentration, attention, memory, and overall mental slowing.

In terms of treatment for open head injuries time is a crucial factor, the sooner treatment is begun, the greater the potential for survival. Prevention and treatment of infections is also crucial because the brain has been exposed to the elements. Necessary surgical procedures will be dependent upon the type of injury incurred. Some fragments of objects that have penetrated the brain may not be able to be removed or removal may involve life-threatening procedures. Open head injury is highly related to epilepsy, with estimates of 80% of patients experiencing seizures within the first 24 hours (Yang & Bernardo, 2000). Improvement of function tends to follow the standard TBI pattern of rapid recovery in the first 1–2 years followed by smaller gains and more accommodation to remaining deficits as time progresses.

closed head injury
impact from an accident or injury causes brain damage but does not penetrate the skull

coup
the initial impact in a traumatic brain injury as an object or event impinges on the skull covering the brain

contrecoup
secondary impact in a traumatic brain injury as the brain ricochets back and forth or side to side within the skull

CLOSED HEAD INJURY

Closed head injury is different from open head injury in that the brain is never exposed to the elements. Even though the brain is not exposed, a closed head injury is still considered a form of severe injury. Closed head injury occurs in two stages. The first stage is the initial impact termed the **coup**. The second stage results from the ricocheting of the brain back and forth or from side to side within the skull and is termed the **contrecoup** (see Figure 4.2).

In closed head injuries, there are several difficulties that come into play. The first is the aforementioned coup in which the force applied to the brain is critical. The force comes into play also when the brain is jostled back and forth during the contrecoup. Stronger force applied to the brain has the potential for greater damage. Primary difficulties include diffuse white matter damage, contusion (bruising), and hemorrhage. Diffuse axonal injury is caused by the acceleration and deceleration of the brain impacting against the skull (Gennarelli & Graham, 2005). Contusions often occur under the frontal and

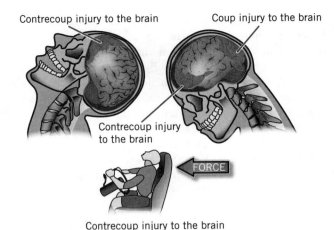

Contrecoup injury to the brain

Coup injury to the brain

Contrecoup injury to the brain

FORCE

Contrecoup injury to the brain

FIGURE 4.2 Coup and contrecoup.

temporal poles where the shearing forces of the brain are impacting on the sharpest and most confined parts of the skull. Contusions can also occur under the point of impact or at the contrecoup. Hemorrhages occur when blood vessels supplying oxygen to the brain are ruptured.

Secondary damage includes injuries resulting from hematomas, cerebral hemorrhage, infection, hydrocephalus, and anoxic damage caused by breathing difficulties or low blood pressure. All of these difficulties may begin at the initial time of injury and lead to secondary damage to the brain. In addition, there may be neurochemical difficulties such as excitotoxicity, cell membrane degradation, cellular edema, and cellular events such as changes in neuropeptides, electrolytes, and excitatory amino acids (Hatton, 2001).

The age group 15–24 is the most likely to sustain closed head injuries. The most common causal factors are moving vehicle accidents, including automobiles, motorcycles, boats, and all-terrain vehicles (ATVs) as the source. Another major source of closed head injury is participating in athletics and, more specifically, in sports that do not require protective headwear such as professional boxing or soccer. Even in sports where protective headwear is required, adequate protection for neurological structures may not be provided. An example of this phenomenon is a football helmet which does not cover the base of the brain or the upper sections of the spinal column. The case study presented in chapter 1 is an example of a closed head injury and illustrates the effects of force on brain tissue.

Neuropsychological difficulties for individuals with closed head injury are similar to those with open head injury except they may be less severe. Typical symptoms include impaired speed of information processing, difficulties with concentration and attention, memory deficits, and problems with reaction time.

Closed head injury patients often experience behavioral and/or personality changes subsequent to the injuries. Family and friends often become aware of the changes before the patient is willing to acknowledge them. In addition, most closed head injury patients experience some form of depression or other emotional difficulty usually because of changes in their life circumstances. Another difficulty is posttraumatic stress disorder (PTSD) if the closed head injury was caused by a trauma. Very often closed head injury patients describe an inability to deal with strong emotions such as anger or rage. Many relationships have experienced severe disruption due to anger management problems on the part of the patient with a closed head injury. Even with the stressors involved with dealing with these emotions, research does not suggest that TBI patients incur a higher rate of divorce (Kreutzer, Marnitz, Hsu, Williams, & Riddick, 2007). Some closed head injury patients have difficulties with the environment because they may look "normal" even though their brain has suffered massive injury. Looking normal implies that patients talk as they usually did with their unique mannerisms, walk normally, and can navigate the environment. However, most closed head injury patients experience a great deal of fatigue and other symptoms already described which are not usually apparent to others. The fact that such individuals look normal but cannot function as they once did may cause many difficulties with employment, social relationships, school, and family. One major difficulty for patients with TBI is often a lack of awareness of their behavioral, cognitive, or physical deficits (Hart, Sherer, Whyte, Polansky, & Novack, 2004). Many closed head injury patients have returned to their previous jobs and/or schooling only to find that they are unable to function as they once did, which leads to feelings of failure and added anger and frustration.

Treatment for closed head injuries is similar to open head injury in terms of the medical needs being prominent. Very important is the need to prevent or control brain swelling. Next, because of the myriad of psychosocial difficulties, it is often helpful to enlist the aid of a therapist or support group. Psychoactive medications may also be necessary for some individuals. Antidepressants have been used to alleviate the depression which may often occur secondary to closed head injury. Atypical antipsychotics and anticonvulsants have been used to help with anger management and behavioral outbursts (Sugden, Kile, Farrimond, Hilty, & Bougeois, 2006).

POSTCONCUSSION SYNDROME

postconcussion syndrome
constellation of physical and psychological symptoms that may occur as a result of a medically verifiable concussion

Another condition considered to be a milder form of closed head injury is termed postconcussion syndrome (see Figure 4.3). This involves the traits and behaviors that exist after an individual has received a TBI caused by a concussion. Although not currently listed in the *Diagnostic and Statistical Manual of Mental Disorders, Fourth Editon, Text Revision* (*DSM-IV-TR*) as a disorder, it is considered a syndrome under study and will probably be included in *DSM-V* along with mild neurocognitive disorder. A concussion is primarily caused by diffuse axonal injury, where axons are damaged or destroyed because of the forces of acceleration and deceleration acting on them and on blood vessels (Bigler, 1990). Symptoms of concussion include loss of consciousness, PTA, and sometimes seizures. In the spectrum of TBI, a concussion is considered mild compared to open or closed head injury. Neuropsychological deficits in postconcussion syndrome include attention deficits, impaired verbal retrieval, and forgetfulness (Gasquoine, 1997). Other symptoms reported by patients include headache, dizziness, irritability, sleep disturbances, and fatigue (Ponsford et al., 2000).

Some researchers have suggested that postconcussion syndrome appears or is embellished in individuals who are consciously or unconsciously looking for secondary gain from their TBI (financial or otherwise). Other researchers suggest that the residual symptoms seen in mild TBI exist due to the significant stress the individual was under at the time of the TBI. Concurrent with this is the supposition that premorbid personality or psychiatric disorders are significant contributors (Ponsford et al., 2000). In addition, the reduced information processing capacity caused by TBI is thought to be a stress-producing factor (Alexander, 1995). Finally, genetic studies also have identified the E4 allele of ApoE thought to relate to the risk for Alzheimer's disease (see chapter 3) as a contributor to the severity of damage of TBI (Teasdale, Nicoll, Murray, & Fiddes, 1997). The supposition is that identification of E4 allele in the patient may point to a more severe outcome.

RESEARCH CRITERIA: POSTCONCUSSIONAL DISORDER

A. A head trauma event that has caused significant cerebral concussion.

Note: The common manifestations of concussion include loss of consciousness, posttraumatic amnesia.

B. Neuropsychological testing or quantified cognitive assessment results showing difficulty in attention (concentrating, shifting focus of attention, performing simultaneous cognitive tasks) or memory.

C. Three (or more) of the following occur shortly after the trauma and last at least three months: easily fatigued, disordered sleep, headache, dizziness, irritability or aggression on little or no provocation, anxiety, depression, or affective lability, personality changes (e.g., social or sexual inappropriateness), apathy or lack of spontaneity.

FIGURE 4.3
Diagnostic criteria for postconcussion syndrome. *Source:* Adapted from the *DSM-IV-TR* (APA, 2000).

Individuals who have received a concussion should be examined by emergency room personnel to determine the severity of the head injury. Several empirically validated treatment protocols are available for postconcussion syndrome (Ponsford et al., 2000). Patients are typically given pain relievers such as nonsteroidal analgesics for headaches and medications to relieve depression, nausea, or dizziness. Rest is advised but is only somewhat effective. An assumption is made that any deficits will rectify themselves with time. A meta-analysis of five studies has shown that a single session treatment involving education about symptoms, attribution of symptoms to benign causes, and reassurance of favorable prognosis was effective in preventing the reemergence of symptoms (Mittenberg, Canyock, Condit, & Patton, 2001).

Due to the manner in which concussion and postconcussion syndromes have been treated or not treated, there have been numerous instances where individuals, particularly young people and athletes, have chosen not to seek medical help and have tried to return directly to their daily lives. At times, the results of returning too early to one's activities involve unexpected failures or inability to perform as one could before the concussion. Athletes in particular are at greater risk for another concussion after they have received a first.

Toxic Conditions

The number and type of substances which can negatively impact the central nervous system are vast. Usual examples include alcohol and other legal and illegal drugs. However, many individuals are surprised when they realize that many products used on a daily basis for personal care or the cleanliness of home or environment could be hazardous. In addition, many toxins in our environment may affect our central nervous system. Examples of the aforementioned categories include aerosol containers which may contain deodorant, shaving lotion, or other personal care products, and detergents in many forms which can be used in kitchen and bath to remove stains, mildew, and mold. Everyday examples of toxins include automobile and bus fumes, smoke from household or business chimneys, and insecticides and herbicides used on lawns and gardens. Not to be overlooked are the toxic effects of medications and medication interactions.

It is usually an infrequent occurrence for an individual to see a clinical neuropsychologist for a toxic condition except in the case of alcohol. However, it must be kept in mind that difficulties with toxic substances can complicate the symptom presentation and differential diagnosis. At this point, the reader is referred back to the case study at the beginning of the chapter. The individuals in the case study were clearly exposed to multiple toxins and also lacked awareness that these substances could be harmful.

ALCOHOL-RELATED DISORDERS

Alcohol stands alone among the conditions considered toxic. It is the only substance in this grouping which has been shown to have both positive protective effects and negative physiological effects. This protective effect is different from the medicinal uses of marijuana by individuals who already have developed a particular difficulty. Studies have shown that alcohol, especially wine, in moderation has protective effects from cardiovascular and cerebrovascular disease (Klatsky, 1994). Drinking in moderation or social drinking is usually defined as one or two drinks in a day. The amount varies by gender, one drink per day for females, two drinks for males where a drink is considered 1 oz of hard liquor, 12 oz of beer, or 6 oz of wine. Research on whether social drinking has any neuropsychological sequelae suggests little impairment. In addition, abstinence from alcohol consumption by social drinkers does not tend to improve memory or cognitive functioning.

Alcohol, however, when not used in moderation may cause moderate to severe difficulties for the central nervous system. There are many and varied definitions and descriptions of alcohol abuse and dependence usually based on the frequency and chronicity of drinking. Alcohol abuse, as described in the *DSM-IV-TR* (American Psychiatric Association, 2000), is defined as the excess use of alcohol for a period of 12 months. During this time, the use of alcohol has been shown to have a negative impact on the individual's social or occupational functioning. Alcohol dependence is defined in *DSM-IV-TR* as the same pattern with the inclusion of tolerance and/or withdrawal. **Tolerance** is defined as needing more of a substance over time to attain the same level of intoxication. **Withdrawal** is a pattern of symptoms that occur after the cessation of substance use. Withdrawal symptoms may include nausea, headache, shakiness, and a desire or craving for the substance.

Binge drinking, defined as drinking large quantities of alcohol in a short period, has become an issue written about extensively in the popular press. Binge drinking appears to be quite pervasive on college campuses for individuals ages 18–22 (Marlatt, 1996). Research is lacking regarding the future, postcollege drinking of those individuals who self-reported binge drinking. However, heavy drinking, in general, declines as students get older and assume adult responsibilities (Jessor, Donovan, & Costa, 1991). Also lacking is information regarding the prevalence of binge drinking within the 18–22 age groups not attending college. However, drinking large quantities of alcohol within a short period can be toxic. The body is not able to metabolize the substance when it is consumed so quickly, and there have been accounts of alcohol poisoning sometimes leading to coma and death. Due to the fact that binge drinking is an underresearched topic, there is little research regarding the neuropsychological implications. What little information that does exist suggests that binge drinkers appear to be less prone to alcohol-related cognitive deficits than those with a heavy daily intake (Sanchez-Craig, 1980). The pattern of binge

tolerance
usually associated with alcohol consumption but can relate to other drugs; the need for more and more of a substance to achieve the same level of intoxication or "high"

withdrawal
symptoms that occur after the cessation of use of a substance; each drug has its own symptoms of withdrawal

binge drinking
the drinking of an excessive amount of alcohol within a short period often with the intent of becoming quickly intoxicated

drinking, whether it more clearly resembles alcohol abuse versus dependence, should be considered and would lead to an understanding of which cognitive and memory deficits to predict.

Binge drinking, especially on high school and college campuses, is a phenomenon that requires preventive as well as treatment considerations. Starting as early as possible, it is advisable to educate young people regarding the effects of alcohol. Many young people engage in binge drinking because it is seen as a rite of passage or peer pressure exerts its influence. Working with young people, the **Drug Abuse Resistance Education (DARE)** program has tried to instill in children the ability to say no to alcohol and to peer pressure. Unfortunately, the literature suggests that while not increasing chemical use, DARE has also not decreased its use (Rosebaum & Hanson, 1998). Many college and university campuses have attempted to deal with these influences by sponsoring chemical-free activities on campus and using various religious or Greek organizations.

Drug Abuse Resistance Education (DARE)
a program developed to assist children and adolescents to respond against peer pressure to consume alcohol or other drugs

Alcohol is a central nervous system depressant and as such depresses or slows the functioning of structures within the central nervous system. Alcohol has a paradoxical effect in that it often produces a feeling of euphoria before the onset of depressive feelings. Researchers often find that this paradox is one reason some individuals develop difficulties with alcohol (Lukas, Mendelson, Benedikt, & Jones, 1986). The positive feeling or euphoria does not continue as one continues to drink but the individual who is drinking may demonstrate poor judgment associated with intoxication and conclude that more will make him feel even better, whereas in reality it leads to depression.

Alcohol is a **neurotoxin** and as such could be considered a poison. Alcohol is metabolized differently than other drugs in a process termed **zero-order kinetics**. It is metabolized at a steady state, approximately one drink per hour regardless of the amount consumed by the person. It is metabolized through several different routes, which explains its effects on multiple central nervous system areas, as well as on multiple organs (Brust, 2000). The effects of alcohol vary based on the age, gender, and race of the individual consuming it in addition to the other situational factors such as food in the stomach and expectations for the effects of alcohol. Females metabolize alcohol more slowly than males because of their body composition and fat distribution. If given the same amount of alcohol, a female will become more intoxicated than a male. Racial differences exist in ability to metabolize alcohol. Asians, particularly Japanese, Chinese, and Korean individuals in 50% of that population, lack the form of aldehyde dehydrogenase that eliminates low levels of the first breakdown product of alcohol, acetaldehyde (American Psychiatric Association, 2000). Usually this causes a flushed face and palpitations when drinking alcohol and may cause these individuals to not imbibe. Within the United States, White and African Americans have similar rates of alcohol abuse and dependence. Latino males have somewhat higher rates and Latino females lower; however, these rates vary by study. It is not a myth that Native Americans and Alaskan Natives have higher rates of chemical dependence with use varying greatly among tribes. This implies that it is a significant difficulty for many Native Americans and Alaskan Natives (SAMHSA, 2007).

neurotoxin
a substance considered to be a poison within the central nervous system

zero-order kinetics
metabolism at a steady state regardless of quantity of substance consumed

Chronic alcohol use may cause multiple cognitive deficits including difficulties with complex visuospatial abilities and psychomotor speed. Well-learned tasks such as arithmetic, language, and attention are not as greatly affected (Rourke & Løberg, 1996). Memory deficits, once thought to be a hallmark of chronic alcohol users, can be severe but are not evident in all alcohol abusers. However, as the memory task increases in complexity there is more of a chance for impairment.

Severe difficulties related to alcohol use include alcoholic dementia and Korsakoff's syndrome. **Alcoholic dementia** involves widespread cognitive deterioration similar to other forms of dementia. The dementia is progressive and involves cognitive and memory

alcoholic dementia
dementia due to alcohol consumption

abilities along with abstract reasoning. It is sometimes difficult to differentiate dementia caused by alcohol use and dementia because of other causes. Abstinence from alcohol use helps clear the diagnostic picture. An individual with dementia caused by alcohol use should recover some abilities with abstinence.

Korsakoff's syndrome
memory and cognitive difficulties due to alcohol consumption and the absence of the vitamin thiamine

Korsakoff's syndrome is characterized by difficulty with short-term memory and other memory deficits. The person may appear to have manic confusion and be unable to clearly state his thoughts. The person also exhibits disoriented eye and limb movements. The cause of these symptoms is significant alcohol intake over a period with subsequent vitamin deficiency. Alcohol interferes with gastrointestinal absorption of the vitamin thiamine. Thiamine deficiency is associated with cognitive and emotional changes. It has been shown that this syndrome can be treated if thiamine is given as soon as possible and alcohol use is curtailed.

There have been many studies looking at the effects of abstinence from alcohol use and subsequent effects. During the initial detoxification period individuals may show a myriad of cognitive and memory deficits. This period usually lasts 1–2 weeks. After 1–2 weeks the beginning of abstinence occurs in which the greatest amount of return of functioning is evident. Subsequently, for the next 3–6 weeks, return of function slows down. Rates of return of functioning after this point are inconsistent, with some studies showing more improvement over time and others showing very little (Unkenstein & Bowden, 1991).

STREET DRUGS (ILLEGAL SUBSTANCES)

The study of illegal substances is much more difficult than the study of alcohol. Alcohol and its effects can be studied in a laboratory setting because it is a legal substance. Alcoholics who are in treatment are often willing to be subjects for studies, whereas individuals using illegal substances may be more hesitant to participate. Very often confounding variables affect the clinical presentation with illegal substances, including criminal activities, which are engaged in to obtain one's drug of choice. Also many drug users are polydrug abusers, and the effects of the various types of drugs are difficult to differentiate. With this in mind, however, many things have been learned regarding the effects of various illegal drugs.

Marijuana

Cannabis or marijuana is the herbal form and hashish is the resinous form of the plant *Cannabis sativa*. The biologically active compound in marijuana is tetrahydrocannabinol (THC). It has psychoactive and physiological effects which vary based on whether the substance is smoked, sniffed, or ingested.

Botanists have determined that cannabis is native to Central Asia. There have been references to cannabis throughout history. It has been used by a plethora of groups throughout time for religious or medicinal purposes. It was not until the 20th century that the production and use of cannabis became illegal in most parts of the world. Marijuana became very popular in the United States during the counterculture movement of the 1960s. It is currently thought to be the most popular illicit drug among younger people with alcohol remaining the number one drug.

Marijuana's effects have been described as pleasant and/or unpleasant often related to variables similar to alcohol, specifically the mental state of the user at the time of use and the expectations of the user in terms of the effects of the drug. Marijuana has the potential to induce hallucinatory experiences and emotional states—some good, some bad—as well as time distortions and memory loss (Lishman, 1997). The intensity of these effects is dose dependent. High doses may result in psychotic-like symptoms (Brust, 1993). Even lesser doses may result in psychotic symptoms in those individuals who have a predisposition or vulnerability to schizophrenia (Leweke, Gerth, & Klosterkolter, 2004).

Marijuana's effect on cognitive abilities is equivocal. Pope and Yurgelun-Todd (2003) found that individuals who initiate use at a younger age (younger than 17) were more likely to develop neuropsychological deficits than those who begin use at a later date. There are studies that show decrements in tasks involving cognitive activities, specifically memory, and those that show no effects. Cannabis is known to act on the hippocampus, an organ associated with memory and learning and impact short-term memory and attention (Lundqvist, 2005). Some studies show personality changes with heavy usage (Brust, 1993). The most common symptoms include emotional blunting, mental sluggishness, apathy, restlessness, mental confusion, and an amotivational syndrome. The studies often have confounding variables such as differences in dosages and background factors of the individual. This problem arises because many studies are based on self-report and not carried out in a laboratory or clinical setting as described earlier. It is difficult to receive approval from human subjects committees at institutions to conduct research using illegal substances, and therefore, self-report is often a common way to obtain data.

As can be seen, there are two sides to the question regarding the effects of marijuana. One side states that there are various cognitive, memory, and emotional effects because of the use of the drug, whereas the other side states these effects do not exist or are not as serious as reported. In addition, there are two sides to the discussion regarding legalization of marijuana, which often refers back to the aforementioned arguments.

The Marijuana Policy Project (2008) states that cannabis is an ideal therapeutic drug for cancer and AIDS patients who often have depression, as well as nausea and weight loss caused by chemotherapy. A difference of opinion was stated on April 20, 2006, when the U.S. Food and Drug Administration (2006) issued an interagency warning against medicinal cannabis, specifically stating the high potential for abuse and that there is no currently accepted medical use (U.S. Food and Drug Administration, 2006). There are also arguments on both sides regarding whether marijuana is a "gateway drug," which implies that it may lead individuals to go from the smoking of marijuana down the path of drug addiction. The most significant and consistent finding is that marijuana has a deleterious effect on reaction time and has been implicated in many traffic accidents (Ramaekers, Berghaus, van Laar, & Drummer, 2003). Research is equivocal regarding withdrawal symptoms with some studies suggesting physiological and psychological withdrawal with heavy use. Other studies suggest little or no withdrawal effects from marijuana. The idea that abstinence from marijuana appears to lead to restoration of any cognitive or memory deficits is related to social use. Heavy users, however, demonstrate poorer performance on decision-making tasks even after 25 days (Bolla, Funderburk, & Cadet, 2000).

Cocaine

Considered a central nervous system stimulant, cocaine is highly addictive due to the "rush," which is experienced through inhalation. The effect is much less when the drug is taken intravenously. Other effects of cocaine include increased alertness and arousal and an increased sense of well-being and confidence, which is often interpreted as positive and may lead to continual use.

Cocaine increases the level of dopamine in the reward circuits in the brain, which leads to craving and a higher threshold for a euphoric reaction to the drug. Beginning use of cocaine may function as an aphrodisiac but with prolonged use lowers libido and may cause impotence (Lukas & Renshaw, 1998). Other reactions to cocaine include paranoia, delusions, and hallucinations and panic attacks. Beginning use of cocaine acts as a pleasure inducer but with repeated use, it damages the brain's reward centers (Dackis &

O'Brien, 2002). Long-term users of cocaine may have many cognitive deficits with memory and concentration difficulties the most significant (Roselli, Ardila, Lubomski, Murray, & King, 2001). Seizures occur with many habitual as well as new users. Hypertension and other symptoms of central nervous system overstimulation such as strokes may occur. Strickland, Miller, Kowell, and Stein (1998) indicate that fMRI imagery shows abnormal metabolism and hypoperfusion both when subjects are using cocaine and in chronic users when abstinent. The neuroimaging findings are consistent with findings of slowed mental processing, memory impairment, and reduced mental flexibility.

Current information indicates withdrawal from cocaine is neither life threatening nor terribly painful. However, symptoms of irritability, restlessness, confusion, sleep disorder, and abnormal muscle movements have been observed. Because both cognitive and memory deficits occur with cocaine use it is difficult to determine the complete rate of return of functioning. Some studies indicate that with long-term use these abilities may not return. Franken, van Strien, Franzek, and van de Wetering (2006) found that cocaine-addicted individuals made more errors on the Erikson flanker task, a cognitive task, and were less likely to correct errors than were a control group. The researchers argued that the results were associated with a compromised dopamine system.

Narcotics

The first opiate drugs were derived from the opium poppy. Heroin, morphine, and codeine are all forms of synthetic derivation. Opiates have been used by many cultures for centuries to ease pain and to produce euphoria. The most likely origin of opiates is the Middle East. Opiates were extremely important within the early Egyptian and Greek cultures. The Ebers Papyrus discussed a remedy using opiates to prevent excessive crying of children. Galen suggested caution in the use of opiates but felt they were an overall cure-all. Paracelsus was one of the early Renaissance supporters of opium as a panacea. Dr. Thomas Sydenham, the father of clinical medicine, was one of the individuals to introduce laudanum, a concoction using opium and other ingredients, which were dissolved in wine. He regarded this to be a general cure-all. English writers and those in high society during the 1800s and 1900s used opium on a daily basis and it was easy and inexpensive to obtain.

In 1806, Fredrick Serturner discovered the synthetic version of opium, which he termed *morphine*. For this discovery, he received the French version of the Nobel Prize in 1831. In 1874, two acetyl groups were attached to the morphine molecule to produce heroin and it was placed on the market in 1898 by Bayer Laboratories. There are very few and mainly inaccurate records regarding the number of people addicted to narcotics at the turn of the 20th century. There does appear to be three groups within the United States which were most susceptible, and included Chinese laborers who worked on the railroad, the average citizen who did not know of the addictive properties and those living in inner-city ghettos.

The Harrison Narcotics Tax Act, which was more of a taxation law than a way to control the spread of the substance, was passed in 1914. Pharmacists and physicians who dealt with narcotics were required to register and pay tax. Narcotics now were only available by prescription. However, this only changed the way that individuals wanting narcotics were able to obtain them and contributed to the increase in cost.

It was not until 1973 that it was discovered that there are specific opiate receptors within the brain (Pert & Snyder, 1973). Soon after this discovery came the finding that the brain produced its own chemicals termed *enkephalins* and endorphins, which fit into these receptors. It became clear that the substances were released during stress or pain. The opiates compete with the naturally occurring endorphins for the receptor sites.

The major medicinal use for narcotics is pain control. Sometimes patients will report that they are still aware of the pain but that it is no longer aversive. Narcotics also have

endorphins
naturally occurring brain hormones which help alleviate pain or lead to a feeling of euphoria

effects on the gastrointestinal system through the ability to counteract diarrhea and were used extensively to control dysentery. Another use of narcotics has been in the control of the cough control center in the medulla through introduction into cough medicine.

Tolerance develops for all of the narcotics and is often a problem for individuals who use the drugs appropriately for pain control. Cross-tolerance also develops; therefore, if an individual is tolerant for one narcotic he or she will be tolerant to all. Narcotics cause physical dependence, which means they cause withdrawal symptoms. Withdrawal is often described as a bad case of the flu or worse. Narcotics also cause psychological dependence. In addition, the use of needles and other paraphernalia involved with the preparation of narcotics may cause the person to feel pleasure at the sight of his or her equipment. Behavioral programs have been developed to wean the individual from drug paraphernalia. Also present when needles are used is the risk of HIV infection and hepatitis.

Excess opiate use may lead to decreased response to stress and decreased memory storage. Death may result because of the ability of narcotics to depress the respiratory center of the brain. Long-term use of opiates may lead to visuospatial and visuomotor difficulties. Mental and physical neglect are often symptoms specific to heroin use. Pau, Lee, and Chan (2002) found that heroin addicts, in comparison to control subjects, exhibited difficulties with impulse control, whereas, attention and mental flexibility in abstinent recovering addicts were not affected. Long-term users of opiates who remain abstinent may recover many lost abilities.

Methamphetamine

Methamphetamine (meth) is currently the most visible drug available. It is visible in the sense that it is readily available, is cheap compared to other drugs, and the target of the media and law enforcement. The drug is easy to make at home. The ingredients and directions are available on the Internet. It causes such a high that "normal" individuals are willing to risk their jobs, families, and friends for the next hit of meth. Meth's effects have been described as similar to several simultaneous orgasms. When taken to excess, meth can give the appearance of psychosis.

Methamphetamine is not a new drug and has a lengthy history. Methamphetamine was part of the National Formulary and the *United States Pharmacopoeia* until the 1940s when its medicinal use was replaced by new medications which were not physically addictive. The new medications which entered the market were methylphenidate (Ritalin) and dextroamphetamine (Dexedrine). Prior to the 1950s methamphetamine had been used to treat attention deficit/hyperactivity disorder. It was used in the 1960s as a stimulant by musical performers. It became very popular in the 1990s with over-the-road truck drivers and others who needed to stay awake and alert for prolonged period. Other professionals potentially at risk are those with a need to say awake at specific periods, such as emergency room personnel, whether doctors or nurses, and air traffic controllers.

The introduction of the Internet made it possible for any individual to manufacture methamphetamine at home. It is a cheap and serious drug that has led to legislation in many states making the ingredients not readily available to minors. Cold medicines and similar products that go into the recipe for methamphetamine are often kept behind the counter at many drug stores. Often individuals steal the ingredients needed to produce methamphetamine. Legislation has led to problems with increased theft. Thus, many individuals, desperate for the money to buy meth, will steal from various places such as construction sites where they can obtain copper to sell for cash. The effects of methamphetamine are astounding, leading to cognitive and memory deficits as well as lack of concern for the daily issues of life, particularly children. Many children have been removed from homes where methamphetamine has been present because of the extreme toxicity of the ingredients used to manufacture methamphetamine. The ingredients used to manufacture methamphetamine are so toxic that when a meth lab is discovered and needs to be taken apart, the individuals who do the work need to wear hazardous material (hazmat) attire.

Methamphetamine is a new phenomenon to study. It is difficult to determine whether an individual can overcome cognitive and memory deficits. However, the prognosis is better the sooner the individual receives treatment.

Phencyclidine and Ketamine

Phencyclidine (PCP) and ketamine are usually categorized under the broader term *hallucinogens*. However, their history and effects are somewhat different from the usual hallucinogens such as LSD and mushrooms. They have been referred to as *dissociative analgesics* relating to the history of the compounds and the effects on patients.

During the 1950s, Parke-Davis and Company investigated a series of drugs in a search for an efficient intravenous anesthetic which did not have the side effects of barbiturates, such as lowered respiration and blood circulation. Animal studies, particularly with monkeys, indicated that PCP was a good analgesic but did not produce muscle relaxation or sleep. Instead of the aforementioned reactions, the animals kept their eyes open and appeared unconcerned. These symptoms were later compared to dissociation.

In 1958, PCP (Sernyl) was first used for surgical anesthesia in humans. The human reactions were similar to those seen in animals in which the analgesic effects were positive without depressing blood circulation or respiration. Humans exhibited a similar dissociative state as was observed in animals. Patients also reported no memory of the procedure.

However, with repeated uses of PCP, other accounts of postsurgical behaviors or **emergence reactions** began to surface. Many accounts were reported of patients who became unmanageable after they emerged from the anesthesia, some even displayed mani-clike behaviors. PCP began to develop the reputation as a drug which induced superhuman strength. There have been many anecdotal stories by emergency room personnel and police personnel regarding the number of individuals needed to restrain someone who has taken PCP. The reason for the need for extra personnel is that the person is anesthetized and does not feel pain when restrained.

Because of the aforementioned difficulties, Sernyl was taken off the market as an investigational drug in 1965. It was sold to another company and subsequently marketed as an animal tranquilizer. It became a drug used in zoos and also an ingredient in tranquilizer guns used to restrain unruly zoo animals.

Even though PCP was no longer legally available, individuals gained access to it through various illegal avenues. During the height of the counterculture movement in 1967, PCP was termed the "peace pill" in San Francisco. It also was readily available in New York under the name "hog" or "trank." In the 1970s, PCP was combined with oregano, parsley, or alfalfa and termed "angel dust." PCP shares something in common with methamphetamine in that it is easy to make and is relatively inexpensive. While it was never as popular as cocaine or other drugs it continues to have an audience. Some users of PCP develop a strong psychological dependence. The predilection toward violence has not been explained but is thought to be a side effect of the suspicion and anesthesia produced by the drug. Individuals do not report feeling violent when taking the drug. PCP activates midbrain dopamine cell firing and stimulates dopamine release. The release of dopamine is the reason for its reinforcing effects. PCP is a difficult drug to stop using because of the reinforcing properties. However, once use is curtailed, it appears that most deficits can be restored.

Ketamine is a dissociative anesthetic chemically related to PCP. It has been in use with humans for 30 years. There is also a related veterinary product available. Ketamine

---

emergence reactions
behaviors exhibited when a drug used for anesthesia is decreasing in the system; common behaviors are dreamlike state, confusion, excitement, and irrational behavior

has more depressive effects than PCP; however, in 12% of patients reports of emergence reactions including delusions and hallucinations, confusion and irrational behavior have occurred.

Ketamine began to develop a reputation as a party drug termed *Special K* or *K* in the late 1990s because of its popularity at raves. In 1999, the Department of Health and Human Service recommended that ketamine become a Schedule III controlled substance. The total number of users or abusers is still unknown. It is thought that some of the abusers are medical or veterinary practitioners who have easy access to the drug through their work. Ketamine works in the same manner as PCP, stimulating the firing of the dopamine neurons in the midbrain and prefrontal cortex. This again leads to the reinforcing effects of the drug. It appears, as is the case with PCP, that once the drug is removed most deleterious effects subside. However, there is a scarcity of research in this area.

SOCIAL DRUGS

Drugs considered social are those that may have a deleterious effect on the central nervous system but in most cases are legal once the individual reaches a certain age.

Caffeine

On a daily basis, more people use caffeine than any other psychoactive drug. Caffeine is one of three substances under the broader category xanthines, the other two substances are theophylline and theobromine. Similar to many of the substances discussed thus far, caffeine has had a long history throughout civilization. As early as 900 AD, an Arabic medical book suggested coffee was a cure-all for any malady. Not the first contrary opinion but one which surfaced much later was voiced in 1674 in England where women objected to the use of coffee and men objected to the women's objections. Coffee was also a matter of economics between Britain and the United States. Coffeehouses became popular in England and France in the mid-1600s. As colonization progressed in the New World, coffee was introduced and became the national drink quickly surpassing tea.

Coffee, however, is not the only beverage or substance that contains caffeine or other xanthines. Many individuals are surprised at the list of substances that have caffeine or other xanthines as a main ingredient (see Figure 4.4). The more common beverages that contain xanthines include various forms of tea, hot or iced, which contain the active ingredient theophylline; cola drinks, which contain caffeine; and cocoa and hot chocolate, which contain theobromide. The beverages that often surprise users because of their caffeine content include root beer, Mellow Yello, Sunkist Orange, and energy drinks. Diet products also contain caffeine unless specifically prepared and labeled caffeine free or decaffeinated. Other products with a significant amount of caffeine include various over-the-counter drugs such as Anacin, Dristan, Dexatrim, and No Doz. Any product having chocolate as an ingredient contains theobromide. Carob, which does not contain xanthines, is an alternative to chocolate.

Xanthines are the oldest central nervous system stimulants known. All have significant effects on the body with caffeine producing the strongest effects. The absorption of caffeine is rapid after oral ingestion. Blood levels reach their peak 30 minutes after ingestion. Maximal effects for the user occur within 2 hours. Cross-tolerance effects exists across xanthines. Loss of tolerance may take up to 2 weeks. Physiological and psychological dependence may develop.

Caffeine and the other xanthines produce their effects by blocking the brain's receptors for the neurotransmitter adenosine. Adenosine produces behavioral sedation

FIGURE 4.4 Caffeine content of various beverages.

12-Ounce Beverage / Caffeine Levels	Milligrams
Red Bull (8.2 oz)	80.0
Jolt	71.2
Pepsi One	55.5
Mountain Dew	55.0
Mountain Dew Code Red	55.0
Diet Mountain Dew	55.0
Kick Citrus	54.0
Mellow Yellow	52.8
Surge	51.0
Tab	46.8
Diet Coke	45.6
Diet Wild Cherry Pepsi	36.0
Diet Pepsi Twist	36.0
Aspen	36.0
Coca-Cola Classic	34.0

8-Ounce Beverage / Caffeine Levels	Milligrams
Coffee, drip	115–175
Coffee, brewed	80–135
Coffee, espresso (2 ounces)	100
Tea, green	15
Hot cocoa	14
Coffee, decaf, brewed	3–4
Coffee, decaf, instant	2–3

in many areas of the brain. The stimulant effects are a result of blocking the receptors for the inhibitory effect. The physiological effects experienced by the subject include increased arousal and alertness and less fatigue and drowsiness. At higher doses, caffeine can affect the autonomic centers of the brain and also increase heart rate and respiration.

Caffeine does cause withdrawal when use is curtailed. Symptoms include headache, jitteriness, confusion, and agitation. After the substance has been completely removed from the body the symptoms abate. Cognitive difficulties caused by the stimulant properties of the xanthines also appear to abate after use is discontinued.

Nicotine

Nicotine is a naturally occurring liquid alkaloid that is colorless and volatile. With oxidation nicotine turns brown and smells like burning tobacco. Nicotine was isolated in 1828 and has been studied extensively.

Nicotine has been shown to be the most addictive of all psychoactive substances (see Figure 4.5). It is a central nervous system stimulant. Nicotine's effects on cognitive and memory tasks vary depending on the study cited. Some studies suggest that nicotine enhances cognitive and memory abilities but used smokers as opposed to nonsmokers as subjects. The question is then raised whether the increase in performance is caused by overcoming withdrawal effects in smokers.

Tobacco is the primary source of nicotine. It has a long history often attributed to the Native Americans who originally inhabited North America before the arrival of Christopher Columbus. Tobacco was then introduced to countries that had colonized the New World. Tobacco was originally used in one of two forms: The individual either took it (used snuff) or drank it (smoked tobacco).

During the mid-1500s, there are accounts of medicinal uses of tobacco for any number of ailments. However, by the 16th century, it was also referred to as a problem that could cause more dysfunctions than it cured.

Over time various forms of tobacco were used, and each type became more or less popular. Snuff and chewing tobacco were used before cigars, with cigarettes being the most recent form of tobacco use. In addition to being a psychoactive substance, tobacco

To rank today's commonly used drugs by their addictiveness, we asked experts to consider two questions: How easy is it to get hooked on these substances and how hard is it to stop using them? Although a person's vulnerability to drug also depends on individual traits — physiology, psychology, and social and economic pressures — these rankings reflect only the addictive potential inherent in the drug.

Nicotine	100
Ice, glass (Methamphetamine smoked)	99
Crack	98
Crystal Meth (Methamphetamine injected)	93
Valium (Diazepam)	85
Quaalude (Methaqualone)	83
Seconal (Secobarbital)	82
Alcohol	81
Heroin	80
Crank (Amphetamine taken nasally)	78
Cocaine	72
Caffeine	68
PCP (Phencyclidine)	57
Marijuana	21
Ecstasy (MDMA)	20
Psilocybin Mushrooms	18
LSD	18
Mescaline	18

Hastings, J. *In Health*, Nov/Dec, 1990.

FIGURE 4.5 Addictiveness of various substances.

was also an important crop for Colonial America. Many states used tobacco as a form of currency and relied on it to support their economy.

In the 1950s, investigation of the safety of tobacco smoking and the relationship between cigarette smoking and cancer began. Filter cigarettes were developed by cigarette companies to convince the public that they were ingesting less nicotine. There has been intense fighting between the tobacco industry, health care companies, insurance companies, and individuals regarding who is to blame when an individual develops cancer due to cigarette smoking or the inhalation of secondhand smoke.

Nicotine is a very effective drug in that 90% of nicotine is absorbed. It is one of the most toxic drugs known. Physiologically, nicotine mimics acetylcholine by acting at several nicotinic subtypes of cholinergic receptor sites. In essence, nicotine first stimulates and then blocks the receptor. Nicotine is the primary reinforcing substance in tobacco. Most smokers smoke at a stable rate, which tends to keep a steady amount of nicotine in their body. Smokers, as stated previously, tend to feel better and concentrate easier when they have nicotine in their system. The reverse appears to be true of nonsmokers who feel worse and have more trouble concentrating when exposed to nicotine.

Nicotine causes withdrawal, which is one of the main reasons that individuals even with serious physical problems continue to smoke. Nicotine is highly addictive and difficult to stop using. Also involved in the difficulty with stopping smoking is weight gain shown in many individuals who stop smoking and the connection between smoking and social behaviors.

Once an individual has stopped smoking many cognitive deficits appear to return to normal. However, smoking has a very high relapse rate.

Environmental and Industrial Neurotoxins

There are more than 800 substances that are known to have potential neurotoxic effects. Some of these potentially toxic substances are common and some are rare. The symptoms of exposure to toxins vary greatly based on the amount of exposure and the amount of time the individual is exposed to the toxin. Many symptoms appear rather quickly, whereas others may not appear until many years after exposure.

SOLVENTS AND FUELS

Exposure to solvents usually occurs in the form of fumes in the environment. There is a continual debate within the United States regarding the effects of environmental fumes and how they affect the central nervous system. The debate becomes very political with each side citing data to back claims for and against greater pollution control standards for these substances.

Acute exposure to solvents may cause an individual to complain of headache, dizziness, fatigue, nausea, and mental confusion. Personality changes such as instability, social withdrawal, and amotivation are also evident. There may be respiratory problems or skin irritations. The severity of dysfunction tends to be associated with the duration and intensity of exposure.

Chronic exposure to solvents is more common in workplace situations and may include substances such as paints, glues, and cleaning fluids. Subjective complaints after chronic exposure include fatigue, memory and concentration problems, sleep disturbances, and sensory and motor disturbances of the extremities. The most common cognitive deficits involve aspects of attention, sensory decrements, and response slowing. Emotional problems include somatic preoccupation, depression, and anxiety. Again, at this juncture, the reader may consider the plight of the individuals in the case study.

One of the major difficulties in investigating exposure to environmental or toxic solvents is that often the individual does not know he or she has been exposed. Many times the individual will seek medical advice and, without realizing the exposure, is diagnosed with a psychiatric disorder.

Treatment for exposure to solvents and fuels is to remove the individual from the toxin as soon as possible. This may be difficult if the toxin is experienced at the place of employment. Class-action lawsuits have been brought against employers who have knowingly exposed workers to toxins. Depending on the length of time exposed to the toxin, memory and cognitive deficits may recover or there may be residual damage. Damage to the peripheral nervous system may not be reversed.

PESTICIDES

More than 1 billion pounds of pesticides are used annually in agriculture in the United States. There are approximately 1 million pesticide handlers who are state certified. Many more people are exposed to pesticides including those who work in fields, pesticide applicators, those individuals who transport food, and food storage personnel.

Even though the family farm is becoming a thing of the past, an estimated 5 million Americans still farm as a primary means of income. Not only the farmers but also their spouses and children are exposed to pesticides. In addition, any migrant or transient laborers who are employed as seasonal farm workers are exposed to pesticides. The total number of individuals who experience pesticide poisoning is not known but it is estimated at 300,000 per year (Office of Technology Assessment, 1990).

Organophosphate and carbamate pesticides have been used widely. Many of the compounds containing them have been banned in recent years. However, in countries outside of the United States the use of organophosphorus pesticides is still prevalent. Research indicates that, particularly in rural regions of the developing world, self-poisoning kills approximately 200,000 persons per year (Eddleston, Buckley, Eyer, & Dawson, 2008). Pesticides used in the U.S. food supply have been a recent concern. The recall of spinach and other vegetables in addition to pet foods leads one to question the safety of the food supply in the United States.

Pesticides lead to many deficits including cognitive and memory difficulties. These may be able to be rectified after the removal of the toxic agent. However, the longer the exposure, the more likely the damage may be permanent. As with any other toxin, the removal of the individual from the source of the pesticide as soon as possible is necessary. Again, this may be very difficult if the person's livelihood is involved.

METALS

Lead and mercury appear to be the metals most likely to affect individuals in the recent past. Lead tends to affect humans through its use in paint, whereas mercury tends to surface in the food supply, specifically after the ingestion of fish.

Lead toxicity may cause an extreme spectrum of cognitive difficulties: attention, memory and learning, visual and verbal abilities, motor and processing speeds, and coordination (Anger, 1992). Those exposed to lead often complain of fatigue, headaches, restlessness, irritability, and poor emotional control. Toxicity usually requires exposure for at least 2 weeks. Children are specifically at risk for lead poisoning. Workers exposed to lead have difficulties that reflect the time and duration of exposure. The same is true of recovery of functions. Other organ systems outside of the central nervous system are also affected by lead exposure or poisoning.

Mercury toxicity, regardless of source, may cause difficulties involving the cerebellum, basal ganglia, primary visual cortex in the occipital lobe, and spinal cord degeneration (Verity & Sarafian, 2000). Even one exposure, if at a high enough dose, can lead to memory and motor dysfunction, cognitive deficits, and death. Chronic low exposure to mercury may lead to visuomotor coordination and construction problems. Also evident may be attention, memory, and reasoning deficits. A surprising fact to many people is that dentists and dental technicians may be exposed to a higher-than-average level of mercury through work and subsequently develop some of the aforementioned difficulties. The research is equivocal regarding whether all deficits can be restored after the toxin is removed from the environment.

GULF WAR SYNDROME

An estimated 1,882 gallons of sarin, a neurotoxic weapon, drifted over the coalition troops near the end of the 1991 Gulf War ("Pentagon Notifying 100,000 Soldiers," 1997). The Pentagon estimated 15,000 service people were exposed, whereas the CIA reported 120,000 troops may have been exposed. The Veterans Administration estimated 7,000 soldiers have Gulf War syndrome. In contrast, an estimated 8,000 American service people complained of Gulf War syndrome of the 700,000 troops involved in the Gulf War. The Gulf War syndrome is a highly politicized topic and the correct number of individuals exposed to toxic nerve gas may never be known. In addition, because it is a much-politicized topic, the effects of exposure to sarin and the amount of return to function may never be known. However, this is a clear example of how thousands of individuals may be exposed to central nervous system toxins without their knowledge and how the toxin may effect them for the rest of their lives.

Oxygen Deprivation

anoxia
complete absence of available
oxygen to the brain

hypoxia
reduced amount of available
oxygen to the brain

The brain requires oxygen and glucose to function. When it is without one or both of these substances, serious impairment may result. Oxygen deprivation longer than 5–10 minutes may be fatal. The complete absence of available oxygen is termed **anoxia**. **Hypoxia** is the term that refers to conditions in which oxygen availability is reduced. During hypoxia glucose is still delivered to the brain and by-products of metabolism are returned (Miyamato & Auer, 2000). The blood supply lacking oxygen is termed **anoxemia**.

MEDICAL EMERGENCIES

Cardiac and respiratory failures are the most common conditions leading to acute oxygen deprivation (DeVolder, Goffinet, Bol, Michel, de Barsy, & Laterre, 1990). Near-drowning accidents, anesthesia, and failed attempts at hanging oneself are other causes of acute oxygen deprivation. The difficulties are more likely to cause brain injury than cases of pure hypoxia (Miyamoto & Auer, 2000).

Almost every person experiencing 5 or more minutes of complete oxygen deprivation or 15 minutes of substantial hypoxia will experience permanent brain damage (Walton, 1993). Many and significant difficulties may occur, including the possibility of coma. Cognitive and memory impairment vary by individual and is related to the amount of oxygen deprivation. Other types of personality impairments may occur and may impair social functions.

HYPOXIA AT HIGH ALTITUDE

The individuals who have been studied in relationship to oxygen deprivation due to altitude are pilots and mountain climbers. Difficulties reported include nausea, headache, and vomiting along with mental slowing, less alertness and affective disturbances such as euphoria or irritability (Lishman, 1997). These difficulties appear to be able to be rectified once oxygen is restored.

CHRONIC OXYGEN DEPRIVATION

There are two main sources of chronic oxygen deprivation: chronic obstructive pulmonary disease (COPD) and sleep apnea. Cigarette smoking is a common cause of COPD. Regardless of the cause, individuals with COPD have various cognitive and memory impairments. Any task that involves complete or complex attention or thinking is likely to be impaired. The difficulties exhibited by COPD patients worsen as the oxygen depletion increases; hence, as the disorder progresses, the symptoms worsen. The difficulties that surface with COPD tend to be permanent.

Sleep apnea is a sleep disorder in which the individual stops breathing while sleeping and awakens 10 or more times per night. This awakening is caused by lack of oxygen to the brain. The individual awakens gasping for air and then returns to sleep. Most people with sleep apnea are sleep deprived. Males and overweight people are more at risk for sleep apnea. Cognitive and memory deficits are related to the amount of time that the individual is without oxygen. With successful treatment of sleep apnea, usually using a continuous positive airway pressure (CPAP) machine, any deficits can be restored.

CARBON MONOXIDE POISONING

Oxygen deprivation occurs in carbon monoxide poisoning as carbon monoxide replaces oxygen in the bloodstream. Carbon monoxide binds to oxygen 200 times more than oxygen. Symptoms of carbon monoxide poisoning include headache, dizziness, fainting, disorientation, and racing heartbeat. Carbon monoxide poisoning may lead to coma or death. The key factor in the treatment of carbon monoxide poisoning is time. The sooner the individual is able to receive oxygen, the better the prognosis. However, in severe cases of carbon monoxide poisoning, simply restoring oxygen is not sufficient. The carboxyhemoglobin level is measured and at a certain level the patient may benefit most from the use of hyperbaric oxygen. Cognition and memory as well as other systemic difficulties may result from carbon monoxide poisoning. However, depending on the length of time, many of these difficulties may be overcome.

Nutritional Deficiencies

MALNUTRITION IN CHILDREN

It is well-known that the first 5 years of life are crucial in the development of the central nervous system. Adequate nutrition implies not only the appropriate quantity of food but also the presence of proteins, carbohydrates, and fats proportional to the age of the child. Vitamins, minerals, and water are also essential for adequate central nervous system functioning.

In children, malnutrition may occur because of poverty, lack of parental knowledge regarding nutrition, or the occurrence of neglect or abuse. Most of the studies indicate that various deficiencies affect mental functioning and imply that the conditions may be irreversible (Grantham-McGregor & Ani, 2001; von Schenk, Bender-Gotze, & Koletzko, 1997; Wasantwisut, 1997; Winick, 1976). Many studies focus on specific nutrients, whereas others focus on overall malnutrition.

NUTRITIONAL DEFICIENCIES IN OLDER ADULTS

As is the case with children, older adults' central nervous systems are more at risk for difficulties. Nutritional difficulties arise for many reasons and many deficiencies are preventable.

Nutritional deficiencies in older adults who do not have any type of systemic difficulty may occur by accident. As the body ages its metabolism slows. Therefore, to maintain the same weight, an individual will need to consume fewer calories. When this is the case, in order to not gain weight, people often by accident leave out food groups that are essential to provide nutrients. Many older adults do not compensate for these missing nutrients by taking vitamins.

Folate is a good example of how a nutrient may be missing by accident and easily rectified. The popular press has made many people aware that it is a necessary nutrient prenatally. However, many people are unaware that folate or folic acid is also necessary throughout life. Folate deficiency may result in mental deterioration including sensory and reflex abnormalities, depressed mood, and impairments of memory and abstract reasoning (Botez, Botez, & Maag, 1984; Lishman, 1997). This problem is avoidable if the individual consumes foods containing folate such as lettuce or other greens, which would add very little to the person's caloric count.

Malnutrition can also occur in older adults whose diet does not include the recommended amount of various nutrients. Disease-free, independent, and financially comfortable adults older than 60 years whose blood levels of vitamin C, riboflavin, vitamin B12, and folic acid were below the recommended level performed in the impaired range on various neuropsychological tests. Greater knowledge of nutrients and their relationships to cognition is essential as the population ages (Riedel & Jorissen, 1998).

Nutritional deficiency and/or malnutrition is a much larger issue for older adults with systemic difficulties. Many difficulties and diseases cause loss of appetite and anorexia. Medications may also have similar effects. Many individuals who are ill and residing in nursing homes or residential care facilities lose their will to survive, develop depression, and fail to maintain adequate nutrition. Dementia with its cognitive and memory difficulties often goes hand-in-hand with nutritional difficulties. These deficits may not be reversible with adequate nutrition.

NUTRITIONAL DIFFICULTIES AND EATING DISORDERS

By the nature of the title, eating disorders involve a difficult and often pathological relationship with food. In addition to the psychological factors contributing to these problems, individuals often develop nutritional or dietary imbalances that have systemic consequences.

Anorexia nervosa and bulimia nervosa often lead to electrolyte imbalances within the body. Various nutrients missing in the diet can have various effects. Lack of adequate weight has also been linked to poor cognitive functioning. The brain uses glucose as its fuel, and without adequate fuel, the individual's thinking may be less than adequate. Anorexic individuals often show difficulties with attention and concentration particularly on complex tasks.

Anorexic women were significantly impaired in every area of neuropsychological functioning except on vigilance tasks (Jones, Duncan, Brouwers, & Mirsky, 1991). It still remains a question whether abilities will return with adequate nutrition (Katzman, Christensen, Young, & Zipursky, 2001).

NUTRITIONAL DIFFICULTIES AND CHEMICAL USE

As mentioned previously, alcohol and various other drugs often have a detrimental effect on nutritional status. Other factors often not considered are the effects of prescription medications or medicine combinations. Any type of medication has the potential to inhibit or exacerbate the effects of a particular nutrient.

Seizures

The discussion of seizures has been divided into two chapters. Epilepsy was covered in chapter 3. Seizures described in this chapter are those that arise as concomitant factors with other disorders.

Any time that the central nervous system suffers an accident or illness there is the potential for concomitant seizures. These seizures may appear in an individual who has never had a seizure prior to central nervous system trauma. It appears that the interference with brain functioning lowers the seizure threshold, which is the cause of the difficulty. The seizures that result could take any form.

Infectious Processes

There are a wide variety of infectious processes that are able to cause an equally wide variety of neuropsychological deficits. Tuberculosis meningitis and measles encephalitis are able to cripple a person or even kill the individual (Gelb, 1990; Lishman, 1997). Many other processes such as general paresis (syphilis) have a long disease course and leave the individual with multiple deficits. As can be seen, each viral process has its own cause and outcome for the individual.

HIV INFECTION AND AIDS

HIV and AIDS have received tremendous media attention for the past several years. Much has been learned regarding the causes and treatment of these disorders, but much still remains unknown. It does not appear clearly why AIDS and HIV began or the exact date. Evidence does suggest that the first individuals to develop this difficulty resided in Africa. The spread of the disease was quick and soon became a worldwide pandemic. It was first thought that HIV and subsequent AIDS were diseases only occurring in the male homosexual population. It soon became evident that women and heterosexuals could develop these difficulties and that it was the transmission of bodily fluid between people which was the cause.

HIV destroys the immune system of the individual. The infectious agent for AIDS is HIV-1. However, HIV-2 has been associated with AIDS especially in Western and Central Africa (Grant & Martin, 1994). HIV and AIDS strike the central nervous system particularly the brain. An individual may develop HIV and appear relatively symptom free for many years. AIDS is defined by the presence of an acute disease state associated with immunological compromise; examples include wasting, fever, diarrhea, opportunistic infections, and neurological difficulty (Collier, Gayle, & Bahls, 1987).

The early stages of the disease very often are symptom free. As stated previously, individuals may live for several years without knowing they are a carrier. This is often how the disease is spread. The disease is variable, however, and some people show symptoms rather rapidly.

Regardless of when symptoms occur, the types of difficulties remain the same. Eventually an individual will have difficulties with opportunistic agents invading the central nervous system. Most individuals will experience some cognitive and memory difficulties. AIDS-related dementia occurs in a portion of the population with this difficulty. The dementia is similar to the dementia described earlier.

Treatment for HIV and AIDS is with antiretroviral therapy and protease inhibitors. If given early enough an individual should escape the dementia. However, any other cognitive or memory deficit may be permanent. Death is then caused by opportunistic viruses, which invade a nonintact central nervous system. Because AIDS is a worldwide problem, the treatment will vary by locale. Hence, the symptom pattern also tends to vary according to the quality of health care.

HERPES SIMPLEX ENCEPHALITIS

This is a relatively rare condition and one with which few people survive without treatment during the early stage (Lishman, 1997). The virus, which causes this difficulty, has a special affinity for the limbic system gray matter and the temporal lobes. Risk factors for this infection are unknown, but 80–90% of adults carry herpes simplex antibodies. The disease can occur at any age during any time of the year.

Due to the hippocampal involvement, the individual displays significant memory difficulty with anterograde amnesia, retrograde amnesia, and social difficulties (O'Connor, Verfaellie, & Cermak, 1995). The difficulties related to the invasion of the limbic system resemble Klüver-Bucy syndrome and include hyperorality, loss of fear, social and personal disinhibition, and affective blunting (Lishman, 1997). The difficulties described tend to be permanent if not treated early. However, if treated early, as many as 30% of individuals will overcome any deficits.

LYME DISEASE

Lyme disease is an infection that is tickborne. It is more prevalent in the northeastern and mid-Atlantic states but is also evident anywhere ticks are able to come in contact with humans. The incubation period is 1–2 weeks, during which a "bull's-eye" rash develops. Following this are flulike symptoms such as fever, headache, and muscle and joint pain.

Neuropsychological difficulties which occur because of Lyme disease include cognitive and memory impairment. Along with these are sleep disturbances, fatigue, and sometimes personality changes. Lyme disease is rarely fatal. Treatment usually includes a relatively long course of antibiotics. Memory difficulties tend to occur and because of the lack of research it is unclear how many individuals recover their lost abilities.

CHRONIC FATIGUE SYNDROME

Chronic fatigue symptom is a controversial difficulty. It is often diagnosed by exception. The individual must display fatigue that is not alleviated by bed rest in addition to sore throat, swollen lymph glands, muscle pain, multijoint pain, and headaches. In addition, there are often memory deficits.

This condition is 4 times more often diagnosed in women than men (Reyes, Gary, & Dobbins, 1997). The causal factor is unknown but there is speculation regarding a link with viruses such as the Epstein-Barr virus. There are cognitive impairments with chronic fatigue syndrome especially involving concentration, impaired learning, and verbal functioning (Barrows, 1995).

Again, due to the lack of research, it is unclear whether the neuropsychological deficits can be rectified. In chronic fatigue syndrome it is particularly difficult to tell because there is no clearly specified treatment for the ailment other than rest.

Summary

The chapter begins with a complex case study that allows the reader to begin to sort through all of the various variables the clinical neuropsychologist must consider in the process of assessment, diagnosis, and rehabilitation.

The first difficulties covered in the chapter are traumatic brain injury. The reader is presented with the similarities and differences encountered with open versus closed head injuries. In addition, the causal factors related to age and behaviors are discussed.

The discussion following relates back to the case example and discusses toxic conditions. Within this discussion are alcohol and other illegal drugs. Also considered are various situations which could be detrimental to the central nervous system and reside in our environment. The reader may be surprised when reading of the many and varied other substances that could be used on a daily basis which could affect the central nervous system. Additionally, the environmental toxins and possibly work-related chemicals are staggering and not dealt well with by current pollution control laws and regulations.

Oxygen deprivation and its effects on the brain is covered next. Also covered are nutritional deficits, seizure disorders secondary to a primary diagnosis, and infectious processes. All of these various difficulties could also affect most individuals and the person may often be unaware of them occurring. By the end of this chapter the reader should be able to differentiate the neurodegenerative difficulties from acquired difficulties.

Questions for Further Study

1. Many closed head injuries could be preventable with the use of protective headgear. Should various sports which do not require it be mandated to use protective headgear?
2. After reading about the effects of various legal and illegal substances, what are your opinions about legalization of them and under what circumstances?
3. Nutritional difficulties are prevalent. Should more foods or beverages be required to fortify their products with vitamins and minerals? Explain.

References

Alexander, M. P. (1995). Mild traumatic brain injury: Pathophysiology, natural history, and clinical management. *Neurology, 45,* 1230–1260.

American Psychiatric Association. (2000). *Diagnostic and statistical manual of mental disorders* (4th ed., text rev.). Washington, DC: Author.

Anger, W. K. (1992). Assessment of neurotoxicity in humans. In H. Tilson & C. Mitchell (Eds.), *Neurotoxicology* (pp. 363–386). New York: Raven Press.

Barrows, D. M. (1995). Functional capacity evaluations of persons with chronic fatigue immune dysfunction syndrome. *American Journal of Occupational Therapy, 49*(4), 327–337.

Bigler, E. D. (1990). Neuropathology of traumatic brain injury. *Traumatic brain injury.* Austin, TX: Pro-Ed.

Bolla, K. I., Funderburk, F. R., & Cadet, J. L. (2000). Differential effects of cocaine and cocaine alcohol on neurocognitive performance. *Neurology, 54*(12), 2285–2292.

Botez, M. I., Botez, T., & Maag, U. (1984). The Wechsler subtests in mild organic brain damage associated with folate deficiency. *Psychological Medicine, 14*(2), 431–437.

The Brady Handgun Violence Prevention Act of 1993, Pub. L. No. 103–159, H.R. 1025, 103rd Congress. (1993).

Brust, J. C. (1993). *Neurological aspects of substance abuse.* Boston: Butterworth: Heinemann.

Brust, J. C. (2000). Ethanol. In P. S. Spencer & H. H. Schaunberg (Eds.), *Experimental and clinical neurotoxicology* (2nd ed., pp. 541–557). New York: Oxford University Press.

Clifton, G. L., Hayes, R. L., Levin, H. S., Michel, M. E., & Choi, S. C. (1992). Outcome measures for clinical trials involving traumatically brain-injured patients: Report of a conference. *Neurosurgery, 31*(5), 975–978.

Cohadon, F., Castel, J. P., Richer, E., Mazaux, J., & Loiseau, H. (2002). *Les traumatises craniens de laccident a la reinsertion* [On mental disease considered in medical, hygienic, and medic-legal terms]. Reuiel-Malmaison, France Reuiel-Malmaison, France: Arnette.

Collier, A. C., Gayle, T. C., & Bahls, F. H. (1987). Clinical manifestations and approach to management of HIV infection and AIDS. *AIDS: A Guide for the Primary Physician, 13,* 27–33.

Dackis, C. A., & O'Brien, C. P. (2002). The neurobiology of drug addiction. In A. K. Asbury, G. M. McKhann, W. I. McDonald, P. J. Goadsby, & J. C. McArthur (Eds.), *Diseases of the nervous system* (3rd ed.). Cambridge, UK: Cambridge University Press.

DeVolder, A. G., Goffinet, A. M., Bol, A., Michel, C., de Barsy, T., & Laterre, C. (1990). Brain glucose metabolism in postanoxic syndrome: Positron emission tomography study. *Archives of Neurology, 47*(2), 197–204.

Eddleston, M., Buckley, N. A., Eyer, P., & Dawson, A. H. (2008). Management of acute organophosphorus pesticide poisoning. *Lancet, 371*(9612), 597–607.

Franken, I. H., van Strien, J. W., Franzek, E. J., & van de Wetering, B. J. (2006). Error-processing deficits in patients with cocaine dependence. *Biological Psychology, 75*(1), 45–51.

Gasquoine, P. G. (1997). Postconcussion symptoms. *Neuropsychology Review, 7*(2), 77–85.

Gelb, L. D. (1990). Infections: Bacteria, fungi, and parasites. In A. L. Pearlman & R. C. Collins (Eds.), *Neurobiology of disease* (pp. 417–434). New York: Oxford University Press.

Gennarelli, T. A., & Graham, D. I. (2005). Neuropathology. In J. M. Silver, T. W. McAllister, & S. C. Yudofsky (Eds.), *Textbook of traumatic brain injury* (pp. 27–50). Washington, DC: American Psychiatric Publishing, Inc.

Grafman, J., Jonas, B. S., Martin, A. Salazar, A. M., Weingartner, H., Ludlow C, et al. (1988). Intellectual function following penetrating head injury in Vietnam veterans. *Brain, 111*(Pt. 1), 169–184.

Grant, I., & Martin, A. (Eds.). (1994). Introduction: Neurocognitive disorders associated with HIV-1 infection. *Neuropsychology of HIV infection.* New York: Oxford University Press.

Grantham-McGregor, S., & Ani, C. (2001). A review of studies on the effect of iron deficiency on cognitive development in children. *Journal of Nutrition, 131*(2S–2), 649S–666S.

Hart, T., Sherer, M., Whyte, J., Polansky, M., & Novack, T. A. (2004). Awareness of behavioral, cognitive, and physical deficits in acute traumatic brain injury. *Archives of Physical Medicine Rehabilitation, 85*(9), 1450–1456.

Harrison Narcotics Tax Act of 1914, 1, 38 Stat. 785. (1914).

Hatton, J. (2001). Pharmacological treatment of traumatic brain injury: A review of agents in development. *CNS Drugs, 15*(7), 553–581.

Jager, T. E., Weiss, H. B., Coben, J. H., & Pepe, P. E. (2000). Traumatic brain injuries evaluated in U.S. emergency departments, 1992–1994. *Academic Emergency Medicine, 7*(2), 134–140.

Jessor, R., Donovan, J. E., & Costa, F. M. (1991). *Beyond adolescence: Problem behavior and young adult development.* New York: Cambridge University Press.

Jones, B. P., Duncan, C. C., Brouwers, P., & Mirsky, A. F. (1991). Cognition in eating disorders. *Journal of Clinical and Experimental Neuropsychology, 13*, 711–728.

Katzman, K. K., Christensen, B., Young, A. R., & Zipursky, R. B. (2001). Starving the brain: Structural abnormalities and cognitive impairment in adolescents with anorexia nervosa. *Seminars in Clinical Neuropsychiatry, 6*(2), 146–152.

King, N. S., & Tyerman, A. (2003). Neuropsychological presentation and treatment of head injury and traumatic brain damage. In P. A. Halligan, U. Kischka & J. C. Marshall (Eds.), *Handbook of clinical neuropsychology* (pp. 487–505). New York: Oxford University Press.

Klatsky, A. L. (1994). Epidemiology of coronary heart disease—Influence of alcohol. *Alcoholism: Clinical and Experimental Research, 18*(1), 88–96.

Kraus, J. F., & Chu, L. D. (2005). Epidemiology. In J. M. Silvers, T. W. McAllister, & S. C. Yudofsky (Eds.), *Textbook of traumatic brain injury* (pp. 3–26). Washington, DC: American Psychiatric Publishing, Inc.

Kreutzer, J. S., Marnitz, J. H., Hsu, N., Williams, K., & Riddick, A. (2007). Marital stability after brain injury: An investigation and analysis. *Neurorehabilitation, 22*, 53–59.

Leweke, F. M., Gerth, C. W., & Klosterkolter, J. (2004). Cannabis-associated psychoses: Current status of research. *CNS Drugs, 18*(13), 895–910.

Lishman, W. A. (1997). *Organic psychiatry* (3rd ed.). Oxford: Blackwell.

Lukas, S. E., Mendelson, J. H., Benedikt, R. A., & Jones, B. (1986). EEG, physiologic and behavioral effects of ethanol administration. *National Institute of Drug Abuse Research Monograph Series, 67,* 209–214. Washington, DC: National Institute of Drug Abuse Research.

Lukas, S. E., & Renshaw, P. F. (1998). Cocaine effects on brain function. In S. T. Higgins & J. L. Katz (Eds.), *Cocaine abuse: Behavior, pharmacology, and clinical applications* (pp. 265–288). New York: Academic Press.

Lundqvist, T. (2005). Cognitive consequences of cannabis use: Comparison with abuse of stimulants and heroin with regard to attention, memory, and executive functions. *Pharmacology, Biochemistry, and Behavior, 81*(2), 319–330.

Marijuana Policy Project. (2008). *Medical marijuana briefing paper—2008.* Marijuana Policy Project.

Marlatt, G. A. (1996). Reducing college student binge drinking: A harm-reduction approach. In R. J. Resnick & R. H. Rozensky (Eds.), *Health psychology through the life span: Practice and research opportunities* (pp. 377–393). Washington, DC: American Psychological Association.

Mittenberg, W., Canyock, E. M., Condit, D., & Patton, C. (2001). Treatment of post-concussion syndrome following mild head injury. *Journal of Clinical and Experimental Neuropsychology, 23*(6), 829–836.

Miyamoto, O., & Auer, R. N. (2000). Hypoxia, hyperoxia, ischemia, and brain necrosis. *Neurology, 54*(2), 362–371.

Naugle, R. I. (1990). Epidemiology of traumatic brain injury in adults. In E. D. Bigler (Ed.), *Traumatic brain injury* (pp. 69–103). Austin, TX: Pro-Ed.

O'Connor, M., Verfaellie, M., & Cermak, L. S. (1995). Clinical differentiation of amnesic subtypes. In A. D. Baddeley, B. A. Wilson, & F. N. Watts (Eds.), *Handbook of memory disorders.* Chichester, UK: John Wiley & Sons, Inc.

Office of Technology Assessment. (1990). *Neurtoxicity: Identifying and controlling poisons of the nervous system, OTA-BA-436.* Washington, DC: U.S. Government Printing Office.

Pau, C. W. H., Lee, T. M. C., & Chan, S. F. (2002). The impact of heroin on frontal executive functions. *Archives of Clinical Neuropsychology, 17,* 663–670.

Pentagon notifying 100,000 soldiers of possible nerve gas exposure. (1997, July 24). Retrieved June 1, 2010, from Cable News Network, Inc. Web site: http://edition.cnn.com/US/9707/24/gulf.war/

Pert, C. B., & Snyder, S. H. (1973). Opiate receptor: Its demonstration in nervous tissue. *Science, 179,* 1742–1747.

Ponsford, J., Willmont, C., Rothwell, A., Cameron, P., Kelly, A. M., Nelms, R., et al. (2000). Factors influencing outcome following mild traumatic brain injury in adults. *Journal of the International Neuropsychological Society, 6*(5), 568–579.

Pope, H. G., & Yurgelun-Todd, D. (2003). Residual cognitive effects of long-term cannabis use. In D. Castle & R. Murray (Eds.), *Marijuana and Madness: Psychiatry and neurobiology* (pp. 198–210). New York: Cambridge University Press.

Ramaekers, J. G., Berghaus, G., van Laar, M., & Drummer, O. H. (2003). Dose related risk of motor vehicle crashes after cannabis use. *Drug and Alcohol Dependence, 73,* 109–119.

Reyes, M., Gary, H. E., & Dobbins, J. G. (1997). Surveillance for chronic fatigue syndrome - four U.S. cities, September 1989 through August 1993 Morbidity and Mortality Weekly Report. *CDC Surveillance Summaries, 46,* 1–13.

Richardson, J. T. E. (2000). *Clinical and neuropsychological aspects of closed head injury* (2nd ed.). London, UK: Taylor and Francis.

Riedel, W. J., & Jorissen, B. L. (1998). Nutrients, age and cognitive function. *Current Opinion in Clinical Nutrition and Metabolic Care, 1,* 579–585.

Rosebaum, D. P., & Hanson, G. S. (1998). Assessing the effects of school based education: A six year multilevel analysis of the Project DARE. *Journal of Crime and Delinquency, 35*(4), 381–412.

Roselli, M., Ardila, A., Lubomski, M., Murray, S., & King, K. (2001). Personality profile and neuropsychological test performance in chronic cocaine abusers. *International Journal of Neuroscience, 110,* 55–72.

Rourke, S. B., & Løberg, T. (1996). Neurobehavioral correlates of alcoholism. In I. Grant & K. M. Adams (Eds.), *Neuropsychological assessment of neuropsychiatric disorders* (pp. 423–485). New York: Oxford University Press.

Public Law S.110–793. S. Res. 793, 110 Cong. (2008) (enacted).

Sanchez-Craig, M. (1980). Drinking pattern as a determinant of alcoholics' performance on the Trail-Making Test. *Journal of Studies on Alcohol, 41,* 1082–1089.

SAMHSA. (2007). Substance use and substance use disorders among American Indians and Alaska Natives. The NSDUH Report. Washington, D.C., Office of Applied Studies.

Sherer, M., Struchen, M. A., Nakase-Thompson, R., & Yablon, S. A. (2005). Comparison of indices of severity of traumatic brain injury. *Journal of the International Neuropsychological Society, 11,* 48.

Strickland, T. L., Miller, B. L., Kowell, A., & Stein, R. (1998). Neurobiology of cocaine-induced organic brain impairment: Contributions from functional imaging. *Neuropsychology Review, 8,* 1–9.

Sugden, S. G., Kile, S. J., Farrimond, D. D., Hilty, D. M., & Bougeois, J. A. (2006). Pharmacological intervention for cognitive deficits and aggression in frontal lobe injury. *Neurorehabilitation, 21*(1), 3–7.

Teasdale, G., & Jennett, B. (1974). Assessment of coma and impaired conciousness: A practical scale. *The Lancet, 2,* 81–84.

Teasdale, G. M., Nicoll, J. A., Murray, G., & Fiddes, M. (1997). Association of apolipoprotein E polymorphism with outcome after head injury. *Lancet, 350,* 1069–1071.

Thurman, D. J., Alverson, C., Dunn, K. A., Guerrero, J., & Sniezek, J. E. (1999). Traumatic brain injury in the United States: A public health perspective. *Journal of Head Trauma Rehabilitation, 14,* 602–615.

Traumatic Brain Injury Act. H.R. Res. 248, 104 Cong. (Ed.). (1996). *(enacted).*

U.S. Food and Drug Administration. (2006). Inter-agency advisory regarding claims that smoked marijuana is a medicine. Retrieved December 20, 2009, from http://www.fda.gov/NewsEvents/Newsroom/PressAnnouncements/2006/ucm108643.htm

Unkenstein, A. E., & Bowden, S. C. (1991). Predicting the course of neuropsychological status in recently abstinent alcoholics: A pilot study. *The Clinical Neuropsychologist, 5,* 24–32.

Verity, M. A., & Sarafian, T. A. (2000). Mercury and mercury compounds. In P. S. Spencer & H. H. Schanky (Eds.), *Experimental and clinical neurotoxicity* (2nd ed., pp. 763–769). New York: Oxford University Press.

von Schenk, U., Bender-Gotze, C., & Koletzko, B. (1997). Persistence of neurological damage induced by dietary vitamin b-12 deficiency in infancy. *Archives of Disease in Childhood, 77,* 137–139.

Walton, J. N. (Ed.). (1993). *Brain's diseases of the nervous system* (10th ed.). Edinburgh: Churchill Livingstone.

Wasantwisut, E. (1997). Nutrition and development: Other micronutrients' effect on growth and cognition. *Southeast Asian Journal of Tropical Medicine and Public Health, 28,* 78–82.

Winick, M. (1976). *Malnutrition and brain development.* New York: Oxford University Press.

Yang, L., & Bernardo, L. S. (2000). Valproate prevents epiliptiform activity and after trauma in an in vitro model in neocortical slices. *Epilepsia, 41,* 1507–1513.

Zhang, J., Jiang, J. Y., Zhong, T., Yu, M., & Zhu, C. (2001). Outcome of 2,284 cases with acute traumatic brain injury. *Journal of Traumatology, 4,* 152–155.

Issues in Clinical Neuropsychological Practice

5

Key Terms

Ethical Principles of Psychologists and Code of Conduct

board of psychology

impaired judgment

dual relationships

mandated reporters

privileged communication

Health Insurance Portability and Accountability Act (HIPAA)

restriction of practice

Department of Health and Human Services

Social Security Disability Insurance (SSDI)

Supplemental Security Income (SSI)

Social Security Administration

workers' compensation

unemployment insurance

short-term disability (STD) insurance

long-term disability (LTD) insurance

premorbid conditions

psychiatrist

psychotropic medications

Learning Objectives

After reading this chapter, the student should be able to understand:

- The Ethical Principles of Psychologists and Code of Conduct and the various sanctions for ethical violations
- The manner in which payments for services may be provided by private insurance programs and government programs
- The role of premorbid patient characteristics and their effects on neuropsychological evaluations and rehabilitation
- The qualities of each individual central nervous system difficulty and its effect on neuropsychological evaluations and rehabilitation
- The role of psychometrists and prescription privileges in neuropsychology

Topical Outline

- Ethical Issues in the Practice of Clinical Neuropsychology
- Ethical Principles of Psychology
- Sanctions for Violation of Ethical Principles
- Availability of Resources

- Patient Characteristics
- Characteristics of Patient's Difficulties
- Qualities of Examination Structure and Examination
- Use of a Psychometrist in Clinical Neuropsychology
- Prescription Privileges for Psychologists

Case Vignette

Tom Swan was referred for a neuropsychological evaluation to determine if there were any residual effects of a traumatic brain injury (TBI) that occurred when he was 16 years old. Tom is enlisting in the military and therefore, his future depends on obtaining a clean bill of health. Tom feels immense pressure to appear "well" because he feels that his future is with the military. Tom is presently 22 years old.

Tom grew up in a chaotic family situation with his mother drinking heavily and having multiple marriages and divorces. Tom does not remember his biological father because his biological parents divorced when he was 3 years old. Although he has tried to make contact with his father, he has had no success. Tom's mother met Tom's first stepfather when Tom was 4 and divorced him when Tom was 6. Tom's first stepfather was verbally abusive and spent very little time with him. After this divorce, Tom's mother had various men live in their home for periods ranging from days to months. Tom's mother married his second stepfather when he was 10 and divorced him when Tom was 16. Tom became very attached to his second stepfather who had served in the military. The second stepfather appears to be the only strong and consistent male figure in Tom's life. Even after that divorce, Tom stayed in contact with his second stepfather and currently gets most of his advice about life from him. It is obvious that Tom has chosen the military because of this man. Once Tom made his decision to try to enter the military, his life became an open book. After becoming aware of Tom's TBI, the military requested any data available regarding Tom's physical and mental status.

Tom sustained the TBI after what appeared to be some kind of altercation. He stated that he was walking down the street with a group of his friends when they were taunted by another group of people they did not know. His group ignored the other group and continued to walk. The other group got into a car and drove away. A short time later the car unexpectedly reappeared and drove up onto the sidewalk striking Tom. Tom fell due to the impact and struck his head on the sidewalk. His friends summoned the police and he was taken to a nearby hospital via ambulance. He did not lose consciousness, but was kept overnight for observation. The medical personnel determined that he had suffered a concussion, considered a mild form of TBI. As was stated in the previous chapter, there are several protocols to treat concussions but most rely on the use of painkillers and rest. Both of these remedies were suggested to Tom. He went back to school a few days later and reported that he had no difficulties. No neuropsychological testing was completed.

When Tom was assessed by the clinical neuropsychologist at the request of the military, he was first interviewed regarding the event that caused the TBI, everything he could remember before and after the TBI, and other symptoms. He was also questioned at length regarding his personal history to determine his premorbid level of functioning and his support system. Neuropsychological testing revealed average intellectual abilities which is consistent with high school grades of B− to C. He did not exhibit any memory deficits. No other difficulties in brain functioning surfaced nor did any emotional sequela that could be attributed to the TBI. The *conclusion from the neuropsychological evaluation was that he had no residual difficulties due to the TBI. The written report sent to the requesting agency stated that Tom was functioning well and appeared completely capable of undertaking military service. Tom had not chosen an area of interest to pursue within the military, therefore addressing issues specifically related to special abilities was not possible.*

The case of Tom is not unique because he falls within the age range most susceptible to traumatic brain injuries, which includes those individuals 15–24 years old. The unique variables in this case are that the referral came from a third party (the military) and that there were serious ramifications of the test results with regard to Tom's future. Even though the military has gone from a draft to a volunteer basis and the entrance requirements may have changed somewhat, once an individual reports a brain injury, any subsequent difficulties are always important. These issues raise questions for the clinical neuropsychologist. How much information should he share with the referral source? Would it hurt or help Tom if his chaotic early family life was divulged? If Tom has no preference whether the information is shared, how does the clinical neuropsychologist decide what is appropriate, advantageous, or disadvantageous information to include in his report? If Tom did not want background information shared but the military requested it, how should the clinical neuropsychologist deal with the situation? All of these questions are related to ethical issues which will be discussed in chapter 5 . Also to be addressed, in a case-by-case basis, are a myriad of other professional issues related to neuropsychological assessment, diagnosis, treatment, and rehabilitation.

Ethical Issues in the Practice of Clinical Neuropsychology

The case example described previously includes many issues which could be considered ethical in nature and which would require some type of judgment on the part of the professional. In any setting where a professional is employed to help with the personal needs or issues of another individual, there is the potential for mistakes or errors. This is the case even though we assume that the professional is attempting to be cognizant of the rights and welfare of the other person.

The field of psychology has developed a code of ethical behavior referred to as the **Ethical Principles of Psychologists and Code of Conduct** (American Psychological Association [APA], 2002) as a way to protect the rights of others and to make sure that no one is unintentionally hurt in the process of being helped by psychologists. All psychologists are encouraged to abide by these standards. However, some areas of psychology, such as clinical, counseling, the school practice of psychology and, in our case, clinical neuropsychology, require a professional practice license that mainly focuses on ethical issues. Other areas covered by the ethics code include research, teaching, supervision of trainees, public service, policy development, social intervention, forensic activities, development of assessment tools, program design and development, and administration (APA, 2002). The Ethics Code applies to any in-person activities as well as those activities completed through the mail, telephone, Internet, and other electronic transmissions. All psychologists who are members or student members of the APA are bound by the ethics code.

Very often state licensing boards use the Ethics Code as the standard for behavior of their members. Some licensing boards adopt the **Association of State and Provincial Psychology Boards (ASPPB)** code of conduct as the basis for their standards for

Ethical Principles of Psychologists and Code of Conduct the ethics code developed by APA in 2002 that strives to reflect both the aspirations and practical aspects of ethical decisions made by members of the psychology profession

board of psychology
a state organization composed of psychologists and public members who determine whether a psychologist is eligible for a license to practice and who enforce the ethics code; it does not have the force of law but can sanction individuals

professional behavior (ASPPB, 2005). ASPPB is the association of all of the psychology licensing boards in the United States and Canada. **Licensing boards** or **boards of psychology** are established at the state level. The responsibilities vary by state but, in general, they are designed to protect the public, not to promote the welfare of psychologists. Boards of psychology grant licenses to psychologists based on proof by the psychologist of adequate education, training, and supervision of clinical hours. In addition, the psychologist must have passed the Examination for Professional Practice in Psychology (EPPP; ASPPB, 2009) and, in some states, other written and oral exams. Licenses to practice are valid for a set number of years and then must be renewed. Dependent on state requirements, in addition to a fee, the psychologist must demonstrate adequate completion of **continuing education credits (CEU)**. The CEUs are designed to ensure that the psychologist remains abreast of current psychological theory and research.

Members of the boards of psychology are psychologists often appointed by the governor or other official, dependent on the state. At least one member of the board is from the general public. The members of the board are volunteers and receive very little compensation. The board evaluates each claim that they receive regarding the behavior of a psychologist and determines whether and what type of sanctions may be invoked. Sanctions for ethical violations will be discussed in a later section of the chapter.

State psychological associations are different in both their scope and focus than are boards of psychology. State organizations often have as their mission the promotion of the science of psychology and its application. These organizations are often seen as the vehicle for the protection of psychologists in various employment situations and often offer advice to members regarding ethical issues. The APA and many state, provincial, and territorial psychological associations (SPTAs) have ethics committees. These associations only have jurisdiction over members of the association, not over all licensees. Ethics committees are able to issue disciplinary notices or remove an individual from the association. Some ethics committees send letters suggesting education in a specific instance as opposed to discipline. In other circumstances, they may refer an issue to the board of psychology (Bennett, Bricklin, Harris, Knapp, VandeCreek, & Younggren, 2006).

The original idea for an ethical code of behavior began with Hippocrates and led to the Hippocratic Oath to which medical doctors must abide. Other disciplines in diverse areas such as nursing, law, and law enforcement have similar codes of conduct. Each code of conduct has specific sanctions, which may be applied for violations of the code. However, an ethics code is not synonymous with law and there are times and/or circumstances when a clinical neuropsychologist must adhere to ethical principles, psychology board requirements, and law. In the case in which the ethics code is the higher standard of conduct, then the clinical neuropsychologist must abide by the code. If there is a conflict between any of the three or between one or more of these and the psychologist's place of employment, the clinical neuropsychologist must inform all concerned regarding his commitment to the code (APA, 2002). In general, being ethical is not always the same as being legal (Bricklin, 2001). Researchers have recently used the term *positive ethics* to refer to ethics as a way to promote patient welfare, as opposed to a way to avoid disciplinary actions (Handelsman, Knapp, & Gottlieb, 2002).

Ethical Principles of Psychology

The Ethical Principles of Psychologists and Code of Conduct was most recently revised and adopted in 2002 by the APA Council of Representatives (Knapp & Vandecreek, 2003). This is the 10th ethics code adopted by the APA. The previous codes were adopted in 1953, 1959, 1963, 1968, 1977, 1979, 1981, 1990, and 1992. Each revision contained some applicable material from the previous code and also information pertinent to the practice of psychology at the time the new code was drafted.

The Ethical Principles of Psychologists and Code of Conduct contain three components (see Figure 5.1). The Preamble and General Principles are aspirational goals to guide psychologists toward the highest ideals of psychology (APA, 2002). The Preamble describes the ethics code and its use. The second section includes the General Principles to which the APA would like its members to adhere. The general principles noted in the APA ethics code include (a) beneficence and nonmalfeasance, (b) integrity, (c) fidelity and responsibility, (d) justice, and (e) respect for peoples' rights and dignity. The general principles are not sanctionable or enforceable rules but are provided to lead psychologists toward basic tenets of social justice. The third section includes all of the ethical standards that, if violated, could be sanctionable (see http://www.apa.org/ethics for the complete ethics code).

The ethical standards are divided into 10 major sections with subsections beneath each major heading. The discussion that follows highlights the general content of each of the 10 sections.

The first ethical standard outlines the procedures involved with resolving ethical issues or complaints. Ethical Standard 1 includes guidelines for reporting ethical issues, including the first step being talking with the offending person. If that does not work, or, for some reason, the person fears the psychologist or the psychologist is in a powerful position vis-à-vis the complainant, the next avenue to pursue is talking with the person's supervisor. If that does not resolve the difficulty, the proper course of action is involving the board of psychology in the state where the psychologist maintains his or her practice. The sequence of reporting is similar whether the person being accused of misbehavior is the psychologist him-/herself or is receiving a complaint from a client or other individual regarding another psychologist. Also included in the first ethical standard are sanctions for psychologists who pursue or engage others to pursue improper complaints and stipulations against retaliation for making a complaint.

Ethical Standard 2 involves providing services in areas where one is competent. This standard discusses only providing services in areas in which one is trained through either graduate study or other appropriate venues. In the case study, one example of violating the standard of competency would involve a person not trained as a clinical neuropsychologist attempting to administer neuropsychological tests and making recommendations about Tom's life. Making sure that one's personal problems do not affect one's professional judgment or abilities is also covered in this standard, which clearly states that a psychologist should not work with clients who have similar issues as the psychologist. For example, if a psychologist was treating a person considering divorce when the psychologist himself or herself was going through a divorce, the psychologist could be unduly affected by his or her own personal issues and be guilty of **impaired judgment**.

Pope and Brown (1996) divided competence into 3 areas: knowledge, technical skills, and emotional competence. As illustrated earlier, any of these areas may cause a clinical neuropsychologist to have difficulties. In the emotional sphere, if the clinical neuropsychologist neglects his or her own self-care, he or she may be more likely to disrespect clients' feelings, experience an array of dysphoric moods, or make clinical mistakes (Pope & Vasquez, 2005). In addition, as the population becomes more diverse, it behooves the clinical neuropsychologist to become competent with as many cultures as possible. However, the fact that the United States has become the home to many diverse groups with various languages, religions, and ethnic and cultural practices may overwhelm the clinical neuropsychologist while practicing with individuals who experience central nervous

impaired judgment
inability to perform the role of a psychologist due to a psychological or physical disability; hence one's judgment is not unbiased

GENERAL PRINCIPLES

Principle A: Beneficence and Nonmaleficence
Principle B: Fidelity and Responsibility
Principle C: Integrity
Principle D: Justice
Principle E: Respect for People's Rights and Dignity

ETHICAL STANDARDS

1. Resolving Ethical Issues
1.01 Misuse of Psychologists' Work
1.02 Conflicts Between Ethics and Law, Regulations, or Other Governing Legal Authority
1.03 Conflicts Between Ethics and Organizational Demands
1.04 Informal Resolution of Ethical Violations
1.05 Reporting Ethical Violations
1.06 Cooperating With Ethics Committees
1.07 Improper Complaints
1.08 Unfair Discrimination Against Complainants and Respondents

2. Competence
2.01 Boundaries of Competence
2.02 Providing Services in Emergencies
2.03 Maintaining Competence
2.04 Bases for Scientific and Professional Judgments
2.05 Delegation of Work to Others
2.06 Personal Problems and Conflicts

3. Human Relations
3.01 Unfair Discrimination
3.02 Sexual Harassment
3.03 Other Harassment
3.04 Avoiding Harm
3.05 Multiple Relationships
3.06 Conflict of Interest
3.07 Third-Party Requests for Services
3.08 Exploitative Relationships
3.09 Cooperation With Other Professionals
3.10 Informed Consent
3.11 Psychological Services Delivered to or Through Organizations
3.12 Interruption of Psychological Services

4. Privacy and Confidentiality
4.01 Maintaining Confidentiality
4.02 Discussing the Limits of Confidentiality
4.03 Recording
4.04 Minimizing Intrusions on Privacy
4.05 Disclosures
4.06 Consultations
4.07 Use of Confidential Information for Didactic or Other Purposes

5. Advertising and Other Public Statements
5.01 Avoidance of False or Deceptive Statements
5.02 Statements by Others
5.03 Descriptions of Workshops and Non-Degree-Granting Educational Programs
5.04 Media Presentations
5.05 Testimonials
5.06 In-Person Solicitation

6. Record Keeping and Fees
6.01 Documentation of Professional and Scientific Work and Maintenance of Records
6.02 Maintenance, Dissemination, and Disposal of Confidential Records of Professional and Scientific Work
6.03 Withholding Records for Nonpayment
6.04 Fees and Financial Arrangements
6.05 Barter With Clients/Patients
6.06 Accuracy in Reports to Payors and Funding Sources
6.07 Referrals and Fees

7. Education and Training
7.01 Design of Education and Training Programs
7.02 Descriptions of Education and Training Programs
7.03 Accuracy in Teaching
7.04 Student Disclosure of Personal Information
7.05 Mandatory Individual or Group Therapy
7.06 Assessing Student and Supervisee Performance
7.07 Sexual Relationships With Students and Supervisees

8. Research and Publication
8.01 Institutional Approval
8.02 Informed Consent to Research
8.03 Informed Consent for Recording Voices and Images in Research
8.04 Client/Patient, Student, and Subordinate Research Participants
8.05 Dispensing With Informed Consent for Research
8.06 Offering Inducements for Research Participation
8.07 Deception in Research
8.08 Debriefing
8.09 Humane Care and Use of Animals in Research
8.10 Reporting Research Results
8.11 Plagiarism
8.12 Publication Credit
8.13 Duplicate Publication of Data
8.14 Sharing Research Data for Verification
8.15 Reviewers

9. Assessment
9.01 Bases of Assessments
9.02 Use of Assessments
9.03 Informed Consent in Assessments
9.04 Release of Test Data
9.05 Test Construction
9.06 Interpreting Assessment Results
9.07 Assessment by Unqualified Persons
9.08 Obsolete Tests and Outdated Test Results
9.09 Test Scoring and Interpretation Services
9.10 Explaining Assessment Results
9.11 Maintaining Test Security

10. Therapy
10.01 Informed Consent to Therapy
10.02 Therapy Involving Couples or Families
10.03 Group Therapy
10.04 Providing Therapy to Those Served by Others
10.05 Sexual Intimacies With Current Therapy Clients/Patients
10.06 Sexual Intimacies With Relatives or Significant Others of Current Therapy Clients/Patients
10.07 Therapy With Former Sexual Partners
10.08 Sexual Intimacies With Former Therapy Clients/Patients
10.09 Interruption of Therapy
10.10 Terminating Therapy

(© 2002 by the American Psychological Association.)

FIGURE 5.1 Ethical Principles of Psychologists and Code of Conduct

system illnesses or injuries. It is therefore suggested that the clinical neuropsychologist follow the APA "Guidelines on Multicultural Education, Training, Research, Practice, and Organizational Change for Psychologists" (APA, 2003) and "Guidelines for Psychotherapy With Lesbian, Gay, and Bisexual Clients" (APA, 2000). The issue of diversity in clinical neuropsychological practice will be further discussed in chapter 6 and throughout the remainder of the text as applicable.

Ethical Standard 3 is a compilation of standards related to human relations. This standard includes provisions directing the professional to be aware of and not engage in any form of discrimination, sexual harassment, or exploitative relationship. Multiple or **dual relationships**, literally defined as having two simultaneous relationships with one person, are discussed and discouraged within this standard. As an example, a clinical neuropsychologist would not be allowed to be the examiner for a client with central nervous system trauma and an employee of the court who may make recommendations regarding monetary awards in the case of a moving vehicle accident. The supposition is that objectivity is lost in a dual relationship. This standard addresses third-party requests for information, as in the case example, and delineates the role of the psychologist and identification of the client and the probable users of the services provided or information obtained. The limits of confidentiality in this type of situation are discussed.

In addition, Ethical Standard 3 discusses the procedures through which a psychologist obtains informed consent for assessment, therapy, or rehabilitation. It is assumed by the ethics code that individuals are competent to give consent for treatment. However, the clinical neuropsychologist may work with individuals with serious mental illnesses, mental retardation, or various central nervous system difficulties which may make understanding difficult. Many individuals have legal guardians who will sign the informed consent form for the client. Research has shown, however, that any additional means that were utilized may facilitate the understanding of treatment on the part of the client. Examples of ways to increase understanding of treatment include use of audiovisual aids, conversations with friends and caregivers, and/or extra time to ask questions (Fischer, 2002; Roberts, 2000). Any additional strategy that allows the client better understanding of the treatment to which he will partake should increase motivation and participation.

Ethical Standard 4 is related solely to privacy and confidentiality. In this standard, the limits on confidentiality, the ways to maintain confidentiality, and the use of disclosures and consultations are discussed. Ultimately, the principle of confidentiality is at the core of any form of treatment and the client must know that everything said remains confidential between himself or herself and the clinical neuropsychologist except in cases of threats of suicide, homicide, child abuse with the client as victim or perpetrator, and abuse of a vulnerable adult with the client as victim or perpetrator. In these circumstances, appropriate authorities such as the police and/or social services may be contacted. When working with a child or adolescent younger than the age of 18, the clinical neuropsychologist must inform the client that his or her parent or legal guardian may have access to the content of therapy and/or records. Informing an individual that a parent or guardian may know of private information may appear to violate the privacy of the child or adolescent or cause the individual to withhold sensitive information. However, many times, parents are more concerned regarding the mental health of their child or adolescent than the content of therapy. In addition to circumstances involved with breaking the confidential relationship, clinical neuropsychologists are also **mandated reporters**. Mandated reporting implies that suspected child abuse must be reported and it is suggested that the clinical neuropsychologist understand the exact law in the state in which he is practicing (VandeCreek &

dual relationships
the situation in which a psychologist is in a professional role with an individual and at the same time in a different type of relationship with the same individual; examples include therapist and teacher or friend and therapist

mandated reporters
professionals, because of their interaction with the public, who must report any physical or sexual abuse of children or vulnerable adults

privileged communication a communication between a patient or client and certain providers of services that may be withheld from a court of law

Knapp, 2001). Confidentiality is extremely important in clinical neuropsychology where many of the patients are vulnerable adults. In these circumstances the patient has fewer individual rights to privacy and consent for treatment must be obtained from a legal guardian.

Often misunderstood is the term privileged communication, which literally refers to the limited right to withhold information from a court. All states have a privileged communication law for psychologists-patients. However, each state varies with some protections being very inclusive and others very limited. It is therefore important that the clinical neuropsychologist know the law in the state in which he or she practices. Clinical neuropsychologists are more likely than other psychologists to be involved in forensic issues regarding their clients particularly if there is a libelous situation that may have caused or contributed to the client's difficulties. It is therefore imperative that clinical neuropsychologists understand their role in the legal system, which often varies by locale. Due to the expanding role of clinical neuropsychologists within the legal system, one researcher stated that practicing clinical neuropsychologists will probably be summoned to testify about the status of a patient at least once during the course of treatment (Bigler, 1986). In addition, a new field of jurisprudence arose in 1991 termed *neurolaw* (Taylor, 1991; Taylor, Harp & Elliott, 1996). **Neurolaw** is a synthesis of medicine, neuropsychology, rehabilitation, and law which relates to medicolegal ramifications of neurological injuries particularly TBI.

The topic of Ethical Standard 5 is advertising and other public statements. This standard addresses false or deceptive advertising, as well as media presentations, testimonials, and other forms of solicitations. Psychologists are limited in their advertising to their highest degree received, their practice specialties, and the insurance companies for whom they are providers.

Ethical Standard 6 involves record keeping and fees. Record keeping involves the use, storage, and maintenance of client records and test data. It protects the records of clients and addresses the conditions of their maintenance. This section is also devoted to financial arrangements and the issues of payment for services and situations involving nonpayment for services.

Health Insurance Portability and Accountability Act (HIPAA) a federal law implemented in 2003 to protect the privacy of individuals' medical and psychological records; it requires various provisions by any provider who uses any electronic medium to send information regarding a patient

At the federal government level, the **Health Insurance Portability and Accountability Act (HIPAA)** of 1996 was implemented in 2003 to protect client privacy particularly with the advances in biotechnology and communication technology. It was included with this standard due to its relationship to record keeping; however, it also relates to various other ethical principles such as the informed consent, psychotherapy notes, forensic services, and psychological testing. In general, HIPAA was enacted to preserve the privacy of an individual's medical (including psychological and neuropsychological) records, medical billing records, client or research databases, and human tissue samples. Health and mental health care providers, health plans, and billing services must follow HIPAA privacy guidelines. HIPAA, because it is a federal program, carries the force of law. However, the reader must keep in mind that while HIPAA is a law, similar implications are also contained within the ethical standards. It is suggested to the reader that he or she become familiar with all of the caveats of HIPAA that are beyond the scope of this chapter. Access to specific guidelines can be made through http://www.hhs.gov/ocr/privacy/.

Education and training are the topics of Ethical Standard 7. This standard addresses the content of educational programs (see chapter 1) as well as ensures the presentation of materials in classes and other situations is done in an unbiased manner. Also addressed here are the topics of sexual harassment and exploitation of students by peers, faculty, staff, and clients and contains clear statements against such behavior.

Ethical Standard 8 has research and publication as its topic. Discussed in this standard are the conditions for conducting research, the consent needed from participants, the care and treatment of both human and animal subjects, and the debriefing after completing research with humans. Publication issues related to credit for participation in research and the provision against plagiarism are also included.

Assessment is the topic of Ethical Standard 9. This standard clearly states that current tests need to be used with appropriate norms for the population tested. In some circumstances, such as a longitudinal study where subjects have been tested multiple times over a long time span, older forms of tests may be used. Issues of diversity may arise during testing. Many tests have been translated and normed on various populations. Other tests have not been translated and an ethical decision must be made regarding the use of an interpreter or the choice of a different type of assessment tool. Also included in this standard are the rights of the client to view and understand the results of the testing. Clients also need to be informed of the results of tests in language they can understand. In the case of children or vulnerable adults, the explanation of testing results is directed toward both the client and his legal guardian.

The final standard discusses all of the variables involved within therapy. The structure of therapy with the roles of the therapist and clients are described. The various forms which therapy can take such as individual, couple, family, and group are also described with a focus on who is the therapy client in each of these circumstances. In clinical neuropsychology, all of these forms of therapy may be used depending on the needs of the individual client. Sexual intimacies with clients are clearly banned by this standard. Furthermore, the therapist should not have friends, relatives, or former intimate partners as clients due to the lack of objectivity that the psychologist would have in these situations.

Sanctions for Violation of Ethical Principles

The Ethical Principles of Psychologists and Code of Conduct were developed by the APA; however, the sanctions that can be administered are imposed by state boards of psychology. Each state's board of psychology may vary regarding its interpretation of the APA Ethics Code or other codes it bases its decisions on. The sanctions vary by the seriousness of the infraction. Minor ethical violations may require a discussion with the board of psychology regarding whether the psychologist was cognizant of the violation or not. Lack of awareness or misunderstanding of an ethical standard is not a legitimate defense in the face of a charge of unethical behavior (APA, 2002). However, education is often the most valuable sanction. Usually, the individual is required to attend a class or read literature pertaining to the infraction and then explain to the board that he has learned the reason why his behavior was not appropriate. An example of a minor infraction in clinical neuropsychology could be making a remark to a client without realizing that it could be construed as sexist or racist. The lack of insight would be the deciding factor for determining the level of sanctions. If the psychologist stated he or she did not know his or her behavior could be offensive, that is very different from a malicious or intentionally hurtful behavior.

The next level of severity could cause the psychologist to not be allowed to practice in a particular area until he can prove that he has overcome or worked through the reason for his inappropriate behavior. An example in clinical neuropsychology could be an individual who completes testing with brain injured individuals while having a person with a TBI in his or her own extended family. Having this background may influence the objectivity of the clinical neuropsychologist possibly resulting in advising the person with the TBI or his or her spouse to divorce because that is what has happened in his or her family. The aforementioned example is considered having personal issues possibly interfering with professional judgment and the board may require that the psychologist not work with TBI clients until appropriate issues have been resolved. The term for this type of sanction is called **restriction of practice**.

The most serious ethical infractions could cause the board to remove the psychologist's license to practice. In a sense, the board has taken away the psychologist's livelihood. An example of a serious infraction within the area of clinical neuropsychology could be a sexual assault on an individual the professional was testing. The board of psychology may also remove a psychologist's license to practice for any conviction of a felony whether it is related to his professional duties or not.

Availability of Resources

Neuropsychological services, similar to services provided by other professionals, are often reimbursed by insurance or other programs. In the example of the case study at the beginning of the chapter, Tom's evaluation was paid for by the military. Tom was fortunate because he did not have to pay for any of the professional services himself. The following discussion of payment has been divided into private insurance and governmental programs. Often individuals without insurance or with limited insurance can receive services through government agencies. This section includes examples of many sources of funding but is by no means an exhaustive list of all the programs available across the country.

PRIVATE INSURANCE PROGRAMS

Each insurance program is different from one another and insurance policies vary substantially. The clinical neuropsychologist should be aware of the differences between these policies and the ramifications for the delivery of services to clients. In addition, many states require insurance vendors to provide coverage for certain services while other states may not do the same. As stated previously, insurance carriers must maintain HIPAA compliance.

To give an example, we will look at a common scenario. A client with central nervous system symptoms visits his medical doctor. The physician cannot determine the difficulty from which the person is suffering and needs more information regarding the person's functioning in areas such as cognition, memory, and attention. The physician then refers the person for a neuropsychological evaluation. The person telephones the clinical neuropsychologist's office and asks for an appointment. The receptionist, at this point, discusses the type of insurance the person has and the cost of the evaluation. If the person is unsure about his or her coverage, he is asked to telephone the insurance carrier. Many insurance companies require a written referral by the physician. Many insurance companies have a limit to the monetary amount they will authorize to be paid for services. Having obtained the information the person can call the clinical neuropsychologist's office again and negotiate the cost and a payment plan if needed. In some circumstances, the receptionist may deal directly with the insurance company as when the client does not understand his coverage.

GOVERNMENT PROGRAMS

In the case where a person has no insurance, is underinsured, or does not have coverage in his policy for clinical neuropsychological services, even with a physician's referral, there are various government programs which may help finance the cost of services. Many people are not aware that there are monies available and often give up when they fall into one of the aforementioned situations. A careful search on the Internet, if available, is a good way to begin to find services. A social worker, if available, is also a person who may help the client access resources. The resources predominately would be available from federal, state, or county funding sources. The federal programs apply across the country. State and county programs will all vary and are often very dissimilar from locale to locale.

There are many programs that are available and each client needs to meet different criteria for each program. The **Substance Abuse and Mental Health Services Administration (SAMHSA)**, a branch of the Department of Health and Human Services (DHHS), handles grants and other funding for individuals who meet criteria for their programs. The **Center for Mental Health Services** (CMHS), a branch of SAMHSA, has many programs from which an individual with central nervous system difficulties could potentially benefit. An example of a program administered by the CMHS is the Comprehensive Community Mental Health Services for Children and Their Families Act. Children with central nervous system difficulties and their families could potentially benefit from this program in paying for assessment and rehabilitation services. With the plethora of services available through DHHS, it might be advantageous to begin a search through DHHS (http://www.hhs.gov/) and work one's way through to the appropriate program for one's needs.

Social Security Disability Insurance (SSDI) and Supplemental Security Income (SSI) are two federal programs that are administered by the Social Security Administration. The services are then delivered through state and local channels. An individual with a central nervous system difficulty could receive funds for living expenses through SSDI if the person has been employed in a job or profession covered by Social Security. Individuals could receive SSDI compensation if they are considered to be disabled according to federal guidelines (http://www.socialsecurity.gov). A neuropsychological exam may be requested to determine if an individual qualifies for SSDI funds. The client would not be responsible to pay for testing which is used to determine eligibility.

SSI is an income supplement program funded by general tax revenues and not by social security taxes. It is designed to help the aged, blind, and/or disabled, and people who have little or no income. The individuals who receive SSI benefits generally have not worked a sufficient amount of time to qualify for traditional Social Security programs. It is designed to provide for the basic needs of food and shelter. SSI usually does not cover assessment or rehabilitation services related to central nervous system difficulties.

Workers' Compensation is a program that is regulated by the individual state. It is designed to protect workers in situations in which they may develop an illness or suffer from an accident that is caused by or related to performance in an employment situation. This also includes situations of harassment. Workers compensation is a right of employment. Individual employers must buy workers compensation insurance and then an employee's claim for worker's compensation would be adjudicated through the insurance carrier. Individuals who sustain central nervous system difficulties could obtain monies to pay for necessary services. Individuals who have central nervous system difficulties and are employed should be able to receive at least partial salary if they become unable to work.

Unemployment insurance is another right of employment and is considered income protection. Monies are removed from an individual's paycheck to fund the program in the event that an individual is no longer employed.

Department of Health and Human Services
the U.S. government's principal agency for protecting the health of all Americans and for providing essential human services, especially for those who are least able to help themselves

Social Security Disability Insurance (SSDI)
one of the three basic protections provided by Social Security; when a worker's earnings are stopped or reduced for a year or more because of a severe impairment, the worker and eligible family members can receive monthly cash benefits from SSDI; benefits continue until the individual dies or is able to work again

Supplemental Security Income (SSI)
a government program that provides economic assistance to persons faced with unemployment, disability, or agedness, financed by assessment of employers and employees

Social Security Administration
an agency of the U.S. government that operates through money obtained from individuals' taxes; it is designed to provide income and insurance upon retirement and also oversees the SSI and SSDI programs

workers' compensation
a program that must be available to employees; if a worker is injured or develops an illness on the job, the employer must provide some compensation

unemployment insurance
a program that an employer must provide to workers in which money is taken out of the worker's salary to use in the event that he or she is unable to work

short-term disability (STD) insurance
an insurance program to replace lost wages when an employee is disabled for a short period

long-term disability (LTD) insurance
an insurance program to replace lost income when an employee is disabled for a long period

Short-term disability (STD) insurance is an insurance program usually offered through one's employer as part of a benefit program. It is not a governmentally required program. It is also possible to purchase it from an insurance carrier. It is used when an individual has a difficulty that precludes employment for a short period. According to the Council for Disability Awareness, 3 in 10 people in the workforce will become disabled before retiring (http://www.disabilitycanhappen.org). Typical STD policies provide an individual with a portion of one's salary, usually 50, 60, or 66.66%, for 13–52 weeks. There are caps or limits on the amount of time one can receive benefits: up to 2 years according to the Insurance Information Institute (http://www.iii.org/).

Long-term disability (LTD) insurance may also be offered through one's employer as a benefit or purchased by the individual. LTD goes into effect after STD has expired or criteria is not met. The average length of time absent from work is 2.5 years (Commissioner's Individual Disability, 1985). LTD may last longer than STD and may last until retirement; however, the individual also does not receive his complete salary.

Government programs such as Medicare, Medicaid, and Medical Assistance are also available for those individuals who meet criteria. These programs may fund assessment and/or treatment for central nervous system difficulties.

Each state also has many programs in place. Examples of programs in the author's home state of Minnesota include the following **waiver programs**. These programs are written to meet federal guidelines and each program includes eligibility requirements specific to the type of disability, funding parameters, and limits, and whether the services are necessary for the recipient's health, welfare, and safety. The client would apply for the program through his or her local county social service agency. Eligibility is determined through a screening process.

The waiver programs are summarized here to give examples:

- *Alternative Care* (AC) is a program that supports certain home and community-based services for older Minnesotans, aged 65 years and older, who are at risk of nursing home placement and have low levels of income and assets (AC is administered by the Department of Human Services [DHS] Aging and Adult Services Division.)
- *Community Alternative Care* (CAC) *Waiver* for chronically ill and medically fragile persons who need the level of care provided in a hospital
- *Community Alternatives for Disabled Individuals (CADI) Waiver* for persons with disabilities who require the level of care provided in a nursing facility
- *Elderly Waiver* (EW) for people older than the age of 65 years who require the level of care provided in a nursing facility (EW is administered by the DHS Aging and Adult Services Division.)
- *Mental Retardation or Related Condition (MR/RC) Waiver* for persons with mental retardation or a related condition who need the level of care provided in an Intermediate Care Facility for Persons with Mental Retardation or Related Conditions (ICF/MR)
- *TBI Waiver* for persons with acquired or traumatic brain injuries who need the level of care provided in a nursing facility that provides specialized (cognitive and behavioral supports) services for persons with brain injury or require neurobehavioral hospitalization (http://www.dhs.state.mn.us/)

Many other states have waiver programs for various central nervous difficulties particularly TBI. New York has a TBI Waiver that is administered through the New York Department of Health (New York Department of Health, 2006). Wisconsin has a Brain Injury Waiver Program in which the individual must also meet criteria for Medicaid (Wisconsin DHS, 2009). Vermont's Division of Disability and Aging Services provide a TBI Program (Vermont Division of Disability and Aging Services, n.d.).

In addition, a Federal a program termed the Tax Equity and Fiscal Responsibility Act (TEFRA; 1982) is for children with disabilities who are living with their parents. TEFRA has income guidelines that must be met and specific services that it will cover.

The final area to cover is military programs for active duty service members, retired individuals, and their families. This is the type of funding that would facilitate the evaluation for our case study. TriCare is a program for active duty service members, National Guard and Reserve members, retirees, their families, survivors, and certain former spouses worldwide. ChampVA is the general medical insurance that allows individuals access to VA services.

Patient Characteristics

After a client has obtained funding for his or her neuropsychological evaluation and/or rehabilitation, the professional needs to take into consideration many individual variables which are discussed here. These variables will surface again as the professional looks at interviewing, testing, rehabilitation, and therapy.

GENDER

The gender of the client is important for many reasons. Several brain structures are slightly different between males and females (see chapter 2); hence, it is important to consider this variable in relationship to central nervous system damage. In summary, females appear to have larger volumes in areas of the brain associated with language function, in medial paralimbic regions, and in some frontal lobe regions. They also have a greater amount of gray matter particularly in Wernicke's area. Males have a larger medial, frontal, and cingulate regions, a larger amygdala, and a larger hypothalamus (Kolb & Whishaw, 2009, pp. 322–323). In addition, many central nervous system difficulties or disorders are more often present in one gender compared to the other. For example, men sustain TBIs twice as frequently as women, except during the age period of those who are older than 65 where women outnumber men (Jager, Weiss, Coben, & Pepe, 2000). Gender is also important in relationship to the level of reported difficulty; females in general tend to be more willing to express physical or mental problems. The expression of feelings is not true for all females, but more a reflection of what types of behaviors have been reinforced by society.

AGE

Age is a factor in testing. Most assessment tools are normed on the 16–65 year old population. Different tests and norms need to be used with younger and older clients. Young children, younger than the age of 5, do not have a fully developed central nervous system and testing may not be totally representative of functioning at very young ages. When working with older adults, it is necessary to separate "normal aging" from the effects of any form of disease process. Normal aging implies a lessening of motor speed, as well as changes in sensory abilities, and needs to be taken into account during testing. For example, in normal aging, motor speed declines more than does language. Many tests have taken age into account as they report standard scores.

Age is also a factor in rehabilitation. Children's rights are different from adults. Because a child is not of legal age, all information pertaining to the child, from the initial contact with the clinical neuropsychologist through any form of assessment, must have the consent of the parent. Confidentiality is also not the same as with adults in that parents have the right to know what their child has said. An example may be a child with central nervous system difficulties whose parents are in the process of divorce. Even though the divorce is not the topic of the evaluation, a parent may inquire whether his or her child has spoken about the topic. The lack of rights compared to adults must be handled carefully to ensure the child is unafraid and as comfortable as possible. Older adults, due to perceived social stigma, may be less likely to seek out services. It is hoped that with the continuing aging of the population, especially the baby boomer generation, the stigma may dissipate and older adults will become more comfortable seeking services.

ETHNICITY

Race and ethnicity are characteristics to consider in evaluation to ensure the client's test results are compared to appropriate norms. If a client's primary language is not English it is important to use a standardized translated test or to use the services of an interpreter. This topic will be discussed in greater detail in chapter 6. Rehabilitation issues may arise because of the perceived lack of usefulness and stigma of these services by a particular client's ethnic group. Some clients prefer to work with people of their own racial or ethnic background; however, the bulk of clinical neuropsychologists at present are Caucasian. The fact that most clinical neuropsychologists are Caucasian may be an issue in both assessment and rehabilitation. An appropriate way around this issue may be a careful introduction to the assessment and rehabilitation process along with an open discussion regarding cultural differences.

PREMORBID INTELLECTUAL LEVEL

premorbid conditions any difficulties that occur before a central nervous system accident or illness

Premorbid refers to the time before the client sustained an injury or incurred an illness that affected her central nervous system. When there are difficulties that are present from birth, there is no premorbid period. The premorbid intellectual level gives the clinical neuropsychologist an idea of the cognitive abilities the individual had prior to the central nervous system trauma. However, many people have never taken a formal IQ test before their central nervous system trauma. Premorbid intellectual information may be gathered from school tests such as the Iowa Tests of Basic Skills, school records, or military records. Individuals who are in school after 2002 will have a standardized measure of intelligence due to the passage of Public Law 107-110 (The No Child Left Behind Act of 2002). This is a controversial legislation and applies to all children including those who are disabled and those in special education classes. Other ways to determine a premorbid level of intellectual functioning include performance on cognitive tests, extrapolation from current reading ability, demographic variables, or a combination of these (Lezak, Howieson, & Loring, 2004). In Tom's case, his premorbid level of functioning was based on his level of academic performance.

PREMORBID PERSONALITY FACTORS

Premorbid personality factors refer to an individual's personality characteristics prior to sustaining a central nervous system difficulty. These characteristics are very important to know in order to separate out the effects of the central nervous system problem from the person's original emotional makeup. The premorbid personality difficulties may include a myriad of factors including anxiety, depression, anger, and/or any diagnosable mental health issue. These issues need to be separated from the effects of central nervous system trauma for treatment planning and rehabilitation.

With any central nervous system difficulty, there is a very good chance that the individual will suffer from depression and/or anxiety. The depression is termed secondary to the central nervous system difficulty. Depression arises because of the person's perceptions of changes in his or her life due to the central nervous system trauma. The actual limitations or abilities are also reasons for the appearance of depressive symptoms. There are also other emotions that are particular to the nature and site of the disability. Anger, frustration and low frustration tolerance, emotional lability, and issues related to poor judgment often appear after a central nervous system difficulty.

SOCIAL SUPPORT NETWORK

An individual's social support network before and after injury or illness is a very important variable to be considered in recovery. Research has continually shown that those individuals with a compassionate and caring support system have a greater likelihood of a positive outcome from rehabilitation (Newcombe, 1982). However, if these individuals are not supportive or helpful, it may make the situation worse for the individual. Difficulties with family, friends, and, particularly, spouses are great after the occurrence of TBI to one of the members of a couple. Hence, evaluation of the social support network will help the clinical neuropsychologist determine if additional social support services are needed as part of the rehabilitation plan.

Characteristics of Patient's Difficulties

After considering the particular demographic and personal factors in an individual's life, the clinical neuropsychologist providing assessment and rehabilitation services must also consider the qualities of the illness or injury to provide appropriate services.

TYPE AND NATURE OF PROBLEM PRESENTED

Earlier chapters covered many of the most common accidents and illnesses that could affect the central nervous system such as the difficulties illustrated in each of the case studies addressed thus far. Each difficulty yields different test patterns and poses different rehabilitation challenges. This, in turn, results in the need to tailor the evaluation to address the specifics of each type of trauma.

If the nature of the individual's difficulties is known at the time of referral, then the assessment may be used as corroboration of the diagnosis and treatment planning may soon take place. If there has been no attempt at determining the nature or extent of the individual's difficulties then, subsequent to assessment, a referral to a neurologist or other medical personnel may be necessary prior to rehabilitation.

TIME SINCE THE ILLNESS OR INJURY

It has been determined from physical medicine and mental health literature that the sooner the client receives treatment, the better the prognosis. If the client has a diagnosed problem, this often is the best route. For example, in an automobile accident, the sooner the victim reaches a hospital, the better the survival rate and, hopefully, the less brain impairment. The military has used this principle in treating mental health difficulties such as posttraumatic stress disorder. Mobile mental health facilities are currently available in the war with Iraq as well as Afghanistan and other active military sites, at the time this book was published.

Time factors into assessment, as well as immediate care of the individual. Often a neuropsychological evaluation is completed before a patient is discharged from a hospital. An evaluation this close to the time of the trauma may not portray an accurate picture of the patient's abilities and disabilities. For the brain to heal itself, as much as possible, it takes approximately 2 years. During this 2-year span, the patient may be extremely fatigued as the majority of energy is directed toward healing the brain. While the brain is actively healing itself, rehabilitation is usually begun. The patient may need to ease into his or her normal activities as opposed to going immediately back to work, school, or other obligations. With all of these factors in mind, it is a general practice to complete a neuropsychological evaluation 6 months after the accident or time of the diagnosis of the illness, at 1 year, and at 2 years, when we can assume that as much healing as possible has taken place (Lezak et al., 2004). Yearly evaluations thereafter are often suggested. However, the determining factors for evaluation are the type of difficulty the individual has sustained and the person's progression or regression in abilities.

Qualities of Examination Structure and Examination

Now that we have considered the personal qualities of the individual, the type of accident or illness he or she has sustained, and the time factors involved, the actual physical layout of the setting for neuropsychological assessment and rehabilitation will be explored. The physical structure will be considered while assuming that the clinical neuropsychologist has control over these variables. If a clinical neuropsychologist is employed in a facility where there is no choice over rooms or in the physical layout of the room, then the professional needs to adapt the available space to meet the needs of the client.

OBTAINING THE BEST PERFORMANCE FROM THE PATIENT

In a neuropsychological evaluation, the professional's objective is to obtain the best measure of the client's abilities. The client may not know or understand the reason for the evaluation. The client may be nervous, confused, or experiencing various emotions as he or she enters the situation. To increase the likelihood that the client will perform well and to help him or her relax, a clear explanation of the reason and the ramifications of the evaluation are necessary. The explanation and instructions for any testing must be in language understandable to the client. Any issues related to confidentiality and issues of when and to whom the information from the evaluation will be sent should be addressed.

To help relax the client, the professional also needs to give clear directions for any assessment task to be completed. It is wise to inform the client to take breaks if he or she needs to and to inform him or her that this is acceptable. Testing may be divided into more than one session if fatigue, concentration, or other issues surface, which may preclude obtaining accurate results, especially because fatigue is often one of the side effects of TBI.

ROOM CHARACTERISTICS: SIZE AND DÉCOR

An assessment or rehabilitation room should be designed to facilitate client comfort and to help the client perform well on all tests. The size of the room is important because too small of a room may cause the client to feel claustrophobic, whereas too large of a room may be intimidating. In general, ideal dimensions for a room are about 12 × 14 ft or the size of a standard office. The colors of the office are similar to the colors used in a counseling setting. Pastels and earth tones tend to have a calming effect. Bright colors such as reds, yellows, and oranges stimulate the central nervous system and may foster anxiety. For example, bright colors are regularly used in fast-food restaurants to encourage people to eat a greater quantity of food and leave quickly.

The décor of the room needs to be comfortable for the client. A desk and chairs are usually necessary for testing purposes. A couch or a few comfortable chairs suitable for a therapy setting with end tables and lamps are very relaxing. Bright or overhead lighting should be avoided as well as any type of ventilation that may cause extraneous sounds and distractions. The fewer stimuli present in a room used in evaluating a person with central nervous system difficulties, the better the performance. Plants, wall decorations, and other objects should be kept to a minimum for the aforementioned reasons.

ACCESSIBILITY TO THOSE WITH DISABILITIES

Assessment and rehabilitation of individuals with central nervous system difficulties is different from any other population. It is essential that the door to the office is wide enough to accommodate a wheelchair. It is also essential that the furniture not get in the way of wheelchair mobility. Testing tables must be at a height that can accommodate a wheelchair if the client does not or cannot transfer to another chair.

It would be advantageous, and in some areas the law may require, that the nearest restroom be handicap accessible. The same is true regarding parking facilities near the office, which must be designated with handicap accessible parking.

QUALITIES OF THE EXAMINER

Clinical neuropsychologists, like every group of professionals, may be male or female, young or old, and of various racial and ethnic groups. Some clients may have a preference for the type of individual they are working with and sometimes this can be accommodated and sometimes not. The clinical neuropsychologist's job is to obtain the best assessment results and use the most effective rehabilitation techniques. In order to do the best job, the professional needs to make the client comfortable. For example, wearing a white coat is synonymous with the medical profession and is discouraged because it may make the client unduly anxious. Dress may be more or less formal depending on the employment situation.

How the professional speaks in terms of voice tone and wording is very important. It is important to never talk down to a client, while at the same time never assuming that the client knows the meaning of professional jargon. It is best to try to speak as one would in casual conversation. Voice tone also needs to be appropriate for the situation, not too loud or too quiet.

Use of a Psychometrist in Clinical Neuropsychology

There are basically two means of completing a neuropsychological evaluation. Clinical neuropsychologists can administer the tests themselves or they can hire a psychometrist to do the testing for them. There are positives and negatives to each approach. Neuropsychological assessment requires a great deal of time, often taking a day or two. If the neuropsychologist is working for this amount of time with one client, he or she is not able to complete rehabilitation with others. The number of evaluations that a clinical neuropsychologist is able to complete has to be balanced with the rehabilitation needs of other clients. The positives of testing patients oneself are that the neuropsychologist is able not only to develop rapport, which will help with therapy and rehabilitation, but also to observe all of the behaviors, verbal and nonverbal exhibited by the client during testing.

There are situations when the sheer volume of patients necessitates the use of a psychometrist. These situations, which involve great numbers of clients, are often in large hospitals such as the Veterans Affairs Medical Centers.

When using a psychometrist it is essential that the individual have proper training in test administration and scoring. The interpretation of results and the interviewing of the patient and family members is still the purview of the clinical neuropsychologist.

The use of a psychometrist in testing has become both accepted and widespread (Brandt & van Gorp, 1999). Sweet, Moberg, and Suchy's survey referred to in chapter 1 shows that between 42 and 69% of clinical neuropsychologists use psychometrists. However, as stated previously, clinical neuropsychologists by self-report more often than not conduct the interview and observe the patient during testing if completed by a psychometrist. Records review, interpretation and report write-ups of test results, patient feedback, and consultation with the referral source are almost always completed by the clinical neuropsychologist (Sweet et al., 2000a).

In order to be employed as a psychometrist, an individual must possess, at the very least, a master's degree. There are some institutions where individuals with bachelor's degrees are hired and then trained by the facilities. However, this practice is ethically questionable and is currently not done as much now as it had been in the past.

Prescription Privileges for Psychologists

psychiatrist
a medical doctor (MD) who specializes in mental health medicine

psychotropic medications
a category of medications used to treat mental health issues; examples include antianxiety, antidepressive, and antipsychotic medications

In the United States, there is a shortage of psychiatrists, particularly in rural areas. **Psychiatrists** are medical specialists who prescribe **psychotropic medications**. **Nurse practitioners** and **physicians' assistants** are also able to prescribe these medications. Where the shortage is extremely great, other medical specialties such as gynecologists and family practitioners are often called on to prescribe psychotropic medication. Many of these medical doctors feel they do not have adequate mental health training for this type of work.

Clinical neuropsychologists and all psychologists involved in health care need to understand basic psychopharmacology (Barnett & Neel, 2000). General knowledge implies an understanding of the central nervous system and the proper use of medications to be able to discuss these issues with patients. It is particularly important due to the fact that 50% of patients in psychotherapy use psychotropic medications (Borkovec, Echemendia, Ragusea, & Ruiz, 2001). It is even more likely that those individuals seen by a clinical neuropsychologist have or will be prescribed psychotropic medication.

In response to the shortage of trained medical personnel, clinical psychologists have been lobbying to obtain prescription privileges. In 1995, the APA Council, at its annual meeting in New York, formally endorsed prescription privileges for appropriately trained psychologists (APA, 1995). In 2000, the APA Insurance Trust announced that in any states where psychologists have prescriptive authority, they would be covered within the practice of psychology (Murray, 2003). Presently, there is a dispute within psychology regarding whether this should happen. The side that is in favor of obtaining prescription privileges states that it would help fill the void of doctors who are able to prescribe psychotropic medications, particularly within rural areas. This is particularly prevalent in clinical neuropsychology in which it may be advisable for the patient to be treated with psychotropic medications soon after assessment. The negative side of the argument states that psychology is a behavioral not biological science. Also, it would alter the amount of time spent in rehabilitation and therapy by psychologists if psychologists began to prescribe.

At the present time, psychologists have the right to prescribe psychotropic medications in Louisiana, New Mexico, Guam, and the military. There is significant training involved for the psychologist to prescribe psychotropic medications, along with practical experience coprescribing with a physician. The issue of prescription privileges will be decided at the state level by state legislatures. At the time of this writing, 5 additional states are considering various proposals for this privilege. The main issue for the clinical neuropsychologist, if prescription privileges become available, is the trade-off between being able to help one's patients more quickly versus potentially being asked to prescribe as a larger part of one's practice.

As this chapter closes we will review the situation of Tom whose referral from neuropsychological evaluation was at the request of a third party. It is clear, at this point, that he was made aware of the ramifications of his evaluation as well as the provisions of informed consent and confidentiality. Tom's evaluation was completed and he was admitted into the military service as he desired. He made the decision that his family life was not something he wanted shared with the referral source and the clinical neuropsychologist honored the request.

Summary

Chapter 5 introduces the reader to the myriad of practical and ethical issues that the clinical neuropsychologist may encounter. A summary of the Ethical Principles of Psychologist and Code of Conduct is included and discussed particularly related to salient issues regarding individuals with central nervous system illness or trauma. Also included are the sanctions for violations of ethical principles. A discussion of payment for services and the many private and government sources of funding are designed to help the reader understand how difficult obtaining services may become. It also serves as a guide for the reader to help clients overcome these difficulties.

The next section of the chapter focuses on patient variables that will affect assessment, diagnosis, and treatment. Salient issues include age, gender, ethnicity, social support, and premorbid intellectual and personality factors. Also included are factors related to the disease or difficulty itself.

A final section addresses professional issues of the use of psychometrists in assessment and prescription privileges for psychologists. Both of these issues have ramifications for the field of clinical neuropsychology. The use of a psychometrist in testing is often determined based on a cost–benefit analysis. The ability of clinical psychologists or clinical neuropsychologists with advanced training obtaining prescription privileges is related to the fundamental position one takes regarding the definition or role of the professional. Also included within this discussion is the lack of prescribers and needs of clients. Neither of these issues has currently been resolved and arguments on either side will continue in the near future.

Questions for Further Study

1. Due to the fact that clinical neuropsychologists often work with patients having medical issues, when and in what context do the two professions intersect?
2. How will the aging of the population affect the ability of clinical neuropsychologists to service all of the people in need?
3. The lack of prescribers for psychotropic medications forces many patients to wait an inordinate amount of time for medication. How would the practice of a clinical neuropsychologist be altered if or when the laws for prescription privileges change?

References

American Psychological Association. (1995). *APA telephone survey of APA members*. (Available from Practice Directorate, APA, 750 First St., N.E., Washington, DC 20002-4242)

American Psychological Association. (2000). Guidelines for psychotherapy with lesbian, gay, and bisexual clients. *American Psychologist, 55,* 1440–1451.

American Psychological Association. (2002). Ethical principles of psychologists and code of conduct. *American Psychologist, 57,* 1060–1073.

American Psychological Association. (2003). Guidelines on Multicultural Education, Training, Research, Practice, and Organizational Change for Psychologists. *American Psychologist, 58,* 377–402.

Association of State and Provincial Psychology Boards. (2005). *ASPPB Code of Conduct.* Retrieved December 26, 2009, from http://www.asppb.net/i4a/pages/index.cfm?pageid=3353

Association of State and Provincial Psychology Boards. (2009). *Examination for Professional Practice in Psychology (EPPP) Information.* Retrieved from http://www.asppb.net/i4a/pages/index.cfm?pageid=3279

Bennett, B. E., Bricklin, P. M., Harris, E., Knapp, S., VandeCreek, L., & Younggren, J. N. (2006). *Assessing and managing risk in psychological practice: An individualized approach* (p. 17). Rockville, MD: The Trust.

Barnett, J. E., & Neel, M. L. (2000). Must all psychologists study psychopharmacology? *Professional Psychology: Research and Practice, 31,* 619–627.

Bigler, E. D. (1986). Forensic issues in neuropsychology. In D. Wedding & A. M. Horton (Eds.), *The neuropsychology handbook* (pp. 526–547). New York: Springer.

Borkovec, C. T., Echemendia, R., Ragusea, S., & Ruiz, M. (2001). The Pennsylvania Practice Research Network and future possibilities for clinically meaningful and scientifically rigorous psychotherapy effectiveness research. *Clinical Psychology: Science and Practice, 81,* 155–167.

Brandt, J., & van Gorp, W. G. (1999). American Academy of Clinical Neuropsychology policy on the use of non-doctoral personnel in conducting clinical neuropsychology evaluations. *The Clinical Neuropsychologist, 13,* 385.

Bricklin, P. (2001). Being ethical: More than obeying the law and avoiding harm. *Journal of Personality Assessment, 77,* 195–202.

Division 44/Committee on Lesbian, Gay, and Bisexual Concerns Joint Task Force on Guidelines for Psychotherapy with Lesbian, Gay, and Bisexual Clients. (2000). Guidelines for psychotherapy with lesbian, gay, and bisexual clients. *American Psychologist, 55,* 1440–1451.

Fischer, C. B. (2002). Respecting and protecting mentally impaired persons in medical research. *Ethics and Behavior, 12,* 279–283.

Handelsman, M., Knapp, S., & Gottlieb, M. (2002). Positive ethics. In C. R. Snyder & S. Lopez (Eds.), *Handbook of positive psychology* (pp. 731–744). New York: Oxford University Press.

H.R. The No Child Left Behind Act of 2001, H.R. Res. 110, 107th Cong., H.R. (2002) (enacted).

H.R. Health Insurance Portability and Accountability Act, H.R. Res. 191, 104 Cong., H.R. (1996) (enacted).

Jager, T. E., Weiss, H. B., Cohen, J. H., & Pepe, P. E. (2000). Traumatic brain injuries evaluated in U.S. emergency departments 1992–1994. *Academic Emergency Medicine, 7*, 134–140.

Knapp, S., & VandeCreek, L. (2003). *A guide to the 2002 revision of the American Psychological Association's ethics code.* Sarasota, FL: Professional Resource Press.

Kolb, B., & Whishaw, I. O. (2009). *Fundamentals of neuropsychology* (6th ed., pp. 322–323). New York: Worth.

Lezak, M., Howieson, D., & Loring, D. (2004). *Neuropsychological assessment* (4th ed.). New York: Oxford University Press.

Murray, B. (2003). A brief history of RxP. *Monitor, 34*(9), 66.

Newcombe, F. (1982). The psychological consequences of closed head injury: Assessment and rehabilitation. *Injury, 14*, 111–136.

New York Department of Health. (2006). *Traumatic brain injury waiver.* Retrieved December 27, 2009, from http://www.health.state.ny.us /health_care/medicaid/program/longterm/tbi.htm

Pope, K., & Brown, L. (1996). *Recovered memories of abuse: Assessment, therapy, forensics.* Washington, DC: American Psychological Association.

Pope, K., & Vasquez, M. (2005). *How to survive and thrive as a therapist: Information, ideas and resources for psychologists in practice.* Washington, DC: American Psychological Association.

Report of the Committee to Recommend New Disability Tables for Valuation. (1985). *Transactions of Society of Actuaries 1985, 37*, 449–466.

Roberts, L. W. (2000). Evidence-based ethics and informed consent in mental dillness research. *Archives of General Psychiatry, 57*, 540–542.

Sweet, J. J., Moberg, P. J., & Suchy, Y. (2000a). Ten-year follow up survey: Part I: Private practices and economics. *The Clinical Neuropsychologist, 14*, 18–31.

Sweet, J. J., Moberg, P. J., & Suchy, Y. (2000b). Ten-year follow-up survey of clinical neuropsychology: Part II. Practices and economics. *The Clinical Neuropsychologists, 14*, 479–495.

Taylor, J. S. (1991). Neurolawyers: Advocates for TBI and SCI survivors. *The Neurolaw Letter, 1*(2), 1.

Taylor, J. S., Harp, J., & Elliot, T. (1991). Neuropsychology and neurolawyers. *Neuropsychology, 5*(4), 293–305.

VandeCreek, L., & Knapp, S. (2001). *Tarasoff and beyond* (3rd ed.). Sarasota, FL: Professional Resource Press.

Vermont Division of Disability and Aging Services. (n.d.). *Traumatic brain injury (TBI) program.* Retrieved December 27, 2009, from http://www.ddas .vermont.gov/ddas-programs/tbi/programs-tbi-default-page

Wisconsin Department of Human Services. (2009). *Brain injury waiver program.* Retrieved December 27, 2009, from http://dhs.wi.gov/bdds/brain.htm

Interviewing in Clinical Neuropsychology

6

Learning Objectives

After reading this chapter, the student should be able to understand:

- The types of referral sources and the presenting complaints as they relate to the interview process
- The characteristics of structured and unstructured interviews and when each should be employed
- The relationship between the interview setting and behaviors of the interviewer and how each affects the interview process
- The language considerations that may be present in the interview process
- The ethnic and cultural characteristics of the client and the interviewer and how each may affect the interview process
- The five phases of the clinical interview

Topical Outline

- Referral Source
- Presenting Complaint
- Structured Interviews
- Unstructured Interviews
- Diagnostic Interviews
- Collateral Interviews
- Interview Setting
- The Interviewer
- Use of a Translator
- Purpose and Outcome of the Interview
- Termination of the Interview
- Use of Interview Forms
- Ethnic and Cultural Issues in Interviewing

Case Vignette

*J*ess was referred to a clinical neuropsychologist by a social worker from his county social services office who had been working with Jess and his girlfriend. The reason for referral was his
anger and frequently abusive behavior toward his girlfriend. The goal was to determine the
type of services which would most appropriately help Jess with his difficulties. Referral to a clinical
neuropsychologist was undertaken for him with the supposition that assessment and rehabilitation
were to be considered as an option. The social worker considered this option because Jess was
in the military and the fact that there is a connection between military service and head injuries
leading to behavioral difficulties.

Jess came in for the initial interview somewhat unhappy about the circumstances surrounding
the referral but willing to cooperate in order to preserve the relationship with his girlfriend. In addition
to a review of the presenting complaint and the social worker's report, the clinical neuropsychologist
spent an hour gathering as much information as possible encompassing all areas of his life.

The following information is in chronological order as best as Jess could remember. Jess told
the clinical neuropsychologist that he grew up in one of the southern states and he described his
family situation as unpleasant. His parents did not get along well with one another and often
displaced their feelings onto the children. Jess, who is presently 41, has an older sister who is now
43 and a younger sister who is now 37. Jess stated that he felt he received more physical abuse than
his sisters, but that they all felt they were emotionally abused.

Jess recalled that, academically, school was easy for him and that he performed very well.
He often felt that school was a place from which to escape the family situation. However, Jess did
have many behavioral problems at school and often fought on the school grounds with boys smaller
than him. Occasionally, when he was particularly daring, he would pick a fight with an older boy.
He described his feelings while fighting as not always being angry or hostile but just a release of
tension. As Jess was involved in more fights, he developed a reputation as a "bully," which caused
his parents to be contacted by the school. Jess's father was not pleased and physically beat his son
for his transgressions. Jess stated that although he could remember his father's abusive behavior,
he could not remember his mother's reactions. However, as Jess described his mother he became
physically tense and avoided eye contact.

After high school Jess enlisted in the military. One of the reasons for enlisting was the high
level of physical activity required in the service. However, he did not stay in the military after
his initial enlistment because he felt a lack of intellectual stimulation. After he left the military
he attended a state college near the town where he grew up. He became quite interested in the
sciences and began to plan a career post-college within the scientific domain. In contrast, he felt
that the arts, particularly theater, caused him to experience emotions which he did not appreciate
nor had the coping capacity for which to deal. In college he became quite well-known as a football
player. As in the past he felt good when he was physically active and aggressive. Jess met his wife
in college and they married soon after graduation. Jess and his wife moved north after he applied
and was accepted into graduate school. Jess took his initial interest in biology and applied it to
his love of animals, which led him to graduate school in veterinary medicine. While in school he
decided to specialize in large animals, such as horses and cows, which he felt would also offer him
the greatest chance of employment in a rural setting. Jess stated that a rural environment would
be less stressful for him. During his time in graduate school he was very competitive with the other
students. In addition to feelings of competition, he also felt a lack of physical release. To compensate for his mounting physical tension he began boxing at the university athletic facility.

Jess's wife worked while he attended classes. Eventually they had two sons, who are now in
their late teens. Jess stated that he knew he was emotionally abusive toward his wife but felt he

could connect it with a lack of an adequate physical outlet. He was also sexually aggressive toward his wife, which she did not encourage or appreciate.

After graduate school they settled in a northern state. Neither Jess nor his wife wanted any contact with his parents because of the history of physical and emotional abuse and the chaotic environment. Jess did keep in contact with his sisters through the mail and over the telephone even though they did not see each other very often. Jess stated that contact with his sisters was the only sense of family that he had. Jess and his wife stayed in contact with her relatives and often visited her family. Even though his wife's family was gracious toward him, Jess stated he never felt totally comfortable. He hypothesized that this was because he was not familiar with the workings of a functional family unit.

Jess opened his own veterinary medicine business soon after graduate school. He became quite successful through working long hours and exerting great physical labor. He employed two veterinary technicians and a receptionist/bookkeeper but did not feel comfortable being part of a larger practice. Jess stated that he wanted to remain in control of his life and not answer to anyone else particularly anyone who could become angry with him. At the same time, Jess's wife met someone else whom she felt was kinder and gentler to her and filed for divorce. Jess was distressed about the divorce and became very angry. Jess did not want to show his angry side to his sons. He talked with a friend who suggested counseling would help and following his friend's advice, he decided to seek assistance regarding his divorce. He indicated to the clinical neuropsychologist that it was good to talk and that the therapist also helped him develop a physical exercise program to help him cope with stress. The exercise program was in addition to boxing, which tended to increase his aggressive feelings. He also stated that the therapist was beginning to help him pursue triggers for his anger, which made him feel stressed. He quit therapy before he could follow through on the causes of his anger. He did not give any reason for quitting therapy to his therapist even though he was contacted to reschedule more appointments.

After his divorce Jess dated periodically until he met his present girlfriend. He stated that they had similar interests, were close in age, and both liked the outdoors. They both were divorced but she had a daughter instead of two sons. After dating for a year, Jess moved in with her on her property in the country. Things went well for quite a while then deteriorated when Jess's girlfriend began to assert herself regarding the activities in which she wanted to participate. During one situation his girlfriend's daughter witnessed an argument which led to objects being thrown. The girlfriend then called the police, which was the impetus for social services involvement. After being notified, a social worker completed separate interviews with Jess and his girlfriend. The social worker determined that Jess's girlfriend should visit with her daughter in neutral surroundings such as the YMCA or a restaurant until the situation between the two adults was rectified. The social worker suggested that couples therapy would be helpful but, first, Jess needed to work on his own issues. Jess stated that he cared deeply for his girlfriend but was also aware that he needed to deal with the cause of his anger before he could go on with the relationship. He agreed with the social worker that military service may have caused or exacerbated his problems with anger.

When evaluating this case study it may appear that Jess is a model client. He is open about his situation and is motivated to change. If we left the initial interview at this point to move on to assessment, diagnosis, therapy, or rehabilitation, we may miss some important issues. This is the topic of the present chapter—interviewing. How does one obtain the information necessary to make appropriate choices for assessment tools to lead to an appropriate diagnosis and subsequently leading to appropriate treatment? Also, what qualities of the interviewer will make this information more or less easy to obtain? In addition, under what circumstances should the interview be conducted to obtain the most accurate representation of the client? Finally, what are the roles of gender and ethnicity in the interview?

For example, after reviewing the information gathered from Jess's interview, the cause of his anger clearly needs to be explored in more depth. Through Jess describing his past, it was revealed that his behavior relates to his mother's treatment of him. If one asked further questions, Jess may recount that he has had vivid nightmares and flashbacks of severe physical abuse at the hands of his mother. Even further questioning, directed appropriately, would allow the clinical neuropsychologist to obtain the symptoms of schizophrenia in Jess's mother. A logical conclusion would be that Jess is likely exhibiting symptoms of posttraumatic stress disorder (PTSD) from his abuse as a child and needs neuropsychological evaluation of his current functioning. This is due to the fact that PTSD may have neurological sequela such as reduced volume in the hippocampal area producing memory impairment. Further interviewing would also reveal that due to his penchant for physical activity, he had been involved in numerous altercations while in the military, which led to a series of concussions. In addition, these concussions had not been treated by any medical personnel. This is an example of how a standard structured interview could be altered to gain more information, which would be crucial to help Jess overcome his difficulties.

Interviewing is part of a larger information gathering process, which is often termed the *assessment process* (Holtz, 1986). The **assessment process** is a structure or flowchart to guide the clinical neuropsychologist in gathering as much information as possible through interview and various forms of testing (see Figure 6.1). The information will subsequently be used to develop a diagnosis which will lead to appropriate treatment and/or rehabilitation. Sattler (2002) described the interview as one of four pillars in the assessment process, the others being formal tests, observation, and informal test procedures. Interviewing in general practice is a skill that can be learned and an art in the manner of delivery. Neuropsychological interviewing is similar to general practice clinical interviewing in that its goal is to obtain the most accurate picture of the individual in all of the areas of his life. Neuropsychological interviewing is different in that it focuses on central nervous system difficulties and disorders in addition to aid other components of a clinical interview. A focus on central nervous system difficulties implies the inclusion of **premorbid functioning** to determine the nature and extent of difficulties both before and after the difficulty and potential **etiological** (causal) factors. Also included in the interview are prenatal and postnatal information to determine the attainment of developmental milestones as well as potential **congenital** (from birth) difficulties.

During the interview, both verbal and nonverbal behaviors are exhibited by the interviewee and are interpreted in various ways by the interviewer. The match or mismatch between the verbal and nonverbal behaviors is often a diagnostic sign. The interviewer must always keep in mind that there are both verbal and nonverbal messages, which he or she sends, that may affect the information obtained based on how they are interpreted by the client.

Neuropsychological interviews are conducted in two main forms: structured and unstructured. Various sources may also refer to these as standardized versus nonstandardized interviews (Gorden, 1987). This chapter will explore both techniques of interviewing and the reasons and appropriate situations for the use of each type. In addition, various interviewing strategies designed for particular diagnostic issues will be explored.

Each type of interview has a referral source, a reason for the referral, and a presenting complaint. Prior to or during the preliminary gathering of information, the clinical neuropsychologist may also have access to various records. The review of records prior to the interview is very important to understand procedures which have already been put into place and/or treatments which have already been undertaken. Record review may happen before the initial interview or after, dependent on the circumstances of each individual case.

assessment process
refers to the methods of assessment or data gathering and related procedures used by the clinical neuropsychologist to reach a clinical diagnosis

premorbid functioning
any difficulties that occur before a central nervous system accident or illness

etiological
causal factor(s) of a disease or disability if it is known

congenital
physical problems present at birth which develop later in life and which can be attributed to genetic causes

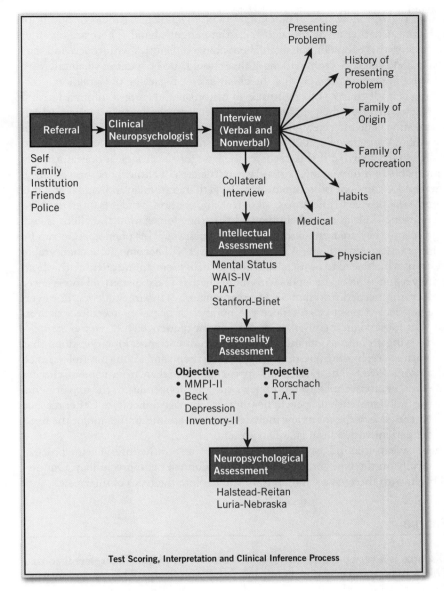

FIGURE 6.1 Flowchart of the assessment process.

In order to view a client's records from another professional, the client must sign a **release of information**. In the situation where the client has a legal guardian, the guardian would sign for record release. The situation is similar for minors where record releases are signed by a parent or guardian. Reynolds (1998) provided a list of the types of records that the clinical neuropsychologist may consider for review dependent on the particular circumstances, which included educational, employment, legal, medical, mental health, substance abuse treatment, and military records. In Jess's case, the clinical neuropsychologist was able, with Jess's permission, to read the social worker's report prior to the initial interview.

Prior to the initiation of the interview, the client is greeted in the waiting room. Confidentiality precludes the use of last names and, often, the person is greeted by first name or is invited into the office by a statement such as "I'm Dr. Smith, I will be meeting

release of information
a form signed by an individual to give permission to a professional to view information from other sources; only competent individuals and adults may sign these forms, parents or legal guardians must sign for minors or those not capable of understanding

with you today, please follow me." The clinical neuropsychologist should decide prior to the introduction whether he or she will shake the patient's hand. There are no strict guidelines regarding this behavior but some clients have difficulties with touch and may shy away from a handshake. A short amount of time should also be spent in small talk with the aim of developing rapport and putting the client at ease regarding the situation.

The interview itself consists of a multitude of historical and current information and an outcome which will follow the culmination of the neuropsychological interview, which often includes testing. The interview and its contents will often determine whether formal testing is possible (Vanderploeg, 2000). Very often students feel lost as they begin to learn the skills of interviewing. If this becomes the case for the reader, it does not imply that one is incapable of interviewing, particularly in the area of clinical neuropsychology. There is a tremendous amount of information to be gathered from an individual and it is often difficult for the novice to encompass all of this information. Students often describe learning interviewing skills as overwhelming and that they forget what the client is currently saying because they are formulating their next question. This phenomenon can be overcome with practice. As with any skill, the interviewer will become more comfortable with the questions which need to be asked and able to focus more on the client with whom he or she is conversing as he or she works with more clients. The experienced interviewer can obtain all of the needed information in approximately 1 hour. Students, however, may need a great deal of practice to reduce the number of questions to collect data in about 1 hour. The most common mistakes made by an inexperienced interviewer are talking too much, trying to help as opposed to gaining information, asking questions that imply yes–no answers, rephrasing questions while asking them, and asking multiple-choice questions (Johnson, 1981). The hour is an approximation taken from general clinical practice. However, neuropsychological interviews may take longer due to the impairments exhibited by the individual such as speech, hearing, or language difficulties. Other reasons which may slow the pace of the interview include the use of an interpreter and/or the need to interview the patient with a legal guardian present.

With these caveats in mind, we will begin the journey into the interviewing process, focusing specifically on the types of issues pertinent to clinical neuropsychology. Our discussion will begin with these issues and then we will explore the types of interview.

Referral Source

referral source
the person or agency initially referring the client for service such as a physician or school; the client may also self-refer

The referral source is a very important part of the interview process. The **referral source** technically refers to how and why the client came to be interviewed. There are many ways by which a person is referred and there are valuable pieces of information that can be learned about the interviewee based on the source of the referral.

The most common source of referral would be the individual himself or herself. The self-referral is the most common in general practice but, when an individual has a central nervous system difficulty, it may be less likely that he or she will be self-referred. Self-referral may imply the individual recognizes there is an issue that needs to be discussed or a problem which needs to be worked on. Self-referral also tends to imply motivation for change. If one calls and seeks an appointment for oneself, it is more likely that he or she will want to change something about his or her circumstances or himself or herself. In the case of an individual who has central nervous system difficulties, he or she may self-refer due to moods or behaviors he or she does not understand or that are embarrassing. In addition, the individual may voice concerns that family, friends, or even colleagues at school or work do not understand how he or she feels or behaves.

Referrals may also come from family or significant others. In the instance of central nervous system difficulties this is often the case. Very often a member of the family or a spouse notices moods or behaviors the individual does not notice or with which he or she does not want to deal. When an individual is asked to go to a professional by a family member or spouse, there is the potential for the individual to feel anger, pressure, shame, and/or many other feelings because one has not initiated this action as one's own. The level of motivation may also be lower because the individual has not chosen to seek help and may feel less control in the situation. Referrals may also give an indication of embarrassment such as in Jess's case in which he appears to embrace the traditional male role, which does not encompass the understanding and/or expression of emotions.

Friends may be an additional source of referral. If friends become involved, it is often the case that family and the spouse have also noticed issues. Friends as a source of referral may be seen as helpful because they are not family or may be seen as a source of the aforementioned emotions. The case study includes an example of this type of referral when Jess's friend referred him for help to manage his anger subsequent to his divorce.

The workplace is also a source of referral particularly in cases of central nervous system functioning. When the employer is involved, it is often because the employee has not been able to live up to his or her responsibilities or is unable to perform adequately in the job situation. With the workplace as a referral source, there are often ultimatums. For example, it may be stated that unless the problem is solved, the employee may be placed on probation or, in the worst case, lose his or her job. The client's school may also be a referral source and the reason for referral may be related to the client's poor performance or absenteeism. Consequences of poor performance may be removal from a class or removal from the academic setting completely.

Referral by a physician is quite often the starting point for an individual with central nervous system difficulties. In this case, the interviewee is more likely to be motivated for help because he/she does not feel the repercussions from the other referral sources. Physicians are often seen as more objective than other referral sources and often looked at as experts or authority figures. In the case of central nervous system difficulties, a referral by a physician may also include a wealth of extra information regarding various symptomatic issues.

The legal system as a source of referral occurs when the individual has broken a law and the court has decided that an interview, assessment, and/or other treatment need to be instigated. There are often quite significant ramifications to the outcome of this type of referral. In the case of a court-ordered interview or assessment, there is often concern regarding the truthfulness of the information provided by the client. In the case of central nervous system difficulties, it may not be intentional lying, but a faulty memory or difficulties with cognitive processes. Motivation tends to be poor with court-ordered referrals because of the lack of control the client has over the process and the larger ramifications involved. An example of the type of ramification may be a client who is placed in assisted living after the interviewer concluded that he or she was unable to care for himself or herself.

Social service referrals, although not part of the legal system, carry substantial weight in the life of the client. If a parent or guardian was referred due to parenting deficits, there is always the fear that children may be removed from the home. In the case study Jess was referred after an altercation which was witnessed by his girlfriend's daughter. The ramifications of the involvement of the social worker may be more serious for Jess's girlfriend in terms of her visitation with her child than for Jess. However, it would be safe to hypothesize that there would be pressure on Jess from his girlfriend to follow through on any recommendations made by the social worker and the clinical neuropsychologist.

Presenting Complaint

At the outset of the interview, before the presenting complaint is even addressed, the client must be made aware of the principles of confidentiality. As stated previously, confidentiality implies privacy for all information except in circumstances of mandated reporting where there is a threat of suicide, homicide, child abuse with the client as victim or perpetrator, or abuse of a vulnerable adult with the client as victim or perpetrator. Many individuals with central nervous system difficulties may have a legal guardian and it is necessary to explain these issues to the guardian. Children also have special issues in that their parents have a right to know what is said during the interview, assessment, and rehabilitation. Requirements may vary by state but there are federal stipulations, which void any confidentiality at any time. For instance, voicing a direct physical threat to the President or top officials of the United States government supersedes any rights to confidentiality. Unfortunately, within the practice of clinical neuropsychology, unsubstantiated threats may happen particularly with clients suffering from a dementing process. In these circumstances, the threat is most often verbal and most likely part of the illness; however, the reporting process remains the same.

presenting complaint
the statement which the client makes as the reason for seeking services from a health care provider

The **presenting complaint** is the reason why the client came for an interview. The presenting complaint is stated in the client's own words such as in a general clinical interview. In some situations, the presenting complaint is the issue that is dealt with in rehabilitation or therapy. In other circumstances, the presenting complaint is not the issue dealt with in treatment but gives an idea how the client views the problem.

When looking at the referral source, one can often determine whether the presenting complaint will be the issue discussed in therapy. Self-referrals often imply that the individual has a sense of awareness regarding issues with which to be dealt. In the case of central nervous system difficulties, self-referral may not imply self-awareness, and the presenting complaint may be quite different from the issue or issues that will be dealt with in treatment.

An example of the aforementioned situation involves the case study at the beginning of the chapter. If the interviewer took Jess's interest in therapy as an indication that he was in touch with issues and focused predominately on the anger that surfaced in the fight which caused the social worker to intervene, all of the issues related to PTSD or traumatic brain injury (TBI) would be missed. In Jess's case, the presenting complaint was important but the interviewer needed to look further for the cause of the anger and potential neuropsychological issues.

As stated previously, there are two major types of interviews, structured and unstructured with various other interviews focusing specifically on individual diagnostic issues. However, there are also many situations or uses for each type of interview which are used by the clinical neuropsychologist to gather different types of information. The next section of the chapter describes the types of interviews and their usage.

Structured Interviews

Structured interviews, as a part of the assessment process, are used when the aim of the interview is to obtain the same type of information from every patient interviewed. All of the questions are the same regardless of the client and the format is the same for all clients (see Figure 6.2).

Structured Interview

Interviewer: Introduce yourself (name, occupation, etc.).

Interviewee: Ask client who they are (name, etc.).

Presenting Complaint: Why are you here? What is it that brought you in today?

Referral: How did you learn of this place (class)? Who sent you?

History of Presenting Complaint: How long have you been interested/concerned about this Topic? Are there certain times that it interests/bothers you?

Personal:
- What are your current interests (hobbies, etc.)?
- What books or articles have you recently read?
- How do you describe your personal strengths and weaknesses?
- If I asked the people that know you best, how would they describe your personal qualities?
- What have been the major influences on your life?
- What are some of your major accomplishments and achievements?
- What people do you most admire?
- What kinds of people/situations are you least tolerant of?
- Give an example of your creativity?
- How do you work under pressure?

Education:
- What is your G.P.A.?
- What courses were your best/worst?
- If you were to start your education over again, what would you do differently?
- What does your degree qualify you to do?
- What experiences and work values led you to your major?
- Do you think extra curricular activities are worth devoting time to?
- Describe the high/low points of your education?
- What changes would you make in your college if you could?

Employment:
- What type of employment are you seeking?
- Where have you worked in the past?
- How did you decide on this particular type of career?
- Have you ever had any difficulties or disagreements with peers, supervisors or employers?
- What kind of person annoys or frustrates you?
- What have you learned from your mistakes?
- How do you schedule your work and manage time?
- How would you describe your ideal job?
- What would you expect to be doing five years from now?
- What are your life goals?
- Describe the ethical issues that could arise on the job and how you might handle them?

Family:
- Where were you born?
- Describe your family situation?
- How many brothers and sisters do you have?
- What was your relationship to your parents like?
- Describe each person in the family situation.

Habits:
- Do you drink alcohol? How much?
- Drugs? Type?
- Cigarettes?

Medical:
- Do you have/had any major illnesses?
- Are you under a physician's care?
- Do you take medication? What type?
- Have you ever had fainting spells/seizures?
- Have you ever hallucinated?
- Have you ever thought about/acted upon suicidal ideation?

FIGURE 6.2 Example of questions from a structured interview used in a college setting.

There are several reasons to employ a structured interview. At times, the referral requires a comparison of the patient's functioning to others. The comparison to others may be to those with central nervous system difficulties, to those with other psychiatric difficulties, and at other times, to those who have no difficulties. Comparison to a standard puts the client's information in context. Many neuropsychological difficulties have specific deficits and present themselves with certain interview and test patterns. Comparison to norm groups may help clarify the diagnosis, prognosis, and treatment of the problem. In addition, a structured interview is often a necessary standard against which to evaluate test data (Lezak, Howieson, & Loring, 2004). Lezak clearly states that blind analysis of test data, in which the clinical neuropsychologist evaluates test scores without an interview, records, or observing the patient may be appropriate as a teaching tool but is inappropriate as a basis for clinical decisions.

There are many parts to a structured interview all dealing with various areas in the patient's environment. The areas covered in a structured interview include the following

blind analysis
the process in which the clinical neuropsychologist evaluates a client's test data without interview information, records, or behavioral observation

as shown in the flowchart for the assessment process and are similar to standard structured clinical interviews. More in-depth questions regarding central nervous system issues are an addendum to these types of interview. The referral source, as described previously, is essential. Next are the verbal and nonverbal behaviors that the client exhibits during the interview. Nonverbal behaviors are all of the behaviors, in addition to verbal expressions, which are exhibited in the interview. An example of nonverbal behavior in Jess's case included his lack of eye contact when discussing his mother compared to talking about other topics. Nonverbal behaviors include physical presence, stance, posture and gait as well as the aforementioned eye contact. Also included are voice tone, gestures, and particularly changes in any of these as topics change. In neuropsychological interviews, nonverbal behaviors often give significant information regarding the patient's condition such as the ability to stand, walk, and speak clearly and articulately, as well as giving information regarding whether the patient understands the question asked of him or her. Nonverbal behavior, however, may vary by culture or ethnic group, which needs to be taken into consideration.

The areas addressed in a structured interview encompass the many and diverse areas of the individual's life space. In addition to the referral source, presenting complaint and nonverbal behaviors are a plethora of areas that could be used to describe an individual. Before addressing the various areas of the interview, it is important to keep in mind that following any negative event, whether it is an accident, illness, or some other circumstance, individuals may attribute symptoms both current and previous to the negative event (Gunstad & Suhr, 2001; Gunstad & Suhr, 2002). Hence, the value of clear and explicit questions when gathering information particularly related to the causal sequence is seen.

History of the presenting complaint refers to a description of any similar symptoms the client has experienced, the length of time experienced, the severity of symptoms and any treatments for those symptoms. This gives information regarding the recurrence of symptoms and the circumstances which may have lead to recurrences. Family history of mental illness of any type gives information regarding symptoms the client may have seen and copied versus symptoms that may have a genetic component. Family history of any central nervous system difficulties is used for a similar purpose. Age of onset of the symptoms and the degree of relationship between client and the person exhibiting the symptoms would be helpful due to the fact that many central nervous system difficulties have familial patterns. Support systems, whether personal such as family or friends, or professional such as therapy, are important for their potential role in recovery. As has been stated in previous chapters, positive support systems help with recovery, whereas negative systems may have adverse effects. School and academic achievement aid to distinguish the premorbid level of functioning of the client versus the present level of functioning. In a similar manner, history of work and job performance give the interviewer information regarding ability to function in a structured employment situation, ability to work with others, and the rate and pace of work the patient is able to accomplish. If the client has had an evaluation that encompasses work-related tasks, particularly tasks that are timed versus untimed, it could be very helpful. These are often referred to as work-sample evaluations and may be completed by a vocational rehabilitation specialist or an agency such as a sheltered workshop. Military service, if applicable, may give similar information as work performance plus the added ability to deal with stress if the person's service was completed during active duty or wartime circumstances. Marital and family information give clues toward whether the individual is capable of forming close or intimate relationships and the qualities of these relationships.

In addition to the standard interview questions, a neuropsychological interview includes questions related to prenatal and postnatal factors. These questions address the development of the central nervous system before and after birth and help determine etiological factors. Also included in a structured neuropsychological interview are questions related to the central nervous system difficulty the patient is experiencing, such as time of onset, symptoms, and any treatment for the symptoms. Dependent on the circumstances, the involvement of medical personnel is crucial. For example, in Jess's case, he sustained a series of concussions without medical intervention, which may have had significant effects on the amount or extent of damage he sustained. In contrast, in the case study in chapter 1, the individual was quickly taken to a hospital, which also impacted the extent and duration of his difficulties. Additional areas, which are generally covered in a neuropsychological interview, include a discussion of any of the following neurological symptoms: headache; alterations in consciousness; abnormal movements; seizures; disturbances of vision; disturbances in perception; pain; muscle weakness; stiffness or paralysis; vertigo; difficulty with auditory perception; difficulty with use of language; bowel, bladder, or genital dysfunction; confusion; decreased intellectual efficiency or memory problems; changes in mood; and emotional regulation (Adams & Jenkins, 1981). Any of these symptoms may point toward a particular difficulty or the etiology of an already diagnosed difficulty.

The main objective of a structured interview is to gain as much information as possible in all areas of a client's life. The questions are formatted, as described earlier, in a similar manner to allow comparison between individuals or between the individual and a standard. All of this information is gathered together to develop a picture of the individual in his life space.

In order to garner this information in the time allotted, the questions posed need to be clear and succinct. A structured interview used in clinical neuropsychology can accomplish this by using the same questions for all clients, as stated previously. The interview, whether structured or in another form, is usually allotted with 1 hour with the caveats discussed earlier for individuals with central nervous system difficulty.

Unstructured Interviews

The term *unstructured interview* is not entirely accurate and is sometimes termed a *semistructured interview*. The interview is designed with the same goal in mind as the structured interview, which is to gain as much information as possible regarding all areas of the patient's life. All of the topics that are covered in a structured interview are also covered in an unstructured interview. These topics include presenting complaint, history of presenting complaint, physical symptoms, emotional symptoms, family issues, social issues, support system, military history, school and employment history, and all of the neuropsychological variables addressed in the previous section.

The difference between an unstructured and a structured interview is that in an unstructured interview, the clinical neuropsychologist has the flexibility to pursue a potential area if it appears to be one of interest or particular concern. In a sense, the unstructured interview violates the ordered procedures of the structured interview and focuses on the information provided by the client. One could compare this to the two main types of neuropsychological test batteries discussed in an earlier chapter. The Halstead-Reitan is a structured assessment approach and yields quantifiable data. The Luria-Nebraska is a client-focused assessment approach that yields more information about the particular client but is less quantifiable and yields less comparable data. There are times when the structure is forsaken to garner more information. In Jess's case, the interview could go from structured to unstructured if the interviewer were to pursue issues related specifically to Jess's mother. In fact, many researchers state that obtaining a history often follows a semistructured, flexible format (Lezak et al., 2004; Stowe, 1998; Vanderploeg, 2000).

Diagnostic Interviews

As stated previously, there are two types of interview, structured and unstructured. The diagnostic interview is designed with the intention of obtaining information to facilitate a diagnosis. It is a form of structured interview with all of the questions given to everyone in a similar fashion. In this manner, it can be determined whether a client's symptoms fit within a particular diagnostic category (see Figure 6.3).

There are several diagnostic interviews that are available on CD or computer. Examples of diagnostic interviews include diagnostic interview scales for symptoms of anxiety, depression, or PTSD. The aim of the interview is to glean information that would help the interviewer determine whether the patient has a particular type of difficulty or another.

Collateral Interviews

collateral interviews interviews conducted with persons familiar with the client to ensure a correct understanding of the client by the clinical neuropsychologist

Interviews with other individuals in addition to the patient are termed **collateral interviews**. The aim of the collateral interview is to determine the authenticity or accuracy of the information given by the client. The same questions are asked of the second person being interviewed as the patient.

Several circumstances would necessitate a collateral interview. Individuals with central nervous system difficulties may not be good behavioral historians and it aids the professional to garner information from a second source. Collateral interviews are often completed with a spouse, significant other, or children. In Jess's case, a collateral interview with his girlfriend may assist the clinical neuropsychologist in ascertaining whether he is an accurate reporter of his life circumstances or has had some memory difficulties. Often, collateral interviews would be helpful with individuals who are not willing or able to participate due to ability, interest, or geographic locale. Jess's mother would be an excellent collateral interview source, however, because of the information he gave regarding her, it is highly unlikely that she would be willing or capable of participating. Due to the fact that she resides far from the client, one may surmise that a telephone interview could be prudent. However, collateral interviews similar to general clinical interviews are almost always completed in person.

Another circumstance that would necessitate a collateral interview would be the involvement of the legal system. As stated previously, individuals who are in legal trouble often fabricate information to keep themselves out of trouble. Individuals with central nervous system difficulties may be involved in legal issues, but the point of the collateral interview would not necessarily be to check on lying but to look for accuracy of information. Collateral interviews always require the permission of the client unless ordered by the court and even in these circumstances an attempt should be made to obtain the client's permission. In certain circumstances the permission is not necessary. An example of the type of situation where permission is not necessary is when a client has a legal guardian due to cognitive or mental deficits and the guardian would determine the appropriateness of the collateral interview.

Identify the relevant trauma: _____

In the past week......	Not at all 0	A little bit 1	Moderately 2	Quite a lot 3	Very much 4
1 How much have you been bothered by unwanted memories, nightmares or reminders of the event?	☐	☐	☐	☐	☐
2 How much effort have you made to avoid thinking or talking about the event, or doing things which remind you of what happened?	☐	☐	☐	☐	☐
3 To what extent have you lost enjoyment for things, kept your distance from people, or found it difficult to experience feelings?	☐	☐	☐	☐	☐
4 How much have you been bothered by poor sleep, poor concentration, jumpiness, irritability or feeling watchful around you?	☐	☐	☐	☐	☐
5 How much have you been bothered by pain, aches, or tiredness?	☐	☐	☐	☐	☐
6 How much would you get upset when stressful events or setbacks happen to you?	☐	☐	☐	☐	☐
7 How much have the above symptoms interfered with your ability to work or carry out daily activities?	☐	☐	☐	☐	☐
8 How much have the above symptoms interfered with your relationships with family or friends?	☐	☐	☐	☐	☐

Total _____

9 How much better do you feel since beginning treatment? (as a percentage)

```
        0              50            100
        |___|___|___|___|___|___|___|___|
     No change                    As well as I could be
```

10 How much have the above symptoms improved since starting treatment?	Worse 5	No change 4	Minimally 3	Much 2	Very much 1
	☐	☐	☐	☐	☐

FIGURE 6.3 Short PTSD Rating Interview (SPRINT) *Source:* Copyright © Davidson, J. R. T., 1997.

Interview Setting

In addition to the information obtained in an interview, the setting of the interview must to be considered. It is very important that the environment be structured to obtain the most accurate information (see Figure 6.4). The interview setting consists of all of the variables involved in the space to be used for the interview including the office location, color of the office, lighting, carpeting, noise, and all other variables, which could enhance or deter the patient's performance.

In terms of privacy, it would be advantageous not to have an office on street level in order that individuals outside of the office could not look in. If there is no choice, then drapes or blinds for privacy should be used. Offices need to be accessible to all who would be interviewed, particularly in cases of central nervous system difficulties when an individual may need to use a cane, crutches, walker, or wheelchair. Therefore, not only the entrance to the building but also doors into offices and transom heights need to be accessible. Also, even though these are usually taken care of by building codes, the restrooms need to be handicap accessible and preferably as close to the interview room as possible.

Colors for an interview office are similar to those chosen for an assessment or rehabilitation office. Pastels and earth tones tend to relax people and put them at ease. Bright colors, particularly reds, yellows, and oranges activate the central nervous system and cause the individual to become tense and work quickly. Color psychologists are aware of these effects and are often hired by fast food companies to use color as a marketing tool.

The office is best if carpeted not only for aesthetic reasons but also for sound abatement. Carpeting helps absorb any noise from other offices nearby. Noise outside of the interview room can be very disturbing and is often a source of difficulties in institutional settings such as hospitals. Lighting is a crucial element used to alleviate the client's anxiety or stress. Bright, overhead, and fluorescent lights are stark and institutional. Track lighting, lamps, and low-voltage overhead lights calm the individual. The use of plants, whether artificial or real, also tends to have a calming effect. In a similar vein, pictures or paintings of tranquil scenes are preferred over abstract or complex art. Pictures of the clinical neuropsychologist's family and friends should be minimized to maintain a professional appearance. Due to the potential for processing difficulties in individuals with central nervous system difficulties, the less stimuli available in the office, the less likely that the client

FIGURE 6.4 Example of an appropriate interview setting. *Source:* Courtesy of Central Minnesota Counseling Center where the author practices.

will become distracted or confused. The interviewer's professional license and degrees are appropriate and should be displayed as should the **Client's Bill of Rights**. The content of the Client's Bill of Rights varies by state but is basically a summary of all of the rights that the client has when using psychological services. It also states that it is possible to file a complaint and the procedure.

Client's Bill of Rights
the statement which must be visibly present in a psychologist's office which describes the client's rights including the right to file a complaint and the process for filing such complaint

The Interviewer

The personal qualities of the interviewer can be very beneficial or very harmful in obtaining appropriate information. Dress, demeanor, and language usage are all factored into making the client comfortable and feeling that it is alright to share information.

The interviewer needs to dress in a professional manner. However, a professional can also be frightening to the potential client due to his or her manner of dress. White laboratory coats are taboo. A large number of people associate the white coat with physicians and various medical procedures. The aim of a clinical neuropsychological interview is to gain as much information as possible without making the client uncomfortable or defensive.

Business casual is a good standard toward which to aim and implies the familiarity of a business setting but also a less formal or friendlier appearance. Specifically, males would be appropriate in pressed slacks, not blue jeans, a dress shirt, and possibly a tie and/or sport coat. Females would be appropriate in a conservative dress, slacks, or skirt with blouse and, possibly, blazer or sweater. Shorts and any type of revealing attire can detract from the interview. Tennis shoes are too informal for clinical neuropsychological interviews as are sandals. The use of perfume or cologne is discouraged in most health care settings due to various difficulties it may cause for patients. The clinical neuropsychologist should use this as a guide and refrain from the use of any personal care products that produce odors. Many personal care products are produced in unscented varieties for this very reason. All of these suggestions for dress are made with the understanding that what is considered appropriate may vary by locale as well as ethnic or cultural customs of the clinical neuropsychologist. It is sometimes difficult for a professional to combine the standards of dress dictated by one's religion or culture and those expected by the employment situation. In addition, there may be dress codes in place at various business sites and health organizations which override any other issue with regard to dress. A professional dress code could address clothing and personal care as described earlier. It may also require professionals to cover any tattoos or remove visible piercings, which could distract from the professional role. However, most dress codes will allow religious or ethnic head ornamentation.

The demeanor of the interviewer implies body language including eye contact, voice tone, and gestures. All individuals have certain mannerisms, which are part of who they are. However, anything that detracts from the interviewee paying attention to the questions at hand could be problematic. Eye contact should be similar to what is acceptable in the larger society. Looking at the client while speaking and then occasionally looking away is polite. Staring at an individual appears threatening. Lack of eye contact gives the impression that the interviewer is not paying attention or may be bored or disinterested. Eye contact, as well as any other mannerisms, may vary by culture and this should always be kept in mind. Good posture is essential. Poor or slouched posture gives the impression that the interviewer may be bored or disinterested.

It has been suggested by many sources that the clinical neuropsychologist should not sit between the client and the door. The reason for this is to allow the client to feel he or she is able to leave the situation if he or she so desires. Clinical experience suggests that this is particularly important if the client has any form of PTSD. However, in situations when the client may appear at all aggressive or angry it may not be wise for the client to be between the clinical neuropsychologist and the door. Many clinics have policies regarding these issues and it is important for the clinical neuropsychologist to be cognizant of the issue both before and during the interview.

Another issue that arises during an interview is the taking of notes. It is almost impossible to accurately remember all of the information that is discussed in an hour interview and, therefore, most clinical neuropsychologists take notes. If the process appears to bother the client, it would be advantageous to discuss it immediately. An alternative to note taking can be an audio recording of the interview, which would require the client's signed consent.

A great deal has been written in the past 10 years regarding the issues of race and ethnicity and the interview and therapy process. As is the case in the general practice of therapy, the interviewer needs to keep in mind that there are many and varied ways to express oneself and that verbal and nonverbal behaviors may vary between groups. It is advised that the student becomes well versed in issues related to the impact of culture on the interview as well as in assessment and rehabilitation.

Use of a Translator

In the course of clinical neuropsychology practices, there are times when the patient does not speak English. In such circumstances, it is essential to employ a translator. The use of an interpreter can be very beneficial or it can be harmful in the interview setting. The reasons for each outcome will be discussed next.

The appropriate use of an interpreter would be in a situation where the client has such difficulties understanding the language used by the interviewer that no reasonable amount of information is gathered. At this point, we will assume the interviewer is speaking English. If the client has a reasonable amount of knowledge of the language, an interpreter may not be necessary and the explanation of a few words may be sufficient.

Many times clients will bring a friend or relative to serve as the interpreter, which is not usually appropriate. A friend or relative may inadvertently answer the questions for the client or possibly change the answer for multiple reasons. LaCalle (1987) warns against the use of friends and family who may be unable to translate accurately or may be protective of the patient.

Due to the aforementioned concerns, it is most appropriate to use the services of someone whose job it is to do interpreting services. Because of the many different languages which are represented in this country, not all areas of the United States will be able to be represented by an interpreting service. However, if the date of the interview is known far enough in advance, usually a translator from a nearby area may be available. In the worst scenario, the clinical neuropsychologist must make the decision between attempting to interview someone where understanding of the examinee's language is poor or referring the client to a professional in another area where a translator is available. The difficulties with the former choice include obtaining incomplete information whereas the later may or may not be an option for the client due to work, transportation, or other issues. Artiola i Frotuny and Mullaney (1998) discuss ethical difficulties that could occur when the clinical neuropsychologist has only a superficial knowledge of the patient's language. They advise the use of an interpretor or making an appropriate referral.

When working with a professional interpreter, it is imperative that the interview questions be directed at the client and that the eye contact and body language also revolve around the client rather than the interpreter. If the interpreter becomes more of a focus than the client, the client may feel that the interview does not really involve him or her and possibly disengage from the process or not report information accurately.

Depending on the culture, the client may trust the interpreter to help provide information that the client is not able to furnish or the client may view the interpreter as an adversary. It would be helpful to know the relationships between the client and the interpreter before the interview. More importantly, it would be advantageous to know the roles that each plays as defined by the culture. Another issue to consider is the relationship between the gender of the client and the gender of the interpreter. In some cultures, this may not be an issue, but in other cultures where males are seen as authority figures, the use of a female interpreter may be problematic.

Purpose and Outcome of the Interview

The purpose or goal of the interview is very important to know before the interview begins. The goal of the interview may be to answer a specific referral question, which may cause the clinical neuropsychologist to choose a specific type of interview. A more broad or general goal for the interview may point toward a more general type interview. The outcome refers to the decision or decisions which will be made based on the data provided by the client. The outcome of the interview also gives the interviewer an indication of the level of motivation of the client in terms of changing one's behaviors. If sanctions are in place based on the client's behavior, the client may be more willing to change or, depending on the circumstances, give the appearance of being willing to change. If there are only negative outcomes no matter the content of the interview then the client may not be motivated.

In some circumstances, the client does not know or is not able to understand the goal or potential outcome of the interview. It is imperative that the interviewer explain it in language the client understands before proceeding with the interview. The culmination of the interview and its outcome may be the beginning of another process for the client such as assessment and/or rehabilitation. Clients with central nervous system difficulties are likely to need to understand the aforementioned areas.

Termination of the Interview

After approximately 1 hour, the interview should begin to come to a culmination. The ability to complete an interview with ease takes great practice with a variety of clients with a multitude of difficulties.

Assuming that the interview was completed with an individual with central nervous system difficulties, many questions may need to be repeated because of cognitive or memory difficulties. At the end of the interview, the outcome or ramifications may also need to be repeated many times. It is crucial that the client leave the interview with information as to the next step in his treatment.

A skilled interviewer will end the interview with questions for the client regarding any additional information that the client could provide that he or she may feel is important. After concluding with this open exchange, the interviewer will summarize the main points covered in the interview. The interviewer may focus on the specific referral question and address information regarding it and/or give a general overview of the interview process.

When the situation is such that the interviewer will continue working with the client through assessment and treatment, the interviewer may ask the client questions regarding his comfort level and ascertain whether any alterations can be made in the situation to further the client's comfort level.

Use of Interview Forms

Researchers have developed several scales that may be administered prior to or subsequent to the interview. The advantage of using these scales is to make sure all necessary information has been gathered. Questionnaires have been developed to provide documentation of information collected during an interview (see Figure 6.5). Clinical neuropsychologists may also develop their own form based on the population they serve. It is important to note that none of the forms have reliability or validity data. They also should not substitute for the interview (Strauss, Sherman, & Spreen, 2006).

Ethnic and Cultural Issues in Interviewing

As has been alluded earlier, the bulk of the literature in psychology and particularly in clinical neuropsychology has been on the age range of 16–65 Caucasian population. It was assumed that the information gained from this group could then be applied to all other groups. This generalization is far from accurate and the past 10–15 years has seen an increasing literature regarding cross-cultural, multicultural, and ethnic issues in mental health. In addition to these issues, which often relate to the use of a translator or a translated test, there is also a large body of literature regarding the evaluation of individuals who are bilingual. Artiola i Frotuny (2008) has written extensively regarding the issues of bilingual clients particularly Spanish/English speakers but also applying bilingual principles to all neuropsychological practice. Myths regarding bilingualism are important for the professional to understand and dispute. The supposition that bilingual individuals are equally proficient in both languages is often false. Very often, a bilingual speaker has a good to excellent command of one language and a less than adequate understanding/speaking of the second. In order to obtain accurate information, it is necessary to ascertain which language is not only preferred but the one in which the client is able to express himself or herself most accurately. Another difficulty is the confusion that occurs when a bilingual speaker may be more or less proficient in two or more languages and/or has little formal education and/or is from a lower socioeconomic status. Education and socioeconomic status often go hand-in-hand with language proficiency; therefore, this apparent mismatch should be further investigated. Language abilities may cause education or work difficulties but the clinical neuropsychologist must separate the differences between language or cognitive impairment and residual effects of incomplete learning of the first or second language.

For this chapter we will focus on issues of diversity in interviewing and return to these issues again as we pursue assessment and rehabilitation. While it may be an impossibility to become well versed in every culture, which is represented in this country and abroad, it still behooves the clinical neuropsychologist to consider ethnic and cultural issues while interviewing.

It has been generally thought that there are four main non-Caucasian ethnic groups within the United States: African American, Hispanic Americans, Asian Americans, and Native Americans. This is only a fraction of the larger ethnic/cultural subgroupings which exist in the United States. When looked at through the lens of urban versus rural; upper, middle, versus lower socioeconomic status; recent immigrant versus first, second, or third generation, one finds various subgroups.

Because of the broad range of individuals and individual differences, let alone ethnic, and cultural differences, we will summarize as best as we can what can be done to address the issue in the clinical neuropsychology interview. As stated by Othmer and Othmer (1994) there are five phases of the clinical interview: (a) warm-up and screening, (b) follow-up on preliminary impressions, (c) psychiatric history and database, (d) diagnosis and feedback, and (e) prognosis and treatment. At each of these stages, Martinez (2000) has suggested ways to incorporate ethnic issues.

During the warm-up and screening phase, the interviewer and patient need to decide on a language in common. As stated previously, there are circumstances in which both the clinical neuropsychologist and the patient speak more than one language. If the two understand languages in common, the choice of language should be based on the comfort of the client. Martinez (2000) suggests that with recent immigrants or elderly minority individuals, native language is a safe choice. As described earlier, an interpreter may be helpful. However, the caveats discussed earlier regarding interpreters need to be kept in mind. The ethnic or cultural background may affect the description of the presenting problem. Various ethnic groups may describe their reason for seeking services as due to medical difficulties whereas others may attribute the need for services as due to familial issues. Additional information from other sources may help the clinical neuropsychologist determine the actual reason for services. The same issue occurs for all of the information garnered in the intake interview, in that in some cultures most information is described in terms of somatic issues, whereas in other cultures familial causes are intertwined into the bulk of information. During the follow-up on preliminary impressions, the practitioner should be aware of his or her own biases in relation to the information garnered from the patient. Martinez (2000) suggests that clinicians step back and evaluate whether any of the information gathered has been tainted or unduly focused on because of any ethnic stereotypes. At the third phase, there needs to be awareness that the information in the history may also be affected by ethnicity. In a cross-cultural interview situation, the clinical neuropsychologist must pay attention to whether symptoms presented are pathological and in need of treatment or are culturally determined behaviors. At the level of diagnosis, it is imperative to consider the cultural presentation of the various diagnostic labels. This is particularly evident with various religions and cultural behaviors. Appendix I of the *Diagnostic and Statistical Manual of Mental Disorders, Fourth Edition, Text Revision* (American Psychiatric Association, 2000) provides an outline for cultural formulation designed to assist the clinical neuropsychologist in evaluating the impact of the individual's culture in symptom presentation. It is suggested that the clinical neuropsychologist be aware of this when working with clients from diverse backgrounds. Finally, closing the interview should be in a manner that the individual understands and can grasp the meaning of the interview findings regardless of ethnicity. The American Psychological Association (1993) has developed guidelines for delivery of services to ethnic, linguistic, and culturally diverse populations. It has also developed guidelines on multicultural education, training, research, practice, and organizational changes for psychologists (American Psychological Association, 2003).

BACKGROUND QUESTIONNAIRE–ADULT
Confidential

The following is a detailed questionnaire on your development, medical history, and current functioning at home and at work. This information will be integrated with the test results to provide a better picture of your abilities as well as any problem areas. Please fill out this questionnaire as completely as possible.

Client's Name: _____ Date: _____
   (If not client, name of person completing this form _____
   Relationship to Client _____)
Home address _____ Work _____
Client's Phone (H)_____ (W) _____
Date of Birth _____ Age_____ Sex _____
Place of Birth _____
Primary Language _____ Secondary Language _____
                               Fluent/Nonfluent (circle one)
Hand used for writing (check one)   ☐ Right   ☐ Left

Medical Diagnosis (if any) (1) _____
                  (2) _____
Who referred you for this evaluation? _____
Briefly describe problem: _____
_____
_____

Date of the accident, injury, or onset of illness _____
What specific questions would you like answered by this evaluation? _____
(1) _____
(2) _____
(3) _____

SYMPTOM SURVEY

For each symptom that applies, place a check mark in the box. Add any comments as needed.

Motor	Rt	Lt	Both	Date of Onset
☐ Headaches				_____
☐ Dizziness				_____
☐ Nausea or vomiting				_____
☐ Excessive fatigue				_____
☐ Urinary incontinence				_____
☐ Bowel problems				_____
☐ Weakness on one side of body (Indicate body part)	__	__	__	_____
☐ Problems with fine motor control	__	__	__	_____
☐ Tremor or shakiness	__	__	__	_____
☐ Tics or strange movements	__	__	__	_____
☐ Balance problems				_____
☐ Often bump into things				_____
☐ Fainting			_____	
☐ Other motor problems _____				

_____

(continued)

FIGURE 6.5 Example of a diagnostic interview. *Source:* Adapted from Straus, Sherman, & Spreen (2006).

Sensory   Rt   Lt   Both   Date of Onset

☐ Loss of feeling/numbness
   (where?)
☐ Tingling or strange skin
   sensations (where?)
☐ Difficulty telling hot from cold
☐ Visual Impairment
☐ Wear glasses ☐ Yes ☐ No
☐ Problems seeing on one side
☐ Sensitivity to bright lights
☐ Blurred vision
☐ See things that are not there
☐ Brief periods of blindness
☐ Need to squint or move
   closer to see clearly ☐ Yes ☐ No
☐ Hearing loss
☐ Wear hearing aid ☐ Yes ☐ No
☐ Ringing in ears
☐ Hear strange sounds
☐ Unaware of things on one
   side of my body
☐ Problems with taste
   (___ Increased ___ Decreased sensitivity)
☐ Problems with smell
   (___ Increased ___ Decreased sensitivity)
☐ Pain (describe)_____
☐ Other sensory problems _____

Problem Solving   Date of Onset

☐ Difficulty figuring out how to do new things
☐ Difficulty figuring out problems that most others can do
☐ Difficulty planning ahead
☐ Difficulty changing a plan or activity when necessary
☐ Difficulty thinking as quickly as needed
☐ Difficulty completing an activity in a reasonable time
☐ Difficulty doing things in the right order (sequencing)

Language and Math Skills   Date of Onset

☐ Difficulty finding the right word
☐ Slurred speech
☐ Odd or unusual speech sounds
☐ Difficulty expressing thoughts
☐ Difficulty understanding what others say
☐ Difficulty understanding what was read
☐ Difficulty writing letters or words (not due to
   motor problems)
☐ Difficulty with math (e.g., balancing checkbook, etc.)
☐ Other languages or math problems _____

Nonverbal Skills   Date of Onset

☐ Difficulty telling right from left
☐ Difficulty drawing or copying
☐ Difficulty dressing (not due to motor problems)
☐ Difficulty doing things I should automatically be able to do
   (e.g., brushing teeth)
☐ Problems finding way around familiar places
☐ Difficulty recognizing objects or people
☐ Parts of my body do not seem as if they belong to me
☐ Decline in musical abilities

(continued)

FIGURE 6.5 *(Continued)*

❏ Not aware of time (e.g., day, season, year) _____
❏ Slow reaction time _____
❏ Other nonverbal problems _____
_____

Awareness and Concentration   Date of Onset
❏ Highly distractible _____
❏ Lose train of thought easily _____
❏ My mind goes blank a lot _____
❏ Difficulty doing more than one thing at a time _____
❏ Easily confused and disoriented _____
❏ Aura (strange feelings) _____
❏ Don't feel very alert or aware of things _____
❏ Tasks require more effort or attention _____

Memory   Date of Onset
❏ Forget where I leave things (e.g., keys, gloves, etc.) _____
❏ Forget names _____
❏ Forget what I should be doing _____
❏ Forget where I am or where I am going _____
❏ Forget recent events (e.g., breakfast) _____
❏ Forget appointments _____
❏ Forget events that happened long ago _____
❏ More reliant on others to remind me of things _____
❏ More reliant on notes to remember things _____
❏ Forget the order of events _____
❏ Forget facts but can remember how to do things _____
❏ Forget faces of people I know (when not present) _____
❏ Other memory problems _____

Mood/Behavior/Personality   Date of Onset
                                    Mild   Moderate   Severe
❏ Sadness or depression   ❏   ❏   ❏   _____
❏ Anxiety or nervousness   ❏   ❏   ❏   _____
❏ Stress   ❏   ❏   ❏   _____
❏ Problems falling asleep ❏ staying asleep ❏ _____
❏ Experience nightmares on a daily/weekly basis _____
❏ Become angry more easily _____
❏ Euphoria (feeling on top of the world) _____
❏ Much more emotional (e.g., cry more easily) _____
❏ Feel as if I just don't care anymore _____
❏ Easily frustrated _____
❏ Doing things automatically (without awareness) _____
❏ Less inhibited (do things I would not do before) _____
❏ Difficulty being spontaneous _____
❏ Energy ❏ loss ❏ increase _____
❏ Appetite ❏ loss ❏ increase _____
❏ Increase ❏ or loss ❏ of weight _____
❏ Sexual interest ❏ increase ❏ decline _____
❏ Lack of interest in pleasurable activities _____
❏ Increase in irritability _____
❏ Increase in aggression _____
❏ Other changes in mood or personality or in how you deal with people
_____
_____

Have others commented to you about changes in your thinking, behavior, personality, or mood?
If yes, who and what have they said? ❏ Yes ❏ No
_____
_____
_____

(continued)

FIGURE 6.5 *(Continued)*

Are you experiencing any problems in the following aspects of your life? If so, please explain:

Marital/Family _____

_____

Financial/Legal _____

Housekeeping/Money Management _____

_____

Driving _____

Overall, my symptoms have developed ☐ slowly ☐ quickly

My symptoms occur ☐ occasionally ☐ often

Over the past six months my symptoms have ☐ improved ☐ stayed the same ☐ worsened

Is there anything you can do (or someone does) that gets the problems to stop or be less intense, less frequent, or shorter? _____

_____

What seems to make the problems worse? _____

_____

In summary, there is ☐ definitely something wrong with me
☐ possibly something wrong with me
☐ nothing wrong with me

What are your goals and aspirations for the future? _____

_____

EARLY HISTORY

You were born: ☐ on time ☐ prematurely ☐ late

Your weight at birth: _____

Were there any problems associated with your birth (e.g., oxygen deprivation, unusual birth position, etc.) or the period afterward (e.g., need for oxygen, convulsions, illness, etc.)? ☐ Yes ☐ No

Describe: _____

Check all that applied to your mother while she was pregnant with you:
☐ Accident
☐ Alcohol use
☐ Cigarette smoking
☐ Drug use (name:_____)
☐ Illness (toxemia, diabetes, high blood pressure, infection, etc.)
☐ Poor nutrition
☐ Psychological problems
☐ Other problems _____

List all medications (prescribed or OTC) that your mother took while pregnant:

_____

Rate your developmental progress as it has been reported to you by checking one description for each area:

	Early	Average	Late
Walking	☐	☐	☐
Language	☐	☐	☐
Toilet training	☐	☐	☐
Overall development	☐	☐	☐

(continued)

FIGURE 6.5 *(Continued)*

As a child, did you have any of these conditions:

- ❑ Attentional problems
- ❑ Clumsiness
- ❑ Developmental delay
- ❑ Hyperactivity
- ❑ Muscle weakness

- ❑ Learning disability
- ❑ Speech problems
- ❑ Hearing problems
- ❑ Frequent ear infections
- ❑ Visual problems

MEDICAL HISTORY

Medical problems **prior** to the onset of current condition

If yes, give date(s) and brief description

- ❑ Head injuries
- ❑ Loss of consciousness
- ❑ Moving vehicle accidents
- ❑ Major falls, sports accidents, or industrial injuries
- ❑ Seizures
- ❑ Stroke
- ❑ Arteriosclerosis
- ❑ Dementia
- ❑ Other brain infection or disorder (meningitis, encephalitis, oxygen deprivation etc.)
- ❑ Diabetes
- ❑ Heart disease
- ❑ Cancer
- ❑ Back or neck injury
- ❑ Serious illnesses/disorder (Immune disorder, cerebral palsy, polio, lung, etc.)
- ❑ Poisoning
- ❑ Exposure toxins (e.g., lead, solvents, chemicals)
- ❑ Major surgeries
- ❑ Psychiatric problems
- ❑ Other

Are you currently taking any medication?

Name	Reason for taking	Dosage	Date started

Are you currently in counseling or under psychiatric care?   ☐ Yes   ☐ No

Please list the date that therapy initiated and name(s) of professional(s) treating you:

Have you ever been in counseling or under psychiatric care?   ☐ Yes   ☐ No
If yes, please list dates of therapy and name(s) of professional(s) who treated you:

Please list all inpatient hospitalizations including the name of the hospital, date of hospitalization, duration, and diagnosis:

(continued)

FIGURE 6.5 *(Continued)*

SUBSTANCE USE HISTORY

I started drinking at age:
☐ less than 10 years old   ☐ 10–15   ☐ 16–19   ☐ 20–21   ☐ over 21

I drink alcohol: ☐ rarely or never   ☐ 1–2 days/week
                         ☐ 3–5 days/week   ☐ daily

I used to drink alcohol but stopped: _____ Date stopped: _____
Preferred type(s) of drinks: _____

Usual number of drinks I have at one time: _____

My last drink was: ☐ less than 24 hours ago   ☐ 24–48 hours ago
                         ☐ over 48 hours ago

Check all that apply:
☐ I can drink more than most people my age and size before I get drunk.
☐ I sometimes get into trouble (fights, legal difficulty, work problems, conflicts with family, accidents, etc.) after drinking (specify): _____
☐ I sometimes black out after drinking.

Please check all the drugs you are now using or have used in the past:

	Presently Using	Used in Past
Amphetamines (including diet pills)	☐	☐
Barbiturates (downers, etc.)	☐	☐
Cocaine or crack	☐	☐
Hallucinogenics (LSD, acid, STP, etc.)	☐	☐
Inhalants (glue, nitrous oxide, etc.)	☐	☐
Marijuana	☐	☐
Opiate narcotics (heroin, morphine, etc.)	☐	☐
PCP (or angel dust)	☐	☐

Others (list)_____

Do you consider yourself dependent on any of the above drugs? ☐ Yes ☐ No
If yes, which one(s): _____

Do you consider yourself dependent on any prescription drugs? ☐ Yes ☐ No
If yes, which one(s):_____

Check all that apply:
☐ I have gone through drug withdrawal.
☐ I have used IV drugs.
☐ I have been in drug treatment.

Has use of drugs ever affected your work performance? _____
Has use of drugs or alcohol ever affected your driving ability? _____
Do you smoke? ☐ Yes ☐ No
If yes, amount per day: _____
Do you drink coffee: ☐ Yes ☐ No
If yes, amount per day: _____

FAMILY HISTORY

The following questions deal with your biological mother, father, brothers, and sisters:
Is your mother alive? ☐ Yes ☐ No
If deceased, what was the cause of her death? _____

Mother's highest level of education: _____
Mother's occupation: _____

(*continued*)

FIGURE 6.5 (*Continued*)

Does your mother have a known or suspected learning disability? ☐ Yes ☐ No
If yes, describe: _____
Is your father alive? ☐ Yes ☐ No
If deceased, what was the cause of his death?

_____
Father's highest level of education: _____
Father's occupation: _____
Does your father have a known or suspected learning disability? ☐ Yes ☐ No
If yes, describe: _____
How many brothers and sisters do you have? _____
What are their ages? _____
Are there any unusual problems (physical, academic, psychological) associated with any of your brothers or sisters?
If yes, describe: _____

Please check all problems that exist(ed) in close biological family members (parents, brothers, sisters, grandparents, aunts, uncles). Note who it is (was) and describe the problem where indicated.

	Who?	Describe
Neurologic disease		
☐ Alzheimer's disease or senility	_____	
☐ Huntington's disease	_____	
☐ Multiple sclerosis	_____	
☐ Parkinson's disease	_____	
☐ Epilepsy or seizures	_____	
☐ Other neurologic disease	_____	_____
Psychiatric illness		
☐ Depression	_____	
☐ Bipolar illness (manic-depression)	_____	
☐ Schizophrenia	_____	
☐ Other	_____	
Other disorders		
☐ Mental retardation	_____	
☐ Speech or language disorder	_____	
☐ Learning problems	_____	_____
☐ Attention problems	_____	_____
☐ Behavior problems	_____	_____
☐ Other major disease or disorder	_____	_____

PERSONAL HISTORY
Marital History

Current marital status: ☐ Single   ☐ Married   ☐ Common-law
                                    ☐ Separated   ☐ Divorced   ☐ Widowed
Years married to current spouse: _____
Dates of previous marriages: From _____ to _____
                                   From _____ to _____
Spouse's name: _____   Age: _____
Spouse's occupation: _____
Spouse's health: ☐ Excellent   ☐ Good   ☐ Poor
Children (include stepchildren)

Name	Age	Gender	Occupation

Who currently lives at home? _____
Do any family members have any significant health concerns/special needs? _____
_____

                                                          (*continued*)

FIGURE 6.5 (*Continued*)

Educational History

	Name of School Attended	Grades and Years Attended	Degree Certifications
Elementary	_____	_____	_____
	_____	_____	_____
High school	_____	_____	_____
	_____	_____	_____
College/university	_____	_____	_____
	_____	_____	_____
	_____	_____	_____
	_____	_____	_____
Trade school	_____	_____	_____
	_____	_____	_____

If a high school diploma was not awarded, did you complete a GED? _____

Were any grades repeated? ☐ Yes ☐ No
Reason: _____
Were there any special problems learning to read, write, or do math? _____
_____

Were you ever in any special class(es) or did you ever receive special services?
☐ Yes ☐ No
If yes, what grade(s) _____ or age? _____
What type of class? _____

How would you describe your usual performance as a student?
☐ A & B   Provide any additional helpful comments about your academic
☐ B & C   performance: _____
☐ C & D   _____
☐ D & F   _____

Military Service
Did you serve in the military? ☐ Yes ☐ No
If yes, what branch? _____ Dates: _____
Certifications/Duties: _____
_____

Did you serve in war time? _____ If so, what arena? _____

Did you receive injuries or were you ever exposed to any dangerous or unusual substances during your service?
☐ Yes ☐ No

If yes, explain: _____

Do you have continuing problems related to your military service? Describe:
_____

Occupational History
Are you currently working? ☐ Yes ☐ No
Current job title: _____
Name of employer: _____
Current responsibilities: _____
Dates of employment: _____
Are you currently experiencing any problems at work? ☐ Yes ☐ No
If yes, describe: _____
_____

Do you see your current work situation as stable? ☐ Yes ☐ No

(continued)

FIGURE 6.5 *(Continued)*

Approximate annual income: Prior to injury or illness _____
After injury or illness _____

Previous employers:

Name	Dates	Duties/position	Reason for leaving

Recreation
Briefly list the types of recreations (e.g., sports, games, hobbies, etc.) that you enjoy:
_____
_____

Are you still able to do these activities? _____
_____

Recent Tests
Check all tests that recently have been done and report any abnormal findings.

	Check if normal	Abnormal findings
❑ Angiography	_____	_____
❑ Blood work	_____	_____
❑ CT scan	_____	_____
❑ MRI	_____	_____
❑ PET scan	_____	_____
❑ SPECT	_____	_____
❑ Skull x-ray	_____	_____
❑ EEG	_____	_____
❑ Neurological exam	_____	_____
❑ Other _____	_____	_____

Identify the physician who is most familiar with your recent problems: _____
_____

Date of last vision exam: _____
Date of last hearing exam: _____

Have you had a prior psychological or neuropsychological exam? ❑ Yes ❑ No
If yes, complete the following:
Name of psychologist: _____
Date: _____
Reason for evaluation: _____
Finding of the evaluation: _____
_____

Please provide any additional information that you feel is relevant to this referral:
_____
_____
_____

Summary

This chapter begins with a case study involving what appears to be a domestic argument between the client and his girlfriend. However, through a methodical intake interview, much more information was ascertained which related to the presenting complaint. The topic for this chapter is interviewing and covers not only the topics within an interview but also the various types of interviews.

In addition to the interviews themselves there are many ethical and procedural issues. Ethical issues covered previously are reviewed and discussed within the context of a one-to-one interview. The personality of the interviewer and the place and circumstances were also discussed. The effects of these on the information gathered is extremely important. In a sense, this chapter discusses not only the interview content but the style of interviewing and its effects.

A very important component to interviewing and to the rest of the assessment process is language. The issues related to whether the client and the clinical neuropsychologist speak and/or understand the same language is discussed. The advantages and disadvantages of an interpreter or translator are also included.

Questions for Further Study

1. Interviews exist in various formats. When is it most advantageous to employ a structured, unstructured, or diagnostic interview?
2. Describe the best possible physical circumstances in which to interview an individual with central nervous system difficulties?
3. Explain the circumstances in which during an interview the services of a translator are the best and the worst option?

References

Adams, R. L., & Jenkins, R. L. (1981). Basic principles of the neuropsychological examination. In C. E. Walker (Ed.), *Clinical practice of psychology* (pp. 244–292). Elmford, NY: Pergamon Press.

American Psychiatric Association. (2000). *Diagnostic and statistical manual of mental disorders* (4th ed., text rev.). Washington, DC: Author.

American Psychological Association. (1993). Guidelines for providers of psychological services to ethnic, linguistic, and culturally diverse populations. *American Psychologist, 48*(1), 45–48.

American Psychological Association. (2003). Guidelines on multicultural education, training, research, practice, and organizational change for psychologists. *American Psychologist, 58*(5), 377–402.

Artiola i Frotuny, L. (2008). Research and practice: Ethical issues with immigrant adults and children. In J. Morgan & J. H. Ricker (Eds.), *Text of clinical neuropsychology* (pp. 960–981). New York: Taylor and Francis.

Artiola i Frotuny, L., & Mullaney, H. A. (1998). Assessing patients whose language you do not know: Can the absurd be ethical? *The Clinical Neuropsychologist, 12,* 113–126.

Connor, K. M., & Davidson, J. R. T. (2001). SPRINT: a brief global assessment of post-traumatic stress disorder. *International Clinical Psychopharmacology, 16,* 279–284.

Gorden, R. L. (1987). *Interviewing: Strategy, techniques, and tactics* (4th ed.). Chicago: Dorsey Press.

Gunstad, J. A., & Suhr, J. A. (2001). Expectation as etiology versus the good old days: Post-concussion syndrome reporting in athletes, headache sufferers, and depressed individuals. *Journal of the International Neuropsychological Society, 7,* 323–333.

Gunstad, J. A., & Suhr, J. A. (2002). Perception of illness: Nonspecificity of postconcussion syndrome symptom expectation. *Journal of the International Neuropsychological Society*, 8, 37–47.

Holtz, J. L. (1986). Assessment Process. Unpublished manuscript.

Johnson, R. W. (1981). Basic interviewing skills. In E. E. Walker (Ed.), *Clinical practice of psychology* (pp. 83–128). Elmford, NY: Pergamon Press.

LaCalle, J. J. (1987). Forensic psychological examinations through an interpreter: Legal and ethical issues. *American Journal of Forensic Psychology*, 5, 29–43.

Lezak, M. D., Howieson, D. B., & Loring, D. W. (2004). *Neuropsychological Assessment* (4th ed.). New York: Oxford University Press.

Martinez, C. (2000). Conducting the cross-cultural clinical interview. In I. Cuellar & F. A. Paniagua (Eds.), *Handbook of multicultural mental health* (311–325). San Diego, CA: Academic Press.

Othmer, E., & Othmer, S. C. (1994). *The clinical interview using DSM-IV Vol. 1* [Fundamentals]. San Diego, CA: American Psychiatric Press.

Reynolds, C. R. (Ed.). (1998). Common sense, clinicians, and actualism in the detection of malingering during head injury litigation. *Detection of malingering during head injury litigation* (pp. 261–286). New York: Plenum Press.

Sattler, J. M. (2002). *Assessment of children: Individual and clinical applications* (4th ed.). San Diego, CA: Sattler.

Stowe, R. M. (1998). Assessment methods in behavioral neurology and neuropsychiatry. In G. Goldstein, P. D. Nussbaus, & S. R. Beers (Eds.), *Neuropsychology* (pp. 437–485). New York: Plenum Press.

Strauss, E., Sherman, E. S., & Spreen, O. (2006). History taking. In E. Strauss, E. S. Sherman, & O. Spreen (Eds.), *A compendium of neuropsychological tests: Administration, norms, and commentary* (pp. 55–74). New York: Oxford University Press.

Vanderploeg, R. D. (2000). Interview and testing: The data collection phase of neuropsychological evaluations. In R. D. Vanderploeg (Ed.), *Clinician's guide to neuropsychological assessment* (pp. 3–38). New Jersey, NJ: Routledge.

Tests of Intellectual Abilities

7

Learning Objectives

After reading this chapter, the student should be able to understand:
- The components of psychometric theory including test construction, reliability, and validity
- The history of intellectual assessment and the important events in its development
- The different theories that attempt to explain the concept of intelligence
- The components of proper test administration
- The characteristics of various individual tests of intelligence

Topical Outline

- Psychometric Theory
- Ethics in Testing and Assessment
- History of Intellectual Assessment
- Definition of Intelligence
- Test Administration
- Individual Tests of Intelligence

Vera was referred by her school counselor for a neuropsychological evaluation. The referral source requested specific information regarding intellectual abilities, the possibility of **attention deficit/hyperactivity disorder** (ADHD), any form of learning disability, and/or any residual cognitive deficits due to a traumatic brain injury (TBI) sustained when the client was 4 years old. The information from the current neuropsychological evaluation would be compared to prior assessments to determine appropriate placement in her academic setting.

Vera is a 14-year-old Caucasian female. She is the middle child of her biological parents. She has an older brother who is 19 and a younger sister who is 10 years old. The family resides in a rural setting close to a metropolitan area. Both parents work in the city and commute daily. The younger children ride the bus to school and the oldest drives himself to his place of employment.

The incident which caused Vera to sustain a TBI was clearly an accident. At the age of 4, she and her brother were playing inside their house while their parents were outside. A sliding patio door, which was to be installed that evening, was leaning against a wall and somehow, in the midst of their play, the door fell and pinned Vera underneath. Her brother ran for help and their parents quickly summoned the paramedics. Everyone present was afraid she would not live through the ordeal. She was unconscious for an indeterminate period of time. At the hospital, the doctors prepared the parents for the worst and asked if they wanted the services of clergy. To everyone's surprise, Vera survived.

The medical diagnosis was a closed head injury with the force of impact on the left hemisphere of the brain. A series of tests including an MRI confirmed the diagnosis. Because the left side of the brain controls the right side of the body, she also developed difficulties walking due to right leg paralysis. Fortunately, she did not sustain any damage to internal organs. Vera began a long road to recovery in the hospital. With the aid of physical therapy, occupational therapy, and speech pathology services, she learned to walk again and recovered the language skills which she had lost. After 2 months in the hospital, Vera returned to her family home. Her parents were fearful and watched her carefully; however, she appeared to be physically intact. Her memory skills appeared somewhat impaired and she appeared to be more easily upset than before the TBI.

When Vera became 5 years old and eligible for kindergarten, her parents sent records to the school and explained her accident. As with any child beginning kindergarten, she was given a preschool evaluation. The school psychologist suggested that Vera be further assessed due to the information provided by Vera's parents. From the assessment and advice from various other professionals, the school psychologist suggested that Vera begin special education classes starting in kindergarten and that she have an **Individual Educational Plan (IEP)**. **Public Law 94-142**, or the **Education for All Handicapped Children Act of 1975**, has provisions for the assessment of all children with handicaps (Public Law 94-142, 1975). There is also the requirement that all children must receive a free and appropriate public education and that all handicapped children have an IEP to achieve particular educational goals (Sattler, 1982). The IEP must be evaluated on a regular basis to determine if goals are being met. From the time the decisions were made when Vera entered the school system until the present, Vera has been taking special education classes. She has excelled in all of her classes to the point that she is currently not challenged and her attention often wanders. The ramifications of the neuropsychological evaluation are whether there is continuing need for special education placement or whether she should be **mainstreamed** into general education classes.

Vera came to the appointment with her mother. It was requested that at least one parent attend the assessment not only because Vera is a minor and needs parental consent for treatment

Individual Educational Plan (IEP)
a plan to address each of the stated needs of the student with specific, concrete, goal-oriented programs

Public Law 94-142, or the Education for All Handicapped Children Act of 1975
a law that states that all children in the United States are entitled to a free and public education in the least restrictive environment

mainstream
the practice of bringing students out of the isolation of special schools and into the "mainstream" of student life; students in special education classes are integrated into the general classroom

but also to supply as much information as possible about Vera's developmental history. Separate interviews were conducted with Vera and her mother. In addition, each individual completed a written interview form, which contained various neurological symptoms and the ability to perform **activities of daily learning**. Information gathered from Vera's mother indicated normal prenatal development, birth, and postnatal achievement of developmental milestones until the time of the accident. Subsequent to the accident, cognitive, memory, and mood difficulties became evident to the family and to the preschool she attended. Vera was described as friendly and eager to be involved with other children. She has had some difficulties with friendships, particularly in the preteen years, because she has difficulty interpreting social cues.

Vera was interviewed prior to testing. She has few memories before the accident which is normal for that age period. She does not remember the accident but does have some memories from the hospital stay. She is not certain whether those are events she actually remembers or are incidents her family told her about. She stated that memory difficulties are the problems which cause her the most difficulty. She indicated that she does well in her classes but that they are too easy for her. She also stated that she would like to be with the other "kids" as she does not want to be labeled as "different."

Behavioral observations from the interview with Vera gave the impression of a typical teenager. She was dressed well and appropriately for the weather. She did not exhibit any behavioral abnormalities or unusual physical mannerisms. She spoke clearly and answered the questions that were asked. Approximately one half hour into the interview her attention began to wander. She appeared to then have difficulty comprehending questions asked of her. Memory difficulties also began to be evident. The changes in concentration appeared to be related to the length of her attention span possibly related to the TBI or could be a symptom of ADHD.

Vera was assessed using the **Wechsler Intelligence Scale for Children-IV (WISC-IV)** to garner an overall measure of intelligence and any evidence of learning difficulties. She was also administered age-appropriate neuropsychological tests to determine any residual deficits due to her TBI. In addition she was administered the **Test of Variables of Attention (TOVA;** Greenberg, Corman, & Kindschi, 1977) to determine if any evidence of ADHD was present. The results of the tests were compiled and conclusions were drawn. These results and conclusions were compared to previous assessments made by the school.

On the WISC-IV Vera received a Full Scale IQ and composite scores within the Borderline range of abilities. This suggests that her intellectual functioning, while not average, is above the cutoff for the classification of mental retardation. Results from the neuropsychological tests indicated a pattern, similar to that from the WISC-IV, that she is functioning at a level less than average but above the level of a brain-impaired subject. Further testing revealed the presence of previously undiagnosed ADHD but no learning disabilities.

These types of results make it difficult to communicate concrete recommendations to the referral source. However, as Vera seemed to be functioning better than was expected and as she has been socially integrated into her school, it was suggested that she attempt taking all of her subjects in the general classroom. The recommendation also follows the intentions of PL-94-142 in that a child is placed in the least restrictive learning environment. It was suggested that her performance be reviewed after a semester to determine how she was functioning within the general classroom. It was also suggested that she be seen by a psychiatrist to determine the need and/or appropriateness of medication for ADHD. Further, it was suggested that both she and her parents obtain the services of a psychologist who specializes in ADHD for both educational information and possible therapy, if needed.

activities of daily learning
activities that any individual does on a daily basis such as personal hygiene, cooking and meal planning, going to work or school, and leisure activities

Wechsler Intelligence Scale for Children-IV (WISC-IV)
the most current form of the Wechsler scales designed for use with children; it yields a Full Scale IQ and composite scores measuring Verbal Comprehension, Perceptual Reasoning, Working Memory, and Processing Speed

Test of Variables of Attention (TOVA)
a computerized test designed to detect symptoms of attention deficit/hyperactivity disorder

There are many issues which need to be addressed for the aforementioned client. In order to obtain data to help make these decisions, the clinical neuropsychologist relies on assessment or testing. Testing, however, cannot be the only factor in making decisions about life choices. In this particular case testing was utilized but a decision was also made based on the best case scenario for the client. In this particular case, her test scores fall in the gray area between "normal" and "brain impaired." However, she was not challenged and was often bored with special education classes and felt stigmatized. Placing her in the general classroom may be difficult for her but it may also increase her self-esteem and allow her not to feel "different." A trial period was suggested to make sure that she was not overwhelmed by the changes in any particular subject. Social functioning would also be assessed at that time.

This chapter focuses on assessment or testing of cognitive abilities. Historically, intelligence was the first of many cognitive abilities to be studied and subsequently assessed. This chapter will review various testing instruments that have been used to measure cognitive abilities. Prior to the introduction of these tests, a short review of psychometrics as it pertains to test construction and usage is presented. This review pertains not only to this chapter but also to the following two chapters, which focus on various other forms of assessment. In addition, a discussion of the testing situation and various person variables similar to the discussion with regard to interviewing will be completed. Following the review will be a brief history of intellectual assessment before we explore the most frequently used tests of intellectual and other cognitive abilities.

Psychometric Theory

In order to understand the tests which will be presented in this and the following chapters, the reader needs to understand the basics involved with test construction and usage. "Traditionally, the function of psychological tests has been to measure differences between individuals or between the abilities of the same individual under different circumstances" (Anastasi & Urbina, 1997, p. 2). In clinical neuropsychology, the use of tests has often been to assess the strengths and weaknesses of a client after an accident or illness, develop a diagnosis, and/or formulate a treatment plan for rehabilitation. The following principles apply regardless of the use of the particular test.

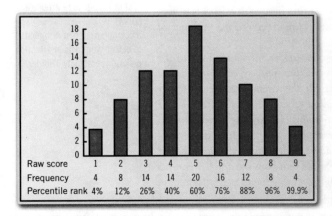

FIGURE 7.1 Test scores expressed as raw scores and as percentiles.

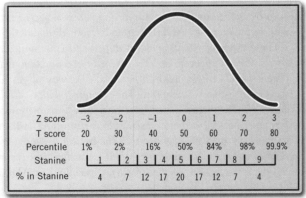

FIGURE 7.2 Linear and area transformation in relation to the normal curve.

TEST CONSTRUCTION

"A psychological test is essentially an objective and standardized measure of a sample of behaviors" (Anastasi & Urbina, 1997, p. 4). In order to obtain this sample of behavior the test must contain items, questions, or tasks which pertain to the behavior in question. Item choice is therefore related to the purpose of the assessment device and implies that the purpose must be clearly articulated.

Test construction is a long and detailed procedure and a complete review of test construction is beyond the scope of this text. For a more extensive explanation of test theory and construction, the reader is referred to Anastasi and Urbina (1997).[1] In brief, the test construction process begins with a **domain** or type of behavior that the researcher desires to sample. For example, a test of intelligence would have as its domain all of the behaviors that were included within the researcher's definition of intelligence. The next step would be generation of test items to measure the concept. After generation of items, the test needs to be given to multiple individuals. Test items will be added and/or deleted as this process progresses based on the usefulness of each item. Many times a **factor analysis** is completed to determine the degree to which each item is related to the construct, which the test purports to measure. **Standardization** is the next step. The manual which accompanies each test details the complete directions for administering each portion of a test in a particular manner which cannot be deviated from without violating standardization. The purpose of having such strict guidelines is to rid the test of any inadvertent error which may be introduced by the examiner or the conditions under which the test was administered. Standardization implies uniformity of procedures in administering and scoring the test.

In conjunction with the standardization of a test is the establishment of **norms**. In order to develop norms, the test must be administered to a group of individuals. The test norms must include the rationale for the choice of the sample. Many tests use a sample of the larger population of the United States often stratified by age, gender, and ethnicity.

After developing norms, scores need to be considered. An individual's scores on tests have no intrinsic value but need to be evaluated compared to other individuals' scores. **Raw scores** can be converted to various scaled scores for ease of interpretation via mathematical computations. An example of a conversion from raw to **scaled score** is the **standard score** derived from the WISC-IV, which was given to the client in the case study. Raw scores are mathematically converted to scaled scores with a **mean** ($\bar{x}$) or average score of 100, and **standard deviation** (sd) or measure of the spread of scores of 15 (see Figure 7.1). The change from raw score to standard score is for ease of interpretation. This conversion follows the **normal curve** or the normal spread of scores around the mean. The normal curve is used due to its mathematical properties (see Figure 7.2). In addition, it is known that most human traits from height and weight to aptitude and personality traits cluster in the middle with fewer individuals further from the mean. Test manuals which are included with the published tests must include all of the aforementioned statistical information. The American Psychological Association (APA) in conjunction with the **American Educational Research Association** and the **National Council on Measurement in Education** have formulated a clear guide entitled *Standards for Educational and Psychological Testing*, which details the information that must be included when developing tests, as well as fairness in testing and testing applications (American Psychological Association, American Educational Research

factor analysis
a statistical procedure in which all of the scores are correlated with one another to determine those variables or factors which account for the most variance in the data

standardization
uniformity of procedure in administering and scoring a test

norms
conversion of the raw scores of the sample group into percentiles in order to construct a normal distribution to allow ranking future test takers

scaled score
a scaled score is a conversion of a participant's raw score on a test or a version of the test to a common scale that allows for a numerical comparison among participants

standard score
any score expressed in units of standard deviations of the distribution of scores in the population, with the mean set at zero

mean
the arithmetic mean of a list of numbers is the sum of all the members of the list divided by the number of items in the list

standard deviation
the square root of the variance; it is usually employed to compare the variability of different groups

normal curve
the normal distribution with a mean of 100 and a standard deviation of 15

---

[1] Anastasi, J., & Urbina, S. (1997). *Psychological testing* (7th ed.). Upper Saddle River, NJ: Prentice Hall.

Association, & the National Council on Measurement in Education, 1999). This document will be described in more detail later in the chapter.

RELIABILITY

In addition to the aforementioned psychometric issues, it is necessary to examine two concepts within test construction, reliability and validity, to aid the reader in understanding the nature of test materials. The **reliability** of a test means its consistency. Test reliability is the consistency of scores obtained by the same individual when retested with the identical test or an equivalent form of the test. A test would be essentially useless if the same person received a different score when taking the same test at a different time. In a more technical sense, measures of test reliability make it possible to estimate what proportion of the total **variance** or differences between test scores is **error variance**. Error variance is not due to errors in taking tests, but is because of characteristics inherent within the tests. The reliability of a test is represented as a **correlation coefficient**, which can range from −1 to +1. Correlation implies that two variables vary together (see Figure 7.3). Correlation does not imply causation. A score of +1 is synonymous with a perfect positive correlation. For example, as X increases, Y increases correspondingly. A negative correlation means that as X increases, Y decreases correspondingly and signifies an inverse relationship. Most correlations vary between +1 and 0 with a reputable test often having a reliability coefficient in the .80's (Anastasi & Urbina, 1997).

There are several forms of reliability. **Test–retest reliability** is obtained by repeating the identical test on two occasions. The reliability coefficient is the correlation between the scores obtained by the same person on the two administrations. The error variance is caused by random fluctuations of performance from Time 1 to Time 2. **Alternate-form reliability** is obtained by having the same person take one form of a test at Time 1 and an equivalent form of the test at Time 2. The correlation between

FIGURE 7.3 Scatter diagrams illustrating correlations of various sizes. Each dot represents one individual's score on two tests, *x* and *y*. In **(A)**, all cases fall on the diagonal and the correlation is perfect (*r* = +1.00). If we know a subject's score on *x*, we know that it will be the same on *y*. In **(B)**, the correlation is 0. Knowing a subject's score on *x*, we cannot predict whether it will be at, above, or below the mean on *y*. In both **(C)** and **(D)**, there is diagonal trend to the scores, so that a high score on *x* is associated with a high score on *y* and a low score on *x* with a low score on *y*, but the relationship is imperfect.

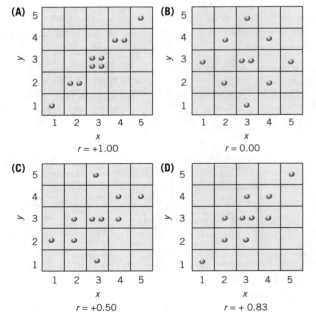

the scores obtained on the two forms is the reliability coefficient. Parallel forms of the test must be evaluated to make sure they truly represent the same domain. **Split-half reliability** is derived by dividing the test into equal portions and correlating the two portions with one another. There are many ways to split a test such as odd numbered items versus even numbered items or the first half of the test versus the second half of the test. The last method of determining reliability includes a single administration of a test and is based on the consistency of responses of all items in the test. The most common procedure for finding **interitem consistency** was developed by Kuder and Richardson (1937). Rather than requiring two half scores, this technique is based on the performance of each item. It can be mathematically shown that the Kuder-Richardson reliability coefficient is the mean of all split-half coefficients resulting from different splittings of the test (Cronbach, 1951). The ordinary split-half coefficient is based on a planned split, which is designed to yield equivalent sets of items. Therefore, "unless the items are highly homogenous, the Kuder-Richardson coefficient will be lower than the split-half coefficient" (Anastasi & Urbina, 1997, p. 98) and the difference between the Kuder-Richardson coefficient and the split-half coefficient serves as a rough index of the heterogeneity of the test.

alternate-form reliability
the same people are tested with one form of a test on one occasion and with another, equivalent form on a second occasion; the correlation between the scores represents the reliability coefficient

split-half reliability
a measure of the reliability of a test based on the correlation between scores on two halves of the test, often the odd- and even-numbered test items

VALIDITY

The validity of a test concerns what the test measures and how well it measures that subject (Anastasi & Urbina, 1997). All procedures, which determine test validity, are fundamentally addressing the question regarding performance on a test and its relationship to some behavioral construct.

Validity is even more critical in test construction than is reliability. A test may be statistically reliable but also possess no relationship to the variables which the test designer purports to study. As with reliability, there are several techniques with which to study validity, including content validity, criterion validity, construct validity, and the use of meta-analysis. Similar to reliability data, validity information is represented as a correlation coefficient. The standard approach is the correlation between the test score and a criterion measure.

Content validity involves a systematic analysis of the actual test items to determine the adequacy of the coverage of the behavior being measured (Maloney & Ward, 1976). There are two decisions that need to be made by the researcher and these are whether items are appropriate for the content area and whether there are enough of various types of items to sample the behavior. Content validity may suffer from subjective factors or bias in choice of items by the researcher.

content validity
the extent to which the items of a test or procedure are in fact a representative sample of that which is to be measured

Content validity is not the same as **face validity**. Face validity is not a correlation between the test and any other measure. Face validity refers to the appearance of the test in terms of the content to be measured to the test taker. Many tests disguise the true information about which they are intended. Face valid tests are clearer in terms of the constructs to be measured which may lead a test taker to not be as truthful in his or her answers if he or she so desires. An example of a face valid test is the Beck Depression Inventory-II (BDI-II; Beck, Steer, & Brown, 1996). The questions on the BDI-II clearly assess depression and if the patient does not desire to deal with this topic, the test may not be an accurate representation of his current mental state.

Criterion validity refers to the effectiveness of the test in predicting extra-test performance or behavior. The criteria vary with the test variable in question. Intelligence tests are often validated against a measure of academic achievement such as grade point average. In the case study, Vera's intelligence test scores were evaluated in comparison to her

criterion validity
the effectiveness of the test in predicting behavioral criteria on which psychologists agree

performance in special education classes. In other cases of central nervous system disease or difficulty, the test scores may be evaluated against current job performance or may be used to predict future job or school performance.

construct validity
refers to whether a scale measures the unobservable social construct (such as "fluid intelligence") that it purports to measure; it is related to the theoretical ideas behind the trait under consideration

Construct validity implies the extent to which the test is able to measure a theoretical construct or trait. Examples of constructs applicable within clinical neuropsychological practice would include processing speed, attention, or concept formation. Each construct is developed to explain and organize observable response consistencies. Correlations between new tests and earlier tests are often used as proof that the new test is valid. Factor analysis, a statistical procedure, is often used to determine the major factors or variables which contribute to the variance between scores and is particularly relevant to construct validity procedures. Measures of **internal consistency** use the total score of the test as the criterion and evaluate each item against the total. Campbell (1960) stated that in order to show construct validity, a test must demonstrate that the test correlates highly with other variables with which it theoretically should and is termed **convergent validation**. The test should also not correlate with variables with which it should differ and is termed **discriminant validation**. Campbell & Fiske (1959) devised a systematic experimental design for the direct evaluation of convergent and discriminant validation, which they termed the **multitrait–multimethod matrix**. The procedure assesses two or more traits by two or more methods.

internal consistency
a measure based on the correlations between different items on the same test (or the same subscale on a larger test); it measures whether several items that propose to measure the same general construct produce similar scores

As time has passed since Cronbach and Meehl (1955) first discussed construct validity and as testing needs have changed so has terminology. Although construct validity was first introduced as a separate type of test validity it has moved in some models to encompass all types of validity (Messick, 1993). In other models, the term has been seen as redundant and been replaced by validity, because all types of validity ultimately conform to the construct measured by the test (Strauss, Sherman, & Spreen, 2006, p. 26).

meta-analysis
the evaluation of multiple studies using factor analytic methodology

A final method that has been used in other sciences and is gaining in use in psychology is **meta-analysis**. It has been in use since the 1970s but is being used more often currently as a substitute for the traditional literature search by test users and developers, mainly because of the large database of available research on current tests (Lipsey & Wilson, 1993). Through considering the findings of several studies and weighing them on the basis of methodological and substantive features of each study, meta-analysis may reveal substantial positive findings (Anastasi & Urbina, 1997). A further feature of meta-analysis is that **effect sizes** are taken into account. Effect sizes are essentially the degree of **statistical significance** in the data or the size of the correlation. Meta-analysis essentially allows the researcher to gain information from previous studies and not sacrifice time completing a study which has already been undertaken.

statistical significance
statistical evidence that there is a difference in the data from a study and is unlikely to have occurred by chance

In addition to the psychometric properties of tests, proper development and usage of these materials are essential. Important decisions have been and continue to be made about individuals based on tests, which are assumed to be not only reliable and valid but also administered appropriately. Referring back to our case study, it is clear that major decisions have been made in Vera's life based on testing materials. In this particular case, it illustrates the reason that test developers must always strive for the highest degree of reliability and validity in their tests.

Ethics in Testing and Assessment

There exist three documents that specify, in detail, the proper construction and development of testing materials. These documents also specify the proper professional use of testing materials.

The American Psychological Association's *Ethical Principles of Psychologists and Code of Conduct* includes specific principles related to competence, privacy and confidentiality, and assessment. Collectively, these statements elaborate upon two basic issues which are technical standards for the development of tests and standards for the professional use of tests. Technical standards are used to evaluate the psychometric properties of the test. Standards regarding professional behavior make it clear that psychologists are personally and professionally responsible for safeguarding the welfare of consumers of psychological tests (Murphy & Davidshofer, 2005).

The second document developed by APA in conjunction with the American Educational Research Association and the National Council on Measurement in Education is termed the *Standards for Educational and Psychological Testing* (1999). This document discusses, in detail, the appropriate technical and professional standards to be followed in construction, evaluation, interpretation, and application of psychological tests.

The third document published by the **International Testing Committee** is entitled *International Guidelines for Test Use* (2000). This document overlaps the other two to a great extent. The main parts include the need for high standards when developing and using tests and also the need for professional behavior when administering, interpreting, and reporting results of testing materials. Taken together, these documents discuss the salient issues regarding test development and usage and also professional behavior by the test administrator. The aforementioned principles apply not only to the tests discussed in the present chapter but also to all tests described in the following two chapters and used and discussed within all of the case studies.

History of Intellectual Assessment

The assessment of intellectual abilities has a long and interesting history and, for that reason, is similar to the study of the brain. The reader will therefore find many of the time periods and issues discussed in relation to the history of brain science are also applicable to the study of intellectual assessment.

The earliest accounts of the use of assessment are from the Chinese Empire. For approximately 2,000 years, the Chinese used some form of assessment for civil service examinations (Bowman, 1989). The Greeks used testing within their educational system. Tests used by the Greeks measured physical as well as intellectual skills (Doyle, 1974). Beginning in the Middle Ages, European universities relied on formal examinations to award degrees and honors (Anastasi & Urbina, 1997).

Moving forward in time, the 19th century was a burgeoning period for the development of tests or assessment devices. World events, as well as developments within the field of psychology, led to these techniques. World events that had major impact on testing included the change in the treatment of individuals with mental disorders. The mental hygiene movement led to individuals with mental disorders being separated from criminals in separate facilities. The development of diagnostic classification systems beginning with Kraepelin led to ways to separate the two populations. Many tests were developed which were designed to separate individuals with various mental illnesses from those with criminal tendencies. Also important was the ability to determine the literacy of mental patients and criminals to determine who was able to benefit from any form of treatment.

Another world event, which helped shape the future of intellectual assessment, was the need of school systems. Beginning in France, then proceeding to other European countries and subsequently to the United States, there was a need to determine the level of ability of students. As has been the case throughout history, there has never been enough space in public schools for students nor enough teachers to educate all potential students. In addition, there has always been the issue regarding the ability levels of students: those who we now would term gifted, those whose abilities fall closer to the norm, and those who may need special education services. Testing in a standardized manner has been used to separate current abilities and predict future benefits from various types of educational strategies. The reader can refer back to the case study for a clear example of this phenomenon.

In addition to diagnosis of mental illnesses and assessment of educational ability and potential, testing has also been used heavily within the military. The period between the end of the 19th century until the early part of the 20th century witnessed the types of abilities necessary for soldiers changing dramatically. The changes were related to the type of technology available, which led to different kinds of abilities necessary for soldiers in different positions. Testing helped to determine the literacy and potential of soldiers as they entered into the service. Testing, later in history, also helped to assess various types of difficulties, which arose from participation in the service. Neuropsychological tests, as suggested previously, were useful to determine the extent of brain impairment caused by warfare. At the present time, the Veterans Administration has recognized that a very large number of soldiers were returning from Iraq and Afghanistan with brain injuries due to the type of warfare and has designated monies for treatment of their difficulties.

In terms of the researchers involved in the development of tests, Jean Esquirol (1772–1840) in 1838 was probably the first to make a distinction between individuals based on testing information. In a two-volume text, he spent more than 100 pages pointing out the differences in types of mental retardation (Anastasi & Urbina, 1997). After many attempts at developing a system to differentiate the levels, he concluded that the individual's use of language provided the most dependable criteria for intellectual level (Esquirol, 1838).

Edward Seguin (1896–1907), also a French physician, spent most of his career trying to educate mentally retarded individuals (Seguin, 1907). He worked heavily with sense discrimination and motor control. One of his major contributions to testing was nonverbal measures of intelligence such as the Seguin Form Board.

Sir Francis Galton (1822–1911) is generally thought to be responsible for instigating or beginning the testing movement. One of Galton's main interests was heredity, possibly because he was related to Charles Darwin and, hence, he realized the need to measure characteristics of related and unrelated individuals. Many of his early measurements were of visual and hearing abilities, muscular strength, reaction time, and other sensorimotor functions. He developed many tests for the assessment of these abilities. Galton (1883) felt that individuals with the best sensory apparatus were the most intelligent. He was also a pioneer in the use of rating scales and questionnaire methods. Further, he has often been credited for his development of statistical methods for analysis of data on individual differences. His work on statistical analysis was carried forward by his eminent student Karl Pearson (1857–1936). The Pearson product–moment correlation coefficient is named for this individual.

James McKeen Cattell (1860–1944), an American, received his doctorate in Leipzig under Wundt's direction. He then returned to the United States and was active establishing experimental psychology laboratories and increasing the use of testing and assessment materials. Cattell, in 1890, was the first to use the term *mental test*. His tests were administered to college students as subjects and contained items similar to those of Galton.

In an article written in France in 1895, Alfred Binet (1857–1911) and Victor Henri (1872–1940) criticized the available tests as too sensory and motor focused (Binet & Henri, 1895). They proposed a group of varied abilities, which they envisioned as essential components of intelligence such as memory, attention, imagination, aesthetics, and many other abilities. In 1904, the French Minister of Public Institutions appointed Binet to the Commission for the Retarded to study the education of retarded children. It was through this appointment and his collaboration with Théodore Simon that the first Binet-Simon scale was developed.

The first test developed by Binet and Simon was known as the 1905 scale and contained 30 items arranged in order of difficulty (Binet & Simon, 1905). This was the first intelligence test to cover a multitude of abilities. The second Binet-Simon test was released in 1908; in this version some tests were added some deleted, and all tests were grouped into age levels. The third version of the Binet-Simon appeared in 1911 the year of Binet's death. After his death, many individuals attempted to improve on the test, the most famous being the Stanford-Binet developed at Stanford University in 1916 by L. M. Terman (1877–1966). The test is now in its fifth revision and will be discussed later in this chapter.

Another individual who was extremely prominent in intellectual assessment was American researcher and theorist David Wechsler (1896–1981). He viewed the Binet scales as too restrictive or unrepresentative of factors that he believed were crucial components of intelligence. Wechsler (1939) was quoted as stating that intelligence comprised the abilities to "think rationally, act purposefully and deal effectively with the environment" (p. 3). After defining intelligence in this manner came the inclusion of not only verbal components to his intelligence scale but also performance components or those tasks that could be completed without verbalizing an answer. The Wechsler Intelligence Scales are currently the most frequently used scales to measure intelligence (Camara, Nathan, & Puente, 2000; Rabin, Barr, & Burton, 2005).

The Binet and Wechsler scales as well as others are considered **individual intelligence tests**. They are administered using one examiner for each client and require up to 2 hours for administration. Other types of tests, such as those described later are **group intelligence tests**. In these tests, many individuals may complete a test at the same time often in a large assembly hall or auditorium.

As indicated previously, the military developed a need for large scale evaluation of incoming soldiers regarding literacy and other potential abilities. The first group tests of intelligence were developed to fill this need. In 1917, as the United States entered World War I, a committee of the APA was formed and developed tests that would be known as the **Army Alpha** and the **Army Beta** (Thorndike, 1997). The former was a general verbal test of intelligence, which consisted of 212 multiple-choice and true–false questions on the following subjects: vocabulary, sentence structure, arithmetic problems, number series, general knowledge, and common sense. The latter was a nonverbal test of intelligence for nonliterate or foreign-language speaking recruits, which minimized verbal knowledge and used only pictures and diagrams. The current Armed Services Vocational Aptitude Battery (ASVAB) is a direct descendent from the first military group tests (Department of Defense, 1968). The current test, however, is less of a measure of intelligence and more of a placement tool to be used to match the recruit's abilities to various positions within the armed forces.

individual intelligence tests intelligence tests administered using one examiner and one examinee

group intelligence tests tests that are administered to individuals in large groups and do not require one-to-one administration; group tests are often used to test large groups of people such as in the military and to save time and manpower through the use of fewer administrators

Definition of Intelligence

Before the evaluation of intelligence tests can begin, the reader must understand the complexity of the concept of intelligence. The IQ score is not synonymous with intelligence. The IQ score is a score on a test purported to measure the concept of intelligence. Intelligence is a concept which has had a history of debate regarding the properties that contribute to this concept.

There are several theories as to what comprises intelligent behavior and, hence, which types of items should appear on a measure of intelligence. At this point, we have learned about Binet's verbal measures of intelligence and Wechsler's verbal and performance measures of intelligence. Many other theorists have examined the content or composition of intelligence.

An early theorist, Charles Spearman (1863–1945), stated in 1904 that intelligence could be explained by a person's standing on a **general intellectual factor** or g (Spearman, 1904). He stated that correlations among test scores can be explained by the fact that different tests provide partial measures of the same general intellectual factor (Murphy & Davidshofer, 2005). The implications of Spearman's ideas include the idea that differences in test performance between individuals are due to differences in the general intelligence, g. It implies that a good intelligence test should be highly loaded with g. Finally, it implies that a good measure of g will successfully predict performance on all cognitively demanding tasks.

Louis Thurstone (1887–1955) disagreed with Spearman's idea of a solitary g factor. He felt that various intelligence tests contained several group factors, which are independent of one another but are all related to g. Thurstone suggested that intelligence could best be understood in terms of seven group factors or primary mental abilities (Thurstone, 1938). The abilities include verbal comprehension, word fluency, number, space, associative memory, perceptual speed, and reasoning. As all of these primary abilities are related to g, it is possible for individuals to have the same level of g but also possess very different abilities. A good intelligence test, according to Thurstone, should measure each of these abilities.

Raymond Cattell (1905–1998) in 1963 described two related but distinct types of general intelligence: fluid and crystallized (Cattell, 1963). **Fluid intelligence** involves the ability to understand relationships and is related to reasoning. **Crystallized intelligence** involves the individual's stored knowledge and skills.

J. P. Guilford's (1897–1987) model of intelligence is very different and does not accept the existence of the general g factor. Guilford (1967) stated that intelligence is organized according to three dimensions: operations, contents, and products. In his theory, there are six types of operations, five types of content, and six types of products, which yield 180 different types of intelligence (Guilford, 1967).

Subsequent to the 1960s, there began an interest in understanding intellectual abilities in an information-processing approach. These theories have been heavily influenced by cognitive psychology and advances in the use and understanding of computers. These approaches tend to understand and evaluate the various mental processes which an individual employed in a given task in a manner similar to how a computer deals with data.

Howard Gardner (1943–present) developed a theory of multiple intelligences based on his observations that adult roles in society require multiple abilities. He defined intelligence as the "ability to solve problems or fashion products that are of consequence to a particular cultural setting or community" (Gardner, 2004, p. 15). In his theory of multiple intelligences he defines seven distinct kinds of categories: (a) linguistic, (b) musical, (c) logical–mathematical, (d) spatial, (e) bodily kinesthetic, (f) interpersonal, and (g) intrapersonal. According to Gardner, each individual is characterized by a unique combination of strong and weak intelligences, which account for individual differences. Gardner (2004) takes into account the effect of culture as well as the functioning of exceptional individuals and those with brain impairment.

Michael L. Anderson has criticized Gardner's theory stating that each of his seven intelligences are not independent of one another. Anderson (1992) states that differences in intelligence result from differences in the "basic processing mechanism" that

---

general intellectual factor or g a construct used in the field of psychology to quantify what is common to the scores of all intelligence tests

fluid intelligence involves novel reasoning and use of information to deal with unfamiliar problems or to gain new types of knowledge

crystallized intelligence refers to acquired skills and knowledge and the use of knowledge in activities such as work or hobbies; it has the advantage of practice

implements thinking, which, in time, yields knowledge. Individuals vary in the speed at which basic processing occurs.

Robert Sternberg (1949–present) developed his triarchic theory of intelligence in 1985 (Sternberg, 1985). Technically, he stated that there exist three separate subtheories, each of which deals with different types or components of intelligence. First, the componential subtheory deals with thought processes and includes metacomponents used to plan, control, monitor, and evaluate processing during problem solving. Performance components carry out problem-solving strategies. Knowledge acquisition components encode, combine, and compare information during the course of problem solving. Second, the experiential subtheory deals with the effects of experience on intelligence. Third, the contextual subtheory considers the effects of the individual's environment and culture on intelligence.

Stephen Ceci (1950–present) developed a theory stating that there exist multiple cognitive potentials (Ceci, 1990). His theory, while similar in having more than one ability, states that the abilities are biologically based and places limits on mental processes. The emergence of these potentials is related to the challenges and opportunities in the individual's environment.

Each one of these theories has been praised and criticized by many researchers. Each of the four more modern theories tend to account for the biological bases of intelligence as well as the environmental and cultural influences. Hence, each deal with the **nature–nurture question** or the extent to which an ability is based on biological factors versus environmental factors. After reviewing many of the older and more modern theories of intellectual ability, we will now proceed to looking at individual tests of intelligence. A thorough review is beyond the scope of this text; however, the most commonly used intellectual assessment devices used by neuropsychologists will be evaluated. For a more extensive explanation of the construction of intelligence tests and other tests of higher order cognitive functioning, the reader is referred to Lezak, Howieson, and Loring (2004).[2] Prior to this, however, will be a discussion of proper test administration.

Test Administration

The proper administration of assessment tools is applicable to tests included within this chapter and also those discussed within chapters 8 and 9. The proper testing procedures and circumstances are similar to those used in interviewing and discussed within chapter 6. Additional issues are included within this section, which apply particularly to the use of testing materials.

Preparation of the patient for testing is essential to alleviate anxiety and increase motivation. Very often testing follows the initial intake interview and, therefore, many ethical issues may have already been discussed. In the situation where testing is delayed or not completed after the interview, many issues may need to be reviewed with the client. As is similar to interviewing, the patient's consent for testing is essential before any procedures are begun. In the case of an individual with a legal guardian or a minor, the person who is responsible for the patient must give the consent. It is most appropriate to discuss the issues verbally and have a written agreement which is signed by the client or parent/guardian. The degree of confidentiality afforded the patient regarding the testing materials

---

[2]Lezak, M. D., Howieson, D. B., & Loring, D. W. (2004). The theory of estimation of test reliability. *Psychometrika*, *2*, 151–160.

and the answers which the patient produces must be discussed. The patient and/or guardian has a right to view the testing responses as well as any report written concerning the client's performance on assessment tools. The client does not have a right to copies of tests administered due to copyright guidelines from test manufacturers. The client has a right to understand the individuals or organizations who may have access to his test results and the potential ramifications of the testing procedures. The guidelines for the aforementioned dissemination may be somewhat different in a forensic arena.

The circumstances in which testing is completed, similar to interviewing, may have an impact on the client's performance. It is very important to limit any form of distraction in the testing situation to allow the client the best opportunity to focus on testing materials to produce as clear and accurate responses as possible. The person of the interviewer and his or her dress and demeanor are also pertinent to a discussion of testing. Overall, the focus should not be on the clinical neuropsychologist or psychometrist but on the client and the testing situation.

In addition to the physical appearance of the testing situation and the professional, there are other issues which need to be taken into account that could affect the ability of the tests to give a representative sample of the client's strengths and weaknesses. Individuals who have central nervous system difficulties may have more and varied issues, which could impede their performance if not taken into consideration or accommodated before the testing session. In the testing circumstance, size of the room doorway, height of the testing table, and/or the need for transfer from wheelchair to other chair must be considered.

Individuals who have hearing difficulties vary from minor, potentially age related, to deficits on either end of the sound wave spectrum, to those who are completely deaf congenitally or due to various deficits. Many individuals who have been deaf from birth have become conversant in American Sign Language and an individual to interpret this may be needed. Other individuals who are deaf due to accident or injury may not, as of yet, learned this language. Most neuropsychological tests which have verbal directions may be interpreted using sign language. However, there are very few norms that have been derived using deaf individuals as subjects; therefore, there are few comparison groups. Individuals who are partially deaf may be able to complete testing with the aid of amplification devices.

Individuals who have vision difficulties may also have difficulties with testing. Visual field cuts may impair the ability to understand the materials, whereas, an individual who is blind may need a reader. The same individual may not be able to accomplish any form of performance task. Those individuals who are color blind, either partially or totally, may also need assistance if coloration is involved with any component of a test.

Considering the various deficits clients may bring to the testing situation, the clinical neuropsychologist must decide between strict adherence to the directions for standard administration of a test or become more flexible using a procedure termed **testing the limits**. The former approach would produce a testing profile which may be comparable to the information provided by the test developer but not an accurate representation of the client's strengths and weaknesses. The latter, while lacking comparability of scores, may more clearly reflect the client's strengths and weaknesses. In testing the limits the client is allowed to complete all items that he or she is capable of regardless of the amount of time it takes. In a sense, the clinical neuropsychologist is assessing the ability to complete a task not the speed of completion.

With all of the aforementioned issues in mind, the clinical neuropsychologist must determine the tests used and the order of presentation. The use of test batteries makes this choice easier and suggests the order of administration. Overall, most clinical neuropsychologists follow the assessment process flowchart beginning with record review (if available), referral, and an initial interview. Usually the next areas assessed are cognitive abilities

testing the limits
a manner of neuropsychological testing that forgoes timing in favor of evaluating the ability of the client; the results generated are not comparable to available norms; often used with clients who have motor disabilities which makes timing a disadvantage in overall score

most often in the form of an intelligence test and then a memory scale or battery. The remainder of testing may be either a neuropsychological test battery or an assortment of individual neuropsychological tests. At times, the referral source may request specific tests due to the circumstances of the client's situation. An example would be a referral from a school regarding the client's ability to function in a particular classroom including an estimate of the client's intelligence and/or other special abilities or deficits. This type of referral is similar to the situation in our case study. In addition, Vera and her mother could benefit from many of the previously discussed principles which could put them both more at ease through the testing process.

Individual Tests of Intelligence

THE BINET SCALES

As noted previously, the Stanford-Binet was originally developed by Alfred Binet and Théodore Simon in 1905. It was a test designed for one-to-one administration, essentially one examiner and one subject. It was a test which predominately measured verbal abilities or those that we tend to think reside within the left side of the brain (see Figure 7.4). There were revisions of the Binet-Simon in 1908 and 1911.

Terman (1916) and others developed the first Stanford-Binet revision of the test. In this test there were an abundance of new and revised items and it thereby did not resemble the original test (Anastasi & Urbina, 1997). The standardization sample was revised using an American sample. The second Stanford-Binet was released in 1937 and included forms L and M (Terman & Merrill, 1937). In this revision, there was difficulty in obtaining a representative sample of the U.S. population. In 1960, a single form of the Stanford-Binet (Form L-M) was released and did not require a restandardization of the test (Terman & Merrill, 1960). In the

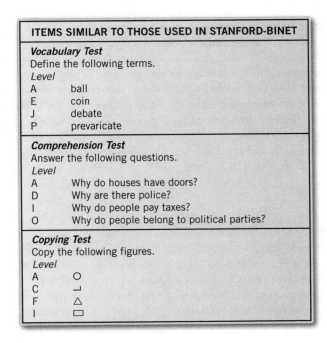

ITEMS SIMILAR TO THOSE USED IN STANFORD-BINET
Vocabulary Test
Define the following terms.
Level
A   ball
E   coin
J   debate
P   prevaricate
Comprehension Test
Answer the following questions.
Level
A   Why do houses have doors?
D   Why are there police?
I   Why do people pay taxes?
O   Why do people belong to political parties?
Copying Test
Copy the following figures.
Level
A   ○
C   ⌐
F   △
I   ▢

FIGURE 7.4 Examples of test items similar to those on the Stanford-Binet intelligence test and test materials.

1973 restandardization of Form L-M, the test remained the same but the norms were derived from current samples and were more updated and representative of the general population (Terman & Merrill, 1973). The current form of the test is the fifth edition Stanford-Binet and includes the most thorough revision (Roid, 2003). As with previous revisions, the fifth edition retains the adaptive testing procedures in which the individual completes only those items whose difficulty level is appropriate for the individual's demonstrated performance level. However, as was the case with the fourth edition (1986), the predominately verbal content was changed to include items relevant to quantitative, spatial, and short-term memory tasks (Delany & Hopkins, 1987; Thorndike, Hagen, & Sattler, 1986).

The current version of the test includes an equal representation of verbal and nonverbal subtests. The Stanford-Binet-V yields a Full Scale IQ (FSIQ), two domain scores (Nonverbal IQ and Verbal IQ), and five factor indices (Fluid Reasoning, Knowledge, Quantitative Reasoning, Visual–Spatial Processing, and Working Memory) based on current factor-analytic Carroll-Horn-Cattell (CHC) theories of intelligence. Unlike previous editions, the means of the IQ and factor index scores are 100 with a standard deviation of 15. The Stanford-Binet-V has been designed to be used with ages 2 through adulthood.

The data in the test manual include information about the test sample, which has changed significantly from the fourth edition. It was renormed on a large representative sample including 4,800 participants ages 2–85 years and older closely matching variables in the 2001 U.S. census.

Reliability was assessed for the Stanford-Binet-V using split-half, test–retest, and interscorer agreement. The reliability coefficients range from mid .80's to high .90's depending on the subtest. In terms of validity, the current Stanford-Binet-V includes multiple components measuring the concept of intelligence. The test contains information regarding intercorrelation and factor analysis of scores, correlation with other intelligence tests, and comparison of performance of previously identified exceptional groups. Studies tend to agree that it is at least as good of a measure of intelligence as any other test available and correlates well with other measures of intelligence including previous versions of the Stanford-Binet (Strauss et al., 2006, p. 265). It also is able to differentiate mentally retarded, gifted, and learning disabled persons. Finally, due to the process of administration, the Stanford-Binet-V also gives interview information. One of the major strengths of the Stanford-Binet-V is the continuity between the various versions of the test and the original test developed by Binet and Simon. The same or similar definitions of intelligence as an ability that involves reasoning, comprehension, and judgment and the age-referenced measurement of intelligence have remained consistent throughout revisions. Becker (2003) stated that each successive revision will do an even better job at maintaining these constructs. One of the deficits in the area of neuropsychology is that the test does not measure processing speed which is often important in differential diagnosis. The test developers have worked extremely hard at eliminating racial or ethnic bias but have not provided data for various groups often seen by neuropsychologists such as individuals with TBI or dementia.

THE WECHSLER SCALES

In comparison to the Stanford-Binet-V, which has one test to encompass all ages with which it is used, David Wechsler developed three separate tests for preschool age children, school age children, and adults. The Wechsler tests have been used as measures of general intelligence, as well as diagnostic tools for brain disease or dysfunction in a clinical neuropsychological context. The adult version of the Wechsler test has been one of the most often used measures in neuropsychological batteries (Rabin et al., 2005). The Wechsler scales have also been used in general clinical practice as a diagnostic tool for mental illness. There have been extensive reviews of the Wechsler scales including thousands of research articles. The adult version of the Wechsler scales has often been considered the gold standard in individual testing (Ivnik et al., 1992; see Figure 7.5).

In developing his scales, Wechsler stated that previous scales had predominantly been developed for children and then adopted for use with adults. He proposed a scale designed specifically for adults with items appropriate for the 18–64 age groups. He also felt the use of the mental age norm was not applicable for adults. The first Wechsler scale was published in 1939 and was termed the Wechsler-Bellevue because Wechsler was employed at Bellevue Hospital in New York City.

In 1949, the Wechsler Intelligence Scale for Children (WISC) was published. It was patterned after the original Wechsler-Bellevue and was considered to be a downward extension of this test (Seashore, Wesman, & Doppelt, 1950). Wechsler had a different philosophy from the Stanford-Binet and began with an adult test to then formulate a children's test. The Wechsler Preschool and Primary Scale of Intelligence (WPPSI) was published in 1967. It was to be used with children 4–6.5 years and somewhat overlapped in age with the WISC.

The Wechsler-Bellevue was replaced by the Wechsler Adult Intelligence Scale (WAIS) in 1955 which contained a more representative sample and gave better reliability information regarding individual subtests. It was supplanted by the WAIS-R in 1981. At that point, the test contained very little information regarding validity.

At the present time, there have been several revisions of each of the Wechsler scales. The WAIS is in its fourth revision (Wechsler, 2008). The WISC is also in its fourth revision (Wechsler, 2003a). The Wechsler Preschool and Primary Test of Infants (WIPPSI) is in its third revision (2002). Each of these tests is still named for Wechsler even though he died in 1981.

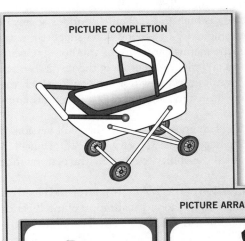

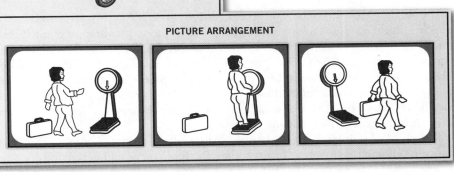

FIGURE 7.5 Items similar to those that might appear on the WAIS-R.

The WISC-IV includes composite scores measuring Verbal Comprehension, Perceptual Reasoning, Working Memory, and Processing Speed in addition to the FSIQ. Matarazzo (2003), in the preface to the test manual, states that the change from verbal and performance IQs (PIQs) to composite scores reflects clinical research, which shows that processing speed, working memory, and fluid reasoning are among the most important cognitive activities to have emerged in the literature. The theoretical background for the changes in the WISC-IV reflects current theories of intelligence based on the factor-analytic work of Carroll (1993; 1997) and Horn and Noll (1997). The CHC model integrates the work of the aforementioned theorists (Flanagan & McGrew, 1997). This model stresses that there are several broad classes of abilities at the higher level (i.e., fluid ability, short-term memory, long-term memory, etc.) and a number of primary abilities at the lower level (i.e., quantitative reasoning, spelling ability, etc.). Due to the fact that these theories stress multiple, sometimes independent factors of intelligence, it is therefore thought that intelligence tests should be composed of multifaceted instruments and techniques.

The change from FSIQ, VIQ, and PIQ to composite scores reflecting a clear theoretical orientation is a dramatic change in the field of intelligence testing. "The first standardized intelligence tests were used by clinicians due to practical concerns and clinical utility not empirically demonstrated rigor" (Spreen, Sheman, & Straus, 2006, p. 98). Because the WISC-IV is used by more psychologists than any other children's intelligence test, the adoption of this new model has been seen as a paradigm shift in the assessment of children. As has been discussed earlier, the Stanford-Binet-V also subscribes to the CHC model. There are many individuals who view the change as an improvement. However, there are critics who desire the traditional VIQ-PIQ dichotomies and those who state that the WISC-IV is more of a hybrid which does not follow strictly the CHC model (Flanagan & Kaufman, 2004).

The norms for the WISC-IV were based on 2,200 children ages 6 years to 16 years 11 months. The group was stratified according to the 2000 U.S. Census data by age, gender, race, parental education, and geographic region. The internal reliability of the WISC-IV is excellent and, in many cases, surpasses that of the WISC-III (Wechsler, 2003b). The test manual states that the test–retest reliability is high to excellent (all index scores in the high .80s to above .90). Sattler and Dummont (2004) found good support for the factor-analytic structure as it was reported in the manual. In terms of validity, it appears that the four separate index scores describe the underlying structure of the test in normal children. Due to the fact that the WISC-IV is not only a new test but one in which the conceptualization of intelligence has changed drastically, additional research on the test and its use with various populations is essential.

The WAIS-III (1997) introduced the idea of composite scores to the adult version of the Wechsler. However, the WAIS-III also included the FSIQ, VIQ, and PIQ. Hence, in a neuropsychological content there still remained the ability to compare the performance on the two sides of the brain.

The WAIS-IV (2008) is the most recent version of the WAIS. It was revised based on 4 years of clinical research looking at the changes in the conceptualization of intelligence and following the introduction of composite scores in the WISC-III. The WAIS-IV is designed for adults ages 16–90. Similar to the WISC-IV and the WAIS-III, it is believed by the authors that the inclusion of the composite scores is a more comprehensive way to measure and evaluate an individual's intelligence. It was thought to be following the earlier described CHC model of cognitive functioning; however, researchers disagree whether it has accomplished that end.

The WAIS-IV intends to update normative data, reduce administration time, enhance psychometric properties by expanding the FSIQ range and improving floors and ceilings, and improve developmental appropriateness with the addition of demonstration and sample items. Improvements include eliminating the Dual IQ/Index IQ score structure and enhancing the measure of working memory, fluid intelligence, and processing speed. Clinical utility is improved with additional special group studies, such as Borderline Intellectual Functioning. It was meant to be co-normed with the WMS-IV. It has 10 subtests to measure the four domains of intelligence. The four domains have index scores to provide a FSIQ score, which is a measure of general intelligence (g). The FSIQ is determined by scores on the 10 subtests in each of the four indices. The four indices are as follows: Verbal Comprehension (VC), Reasoning (R), Working Memory (WM), and Processing Speed (PS).

Verbal Comprehension is designed to measure a person's general verbal skills, including the understanding of words and similarities. The Verbal Comprehension subtests include Vocabulary, Similarities, and Information (measures crystallized intelligence). Working Memory tests are designed to measure the ability to temporarily retain information, problem solving skills, and attention. The Working Memory subtests include Arithmetic and Digit Span. The Perceptual Reasoning tests are designed to measure nonverbal reasoning and visual–motor coordination. The Perceptual Reasoning subtests include Block Design, Matrix Reasoning, and Visual Puzzles. The Processing Speed tests are designed to measure a person's ability to process visual information quickly, attention, and planning. The Processing Speed subtests include Symbol Search and Coding. Picture Arrangement, Object Assembly, Coding Recall, and Coding Copy, which were part of the WAIS-III, have been removed from the WAIS-IV. A General Ability Index (GAI) score is a cumulative score of the six subtests in the Verbal Comprehension and Perceptual Reasoning scales.

The normative sample was 2,200, with 200 participants per age group for ages 16–69, and 100 participants per age group from ages 70–90. The sample stratification was based on gender, ethnicity, education level, and region to provide the highest reliability of results. The reliability and validity of the WAIS-IV was indicated within the interpretative manual for all of the subtests, components, and various combinations of scores. The test developers state that the WAIS-IV is sound with reference to both reliability and validity.

The Wechsler scales have been used not only alone but also in conjunction with other tests in neuropsychological batteries since the inception of the field of neuropsychology. The change in the structure of the Wechsler scales at the same time as the change in the formulation and understanding of cognitive processes particularly using CHC model will be discussed further in chapter 9.

As we return to the case study, it has been very clear that the use of intelligence tests and other forms of assessment has had a large effect on the life of Vera. Due to the fact that such significant decisions may be made in an individual's life using test data, it is essential that the tests are constructed well with adequate reliability and validity and appropriate norms from the groups for which it is intended to be used.

Vera's placement was based on her test scores and other important information from her teachers and family. Subsequent to her neuropsychological evaluation, she began taking classes in the regular classroom and at first was somewhat intimidated. However, the students were welcoming and assisted her as she adjusted to the new learning environment. As of this writing, she has come to function adequately academically. Emotionally she feels much better about herself and her abilities. She has also been making plans to attend technical or junior college once she graduates from high school. The change in Vera's emotional state has made it less stressful for her entire family.

Summary

This chapter began with a case study illustrating the use of an intelligence test to garner information regarding the client's cognitive abilities and also to ascertain diagnostic clues for potential disabilities. Contained within the case study are various ethical and procedural issues that will surface in many clinical neuropsychological testing situations. Examples given in the case study include the fact that the client has a legal guardian because she is a minor and also disabled, has sustained central nervous system trauma, and suffers from various residual deficits.

The chapter continues with review of psychometric theory. The topic is covered to acquaint the reader with the terminology, particularly reliability and validity and how they must be reported in test manuals. Following the psychometric issues are ethical issues in testing.

The next section of the chapter involves a history of intellectual assessment particularly involving social, economic, and world events and how they shaped the appearance of assessment tools. Implied here are the decisions that must be made whenever individuals are grouped together based on any type of ability. Theories of intelligence or cognitive ability are also covered in this section followed by various definitions of intelligence.

Prior to the discussion of the tests themselves, is a review of issues regarding the testing situation and the person of the administrator. Special considerations in testing are also covered with the aim being comfort of the client to obtain the most accurate evaluation of his or her cognitive abilities. The chapter closes with a review of the most often used individually administered intelligence scales for children and adults. Included within this discussion is the current debate that has arisen due to changes in the construct of intelligence and how that relates to neuropsychological assessment.

Questions for Further Study

1. Explain the socio-political ramifications of intelligence test scores.
2. What is the ethical conflict regarding the release of test forms really about? Why is this a forensic issue?
3. With the introduction of the CHC model of cognitive functioning, are all tests not using it somewhat obsolete? Has the CHC construct been adequately tested?

References

American Psychological Association, American Educational Research Association, & the National Council on Measurement in Education. (1999). *Standards for educational and psychological testing.* Washington, DC: American Psychological Association.

Anastasi, J., & Urbina, S. (1997). *Psychological testing* (7th ed.). Upper Saddle River, NJ: Prentice Hall.

Anderson, M. (1992). *Intelligence and development: A cognitive theory.* Oxford, UK: Blackwell.

Beck, A. T., Steer, R. A., & Brown, G. F. (1996). *Beck Depression Inventory* (2nd ed.) San Antonio, TX: The Psychological Corporation.

Becker, K. A. (2003). *History of the Stanford-Binet intelligence scales: Content and psychometrics. Stanford-Binet intelligence scales* (5th ed.). Assessment Service Bulletin No. 1. Itasca, IL: Riverside.

Binet, A., & Henri, V. (1895). La psychologie individuelle [Individual psychology]. *L'Année Psychologique, 2,* 411–463.

Binet, A., & Simon, T. H. (1905). Methodes nouvelles pour le diagnostic du niveau intellectuel de anormaux. [New methods for diagnosing abnormal intellectual levels] *L'Année Psycologique, 11,* 191–244.

Bowman, M. L. (1989). Testing individual differences in ancient China. *American Psychologist, 44,* 576–578.

Camara, W. J., Nathan, J. S., & Puente, A. E. (2000). Psychological test usage: Implications in professional practice. *Professional Psychology: Research and Practice, 31,* 141–154.

Campbell, D. T. (1960). Recommendations for APA test standards regarding contruct, trait, and discriminant validity. *American Psychologist, 15,* 546–555.

Campbell, D. T., & Fiske, D. W. (1959). Convergent and discriminant validation by the multitrait-multimethod matrix. *Psychological Bulletin, 56,* 81–105.

Carroll, J. B. (1993). *Human cognitive abilities: A survey of factor analytic studies.* Cambridge, MA: Cambridge University Press.

Carroll, J. B. (1997). The three-stratum theory of cognitive abilities. In D. P. Flanagan, J. L. Genshaft, & P. L. Harrison (Eds), *Contemporary intellectual assessment: Theories, tests, and issues* (pp. 122–130). New York: Guilford.

Cattell, J. M. (1890). Mental tests and measurements. *Mind, 15,* 373–381.

Cattell, R. B. (1963). Theory of fluid and crystallized intelligence: A critical experiment. *Journal of Educational Psychology, 54,* 1–22.

Ceci, S. J. (1990). *On intelligence…more or less: A bio-ecological treatise on intellectual development.* Englewood Cliffs, NJ: Prentice Hall.

Cronbach, J. L. (1951). Coefficient alpha and the internal structure of tests. *Psychometrika, 16,* 297–334.

Cronbach, L., & Meehl, P. E. (1955). Construct validity in psychological tests. *Psychological Bulletin, 52,* 281–302.

Delany, E., & Hopkins, T. (1987). Stanford-Binet: Intelligence Scale-examiner's handbook: An expanded guide for fourth edition users. Chicago: Riverside.

Department of Defense. (1968). Armed Services Vocational Aptitude Battery (ASBVAB), Washington, DC: Department of Defense.

Doyle, K. O., Jr. (1974). Theory and practice of ability testing in ancient Greece. *Journal of the History of the Behavioral Sciences, 10,* 202–212.

Esquirol, J. E. (1838). *Des malodies mentales considered, sous les rapports medical, hyienque, et medico-legal* [Mental maladies considered, under medical reports, health, and medical-legal]. Paris: Bailliere.

Flanagan, D. P., & McGrew, K. S. (1997). A cross-battery approach in assessing and interpretation cognitive abilities: Narrowing the gap between practice and cognitive science. In D. P. Flanagan & J. L. Genshaft (Eds.), *Contemporary intellectual assessment: Theories, tests, and issues* (pp. 314–325). New York: Guilford.

Flanagan, D. P., & Kaufman, A. S. (2004). *Essentials of WISC-IV assessment.* Hoboken, NJ: John Wiley & Sons, Inc.

Gardner, H. (2004). *Frames of mind: The theory of multiple intelligences.* New York: Basic Books.

Galton, F. (1883). Inquires into human faculty and its development. London, UK: Macmillan.

Greenberg, L. M., Corman, C. L., & Kindschi, C. L. (1977). *Test of Variables of Attention (TOVA) Version 7.03.* Los Alamitos, CA: Universal Attention Disorders, Inc.

Guilford, J. P. (1967). The nature of human intelligence. New York: McGraw-Hill.

Horn, J. L., & Noll, J. (1997). Human cognitive capabilities. In D. P. Flanagan & J. L. Genshoft (Eds.), *Contemporary intellectual assessment: Theories, tests and issues* (pp. 53–91). New York: Guilford Press.

International guidelines for test use. (2000). New York: International Testing Commission.

Ivnik, R. J., Malec, J. F., Smith, G. E., Tangalos, E. G., Peterson, R. C., Kokmen, E., et al. (1992). Mayo's older American normative studies: WAIS-R norms for ages 56–97. *The Clinical Neuropsychologist, 6* (Suppl.), 1–30.

Kuder, G. F., & Richardson, M. W. (1937). The theory of estimation of test reliability. *Psychometrika, 2,* 151–160.

Lezak, M. D., Howieson, D. B., & Loring, D. W. (2004). *Neuropsychological assessment* (4th ed.). New York: University Press.

Lipsey, M. W., & Wilson, D. B. (1993). The efficacy of psychological educational and behavioral treatment: Confirmation from meta-analysis. *American Psychologist, 48,* 1181–1209.

Maloney, M. P., & Ward, M. P. (1976). *Psychological assessment: A conceptual approach.* New York: Oxford University Press.

Matarazzo, J. D. (2003). *Preface to Weschsler Intelligence Score for Children-IV.* San Antonio, TX: The Psychological Corporation.

Messick, S. (1993). Validity. In R. L. Linn (Ed), *Educational measurement* (3rd ed., pp. 13–103). New York: Macmillan.

Murphy, K. R., & Davidshofer, C. O. (2005). *Psychological testing: Principles and applications* (6th ed.). Upper Saddle River, N.J Pearson Prentice Hall.

Public Law 94-142 Education for all Handicapped Children Act of 1975. (1975).

Rabin, L. A., Barr, W. B., & Burton, L. A. (2005). Assessment practices of clinical neuropsychologists in the United States and Canada: A survey of INS, NAN, and APA Division 40 members. *Archives of Clinical Neuropsychology, 20,* 33–66.

Roid, G. H. (2003). *Stanford-Binet Intelligence Scale* (5th ed.). Itasca, IL: Riverside.

Sattler, J. M. (1982). *Assessment of children's intelligence and special abilities* (2nd ed.). Boston: Allyn & Bacon.

Sattler, J. M., & Dummont, R. (2004), *Assessment of Childrens WISC-IV and WPPSI-III supplement.* San Diego: Jerome M. Sattler Publishing, Inc.

Seashore, H. G., Wesman, A. G., & Doppelt, J. E. (1950). The standardization of the Wechsler Intelligence Scale for Children. *Journal of Consulting Psychology, 14,* 99–110.

Seguin, E. (1907). *Idiocy: Its treatment by the physiological method.* New York: Columbia University, Bureau of Publication.

Spearman, C. (1904). "General intelligence" objectively determined and measured. *American Journal of Psychology, 15,* 201–293.

Sternberg, R. (1985). *Beyond IQ: A triarchic theory of human intelligence.* Cambridge, England: Cambridge University Press.

Strauss, E., Sherman, E., & Spreen, O. (2006). *A compendium of neuropsychological tests: Administration norms and commentary* (pp. 17). New York: Oxford University Press.

Terman, L. M. (1916). The measurement of intelligence. Boston: Houghton Miflin.

Terman, L. M., & Merrill, M. A. (1937). *Measuring intelligence: A guide to the administration of the new revised Stanford-Binet Tests of Intelligence.* Boston: Houghton Mifflin.

Terman, L. M., & Merrill, M. A. (1960). *Stanford-Binet Intelligence Scale: Form L-M.* Boston: Houghton Mifflin.

Terman, L. M., & Merrill, M. A. (1973). *Stanford-Binet Intelligence Scale: Manual for the third review Form L-M* (1972 norms tables by R. L. Thorndike). Boston: Houghton Mifflin.

Thorndike, R. L., Hagen, E. P., & Sattler, J. M. (1986). *Stanford-Binet Intelligence Scale-Fourth Edition guide for administering and scoring.* Itasca, IL: Riverside Publishing.

Thorndike, R. M. (1997). The early history of intelligence testing. In D. P. Flanagin, J. L. Genshaft, & P. L. Harrison (Eds.), *Contemporary Intellectual Assessment: Thesis, tests and issues* (pp. 3–16). New York: Guilford Press.

Thurston, L. L. (1938). Primary mental abilities. *Psychometric monographs,* No. 1.

Wechsler, D. (1939). The measurement of adult intelligence. Baltimore, MD: Williams & Wilkins.

Wechsler, D. (1958). The measurement and appraisal of adult intelligence. Baltimore, MD: Williams and Wilkins.

Wechsler, D. (2003a). The Wechsler Intelligence scale for children. San Antonio, TX: The Psychological Corporation.

Wechsler, D. (2003b). WISC-IV technical and interpretation manual. San Antonio, TX: The Psychological Corporation.

Wechsler, D. (2008). *The measurement and appraisal of adult intelligence.* San Antonio, TX: The Psychological Corporation.

Tests of Memory Functioning

8

Learning Objectives

After reading this chapter, the student should be able to understand:

- The three types of memory and their functions
- The types and characteristics of memory deficits
- The various tests used to assess attention and concentration
- The various tests used to assess short-term and long-term memory
- The characteristics of various memory assessment batteries

Topical Outline

Joseph is a 64-year-old White male who is currently being seen by the clinical neuropsychologist for depression and post-traumatic stress disorder. The depressive symptoms are long standing and relate to a general lack of satisfaction with his life and a lack of purpose regarding his future. The post-traumatic stress symptoms relate to instances of alleged physical and emotional abuse at the hands of his father while he was a young child. Within the past year, he has been dealing with self-described memory issues, which are his main concern at the present time.

Joseph is the eldest child of his biological parents. He has three younger sisters, ages 58 (now deceased), 53, and 52. His parents are still living and in their late 80s. His father was recently hospitalized for heart difficulties and his mother has been suffering from symptoms similar to those of Alzheimer's type dementia. Joseph's youngest sister stayed with their mother because it was felt she should not be living alone while her husband was in the hospital.

Joseph described his early life as somewhat chaotic. His father was in the military and they were stationed at three different locations across the United States before settling in the upper Midwest. Joseph's father obtained employment outside of the military and his parents began to have more children. Joseph stated that the family environment became more comfortable after the birth of his sisters. However, even with his father being home more, he never developed a "close" relationship with him and felt that he was always much closer to his mother.

Joseph was an average student throughout school. He neither disliked school nor found it particularly interesting. After completing high school, Joseph enlisted in the Navy to avoid being drafted. The United States was heavily involved in the Vietnam conflict at that time. Joseph was sent for basic training in Newport News, Rhode Island. After basic training, he was assigned to a supply ship that traveled to deliver supplies and commodities to other ships. He was a supply clerk, which meant that he kept track of the number and type of items that were delivered to the various other vessels. This is a task that requires an individual to have adequate memory skills. Joseph stated that he enjoyed his tour of duty in the Navy and was able to visit many places such as Italy, Spain, and the Far East.

After his tour of duty Joseph returned to his hometown. He was aware of the protests against Vietnam veterans and the Vietnam conflict but felt very disconnected from the issue because he had volunteered rather than been drafted and he had also not experienced any combat or particularly dangerous circumstances. Compared to others who were involved in the service at that point in history, he stated that he felt his return home was much easier. After the service, he went to work as a bartender, lived at his parent's home, and spent most of his time "dating."

After several years of nonserious dating, he met and married his wife. Joseph stated that he did not love her but was eager for companionship and wanted to have a family. They eventually had two children, both girls, who are presently 28 and 30 years old. The marriage was rocky because Joseph was not always employed full time, which necessitated his wife being the primary financial supporter of the family. He also admitted that he had difficulties with gambling and drinking, although he stated that they are not current problems. Throughout the marriage, he admits to having had several affairs. As time passed, things became worse for the couple and Joseph filed for divorce approximately 10 years ago. He and his ex-wife became better friends after the divorce and were able to spend their time together without fighting.

Sometime after the divorce, Joseph ran into an old acquaintance who informed him that one of Joseph's previous girlfriends had died. This then became the focus of his therapy for a long period of time. He stated that he had not remembered this woman since he left her. He apparently knew the woman before he entered the Navy and when he returned there were plans to marry. He also stated that she had become pregnant. He spent a great deal of time trying to understand *how he could have "forgotten" about her and the child. He came to understand that the memory loss was due to the trauma of not only the pregnancy but also the fact that he left her and went on with his life. Joseph shared this amazing story with his ex-wife and daughters. One daughter was so curious she found the woman's identity and discovered that she had given birth to a son and contacted him. He was not interested in knowing Joseph and had found out about him in the deathbed confession of his mother.*

From the time of the discovery of the ex-girlfriend's death until the present, Joseph has been struggling with how it could be possible to forget all of this information. For a period of time, he sought out the help of the Church and tried to understand that maybe he needed to be forgiven to obtain his missing memory. He also tried and was unsuccessful at using hypnosis to retrieve any of his missing memory.

In Joseph's description, it was "as if a door closed" and he had no memory after a particular day when he went to see his girlfriend. Discussions with him revealed that he did know that they had broken up and that she had written him several letters trying to get back together, which Joseph's mother had destroyed or hidden. Joseph stated that he knew she had sent a letter, was on his way to get back together with the woman, and for some reason it never happened. After that, he then went on with his life and did not think of the girlfriend or their child until he was informed of her death.

After trying to recapture these memories for a long time, he became more depressed than when he initially entered therapy. He took more medications (anxiolytics and antidepressants) than previously. He ate less, slept more, and felt a general sense of estrangement from life. The original referral question or issue was not the severe memory deficit as just described in his history. However, the concern at the present time regards attention, concentration, and the ability to keep items in short-term or working memory. He describes himself as extremely forgetful and is concerned that this may be a symptom of some other difficulty. He also is aware that some of the memory symptoms may be related to the increase in his level of depression but states that he also wants to investigate other causes. He is also aware that his mounting level of anxiety may make the memory deficits worse.

This is a very unique and interesting case study. Described here is a typical memory loss potentially related to aging, physical or mental deterioration, or some other difficulty. In Joseph's case, exacerbations of an already existing depression and post-traumatic stress difficulties could be the cause. In addition, there is a 40-year memory loss for a particularly significant relationship and the causes of its demise.

The clinical neuropsychologist treating this individual has the difficult task of ascertaining the causal factors for each of these types of memory difficulties and for determining whether there is any connection between the two problems. Also, the clinical neuropsychologist needs to take into consideration the role of the preexisting depression and post-traumatic stress symptoms. Finally, the clinical neuropsychologist must take into account any undiagnosed medical problems or effects of medications which may have caused his memory difficulties.

Introduction

Memory, in a sense, is our only way of keeping track of ourselves as we progress through our lives and our world. Memory is our way of understanding how things work and of not having to relearn these things once we know them. For example, without any trauma or illness, once we know how to brush our teeth or ride a bicycle, we usually will be able to do those tasks repeatedly without help. Memory is also our personal store of events that have happened to us, as well as socially and culturally, how things happen in the world. Personal memories would include any events, significant or not, that have happened in our lives and have been part of who we are. Examples of social or cultural memories include how individuals dine in a restaurant or partake of religious rites or even how a parade functions. It is very difficult for most of us to imagine a life without memory. Hence, it is one of the reasons that when memory begins to fade, for various reasons, individuals often become irate or incensed. Throughout this chapter, we will focus on the topic of memory. The types of memory and how they function will be our starting point. It will become very clear as we pursue the types of memory and the theories that purport to explain them that memory is a volatile topic which leads to many and varied competing ideas regarding its function. After developing a rudimentary knowledge of memory, we will pursue difficulties individuals have with their memory. The remainder of the chapter will then focus on the types of memory tests which a clinical neuropsychologist employs to assess memory difficulties. As with the previous chapter on intelligence testing, ethical issues and issues in the use of testing materials are also salient with memory testing.

Types of Memory and Their Functions

declarative or explicit memory
the aspect of human memory that deals with factual material that is conscious and can be discussed or declared

nondeclarative or implicit memory
memory that tends to be non-conscious or lacks awareness

semantic memory
memory for meaning without reference to the time and place of learning

episodic memory
memory for specific experiences that can be defined in terms of time and space

item-specific implicit memory
unconscious memory from specific events

procedural memory
long-term memory of skills and procedures or how-to-do-it knowledge; a form of implicit memory

There exist various types of memory, as illustrated within the case study. There are also many theories as to the role of memory. How memory functions and which brain structures are involved has been the topic of extensive research. Lezak, Howieson, and Loring (2004) state that despite the plethora of theories about memory stages, there really are only three stores that need to be addressed clinically: sensory memory or registration, short-term or working memory (also termed *intermediate memory*), and long-term memory. Other researchers believe that short-term memory and working memory are not synonymous and that working memory involves more control processes or active involvement (Baddeley, 1992). In a sense, short-term memory is viewed as a passive form of memory, whereas working memory is viewed as an active form. Each of these will be described further. Within the tripartite schema, long-term memory is often divided into two sections termed *declarative* and *nondeclarative* memory. **Declarative** or **explicit memory** is the division that deals with facts and events and is available to consciousness. **Nondeclarative** or **implicit memory** is thought to be unconscious (Squire & Knowlton, 2000). Other researchers, particularly when defining memory difficulties in a clinical sense, further divide declarative memory into **semantic** (fact memory) and **episodic** (personal information) and nondeclarative memory into **item-specific implicit memory** and **procedural memory** (Baddeley, 2002).

There are many other issues that are related to the memory process. Hence, we will be pursuing issues related the stages of memory: encoding, storage, and retrieval. The process through which memories are transferred from short-term or working memory into long-term memory or the storage phase is a major research topic. Another major topic in the field of memory research is the means by which information is retrieved from long-term memory. Finally, difficulties which an individual may suffer with memory include deficits caused by illness or injury and also those that have a psychogenic cause, which is often due to psychological trauma. The case study at the beginning of the chapter includes multiple examples of memory difficulties which will be described throughout the chapter.

SENSORY MEMORY

Sensory memory or **registration** is the first stage of the memory process. It holds a large amount of sensory information for a very brief period, usually thought to be a matter of seconds (Vallar & Papagno, 2002). Some researchers do not refer to this as a stage of memory because it refers to information brought in by the senses and held there until perceptions are formed. In general terminology, the first impression of a stimulus is referred to as **iconic memory** if it is a visual image and **echoic memory** if it is an auditory stimulus. Iconic memory may last up to 200 milliseconds whereas echoic memory may last up to 2,000 milliseconds (Fuster, 1995). This material may then move to working memory.

IMMEDIATE, SHORT-TERM, OR WORKING MEMORY

Short-term or **working memory** holds information received from the senses for a limited amount of time (see Figure 8.1). Lezak et al. (2004) suggests that this can be equated with simple, immediate span of attention. **Immediate memory** has been described as having the capacity of 7 ± 2 U (Miller, 1956). Immediate memory is of sufficient duration to allow a person to respond to ongoing events when more enduring forms of memory have been lost (Talland, 1965). Hence, an individual may suffer from long-term memory difficulties but be capable of remembering a telephone number.

It has often been thought that immediate memory is one system. However, researchers have begun to show that there is more than one system which operates in working memory. Vallar and Papagno (2002) suggest that there exist two subsystems, one termed the **phonological loop** for processing language and the other termed the **visuospatial sketch pad** for visuospatial data. Their research follows the original research of Baddeley and Hitch (1974). Baddeley and Hitch suggested a multicomponent model of working memory which contained two "slave systems," which were responsible for short-term maintenance of information, and a "central executive," which was responsible for supervision of information and the coordination of the slave systems. The slave systems are the aforementioned

sensory memory or registration
the ability to retain impressions of sensory-based information after the original stimulus has ceased

working memory
once referred to as short-term memory, this is the second stage of memory in which several bits of information can be stored for a brief period; it is thought to be more active than passive short-term memory

phonological loop
from Baddeley and Hitch's model of working memory; deals with sound and consists of two parts: short-term phonological storage with auditory memory traces and an articulatory rehearsal component that can review the memory traces

visuospatial sketch pad
a portion of working memory assumed to hold information about what we see and to be the mechanism for the temporary storage and manipulation of spatial and visual information such as shapes, colors, or location of items in space

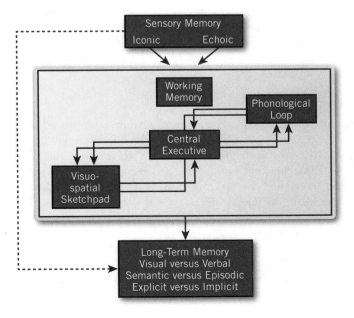

FIGURE 8.1 The working memory model. *Source:* Adapted from Baddeley & Hitch (1974).

phonological loop and the visuospatial sketch pad. Baddeley (2000) has recently included a fourth component to the schema, the **episodic buffer**. This is a temporary and limited capacity storage system which functions to hold and integrate information from different modalities (i.e., visual and auditory) through connection with long-term memory.

In 1949, Hebb in his seminal research stated that immediate memory is maintained in **reverberating neural circuits**, which are described as self-contained networks that sustain a nerve impulse by channeling it repeatedly through the same network. Research following Hebb has supported his original ideas. It appears that information will completely disappear if it is not converted into a stronger biochemical organization that allows it to be placed into long-term memory.

LONG-TERM MEMORY

Long-term memory is actually the acquiring of new information. Some researchers consider that the inclusion of information within long-term memory as synonymous with learning. **Consolidation** is the term used for the process in which information is stored in long-term memory. Consolidation may happen quickly or may take time. It may also happen without active involvement. Before the cognitive revolution in neuroscience beginning in the 1980s, it was assumed that most memory consolidation occurred within 30 minutes. However, with a greater understanding of the biochemical pathways involved with memory consolidation, an exact amount of time cannot be clearly stated and some researchers suggest that two time periods are critical (Igaz, Vianna, Medina, & Izquierdo, 2002). Learning is often thought to involve a more active process than consolidation. However, some **incidental learning** may happen without much effort. Incidental learning could be described as the acquiring of information without conscious thought.

Process of Memory Functioning

SENSORY MEMORY

As stated previously, sensory memory holds sensory impressions, either visual or auditory, for a brief period. Either the information is paid attention to and processed into working memory or it quickly decays. Attention, concentration, and rehearsal appear to be the primary means for information to transfer from sensory memory to working memory.

WORKING MEMORY

Information which is attended to in sensory memory may then move onto working memory. It is from here that a number of processes must come into play for the information to move forward into long-term memory. **Rehearsal** is the mental repetition which causes information to remain in working memory for sufficient time until it may be processed and sent to long-term memory. Information about the brain structures which are most involved with rehearsal comes from lesion experiments on animals and imagery studies with humans. The brain structures (see Figure 8.2) most involved in the rehearsal process or in transferring information from working memory to long-term memory include the prefrontal cortex (Fuster, 1973), the posterior parietal cortex, the thalamus, the caudate, and the globus pallidus (Ashby, Ell, Valentin, & Casale, 2005). The actual process by which the information moves from working memory to long-term memory in the aforementioned areas is through physical changes in the structure of neurons.

episodic buffer
the fourth component to Baddeley's working memory system; a temporary and limited storage system to hold and integrate information from various modalities

consolidation
the process through which information is stored in long-term memory

rehearsal
involves repetition of information which allows it to remain in working memory long enough to be transferred to long-term memory

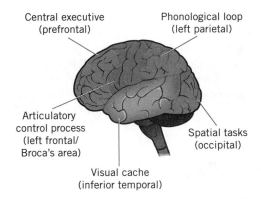

FIGURE 8.2 Brain areas involved in working memory. *Source:* Adapted from Kolb, B., and Whishaw, I.Q. (2003). *Fundamentals of Human Neuropsychology*. New York: Worth Publishers.

LONG-TERM MEMORY

As previously discussed, long-term memory involves consolidation and learning (see Figure 8.3). The individual must turn the very briefly presented information into something which has meaning and enough connections so that it can be retrieved. The brain stores long-term information by growing additional synapses between neurons (Kandel, 2001). Although the brain has approximately 10^{15} synapses, experiments have shown that the cumulative amount of data stored in the brain during an average 70-year life span is only 125 megabytes, much less than the 100 terabytes hypothesized with 10^{15} synapses (Landauer, 1986).

There exist three main interconnected constellations of brain structures that operate in long-term memory. These three memory centers are the medial temporal lobes around the hippocampus, the diencephalon, and the basal forebrain.

The classic case of a man with the initials H. M. should help with the understanding of how various structures affect the memory process. H. M.'s life was almost completely disrupted by serious epileptic seizures. At the hands of surgeon Wilder Penfield, H. M. sustained the bilateral removal of an 8-cm length of the medial temporal lobes. This is an area

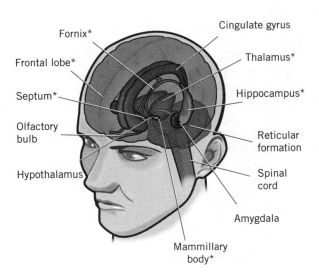

FIGURE 8.3 Diagram of the limbic system and related structures. Areas indicated with an asterisk are known to be associated with memory function.

that is closely connected to the hippocampus. The surgery had no effect on his reasoning ability or his ability to repeat a short series of digits. However, as Brenda Milner (1966) described, H. M. was not able to remember her after she left the room, even though he had spent half of the day with her. If his attention was not on a particular word, he was not able to remember the material. He sustained severe retrograde and anterograde amnesia as a result of the surgery. This was a controversial finding at the time, but many years later Mortimer Mishkin (1978) showed a similar memory deficit in macaque monkeys with bilateral medial temporal lobe lesions.

Retrieval of Information From Long-Term Memory

Once information has been stored in long-term memory, the next objective is to be able to retrieve it when needed. The two major processes to retrieve information involve recall and recognition. The more connections that are able to be formed with the information to be retrieved, the easier it will be for it to be grasped from memory.

recognition
the presentation of cues to help an individual remember

Recognition is often an easier way to obtain information from long-term memory. It involves presenting cues and assuming that these will aid the individual in retrieving the correct information. A multiple-choice exam is an example of a recognition task. A stem or question is posed and several answers are presented. The student is usually able to dismiss half of the answers as not plausible and then work with the remaining using the cues presented by the question to ascertain the correct answer.

recall
retrieval of information from long-term memory without any cues

Recall or free recall is the process in which an individual tries to grasp the information in long-term memory without any cues. An essay test is often thought to be an example of a free recall task.

Difficulties With Memory

AMNESIA

amnesia
total or partial loss of memory that can be associated with brain damage, a dissociative disorder, or hypnosis

The inability to remember certain events or circumstances is termed **amnesia**. Amnesia may be due to an accident such as traumatic brain injury (TBI) or illnesses such as chronic alcoholism. Psychological trauma may also be a cause of amnesia and is apparent in the case study at the beginning of the chapter. Amnesia without any other cognitive deficits is termed **dissociative amnesia** and would be the term used for Joseph's 40-year memory lapse regarding his girlfriend and child.

retrograde amnesia
disorder of memory characterized by an inability to retain old, long-term memories, generally for a specific period extending back from the onset of the disorder

If an individual receives trauma to the brain, memory loss may appear in two forms, which are termed *retrograde* and *anterograde* amnesia. **Retrograde amnesia** relates to memory loss of material learned before the trauma. Dependent on the severity, the individual may lose almost all or some of his declarative memory. The most common pattern is loss of months or years before the trauma but some intact memory for older information.

anterograde amnesia
memory difficulty occurring after some type of trauma where the person loses the ability to learn new material

Anterograde amnesia is the opposite type of memory problem in that it occurs after the trauma. In a very serious situation an individual may be unable to learn any new information. In less serious situations, learning may be slower and require a great deal of repetition.

Most individuals who suffer from brain impairment usually sustain a combination of retrograde and anterograde amnesia. If one were to return to the case study from the first chapter of this text, the man who sustained a car accident would be a classic example of a situation in which both forms of amnesia may have occurred.

Transient global amnesia is a form of amnesia that includes both retrograde and anterograde amnesia factors. It lasts for a much shorter period, anywhere between minutes to days. Causal factors for this form of amnesia could include a concussion from a sports accident or a brief cerebral ischemia. Other causes may include physical or emotional stress, the effects of drugs, cold showers, or sexual activity due to these factors affect cerebral blood flow.

Tests of Memory Impairment

Now that the reader has gained a rudimentary understanding of the types of memory, the processes that occur during encoding, storage, and retrieval, and the various difficulties that occur with memory, it is time to move forward to assessment. All of the psychometric properties described in an earlier chapter apply to memory assessment instruments.

Memory assessment in clinical neuropsychology is often part of a broader or more in-depth assessment. Occasionally, such as in the case study, an individual has circumscribed memory deficits that need to be addressed and assessed. A clinical neuropsychologist has the choice in memory assessment to use a standard memory test battery or an individual test of memory ability. As stated previously all of these tests must be administered in a standardized fashion and the examiner must uphold the ethics of the profession. In addition, the issues related to the testing situation and the personal qualities of the examiner also apply with the goal of assessment always being obtaining the best picture of the client's strengths and weaknesses.

The two most commonly used memory batteries are the Wechsler Memory Scale-IV (WMS-IV; Wechsler, 2008) and the Memory Assessment Scale (MAS; Williams, 1991). Other memory batteries which are not used as frequently in neuropsychology will also be included in this chapter. There are many individual memory scales that may be used to test memory as a solitary deficit or that may be combined into a larger battery.

Before looking at each of the batteries and individual tests of memory abilities, the reader is reminded that record review, evaluation of the referral question, a clinical interview, observation, and discussion with family members are also of great clinical utility. Also, it is critical to note that attention, concentration, and motivation are factors in all forms of memory assessment. Available tests of these attributes will be covered prior to the memory tests section.

Tests of Attention and Concentration

ORIENTATION

Orientation is the ability to be aware of oneself in relationship to the surroundings in which one is located. It requires an individual to maintain attention and have adequate perceptual abilities and memory skills. Difficulties with orientation may be one of the first neuropsychological indicators of brain impairment. Orientation difficulties for time and place are the most common and occur with many types of brain difficulty such as in widespread cortical impairment (i.e., Alzheimer's type dementia) or in more circumscribed lesions to the limbic system (i.e., Korsokoff's psychosis). In juxtaposition, when cognitive difficulties are mild, orientation may remain intact. Hence, while impaired orientation may be strongly suggestive of brain difficulties, good orientation is not an indication of cognitive or attentional competence (Varney & Shephard, 1991).

Questions regarding an individual's orientation to time, place, and person in addition to other personal data are components of all types of mental status examinations. Many individual tests of memory as well as memory test batteries contain questions related to orientation. Hence, there usually is not a section devoted to orientation specifically within a neuropsychological evaluation. There exist a few tests, however, which may be used when the individual's orientation abilities are in question. As the reader peruses the measures of orientation, it will become apparent that very little information is available regarding the reliability and validity of these tests.

AWARENESS INTERVIEW

The Awareness Interview (Anderson & Tranel, 1989) was developed to determine an individual's orientation in various spheres. It is a structured interview (the reader is referred to Chapter 6 for information on structured interviews), which consists of questions pertaining to person, place, time, and the patient's awareness of any difficulties with his motor skills, thinking, speech, and memory. The interview provides a graded scoring schedule for evaluation of overall severity of awareness problems and provides useful wording of the questions neuropsychologists should ask in evaluating orientation and awareness. Lezak et al. (2004) reported that the 3-point ratings for each item could be subjective. However, the authors reported a high ($r = .92$) interrater reliability coefficient (Anderson & Tranel, 1989). High awareness scores correlate with good functioning in activities of daily living (LaBuda & Lichtenberg, 1999).

TEMPORAL ORIENTATION TEST

The Temporal Orientation Test was developed by Benton, Sivan, Hamsher, Varney, and Spreen (1994) to detect any errors in day, month, year, day of the week, and present clock time. It is scored through a system, which differentially weighs errors within each of the five time categories and subtracts the total error score from 100. In the original subject group of 60 patients with brain disease and 110 control subjects, any loss of greater than 5 score points indicated significant temporal disorientation (Eslinger, Damasio, & Benton, 1984). In one study, only 4% of the elderly control subjects (ages 60–88) received an error score greater than 2 (Eslinger, Damasio, Benton, & Van Allen, 1985).

PERSONAL ORIENTATION TEST

The Personal Orientation Test was developed by Semmes, Weinstein, Ghent, and Teuber (1963) and Weinstein (1964) to evaluate a person's ability to deal with personal body parts within space. The test asks the subject to (a) touch parts of his or her body named by the examiner, (b) name parts of his or her body touched by the examiner, (c) touch parts of the examiner's body the examiner names, (d) touch his or her body in imitation of the examiner, and (e) touch his or her body according to numbered schematic diagrams. There is also a sixth test in which the subject is asked to move objects seen and felt.

In a comparison of individuals with left and right hemisphere damage, those patients with left hemisphere damage had greater difficulty following verbal directions. Patients with right hemisphere damage tended to ignore the left side of their body or objects presented to their left side (Raghaven, 1961).

FINGER LOCALIZATION TEST

The Finger Localization Test was developed by Benton et al. (1994) to examine finger agnosia. Deficits with finger recognition may be attributed to many causes. Difficulty with only one hand may reflect a sensory deficit whereas difficulties with both hands more often points toward finger agnosia and may occur with lesions to either side of the brain (Denburg & Tranel, 2003). The Finger Localization Test has three parts consisting of the following: Part A has the patient identify his fingers when touched one at a time by the examiner, Part B shields the hand as the same task is performed, and Part C involves touching two fingers simultaneously. Ten trials are given for each hand for each of the three conditions. According to the test developers, 7–9 errors is considered borderline performance, 10–12 errors is moderately defective, and 13 or more errors is defective.

STANDARDIZED ROAD MAP TEST OF DIRECTION SENSE

This is an easily administered test of right–left orientation developed by Money (1976). The test consists of a practice example followed by the examiner tracing a dotted pathway with a pencil and asking the patient to state the direction, right or left, taken at each turn. Lezak et al. (2004) states that there are no norms available for persons older than 18 years of age; however, a cutoff of 10 errors out of 32 points is recommended regardless of the age. Men perform better than women on this test until the elderly years. Both control and brain-impaired subjects tend to have less than 10 errors, hence more errors is a clear sign of impaired right–left orientation (Vingerhoets, Lannoo, & Bauwens, 1996).

MENTAL REORIENTATION TEST

This test was developed by Ratcliff (1979) to identify difficulties in spatial transformations. Small figures of men are presented in each of four positions and each are shown eight times. The patient's task is to name which of the stimuli's hands holds a black disc. In all subjects, there were fewer errors when the figure was presented in an upright rather than inverted position not dependent on whether the figure was placed facing forward or backward.

FARGO MAP TEST

Difficulty in topographical orientation is the subject of this test developed by Beatty (1988). This test involves knowledge of the map of the United States and other specific areas that the patient may have learned in the past and also gained from living in various areas. The test is designed to measure recent and remote spatial memory and visuospatial orientation. After obtaining personal information from the patient regarding where he or she has lived, he or she then locates from 12–16 designated target items on a map of the United States and 17 regional outline maps. A near correct location receives a score of 1; a less precise approximation earns .5; and a complete failure receives a 0. This test obviously is biased against those who have not lived in the United States or have not studied its geography.

ATTENTION, CONCENTRATION, AND TRACKING

Attention, concentration, and tracking of information are very difficult to separate in a clinical sense. In terms of a definition of these difficulties, attentional problems may surface as distractibility or inability to focus on a topic even though the individual is trying. Good attention is a prerequisite for concentration and mental tracking. Concentration problems may be due to an attentional problem or the inability to maintain focus or both. Mental tracking may be impaired by attentional or concentration difficulties.

Clinical neuropsychologists must focus on an individual's behavior as well as performance on tests to determine whether a difficulty is due to a simple attention problem or a more complex difficulty with concentration or mental tracking.

REACTION TIME

Slowed processing speed often is at the root of attention deficits. Reaction time tests are a means of measuring processing speed and understanding the nature of attention deficits. Reaction time may be slowed by any of the difficulties, which have been covered in chapters 3 and 4. Reaction time may be measured through any of the tasks which have timed components.

VIGILANCE

Vigilance tests measure the ability to sustain and focus attention. Most tests involve stimuli being presented sequentially. The subject is told to respond when a given number or letter, a given stimulus pattern, or an item is presented. The following tests all may be used as measures of vigilance, attention, and concentration. As seen with the tests of awareness, very little psychometric data are available.

CONTINUOUS PERFORMANCE TESTS

There are several forms of the Continuous Performance Test (CPT). Rosvold, Mirsky, Sarason, Bransome, & Beck (1956) developed the CPT-I, and Conners (1992) developed the CPT-II both of which are now administered on a computer (Klecker, 2008). The CPT-II has five versions extant for use with various computer formats. On the CPT-I, random letters of the alphabet appear on the computer screen and the subject is asked to respond when X occurs or when X occurs followed by A. Errors on this test may occur for reasons other than attention difficulties and therefore may not help with sorting out the causes of the difficulty.

On the CPT-II, the subject is to respond every time a letter other than X appears; the test allows for errors of omission and commission, hence, reversing the targets. The CPT-II is also a good measure of the ability to sustain attention as it takes 14 minutes and is a monotonous task. The test measures response speed as well as accuracy of responses. The Conners' version provides normative data for 378 individuals with attention deficit/hyperactivity disorder (ADHD) and 223 adults with neurological impairment. In addition, a sample of 1,920 control subjects is included. The split-half reliability procedure is very difficult to follow and the correlations are nearly impossible to interpret. It is also criticized for allowing the examiner to interrupt the test to answer questions which may invalidate the test (Klecker, 2008).

The third form of the CPT was developed by Cicerone (1997) and is an auditory version. Subjects listen to letters read one per second and respond by tapping their finger when the target letter is produced.

DIGIT SPAN TEST

The Digit Span Test, which is included in the Wechsler Adult Intelligence Scale-IV (Wechsler, 2008), is the format used most often to measure span of immediate auditory memory. The test has seven pairs of random number sequences that are read to the subject and represented in Digits Forward in the forward direction and in reverse order in Digits Backward. The two subtests involve different mental activities and are affected differently by brain damage (Banken, 1985). The psychometrics of this test are included within the section on memory test batteries. Lezak et al. (2004) draw attention to the problem of combining Digits Forward and Digits Backward. There is a potential for significant loss of data because they measure two separate deficits in brain-impaired individuals. Digits Forward measures efficiency of attention or freedom from distractibility and less of what is usually considered memory. Digits Backward is a task that measures mental tracking or the ability to hold information in the mind while performing a mental operation.

KNOX CUBE TEST–REVISED

This test was originally developed in 1915 to evaluate mental impairment of immigrants. It is a test of visual forward span originally included within the Arthur Point Scales of Performance Battery (Arthur, 1947). The Knox Cube Test–Revised (KCT-R) in its most recent revision (Stone, 2002) is designed to measure attention span and short-term memory. This task was designed to eliminate the use of words and their ability to detract from the underlying knowledge of the subject. The subject uses a 1-in. cube to duplicate the examiner's demonstration of increasingly complex and larger series of taps on four 1-in. cubes fastened to a wooden base.

The psychometrics of this test are poor as is the standardization sample. Reviewers also take issue with the authors stating that it is a test of short-term memory when it clearly tests visual or visuospatial memory (Callahan, 2005).

TEST OF VARIABLES OF ATTENTION

The Test of Variables of Attention (TOVA) is a computerized continuous performance test (CPT) using visual and auditory stimuli to assess attention. It was originally known as the Minnesota Computer Assessment (Greenberg, 1985). There are several versions: a visual CPT (TOVA), an auditory CPT (TOVA-A), and a screening or preschool version, which is part of the standard TPVA (Greenberg, 1988–2000). This test has multiple diagnostic uses in addition to separating attention versus memory problems. The test is most often used to assess ADHD.

The test takes 21.6 minutes to complete with one stimulus presented for 100 milliseconds every 2 seconds. Responses, nonresponses, and reaction time are automatically recorded. The TOVA was normed on 1,596 people ranging in age from 4–80 years old, 99% of whom were Caucasian and all from Minnesota, which restricts generalizations to racial/ethnic minorities. The test–retest reliability information is minimal. The test appears to be face valid but contains little information regarding content validity (Loew, Whiston, & Kane, 2001).

VIGIL CONTINUOUS PERFORMANCE TEST

The Vigil Continuous Performance Test was developed to measure a person's ability to concentrate on a single or relatively complex task over time (Rosvold, 1956). The Vigil is a proprietary version of the CPT developed by Rosvold. The Vigil is similar to other continuous performance tests in that the subject is to respond when the target letter *K* appears on the computer screen. A second condition has the subject respond only when *K* is preceded by *A*. The Vigil produces hit rates, false alarm rates, errors of commission, errors of omission, and perseverations.

The Vigil was standardized on 324 individuals between the ages of 6 and 90. The sample was very poorly described in the manual. Reliability and validity are equally poor and make it difficult for the test user to make adequate comparisons between subject and norm groups (Kush, 2005).

PACED AUDITORY SERIAL ADDITION TEST

This test was developed by Gronwall (1977) as a measure of central information processing similar to tasks of reaction time and divided attention. The test has several versions, and in each, the number of items is different. There is also a children's version. In general, the test asks the subject to add 60 pairs of randomized digits so that each is added to the digit immediately preceding it. The interstimulus interval changes at the end of each trial. The Paced Auditory Serial Addition Test (PASAT) thus incrementally increases processing demands over trials by increasing the speed of stimulus input and decreasing the available response time. The task is presented on tape or computer; therefore, the subject must keep pace with the tape or computer in addition to doing the tasks. Most subjects, whether they are controls or brain impaired, find this task to be very stressful. The PASAT has a long history as a measure of processing speed, divided attention, and working memory and it has been proven sensitive to various neurocognitive deficits. The test has multiple versions with multiple modality types, number of items per trial, interstimulus intervals, and digit item lists. There are also multiple normative databases available. Strauss, Sherman, and Spreen (2006) suggest that the PASAT-200, PASAT-100, and PASAT-50 created by Diehr et al. (Diehr, Heaton, Miller, & Grant, 1998; Diehr et al., 2003) have the most impressive databases available due to their ability to adjust for demographic variation. A negative comment on the test is that it requires the patient to have a command of mathematics, which may also imply higher education, which may exclude many individuals who could benefit from the test.

Tests of Short-Term or Working Memory and Long-Term Memory

Now that we have reviewed tests of orientation, attention, mental tracking, and the reader understands the necessity for separating difficulties within these modalities from memory deficits, we will move on to tests designed specifically to measure short-term or working memory and tests to measure long-term memory. There are many tests available which purport to test memory abilities.

Lezak et al. (2004) in their extensive review of neuropsychological tests state that an adequate assessment of memory includes all of the following: (a) orientation to time and place, (b) prose recall to examine learning and retention of meaningful information, (c) rote learning, (d) visuospatial memory, (e) remote memory, and (f) personal or autobiographical information. They also state that tests designed to measure learning should include one or more trials following a delay period including distraction tasks to prevent rehearsal. Finally, they suggest that when assessing memory the examiner should also compare aspects of cognition that are not heavily dependent on memory with memory performance. In order to assess all of the aforementioned types of memory it is often necessary to employ more than one test or to use a battery. However, as each individual to be assessed and the referral question for him or her is different, this must be kept in mind as the clinical neuropsychologist chooses a form of assessment. In addition, not all tests are as commonly used, and those that are used less often may contain less information regarding deficit patterns of individuals with various forms of memory problems. Finally, as stated earlier, some tests are more psychometrically sound and the clinical neuropsychologist must weigh that against the referral question.

Individual Tests of Long-Term Memory

VERBAL AUTOMATISMS

As Lezak et al. (2004) states, material learned by rote in early childhood and frequently used throughout life is normally recalled so effortlessly that it is termed an **automatism**. Tests that measure automatisms do not exist, but the neuropsychologist may assess this by asking the patient to repeat the alphabet, the days of the week, or other well-known and used lists. More than a single error often indicates brain dysfunction.

REY AUDITORY VERBAL LEARNING TEST

The Rey Auditory Verbal Learning Test (RAVLT), also referred to as the Auditory Verbal Learning Test, was developed by Rey (1964) in France. It is a brief pencil and paper test that measures immediate memory span, new learning, susceptibility to interference, and recognition memory. It has been translated into English and four other languages. It is not possible to purchase the test, but a manual is available from Western Psychological Services, which describes and gives psychometric data from numerous studies (Schmidt, 1996).

The test consists of a list of 15 nouns (List A) that are read aloud for five consecutive trials with each trial being followed by free recall of the words. After List A, a second list (List B) is presented for interference. Next, a delayed recall of List A is tested and then at 20 minutes another delay test is administered. Finally, a story that uses words from List A is presented orally or in written form, and the subject must recognize words from List A. The score of each trial is the number of items correctly recalled. Scores for Trials 1–5 may be used to show a learning curve. Also available are words recalled immediately after interference, at 20-minute delay, and words recognized from the story. Geffen, Hoar, O'Hanlon, Clark, & Geffen (1990) have also calculated other memory indices, which may be helpful to examine memory function.

Reliability and validity estimates are listed in the test manual based on various studies conducted with different sample groups. Test–retest reliability estimates range from .12–.86 and the test–retest intervals ranged from 6 days to 3 years (Mackler & Schmidt, 1996).

Norms have also been drawn from several studies and are therefore not straightforward. The clinical neuropsychologist needs to match the individual tested as closely as possible to the most appropriate norm group. Strauss et al. (2006) in their review state that RAVLT scores decrease with advancing age, recall is better with higher

IQ levels, and females outperform males on the recall but not the recognition trials. They also suggest that data for subjects grouped by age, sex, and intellectual level need to be gathered.

CALIFORNIA VERBAL LEARNING TEST II

The California Verbal Learning Test II (CVLT-II) is the second revision (2000) of an individually administered test of strategies and processes involved in learning and remembering information (Delis, Kramer, Kaplan, & Ober, 2000). This test is similar to the RAVLT in that it involves retention of word lists but reviewers have stated that the presentation of information in the CVLT-II is much better and the psychometrics are definitely much better.

There are three forms of the CVLT-II and the directions are the same for each form. The test contains two lists of 16 words each from four categories (e.g., furniture, vegetables, ways of traveling, and animals). List A is the primary list and List B is an interference task. These two forms consist of five immediate free recall trials of List A, an immediate free recall trail of List B, short delay free and cued recall trails of List A, long delay free and cued recall of List A, long delay yes–no recognition trial of List A, and an optional long delay forced-choice recognition trail of List A (Hubley, 2005).

The CVLT-II can be scored by hand or computer; however, the computer is able to generate a tremendous number of scores. Raw and standardized scores are available for 27 commonly used measures in the Core Report, 66 measures in the Expanded Report, and more than 260 measures in the Research Report. The standardization sample consists of 1,087 adults (565 females, 522 males) ages 16–89 who were matched to the March 1999 U.S. Census demographics. It is a much better sample than in the original version as discussed by Elwood (1995). Estimates for internal consistency are higher than .80. Criticism has been raised about the stability estimates because the retest interval ranged from 9–49 days and the correlations between the forms were no higher than .79. The key strength of the test is that it allows the learning and remembering of a word list that uses categories and incorporates an interference task. The CVLT/CVLT-II is among the top three memory assessment instruments used by neuropsychologists (Rabin, Barr, & Burton, 2005).

REY COMPLEX FIGURE TEST AND RECOGNITION TRIAL (RCFT) (MEYERS VERSION)

The original Rey-Osterrieth Complex Figure Test was designed as a measure of visuospatial constructional ability and visual memory. The Meyers and Meyers (1995) version has the same intention but includes a recognition trial and more complete psychometrics.

The original Rey Complex Figure Test (Rey, 1941) and the Rey-Osterrieth Complex Figure Test, which came after it, have a 60-year history. In that amount of time, the figure to be copied has been somewhat distorted and at one point interspersed with a figure designed by Taylor (1969). Also, the reliability and validity has been suspect because there are many ways in which the test was administered, all without informing the subject of a recall component and varying in the amount of time between initial presentation and recall.

The Meyers and Meyers (1995b) version includes the original Rey design. The subject copies the design from the model presented without being told of a recall component. It is then redrawn after a 3-minute delay and a 30-minute delay. In the recognition trial the correct design elements are selected from a group of options. The norms for the test were composed of 601 subjects screened for learning disabilities, substance abuse, psychiatric disorders, and depression. The age range was from 18–89 years. Interrater reliability ranged from .93–.97. Convergent and discriminant validity were highly correlated at .881 (Meyers & Meyers, 1995a).

BENTON VISUAL RETENTION TEST, FIFTH EDITION

This is the fifth edition of the Benton Visual Retention Test (BVRT) and is designed to be a brief measure of visuospatial perception, construction, and memory (Sivan, 1992). There are four methods of administration for this test, three in a drawing mode, and one in a multiple-choice format. In the drawing administrations A and B, the subject views each design for 10 seconds (A) or 5 seconds (B) before drawing it on his own. In D, a 15-second delay is employed before the subject reproduces the design. C is a simple copy trial. Scoring is not complicated. The Number Correct score is the number of the 10 designs, which are either correct or incorrect. The Number Error score is the total number of errors and their type. The errors may include omissions, distortions, perseverations, rotations, misplacements, and size errors. Interscorer reliability in total scores on administration is .90–.97 for the correct number and .94–.98 for Number Error score. There is no information in the manual regarding test–retest reliability. In the multiple-choice format, the subject is shown each of 15 cards, which display one to three geometric figures for 10 seconds. After each exposure, the subject is shown a multiple-choice card with a form similar in structure that the subject must choose verbally or by pointing as having been in the original presentation. Scoring procedures allow for both a quantitative and qualitative analysis of the subject's ability.

Memory Assessment Batteries

WECHSLER MEMORY SCALE-IV

The WMS-IV is the memory battery used most frequently by clinical neuropsychologists to develop a basic picture of the memory strengths and weaknesses of the client. It is the fourth revision of the WMS. Many changes are apparent within the WMS-IV, which the technical manual describes in detail with reference to current research. The WMS-IV was designed in collaboration with the Wechsler Adult Intelligence Scale-IV (WAIS-IV) and it is assumed that both tests will be used in the same assessment. Hence, the test preparers have devoted considerable space in their technical manual to the interpretation of differences between WMS-IV and WAIS-IV scores. This procedure was most likely the result of feedback that a plethora of professionals had become familiar with the use of WMS-III and WAIS-III discrepancies as diagnostic indicators.

In its development, the WMS-IV has been designed to measure different memory functions, similar to the changes in the WAIS-IV from the WAIS-III. The updated version includes demographically adjusted norms, additional subtests for neurological and older adult assessment, and measures of independent living. The WMS-IV intends to reduce testing time for older adults, decrease confounding factors by using contrast scores to partial out confounding cognitive effects, improve the assessment of working memory by focusing on visual working memory creating subtests with minimal verbalization, and eliminate subtest overlap with the WAIS-IV. The difficulty level was also increased for the younger age groups.

Four subtests were added to the WMS-IV. They include Spatial Addition, Symbol Span, Design Memory, and the Brief Cognitive Status Exam. The Brief Cognitive

Status Exam is used as a preliminary assessment for cognitive impairment. It includes Temporal Orientation, Mental Control, Clock Drawing, Memory, Inhibitory Control, and Verbal Productivity.

Design Memory replaces Family Pictures and Faces. This test is developed to differentiate visual spatial from visual details. The Spatial Addition was developed as a measure of spatial working memory, requiring both storage and manipulation of visual spatial information. It was developed to replace the Spatial Scan subtest. The Symbol Span subtest was developed as a visual analog to the Digit Span subtest. The symbols are visualized rather than being read verbally from the page.

Modifications were made to three existing subtests: Logical Memory, Verbal Paired Associates, and Visual Reproduction. The Logical Memory has scaled scores for Immediate Memory and Delayed Memory, and Delayed Recognition is scored as a cumulative percentage. The contrast scores are Immediate versus Delayed and Recognition versus Delayed.

The Verbal Paired Associates added easier items and added a free recall condition after the recognition trial. Immediate Learning, Delayed, and Delayed Free Recall are all scaled scores, whereas the Delayed Recognition is scored as a cumulative percentage. Again, the scores are contrasted by Immediate versus Delayed and Recognition versus Delayed.

The Visual Reproduction subtest uses the same five items as in the WMS-III, but new scoring rules allow for faster and easier recording and reduces guessing. Immediate Recall and Delayed Recall are scaled scores, and the Delayed Recognition is a cumulative percentage. Contrast scores include Immediate versus Delayed, Delayed Recognition versus Delayed, and Copy versus Immediate.

Eight subtests were eliminated: Information and Orientation, Spatial Span, Mental Control, Faces, Digit Span, Family Pictures, Letter–Number Sequencing, and Word List. Digit Span and Letter–Number Sequencing already appear in the WAIS-IV, and the Mental Control and Information and Orientation subtests were incorporated into the Brief Cognitive Status Exam subtest.

An individual's performance is reported on five index scores: Auditory Memory, Visual Memory, Visual Working Memory, Immediate Memory, and Delayed Memory. These index scores are then contrasted: Immediate versus Delayed, Auditory Memory versus Visual Memory, Visual Working Memory versus WAIS-IV Working Memory, Auditory Memory versus WAIS IV Working Memory. The WAIS-IV General Ability Index is also contrasted to each of the WMS-IV five index scores.

Scores are now derived for the Older Adult Battery (ages 65–90) and Adult Battery (ages 16–69). The Older Adult Battery has fewer subtests and they are shortened. Classification tables translate the total scores into Average, Low, Moderately Low, and Very Low. The WMS-IV normative sample was $N = 1,400$; 100 participants per every age for ages 16–69; and 100 participants per every age for ages 65–90. The sample stratification accounted for gender, education level, ethnicity, and region.

MEMORY ASSESSMENT SCALE

The MAS was developed in 1991 by Williams. It is an individually administered battery of tasks, which assesses three areas of cognitive functioning: (a) attention, concentration, and short-term memory; (b) learning and immediate memory; and (c) memory following a delay (MAS, p. 3). Within each area, verbal and nonverbal tasks are used to measure material specific (verbal versus visuospatial) memory abilities. The tests employ both recall and recognition formats. This test is often seen as an alternative to the WMS-IV based on the needs of the client, the referral question, and theoretical orientation of the neuropsychologist.

The MAS was developed through research on amnesic disorders. It was also responding to the practical limitations placed on the clinical neuropsychologist and is designed to be completed in 1 hour. The MAS is composed of 12 subtests based on seven memory tasks. Five of the subtests measure memory functioning after brief or extended delay. The MAS subtests in order include: (a) List Learning, (b) Prose Memory, (c) List Recall, (d) Verbal Span, (e) Visual Span, (f) Visual Recognition, (g) Visual Reproduction, (h) Names-Faces, (i) Delayed List Recall, (j) Delayed Prose Meaning, (k) Delayed Visual Recognition, and (l) Delayed Names-Faces Recall.

The manual includes detailed scoring instructions. Raw scores are converted to standard scores with a mean of 10 and a standard deviation of 3. The MAS gives three scoring scales: Short-Term Memory, Verbal Memory, and Visual Memory. A Global Memory Scale score is computed from the Verbal and Visual Memory Scoring scores. Considering the changes in the Wechsler scales reflecting new and increased understanding of memory functioning, these scales may be somewhat out-of-date.

The MAS is normed on 843 adults, ages 18–90 years without neurological difficulties and based on the prospective U.S. census of 1995 demographics. Test–retest reliability was estimated using generalizability theory, similar to the Wechsler. Generalizability coefficients for the subtests range from .70–.95. Validity estimates appear to be adequate but reflect a very small sample size.

RIVERMEAD BEHAVIORAL MEMORY TEST (SECOND EDITION)

Wilson, Cockburn, and Baddeley (2003) developed the Rivermead Behavioral Memory Test (RBMT) is an attempt to evaluate memory as it is used in day-to-day life. Hence, this test is atheoretical and based on tasks that an individual would need to accomplish in the real world. The test has 12 tasks that are similar to everyday situations. The tasks include remembering a person's first and last name, recalling a hidden belonging, remembering an appointment, face recognition, remembering a short story, picture recognition, remembering a new route, delivering a message, and answering orientation questions. Remembering a short story and a new route have immediate and delayed recall tasks.

The RBMT has four parallel forms with relatively high correlations between them except for Form D (Paolo, 2001). The age range in which norms are available between 11 and 94 and there is a children's version for use between 5 and 10 years old. The standardization sample consisted of 188 healthy people ages 16–69 and 176 brain-impaired individuals. The correlations with other tests of memory suggest that it measures what it purports to measure. Evaluations of the test suggest that it has good ecological validity and is a good addition to the more standard memory tests.

LEARNING AND MEMORY BATTERY

Tombaugh and Schmidt (1992) developed this memory battery within an information-processing framework. The choice of subtests was based on the research literature of which memory functions were anatomically and functionally distinct as well as clinically useful. Many of the subtests were derived from already existing memory tests.

The tests consist of seven subtests, three of which are verbal (Paragraph Learning, Word List, and Word Pass), two are numerical (Digit Span and Super Span Digit) and two are visual (Simple and Complex Figures). The administration time can be as long as 90 minutes; however, each individual subtest may be given separately and produces normative data.

The normative sample included 480 individuals ages 20–79 with no neurological disease or trauma. Subtest reliabilities obtained through coefficient alpha range from .62–.95. Subtest reliabilities obtained through split-half coefficients ranged from .76–.96. To assess concurrent validity, the Learning and Memory Battery (LAMB) was compared to other memory assessment tests and was only mildly successful (.17–.59; Long & van Gorp, 1996).

As we return to Joseph, it was clear that he needed a memory evaluation to begin work toward understanding his short- and long-term memory deficits. Many of the tests evaluated could suffice in determining that he has difficulty with attention and concentration, possibly caused by anxiety, which was impeding his ability to retain information. A more thorough memory evaluation using the WMS-IV and the WAIS-IV gave an indication of the extent of his memory deficits. Compared to his overall Full Scale IQ (FSIQ), which fell within the average range, his memory scores were much lower. A program of memory rehabilitation was begun with the aid of the clinical neuropsychologist. He also began to pursue the psychological factors related to the long-term memory loss of information related to his previous girlfriend and son. Through many therapy sessions, he began to understand that the shame and guilt he felt and that these emotions were strong enough to cause him to try to actively forget the situation. Active forgetting caused him to not form good connections to the information as it was being consolidated. However, with the introduction of various cues provided by others who were involved in his life at the time, he has begun to remember more details even though they cause him to feel shame and remorse over his actions.

Summary

The chapter begins with a complex case study describing two types of memory deficits, short-term memory and a 40-year memory gap for personal information. Following the case study is a review of the types of memory: sensory memory, short-term or working memory and long-term memory, and three stages of memory: encoding, storage, and retrieval. The current understanding of the structures involved with each type of memory is the next topic covered. The memory components are followed by an introduction to memory deficits such as the various forms of amnesia. The testing section begins with tests of attention, concentration, and mental tracking, which are often evaluated when memory impairment is suspected. It is important to distinguish between any of the deficits and various forms of memory difficulties. The remainder of the chapter involves a discussion of the individual tests of memory and memory test batteries. The conclusion of the chapter is a positive outcome for the individual in the case study.

Questions for Further Study

1. Explain the issues within the field of neuropsychology regarding the differences between short-term and working memory.
2. In a case of brain injury or illness, which type or types of tests should be given first: measures of attention, concentration, or memory?
3. The WMS-IV is designed to be used in conjunction with the WAIS-IV. Does this cause any concern for the neuropsychologist?

References

Anderson, S. W., & Tranel, D. (1989). Awareness of disease states following cerebral infarction, dementia, and head trauma: Standardized assessment. *The Clinical Neuropsychologist, 3,* 327–339.

Arthur, G. (1947). *A point scale of performance tests* (Rev. Form II). New York: Psychological Corporation.

Ashby, F. G., Ell, S. W., Valentin, V. V., & Casale, M. B. (2005). FROST: A distributed neurocomputational model of working memory maintenance. *Journal of Cognitive Neuroscience, 17*(11), 1728–1743.

Atkinson, R. C., & Shiffrin, R. M. (1968). Human memory: A proposed system and its control processes. In K. W. Spence & J. T. Spence (Eds.), *The psychology of learning and memory advances in research and theory* (Vol. 2, pp. 82–89). New York: Academic Press.

Baddeley, A. D. (1992). Working memory. *Science, 255,* 556–559.

Baddeley, A. D. (2000). The episodic buffer: A new component of working memory? *Trends in Cognitive Sciences, 4,* 417–423.

Baddeley, A. D. (Ed.). (2002). The psychology of memory. In M. D. Kopelma & B. A. Wilson (Eds.), *The handbook of memory disorders.* Chichester, UK: John Wiley & Sons, Inc.

Baddeley, A. D., & Hitch, G. J. (1974). Working memory. In G. A. Bower (Ed.), *The psychology of learning and motivation: Advances in research and theory* (Vol. 8, pp. 47–89). New York: Academic Press.

Banken, J. A. (1985). Clinical utility of considering digits forward and digits backward as separate components of the Wechsler Adult Intelligence Scale-Revised. *Journal of Clinical Psychology, 41,* 686–691.

Beatty, W. W. (1988). The fargo map test: A standardized method for assessing remote memory for visuospatial information. *Journal of Clinical Psychology, 44*(1), 61–67.

Benton, A. L., Sivan, A. B., Hamsher, K., Varney, N. R., & Spreen, O. (1994). *Contributions to neuropsychological assessment. A clinical manual* (2nd ed.). New York: Oxford University Press.

Callahan, C. M. (2005). Review of the Knox Cube Test, Revised. In R. A. Spies & B. S. Plake (Eds.), *The sixteenth mental measurements yearbook.* Lincoln, NE: Buros Institute of Mental Measurements.

Cicerone, K. D. (1997). Clinical sensitivity of four measures of attention to mild traumatic brain injury. *The Clinical Neuropsychologist, 11,* 266–272.

Conners, C. K. (1992). *Conners' Continuous Performance Test.* Toronto, OH: Multi-Health Systems.

Denburg, N. L., & Tranel, D. (2003). Acalculia and disturbances of body schema. In K. M. Heilman & E. Valenstein (Eds.), *Clinical neuropsychology* (4th ed, pp. 161–184.). New York: Oxford University Press.

Delis, D. C., Kramer, J. H., Kaplan, E., & Ober, B. A. (2000). *California Verbal Learning Test (CVLT-II)* (2nd ed.). San Antonio, TX: Psychologist Corporation.

Diehr, M. C., Cherner, M., Wolfson, T. J., Miller, S. W., Grant, I., Heaton, R. K., et al. (2003). The 50 and 100 item short forms of the Paced Auditory Serial Addition Task (PASAT): Demographically corrected norms and comparisons with the full PASAT in normal and clinical samples. *Journal of Clinical and Experimental Neuropsychology, 25*(4), 571–585.

Diehr, M. C., Heaton, R. K., Miller, W., & Grant, I. (1998). The Paced Auditory Serial Addition Task (PASAT): Norms for age, education, and ethnicity. *Assessment, 5*(4), 375–387.

Elwood, R. W. (1995). The California Verbal Learning Test: Psychometric characteristics and clinical application. *Neuropsychology Review, 5,* 173–201.

Eslinger, P. J., Damasio, A. R., & Benton, A. L. (1984). *The Iowa Screening Battery for Mental Decline.* Iowa City: University of Iowa.

Eslinger, P. J., Damasio, A. R., Benton, A. L., & Van Allen, M. (1985). Neuropsychological detection of abnormal mental decline in older persons. *Journal of the American Medical Association, 253*(5), 670–674.

Fuster, J. M. (1973). Unit-activity in prefrontal cortex during delayed-response performance neuronal correlates of transient memory. *Journal of Neuropsychology, 36,* 61–78.

Fuster, J. M. (1995). *Memory in the cerebral cortex: An empirical approach to neural networks in human and non-human primates.* Cambridge, MA: MIT Press.

Geffen, G., Hoar, K. J., O'Hanlon, A. P., Clark, C. R., & Geffen, L. B. (1990). Performance measures of 16 to 86-year-old males and females on the Auditory Verbal Learning Test. *Clinical Neuropsychologist, 4,* 45–63.

Greenberg, L. M. (1985). Minnesota Computer Assessment Manual. Minneapolis, MN: University of Minnesota Press.

Greenberg, L. M. (1988–2000). TOVA Continuous Performance Test. Los Alamitos, CA: Universal Attention Disorders.

Gronwall, D. M. A. (1977). Paced Auditory Serial-Addition Task: A measure of recovery from concussion. *Perceptual and Motor Skills, 44,* 367–373.

Hebb, D. O. (1949). *The organization of behavior.* New York: John Wiley & Sons, Inc.

Hubley, A. M. (2005). [Review of the California Verbal Learning Test II (CVLT-II)]. In R. A. Spies & B. S. Plake (Eds.), *The Sixteenth mental measurements yearbook.* Lincoln, NE: Buros Institute of Mental Measurements.

Igaz, L. M., Vianna, M. R., Medina, J. H., & Izquierdo, I. (2002). Two time periods of hippocampal mRNA synthesis are required for memory consolidation of fear-motivated learning. *Journal of Neuroscience, 22*(15), 6781–6789.

Kandel, E. R. (2001). The molecular biology of memory storage: A dialogue between gene and synapses. *Science, 294*(5544), 1030–1038.

Klecker, B. M. (2008). Conners' Continuous Performance Test II. In B. S. Plake, J. C. Impara, & R. A. Spies (Eds.), *The mental measurements yearbook database.* Lincoln, NE: The Buros Institute of Mental Measurement.

Kush, J. C. (2005). Vigil Continuous Performance Test. In R. A. Spies & B. S. Plake (Eds.), *The sixteenth mental measurements yearbook* [Electronic version]. Retrieved December 20, 2009, from the Buros Institute's Test Reviews Online Web site: http://www.unl.edu/buros

LaBuda, J., & Lichtenberg, P. (1999). The role of cognition, depression, and awareness of deficit in predicting geriatric rehabilitation patients IADL performance. *The Clinical Neuropsychologist, 13,* 258–267.

Landauer, T. K. (1986). How much do people remember? Some estimates of the quality of learned information in long-term memory. *Cognitive Science: A Multidiscipline Journal, 10,* 477–493.

Lezak, M. D., Howieson, D. B., & Loring, D. W. (2004). Neuropsychological Assessment (4th ed.). New York: Oxford University Press.

Loew, S., Whiston, S. C., & Kane, H. (2001). [Review of Test of Variables of Attention]. In B. S. Plake, J. C. Impara, & R. A. Spies (Eds.), *The fourteenth mental measurement yearbook.* Lincoln, NE: Buros Institute of Mental Measurements.

Long, C. J., & van Gorp, W. G. (1996) [Review of Learning and Memory Battery]. In B. S. Plake, J. C. Impara, & R. A. Spies (Eds.), *The fourteenth mental measurements yearbook.* Lincoln, NE: Buros Institute of Mental Measurements.

Mackler, K., & Schmidt, M. (1996). [Review of Rey Auditory Verbal Learning Test]. In B. S. Plake, J. C. Impara, & R. A. Spies (Eds.), *The fourteenth mental measurements yearbook.* Lincoln, NE: Buros Institute of Mental Measurements.

Meyers, J., & Meyers, K. (1995a). *Manual for Rey Complex Figure Test and Recognition Trial.* Odessa, FL: Psychological Assessment Resources.

Meyers, J., & Meyers, K. (1995b). *Rey Complex Figure Test and Recognition Trial.* Odessa, FL: Psychological Assessment Resources.

Miller, G. A. (1956). The magical number seven, plus or minus two: Some limits on our capacity for processing information. *Psychological Review, 63,* 81–97.

Milner, B. (1966). Amnesia following operation on the temporal lobes. In C. W. M. Whitley & O. L. Zangwill (Eds.), *Amnesia.* (pp. 109–133) London, UK: Butterworths.

Mishkin, M. (1978). Memory in monkeys severely impaired by combined but not separate removal of the amygdala and hippocampus. *Nature, 273*(5660), 297–298.

Money, J. (1976). *A standardized road map test of direction sense. Manual.* San Rafael, CA: Academic Therapy Publications.

Paolo, A. M. (2001). The Rivermead Behavioural Memory Test. In B. S. Plake & J. C. Impara (Eds.), *The fourteenth mental measurements yearbook* (pp.). Lincoln, NE: Buros Institute of Mental Measurement.

Rabin, L. A., Barr, W. B., & Burton, L. A. (2005), Assessment practices of clinical neuropsychologists in the United States and Canada: A survey of INS, NAN, and APA Division 40 members. *Archives of Clinical Neuropsychology, 20,* 33–66.

Raghaven, S. (1961). *A comparison of the performance of right and left hemispheres on verbal and nonverbal body image tasks.* Northhampton, MA: Smith College Thesis.

Ratcliff, G. (1979). Spatial thought, mental rotation and the right cerebral hemisphere. *Neuropsychologia, 17,* 49–54.

Rey, A. (1941). L'examen psychologique dans les cas d'encephalopathie traumatique [The psychological examination in cases of traumatic encephalopathy]. *Archieves de Psychologic, 28,* 286–340.

Rey, A. (1964). *L'examen clinique en psychologie* [Clinical psychology]. Paris: Presses Universitaires de France.

Rosvold, H. E., Mirsky, A. F., Sarason, I., Bransome, E. D., & Beck, L. H. (1956). A continuous test of brain damage. *Journal of Consulting Psychology, 41,* 521–527.

Schmidt, M. (1996). *Rey Auditory Verbal Learning Test. A handbook.* Los Angeles: Western Psychological Services.

Semmes, J., Weinstein, S., Ghent, L., & Teuber, H. L. (1963). Correlates of impaired orientation in personal and extrapersonal space. *Brain, 86,* 747–772.

Sivan, A. B. (1992). *Benton Visual Retention Test* (5th ed.). San Antonio, TX: Psychological Corporation.

Strauss, E., Sherman, E., & Spreen, O. (2006). *A compendium of neuropsychological tests: Administration, norms and commentary* (3rd ed.). New York: Oxford University Press.

Squire, L. R. (1987). *Memory and brain.* New York: Oxford University Press.

Squire, L. R., Knowlton, B. S. (2000). The medial temporal lobe, the hippocampus, and the memory systems in the brain. In M. S. Gazzaniga (Ed.), *The new cognitive neurosciences* (2nd ed.). Cambridge, MA: MIT Press.

Stone, M. (2002). *Knox's Cube Test, revised.* Wood Dale, IL: Stoelting Co.

Talland, G. A. (1965). *Deranged memory.* New York: Academic Press.

Taylor, L. B. (1969). Localization of cerebral lesions by psychological testing. *Clinical Neurosurgery, 16,* 269–287.

Tombaugh, T. N., & Schmidt, J. P. (1992). The Learning and Memory Battery (LAMB): Development and standardization. *Psychological Assessment, 4,* 193–206.

Vallar, G., & Papagno, C. (2002). Neuropsychological impairments in short-term memory. In A. D. Baddeley, M. D. Kopelma, & B. A. Wilson (Eds.), *Handbook of memory disorders* (2nd ed., pp. 249–270). Chichester, UK: John Wiley & Sons, Inc.

Varney, N. R., & Shephard, J. S. (1991). Predicting short-term memory on the basis of temporal orientation. *Neuropsychology, 5,* 13–17.

Vingerhoets, G., Lannoo, E., & Bauwens, S. (1996). Analysis of the Money Road-Map Test performance in normal and brain-damaged subjects. *Archives of Clinical Neuropsychology, 11,* 1–9.

Wechsler, D. (2008). *Wechsler Memory Scale, manual* (4th ed.). San Antonio, TX: The Psychological Corporation.

Weinstein, S. (1964). Deficits concommittant with aphasia or lesions of either cerebral hemisphere. *Cortex, 1,* 154–169.

Williams, J. M. (1991). *Memory Assessment Scales.* Odessa, FL: Psychological Assessment Resources.

Wilson, B. A., Cockburn, J., & Baddeley, A. (2003). *The Rivermead Behavioral Memory Test-II.* Bury St. Edmunds, UK: Thames Valley Test.

Neuropsychological Test Batteries

9

Learning Objectives

After reading this chapter, the student should be able to understand:

- The characteristics and components of the Halstead-Reitan Neuropsychological Test Battery
- The characteristics and components of other neuropsychological batteries including Luria's Neuropsychological Investigation, the Luria-Nebraska Neuropsychological Battery, the Boston Process Approach, the Kaplan Baycrest Neurocognitive Assessment, the Delis-Kaplan Executive Function System, the Neuropsychological Assessment Battery, and the Dean-Woodcock Neuropsychological Battery
- The characteristics of fixed, flexible, and process-oriented neuropsychological batteries
- The field of forensic clinical neuropsychology

Amanda was referred for a neuropsychological evaluation by her primary care physician. She went to her doctor because she felt she needed to be treated for depression. She had been experiencing multiple and varied symptoms for the past several months. After speaking with her doctor it surfaced that she was having anger outbursts, anxiety attacks, trouble sleeping at times, feeling excessively tired, and being more sexually active than she was previously. Knowing that Amanda had been in a motor vehicle accident 6 months prior to the current visit, the physician suggested that she may be experiencing difficulties related to the accident.

Amanda is presently 19 years old. She is the older of two children born to her biological parents. Her brother is 17. Their parents were divorced when the children were very young. Both Amanda and her brother have good relationships with their father, stepmother, and stepsiblings who all reside approximately 150 miles away. Their mother is also remarried and Amanda's brother lives with them while finishing high school. Amanda was in the process of moving out of the family home when she was in the motor vehicle accident. At present she has an apartment but is not comfortable alone all of the time. Her mother also feels that she may be overspending and not be able to pay her rent or other bills. Amanda is currently attending the local community college and is unsure regarding her choice of major. At this time she describes her grades as "poor."

Amanda had what she described as a "normal" childhood considering the divorce of her parents. She did not feel that either parent tried to sabotage the relationship that she and her brother had with the other. She was an average student throughout elementary and secondary school. She liked athletics and participated in several sports. She did not describe herself as one of the "popular" kids but she also stated that she did have friends and also had experiences with boyfriends. She and her boyfriend at the time of the accident were sexually active. Amanda also admitted that she had experimented with alcohol and marijuana.

The accident which led her to the neuropsychological evaluation happened the summer after her graduation when she had moved into her own apartment, but before she began the community college. Approximately 6 months had elapsed since the accident occurred until she was referred. As is often the case, she is unsure how much she remembered from the accident and how much was told to her by the other person involved and the amount of information she read in the police report or her town's newspaper. The account that Amanda recalls is that she was driving home before midnight on dry pavement on a county highway. She was not intoxicated at the time. She recalls that she saw something in the road but before she could swerve to avoid it, her car hit what she thought was a "bunny." She was devastated and stopped as soon as she could to help the animal. However, she parked her car in the opposing traffic lane with her lights on so that they illuminated the area around the animal. She very graphically and with much emotion explained how she watched the rabbit die and that it was her fault. In the meantime a truck came toward her car and saw that the vehicle was in the wrong lane. Trying to avoid hitting the car the driver of the truck swerved into the other lane and hit Amanda. The truck driver stated that he could not see that anyone was in his path. Amanda was apparently carried a few yards on the hood of the truck and landed at the side of the road in the brush. As soon as the truck driver felt that he had hit something he came to a stop. He was startled to find he had hit a person because he thought it must have been a deer.

Using his cell phone the truck driver summoned the police and an ambulance was called. Due to the fact that it was by then early morning it took some time for help to come. It is not clear how long, if at all, that Amanda was unconscious. When help did arrive, Amanda was combative, swearing, and very upset. Interspersed with profanities came tears and the story of the rabbit. It was apparent to the paramedics that she needed immediate assistance, and after radioing for advice from their supervisors, they transported Amanda to the closest metropolitan area hospital rather than the small local hospital. In addition to her peculiar behavior, it was apparent that Amanda had broken at least one leg and several ribs.

Amanda went directly to the emergency room and had to be sedated to be examined. She was admitted with a leg broken in several places, several broken ribs, numerous lacerations, and a closed head injury due to the accident. Her family was notified that she was in serious but stable condition. All of her family members came to visit her, including her grandparents who lived an hour away, but she stated she did not remember anything about the week she was in the hospital. She described behaviors that she was told she exhibited, which made her embarrassed, such as using profanity with the staff and her family. She also tried to leave the ward in her wheelchair on several occasions.

A very brief mental status examination was given to her after a week in the hospital. She passed the exam knowing much more about the circumstances of her hospitalization by that point in time. She was examined by a staff neurologist who described her as healing well and that she could return home to recuperate. Both Amanda and her mother stated that no one gave them any information regarding what to expect after sustaining a head injury.

Amanda stayed the summer with her mother, stepfather, and brother. Her leg healed well; however, she was very depressed and angry all of the time. Soon after the accident, her boyfriend ended their relationship. In addition, friends she had known most of her life did not want to be around her. As the time came for school to begin Amanda moved back to her apartment with her mother's help and began to prepare to enter college. However, emotionally she did not feel as excited as she previously had felt about the new semester.

Amanda started school with a full schedule of classes. She soon found that subjects which were easy in high school were much more difficult than she had expected. She became more angry and depressed and found it very difficult to complete homework.

As all of these things were happening to her, Amanda's mother hired an attorney to help deal with the motor vehicle accident. The police report stated that both parties were at fault for the accident and neither were assigned a percentage of blame. Because there was no assignment of fault, Amanda's mother felt that they may be able to receive some money to help pay medical bills. The truck driver also had been contacting Amanda and wanted to meet with her and explain what he thought had happened. He stated that he felt that staying out of a court situation would be best and he would like to end things without any bad feelings.

At this point, the clinical neuropsychologist must decide the type of assessment that would be best for Amanda. It is clear that she has multiple difficulties surfacing after the accident and she would benefit from a full neuropsychological evaluation that could include an intellectual assessment and a memory assessment in addition to evaluation of all the other symptoms described to the primary care physician. The question for the clinical neuropsychologist then becomes which type of battery would give the best picture of Amanda's strengths and weaknesses. There are many batteries available, some are flexible and tailored to the needs of the client, and some are given in a very standardized manner in order to ensure comparability to norm groups. In addition to choosing the battery that is best for Amanda, the clinical neuropsychologist has gained information that Amanda is struggling in school and, hence, the assessment results may pertain to that situation. The hiring of an attorney by her mother and the interest of the truck driver in speaking with her alert the clinical neuropsychologist that whatever assessment is completed may be brought into a court situation. This knowledge may impact the choice of test battery. Finally, there is a question of lack of information given at the time of discharge as reported by Amanda and her mother. The clinical neuropsychologist may need to sort out whether this is negligence on the part of the physician or lack of understanding of instructions in an emotional situation on the part of the patient and her family.

Introduction

As has been discussed in the previous two chapters, there are many assessment tools available to evaluate the same attribute, whether it is intelligence, memory, or overall cognitive functioning. The clinical neuropsychologist, knowing this, must look at all of the choices available and make an informed decision regarding assessment tools. The focus of the chapter is to introduce the reader to the various types of test batteries. As stated previously, test theory and construction apply to all tests discussed. All of the ethical issues discussed earlier also apply to the use of the test batteries. The change in the role of the clinical neuropsychologist, as discussed in previous chapters, from one of primarily diagnosis to more focused on corroborating an already formal diagnosis and looking at strengths and weaknesses of the client in relationship to rehabilitation may also affect the type of assessment battery chosen. Finally, as is the situation in this case study, many situations within neuropsychological assessment contain legal or **forensic** issues; hence, a section of this chapter will be devoted to legal issues within clinical neuropsychology.

Halstead-Reitan Neuropsychological Test Battery

As was discussed previously, **test batteries** are groupings of tests brought together to serve some specific purpose which is usually related to the theoretical orientation of the developer. Ward Halstead first began his investigation of what would later be called the *Halstead-Reitan Neuropsychological Test Battery* while he was working at the University of Chicago in 1935. The battery was based on experimental psychology procedures, first used by Halstead to investigate the human abilities which were compromised by brain injury. Halstead was working predominantly with neurological patients and wanted a way to be able to diagnose patients based on their behavioral performance. Halstead wanted to use a format which could be administered to any subject and then be compared to others who had taken the same instrument to compare abilities. Hence, Halstead's tests required a **standardized administration** by the clinical neuropsychologist. It is also a **fixed battery** of tests, in that the same tests are given to all subjects and there is no room for flexibility based on any of the circumstances of the client, the situation, or the referral question. The advantages of a fixed test battery are that the clinical neuropsychologist has a consistent base of information about an enormous number of individuals with various types of difficulties as a basis of comparison. This data pool allows the clinical neuropsychologist to compare test results between individuals with like symptomology. It is then possible to make statements regarding course and rehabilitative strategies. Also, using a fixed battery allows for further research regarding the aforementioned topics. The negative aspects of a fixed test battery are the lack of flexibility that is inherent in a **flexible battery** tailored to the client. A flexible battery (to be discussed in greater depth later) can be altered based on the progress of the client through the various subtests.

The original idea that prompted Halstead to develop his battery was the concept of biological intelligence, which he described as the adaptive capacity of the brain dependent

forensic
within the context of clinical neuropsychology, it relates to use of neuropsychological tests by the examiner to produce objective evaluation within criminal and civil matters

test batteries
groupings of tests brought together to serve a specific purpose

standardized administration
a consistent test format that allows the test to be administered to any subject and results compared to other subjects who have taken the test

fixed battery
when the same tests are given to all subjects in a study eliminating variable circumstances

flexible battery
a series of tests that are altered based on the individual being tested

on its organic integrity and assumed to be related to frontal lobe functioning (Halstead, 1947). Halstead factor analyzed the test results from his battery and proposed a four-factor model of neuropsychological ability. The factors include a central integrative field factor, an abstraction factor, a power factor, and a directional factor (Halstead, 1947).

Halstead's graduate student Ralph Reitan added the Wechsler Intelligence Scale, measures of aphasia, constructional dyspraxia, sensory–perceptual functioning, grip strength, the Trail Making Tests, and the Minnesota Multiphasic Personality Inventory (MMPI) to the original test battery (Horton & Wedding, 1984). These additions allowed the new Halstead-Reitan Neuropsychological Test Battery to be considered a clinical brain damage assessment battery (Reitan & Davidson, 1974).

The Halstead-Reitan has been the single fixed neuropsychological test battery most often used in neuropsychological, neurosurgical, rehabilitation, and psychiatric settings (Guilmette, Faust, Hart, & Arkes, 1990). The reason the test has been so well received is due to the extensive body of research conducted by Reitan and his colleagues demonstrating the validity of the battery in assessing brain damage (Reitan & Wolfson, 1986).

The tests which are commonly thought to comprise the Halstead-Reitan Neuropsychological Test Battery include the Category Test, Tactile Performance Test (TPT), Speech Sounds Perception Test, Rhythm Test, Trail Making Test, Finger-Tapping Test, Reitan-Indiana Aphasia Screening Test, Reitan-Kløve Sensory Perceptual Examination, Reitan-Kløve Lateral Dominance Examination, and Strength of Grip.

CATEGORY TEST

The Category Test is believed by many to be the Halstead-Reitan Neuropsychological Test Battery subtest most sensitive to brain damage (Reitan & Wolfson, 1993). It is almost as sensitive as the full Halstead-Reitan battery in detecting the presence or absence of neurological damage (Adams & Trenton, 1981). The test is a relatively complex visual concept formation test that measures the subject's ability to learn general abstraction principles and also profit from feedback regarding his or her performance. The original test was administered using a slide projector but is now delivered through a booklet format or using the computer. The test contains seven subtests with 208 items. The subject is to reason how the stimulus materials make him or her think of a number between one and four. The subject is given one choice and then receives feedback regarding whether his or her answer was correct or incorrect. Each subtest becomes progressively more difficult until Subtest 7, which is a composite of all the other subtests. The subject's score is considered to be normal if he receives fewer than 50 errors. The odd–even split-half method and coefficient alpha have been used to calculate internal consistency with high reliability coefficients obtained from the total score for samples of normal and brain-damaged adults (Lopez, Charter, & Newman, 2000). Test–retest reliabilities varied greatly from a short 3-week interval to a longer interval with scores ranging from 0.60 to 0.85 (Bornstein, Baker, & Douglas, 1987; Dikmen, Heaton, Grant, & Temkin, 1999). Scores on the Category Test have been compared to most other measures of intelligence, memory, and higher order functioning. The most significant finding is in the comparison to the Wisconsin Card Sorting Test (WCST) which has shown that the two tests are not identical (Adams et al., 1995) and shows only modest common variance (Goldstein & Watson, 1989). The choice between these two tests often is dependent on the referral question. Neuropsychologists often look not only at the score but also the pattern of answers and the use of feedback by the patient to evaluate the person's higher order thinking abilities.

TACTILE PERFORMANCE TEST

The TPT is a variation of the Seguin-Goddard Form Board. The blindfolded subject is positioned in front of a form board that has spaces for 10 geometric figures. With the figures placed in front of him or her, the subject begins, using his or her dominant hand, to insert each figure into its appropriate space. The subject next uses his or her nondominant hand and then both hands together. Each trial is timed and total time is the sum of each trial. After the subject completes all trials, the form board is removed and the subject removes the blindfold. He or she is then asked to draw a replica of the board as he or she recalls it, both in terms of the number of stimuli and their placement. From this test, several scores are collected, which include total time, memory, and location, each of which is added into Halstead's impairment index (to be discussed later). Total time is considered to be in the impaired range if it is beyond 15 minutes, 7 seconds. Memory for the designs is impaired if it is 5 or below and localization for the designs is impaired if it is 4 or below. The TPT assesses the integration of tactile and kinesthetic feedback, performance skills, and spatial memory. In addition, lateralization of difficulty may be inferred from the difference between performances with each hand. Although the TPT has been used for many years as part of the Halstead-Reitan test battery, Lezak, Howieson, and Loring (2004) stated that the task is time-consuming and may give little new information in return. They also discussed that the blindfold is stressful for the subject for such a prolonged period of time. Reliability estimates for the TPT have varied greatly by study.

SPEECH SOUNDS PERCEPTION TEST

The Speech Sounds Perception Test has the subject listen to 60 tape-recorded nonsense words that are variants of the "ee" sound and choose which one is heard. The assumption is that this is a measure of left hemisphere functioning which involves the ability to maintain attention, perceive the spoken stimulus through hearing, and relate the perception through vision to the correct configuration of letters on the test form. Eight errors or more is considered to fall within the brain-impaired range.

Test–retest correlations rarely fell below .60 and most were above it (Goldstein & Watson, 1989). Due to the fact that this is an auditory test, patient performance tended to decrease with age. There is a shorter form Speech Sounds Perception Test-30, which uses the first three series of stimuli. However, it has a lower reliability than the full test, leading researchers to recommend the use of the 60-item test (Charter & Dobbs, 1998).

RHYTHM TEST

The Rhythm Test was taken from the Seashore Tests of Musical Talent (Reitan & Wolfson, 1993). It involves 30 pairs of rhythmic patterns presented auditorially in which the subject is to respond whether the pairs are the same or different. The subject is not cued when each presentation begins; therefore, he or she must maintain adequate attention. The test measures auditory memory, rhythmic discrimination, and attention ability. The raw error score is translated into a ranked score. A ranked score of 6 or above is indicative of brain impairment.

Test–retest differences are small (McCaffrey, Duff, & Westervelt, 2000). However, Charter and Webster (1997) reported a reliability coefficient of .78, that many of the items were too easy, and that the Seashore Rhythm test was not a psychometrically sound instrument.

TRAIL MAKING TEST

This test was originally part of the Army Individual Test Battery (1944) and is now in the public domain and may be copied without permission. The Trail Making Test is composed of two components labeled Trails A and Trails B. Each is a sequencing task with B more difficult than A. In Trails A, the subject draws a line to connect 25 numbered circles in the correct order. Time is recorded as well as errors; however, the clinical neuropsychologist is allowed to verbalize when an error is committed. Trails B is more complex and has the subject draw a line, which connects alternately sequential alphabetic and numeric items, such as 1, A, 2, B, 3, C, and so forth. The test is a measure of visual tracking, set-shifting, and sequencing ability. Trails Part B, along with the Category Test, TPT Localization, and the Halstead Impairment Index (HII), has been considered one of the four best general indicators of cerebral dysfunction (Russel, Neuringer, & Goldstein, 1970).

The scores on the test are the seconds that it takes the subject to complete Trails A and Trails B, respectively. Also recorded is the number of errors. The cutoff score for Part A is between 39 and 40 seconds and between 91 and 92 seconds for Part B (Reitan, 1986). Hence, those scoring over the time limit are considered to be impaired.

There has been a large amount of research completed on the Trail Making Test with at least 46 different studies generating normative data (Mitrushina, Boone, Razani, & D'Elia, 2005). Test–retest reliability estimates have varied somewhat between Trails A and Trails B and are dependent on age group. One of the most recent studies (Levine, Miller, Becker, Seines, & Cohen, 2004) used a well-educated, mostly Caucasian sample of male subjects with results of .70 for Parts A and B. Parts A and B correlate modestly well with each other (r = .31 − .6) suggesting that they measure similar although somewhat different functions (Heilbronner, Henry, Buck, Adams, & Fogle, 1991). The Trail Making Test is one of the five measures most commonly used by neuropsychologists (Rabin, Barr, & Burton, 2005). As a measure of attention, it ranks among the most often used instruments and in the area of executive functioning it ranks fourth (Rabin et al.).

FINGER TAPPING TEST

This is a test of motor speed in which the subject uses a key counter mounted on a board. There are five 10-second tapping trials for each hand. The average number of taps for five trials comprises the score for each hand. This test also serves as a measure of laterality when comparing the performance between hands. In right-handed subjects, performance with the dominant hand is assumed to be 10% better than with the nondominant hand. The same is not always the case with left-handed subjects. There are cases where the reverse is true in left-handers (Jarvis & Barth, 1994). The original cutoff scores for impairment supplied by Halstead were 50 or less taps for the five taps for the dominant hand and 44 or less for the five taps for the nondominant hand. Bornstein, Paniak, and O'Brien (1987) suggested lowering the cutoff scores to 33 or less and 32 or less for men's dominant and nondominant hands, respectively, and 20 or less and 25 or less for women. These changes were suggested due to research which shows a gender difference in performance, as well as aging effects. Reliability coefficients ranging from .58–.93 have been reported by both normal and patient samples (Strauss, Sherman, & Spreen, 2006). Reitan and Wolfson (1996) suggested finger tapping is a pure measure of mental functioning. However, cognitive factors also contribute, and Prigatano and Borgaro (2003) suggest that qualitative features of the test may also be diagnostic.

REITAN-INDIANA APHASIA SCREENING TEST

This test is a modification of the Halstead-Wepman Aphasia Screening Test (Reitan & Wolfson, 1993). Many symptoms of aphasia may be gleaned from this brief screening test, such as difficulties with reading, spelling, naming, arithmetic, and/or repeating words and phrases. Also included are nonlanguage skills such as drawing and following directions to check for left–right confusion. Any errors on this test are considered to be an indication of the possible presence of aphasia. However, Lezak et al. (2004) stated that if one goes by scores alone, the test cannot qualify for aphasia screening. Lezak et al. also discussed the misuse that may happen as new examiners overpathologize from a single error. There does not appear to be any reliability or validity data available for this test.

REITAN-KLØVE SENSORY PERCEPTUAL EXAMINATION

This test is an adaption of a standard neurological exam. It focuses on the functioning of the various cranial nerves that relate to visual, auditory, and tactile sensory and perceptual functioning. The test evaluates bilateral sensory stimulation after it is determined that unilateral stimulation is intact. In order to evaluate tactile functioning, the hands are touched one at a time and then both hands are touched. Contralateral face–hand stimulation is also used with single and double simultaneous stimulation. An auditory stimulus is achieved by the examiner rubbing his or her fingers together quickly and sharply while standing behind the subject. Conditions involve dominant versus nondominant ear and also stimulation of both at the same time. The visual examination is conducted by having the subject focus on the examiner's nose while he or she makes discrete hand movements to check the visual field of the subject.

Errors in any of these modalities may be indicative of brain dysfunction. It is also important to make sure the subject's senses are intact before beginning the exam. There are no available reliability or validity data on this test.

REITAN-KLØVE LATERAL DOMINANCE EXAMINATION

The neuropsychologist assesses dominance through asking the patient various questions that elicit use of hand, foot, and eye. Lateral dominance helps in the interpretation of Finger-Tapping, Strength of Grip, and Tactile Performance Test. This test also contains no validity or reliability data.

STRENGTH OF GRIP

This test assesses differences in hand strength with the assumption that lateralized brain damage may affect strength of the contralateral hand. The grip strength is assessed though the use of a Smedly hand dynamometer. The subject squeezes the dynamometer twice with each hand, alternating hands. The score is the mean strength of grip measured in pounds for each hand. Gender differences appear on this test, as well as within-gender differences. Men have a greater grip strength overall than women. However, some studies show men's abilities declining after age 40 (Fromm-Auch & Yudall, 1983) while other studies show a decline after age 60 (Mitrushina, Boone, & D'Eli, 1999). Reliability coefficients ranges from .52–.96 with most greater than .70 have been reported for both normal and neurologically impaired individuals (Strauss et al., 2006). In terms of validity, grip strength evaluates sensorimotor abilities and is used in neuropsychological evaluations to assess gross and subtle motor impairment.

ADDITIONAL TESTS

The Halstead-Reitan Neuropsychological Test Battery generally employs a measure of intelligence, usually a Wechsler test, which would currently be the Wechsler Adult Intelligence Scale-IV (WAIS-IV), and a memory battery, which would be the Wechsler Memory Scale-IV (WMS-IV), both of which are designed to be used together. A measure of academic achievement may be included, which is usually the Wide Range Achievement Test-3. Finally, an objective personality test such as the MMPI-2 or sometimes the Millon Clinical Multiaxial Inventory (MCMI-III) is included.

HALSTEAD-REITAN NEUROPSYCHOLOGICAL TEST BATTERY: SUMMARY MEASURES

Due to the fact that the Halstead-Reitan has essentially been the first neuropsychological assessment battery and that it has been administered in a standardized manner, it has engendered a plethora of a research. Much of the research relates to separation of diagnostic groups based on test scores. However, additional information is available for the various summary indices that may be generated from the battery. The indices that are extant include the Halstead Impairment Index (HII), a linear composite of seven neuropsychological test scores (Halstead, 1947); the Average Impairment Rating (AIR), a weighted average of 12 selected subtest scores; the General Neuropsychological Deficit Scale (GNDS), a total of weighted scores from 42 measures (Reitan & Wolfson, 1988); the Short-Form Impairment Index, a total of 3 neuropsychological test scores (Horton, Anilane, Slone, & Shapiro, 1986); the Alternative Impairment Index, a total of 7 neuropsychological test scores (Horton, 1995); and the Global Deficit Score (GDS), a mean of 21 demographically corrected test scores (Heaton, Miller, Taylor, & Grant, 2004).

The HII was developed by Halstead based on the premise that a linear composite of test scores was more sensitive to brain damage than a single test. The scores range from 0 (*no evidence of brain damage*) to 1.0 (*severe brain damage*). Halstead used 10 tests to produce the index, whereas Reitan's use of seven subtests is the current approach. The seven tests include the Category Test, the Rhythm Test, the Speech Sounds Perception Test, the Finger-Tapping Test, and Total Time, Memory, and Localization for the Tactile Perception Test. The cut-off score for Halstead was 0.5. For Reitan the cut-off became 0.4 for patients with measured IQ of 100 or better, and 0.5 for those with a measured IQ less than 100. Research led to the modification noting that there exists a significant relationship between intelligence and HII (Reitan, 1985).

AIR uses weighted scores to calculate an average summary measure of brain impairment. It addresses the critique of the HII using a dichotomous cut-off scores. The AIR averages the weighted scores of the following 12 tests: the Category Test, TPT (time, memory, and localization), Rhythm Test, Speech Sounds Perception Test, Finger-Tapping Test, Trails B, Digit Symbol from the Wechsler, and weighted rated scores for Aphasia Screening Test and Spatial Relations.

The General Neuropsychological Deficit Score (GNDS) uses 42 separate test variables from the Halstead-Reitan Neuropsychological Test Battery. The test variables are arranged according to Reitan's methods of inference (Horton & Wedding, 1984). The groupings include test scores that demonstrate the patient's level of performance, specific deficits, pathognomic signs, patterns of performance, and comparisons of the two sides of the patient's body on motor and sensory–perceptual means. Research has indicated fairly impressive hit rates (Wolfson & Reitan, 1995).

The Short Form Impairment Index (SFII) is composed of scores from the Trail Making Test Part B and Block Design and Coding Subtests of the Wechsler. The SFII will need to be changed as the WAIS-IV has changed its manner of conceptualizing intelligence.

The Alternate Impairment Index (AII) includes scores from the Category Test, Rhythm Test, Speech Sounds Perception Test, Finger Tapping and Trail Making Test Parts A and B. This is designed to be used when time and money preclude the use of the entire Halstead-Reitan Neuropsychological Test Battery.

The Global Deficit Scale (GDS) is drawn from 21 test scores from the expanded Halstead-Reitan Neuropsychological Test Battery, which are demographically corrected for age, education, gender, and ethnicity. The 21 measures include the Category Test, Trail Making Parts A and B, Tactile Performance Test (total time, memory, and localization), Rhythm Test, Speech Sounds Perception Test, Digit Vigilance Test (time and error components), Story Memory Test (learning and delayed recall components), Figure Memory Test (learning and delayed recall components), Aphasia Screening Test, Boston Naming Test, Thurston Word Fluency Test, Spatial Relations, Sensory-Perceptual-Total, Finger-Tapping-worst hand and Grooved Pegboard-worst hand.

Reviews of the Halstead-Reitan Neuropsychological Test Battery manual indicate that it describes the subtests well and how they were developed, but there are several difficulties with the manual (Dean & Meier, 1985). One in particular that stands out is that it relies on the tremendous research literature that has accumulated within the past 30–40 years to establish the reliability and validity of the battery. Instead of completing research themselves to demonstrate the reliability and validity of the test battery, the authors include within the manual references to other researchers who have utilized the test battery with individuals with a variety of central nervous system difficulties. Further, it is criticized in that it should supply individual reliability and validity data for each of the subtests that are included in this text when available and not in the overall battery.

A large body of research indicates that the battery is sensitive to cortical dysfunctions (Boll, 1981). It is able to discriminate normal controls from patients with brain damage with accuracy (84–98%). Reitan and associates (Dikmen & Reitan, 1977; Reed & Reitan, 1963) have produced data favoring brain damage localization with the battery for acute lesions rather than more chronic. After excluding individuals with a diagnosis of schizophrenia, many researchers have shown the battery is able to distinguish patients with specific organic pathology from those with other psychiatric disorders (Heaton & Crowley, 1981).

In summary, the battery has a large body of research describing its ability to separate patients into certain groups based on test scores. It suffers in that, to interpret the data presented, the clinical neuropsychologist must be extremely familiar with the battery to interpret the pattern of test results produced by the patient. It is also criticized due to the lack of the aforementioned reliability and validity information which this text has included for the individual subtests when available. The Halstead-Reitan Neuropsychological Test Battery also lacks studies that demonstrate its ecological validity.

Luria's Neuropsychological Investigation

This test battery was based on Luria's original ideas regarding brain functioning. It was compiled into the form of a battery and termed *Luria's Neuropsychological Investigation* in his honor (Christensen, 1989, 1979). His ideas are contained within the works *Higher Cortical Functions in Man* (1966) and *The Working Brain* (1969/1973), which cover the range of neurosensory and cognitive functions he studied. A. L. Christiansen translated the works from the original Russian. She brought his ideas together into a single set of materials comprising a text, a manual of instructions, and test cards. Christensen made

Luria's ideas readily available by reproducing his techniques in card form using his detailed directions for administration. She also presented the items in a framework that follows Luria's conceptualization of the roles and relationships of the brain's cortical functions and guides the course of the examination (Lezak et al., 2004).

The material based on Luria's works includes the following 10 sections related to specific functions: motor functions, acoustico-motor organization, higher cutaneous and kinesthetic functions, higher visual functions, impressive (receptive) speech, expressive speech, writing and reading, arithmetic skill, -mnestic processes, and investigation of intellectual processes (Luria, 1966). In order to test these various cortical functions, he used many familiar tests such as Kohs Blocks, Raven's Matrices, and Gottschaldt's Hidden Figures. Many of Luria's tasks are also similar to items contained on tests of mental abilities or speech disorders. Some of the items he employed come directly from the mental status examination, whereas some items are those used in a neurological examination. Luria also included tasks he developed including a series of tasks involving speech regulation of the motor act and conflict commands to which the subject makes a hand response that is the opposite of the examiner's movement (i.e., tap once when the examiner taps twice and vice versa) and go/no go instructions to test the subject's ability to respond to one cue and withhold response to another (i.e., squeeze the examiner's hand at the word *red*; do nothing at the word *green*). Many of these tasks are particularly sensitive to frontal lobe damage (Truelle, LeGall, & Joseph, 1995).

The distinct feature of this type of battery is that it is not fixed and may be altered dependent on the needs of the client. Christiansen pointed out the need to be able to respond to the patient's capacity even though it may be at the expense of standardization procedures. Luria's approach is truly a **qualitative form of neuropsychological assessment**. This type of battery has clear strengths and weaknesses. The strengths include that it is relatively inexpensive, flexible, and brief to administer. The weaknesses include that it is not a comprehensive battery that is able to answer all neuropsychological questions. It clearly lacks tests of attention, concentration, and medical history. Some of the tests included are things most adults are capable of doing and do a poor job of separating more serious from less serious difficulties. Many clinical neuropsychologists will use parts of the battery and include supplemental testing as needed.

> **qualitative form of neuropsychological assessment**
> a battery of tests that is not fixed and is altered based on the needs of the client

Luria had developed a scoring system for his assessment approach, which has been translated from one of his teaching pamphlets and was used for many years in his Moscow clinics (Tupper, 1999). A 6-point scoring system that is designed to give information regarding the qualitative features of patient performance is also available (Glozman, 1999).

The Luria-Nebraska Neuropsychological Battery

Golden, Purisch, and Hammeke (1985) developed this battery whose title is somewhat of a misnomer. The test developers state that it was designed "to diagnose general and specific cognitive deficits, including lateralization and localization of focal brain impairments and to aid in the planning and evaluation of rehabilitation programs" (Golden et al., 1991, p. 1). The test battery is available in Forms I and II. In the previous section, Christiansen's work translating Luria's ideas and procedures has been heralded as being true to Luria's original ideas. Spiers (1981) stated that the incorporation of items drawn from Luria's work into a standardized test should not be interpreted to mean that the test is an operational or standardization of Luria's method. Hence, while it may be an appropriate test for certain usages, there have been questions regarding the use of Luria's name and whether the battery truly represents his ideas regarding cortical functions. Secondly, there are questions regarding the methodology employed by Golden et al. (1991).

In order to develop the battery, Golden and his associates selected items from Christiansen's manual on the basis of whether the items discriminated between normal subjects and an unspecified group of neurologically impaired patients (Lezak et al., 2004). They were placed within the test battery in a manner similar to Christensen's with the only difference being that Reading and Writing became separate scales. In Form II, an Immediate Memory scale is included. Although they are purported to be parallel forms, Form I contains 269 items using Christensen's stimulus cards, Form II contains 279 and uses cards developed in the United States; hence, they cannot be truly called parallel due to the differences in items, but are similar forms. Forms I and II have 84 common items and Form II contains the additional memory scale. Form II can only be scored on the computer, whereas, Form I may be scored by hand, which saves the examiner and patient money and time to receive a report back from a testing company.

Instead of scores on subtests, each item is given a score of 0 (*normal performance*), 1 (*mildly dysfunctional*) or 2 (*severely dysfunctional*). Raw scores for item clusters may be converted to scale scores for general areas: Clinical scales, Summary scales, Localization scales, and Factor scales.

Raw scores for each scale are converted to a T score with a mean of 50 and a standard deviation of 10. Similar to the MMPI-II, the Luria-Nebraska Neuropsychological Battery (LNNB) has abandoned the name of the scales due to overlap between items, which renders the titles meaningless and now refers to the scales as C1–C12 on Form I and C1–C13 on Form II. Five summary scores, now referred to by a number–letter code are composed of items from the clinical scales: Pathognomonic, Right Hemisphere, Left Hemisphere, Profile Elevation, and Impairment.

The LNNB was designed as a way to separate normal controls from those individuals with brain impairment. However, since its introduction, this battery has generated more research and clinical debate than most other tests within clinical neuropsychology. The first issue relates to the aforementioned question regarding whether it is a true and accurate representation of how Luria would have assessed his patients. The second question relates to the psychometrics that the test developers have included within the test manual. Form I was standardized on very few subjects, 50 hospitalized for a variety of medical problems, infectious diseases, and chronic pain; and Form II was standardized on 51 normal individuals (Golden, Purisch, & Hammeke, 1991). The critical level, which gives the cutting score value for the clinical scales plus Writing/Arithmetic and the Pathognomonic scales, is found by multiplying the subjects' age by .214 for every year between 25 and 70. The age correction assumes a simple linear increase in number of errors in every examined function or skill which Lezak et al. (2004) states goes against any responsible study made concerning cognitive changes with aging. This is quite a strong statement regarding the psychometrics of this battery. The manual itself reports reliability estimates, which, again, have been questioned by researchers due to their sample size and composition. It has also been stated that researchers working outside of the Golden et al. group have not been able to replicate their findings (Lezak et al., 2004).

The Boston Process Approach

process approach
testing based on understanding the qualitative nature behind clinical psychometric instruments

A **process approach** is based on a desire to understand the qualitative nature of the behavior assessed by clinical psychometric instruments. Led by Edith Kaplan, the Boston group began looking at various forms of apraxia followed by an evaluation of the reasons why individuals passed or failed various items on the Wechsler Adult Intelligence Scale and the Wechsler Memory Scale.

In addition to evaluating already existing measures other tests were developed, such as to assess parietal lobe functions. Also, the Boston Diagnostic Aphasia Examination (Goodglass & Kaplan, 1972) allows the precise characterization of the breakdown of language using a series of finely grained quantitative scales. As time passed, the Boston group adopted and integrated a collection of core and satellite tests into the Boston Process Approach. The Boston group also stressed that many of the traditional clinical tests that had been designed for other purposes such as tests of personality (i.e., the Rorschach test), cognitive development (i.e., the Bender-Gestalt Test), and cognitive functions (i.e., WMS; Sequin-Goddard Formboard) were also sensitive to brain damage in both adults and children (Milberg, Hebben, & Kaplan, 1986).

The Boston Process Approach uses a core set of tests for most subjects but it is not considered to be a battery because the techniques may be altered to assess the pattern of intact and impaired functions. In a sense, it starts out as a fixed battery of tests but may be altered to determine the reasons why a subject is impaired. It also uses a testing the limits paradigm in order to further evaluate the qualitative aspects of the patient's performance. For example, a subject may not be able to complete a task in the given time because of motor impairments. However, if the time is extended he or she may do very well. The ability to vary the time helps the clinical neuropsychologist differentiate between subjects who cannot complete the test due to the time constraints from those who do not understand the directions or do not have the skills necessary to complete the task. The only limits that the Boston group employs are the examiner's knowledge of available tests and his or her ingenuity in creating new measures for potential deficit areas (Milberg, Cummings, Goodglass, & Kaplan, 1979).

The Boston group felt it was necessary to modify many original test measures to facilitate the collection of data about individual cognitive strategies. The following list includes the most often used tests to measure six core functions:

testing the limits
a manner of testing that foregoes timing in favor of evaluating the ability of a client; often used with clients who have motor disabilities

1. Intellectual and Conceptual Functions
    *   WAIS-IV (Wechsler, 2008)
    *   Standard Progressive Matrices (Raven, 1960)
    *   Shipley Institute of Living Scale-Revised (Zachary, 1986)
    *   WCST (Grant & Berg, 1948)
    *   Proverbs Test (Gorham, 1956)
2. Memory Functions
    *   WMS (Wechsler, 2009)
    *   Rey Auditory–Verbal Learning Test (Rey, 1964)
    *   Rey-Osterrieth Complex Figure Test (Osterreith & Rey, 1944)
    *   Benton Visual Recognition Test (multiple choice form; Benton, 1950)
    *   Consonant Trigrams Test (Butters & Grady, 1977)
    *   Cowboy Story Reading Memory Test (Talland, 1965)
    *   Corsi Blocks (Milner, 1971)
3. Language Functions
    *   Narrative Writing Sample (Goodglass & Kaplan, 1972)
    *   Tests of Verbal Fluency (Word-List Generation; Thurstone, 1938)
4. Visuo-Perceptual Functions
    *   Cow and Circle Experimental Test (Palmer & Kaplan, 1985)
    *   Automobile Puzzle (Wechsler, 1974)
    *   Parietal Lobe Battery (Goodglass & Kaplan, 1972)
    *   Hooper Visual Organization Test (Hooper, 1958)

5. Academic Skills
   - Wide Range Achievement Test (Jastak & Jastak, 1978)
6. Self-Control and Motor Functions
   - Porteus Maze Test (Porteus, 1965)
   - Stroop Color–Word Interference Test (Stroop, 1935)
   - Luria Three-Step Motor Program (Christensen, 1975)
   - Finger Tapping (Halstead, 1947)

This list does not imply that all of the tests are given to each patient. However, the Boston group states that these particular tests are sensitive measures of the six categories on which they focused. They have also modified the original test measures to collect data about individual cognitive strategies. An attempt was made to make modifications that did not interfere with the standardized administration of the tests. Thus, it is still possible to obtain reliable data and generalize to the norms because most modifications involve techniques of data collection rather than changes in test procedures. An example would be the testing of limits procedure discussed earlier. Other changes include pushing a patient beyond an I-don't-know response, encouraging a patient who appears unmotivated and modifying time limits. The goal is to remove obstacles so that a true picture of abilities and disabilities of the client is gained. According to the developers of this approach, changing the manner in which some of the tests are administered does not affect the test's usefulness in diagnosis for detection and localization of cortical lesions (Milberg et al., 1986). Some researchers (Heaton & Crowley, 1981) have suggested that the extra qualitative data have increased the **hit rate** compared to a psychometric formula based on level of performance. Also, according to the developers of the process, the greatest neuropsychological advantage of this approach is in treatment planning, particularly in terms of more precise investigation of functions available and the patient's strengths and weaknesses.

hit rate
successful result

Kaplan Baycrest Neurocognitive Assessment

The Kaplan Baycrest Neurocognitive Assessment (KBNA) was developed to be a comprehensive test of neuropsychological functioning. Its development was driven by concerns that clinical neuropsychologists had a tendency to rely on brief tests of cognitive functioning and/or nonstandardized mental-status exams. In addition, it addresses the paucity of norms for subjects older than the age of 55. The authors also claim that the test may be administered in as little as 2 hours.

Building on the ideas that went into the development of the Boston Process Approach, Leach, Kaplan, Rewilak, Richards, and Proulx (2000) developed a neurocognitve approach that contains 25 subtests. The similarities between this assessment battery and the Boston Process Approach is that it includes multiple measures, many of which are already extant in the literature and includes procedures for evaluating both qualitative and quantitative information. The authors state that the battery is grounded in behavioral neurology and was developed to assist in the localization and etiology of neurological dysfunctions.

The KBNA is organized according to six areas of cognitive functioning, which include Attention/Concentration, Declarative Memory, Visuoconstruction/Visoperception, Praxis, Language, and Reasoning/Problem Solving. The domains are represented by seven indices: Attention/Concentration, Memory-Immediate Recall, Memory-Delayed Recall, Memory-Delayed Recognition, Spatial Processing, Verbal Fluency, and Reasoning/Conceptual Shifting. These indices then contribute to a total index that provides an overall estimate of neurocognitive ability.

Attention/Concentration is composed of the Sequences and Spatial Location subtests. Memory-Immediate Recall is made up of Word-Lists 1 Recall and Complex Figure 1 Recall. Memory-Delayed Recall is composed of Word-List 2 Recall and Complex Figure 2 Recall. Memory-Delayed Recognition also includes Word-List 2 Recognition and Complex Figure 2 Recognition in addition to target words from Word-List 1 and identifying and drawing parts of the complex figure in Complex Figure 1. Spatial Processing is made up of Complex Figure 1 and clocks. Verbal Fluency includes Verbal Fluency Phoneme and Semantic Scores. Reasoning/Conceptual Shifting contains Practical Problem Solving and Conceptual Shifting. The total index is the sum of all of the previous indices. All subtests must be given to every subject to determine the indices.

Fifteen additional tests are included to provide qualitative information regarding the functioning of the individual. These tests include Orientation, Repetition, Auditory Comprehension, Auditory Signal Detection, Symbol Cancellation, Motor Programming, Praxis, Expression of Emotions, Picture Naming, Picture Description-Oral, Picture Description-Written, Reading Single Words, Sentence-Reading, Arithmetic, Numbers, and Picture Recognition.

The authors state that the KBNA was normed using a standardization sample of 700 adults, 100 in each age group, which reflected the 1999 U.S. Census demographic characteristics. Reliability data suggest internal consistency of the subtests ranging from .645–.90. There are very little validity data available.

The strengths of this test are that it may be completed in a short amount of time, it is updated compared to many older neuropsychological batteries, and it includes both quantitative and qualitative information. The weakness is that the manual includes very little reliability and validity information and the complexity of the test requires experienced professionals to administer the test and interpret results.

Delis-Kaplan Executive Function System

The Delis-Kaplan Executive Function System (D-KEFS) is a neuropsychological test battery developed by Delis, Kaplan, and Kramer (2001) to assess higher order cognitive abilities usually described as executive control functions and thought to reside within the frontal lobes. The battery is composed of nine individually administered and scored tests that may be given as a group or certain tests may be selected based on the needs of the patient. The nine tests include the following: Trail Making Test, Verbal Fluency Test, Color–Word Interference Test, Sorting Test, Twenty Questions Test, Word Context Test, Design Fluency Test, Tower Test, and Proverbs Test. As may be seen, some of these are extant neuropsychological tests that the authors have improved on and some are completely new tests.

Scoring and interpretation of these tests is based on the cognitive process theoretical approach to clinical neuropsychology, which was originally discussed within the section on the Boston Process Approach. Hence, this test also produces quantitative and qualitative information for each of the nine subtests. All of the raw scores are converted to age-corrected scale scores with a mean of 10 and a standard deviation of 3.

The D-KEFS was standardized on a stratified sample of 1,750 individuals, 700 children between the ages of 8 and 15 years, 700 individuals between the ages 16 and 59 and 350 individuals between ages 60 and 89 years. Reviews of this test state that several classes of reliability estimates were employed. Internal consistency reliability for some of the subtests was quite high whereas for others it was somewhat lower. The authors fail to present much data with regard to validity. While it lacks some information on psychometrics, according to reviews, this test appears to be a valuable tool to assess executive functions compared to many of the older neuropsychological test batteries (Dugbartey & Ramsden, 2003).

Neuropsychological Assessment Battery

The Neuropsychological Assessment Battery (NAB) developed by Stern and White (2003) is a relatively new battery designed to assess an array of cognitive skills and functions in adults with known or suspected disorders of the central nervous system. The choice of content for the battery was based on an extensive survey (Stern & White, 2000) of practicing clinical neuropsychologists regarding the importance of 79 specific neuropsychological functions derived from the literature. The NAB also includes suggestions from an advisory council of six prominent neuropsychologists and a language/aphasia consultant.

The NAB has two equivalent forms and each form contains 36 neuropsychological tests, organized into six modules: Screening, Attention, Language, Memory, Spatial, and Executive Functioning. The Attention Module consists of six subtests involving the Orientation, Digits Forward and Digits Backward, Dots, Numbers, and Letters Test, and Driving Scenes. The Language Module comprises six subtests involving Oral Production, Auditory Comprehension (varied formats), Naming, Reading Comprehension, Writing, and Bill Payment. The Memory Module includes 10 subtests involving Word List Learning with delayed recall and recognition trials, Shape Learning with delayed recognition trials in two formats, Story Learning with delayed recall trials, and Daily Living Memory with delayed recall and recognition trials. The Spatial Module consists of four subtests involving Visual Discrimination, Design Construction, Figure Drawing with immediate recall, and Map Reading. The Executive Functioning Module includes four subtests involving Mazes, Judgment, Categories, and Word Generation. The Screening Module consists of 12 subtests including two subtests derived from the Attention Module, two subtests derived from the Language Module, two subtests derived from the Spatial Module, four subtests derived from the Memory Module, and two subtests derived from the Executive Functions Module.

The Screening Module may be used alone as a screening tool or used to determine whether further assessment in each area is needed. Each of the other modules may be given together as part of a total battery or some be given and scored separately.

The NAB manual provides extensive reliability and validity data on each of the modules as well as for the total battery. Raw scores from each of the subtests are converted to Z scores, T scores, and/or percentile ranks based on normative samples consisting of either a demographically corrected sample or a U.S. Census matched sample. Standard scores for selected subtests are summed to create a composite score that is converted to a standard score and percentile rank. Composite scores for the Screening Module are used to determine if assessment with the respective Main Module is necessary.

ecological validity
the functional and predictive relationship between a patient's performance on a particular test or battery and his or her behavior at home, work, school or in the community

Each of the main modules includes one test that is designed to be more **ecologically valid** than traditional neuropsychological tests. These subtests reflect cognitive processes as they apply to real world activities. These subtests include Driving Scenes, Bill Payment, Daily Living Memory, Map Reading, and Judgment.

The advantages of this battery are that each module may be used separately or combined into a larger battery. The screening module may also be used separately. This battery includes a fairly large amount of psychometric and normative data. Finally, the battery includes ecologically valid items that are generally needed in assessment of individuals with central nervous system difficulties.

Lezak et al. (2004) state that the downfall of the battery is its newness as there is very little research supporting its claims. However, Lezak et al. also state that with further research, the chances appear good that it will meet its goals and enter into the standard clinical neuropsychological assessment repertory.

Dean-Woodcock Neuropsychological Battery

The Dean-Woodcock Neuropsychological Battery (DWNB; Dean & Woodcock, 2003) is a relatively new battery that consists of the Dean-Woodcock Sensory Motor Battery (DWSMB), a Structured Neuropsychological Interview, and an Emotional Status Examination. Many of the items on these three tests are familiar to clinical neuropsychologists because they are from other extant neuropsychological interviews.

The DWNB is one component of the Dean-Woodcock Neuropsychological Assessment System (DWNAS). The DWNAS includes the DWNB along with the Woodcock-Johnson III Tests of Cognitive Abilities (Woodcock, McGrew, & Malther, 2001b) and the Woodcock-Johnson Test of Achievement (Woodcock, McGrew, & Malther, 2001a).

The first component of the DWNB is the DWSMB, which is the most comprehensive part of this instrument. Ten of the 18 DWSMB subtests measure motor functioning and the remaining eight subtests measure sensory functions such as visual, auditory, and tactile perception. A set of interview materials provide the examiner with additional information, such as the client's motivation, attention, emotional problems, and medical disorders that may contribute to their performance on certain measures. The final component, an Emotional Status Examination, is used to explore signs and symptoms of psychiatric disorders. This protocol contains two parts: the examination conducted with the client and a section on clinical observations and impressions that is completed by the examiner.

The DWSMB can be administered in 30–45 minutes. The Structured Neuropsychological Interview and the Emotional Status Examination each take about 30 minutes. The DWNB was normed on a sample of 1,011 individuals ages 2–95 and was closely matched to the demographic variables of the U.S. 2000 Census. In the sample, there were 233 children ages 2–10, 265 adolescents and younger adults ages 11–24, and 513 adults ages 25–95.

Reliability for the DWSMB was estimated using interrater agreement and split-half methods. Correlations ranged from 0.45–1.00. Reliability and validity data are lacking for the interview and emotional status examination.

The advantages of the DWNB are that it is included with two other batteries for the clinical neuropsychologist to develop a clear picture of the patient's strengths and weaknesses, and, in addition, the DWSMB exhibits good reliability and excellent normative data. The disadvantages of the battery include lack of psychometric information for the interview and emotional status examination.

Returning to our case study, many issues may arise in the decision as to which test battery to administer to Amanda. She appears to need a thorough assessment to evaluate her cognitive, memory, attention, concentration, and multiple other areas of functioning. She is in school and the results of her evaluation may have ramifications regarding the classes she chooses and any extra help that she receives. She is also beginning a process of litigation that would require a test battery that has a plethora of data available be credible in a court situation. The decision was made to use the Wechsler Adult Intelligence Scale-IV and Wechsler Memory Scale-IV due to the information that could be gleaned from them and the psychometrics available.

The WAIS-IV and the WMS-IV were designed to be used together and that was seen as an advantage to compare her abilities between the two tests. The clinical neuropsychologist then evaluated and employed the most psychometrically strong instruments to measure attention, concentration, and higher order cognitive abilities and completed his battery with them.

Forensic Clinical Neuropsychology

Following this review of the various types of neuropsychological test batteries that are extant in the literature, we will now discuss another area that the clinical neuropsychologist may need to consider, which has been referred to earlier in the text. Recently, clinical neuropsychologists are increasingly becoming involved within the forensic arena. This implies that the clinical neuropsychologist may need to present his or her report and recommendations regarding a patient in a situation that involves legal ramifications. Forensic clinical neuropsychology is now considered to be a subspecialty of clinical neuropsychology that directly applies neuropsychological principles and practices to matters that pertain to legal decision making. Practitioners of forensic clinical neuropsychology are trained as clinical neuropsychologists and, subsequently, specialize in the forensic application of their knowledge and skills (Hom, 2003).

Whether the clinical neuropsychologist determines that a fixed, flexible, or process-oriented battery is appropriate for the client, in a forensic setting, other issues often surface. Some of these issues may point the clinical neuropsychologist toward a certain type of test battery. Key among the issues is the psychometrics of the test battery. The clinical neuropsychologist is dependent on the battery plus his or her clinical judgment to make recommendations that have great ramifications in forensic setting. For example, the case study at the beginning of the chapter involves a young person who was involved in a motor vehicle accident. In this particular case, the client's mother stated that she was employing an attorney in order to possibly recoup money for outstanding medical bills. Due to the circumstances, the fact that there was more than one person involved and that each produces a somewhat dissimilar accounting of the event leads the clinical neuropsychologist to be very careful with his interview and assessment. Particular to this issue, but also often involved with forensic clinical neuropsychology, is the degree of memory impairment experienced by the client. Also of importance is the amount of time the client may have been unconscious as having an impact on the ability of that client to accurately describe circumstances of the accident or injury. Also related is the motivation of all individuals involved. Many individuals may honestly want to divide blame versus others who may claim disability benefits, have apparent secondary gain, or even be malingering.

The area of forensic clinical neuropsychology encompasses both criminal and civil litigation. As more and more clinical neuropsychologists become involved in forensics, both types of cases could be encountered. However, in general terms, there are more referrals for civil than criminal evaluation. As was discussed in the chapter on ethics, a current controversy in clinical neuropsychology is the release of raw test data in a forensic situation. At the time of this writing, the issue has not been settled but the reader is referred to the Ethical Principles of Psychologists and Code of Conduct and the Health Insurance Portability and Accountability Act (HIPAA) guidelines.

In the area of criminal evaluations, many of the referrals relate to the competency of the individual to stand trial. The clinical neuropsychologist in these circumstances would most often be an officer of the court and the aim of the evaluation is to render an objective assessment regarding the mental functioning of the individual through interview and the use of testing procedures. Competency to stand trial occurs through all phases of the criminal judicial process from the first contact a suspect has with law enforcement to the time of sentencing and even the point of execution in capital cases (Grisso, 1988).

Neuropsychological evaluations in criminal cases have enormous ramifications on an individual's life; hence, it is essential that as much data be gained as possible. Information from many areas in addition to interview and testing data is suggested (i.e., medical records, collateral interviews with other individuals, etc.). It is also essential that the clinical neuropsychologist be conversant with the legal system and the role he or she will have in the process. Finally, the clinical neuropsychologist needs to keep in mind that a defendant in a criminal case may not be cooperative and may deliberately distort the test results.

Civil cases tend to have different types of referral questions than do criminal cases. There is less concern about the competency issue and more concern regarding the presence of brain dysfunction and whether the dysfunction results from the event under question. Very often, the question is also raised regarding the premorbid functioning of the individual versus the person's current strengths and weaknesses. As stated previously, some of the most important civil issues could relate to recovering damages to pay medical bills, lost wages, or possible disability issues.

As we close our discussion of neuropsychological test batteries, we return to our case study. Amanda was assessed by the clinical neuropsychologist and the report was submitted to an arbitrator whom Amanda's mother and the truck driver had agreed to employ to settle their issues. Neither party was interested in pursuing a protracted legal battle. It appeared to both sides that both parties were at fault. Because Amanda was eligible and had been receiving Social Security Disability Insurance (SSDI) benefits, there was no need for the truck driver to assume any medical bills. Each individual agreed to assume responsibility for their own vehicle. The negative outcome of the situation for Amanda is that she continues to experience emotional sequela to her head injury as well as some concentration and attention difficulties. With the assistance of cognitive rehabilitation, these difficulties are slowly and gradually abating. However, she is aware that for the remainder of her life, she may be more tired on exertion than other individuals and that the use of alcohol and other substances may affect her more strongly than it had premorbidly.

Summary

The chapter began with a case study that addresses the issues involved for a young woman who was in a moving vehicle accident. These issues involved appropriate assessment and how it could be chosen with the caveat that school, work, and litigation could all be involved.

The chapter's focus was on the various types of neuropsychological batteries that are available. Definitions of fixed, flexible, and process-oriented batteries were included. The most often used neuropsychological test batteries were described and their psychometrics were reviewed.

The chapter ended with a short review of forensic neuropsychology. This section was included due to the fact that more and more clinical neuropsychologists are practicing as expert witnesses in both criminal and civil litigation.

Questions for Further Study

1. How will neuropsychological test batteries change as technology changes?
2. What are the ramifications of the ethical issues raised regarding the release of raw test data?
3. Are there circumstances in which none of the available test batteries would be able to answer the referral question? Is this related to ecological validity?

References

Adams, K. M., Gilman, S., Koeppe, R., Klaine, K., Junck, L., Lohman, M., et al. (1995). Correlations of neuropsychological function with cerebral metabolism rate in subdivisions of frontal lobes of older alcoholic patients measured with [−1-8F] fluorodeoxyglucose and positron emission tomography. *Neuropsychology, 9,* 275–280.

Adams, R. L., & Trenton, S. L. (1981). Development of a paper-and-pen form of the Halstead Category Test. *Journal of Consulting and Clinical Psychology, 49,* 298–299.

Army Individual Test Battery. (1944) *Manual of directions and scoring.* Washington DC: War Department, Adjutant General's Office.

Benton, A. L. (1950). A multiple choice type of visual retention test. *Archives Neurological Psychiatry, 64,* 699–707.

Boll, T. J. (1981). The Halstead-Reitan Neuropsychology Battery. In S. B. Filskov & T. J. Boll (Eds.), *Handbook of clinical neuropsychology* (pp. 577–607). New York, NY: John Wiley & Sons, Inc.

Bornstein, R. A., Baker, R. B., & Douglas, A. B. (1987). Short-term test-retest reliability of the Halstead-Reitan Battery in a normal sample. *The Journal of Nervous and Mental Diseases, 175,* 229–232.

Bornstein, R. A., Paniak, C., & O'Brien, W. (1987). Preliminary data on classification of normal and brain-damaged elderly subjects. *Developmental Neuropsychology, 4,* 315–323.

Butters, N., & Grady, M. (1977). Effects of predistractor delays on the short-term memory performance of patients with Korsakoff's and Huntington's Disease. *Neuropsychologia, 13,* 701–705.

Charter, R. A., & Dobbs, S. M. (1998). Long and short forms of the Speech Sounds Perception Test: Item analysis and age and education correlations. *The Clinical Neuropsychologist, 12,* 213–216.

Charter, R. A., & Webster, J. S. (1997). Psychometric structure of the Seashore Rhythm Test. *The Clinical Neuropsychologist, 11,* 167–173.

Christensen, A. L. (1975). *Luria's neuropsychological investigation: Text, manual, and test cards.* New York: Spectrum.

Christensen, A. L. (1979). *Luria's neuropsychological investigation* (2nd ed.). Copenhagen, Denmark: Munksgaard.

Christensen, A. L. (1989). The neuropsychological investigation as a therapeutic and rehabilitative technique. In D. W. Ellis & A. L. Christensen (Eds.), *Neuropsychological treatment after brain damage* (pp. 127–156). Norwall, MA: Kluwer.

Dean, R. S., & Woodcock, R. W. (2003). *Dean-Woodcock Neuropsychological Battery.* Itasca, IL: Riverside Publishing.

Dean, R. S., & Meier, M. J. (1985). [Review of the Halstead-Reitan Neuropsychological Test Battery]. In J. V. Mitchel (Ed.), *The ninth mental measurements yearbook.* Lincoln, NE: Buros Institute of Mental Measurements.

Delis, D. C., Kaplan, E., & Kramer, J. H. (2001). *The Delis Kaplan executive function system.* San Antonio, TX: The Psychological Corporation.

Dikmen, S. J., & Reitan, R. M. (1977). Emotional sequalae of head injury. *Annals of Neurology, 2,* 492.

Dikmen, S. S., Heaton, R. K., Grant, I., & Temkin, N. R. (1999). Test-retest reliability and practice effects of the expanded Halstead-Reitan neuropsychological test battery. *Journal of the International Neuropsychological Society, 5,* 346–356.

Dugbartey, A., & Ramsden, P. (2003). [Review of the Delis-Kaplan Executive Function System]. In B. S. Plake, J. C. Impara & R. A. Spies (Eds.), *The fifteenth mental measurements yearbook.* Lincoln, NE: Buros Institute of Mental Measurements.

Fromm-Auch, P., & Yudall, L. T. (1983). Normative data for the Halstead-Reitan neuropsychological tests. *Journal of Clinical Neuropsychology, 5,* 221–230.

Glozman, J. M. (1999). Quantitative and qualitative integration of Luria's procedures. *Neuropsychology Review, 9,* 23–32.

Golden, C. J., Purisch, A. D., & Hammeke, T. A. (1985). *Luria Nebraska Neuropsychological Battery: Forms I and II Manual.* Los Angeles: Western Psychological Services.

Golden, C. J., Purisch, A. D., & Hammeke, T. A. (1991). *Luria Nebraska Neuropsychological Battery: Forms I and II*. Los Angeles: Western Psychological Services.

Goldstein, C., & Watson, J. R. (1989). Test-retest reliability of the Halstead-Reitan Battery and the WAIS in a neuropsychiatric population. *The Clinical Neuropsychologist, 3*, 265–273.

Goodglass, H., & Kaplan, E. (1972). *The assessment of aphasia and related disorders*. Philadelphia: Lea & Febinger.

Gorham, D. R. (1956). *Proverbs test*. Missoula, MT: Psychological Test Specialists.

Grant, D. A., & Berg, E. A. (1948). A behavioral analysis of degree of reinforcement and ease of shifting to new responses in a Weigl-type card sorting program. *Journal of Experimental Psychology, 38*, 404–411.

Grisso, T. (1988). *Competency to stand trial evaluations: A manual for practice*. Sarasota, FL: Professsional Research Exchange.

Guilmette, T. J., Faust, D., Hart, K. J., & Arkes, H. K. (1990). A national survey of psychologists who offer neuropsychological services. *Archives of Clinical Neuropsychology, 5*, 373–392.

Halstead, W. C. (1947). *Brain and intelligence: A quantitative study of the frontal lobes*. Chicago: University of Chicago Press.

Heaton, R. K., & Crowley, T. J. (1981). Effects of psychiatric disorders and their somatic treatments on neuropsychological test results. In S. B. Filskov & T. J. Boll (Eds.), *Handbook of clinical neuropsychology* (pp. 481–525). New York: John Wiley & Sons, Inc.

Heaton, R. K., Miller, S. W., Taylor, M. J., & Grant, I. (2004). *Revised comprehensive norms for an expanded Halstead-Reitan Battery*. Odessa, FL: Psychological Assessment Resources.

Heilbronner, R. L., Henry, G. K., Buck, P., Adams, R. L., & Fogle, T. (1991). Lateralized brain damage and performance of Trail Making A and B, Digit Span Forward and Backward and TPT memory and location. *Archives of Clinical Neuropsychology, 6*, 251–258.

Hom, J. (2003). Forensic neuropsychology: Are we there yet? *Archives of Clinical Neuropsychology, 18*, 827–846.

Hooper, H. E. (1958). *The Hooper Visual Organization Test Manual*. Los Angeles: Western Psychological Services.

Horton, A. M., & Wedding, D. (1984). *Clinical and behavioral neuropsychology*. New York: Praeger.

Horton, A. M. (2008). The Halstead-Reitan Neuropsychology Test Battery: Past, present and future. In D. Wedding & A. M. Horton (Eds.), *The neuropsychology handbook* (pp. 253–280). New York: Springer Publishing Company.

Horton, A. M., Jr. (1995). Alternative Impairment Index: A measure of neuropsychological deficit. *Perceptual and Motor Skills, 80*, 336–338.

Horton, A. M., Jr., Anilane, J., Slone, D., & Shapiro, G. (1986). Development and cross-validation of a short-form impairment index. *Archives of Clinical Neuropsychology, 1*, 243–246.

Jarvis, P. E., & Barth, J. T. (1994). *Halstead-Reitan Test Battery: An interpretive guide* (2nd ed.). Odessa, FL: Psychological Assessment Resources.

Jastak, J. F., & Jastak, S. R. (1978). *The wide range achievement test manual* (revised). Los Angeles: Western Psychological Services.

Leach, L., Kaplan, E., Rewilak, D., Richards, B., & Proulx, G. B. (2000). *Kaplan Baycrest Neurocognitive Assessment*. San Antonio, TX: Psychological Corporation.

Levine, A., Miller, E., Becker, J., Seines, O., Cohen, B. (2004). Normative data for determining significance of test-retest differences on eight common neuropsychological instruments. *The Clinical Neuropsychologist, 18*, 373–384.

Lezak, M. D., Howieson, D. B., & Loring, D. W. (2004). *Neuropsychological assessment* (4th ed.). New York: Oxford University Press.

Lopez, M. N., Charter, R. A., & Newman, J. R. (2000). Psychometric properties of the Halsted Category Test. *The Clinical Neuropsychologist, 14*, 157–161.

Luria, A. L. (1966). *Higher cortical functions in man*. New York: Basic Books.

Luria, A. L. (1973). *The working brain: An introduction to neuropsychology* (B. Haigh, Trans.). New York: Basic Books. (Original work published 1969)

McCaffrey, R. J., Duff, K., & Westervelt, H. (2000). *Practitioner's guide to evaluating change with intellectual assessment instruments*. New York: Kluwer Academic/Plenum Press.

Milberg, W., Cummings, J., Goodglass, H., & Kaplan, E. (1979). Case report: A global sequential processing disorder following head injury: A possible role for the right hemisphere in serial order behavior. *Journal of Clinical Neuropsychology, 3,* 213–225.

Milberg,, W. P., Hebben, N., & Kaplan, E. (1986). The Boston Process Approach to neuropsychological assessment. In I. Grant & K. M. Adams (Eds.), *Neuropsychological assessment of neuropsychological disorders* (pp. 65–86). New York: Oxford University Press.

Milner, B. (1971). Interhemispheric differences in the localization of psychological processes in man. *British Medial Bulletin, 27,* 272–277.

Mitrushina, M. N., Boone, K. B., & D'Eli. (1999). *Handbook of normative data for neuropsychological assessment.* New York: Oxford University Press.

Mitrushina, M. N., Boone, K. B., Razani, J., & D'Elia, L. (2005). *Handbook of normative data for neuropsychological assessment* (2nd ed.). New York: Oxford University Press.

Osterreith, P., & Rey, A. (1944). Le test de copie d'une figure complexe [The test of copying a complex figure]. *Archives de Psychologie, 30,* 206–356.

Palmer, P., & Kaplan, E. (1985). The cow and circle experimental test (available from E. Kaplan). Unpublished test.

Porteus, S. D. (1965). *Porteus maze test.* Palo Alto, CA: Pacific Books.

Prigatano, G. P., & Borgaro, S. P. (2003). Qualitative features of finger movement during the Halstead-Reitan Finger Oscillation Test following traumatic brain injury. *Journal of the International Neuropsychological Society, 9,* 128–133.

Rabin, L. A., Barr, W. B., & Burton, L. A. (2005). Assessment practices of clinical neuropsychologists in the United States and Canada: A survey of INS, NAN, and APA Division 40 members. *Archives of Clinical Neuropsychology, 20,* 33–66.

Raven, J. C. (1960). *Guide to the standard progressive matrices.* London, UK: H. K. Lewis.

Reed, H. B. C., & Reitan, R. M. (1963). Intelligence test performances of brain damaged subjects with lateralized motor deficits. *Journal of Consulting Psychology, 27,* 102–106.

Reitan, R. M. (1985). Relationships between measures of brain functions and general intelligence. *Journal of Clinical Psychology, 41,* 245–253.

Reitan, R. M. (1986). *Trail making test: Manual for administration and scoring.* Tucson, AZ: Reitan Neuropsychology Laboratory.

Reitan, R. M. & Davidson. (1974). *Clinical Neuropsychology: Current status and applications.* New York: Winston/Wiley.

Reitan, R. M., & Wolfson, D. (1986). The Halstead-Reitan Neuropsychology Test Battery. In D. Wedding & A. M. Horton (Eds.), *The neuropsychology handbook.* New York: Springer Publishing Company.

Reitan, R. M., & Wolfson, D. (1988). *Traumatic brain injury: Vol. 2.* Recovery and rehabilitation. Tucson, AZ: Neuropsychology Press.

Reitan, R. M, & Wolfson, D. (1993). *The Halstead-Reitan Neuropsychological Test Battery: Theory and clinical interpretation* (2nd ed.). Tucson, AZ: Neuropsychology Press.

Reitan, R. M., & Wolfson, D. (1996). Relationships between specific and general tests of cerebral functioning. *The Clinical Neuropsychologist, 10,* 37–42.

Rey, A. (1964). *L'Examen clinique en psychologie* [The clinical examination in psychology]. Paris: Presses Universitaires de France.

Russel, E. W., Neuringer, C., & Goldstein, G. (1970). *Assessment of brain damage: A neuropsychological key approach.* New York: John Wiley & Sons, Inc.

Spiers, P. A. (1981). Have they come to praise Luria or to bury him? The Luria-Nebraska Battery Controversy. *Journal of Consulting and Clinical Psychology, 49,* 331–341.

Stern, R. A., & White, T. (2000). Survey of neuropsychological assessment practices. *Journal of the International Neuropsychological Society, 6,* 137.

Stern, R. A., & White, T. (2003). *Neuropsychological Assessment Battery.* Lutz, FL: Psychological Assessment Resources.

Strauss, E., Sherman, E. S., & Spreen, O. (Eds.) (2006). *A compendium of neuropsychological tests.* New York: Oxford University Press.

Stroop, J. R. (1935). Studies of interference in serial verbal reactions. *Journal of Experimental Psychology, 18,* 643–662.

Talland, G. A. (1965). *Deranged memory*. New York: Academic Press.

Thurstone, L. L. (1938). *Primary mental abilities*. Chicago: University of Chicago Press.

Truelle, J. L., LeGall, D., & Joseph, P. A. (1995). Movement disturbances following frontal lobe lesions. *Neuropsychiatry, Neuropsychology, and Behavioral Neurology, 8*, 14–19.

Tupper, D. E. (1999). Introduction: Alexander Luria's continuing influence on worldwide neuropsychology. *Neuropsychology Review, 9*, 1–7.

Wechsler, D. A. (1945). A standardized memory scale for clinical use. *Journal of Psychology, 19*, 87–95.

Wechsler, D. A. (1974). *Wechsler Intelligence Scale for Children-Revised*. New York: Psychological Corporation.

Wechsler, D. A. (1981). *Wechsler Adult Intelligence Scale-Revised*. New York: Psychological Corporation.

Wechsler, D. (2008). *Wechsler Adult Intelligence Scale-Fourth Edition: Technical and interpretive manual*. San Antonio, TX: Pearson Assessment.

Wechsler, D. (2009). *Wechsler Memory Scale-Fourth Edition*. San Antonio, TX: Pearson Assessment.

Wolfson, D., & Reitan, R. M. (1995). Cross-validation of the General Neuropsychology Deficit Scale (GNDS). *Archives of Clinical Neuropsychology, 10*, 125–131.

Woodcock, R. N., McGrew, K. S., & Malther, N. (2001a). *Woodcock-Johnson III Test of Achievement*. Itasca, IL: Riverside Publishing.

Woodcock, R. N., McGrew, K. S., & Malther, N. (2001b). *Woodcock-Johnson III Tests of Cognitive Ability*. Itasca, IL: Riverside Publishing.

Zachary, R. A. (1986). *Shipley Institute of Living Scale: Revised manual*. Los Angeles: Western Psychological Service.

Differential Diagnosis

10

Learning Objectives

After reading this chapter, the student should be able to understand:

- The concept of differential diagnosis and its importance in determining treatment plans, communicating with other professionals, and for reimbursement purposes
- The history and current status of the *Diagnostic and Statistical Manual of Mental Disorders (DSM)* as well as its relationship to the *International Classification of Diseases (ICD)*
- The multiaxial system of the *DSM* and how the axes aid in differential diagnosis and treatment planning
- The disorders encompassed within the five axes of the *DSM*
- The coding system used in the *DSM* and its purpose in relationship to insurance and reimbursement

Topical Outline

Case Vignette

*L*ori is a 35-year-old White female. She was referred for psychotherapy by a previous therapist who felt that she (the therapist) was not able to provide all of the services that Lori needed. Lori had been seen in therapy by the referring therapist for approximately 1 year and a summary of treatment goals indicated that she had multiple issues which included appropriate friendships, independent living, financial responsibility, and developing assertiveness skills. She also needs assistance coping with central nervous system difficulties which include epilepsy and borderline intellectual functioning.

Lori has had two other previous therapists whose notes also included similar goals, such as setting appropriate boundaries and not misusing support services (i.e., frequent emergency room visits and telephone calls for nonemergency reasons). Hence, it is clear that she has not mastered living as an adult in the community. In addition to three female therapists, Lori receives services from a man who is a senior county social worker, and various male and female county employees who help her with living skills, budgeting, getting to appointments, and so forth. She also has county-funded male and female drivers who take her to medical and psychological appointments. Lori does not drive due to her epilepsy, which has not been totally controlled by medicine. Completing the treatment team, Lori has had a male psychiatrist and is currently working with a female psychiatrist, a male neurologist, and a female primary care physician. The listing of professionals gives the reader an idea not only of the myriad of services which she needs but also that she has worked with professionals of both gender and has had difficulty with both.

In terms of personal history, Lori is the third of four children born to her biological parents. She has two older brothers, 37 and 39 years old both of whom are married and have children and one younger brother, 31 who is single. All of her siblings are functioning well in the community and none has central nervous system difficulties. Her parents are retired and living in their own home approximately 45 miles away from Lori.

Lori is a high school graduate who completed many of her classes in special education. It is unclear from the referral source whether testing was completed in order to place her in these classes and Lori does not recall. Requests for information from the school could not uncover the information because at that time, placement may not have been based on testing. As best as she could recall after high school graduation she had a seizure but does not remember the experience. She awoke in the hospital and was told by her mother that the physician felt she was suffering from epilepsy and prescribed phenobarbital. Lori was very unhappy about the episode. Her mother was concerned both about the seizure and also about Lori's planned move out of the home. Lori let her mother talk her into staying at home with her parents. Lori became very despondent regarding her situation and began to isolate herself. A few months later Lori was admitted into a state hospital for what she described as suicidal ideation. However, she indicated she was not seriously suicidal but more upset about having seizures. She spent 3 months in the hospital and was then released to her parents' care and enrolled in a partial care program at her local community mental health center for several months. **Partial care** is a program designed to help individuals transfer from a hospital-based program to living on one's own or in a group setting. Partial Care programs usually offer breakfast and lunch that the participants help prepare, in addition to classes, which are oriented toward development of independent living skills. Also included may be group and/or individual therapy.

After several months, Lori convinced her parents that she was doing well and they agreed she could live on her own in the community. She moved into a one-bedroom apartment in a small community 45 miles away from her parents. She began receiving county social services sometime after her move. As best as she could recall, the county services were invoked as part of

partial care
a program, often administered by a county mental health center, that is used as a transitional program for individuals who are going from hospitalization to independent or semi-independent living

*the aftercare plan developed by her local Community Mental Health Center. An **aftercare plan** is developed to provide an individual with community-based services as one transitions to living on his or her own. Often the services include assistance with transportation, meal planning, budgeting, and financial assistance.*

*Lori has attempted to work in the community many times in various positions but she often has trouble with undertaking the task she is to complete or has difficulties with coworkers. She has had difficulties with both males and females and often has unrealistic expectations of relationships with individuals. After many years of attempting employment, Lori began volunteer work at the local hospital. In this capacity, she feels better treated because as she stated, "I don't have to be there" and "the people are grateful for whatever I do." Hence, she feels that she is praised and valued for whatever she is capable of doing. Her parents, however, would like her to be working and not relying on government services, which "cost taxpayers' money." Since she left home, she describes an estranged relationship with her family and feels her parents do not treat her as well as they treat her brothers or allow her the freedom that her brothers have. She admits this bothers her a great deal, even though her parents are not her legal guardians and she has not been judged to be incompetent to manage her own affairs. However, it soon becomes apparent when speaking with her that Lori could be considered to be a **vulnerable adult**. The legal definition of vulnerable adult varies by state but usually implies someone who for physical or mental health reasons may be an easy victim of unscrupulous individuals or may have difficulty living on one's own in the community.*

Lori has had very poor and erratic relationships with men. She appears to make poor choices with regard to whom to trust and whom to allow in her apartment. While she states that she has never been sexually assaulted, she does admit to having intercourse in circumstances or with people that she would rather not have. Hence, by most legal definitions, she has been sexually violated. She also has a pattern of loaning money to others even when she is relatively sure that the money will never be returned. She appears to be easily swayed by whatever the person says is the reason to borrow money or she may have been under some form of coercion. Due to some of the difficulties she has had with relationships, she states that she is often nervous, has trouble sleeping, and has nightmares. She has been prescribed medication for sleep (trazodone [Desyrel]) and an antidepressant (paroxetine [Paxil]) that also has properties to alleviate anxiety. She has been told by all of the professionals that she should be very careful taking her medications and refrain from chemical use permanently because she has epilepsy. However, under stress, she admitted that she likes to consume wine coolers. Although these are not strong alcoholic beverages, she should not consume any type of alcohol. She is also unclear or evasive about the quantity she consumes, which makes it difficult to determine if this is a significant problem for her or not.

aftercare plan
a treatment plan for individuals who are residing in the community to ensure they have all of their needs provided

vulnerable adult
an individual who, because of physical or mental difficulties or both, is determined to not be able to care for him- or herself and his or her affairs in the community

Clearly, one of the most important issues for Lori to work on in therapy is making appropriate choices, whether in relationships, financial situations, employment, volunteer work, and particularly in chemical use. The clinical neuropsychologist who works with Lori will need to prioritize which issues should be addressed in the appropriate order based on a differential diagnosis of her difficulties. Lori has many issues, all of which have roots in central nervous system functioning. Extant records (i.e., medical, school, social services, etc.) gave information already discussed regarding special education courses but no testing information. Medical records indicate that she has been treated for seizures beginning after high school. Once she was on her own she began to go from doctor to doctor not agreeing with various treatments or feeling that the doctor did not care enough about her. Records from social service providers indicate that she has been referred to as a very difficult client with whom to work. She is described as very demanding and having inappropriate boundaries. She has been switched between social workers many times. Until the present referral, there has been no formal assessment completed beyond one intelligence test which was requested by a social worker. The intelligence test stated that her abilities fell within the borderline level of functioning.

The clinical neuropsychologist who she was referred to gathered all of this information and the particulars of the case and decided that a well-standardized battery of tests would help develop a picture of Lori's strengths and weakness. She was administered the Halstead-Reitan Neuropsychological Test Battery (HRTB) over 2 days to prevent fatigue. Given the information regarding the difficulties inherent with the HRTB, it was chosen due to the fact that it had a wealth of comparison norms and was also a fixed battery. With a client who exhibits weak boundaries it would be difficult to employ a flexible battery which may not be rigid enough to keep her focused. Intake interview information revealed a young woman who was very needy, dependent, and somewhat histrionic. It was debatable whether her accounts of information were true and/or accurate; however, she would not allow the clinical neuropsychologist to speak to anyone else to verify the information. After the information was gathered and compared to available historical information, the clinical neuropsychologist produced the following five-axis diagnosis based on the *Diagnostic and Statistical Manual of Mental Disorders, Fourth Edition–Text Revision* (*DSM-IV-TR*; American Psychiatric Association [APA], 2000).

- Axis I—300.4 Dysthymic Disorder
  309.81 Posttraumatic Stress Disorder (provisional)
  305.00 Alcohol Abuse (provisional)
- Axis II—V62.89 Borderline Intellectual Functioning
  301.83 Borderline Personality Disorder
- Axis III—Epilepsy
- Axis IV—Poor Social Relationships, Financial Difficulties, Employment Difficulties, Family Difficulties
- Axis V—Global Assessment of Functioning (GAF) = 50

Introduction

The current chapter contains the basics for developing a differential diagnosis within the area of clinical neuropsychology. The aforementioned diagnostic schema illustrated via the case study is an example that will be used throughout the chapter. The reader will be introduced to the *DSM-IV-TR* (APA, 2000) and its history from the time the first diagnostic manual was published. The reasons for and uses of a diagnostic nomenclature or categorization system will be provided. In addition to the basics of applying a diagnosis, there will also be a discussion of how one separates various diagnostic groupings that often have similar symptoms.

Difficulties in Differential Diagnosis

According to Lezak, Howieson, and Loring (2004), one of the most common issues which a clinical neuropsychologist faces is that brain disease may be manifested in an emotional or personality disturbance, or conversely that behavioral deterioration or cognitive complaints may have a psychological rather than a neurological basis. However, with newer technologies and research, it has become clear that the central nervous system affects any and all functions of the person. The clinical neuropsychologist is thus faced with the task of determining the appropriate course of action or declaring which area, neurological or psychological, should be treated first. In addition, the causal pattern must be determined for appropriate treatment.

In the case study it is very important to determine the specific difficulties Lori is experiencing, as well as determining the course and prognosis for her difficulties. All of this is part of any differential diagnostic process. Another important issue in differential diagnosis is to determine the preexisting difficulties or circumstances that may have been in place before the central nervous system difficulty occurred. These premorbid factors may help or hinder any form of treatment or rehabilitation.

Development of the Diagnostic System

In order to develop an appropriate treatment or rehabilitation plan a clinical neuropsychologist must understand the difficulty from which the client is suffering. A *diagnostic label* is a term applied to a group of symptoms which tend to occur together and therefore may be referred to as a **syndrome**. The application of a diagnostic label to a group of symptoms began in the field of medicine when physicians needed to understand the particular ailment from which a patient was suffering before any treatment began. The alternative to having an accurate diagnosis could be disastrous, possibly causing unnecessary procedures or surgeries. Even with careful application of diagnoses, there are often cases of medical mistakes which make it even more critical to be particularly careful in the diagnostic process.

syndrome
a group of symptoms that tend to occur together and therefore receive a diagnostic label

The *DSM* is published by the APA and is considered a medical text. It is patterned after the *International Classification of Diseases* (ICD) published by the World Health Organization (WHO). The current version is the *ICD-10* published in 1992 with, a clinical modification published in 2004. The *ICD*, in all of its versions, lists symptoms with an overarching term used to describe the syndrome. All known medical difficulties and mental disorders are listed in the *ICD*. The *DSM* includes the symptoms of various psychiatric disorders including the current term for the particular difficulty. In addition, it includes further information regarding incidence, prevalence, sex ratio, familial pattern, and differential diagnostic features. All of these additional features are not included within the *ICD*. The *DSM* uses the same code numbers as the *ICD* for purposes of medical record keeping.

The primary use of the *DSM* is for the clinical neuropsychologist or other professional to apply the appropriate term to the client's symptoms in order to ensure appropriate treatment. The other reasons why an appropriate diagnosis is useful include communication among professionals, research, and insurance payments. Many insurance companies will not pay for a client's services without a diagnostic label.

Even though the need is great to diagnose the appropriate difficulty within the individual, the original impetus for the development of a diagnostic schema in the United States came from a need to collect statistical information. The reason for needing to know the number of individuals with difficulties was to determine the amount of money that would be allocated from the federal government for services for them. The 1840 census was the first time that a psychiatric category was included and was termed *idiocy/insanity*. By the 1880 census, seven categories of mental illness were distinguished: mania, melancholia, monomania, paresis, dementia, dipsomania, and epilepsy (APA, 2000). In 1917, the Committee on Statistics of the APA in conjunction with the National Commission on Mental Hygiene formulated a plan that was adopted by the Bureau of the Census for gathering uniform statistics across mental hospitals. Subsequently, the APA collaborated with the New York Academy of Medicine to develop a nationally acceptable psychiatric nomenclature that would be incorporated within the first edition of the American Medical Association's Standard Classified Nomenclature of Disease. This was used primarily to diagnose patients with severe psychiatric and neurological disorders. A broader nomenclature was later developed by the U.S. Army and modified by the Veterans Administration to better incorporate the outpatient presentations of World War II service members and veterans. At that point in time the *ICD* was in its sixth edition and included a section regarding mental disorders.

The APA published the first *DSM* in 1952 patterned after the *ICD-6*. *DSM-I* contained a glossary of descriptions of the diagnostic categories and was the first official manual of mental disorders to focus on clinical utility (APA, 2000). The term *reaction* was used throughout the first *DSM* and reflected Adolph Meyer's (one of the original authors) psychobiological view that mental disorders represented reactions of the personality to psychological, social, and biological factors.

The first revision, *DSM-II*, published in 1968, was similar to the original *DSM* except that it did not include the word *reaction*. At the same time there was widespread nonacceptance of the *ICD-6* and *ICD-7*. The *ICD-6* was greatly influenced by the Veterans' Administration and included 10 categories for psychosis, 9 for psychoneurosis, and 7 for disorders of character, behavior, and intelligence. Both *ICD-6* and *ICD-7* were thought to lack specific diagnostic criteria. Hence, the WHO sponsored a comprehensive review of diagnostic issues conducted by the British psychologist Stengel. However, none of his conclusions were included with *DSM-II*. Stengel touted the need for explicit definitions as a means for reliable clinical diagnosis (APA, 2000).

The next revision, *DSM-III*, which was published in 1980, was coordinated with the development of the ninth version of the *ICD*, which had been published in 1975. *DSM-III* was quite different from its predecessors in that it contained explicit diagnostic criteria, a multiaxial system, and a descriptive approach that attempted to be neutral regarding theories of etiology (APA, 2000). Even though *DSM-III* was quite different from previous diagnostic schemas, it still contained criteria that were not clear in some circumstances. Therefore, the *DSM-III-R* was published in 1987. Significant changes during the period between *DSM-III* and *DSM-III-R* included the inclusion of Posttraumatic Stress Disorder (PTSD), an anxiety-based disorder, and the exclusion of homosexuality except in the case of **ego-dystonic** circumstances (situations in which the individual did not desire to be homosexual).

DSM-IV benefited greatly from the type of literature reviews and field trials that were conducted before the publication of *DSM-III* and *DSM-III-R*. Hence, the goal of the *DSM-IV* literature review was to provide comprehensive and unbiased information and to ensure that *DSM-IV* reflected the best available clinical and research literature. *DSM-IV* was published in 1994. As time has passed, there has been a special effort to consider the effects of ethnic and cultural considerations in diagnosis. Differential diagnosis may be particularly challenging when a clinical neuropsychologist from one ethnic or cultural group uses the diagnostic manual to evaluate an individual from another ethnic or cultural group. In a similar vein, it may be difficult to evaluate women as the majority clinical neuropsychologists at the present time are men.

The *DSM-IV* includes three types of information specifically related to cultural considerations: (a) a discussion in the text of cultural variation in the clinical presentation of various disorders, (b) a description of **culture-bound** syndromes that are not included in the *DSM* but are included within Appendix I, and (c) an outline for cultural formulations designed to assist the clinical neuropsychologist in evaluating and reporting the input of the individual's culture (APA, 2000, Appendix I).

DSM-IV-TR was published in 2000 as an intermediary step between *DSM-IV* and the soon-to-be-published *DSM-V*. The *TR* in this designation stands for *Text Revision*. *DSM-IV-TR* includes all of the features described in *DSM-IV*. The goals for *DSM-IV-TR* included correcting any factual errors identified in the *DSM-IV* text, making sure the information is up-to-date, making any changes that reflect new information available since the publication of *DSM-IV*, making any changes that would increase its educational value, and updating *ICD-9-Clinical Modification* (CM) codes, which have been changed. All changes are in the text, and there were no new disorders, subtypes, or appendices added to the *DSM-IV-TR*.

Axes of the *Diagnostic and Statistical Manual of Mental Disorders*

The student will need a frame of reference to begin his or her understanding of differential diagnosis. This text will use *DSM-IV-TR* with the caveat that by the time of publication, *DSM-V* may be the standard for practice. The axes will not be changed, however, the inclusion or exclusion of various disorders will certainly occur, as will other adjustments be made similar to those described when the diagnostic manual went from *DSM-IV* to *DSM-IV-TR*. The term **axis** refers to one of the five areas in which information is placed, which will help the professional develop a clearer picture of the individual. *DSM-IV-TR* is a **multiaxial system**, which means that it contains different information on each axis all of which is included to aid in treatment planning and to predict outcome (APA, 2000). As a word of caution, beginning clinical neuropsychologists and other professionals tend to overdiagnose as they are learning the **nomenclature**. Nomenclature describes the names and labels that make up the **nosology**, which is the classification system. It is very important that all required symptoms be present for the particular diagnostic category before a label is applied.

The beginning section of *DSM-IV-TR* is entitled "Disorders Usually First Diagnosed in Infancy, Childhood, or Adolescence" (APA, 2000). Not all of the disorders in this category are apparent during those years and may therefore be diagnosed in adulthood (i.e., Attention Deficit/Hyperactivity Disorder [ADHD]). In addition, many disorders listed later in the *DSM* (i.e., depression or schizophrenia) may be diagnosed during the childhood years. The next three sections, "Delirium, Dementia, Amnesia, and Other Cognitive Disorders"; "Mental Disorders Due to a General Medical Condition"; and "Substance-Related Disorders," are listed in the order they are due to the historical artifact that in *DSM-III-R*, they were all listed under the single-term *organic mental syndromes and disorders* (APA, 2000). The implication was that these disorders had a biological basis and other disorders did not. Current research suggests that this is not the case. However, for example in terms of differential diagnosis, it is important to rule out substance-related causes of depressed mood before applying a diagnosis of Major Depressive Disorder. In the *DSM-IV-TR*, the complete list of the Mental Disorders due to Medical Condition and Substance-Related Disorders appears in these sections, whereas the text and criteria for these disorders are placed in the diagnostic sections with the disorder with which they share **phenomenology** (APA, 2000). The remaining sections group disorders based on their shared phenomenological features. The following is a list of the syndromes within which all of the Axis I disorders fall (APA, 2000):

- Disorders Usually First Diagnosed in Infancy, Childhood, or Adolescence (excluding Mental Retardation, which is diagnosed on Axis II)
- Delirium, Dementia, and Amnesia and other cognitive disorders

axis
in the *DSM* diagnostic schema, an axis is where information is recorded regarding a specific diagnosis or the medical and social information regarding the overall functioning of the individual

multiaxial system
this term refers particularly to the *DSM* and its use in diagnosis; multiaxial implies that information is recorded regarding multiple issues that relate ultimately to treatment of the individual

- Mental Disorders due to Medical Condition
- Substance-Related Disorders
- Schizophrenia and other Psychotic Disorders
- Mood Disorders
- Anxiety Disorders
- Somatoform Disorders
- Factitious Disorders
- Dissociative Disorders
- Sexual and Gender Identity Disorders
- Eating Disorders
- Sleep Disorders
- Impulse-Control Disorders Not Otherwise Classified
- Adjustment Disorders
- Personality Disorders
- Other conditions that may be a focus of clinical attention

AXIS I

Axis I of the diagnostic nomenclature includes clinical syndromes and V codes. Clinical syndromes are the set of symptoms that through research have been determined to coexist on a regular basis and hence have been given a label (i.e., Schizophrenia or Bipolar I Disorder). An individual may be diagnosed with one or more disorders on Axis I, or there may not be any Axis I difficulties apparent. The individual in our case study was diagnosed with two Axis I difficulties. V codes are issues that need to be addressed in rehabilitation, treatment, or therapy but tend not to be viewed as mental disorders and are technically referred to as other conditions that may be a focus of clinical attention. Examples of V codes include academic problems, malingering, or religious or spiritual problems. Clinical syndromes and V codes are listed on Axis I in the order of importance for treatment. If no Axis I disorder is present, it should be coded as V 71.09 or if an Axis I diagnosis is **deferred** it should be coded as 799.9 (APA, 2000). Deferring a diagnosis implies that the diagnosis is provisional or time limited until other information is gathered, which would lead to a clearer determination if the condition existed.

Disorders Usually First Evident in Infancy, Childhood, or Adolescence

Differential diagnosis of each of the 16 classes of disorders will now be discussed. As stated previously, the category disorders usually first diagnosed in infancy, childhood, or adolescence is the first grouping. Learning Disorders are difficulties with academic functioning in which the individual performs below what would be expected at given age, education, and measured intelligence. These difficulties include (a) Reading Disorder, (b) Mathematics Disorder, (c) Disorder of Written Expression, and (d) Learning Disorder Not Otherwise Specified (NOS). In terms of differential diagnosis, it is important to note that Learning Disorders are different from normal variations in academic ability and are not due to lack of opportunity, poor teaching, or cultural difficulties (National Joint Committee on Learning Disability, 1990). Learning Disorders are not synonymous with lowered intelligence; however, many individuals with these difficulties sustain lowered IQ when they are tested (Gregg, Hoy, & Gay, 1996). A new approach called *response to intervention* screens children who do not respond well to proven intervention strategies at an early age before the Learning Disorder causes significant difficulties (Compton, Fuchs, Fuchs, & Bryant, 2006). Vision and hearing difficulties must be separated from Learning Disorders as well as mental retardation. Learning Disorders may be diagnosed in conjunction with Pervasive Developmental Disorders

(PDD) only when the individual's level of performance is below what is expected for a given intellectual functioning and schooling. Individuals with Communication Disorders may also have Learning Disorders but it may be very difficult to assess. Learning Disorders often occur together, therefore, there may be multiple diagnoses within this group.

Motor Skills Disorder comprises Developmental Coordination Disorder, which is defined as motor coordination that is substantially lower than would be expected for age and measured intelligence. Motor Skills Disorder must be separated from coordination problems due to neurological disorders and mental retardation. This diagnosis is not appropriate if the criteria are met for PDD. Children who have ADHD are often climbing, falling, or knocking things over but this is usually due to distractibility and impulsivity.

Communication Disorders include difficulties with speech or language and include (a) Expressive Language Disorder, (b) Mixed Receptive Expressive Language Disorder, (d) Phonological Disorder, Stuttering, and (d) Communicative Disorder NOS. Each of the Communication Disorders needs to be separated from one another based on symptoms present. Communication Disorders are not diagnosed if criteria are met for PDD. Difficulties with communication may also occur because of mental retardation, hearing or other sensory deficit, or severe environmental deprivation. Selective mutism may appear as a Communication Disorder but the person should not be diagnosed if they are able to communicate in any setting. A Communication Disorder may be related to a general medical condition but only if it continues beyond the usual recovery period for the particular medical condition.

PDD are severe difficulties that include deficits in reciprocal social interaction, impairment in communication and the presence of stereotypical behavioral interests and activity (Durand, 2005). Autistic Disorder is the most commonly diagnosed PDD. The exact figures for autism are controversial with early research suggesting a rate of 2–20 in 10,000 to divergent estimates as high as 1 in every 500 births (Shattuck, 2006). Autism includes symptoms of qualitative impairment in social interaction (at least two of the following: impairment in the use of multiple nonverbal behaviors, failure to develop peer relationships at appropriate developmental level, lack of sharing of interests, lack of social or emotional reciprocity); impairment in communication (at least one of the following: delay or lack of spoken speech, inability to sustain conversation, stereotyped or repetitive language, or lack of make-believe play); and a restrictive and/or repetitive pattern of behavior (at least one of the following: preoccupation with stereotypic interests, inflexible routines, stereotyped and repetitive motor mannerisms, or preoccupation with objects). The onset is before 3 years of age and occurs more often in boys than girls.

Rett's Disorder is a difficulty diagnosed only in girls. There exists normal prenatal and postnatal development, normal psychomotor development through 5 months, and normal head circumference. Subsequent to 5 months, there is deceleration of head growth, loss of previously acquired hand movements, loss of social engagement, poor coordination, and severely impaired expressive and receptive language development. The person with childhood disintegrative disorder evidences normal development for the first 2 years. Before age 10, there is loss of previously acquired skills in two of the following areas: expressive or receptive language, social skills or adaptive behavior, bowel or bladder control, or play and motor skills.

There are also abnormalities in functioning in two of the following areas: interaction, communication, restricted, repetitive, or stereotyped behavior.

Childhood Disintegrative Disorder is diagnosed more often in boys. Asperger's Disorder has often been difficult to separate from Autistic Disorder; however, very often children with Asperger's Disorder are able to function much better in their environment. Symptoms include impairment in social interaction and restrictive, repetitive, or stereotyped behavior. There is no delay in language nor is there a significant delay in cognitive development with IQ scores usually falling within the average range (Volkman, Klin, & Schultz, 2005).

Several very successful or famous individuals are thought to have suffered from Asperger's Disorder. The following are the diagnostic categories that often need to be separated from PDD: Schizophrenia with Childhood Onset, Selective Mutism, Language Disorders, Mental Retardation, Stereotypic Movement Disorders, or ADHD.

Attention Deficit and Disruptive Behavior Disorders include difficulties that often include behaviors that are not socially acceptable, violate social rules and norms, or may be negative, hostile, and/or threatening. The group of difficulties includes (a) ADHD including problems with inattention, (b) Hyperactivity–Impulsivity or both, (c) Conduct Disorder, (d) Oppositional Defiant Disorder, (e) ADHD NOS, and (f) Disruptive Behavior Disorder NOS. The symptoms of the aforementioned difficulties need to be separated from (a) Mental Retardation, (b) Stereotypic Movement Disorders, (b) Mood or Anxiety Disorders, (c) PDD, (d) Psychotic Disorder, or (e) a Substance-Related Disorder. Disorders in this category may be comorbid, therefore the clinical neuropsychologist may expect more than one diagnosis within this group (Wilens et al., 2002).

Feeding and eating disorders of infancy or early childhood involve persistent difficulties in feeding and eating and include (a) Pica, (b) Rumination Disorder, and (c) Feeding Disorders of Infancy or Early Childhood. Anorexia Nervosa and Bulimic Nervosa are included within a later part of the *DSM*. Mouthing or eating of nonnutritive substances is relatively common at a very young age and may not indicate the presence of a disorder. Pica is separated from the other eating disorders by an inappropriate consumption of nonnutritive substances such as paint or human feces. Differential diagnosis needs to be made with PDD, Schizophrenia, and neurological or other medical difficulties.

Tic Disorders are distinguished by vocal and motor tics. The specific disorders include (a) Tourette's Disorder, (b) Chronic Motor or Vocal tic Disorder, (c) Transient Tic Disorder, and (d) Tic Disorder NOS. Tic Disorders must be separated from other types of abnormal movements that may accompany general medical conditions (i.e., Huntington's disease, stroke, and abnormal movements that are caused by the direct effects of a substance).

Elimination Disorders include Encopresis, which is the passage of feces at inappropriate time or in inappropriate places, and Enuresis, which is the repeated voiding of urine at inappropriate time or in inappropriate places. These symptoms must be separated from those caused by a general medical condition.

Other Disorders of Infancy, Childhood, or Adolescence is a catchall category for difficulties that do not fit within the other groupings. Separation Anxiety Disorder is excessive anxiety concerning separation from home or those to whom the child is attached and the concern is inappropriate for age. The child fears that something will happen to the primary caretaker or to himself or herself. The fear can result in not being able to sleep alone, nightmares, physical symptoms, and anxiety (Barlow, Pincus, Heinrichs, & Choate, 2003). A differential diagnosis needs to separate this disorder from PDD, Schizophrenia, and other psychotic disorders. Separation Anxiety Disorders also need to be separated from each of the anxiety-based disorders. Selective Mutism is the refusal to speak in social situations despite speaking in other situations. Differential diagnosis involves separation from Communication Disorders, PDD, Schizophrenia, and Mental Retardation. Reactive attachment Disorder of infancy or early childhood is characterized by disturbed and developmentally inappropriate social relations usually caused by severely deficient care. This is often thought to occur early in life due to an insecure or ambivalent attachment to the primary caregiver (Davison & Neale, 1997). Differential diagnosis must be made between this and Mental Retardation, PDD, Social Phobia, and ADHD. Stereotypic Movement Disorder is a pattern of repetitive, appearing to be driven, nonfunctional motor behavior that interferes with normal activity. Differential diagnosis needs to be made between this disorder and Mental Retardation and PDD. Obsessive–Compulsive Disorder and Tic Disorders may also appear similar. Finally, any movement or self-injury that may be caused by medication needs to be ruled out. Disorders of Infancy, Childhood, or Adolescence NOS is a category for coding disorders that have apparent early onset of symptoms but do not fit a clear diagnostic pattern. Mental Retardation is included within this category but will be discussed later in the chapter because it is coded on Axis II.

As a category, Disorders First Evident in Infancy and Childhood covers a broad array of behaviors. Typically, the behaviors that cause a diagnosis to be made are when there is an exacerbation of normal behaviors such as excess movement in ADHD, absence of expected behaviors such as in selective mutism, or behavior that does not occur in a normal child, such as hand flapping in autism. In our case study, it is possible that Lori may have a form of learning disorder but it is difficult to diagnose based on the information available. This illustrates how important it is for the clinical neuropsychologist to garner as much historical information as possible in addition to completing a neuropsychological assessment as soon as possible. If she had been suffering from a Learning Disorder she may have been helped further in the special education courses if it had been diagnosed.

Delirium, Dementia, and Amnestic and Other Cognitive Disorders

Each disorder within this section presents with a significant deficit in cognition that is quite different from the previous level of the individual's functioning. The etiology is a general medical condition, a substance, or a combination of these factors. As stated previously, these disorders were referred to as organic mental syndromes and disorders in *DSM-III-R* (APA, 2000).

Delirium is a disturbance of consciousness and a change in cognition that develops within a short period. The disturbance in consciousness presents itself as a lack of awareness of the environment and an inability to focus, sustain, or shift attention. The cognitive disturbances may include memory impairment, disorientation, or language disturbances. There exist four types of Delirium based on presumed etiology: Delirium due to Medical Condition, Substance-Induced Delirium, Delirium Due to Multiple Etiologies, and Delirium NOS. The Delirium must not be better characterized by dementia. Research suggests Delirium is most often presented in older adults, people undergoing medical procedures, patients with cancer, and people with AIDS (Bourgeois, Seaman, & Servis, 2003).

The most common differential diagnostic issue is separating cases of delirium from those of dementia. It is possible that both may coexist and it is difficult to separate the two because both may have memory deficits as significant symptoms. In delirium, the onset of symptoms is much more rapid than in dementia where the symptoms may appear gradually over a period of time. The type of delirium that is diagnosed is caused by the etiological factors involved. Delirium, which includes delusions, hallucinations, or agitation, must be separated from Brief Psychotic Disorder, Schizophrenia, Schizophreniform Disorder, other Psychotic Disorders, and Mood Disorders with Psychotic Features. Also, delirium needs to be separated from anxiety and mood disorders as well as Acute Stress Disorder.

Dementia is characterized by the development of multiple cognitive difficulties, including memory impairment that are caused by the direct physiological effect of a general medical condition, effects of a substance, or multiple etiology. The following are the types of dementias (APA, 2000): Dementia of the Alzheimer's Type; Vascular Dementia; Dementia Due to HIV Disease; Dementia Due to Head Trauma; Dementia due to Parkinson's Disease; Dementia due to Huntington's Disease; Dementia due to Pick's Disease; Dementia due to Creutzfeldt-Jakob Disease; Dementia due to Medical Conditions; Substance-Induced Persisting Dementia; and Dementia due to Multiple Etiologies.

The main feature of dementia is the development of multiple cognitive deficits that include memory impairment and at least one of the following: aphasia, apraxia, agnosia, or a disturbance in executive functioning.

There tends to be stages in the deterioration of cognitive functioning. In the early stages, the individual is often aware of his or her cognitive decline and there may be emotional changes that occur as well. Emotional changes may also occur as a consequence of knowing that one is deteriorating cognitivity. Common emotions include depression, agitation, aggression, and apathy (Neurroschi, Kolevzon, Sammuels, & Marin, 2005). These deficits are severe enough to cause difficulties with social or occupational functioning. As stated earlier, memory deficits occur with both dementia and delirium and the memory deficits need to be evaluated and may help differentiate between the two. Delirium may occur with dementia in which case both are diagnosed. Amnestic Disorder also has serious memory deficits as a symptom but lacks other cognitive difficulties. The etiology of the dementia determines the specific dementia diagnosis. Mental Retardation has as a symptom subaverage general intellectual functioning but no significant memory impairment which helps in this differential diagnosis. Schizophrenia and Major Depressive Disorder also have symptoms of memory difficulties as part of their diagnosis and need to be differentiated. Often a differential diagnosis between dementia and any form of Mood Disorder may be very difficult, particularly in the older adults (Zubenko, 2000).

Amnestic Disorders are disorders that have as their principle symptom a disturbance in memory that is either due to the direct physiological effects of a general medical condition or the persisting effects of a substance. The types of amnestic disorders include (a) Amnestic Disorders due to Medical Conditions, (b) Substance-Induced Persisting Amnestic Disorder, and (c) Amnestic Disorder NOS. Individuals with the amnestic disorders are unable to learn new information or are unable to recall past information. The disturbance is severe enough to cause social or occupational functioning and is not due to dementia or delirium. Differential diagnosis from dementia and delirium that have memory loss as a symptom is a starting point. Amnestic disorders need to be distinguished from Dissociative Amnesia and other dissociative disorders. The later usually does not have any deficits in learning or recalling new information but more often the individual forgets trauma-laden experiences. Memory impairment due to intoxication or withdrawal from a substance also needs to be ruled out.

Cognitive Disorder NOS is a category for symptoms of cognitive dysfunction because of the direct physiological effect of a general medical caution. However, the symptoms are not criteria for any of the aforementioned difficulties.

Individuals who have Cognitive Disorder NOS may have a mixture of symptoms that would include difficulties with attention, concentration, memory, executive functioning, and so forth. Because this is such a broad category, individuals who are diagnosed with this disorder may appear very dissimilar from one another. The vagaries of this category and the lack of other specifically cognitive diagnostic categories is the cause for the inclusion within the *DSM-V*, when it is released, of postconcussion syndrome and mild neurocognitive disorder (APA, 2000).

Mental Disorders Due to Medical Condition

Mental Disorders due to Medical Condition are described as mental symptoms which are a direct physiological consequence of a general medical condition. The general medical condition is coded on Axis III (APA, 2000).

Criteria for three of the disorders, Catatonic Disorders due to Medical Condition, Personality Change due to Medical Condition, and Mental Disorders NOS due to Medical Condition are included here. Other difficulties due to general medical conditions are listed in other sections of the *DSM-IV-TR*. These include the following (APA, 2000): delirium due to a general medical condition included in the "Delirium, Dementia, and Amnestic and Other Cognitive Disorders" section; dementia due to a general medical condition included in the "Delirium, Dementia, and Amnestic and Other Cognitive Disorders" section; amnestic disorder due to a general medical condition included in the "Delirium, Dementia, and Amnestic and Other Cognitive Disorders" section; psychotic disorder due to a general medical condition included in the "Schizophrenia and Other Psychotic Disorders" section; Mood Disorder due to Medical Condition included in the "Mood Disorders" section; anxiety disorder due to a general medical condition are included in the "Anxiety Disorders" section; sexual dysfunction due to a general medical condition included in the "Sexual and Gender Identity Disorders" section; and sleep disorder due to a general medical condition included in the "Sleep Disorders" section.

Two criteria must be present for the diagnosis of mental disorders due to a general medical condition to be made. The difficulty is etiologically related to the medical condition through a physiological mechanism and the condition is not better accounted for by another mental disorder. In terms of differential diagnosis, the difficulty needs to be distinguished from a primary mental disorder, a substance-induced disorder, or the combined effects of both. Catatonic disorder due to a general medical condition is characterized as catatonia due to a general medical condition. **Catatonia** has any of the following as symptoms: Motor immobility; Excessive motor activity; Extreme negativism or mutism, peculiarities of voluntary movement; **Echolalia** (repetition of a word or phrase spoken by another person); or **Echopraxia** (repetition or imitation of the movements of another person).

catatonia
motor abnormalities including involuntary or excessive motor activity with no goal or direction; the term is used in relation to schizophrenia

echolalia
senseless repetition of a word or phrase spoken by another person

echopraxia
repetition by imitation of the movements of another person

Personality change due to a general medical condition is a persistent personality disturbance due to a general medical condition. The personality difficulty is a change from the individual's previous characteristic premorbid pattern. It is coded on Axis I even though it may appear similar to the Axis II Personality Disorders. There are several subtypes, which include: labile type, used if the predominant feature is affective lability; disinhibited type, used if the predominant feature is poor impulse control; aggressive type, used if the predominant feature is aggressive behavior; apathetic type, used if the predominant feature is marked apathy and indifference; paranoid type, used if the predominant feature is suspiciousness or paranoid ideation; and other type, used for presentations not characterized by any of the mentioned subtypes; and combined type, used if more than one feature predominates in the clinical subtypes.

Mental Disorders NOS due to a general medical condition is a residual category used when it is an apparent difficulty caused by a general medical condition but the criteria are not met for a specific mental disorder due to a general medical condition.

At this point, the reader may have decided that Lori may have an unusual personality and guess that she has a form of personality change due to general medical condition. It is a difficult diagnosis to make because she does exhibit symptoms of Personality Disorder but it is not described whether these are due to her medical problems or are predominantly psychological in nature. In addition, it is not clear if she have these symptoms all of the time or if they appear only when she has seizures. This diagnostic issue will become clearer after we cover Personality Disorders.

Substance-Related and Substance-Induced Disorders

The Substance-Related Disorders include difficulties related to the taking of a drug abuse, the side effects of a medication, and/or toxin exposure. The *DSM-IV-TR* contains 11 classes of substances of abuse (APA, 2000): alcohol, amphetamine or similarly acting sympathomimetics, caffeine, cannabis, cocaine, hallucinogens, inhalants, nicotine, opioids, phencyclidine (PCP) or a similarly acting arylcyclohexamines, and sedatives, hypnotics, or anxiolytics.

Substance-Related Disorders are divided into Substance-Use Disorders (abuse and dependence) and Substance-Induced Disorders (intoxication, delirium, and withdrawal). Medications that may cause Substance-Related Disorders include but are not limited to anesthetics and analgesics, anticholinergic agents, anticonvulsants, antihistamines, antihypertensive and cardiovascular medications, antimicrobial medications, antiparkinsonian medications, chemotherapeutic agents, corticosteroids, gastrointestinal medications, muscle relaxants, nonsteroidal anti-inflammatory medications, other over-the-counter medications, antidepressant medications, and disulfiram (APA, 2000). Toxic substances that may cause Substance-Related Disorders include but are not limited to heavy metals (i.e., lead or aluminum), rat poisons containing strychnine, pesticides containing nicotine, or acetylcholinesterase inhibitors, nerve gases, ethylene glycol (antifreeze), carbon monoxide, and carbon dioxide (APA, 2000). The volatile substances (i.e., fuel, paint) are classified as inhalants if they are used for the purpose of becoming intoxicated. They are considered toxins if exposure is accidental or part of unintentional poisoning. Impairments in cognition or mood are the most common symptoms associated with toxic substances, although anxiety, hallucinations, delusions, or seizures may also result.

Substance dependence is a pattern of repeated use that can lead to tolerance, withdrawal, and compulsive drug-taking behavior. According to *DSM-IV-TR* (APA, 2000), substance dependence may be applied to every class of substances except caffeine. Dependence is defined by at least three or more of the following symptoms evident within a 12-month period: tolerance (the substance is taken in larger amounts or over a longer period than intended); withdrawal (physiological or psychological symptoms that occur in the absence of the substance); desire or unsuccessful efforts to control use; time is spent to obtain or recover from the substance; social, occupational, or recreational activities are given up for the substance; and substance use is continued even though a physical or psychological difficulty occurs because of its use.

Specifiers include (a) with physiological dependence or (b) without physiological dependence. After 1 month of no dependence or abuse, the following specifiers may be applied: (a) early full remission, (b) early partial remission, (c) sustained full remission, (d) sustained partial remission, (e) on agonist therapy, and (f) in controlled environment.

Substance abuse is defined as displaying one or more of the following symptoms as a result of the use of a substance: (a) failure to fulfill major role objectives, (b) repeated substance use in a situation that could be dangerous, (c) repeated legal problems, and/or (d) use despite persistent or recurrent social or interpersonal problems, all within the past 12 months. These symptoms do not meet the criteria for dependence.

Substance intoxication is defined as maladaptive behavior or psychological changes associated with the direct physiological effects of a substance. The symptoms are not caused by a general medical condition and not better accounted for by another mental disorder.

Substance withdrawal is a pattern of physiological and cognitive features that is caused by the cessation or reduction in heavy and prolonged usage. Usually there are social, occupational, or other difficulties. The symptoms are not caused by any general medical condition nor are they better explained by another mental disorder. Withdrawal is often associated with substance dependence.

Differential diagnosis for substance-related disorders is difficult partially because each class of substance has its own symptoms. Multiple diagnoses of substance-related disorders is possible if all criteria are met for each diagnosis. Multiple diagnoses are often apparent and termed **polydrug** abuse in the treatment literature. The main diagnostic issues are between dependence and abuse and intoxication and withdrawal. In addition, the symptom pattern

polydrug
the use of multiple substances at the same time; also may refer to individuals who use more than one substance but do not combine them or use them at the same time but may be abusing or dependent upon one or all of the substances

must not be better explained by any of the earlier mentioned substance-induced psychological difficulties. In addition, there may be separate diagnoses of Substance-Related Disorders and other mental disorders. Many times, in the course of various difficulties, an individual may self-medicate to try to alleviate various symptoms. Another difficulty is that many of the substances are illegal or only legal at a certain age; hence, it is difficult to determine the exact amount of a substance an individual may consume. Finally, within the area of treatment most programs are abstinence based; however, alcohol treatment also has programs for controlled use that have been highly controversial (Pendery, Maltzman, & West, 1982). These programs for many reasons, which are discussed throughout this text, may not be appropriate for individuals with central nervous system difficulties.

As may be seen with the case study, Lori has occasionally consumed wine coolers when she was upset and not able to deal with her feelings. Her pattern of consumption would most likely fit the definition of alcohol abuse if she was diagnosed because there is no evidence of tolerance, withdrawal, or other more severe problems. However, if the pattern continued or she began to experience tolerance or withdrawal, she may be diagnosed with alcohol dependence.

Schizophrenia and Other Psychotic Disorders

The difficulties within this section are termed *Thought Disorders* because the predominant symptoms focus on how the individual thinks or conceptualizes information that he or she receives from the outside world through his or her senses. All of the difficulties occur in individuals who have had a period of what would be considered normal functioning. A **prodrome** often occurs as the behavior tends to develop usually under stress. Up to 85% of the people who later develop schizophrenia go through a prodromal phase (Murray & Brammon, 2005).

Schizophrenia is a term used for a group of signs and symptoms (both positive and negative) that have been present for most of the time during a 1-month period. **Positive symptoms** are symptoms beyond normal emotions. **Negative symptoms** are the absence of normal expressions or feelings. Some signs of the disorder must persist for at least 6 months. The *DSM IV-TR* (APA, 2000) states that two or more of the following positive symptoms must be present for a diagnosis:, hallucinations, disorganized speech, grossly disorganized or catatonic behavior (motor behavior that is excessively rigid or malleable often termed *waxy flexibility*), or negative symptoms such as **affective flattening** (no change in mood state based on circumstances), **alogia** (lack of logical thought or speech), or **avolition** (lack of motivation or interest). Subsequent to the onset of symptoms, one or more areas of functioning (work, school, etc.) must have declined. Hence, individuals with Schizophrenia have a downward course in their functioning often from what would appear to be normal functioning. There are several subtypes of Schizophrenia based on the content of the symptoms. Catatonic Type is assigned when catatonic symptoms are present. Disorganized Type is assigned whenever disorganized speech and behavior or flat and inappropriate affect are present. Paranoid Type is assigned when the symptom content focuses on unsubstantiated persecution. Undifferentiated Type is assigned when Schizophrenia is apparent but the symptoms do not meet the criteria for the other subtypes. Residual Type is assigned when there is evidence of a disturbance, but criteria for the active phase is no longer met. There are many general medical conditions that may have symptoms of psychosis and need to be differentially diagnosed from Schizophrenia. These conditions include Psychotic Disorder due to medical condition, substance-induced delirium, or dementia. Many substances have symptoms similar to Schizophrenia and the clinical neuropsychologist should observe the patient in a detoxified state, if at all possible, to determine the diagnosis. Differentiating Mood Disorder with Psychotic Features is very

prodrome
an early or premonitory sign or symptom of a disorder; a prodrome occurs for most individuals who experience schizophrenia

positive symptoms
an excess or distortion of normal function; examples include the delusions or hallucinations of schizophrenia

negative symptoms
diminution or loss of normal functions; examples include restriction of emotion or motivation in schizophrenia

affective flattening
absence or near absence of any signs of emotional expression either positive or negative

alogia
impoverishment in thinking; very concrete answers to questions and lack of spontaneous speech; a term used in relation to schizophrenia

avolition
the inability to initiate and persist in goal-directed activity

difficult because mood disturbances may occur during the prodromal, active, and residual phases of Schizophrenia. If the psychotic features occur only during the course of mood disturbances, then a diagnosis of Mood Disorder is appropriate. PDD share symptoms of language, affective, and interpersonal difficulties; however, PDD is usually evident early in life most often before the age of 3. Early or childhood onset of Schizophrenia is rare, however, it must be separated from the disorganized speech of a Communication Disorder and the disorganized behavior from ADHD. Schizophrenia shares many features with Paranoid, Schizoid, and Schizotypic Personality Disorders and they may be diagnosed as preceding schizophrenia.

Schizophreniform Disorder shows the same symptoms of Schizophrenia; however, the duration of the illness (including prodromal, active, and residual phases) is at least 1 month but less than 6 months, and the individual does not need to exhibit difficulties in social or occupational functioning. Specifiers include (a) with good prognostic features or (b) without good prognostic features. Examples of good prognostic features are good premorbid social and occupational functioning. Because the symptoms are similar to schizophrenia, the difficulties in differential diagnosis are similar to those listed for schizophrenia.

Schizoaffective Disorder includes the symptoms of Schizophrenia in addition to symptoms of major depression, mania, or both (refer to section for symptoms) at the same time. There must also be a period of at least 2 weeks when delusions or hallucinations are present without a mood disturbance. Differential diagnosis is similar to schizophrenia with the need to rule out difficulties due to a general medical condition or due to dementia or delirium. Schizoaffective Disorder needs to be differentiated from an episode of schizophrenia without mood difficulties and from mood disorders with psychotic features.

Delusional Disorder involves the presence of one or more **nonbizarre delusions** (false beliefs that are held by the individual even when there is evidence to the contrary) that exist for at least 1 month. There are several different subtypes of Delusional Disorder, which include the following:

- Erotomanic Type Delusional Disorder is when the delusion is that another person is in love with the patient
- Grandiose Type Delusional Disorder exists when the delusion is the conviction of having a great talent or insight or of or having made some important discovery
- Jealous Type Delusional Disorder applies when the theme of the delusion is that the patient's spouse or lover is unfaithful
- Persecutory Type Delusional Disorder occurs when the delusion's content includes being conspired against, cheated, spied upon, followed, poisoned or drugged, maliciously maligned, harassed, or obstructed in the pursuit of long-term goals
- Somatic Type Delusional Disorder is evident when the delusional theme is bodily functions or sensations
- Mixed Type Delusional Disorder is used when no one theme appears in the delusions
- Unspecified Type Delusional disorder is used when the main theme of the delusion cannot be determined. The differential diagnostic issues are similar to those of Schizophrenia

Brief Psychotic Episode is the sudden onset of at least one of the positive symptoms of Schizophrenia, which include delusions, hallucination, disorganized speech, or disorganized or catatonic behavior. The symptoms must exist for at least 1 day but for less than 1 month. Differential diagnosis is similar to Schizophrenia.

Shared Psychotic Disorder (folie á deux) is the appearance of a delusion within an individual who is closely involved with another individual who has a Psychotic Disorder with Prominent Delusions. The second individual begins to share all or part of the delusion.

The person who shares the delusion usually is married to or has been living with the person with the psychotic disorder for a long period often in isolation. Shared Psychotic Disorder may occur with more than one person. It is not usually difficult to diagnose this difficulty.

Psychotic Disorder due to Medical Condition entails symptoms similar to schizophrenia that are etiologically related to a general medical condition. The medical condition is evident from history, physical examination, or laboratory findings. This diagnosis is not given if symptoms occur during delirium but may be an additional diagnosis with dementia. Other disorders that need to be ruled out include Substance-Induced Psychotic Disorder or a Primary Psychotic Disorder or Primary Mood Disorder.

Substance-Induced Psychotic Disorders are symptoms of delusions or hallucinations that are clearly related to the direct physiological affects of a substance. Differential diagnosis needs to be made between the aforementioned symptoms and those of substance intoxication and substance withdrawal. In addition, a Primary Psychotic Disorder is differentiated based on the use of a substance. Excessive use of amphetamines needs to be separated from schizophrenia because a heavy amphetamine user may look and act very similar to an individual who is suffering from schizophrenia (Jaffe, Rawson, & Ling, 2005).

Psychotic Disorder NOS is a diagnostic category that is employed when there is inadequate information or contradictory information, or symptoms do not clearly fit a particular psychotic disorder.

Comparing the various symptoms and the issues presented by Lori, one becomes aware that she does not suffer from a thought disorder. Lori is in touch with reality but clearly has other issues that cause her to have difficulties living in this community and with interpersonal relationships.

Mood Disorders

The difficulties in this section are termed Mood or Affective Disorders because the predominant symptoms have to do with fluctuations or changes in mood from what is considered the normal state for the individual. In clinical practice, mood disorders have often been referred to as the common cold of mental health because they are the symptoms which often cause the most people to come in for therapy. However, at present, Mood Disorders are rivaled by the number of Anxiety Disorders that are present at clinics. Additionally, many times there is a combination presentation of anxiety and mood symptoms (Brown, Campbell, Lehman, Grisham, & Mancill, 2001). A Mixed Anxiety Depressive Disorder is suggested as one of the categories for further research and/or inclusion in the next version of the *DSM* (APA, 2000).

Major Depressive Disorder is characterized as one or more major depressive episodes without a history of mania, mixed, or hypomanic episodes. Symptoms for major depressive episode include evidence of at least five of the following for at least 2 weeks: weight gain or weight loss, insomnia or hypersomnia, psychomotor agitation or retardation, fatigue, feelings of worthlessness or guilt, difficulty in concentration, or recurrent thoughts of death. Depressed mood or loss of interest or pleasure must also be present. The symptoms cause significant impairment in social or occupational functioning. If criteria are met for major depressive episode, the following specifiers are used: (a) mild, (b) moderate, (c) severe without psychotic features, (d) severe with psychotic features, (e) chronic with catatonic features, (f) with **melancholia** (a distinct type of depression that is usually worse in the morning, includes early morning awakening, psychomotor retardation or agitation, anorexia, or excessive or inappropriate guilt), (g) with atypical features, or (h) with **postpartum** onset (onset within 4 weeks after giving birth). Major Depressive Disorder is differentially diagnosed from mood disorders caused by substance abuse or medical conditions.

The diagnosis of dementia versus Major Depressive Disorder, particularly in older adults, is often difficult to make and may require additional information (Delano-Wood & Abeles, 2005). ADHD has symptoms of distractibility and low frustration tolerance; hence, both may be diagnosed. Periods of normal sadness need to be separated from Major Depressive Disorder as well as from the effects of bereavement.

Dysthymic Disorder is a difficulty in which the individual evidences a chronically depressed mood for most of the day more days than not for at least 2 years. Two or more of the following symptoms are evident: poor appetite or overeating, insomnia or hypersomnia, fatigue, low self-esteem, poor concentration, or feelings of hopelessness. The symptoms do not abate for more than 2 months at a time. Specifiers include (a) early onset if symptoms occur before age 21, (b) late onset if symptoms occur after 21, or (c) with atypical features, which includes the following symptoms within the past 2 weeks: **mood reactivity** (the capacity to be cheered up when presented with positive events) and two of the following: increased appetite or weight gain, hypersomnia, leaden paralysis, and extreme sensitivity to perceived rejection. Differential diagnostic issues are similar to those with Major Depressive Disorder. Depressive Disorder NOS is a category that includes depressive features that do not meet the criteria for other depressive disorders.

Bipolar I Disorder is characterized by one or more manic episodes or mixed episodes. Sometimes individuals have also had one or more major depressive episodes. A manic episode is an abnormally elevated, expansive, or irritable mood lasting at least 1 week. Three or more of the following symptoms occur: inflated self-esteem or grandiosity, decreased need for sleep, more talkative, flight of ideas, distractibility, increase in goal-directed activity, excessive involvement in pleasurable activities that have a high potential for painful consequences. These symptoms cause significant social or occupational difficulties. The following specifiers are included if criteria are met for a manic episode: (a) mild, (b) moderate, (c) severe without psychotic features, (d) severe with psychotic features, (e) with catatonic features, or (f) with postpartum onset. Bipolar I Disorder needs to be differentially diagnosed from difficulties because of a general medical condition or substance-induced difficulty. Also, Bipolar I Disorder does not involve hypomanic episodes. ADHD has many similar qualities as a manic episode but the age of onset is usually earlier.

Bipolar II Disorder is a pattern that is characterized by one or more major depressive episodes and at least one hypomanic episode. A hypomanic episode is similar to a manic episode but occurs for at least 4 days and symptoms are different from the usual nondepressed mood. The specifiers hypomanic or depressed indicate the current quality of the episode. Differential diagnosis is similar to a Major Depressive Disorder and Bipolar I Disorder.

Cyclothymic Disorder is a pattern of fluctuating mood disturbance involving many periods of hypomanic and depressed symptoms. The symptoms are not severe enough for major depression disorder nor Bipolar I Disorder. Symptoms must occur for at least 2 years with not more than 2 months symptom free. Differential diagnostic issues are similar to those for major depression disorder, Bipolar I and II Disorders. Bipolar Disorder NOS is a category for difficulties with symptoms of Bipolar I or II, but does not meet the criteria. The differential diagnostic issues are similar to those already stated.

Mood Disorder due to Medical Condition is a diagnosis used when there exist symptoms of major depression or bipolar disorder that are directly related to a general medical condition. The differential diagnostic issue is to verify through laboratory tests or physical exam that a general medical condition exists and that the mood symptoms are not due to a general psychological difficulty or substance-related difficulty. Substance-Induced Mood Disorder is similar to the aforementioned difficulty with the use of a substance or withdrawal from a substance as the etiological factor. However, the differential diagnostic issues relate to ruling out general medical conditions and other psychological difficulties. Mood Disorders NOS is used when criteria are not met for a specific mood disorder and it is difficult to choose between Depression Disorders NOS and Bipolar Disorder NOS.

As we look again at Lori's case study, it appears that she has had periods when she was sad. She was hospitalized for suicidal ideation, which is the most lethal symptom of major depression. These symptoms appear to be in the past so that even though she could previously be diagnosed with a major depression, it does not appear to be prominent at the present time. However, the clinical neuropsychologist diagnosed her with Dysthymic Disorder because she appeared to have a steady state of low-grade depression.

Anxiety Disorders

Disorders in this section have the affective state of anxiety as their main symptom. It surfaces in many ways and is distinguished from the emotion of fear that tends to be focused on a particular object or situation.

Panic Disorder without Agoraphobia is the presence of more than one unexpected panic attack within 1 month followed by one of the following: concern about having additional attacks or consequences of the attack or a change in behavior due to the attack. A panic attack is a period of intense fear in which four or more of the following symptoms develop abruptly and reach a peak within 10 minutes: palpitations, sweating, trembling, shortness of breath, feeling of choking, chest pain, nausea, dizziness, fear of losing control, fear of dying, **parathesis** (numbness or tingling sensations), chills, or hot flashes.

There are three types of panic attacks termed *unexpected* (uncued), *situationally based* (cued), and *situationally predisposed*. **Agoraphobia** is defined as being in places or situations from which escape might be difficult or embarrassing if a panic attack would occur. The anxiety leads to avoidance of various situations. Panic Disorder is not diagnosed if the symptoms are due to a general medical condition or substance use or withdrawal. Panic Disorder needs to be differentiated from other anxiety and psychotic disorders that have panic attacks as symptoms. Panic disorders specifically have symptoms of unexpected panic attacks as opposed to situationally bound or cued attacks such as in other anxiety disorders. Agoraphobic avoidance is caused by fear of another panic attack, which is not similar to avoidance in other anxiety disorders.

Panic Disorder with Agoraphobia is a diagnosis of the aforementioned panic attacks with the symptoms of agoraphobia. The differential diagnostic issues are similar.

Agoraphobia without History of Panic Disorder is a difficulty with symptoms similar to Panic Disorder with Agoraphobia except that the fear is of the possibility of panic-like symptoms occurring. This diagnosis is not made if the individual has panic disorder or a general medical condition that causes any symptoms. Any form of phobia or mood disorder also needs to be ruled out.

Specific phobia is a marked fear of an object or situation that causes an anxiety response that interferes with social or occupational functioning. The fear is recognized by the individual to be out of proportion to the stimulus. In response, the person avoids any situation that involves the phobic object. The following subtypes indicate the content of the phobia: animal type, natural environment type, blood-injection-injury type, situational type, or other type. Differential diagnosis of specific phobia from Panic Disorder with Agoraphobia may be difficult because both may include panic attacks and avoidance of similar types of situations. Specific Phobia and Social Phobia are differentiated based on the focus of the fears. In PTSD, the avoidance behavior follows a life-threatening situation and contains other features. In Obsessive–Compulsive Disorder, the avoidance is related to the content of the obsession. Individuals with hypochondriasis are preoccupied with fears of having a disease whereas individuals with a specific phobia fear getting a disease.

agoraphobia
fear of situations in which escape is often not possible; very often occurs after an individual experiences a panic attack

Social phobia (Social Anxiety Disorder) is a clear and persistent fear of social or performance situations where embarrassment may occur. Exposure to such a situation leads to an immediate anxiety response. The anxiety often leads to avoidance behaviors. Adults know their anxiety is out of proportion but that may not be the case with children. Social Phobia interferes with social or occupational functioning. The specifier Generalized is used when the fears are related to most social situations. Differential diagnosis is often difficult between individuals who have social phobia and individuals who have panic attacks. However, most individuals with social phobia avoid social situations but do not have unexpected panic attacks. Other anxiety difficulties that need to be ruled out include Panic Disorder with or without Agoraphobia, Generalized Anxiety Disorder, or specific phobia. Also to be ruled out are PDD, Schizoid Personality Disorder, and Avoidant Personality Disorder.

obsessions
intrusive and often nonsensical thoughts, images, or urges that the individual tries to suppress or resist

compulsions
behavioral patterns such as washing or counting used to suppress aberrant thoughts

Obsessive–Compulsive Disorder requires two discrete sets of symptoms for a diagnosis. **Obsessions** are recurrent and persistent thoughts, images, or impulses that the person tries to ignore but remain intrusive and cause anxiety. **Compulsions** are repetitive behaviors such as washing, ordering, or checking that the person feels driven to do and are designed to rid themselves of the obsessional thoughts. Most individuals know that the obsessions and compulsions are excessive. A specifier for this pattern is with poor insight—when the individual does not recognize that the obsessions or compulsions are excessive. Differential Diagnosis needs to be made from any form of Anxiety Disorder due to Medical Condition or a Substance-Induced Anxiety Disorder. Other difficulties that may have similar symptoms are body dysmorphic disorder, trichotillomania, and/or specific or social phobia. Worry but not to the extent described, is also a symptom of major depressive episode, Generalized Anxiety Disorder, Hypochondriasis, delirium, Schizophrenia, Tic Disorder, eating disorders, and Pathological Gambling.

flashbacks
the recurrence of a memory, feeling, or a perceptual experience from the past

PTSD is a group of symptoms that occur as a result of an experience that is thought to be outside of the realm of normal human experience (i.e., war, sexual assault). The individual usually feels that he or she will sustain great harm or that his or her life is in danger. The person's response involves fear and the event is reexperienced in one or more of the following ways: distressing recollections of the event; distressing dreams; **flashbacks** (a sense of actually reliving the experience); or distress when exposed to external or internal cues that resemble the event and/or intense reaction to symbolic representations of the event.

Avoidance of stimuli associated with the trauma is indicated by three or more of the following: avoidance of thoughts, feelings or conversations associated with the trauma, avoidance of people and places associated with the trauma, inability to recall important aspects of the trauma, diminished interest in activities, feelings of detachment from others, restricted range of affect, or a sense of a foreshortened future.

Symptoms of increased arousal include two or more of the following: difficulty falling or staying asleep, irritable or angry outbursts, difficulty concentrating, hypervigilance, or exaggerated startle response. Specifiers include (a) acute, (b) chronic, or (c) with delayed onset. As has been stated earlier, individuals who have PTSD have been shown to have structural brain changes due to the trauma (van der Kolk, 2002). Individuals who work with others who develop PTSD are beginning to be labeled as having secondary PTSD. Examples include first responders such as firefighters, police officers, emergency room personnel, and psychologists. Acute Stress Disorder is differentiated based on the onset of symptoms occurring within 4 weeks of the trauma. In Obsessive–Compulsive Disorder, there are intrusive thoughts but they are experienced as inappropriate and not related to a trauma. Flashbacks of PTSD must be separated from the perceptual distortions of schizophrenia or any other psychotic disorder.

dissociation
a disruption in the usually integrated functioning of identity or perception of an event

Acute Stress Disorder is described as having anxiety, **dissociation** (separation from reality), and other symptoms that occur within 1 month after an extreme stressor. Most symptoms are similar to PTSD. A diagnosis of this disorder must rule out any Mental Disorder due to Medical Condition or any form of Substance-Related Disorder.

Generalized Anxiety Disorder is characterized as excessive anxiety more days than not for a period of at least 6 months during which time the person finds it difficult to control the worry. Three or more of the following symptoms must be present for the diagnosis: restlessness, easily fatigued, difficulty concentrating, irritability, muscle tenseness, or sleep disturbances. The anxiety is great enough to cause difficulty with social or occupational functioning. Differential diagnosis is made from any Anxiety Disorder due to Medical Condition or substance induced. Also, any other anxiety or mood disorders should be ruled out. Generalized Anxiety Disorder with its **free-floating anxiety** (not related to a particular event or topic) is only diagnosed when the other anxiety disorders do not account for the anxiety.

Anxiety Disorder due to Medical Condition is made if anxiety, panic attacks, or obsessions or compulsions are evidenced and etiologically related to a general medical condition. Specifiers include (a) with generalized anxiety, (b) with panic attacks, and (c) with obsessive–compulsive symptoms. This diagnosis is not given if the symptoms are better described by delirium, dementia, or a Substance-Induced Anxiety Disorder.

Substance-Induced Anxiety Disorder has symptoms similar to the aforementioned difficulty with the etiological factor being the use of a substance. Specifiers include (a) with generalized anxiety, (b) with panic attacks, (c) with obsessive–compulsive symptoms, or (d) with phobic symptoms. Specifiers also indicate whether these symptoms occur with onset during intoxication or with onset during withdrawal. The main differential diagnostic issue is between this disorder and Anxiety Disorder due to Medical Condition. Anxiety Disorder NOS is a category used for symptoms of anxiety that do not fit the criteria for any particular anxiety disorder.

Anxiety is a feeling state which most individuals will admit experiencing from time to time. A diagnosis of anxiety is an exacerbation of this normal experience. Lori, through her sexual encounters, may have developed symptoms similar to those of PTSD. Without further information, it is difficult to determine whether she has experienced enough symptoms for a diagnosis, hence, it was diagnosed provisionally.

free-floating anxiety
usually refers to anxiety; with the lack of a specific situation or object that causes the anxiety; the feeling is that the anxiety is always there

Somatoform Disorders

Somatoform Disorders are a group of difficulties in which the psychological problem is shown through physical symptoms with little awareness on the part of the patient. Somatization Disorder is characterized by a history of physical complaints that begin before age 30, occur over a period of years, and result in treatment being sought or in impaired social or occupational functioning. The following must be present for a diagnosis: four pain symptoms (in at least 4 different sites or involving at least 4 functions), and two gastrointestinal other than pain (one sexual and one pseudoneurological not limited to pain). The aforementioned symptoms cannot be appropriately explained by a general medical condition or the effects of a substance. A differential diagnostic issue with this disorder is with so many nonspecific symptoms there may be overlap with many general medical conditions. Indicators of somatization include multiple organ involvement, early onset, chronic course, and lack of laboratory abnormalities, which would suggest disease. Schizophrenia with Somatic Delusions needs to be ruled out. Many of the anxiety and mood disorders have physical symptoms as part of their presentation and also need to be ruled out. Individuals with factitious disorder with predominately physical signs and symptoms and malingering have physical symptoms that are intentionally produced and need to be separated from somatization disorder. Undifferentiated Somatoform Disorder is a residual category for persistent somatoform symptoms that do not meet the criteria for somatization disorder. Differential diagnostic issues are similar to those for Somatization Disorder.

Conversion Disorder includes one or more symptoms involving voluntary motor or sensory functions that appear to be caused by a neurological difficulty or a general medical condition. The instigation of the symptoms is associated with psychological functioning and usually preceded by conflict or stress. The symptoms are not intentionally produced and cannot be adequately explained by a general medical condition, use of a substance, or culturally sanctioned behavior. The symptoms cause social or emotional difficulties. There are several subtypes that describe the nature of the symptoms: with motor symptoms or deficits, with sensory symptoms or deficits, with seizures or convulsions, and with mixed presentation. The main differential diagnostic issue is between conversion symptoms and occult neurological or other medical conditions or substance induced difficulties. Depending on the symptoms presented, the following difficulties need to be ruled out: (a) Somatization Disorder, (b) any other psychotic disorder, (c) Anxiety Disorder, or (d) Mood Disorder. Symptoms in Factitious Disorder or malingering are intentionally produced.

Pain disorder is characterized by pain in one or more body areas that is serious enough to cause the person to seek assistance and cause difficulties in social or occupational functioning. Psychological factors are thought to play a significant role in the onset, severity, exacerbation, or maintenance of the pain. The symptoms are not intentionally produced. The following subtypes relate to the etiology and maintenance of the pain: Pain Disorder Associated with Psychological Factors or Pain Disorder Associated with Both Psychological Factors and Medical Condition. Specifiers are acute or chronic. The major differential diagnostic issues include separation from other somatoform disorders and malingering or factitious disorder.

Hypochondriasis is the preoccupation with the fear of having or the idea that one has a serious diseases based on misinterpretation of bodily symptoms. This occurs even when there has been medical evaluation and reassurance. The difficulty must occur for at least 6 months and leads to social or occupational difficulties. The specifier for this difficulty is with poor insight if the person does not realize that the concern is out of proportion. Differential diagnosis from a general medical condition is necessary because it is possible that an underlying medical condition exists. Concern about health or illness is apparent in Generalized Anxiety Disorder and with some individuals with major depressive episode.

Body Dysmorphic Disorder is a preoccupation with an imagined or grossly exaggerated defect in appearance. The concern causes difficulty in social or occupational areas. Individuals with this disorder may partake of multiple plastic surgery procedures but are never satisfied with the results (Miller, 2005). This difficulty needs to be differentiated from normal concern about appearance and from healthy exercising and eating disorders. The following are other disorders that may have somewhat similar symptoms: Gender Identity Disorder, Major Depressive Disorder, Avoidant Personality Disorder, Social Phobia, Obsessive–Compulsive Disorder, trichotillomania, Delusional Disorder, and somatic types.

Somatoform Disorder NOS is used for somatoform symptoms that do not meet the criteria for somatoform disorders.

There does not appear to be any indication that Lori is suffering from any form of somatoform difficulty. Her medical difficulty of epilepsy is clearly a central nervous system difficulty.

Factitious Disorders

A Factitious Disorder is the unintentional production of a physical or psychological symptom to assume the sick role. External incentives such as economic gain are not present. There are three subtypes: with predominately psychological signs and symptoms, with predominantly physical signs and symptoms, and with combined psychological and physical signs and symptoms. The differential diagnostic issues for Factitious Disorder include making sure the individual does not have any "real" medical or mental disorder. In Somatoform Disorders, physical complaints are evident but not intentional, whereas in Factitious Disorder, the symptoms are intentional and relate to secondary gain. Factitious Disorder NOS is diagnosed when the person exhibits factitious symptoms but they do not meet the criteria for the aforementioned difficulty.

Lori does not appear to have any form of factitious disorder. The case study indicates that there may be some indication of diminished intellectual abilities that could argue against her ability to generate such symptoms.

Dissociative Disorders

Dissociative Disorders include a group of different difficulties in which the functions of consciousness, memory, identity, or perception are impaired.

Dissociative Amnesia is a difficulty in which an individual experiences the inability to recall important personal information that is usually the result of a stressful event. It cannot be explained as normal forgetfulness and causes social or occupational functioning difficulty. There are several different types of Dissociative Amnesias each involving a particular type of forgetting. In localized amnesia, the individual fails to recall events around a particular period. In selective amnesia, the person may recall some but not all events during a particular period. In generalized amnesia, the person fails to recall his whole life. In continuous amnesia, the individual is not able to recall events after a specific period to the present. Specialized amnesia is a loss of memory for certain categories of information. The last three types are the least common. Dissociative Amnesia needs to be separated from amnesia due to a general medical condition particularly amnestic disorder due to brain injury. Delirium and dementia also have periods of memory failure but they are embedded in a larger clinical picture. Substance-induced amnesia occurs only with the ingestion of a substance. Dissociative Amnesia is not diagnosed if the memory lapse is part of a broader pattern of PTSD or Acute Stress Disorder. Malingered amnesia includes clear secondary gain.

Dissociative Fugue is sudden unexpected travel away from one's usual place of work or home without memory of one's past. Personal identity may be confused or a new identity may be assumed. This difficulty is usually etiologically related to stress or trauma. Dissociative Fugue needs to be differentiated from the physiological consequences of a general medical disorder. Complex partial seizures usually may be differentiated based on an aura or other perceptual abnormality. Fugue also must be differentiated from the direct effects of substance use. If another dissociative disorder or manic episode better explains symptoms, then fugue should not be diagnosed. Roaming behavior may occur in schizophrenia but loss of memory for it may be difficult to determine. Malingering fugue states occur when individuals are trying to avoid or escape from legal, financial, or other personal difficulties.

Dissociative Identity Disorder (DID) is the presence of two or more distinct identities or personalities that change in terms of which controls behavior. This difficulty has previously been referred to as Multiple Personality Disorder (MPD). There tends to be lack of memory for information when one personality replaces the other. Changes in personality are often caused by stressful events. Very often the histories of individuals with DID include incidence of very severe physical or sexual abuse. It needs to be noted that this is a highly controversial diagnosis within the mental health community, as is the extent of abusive behavior as the etiological factor. DID needs to be differentiated from the effects of a general medical condition, substance use, or a symptom caused by complex partial seizures. DID takes precedence over the other dissociative disorders. The following disorders have some similar symptoms and need to be carefully ruled out: Schizophrenia and other Pychotic Disorders, Bipolar Disorder, Anxiety Disorder, Somatization Disorder, Personality Disorder, Malingering, and Factitious Disorders.

Depersonalization Disorder is the persistent and recurrent experiences of feeling detached from one's mental processes and/or body. In this state, reality testing remains intact, however, social or occupational difficulties occur. Depersonalization must be separated from symptoms due to a general medical condition or use or withdrawal from a substance. Anxiety disorders are the primary difficulty that must be ruled out for this diagnosis, particularly those that contain any form of panic. Dissociative Disorder NOS is used when dissociative features exist but do not meet the criteria for any particular type.

Again, referring to Lori's case, it does not appear that she has experienced any somatoform or dissociative disorders. However, the reader should begin to see that there are some symptoms in common and possible diagnostic issues between PTSD and dissociative disorders.

Sexual and Gender Identity Disorders

Difficulties in this section relate to the broadly defined category of sexual functioning. Included here are difficulties with sexual functioning, object choice, and comfort within one's own gender. In addition, this diagnostic area has an interface with legal definitions of appropriate behavior.

Sexual dysfunctions may occur in any of the four phases of the sexual response cycle: desire, excitement, orgasm, or resolution. In all of these difficulties, there needs to be ruled out causes due to a general medical condition or the use of a substance. There are two subtypes which may be used with all of the difficulties that indicate time of onset, lifelong type, or acquired type. There are two types of situational specifiers, generalized type referring to the difficulty not being specific to a situation or partner and situational type referring to the difficulty occurring in only certain circumstances. The subtypes are used to indicate etiological factors due to psychological factors or combined factors.

Hypoactive Sexual Desire Disorder includes the absence of sexual fantasies or interest in sexual activity. This difficulty causes distress or interpersonal difficulty. This disorder must be differentiated from other Axis I difficulties that have inhibited sexual desire as a symptom.

Sexual Aversion Disorder is the aversion to sexual activity and the avoidance of genital contact with a partner. This causes distress and/or interpersonal difficulty. This difficulty needs to be differentiated from other Axis I disorders that may have lack of sexual interest as symptoms and specific phobia.

Female Sexual Arousal Disorder is the inability to attain or maintain adequate lubrication and swelling for sexual intercourse to occur. This difficulty causes distress and/or interpersonal difficulty. Any other Axis I difficulty with similar symptoms should be ruled out as should occasional problems with sexual arousal.

Male Erectile Disorder is the persistent inability to maintain an erection until the completion of intercourse. This causes distress or interpersonal difficulty. The disorder may occur in conjunction with another sexual dysfunction or may be better accounted for by another Axis I disorder that has sexual difficulties as symptoms. Also needing to be ruled out are occasional problems with erection, which occur in most males.

Female Orgasmic Disorder is the recurrent difficulty or absence of orgasm following a normal sexual excitement phase. Age, sexual experience, and adequacy of sexual stimulation must be taken into account. This difficulty causes distress or interpersonal difficulty. Other Axis I difficulties with these symptoms as well as occasional orgasmic problems need to be ruled out. Women who have been raped or sexually abused may be more likely to have difficulties with orgasm (Logan, Walker, Jordan, & Leukefeld, 2006). In general, it is not uncommon for women to not be able to achieve orgasm but this difficulty is relatively rare in men (Stock, 1993). Male Orgasmic Disorder is similar to the aforementioned difficulty in females. The same differential diagnostic criteria apply.

Premature Ejaculation is recurrent ejaculation with minimal stimulation before, on, or shortly after penetration and before the person desires. Age, novelty of sexual situation, and frequency of sexual activity need to be considered. This causes distress or interpersonal difficulty. Compared to the frequency of inhibited orgasm, Premature Ejaculation appears to be quite common (Althof, 2006).

Dyspareunia is genital pain associated with intercourse and applies to males or females. This difficulty causes distress or interpersonal difficulty. This difficulty needs to be differentiated from any other Axis I difficulty with similar symptoms or occasional pain associated with sexual intercourse. Vaginismus is the involuntary spasms of the muscles of the outer third of the vagina during intercourse. It causes marked distress or interpersonal difficulty. Both of the difficulties tend to occur with greater frequency in cases of rape or sexual abuse (Logan et al., 2006).

Sexual dysfunctions due to a general medical condition can be any of the aforementioned sexual difficulties which cause marked distress or interpersonal difficulty. There is evidence from history, physical examination, or laboratory findings that the etiology is a general medical condition. The general medical condition is coded on Axis III. Differential diagnosis would be similar to each of those listed with the particular difficulties.

Paraphilias. As a group, paraphilias involve recurrent, intense, sexually arousing fantasies, urges, or behaviors that occur during at least a 6-month period. The object of these activities includes nonhuman objects, the suffering of self or partner, or children. The object or images of the object must be present for sexual gratification the majority of the time. Some of these difficulties may lead the individual into difficulties with the legal establishment. It is unusual for an individual to have only one paraphilia and often two, three, or four may coexist (Abel et al., 1987). For each of the paraphilias, a differential diagnosis needs to be made between the paraphilia and nonpathological use of sexual fantasies, behaviors, or objects as a stimulus for sexual excitement in individuals without a paraphilia. Paraphilias are only diagnosed when they cause significant distress or impairment. The following difficulties may have a decrease in judgment, social skills, or impulse control that in only rare instances lead to unusual sexual behavior: mental retardation, dementia, personality change due to a general medical condition, substance intoxication, manic episode, and schizophrenia.

Exhibitionism involves the recurrent, sexually arousing fantasies, urges, or behaviors of exposing one's genitals to an unsuspecting stranger. This particular behavior must exist for at least 6 months. The person has either acted on these urges or they cause distress or interpersonal difficulty. Voyeurism involves observing others, usually unknown persons, who are naked, in the process of undressing, or engaging in sexual activity. This difficulty must occur for 6 months and must either be acted on or the urges or fantasies must cause distress or impairment in functioning in many areas. Langstron and Seto (2006) surveyed a random sample of Swedish citizens and found 31% reported being sexually aroused by exposing their genitals to a stranger. They also found 7.7% reported being aroused by spying on others having sex.

Fetishism is the intense sexually arousing fantasies, sexual urges, or behaviors involving the use of nonhuman objects. This behavior must exist for a period of at least 6 months. The behavior causes significant distress or impairment in social or occupational functions.

Frotteurism involves touching or rubbing against a nonconsenting person and occurs in crowded places from which the nonconsenting individual cannot easily leave. This activity occurs for at least 6 months and involves sexually arousing fantasies, sexual urges, or behaviors. The person has acted on the urges or they cause distress or interpersonal difficulty.

Pedophilia involves sexual activity with a prepubescent child. The perpetrator must be at least 16 years of age and at least 5 years older than the child. The person has acted on fantasies or they cause distress and interpersonal difficulties. There are several specifiers to this disorder: (a) sexually attracted to males, (b) sexually attracted to females, (c) sexually attracted to both (attracted to children), (d) limited to incest, (e) exclusive type, and (f) nonexclusive type.

Sexual Masochism involves the act or fantasy of being humiliated, beaten, bound, or otherwise made to suffer. This behavior causes distress or impairment in social, occupational, or other areas of functioning. Sexual Sadism is the act or fantasy in which the psychological or physical suffering of the victim is sexually exciting. The person has either acted on these impulses with a nonconsenting person or the urges or fantasies cause distress or interpersonal difficulty.

Transvestic Fetishism is diagnosed only in heterosexual males. It involves a period of at least 6 months when there are fantasies, sexual urges, or behaviors involving cross-dressing. This pattern causes distress or impairment in functioning in many areas. Transvestism Fetishism is not diagnosed if it occurs during the course of Gender Identity Disorder. A specifier is with gender dysphoria if the person has problems with gender role or identity.

Paraphillias NOS is a category for paraphillic activity that does not meet the criteria for the aforementioned categories.

Gender Identity Disorder. Gender Identity Disorder is a strong and persistent cross-gender identification meaning the desire to be or the insistence that one is the opposite sex. There is also discomfort with one's own gender assignment. This causes significant distress or interpersonal difficulty. Boys tend to dress in the stereotypic clothes of the opposite gender and do stereotypic tasks of the opposite gender. Girls have intense dislike for stereotypic girl activities. Adults may exhibit strong aversion to their gender. This diagnosis is not used if the individual has a physical **intersex** condition at the same time. The disorder is coded based on age and called Gender Identity Disorder in Children or Gender Identity Disorder in Adolescents or Adults. Specifiers for this disorder include (a) sexually attracted to males, (b) sexually attracted to females, (c) sexually attracted to both, and (d) sexually attracted to neither. Differential diagnosis must be made between Gender Identity Disorder and nonconformity to stereotypic sex-role behaviors usually by the extent and pervasiveness of the behavior. In Transvestic fetishism, the cross-dressing is for sexual excitement. Some individuals with schizophrenia insist that they are a member of the opposite gender but that may be ruled out due to obvious schizophrenic symptoms.

Gender Disorder NOS is a category for gender identity behavior that do not fit the criteria for Gender Identity Disorder. Sexual disorder NOS is coded when a sexual difficulty occurs but the symptoms do not meet the criteria for sexual dysfunction or paraphillia.

Lori does not complain or exhibit any of the difficulties that have been discussed in this section. However, sexual difficulties are a symptom of mood disorders and that needs to be kept in mind for diagnostic purposes since she has been diagnosed with Dysthymic Disorder. Sexual difficulties are also a symptom of PTSD which has been provisionally diagnosed.

Eating Disorders

Difficulties within this category involve the voluntary change in eating habits. These difficulties do not occur as a result of medical conditions, medications, or central nervous system difficulties.

Anorexia Nervosa is diagnosed when an individual exhibits the symptoms of failure to maintain at least a minimally normal weight (85% of what is considered normal for height and age), is afraid of gaining weight, and has a significant misperception of one's body and its size or shape. In females, there has been the absence of at least three successive menstrual periods. Specifiers include (a) restricting type or (b) binge-eating/purging type. Differential diagnosis should be made between Anorexia Nervosa and other general medical conditions particularly when the disorder occurs after the age of 40. Major depression may lead to weight loss but without the desire to do so or body image difficulties. Schizophrenic individuals may have unusual eating behavior but do not show fear of weight gain. Some of the symptoms of Anorexia Nervosa are also present in the diagnoses of social phobia, Obsessive–Compulsive Disorder, and Body Dysmorphic Disorder.

Bulimia Nervosa is a pattern of binge eating and inappropriate methods (self-induced vomiting/laxatives, diuretics, exercise, fasting, or excessive exercise) to ensure against weight gain. For a diagnosis, these behaviors must occur at least twice a week for 3 months. A binge is defined as eating a larger than normal amount of food during a particular period of time. The person also feels a sense of lack of control during the episode of binging. Bulimia Nervosa is separated into purging type and nonpurging type. When binge-eating behavior occurs only during periods of anorexic nervosa, Bulimia Nervosa is not diagnosed. Neurological or general medical conditions where eating behavior is disturbed need to be differentially diagnosed from Bulimia Nervosa. Individuals with major depression with atypical symptoms often overeat but do not have the body preoccupation. Binge-eating behavior could be considered part of the impulsive behavior of Borderline Personality Disorder; hence, both diagnoses may coexist.

Eating disorders NOS is a category of disorder of eating that does not meet the criteria for any specific eating disorder. From what has been revealed to this, point Lori has not evidenced any symptoms of an eating disorder.

Sleep Disorders

Sleep disorders are categorized into four major groups. Primary sleep disorders are those that are not etiologically due to a general medical condition, another mental disorder, or substance use. They are divided into Dyssomnias (difficulty with the amount, quality, or timing of sleep) and Parasomnias (arousal events during sleep). The other three categories are Sleep Disorder Related to Another Mental Disorder, Sleep Disorder due to Medical Condition, and Substance-Induced Sleep Disorder.

Dyssomnias. Primary Insomnia is the difficulty in which the individual has trouble initiating or maintaining sleep or maintaining restorative sleep for at least 1 month. This causes distress or impairment in social or occupational functioning. Differential diagnosis must be made between Primary Insomnia and the other parasomnias in addition to Primary Insomnia caused by medical, substance use, or other mental disorder.

Primary Hypersomnia is excessive sleepiness for at least 1 month, which causes marked distress or difficulty with social or occupational functioning. The specifier of recurrent is used if excessive sleepiness periods that last at least 3 days occur several times a year for at least 2 years. This disorder needs to be differentially diagnosed from an inadequate amount of nocturnal sleep, which may lead to daytime sleepiness. Also, other parasomnias need to be ruled out.

Narcolepsy is characterized by repeated irresistible attacks of nonrefreshing sleep, **cataplexy** (episodes of sudden bilateral loss of muscle tone resulting in the individual collapsing often accompanied by intense emotion), and intrusion of rapid eye movement (REM) sleep into the transition between sleep and wakefulness evidenced by **hypnopompic** (just after awakening) or **hypnogogic** (just before falling asleep) hallucinations or sleep paralysis at the beginning or end of sleep episodes. The sleep attacks occur daily for a period of at least 3 months. Narcolepsy must be differentiated from normal variations in sleep, sleep deprivation, and other sleep disorders. All of these may have symptoms of excessive sleepiness but not the immediate attacks with the attendant cataplexy or hallucinations.

Breathing-Related Sleep Disorder is characterized as sleep disruption, leading to extreme sleepiness or insomnia that is caused by a sleep-related breathing disorder (i.e., **sleep apnea** [episodes of breathing cessation] or **central alveolar hypoventilation syndrome** [abnormal blood oxygen and carbon dioxide levels]). There are three forms of Breathing-Related Sleep Disorders: obstructive sleep apnea syndrome, central sleep apnea syndrome, and central alveolar hypoventilation syndrome. The cause of Breathing-Related Sleep Disorders is coded on Axis III. Many of the sleep disorders may have sleepiness as a symptom but Breathing-Related Sleep Disorders involve characteristic snoring and or gasping for breath upon awakening. There are individuals, however, who snore but do not have Breathing-Related Sleep Disorders and those may be differentiated based on the presenting complaint. Nocturnal panic attacks may include symptoms of gasping or choking but do not show any of the physical signs such as apnea on polysomnography. Children with ADHD may exhibit symptoms of apnea and, hence, need to be dually diagnosed.

Circadian Rhythm Sleep Disorder is a recurrent pattern of sleep disruption leading to excessive sleepiness or insomnia due to a sleep–wake schedule which is caused by the person's environment or his or her circadian sleep–wake pattern. The pattern causes distress or difficulty in social or occupational functioning. Four specifiers exist for this difficulty: (a) delayed sleep phase type, (b) jet lag type, (c) shift work type, and (d) unspecified type. Circadian Rhythm Sleep Disorder must be differentiated from normal patterns of sleep and normal adjustments following changes in schedules. The key factor is how quickly an adjustment is made and the degree of social or occupational impairment. In addition, the sleep adjustment must not be a symptom of another dyssomnia.

Dyssomnia NOS is diagnosed when there exists sleeping difficulties that do not meet the criteria of any particular dyssomnia.

Parasomnias. Parasomnias are unusual behavioral or physiological events that occur during sleep, specific sleep stages, or sleep–wake transitions. Parasomnias involve activation of the autonomic nervous system, motor system, or cognitive processes during sleep or sleep–wake transitions. Nightmare Disorder is a pattern of repeated awakenings from sleep or naps with detailed recall of frightening dreams often involving survival issues. The majority of these dreams occur during the second half of the sleep period. The nightmares do not always occur during REM sleep. The person quickly becomes oriented and alert once awakened. The experience causes distress or social or occupational difficulty. Nightmare Disorder needs to be differentiated from other parasomnias, particularly sleep terror disorder in which the difficulty occurs during the early part of the sleep period and the person has less recall of the dream. Panic attacks may also lead to nocturnal awakening with autonomic reactivity but usually there is no record of nightmare type material.

Sleep Terror Disorder is a pattern of abrupt awakening from sleep usually during the first third of the sleeping period. The person awakes with a panicky scream, autonomic arousal, and fear which are usually unresponsive to comforting by others. There is usually no dream recall and also amnesia for the episode. The difficulty causes distress or difficulty in social or occupational functioning. Sleep Terror Disorder needs to be differentiated from other sleep disorders that may cause awakenings. Particularly difficult to differentially diagnosis is between Sleep Terror Disorder and Parasomnia NOS in which the individual may be experiencing REM sleep behavior disorder in which he or she experiences fear, motor activity, and has the potential for injury (Schenk, Bundlie, & Ettinger, 1986; Schenk, Bundlie, Patterson, & Mahowald, 1987). Seizures that occur during sleep may also cause similar awakenings and fear. Finally, panic disorders may cause awakening and fearfulness but the individual does not exhibit the other symptoms of sleep terror disorder.

Sleepwalking Disorder is a pattern of arising from sleep and walking about usually occurring during the first part of the sleep period. The person usually has a blank facial expression and is relatively nonresponsive to communication from others while sleepwalking. Once the person is awake, he or she has amnesia for the episode and no impairment of mental ability or behavior. The difficulty causes distress or social or occupational impairment. Sleepwalking Disorder needs to be separated from an occasional nonsignificant sleepwalking episode in children. Other dyssomnias or parasomnias may include arousals but usually do not include actual motor behaviors.

Parasomnia NOS is a category diagnosed when an abnormal behavior or physiological event occurs during sleep or sleep–wake transitions but does not meet criteria for a specific parasomnia.

Sleep Disorder Related to Another Mental Disorder is diagnosed when a known mental difficulty causes the sleep disorder. The two sleep disorders diagnosed are Insomnia Related to Another Mental Disorder and Hypersomnia Related to Another Mental Disorder. The symptoms and differential criteria are similar to those discussed previously. These diagnoses are made in addition to another mental disorder only when the insomnia or hypersomnia is serious enough to warrant separate consideration as opposed to a symptom to another mental disorder.

Sleep Disorder due to Medical Condition is diagnosed when there is a sleep disturbance that requires clinical attention and it is evident from history, physical examination, or laboratory findings that the etiology is a medical condition. This is not diagnosed if it is caused by delirium, Breathing-Related Sleep Disorder, or narcolepsy. It causes distress or problems with social or occupational functioning. The general medical condition is coded on Axis III. There are four specifiers, which include (a) insomnia type, (b) hypersomnia type, (c) parasomnia type, and (d) mixed type. The symptoms are similar to those already discussed as are the differential diagnostic issues.

Substance-Induced Sleep Disorder is a sleep disturbance that is severe enough for clinical attention that is shown through history, physical examination, or laboratory findings to be etiologically related to the use or withdrawal from a substance. It does not occur only during delirium and causes distress or impairment in social or occupational functioning. Specifiers include the same as the previous diagnostic category and with onset during intoxication or with onset during withdrawal.

Lori has revealed that she has had periods when she has had trouble sleeping and has had nightmares. She has also been prescribed medication for sleep. It appears, however, that the sleep difficulties are related to the stressor which is the cause of her PTSD symptoms. In diagnosis, if one diagnosis can account for the symptoms of another, then both do not need to be included.

Impulse Disorders-Control Disorders Not Elsewhere Classified

These disorders as a group involve problems of impulse control. The person has difficulty with an impulse, drive, or temptation to perform an act that is harmful to the person or to others. The person usually feels tense or anxious before the act and then experiences pleasure or relief at the time of committing the act. Afterward, the person may feel guilt or regret.

Intermittent Explosive Disorder is described as several episodes of failure to resist aggressive impulses that lead to assault or destruction of property. The aggressiveness is out of proportion to the perceived precipitating stresses. Several disorders have aggressive symptoms. Intermittent Explosive Disorder should not be diagnosed if aggressive behavior occurs only during delirium, dementia, or when the behavior is due to a general medical disorder or substance use or withdrawal. The diagnosis should also be separated from aggressive or erratic behavior due to Oppositional Defiant Disorder, Conduct Disorder, Antisocial Personality Disorder, Borderline Personality Disorder, a manic episode, or Schizophrenia. Anger attacks or sudden anger outbursts with autonomic arousal may occur in Major Depressive Disorder or Panic Disorder. Finally, this disorder needs to be differentiated from anger as a normal reaction to life events.

Kleptomania is a failure to resist impulses to take objects that are not needed for personal use or monetary value. The individual feels tension before committing the theft and pleasure or relief at the time of committing the theft. Stealing is not an expression of anger or in response to delirium or a hallucination. Ordinary stealing in comparison is deliberate and motivated by the worth of the object. Antisocial Personality Disorder and Conduct Disorder may exhibit stealing as part of a general antisocial pattern of behavior.

Pyromania is deliberate and purposeful fire setting on more than one occasion. There exists tension before the act and pleasure or relief after. There also exists fascination with fire and its situational context. The fire setting is not for monetary gain or political reasons. Pyromania must be differentiated from developmental experimentation with fire in childhood. Also, Pyromania is not for profit, sabotage, or revenge, or to make a political statement. A separate diagnosis of pyromania is not given when it is a part of conduct disorder, a manic episode, Antisocial Personality Disorder, or due to impaired judgment with dementia, mental retardation, or substance intoxication.

Pathological Gambling is recurrent maladaptive gambling behavior indicated by five or more of the following symptoms: preoccupation with gambling; gambling with increasing amounts of money; unsuccessful attempts to quit; restlessness and irritability when tries to cut down; gambles to escape problems; gambles after losing money; lies to family or to others; has committed illegal acts to obtain money to gamble; has lost job or other opportunities because of gambling; or relies on others to support gambling habit.

The gambling behavior is not due to a manic episode. Pathological Gambling is differentiated from social gambling or gambling by professionals.

Trichotillomania is the recurrent pulling out of one's hair causing noticeable hair loss. Tension builds before the pulling of hair and subsides or is relieved afterward. The behavior causes distress or social or occupational difficulty. This difficulty should be differentiated from Obsessive–Compulsive Disorder, stereotypic movement disorders, and factitious disorder with predominately physical signs and symptoms.

Impulse Control Disorder NOS is diagnosed if there is difficulty with impulse control but it does not meet criteria for the aforementioned disorders.

Lori's behavior does not reflect any of the Impulse Control Disorders. However, her emotions appear to be related to impulses but that is not part of the diagnostic pattern.

Adjustment Disorders

Adjustment Disorders are characterized by the development of emotional or behavioral symptoms in response to an identifiable stressor within 3 months of the onset of the stressor. There is an either social or occupational functioning difficulty. The symptoms are not due to bereavement. After the stressor terminates, the symptoms do not last more than 6 months. Specifiers are acute or chronic. Subtypes include (a) with depressed mood, (b) with anxiety, (c) with anxiety and depressed mood, (d) with disturbance of conduct, (e) with mixed disturbance of emotion and conduct, and (f) unspecified. This is a residual category used when the symptoms do not meet the criteria for another Axis I disorder.

In the case study, it is possible to state that some of Lori's difficulties may fit the criteria for Adjustment Disorders. However, her difficulties last longer and are more pervasive than is the case with Adjustment Disorders.

Other Conditions That May Be a Focus of Clinical Attention

Psychological factors affecting medical condition involve a general medical condition that is coded on Axis III and psychological feelings that have done one of the following: influenced the course of the condition; interfered with the treatment of the condition; constituted additional health risks for the person; or caused, precipitated, or exacerbated symptoms.

The coding involves the nature of the psychological factors and is termed one of the following (APA, 2000): Mental Disorder Affecting [indicate the general medical condition]; Psychological Symptoms Affecting [indicate the general medical condition]; Personality Traits or Coping Style Affecting [indicate the general medical condition]; Maladaptive Health Behavior Affecting [indicate the general medical condition]; Stress-Related Physiological Response Affecting [indicate the general medical condition]; or Other Unspecified Psychological Factors Affecting [indicate the general medical condition].

Medication-Induced Movement Disorders are diagnosed because of the frequent importance in the management of medication of medical disorders or general medical conditions and the need for differential diagnosis from Axis I disorders. The following have as an etiology some type of neuroleptic medication: neuroleptic-induced parkinsonism; neuroleptic-malignant syndrome; neuroleptic-induced acute dystonia; neuroleptic-induced acute akathisia; neuroleptic-induced tardive dyskinesia; medication-induced postural tremor; medication-induced movement disorder NOS; and adverse effects of medications NOS.

V Codes

Relational Problems. Relational problems include patterns of interaction between or among members of a relational unit that are associated with clearly significant impairment in functioning or symptoms among one or more of a relational unit or impairment in the functioning of a relational unit itself. These problems are included because they are of clinical interest but are not generally thought to be mental disorders. However, they may exacerbate a mental and medical disorder in one of the participants or may exist at the same time as one or more individuals in the relational unit exhibits a medical or mental disease. They are coded on Axis I when they are the focus of clinical attention and on Axis IV when they are considered environmental stressors. The following are often referred to as V codes (APA, 2000): Relational Problem Related To A Mental Disorder Or General Medical Condition; Parent–Child Relational Problem; Partner Relational Problem; Sibling Relational Problem; and Relational Problem NOS.

Problems Related to Abuse or Neglect. Problems Related to Abuse or Neglect is a category used when the issue comes to attention and requires treatment. This V code may apply to the perpetrator or the victim and includes the following: physical abuse of a child, sexual abuse of a child, neglect of a child, physical abuse of an adult, or sexual abuse of an adult.

Additional Conditions That May Be a Focus of Clinical Attention. The following are various types of difficulties diagnosed as V codes that may require clinical attention but not all have psychological etiology. These various difficulties include the following: noncompliance with treatment, malingering, adult antisocial behavior, child or adolescent antisocial behavior, borderline intellectual functioning, age-related cognitive decline, bereavement, academic problem, occupational problem, identity problem, religious or spiritual problems, academic problem, and phase of life problem.

AXIS II

Axis II contains Personality Disorders and Mental Retardation. These two categories are coded on a special axis because they are unique in terms of early onset, chronic course, and nonamenability to treatment. There are ten Personality Disorders that are often clustered into three groups. There are four levels of Mental Retardation which are usually evident from birth. If an Axis II diagnosis is the principal reason for treatment it should be followed by Principal Diagnosis or Reason for Visit (APA, 2000). If no Axis II disorder is present, it should be coded as V 71.09, or if a diagnosis is deferred, it should be coded as V 799.9 (APA, 2000).

Personality Disorders

A personality disorder is an "enduring pattern of inner experience and behavior that deviates markedly from the expectations of the individual's culture, is pervasive and inflexible, has an onset in adolescence or early adulthood, is stable over time, and leads to distress or impairment" (APA, 2000, p. 685). The following is a brief description of each of the ten personality disorders.

Cluster A includes three personality disorders. Paranoid Personality Disorder is a pattern of distrust and suspiciousness such that other's motives are interpreted as malevolent. Schizoid Personality Disorder is a pattern of detachment from social relationships and a restricted range of emotional expression. Schizotypal Personality Disorder is a pattern of acute discomfort in close relationships, cognitive or perceptual distortions, and eccentricities of behavior. Individuals with Cluster A Personality Disorders are often thought to be odd or unusual in their behavior. Individuals with these types of Personality Disorders tend to avoid relationships with others.

Cluster B includes four Personality Disorders. Antisocial Personality Disorder is a pattern of disregard for, and violation of, the rights of others. Borderline Personality Disorder is a pattern of instability in interpersonal relationships, self-image, affect, and marked impulsivity. Histrionic Personality disorder is a pattern of excessive emotionality and attention seeking. Narcissistic Personality Disorder is a pattern of grandiosity, need for admiration, and lack of empathy. Individuals with these types of Personality Disorders tend to seek out relationships with others to have their needs met without reciprocal concern for the other party.

Cluster C includes three personality disorders. Avoidant Personality Disorder is a pattern of social inhibition, feelings of inadequacy, and hypersensitivity to negative evaluation. Dependent Personality Disorder is a pattern of submissive and clinging behavior related to an excessive need to be taken cared for. Obsessive–Compulsive Personality Disorder is a pattern of preoccupation with orderliness, perfectionism, and control. Individuals with these types of Personality Disorders tend to seek out relationships and are often taken advantage of by others.

When diagnosing a personality disorder, the individual's cultural, ethnic, and social background must be kept in perspective. Personality disorders should not be confused with problems associated with acculturation following immigration or customs and habits that arise from religious or political values held by the individual. Personality disorders may be diagnosed in children or adolescents in circumstances where the individual's difficulties may not be attributable to a developmental stage or an Axis I disorder.

In terms of a differential diagnosis, many of the symptoms of Personality Disorders are also symptoms of Axis I difficulties. It is often difficult to determine whether a Personality Disorder should be diagnosed when there are symptoms of an Axis I disorder which is of long-lasting course such as Dysthymic Disorder. During an episode of a Mood Disorder or Anxiety Disorder, it is often difficult to separate Personality Disorder symptoms until the episode abates. If an individual has been exposed to an extreme stressor and personality changes then emerge and persist, a diagnosis of PTSD should be considered. If an individual has a substance-related disorder, it is important to not diagnose a Personality Disorder based on symptoms that emerge solely when the individual is under the influence of chemicals or during withdrawal. An individual who exhibits symptoms of a Personality Disorder which appears only after brain damage (i.e., brain tumor) should be diagnosed as having Personality Change due to a Medical Condition.

Mental Retardation

The second set of difficulties coded on Axis II are mental retardation. The essential feature of mental retardation is significantly subaverage general intellectual functioning as measured on a standardized intelligence test. It is accompanied by significant limitations in adaptive functioning in at least two of the following skill areas: communication, self-care, home living, social/interpersonal skills, use of community resources, self-direction, functional academic skills, work, leisure, health, or safety.

The onset must occur before age 18 years. *Intellectual functioning* is defined by the concept of intelligence quotient (IQ) obtained from one of the standardized individually administered intelligence scales. *Adaptive functioning* refers to the ability of the individual to cope with common life demands. Information regarding the individual's ability to deal with these life demands may be assessed by parents, teachers, or others who interact with the individual. The major tests available for this purpose are the Vineland Adaptive Behavior Scales-II (Sparrow, Cicchettim, & Balla, 2006) and the American Association on Mental Retardation Adaptive Behavior Scale (Lambert, Nihiri, & Leland, 1993). Four degrees of severity of mental retardation may be specified based on levels of intellectual impairment. A diagnosis of mental retardation, however, is never made solely based on an IQ score and always includes the ability to function in the environment (see Figure 10.1).

In terms of differential diagnosis, anytime the criteria are met, a diagnosis should be applied regardless of whether there is the presence of another disorder. In learning disorders and communication disorders, the difficulty is in a specific area rather than overall as in mental retardation. In pervasive development disorders, there is qualitative impairment in the development of reciprocal social interaction and verbal and nonverbal social communication skills. Mental retardation often accompanies these disorders. If symptoms of mental retardation appear after a period of normal development, a diagnosis of dementia may be merited, but it is not common in children.

SEVERITY OF MENTAL RETARDATION WITH IQ SCORES	
Mental Retardation	*IQ Level*
317 Mild	50–55 to approximately 70
318.0 Moderate	35–40 to 50–55
318.1 Severe	20–25 to 35–40
318.2 Profound	Below 20 or 25

FIGURE 10.1 Severity of mental retardation from IQ scores. *Source:* Adapted from *DSM-IV-TR* (APA, 2000).

Beginning students often find it helpful when attempting to determine which difficulty is coded on a particular axis to begin with Axis II. If a particular diagnostic syndrome is not a Personality Disorder or Mental Retardation, by default it is coded on Axis I. It is possible to have no diagnosis on Axis II or multiple diagnoses. The number of diagnoses is again limited in terms of the necessity for treatment. If an individual has no diagnosable difficulty on Axis I or II, then there is no reason to continue and the client has no diagnosable difficulties that could benefit from treatment at this time.

AXIS III

Axis III contains medical conditions or difficulties. The medical conditions must be diagnosed by a medical professional not simply reported by the client (see Figure 10.2). The reason for this is that the client may be reporting physical symptoms which are technically symptoms of an Axis I or II disorder. An example would be racing heartbeat or heart palpitations, which may be self-reported as symptoms of a heart attack but may also be symptoms of panic disorder, which would be coded on Axis I. The implication is that the clinical neuropsychologist does not want to treat medical problems with talk therapy or treatment and vice versa. An examination by a physician is often required when there is confusion whether the symptom is physiological or psychological.

Medications are not coded on Axis III. There are many medications which have side effects which mimic symptoms of mental disorders and hence, the clinical neuropsychologist needs to know those the client is taking. Often a client will be taking multiple medications that may interact and cause further difficulties. Many medications have addictive properties; hence, it is also necessary to determine if the client is taking the medications as prescribed.

AXIS IV

Axis IV, similar to Axis III, is an additional axis introduced with *DSM-III* and is a place to record the stressors in a client's life (see Figure 10.3). The stressors that are listed on this axis are those events that would cause anyone difficulty. The clinical neuropsychologist needs to

FIGURE 10.2
General medical conditions from the *DSM-IV-TR*. *Source:* Adapted from *DSM-IV-TR* (APA, 2000).

Axis III
GENERAL MEDICAL CONDITIONS

- Infectious and Parasitic Diseases
- Neoplasms
- Endocrine, Nutritional, and Metabolic Diseases and Immunity Disorders
- Blood and Blood–Forming Organs Diseases
- Nervous Systems and Sense Organs Diseases
- Circulatory System Diseases
- Respiratory System Diseases
- Digestive System Diseases
- Genitourinary System Diseases
- Complications of Pregnancy, Childbirth, and the Puerperium
- Skin and Subcutaneous Tissue Diseases
- Musculoskeletal System and Connective Tissue Diseases
- Congenital Anomalies
- Certain Conditions Originating in the Perinatal Period
- Symptoms, Signs, and Ill-Defined Conditions
- Injury and Poisoning

Axis IV
PSYCHOSOCIAL AND ENVIRONMENTAL PROBLEMS

- Problems with the primary support group
- Problems related to the social environment
- Educational problems
- Occupational problems
- Housing problems
- Access to health care problems
- Legal system interaction problems
- Other psychosocial and environmental problems

FIGURE 10.3 Axis IV psychosocial and environmental problems from the *DSM-IV-TR*. *Source:* Adapted from *DSM-IV-TR* (APA, 2000).

sort out the symptoms of an Axis I or II difficulty from the stressors. The stressors which are recorded in the client's life give the professional information for treatment planning.

AXIS V

Axis V is the GAF. It is a ranking from 0–100 which gives an indication of the level of psychological functioning of the individual (see Figure 10.4). This gives significant information regarding the coping strategies of the individual particularly in relation to the level of stressors. Students also find this axis to be particularly difficult as it often seems arbitrary. However, with practice, it becomes clearer that certain patients with certain symptoms and levels of functioning have a certain GAF.

CODING

Knowing the syndrome or difficulty which is diagnosed on each axis is only the beginning of differential diagnosis. To begin, the word coding has been used throughout the past few pages. Coding means the application of a particular diagnostic category along with a standard code number. These numbers are called **Current Procedural Terminology (CPT)** codes. All *DSM-IV-TR* disorders have code numbers that originate from the *ICD-10-CM*. For some diagnoses, further specification is needed. The use of diagnostic codes is a basic in medical record keeping. Codes are often required to report diagnostic information to third parties such as governmental agencies, private insurers, and the WHO. The Health Care Financing Administration requires diagnostic codes for the purpose of reimbursement under the Medicare system.

Subtypes and specifiers are provided for increased specificity. Subtypes define mutually exclusive and jointly exhaustive phenomenological subgroupings within a diagnosis. An example is Delusional Disorders that is subtyped based on the content of the delusions and includes seven subtypes (Erotomanic Types, Grandiose Type, Jealous Type, Persecutory Type, Somatic Type, Mixed Type, and Unspecified Type).

Specifiers are not intended to be mutually exclusive or jointly exhaustive. Specifiers provide an opportunity to define a more homogenous subgrouping of individuals with a disorder who share certain features. An example would be Major Depressive Disorder with melancholic features. There are several course specifiers related to the severity of the disorder which include mild, moderate, severe, in partial remission, in full remission, and with prior history.

In addition to difficulties with differential diagnosis or the determining of which is the correct diagnosis to describe the symptom pattern is the issue of comorbidity.

coding
application of a diagnostic category along with a code number; this is often completed for medical records purposes or insurance reimbursement

Current Procedural Terminology (CPT)
code numbers that were developed by the *ICD* and used in the *DSM* to signify a particular diagnosis. Using the same CPT codes allows for ease in medical records and insurance reimbursement

subtypes
used to define mutually exclusive and exhaustive subgroupings within a diagnosis

specifiers
used to define a more homogeneous subgrouping of individuals with a disorder who share certain common features

comorbidity
two or more diagnostic categories that tend to occur at the same time within the individual

FIGURE 10.4 Global Assessment of Functioning (GAF) *Source:* Adapted from the *DSM-IV-TR* (APA, 2000).

Consider psychological, social, and occupational functioning on a hypothetical continuum of mental health–illness. Do not include impairment in functioning due to physical (or environmental) limitations.

Code

100–91*
Superior functioning in a wide range of activities, is sought out by others because of many positive qualities. No symptoms.

90–81
Absent or minimal symptoms, good functioning in all areas, interested and involved in a wide range of activities, generally satisfied with life, no more than everyday problems or concerns.

80–71
If symptoms are present, they are transient and expected reactions to psychosocial stressors; any impairment in social, occupational, or school functioning is slight.

70–61
Some mild symptoms (e.g., mild insomnia) OR some difficulty in social, occupational, or school functioning but generally functioning fairly well, has some meaningful interpersonal relationships.

60–51
Moderate symptoms (e.g., flat affect, occasional panic attacks) OR moderate difficulty in social, occupational, or school functioning (e.g., few friends).

50–41
Serious symptoms such as suicidal thoughts OR any serious impairment in social, occupational, or school functioning (e.g., no friends, unable to keep a job).

40–31
Some impairment in reality testing or communication (e.g., speech is sometimes illogical, obscure, or irrelevant) OR major impairment in several areas, such as work, school, family relationships, judgment.

30–21
Behavior is considerably influenced by delusions or hallucinations OR serious impairment in communication or judgment (e.g., acts grossly inappropriately, suicidal preoccupation) OR inability to function in almost all areas (e.g., no job, home, or friends).

20–11
Some danger of hurting self or others (e.g., suicide attempts without clear expectation of death; frequently violent; manic excitement) OR occasionally fails to maintain minimal personal hygiene OR gross impairment in communication (e.g., incoherent or mute).

10–01
Persistent danger of severely hurting self or others OR persistent inability to maintain minimal personal hygiene OR serious suicidal acts with clear expectation of death.

0
Inadequate Information

(* Use intermediate codes when appropriate; e.g., 45, 68, 72.)

Comorbidity means that a particular diagnosis tends to coexist quite often with another diagnosis. A classic example is the incidence within the general clinical population of depressive disorders and anxiety disorders. These disorders tend to coexist with such frequency that most clinicians ask the question regarding symptoms of one when the other is the presenting complaint. In the forthcoming *DSM-V* there will be a diagnostic category that includes symptoms of each (APA, 2000). In clinical neuropsychology, very often depression is comorbid with other diagnoses often as a reaction to central nervous system disease or difficulty.

As discussed previously, differential diagnosis of central nervous system difficulties is often made difficult due to the overlap of symptoms. Very often a single symptom may be contained within the list of symptoms necessary for multiple diagnoses. As an example, lack of sleep may be a symptom of several sleeping disorders, depression, or a number of difficulties that have biochemical or endocrinological causes.

Perhaps the best way to begin to understand the process of separating the symptoms for diagnosis is to again look at the case study of Lori at the beginning of the chapter. Clearly one of the diagnoses with which she must cope is epilepsy. It would be coded on Axis III because it is a medical disorder and has been diagnosed by a physician. Another difficulty that has solid grounding in assessment is borderline intellectual functioning based on testing and coded on Axis I.

She appears to suffer from multiple difficulties in her relationships with other people. Due to this symptom, the clinical neuropsychologist would immediately consider an Axis II difficulty in the Personality Disorder category. The next step would be to list the types of relationships and their issues. Because many of her relationships appear to be erratic, this points to Cluster B Personality Disorders or those in which the individual has more contact with others than in Cluster A and also the relationships are more dramatic than in Cluster C. Looking through the symptoms it appears Borderline Personality Disorder is the most likely fit with her symptom presentation. The following describes the diagnostic features necessary for Borderline Personality Disorder within *DSM-IV-TR*.

A pervasive pattern of instability of interpersonal relationships, self-image, and affect, and marked impulsivity beginning by early adulthood and present in various contexts, as indicated by five (or more) of the following (APA, 2000): Frantic efforts to avoid real or imagined abandonment. Note: Do not include suicidal or self-mutilating behavior covered in Criterion 5; a pattern of unstable and intense interpersonal relationships characterized by alternating between extremes of idealization and devaluation; identity disturbance: markedly and persistently unstable self-image or sense of self; impulsivity in at least two areas that are potentially self-damaging (e.g., spending, sex, substance abuse, reckless driving, binge eating). Note: Do not include suicidal or self-mutilating behavior covered in Criterion 5; recurrent suicidal behavior, gestures, or threats, or self-mutilating behavior; affective instability due to a marked reactivity of mood (e.g., intense episodic dysphoria, irritability, or anxiety usually lasting a few hours and only rarely more than a few days); chronic feelings of emptiness; inappropriate, intense anger or difficulty controlling anger (e.g., frequent displays of temper, constant anger, recurrent physical fights); and transient, stress-related paranoid ideation or severe dissociative symptoms.

In addition, she has symptoms that are clearly depressive, not extremely severe but of long-standing duration. This leads to the Axis I diagnosis of Dysthymic Disorder. The two remaining difficulties, PTSD and alcohol abuse, are listed provisionally due to lack of sufficient data. It may be assumed that through intake, assessment, and therapy, the clinical neuropsychologist will garner enough information to determine whether these diagnoses should be included and the word ***provisional*** would then be removed from her diagnostic schema. Lori has multiple stressors that would be coded on Axis IV. These stressors need to be events or circumstances that would stress anyone and not symptoms of Axis I or Axis II disorders. This is often difficult for the student to separate when beginning diagnosing. Finally, Lori has been given a GAF score of 50. The clinical neuropsychologist compared her level of functioning with examples that were given in the *DSM*. The practicing clinical neuropsychologist has seen many clients who have presented various symptoms, which makes it easier to determine the GAF. Beginning diagnosticians often refer to Axis V as the most arbitrary and difficult axis to learn.

provisional
a diagnostic qualifier added to the diagnosis when there is presently not enough information to state clearly that the diagnosis exists; assumption is that information will be gathered over time to remove the term from the diagnosis

Summary

The chapter began with a case study in which the client evidenced multiple difficulties which were in need of treatment. Two of her difficulties were diagnosed based on medical tests (epilepsy) and assessment tools (borderline intellectual functioning). The other diagnoses were more difficult to determine and required further information from interview, further testing, and other sources that in this case were not available or not allowed to be contacted by the client. After accumulation of as much data as possible, a final diagnostic schema was settled upon which was needed for a treatment plan for rehabilitation.

This chapter is concerned with all of the issues involved in differential diagnosis or the determination of the appropriate diagnosis for the client's set of symptoms. The process of differential diagnosis may be very straightforward or it may be quite complex, as in the case study. It is important for the clinical neuropsychologist to have a clear grasp of the process because four functions are based on the appropriate diagnosis: the most effective rehabilitation or treatment, communication among professionals, further research, and insurance reimbursement for service.

This chapter begins with a short history of the diagnostic process. Included here is the relationship between the *DSM* (APA, 2000) and the *ICD* (WHO, 2004). The *DSM* is the most often utilized diagnostic schema for mental health issues worldwide.

Each of the five axes of the *DSM* are covered in detail with the most often encountered difficult diagnostic issues. Axes I of the *DSM* includes clinical syndromes and V codes. Axis II includes ten personality disorders and four levels of mental retardation. Axis III includes medical disorders when they have been diagnosed by a physician. Axis IV includes psychosocial stressors that are not symptoms of an Axis I or II difficulty. Axis V includes the GAF in a numeric form describing how well the client functions in the larger society.

In addition to the *DSM*, the chapter discusses issues related to the process and use of coding. Coding is used predominately within medical records and insurance reimbursement.

Questions for Further Study

1. Depression is often comorbid with central nervous system difficulties. Are there other diagnoses which could be more common in these circumstances?
2. The individual in the case study evidenced multiple diagnoses. Would this individual require a separate form of treatment or rehabilitation for each? Explain your answer.
3. Explain the pros and cons related to informing the client regarding his or her particular diagnosis.

References

Abel, G. G., Becker, J. V., Cunningham-Rathes, J., Mittleman, M., Murphey, W. E., & Rouleau, J. L. (1987). Self-reported sex crimes of nonincarcerated populations. *Journal of Interpersonal Violence, 2*, 3–25.

Althof, S. (2006). The psychology of premature ejaculation: Therapies and competencies. *Journal of Sexual Medicine, 3*, 324–331.

American Psychiatric Association. (2000). *Diagnostic and statistical manual of mental disorders* (4th ed, text rev..). Washington, DC: American Psychiatric Association.

Barlow, D. H., Pincus, D. B., Heinrichs, N., & Choate, M. (2003). Anxiety disorders: A lifespan developmental perspective. In I. Weiner (Ed.), *Comprehensive textbook of psychology* (Vol. 8, pp. 119–148). New York: John Wiley & Sons, Inc.

Bourgeois, J. A., Seaman, J. S., & Servis, M. I. (2003). Delirium, dementia, and amnestic disorder. In R. E. Hales & S. C. Yudofsky (Eds.), *Textbook of clinical psychiatry* (pp. 259–308). Washington, DC: American Psychiatric Press.

Brown, T. A., Campbell, L. A., Lehman, C. L., Grisham, J. R., & Mancill, R. B. (2001). Current and lifetime comorbidity of the DSM-IV anxiety and mood disorders in a large clinical sample. *Journal of Abnormal Psychology, 110*(4), 585–589

Compton, D. L., Fuchs, D., Fuchs, L. S., & Bryant, J. (2006). Selecting at-risk readers in first grade for early intervention: A two-year longitudinal study of decision rules and procedures. *Journal of Educational Psychology, 98*, 394–409.

Davison, G., & Neale, J. (1997). *Abnormal psychology.* New York: John Wiley & Sons.

Delano-Wood, L., & Abeles, N. (2005). Late-life depression: Detection, risk, reduction, and somatic intervention. *Clinical Psychology: Science and Practice, 12*, 207–217.

Durand, V. M. (2005). Past, present, and emerging disorders in education. In D. Zager (Ed.), *Autism: Identifying educational treatment* (3rd ed., pp. 89–110). Hillsdale, NJ: Erlbaum.

Gregg, N., Hoy, C., & Gay, A. F. (Eds.). (1996). *Adults with learning disabilities* (pp. 329–367). New York: Guilford Press.

Jaffe, J. H. L., Rawson, R. A., & Ling, W. (2005). Amphetamine or (amphetamine like) related disorders. In B. J. Sadock & V. A. Sadock (Eds.), *Kaplan & Sadock's comprehensive textbook of psychiatry* (pp. 1188–1200). Philadelphia: Lippincott, Williams and Wilkins.

Lambert, N., Nihiri, K., Leland, H. (1993). *Adaptive Behavior Scale-School* (2nd ed.). Columbia, MO: Hawthorne Educational Services, Inc.

Langstron, N., & Seto, M. (2006). Exhibitionistic and voyeuristic in a Swedish national population survey. *Archives of Sexual Behavior, 35*, 427–435.

Lezak, M. D., Howieson, D. B., & Loring, D. W. (2004). *Neuropsychological assessment* (4th ed.). New York: Oxford University Press.

Logan, T. K., Walker, R., Jordan, C. E., & Leukefeld, C. G. (2006). *Women and victimization: Contributing factors, interventions, and implications.* Washington, DC: American Psychiatric Association.

Miller, M. (2005). What is body dysmorphic disorder? *Harvard Mental Health Letter*, p. 8.

Murray, R. M., & Brammon, E. (2005). Developmental model of schizophrenia. In B. J. Sadock & V. A. Sadock (Eds.), *Kaplan and Sadock's comprehensive textbook of psychiatry* (pp. 1383–1396). Philadelphia: Lippincott, Williams and Wilkins.

National Joint Committee on Learning Disability. (1990). Operationalizing the NJCLD definition of learning disabilities for ongoing assessment in schools: A report from the National Joint Committee on Learning Disability Perspectives. *The International Dyslexia Association, 23*(4), 29.

Neurroschi, J. A., Kolevzon, A., Sammuels, S. C., & Marin, D. B. (2005). In B. J. Kaplan & V. A. Sadock (Eds.), *Kaplan and Sadock's comprehensive textbook of psychiatry* (pp. 1068–1093). Philadelphia: Lippincott, Williams and Wilkins.

Pendery, M. L., Maltzman, I. M., & West, I. J. (1982). Controlled drinking by alcoholics? New findings and a reevaluation of a major affirmative study. *Science, 217*, 169–175.

Schenk, C. H., Bundlie, S. R., & Ettinger, M. G. (1986). Chronic behavioral disorders of human REM sleep: a new category of parasomnia. *Sleep, 9*(2), 293–308.

Schenk, C. H., Bundlie, S. R., Patterson, A. L., & Mahowald, M. N. (1987). Rapid eye movement sleep behavior disorder. *Journal of American Medical Association, 257*(13), 1786–1789.

Shattuck, P. T. (2006). The contribution of diagnostic substitution to the growing administration prevalence of autism in U.S. Special Education. *Pediatrics, 117*, 1028–1037.

Sparrow, S. S., Cicchettim, D. V., & Balla, D. A. (2006). *Vineland Adaptive Behavior Scales-Second Edition.* Toronto, ON: Pearson Canada Assessment, Inc.

Stock, W. (1993). Inhibited female orgasm. In W. O'Donahue & J. H. Greer (Eds.), *Handbook of sexual dysfunction: Assessment and treatment* (pp. 253–277). Boston: Allyn and Bacon.

van der Kolk, B. A. (2002). Posttraumatic therapy in the age of neuroscience. *Psychoanalytic Dialogues, 12*(3), 381–392.

Volkman, F. R., Klin, A., & Schultz, R. T. (2005). Pervasive Developmental Disorders. In B. J. Sadock & V. A. Sadock (Eds.), *Kaplan and Sadock's comprehensive textbook of psychiatry* (pp. 3164–3182). Philadelphia: Lippincott, Williams and Wilkins.

Wilens, T. E., Biederman, J., Brown, S., Tanguay, S., Monuteaux, M. C., Blake, C., & Spencer, T. J. (2002). Psychiatric comorbidity and functioning clinically referred preschool children and school-age youths with ADHD. *Journal of the American Academy of Child and Adolescence Psychiatry, 41*(3), 262–268.

World Health Organization. (1992). *International classification of diseases* (10th ed.). Los Angeles: Practice Management Information Corporation.

World Health Organization. (2004). *International classification of diseases* (10-CM). Los Angeles: Practice Management Information Corporation.

Zubenko, G. S. (2000). Neurobiology of major depression in Alzheimer's disease. *International Psychogeriatrics, 12*(Suppl. 1), 217–230.

Prognosis and Treatment Planning

11

Learning Objectives

After reading this chapter, the student should be able to understand:

- The concept of prognosis and how it relates to an individual's treatment plan
- How premorbid patient variables affect a patient's prognosis and the clinician's treatment plan
- The nature and course of an injury and how it relates to a patient's prognosis and treatment plan
- The manner in which a patient recovers, with and without treatment, and ways the clinician can enhance recovery
- The neuropsychologist's role regarding cognitive injuries and forensic issues

Topical Outline

- Premorbid Patient Factors
- Types of Difficulties Expressed by the Patient
- Ways to Enhance Recovery
- Forensic Issues in Prognosis and Treatment Planning

Timmy is a 17-year-old White male who was referred for neuropsychological evaluation and treatment planning by his neurologist. The major referral question is the extent to which he will recover any cognitive or memory functions which he may have lost and his ability to return to school post-trauma. Also requested was an estimate of prognosis and treatment planning issues particularly focusing on aids which he will need if and when he returns to school. Many of these aids could be requested and then paid for by monies available through various government programs.

Historical information was gleaned from interviews with both Timmy and his parents. Timmy is the oldest boy born to his biological parents. He has two older sisters and two younger brothers. Both of his sisters have central nervous system difficulties which were evident from birth. The eldest sister has multiple sclerosis and the younger has scoliosis. The brothers do not have any central nervous system difficulties. The parents are married and it appears from verbal report that the father drinks heavily. The family is of upper middle-class standing with both parents working. Neither parent is college educated nor do they stress post-secondary education for their children. However, they have stressed the attainment of good grades and athletic ability throughout elementary and secondary school. All of the children have attended private parochial schools beginning with kindergarten. The parents are in their 60s and plan to retire within the next few years. This plan may change due to Timmy's difficulties and needs.

The difficulty which caused Timmy to be seen was an accident that happened at the parent's lake cabin. Timmy and his friends were swimming and diving in the lake. At the time of the traumatic event, Timmy stated that it was his turn to dive off the dock into the lake. Prior to Timmy's turn, all of the boys had taken turns diving into the lake without paying attention to the water level or any submerged objects. Timmy apparently dove into the lake and hit a large submerged rock which instantaneously rendered him unconscious. When he did not come to the surface after his dive, his friends dove in after him, fortunately none of them hit the rock. It took three of his friends to pull him to shore and they then proceeded to revive him. One of the boys was able to use cardiopulmonary resuscitation (CPR) techniques, which he had learned in the Boy Scouts to help Timmy regain consciousness. Timmy stated that he did not remember anything after starting his dive until he arrived at a hospital in a major metropolitan area 200 miles from the cabin. Even though he regained consciousness sooner than that, he had no memory before the events at the hospital.

While these events were occurring, the noise and confusion caused Timmy's parents to come running from the cabin only to see what appeared to be a lifeless body being pulled from the water. Timmy's mother cried and wailed while his father checked with the other boys for the cause of the accident. In the midst of the commotion, one of the boys ran to get his cell phone to call for any emergency assistance which was available in the area. Because it was a rural area the Sheriff was the first responder to the call. Once he arrived, the Sheriff summoned the town volunteer firefighters who also served as paramedics. The firefighters had been trained in life support and other advanced techniques which they used to help numerous tourists during the winter when they had fallen through the ice while ice fishing. The firefighters were wary of moving Timmy particularly because he did not appear to be able to move his legs on his own. They telephoned the nearest trauma center, which stated that not moving Timmy was the best course of action. They also stated that a helicopter would be sent as soon as possible to airlift Timmy to the nearest trauma center. All of the information was relayed to the parents who expressed both relief and fear regarding the plight of their son. While everyone waited for the helicopter to arrive, the Sheriff interviewed each of the boys regarding what they saw and how each understood the events transpiring. Although Timmy had regained consciousness, the Sheriff did not attempt to interview him at that time. The consensus was that Timmy took his turn and dove into the water. The boys had not *looked for any submerged objects before they began diving nor had they ever done that in the past. The Sheriff told the parents that an accident such as this was waiting to happen considering the lack of precautions. While discussing the circumstances with Timmy's father, the Sheriff smelled alcohol on his breath. Due to the smell and the fact that he had no reason to question the father, the sheriff asked the paramedics to take the boys blood alcohol levels as a precaution because liquor could have been a factor in the accident. All of the boys' would eventually test positive for alcohol use but not to the extent that they were over the legal limit. However, the fact that the boys were all minors eventually led all of them to receive minor consumption citations.*

Within an hour, the helicopter arrived to transport Timmy to a regional trauma center. On board the helicopter were two trauma nurses and the pilot. The nurses stated that the best thing that had happened was that no one had tried to move Timmy after he was removed from the water. With the help of the local paramedics, the nurses were able to secure Timmy on a board which immobilized his head and spinal column. At this point, the nurses were unable to give the parents any indication of the extent of Timmy's injuries. They also stated that there was not room for the parents to get to the hospital via the helicopter. The Sheriff spoke very frankly with Timmy's father regarding the alcohol smell and suggested that either the parents wait until another relative could drive them to the hospital or his wife should do the driving. The parents decided to ask the next door neighbor, who was also the father of one of the boys, to drive them.

Once the helicopter was airborne, the nurses quickly evaluated Timmy's vital signs and relayed them to the hospital. They also completed a review of systems and determined that Timmy was not able to move his legs and the lower part of his torso. The nurses suspected that he had severed his spinal cord at the level of his sternum but did not relay the information to Timmy. The nurses also suspected that Timmy had received a concussion or more serious form of closed head injury because the impact on the rock rendered him unconscious. With instructions from the hospital, the nurses administered pain medication and anticonvulsants.

Upon arrival at the hospital, the helicopter was met by hospital personnel and a stretcher that quickly took Timmy to the emergency room. The doctor in charge examined him and determined that his spinal cord had been severed. The doctor felt that the best course of action was to try to surgically intervene to determine if any portion of the spinal cord was still attached and could be repaired. He next called to prepare the operating room. At this time, the doctor was more concerned about the spinal cord injuries and paralysis than any head injury. Because Timmy was a minor his parents needed to be the ones to consent for surgery. Fortunately, the nurses had taken their cell phone number and reached them quickly. Once contacted, the parents gave verbal consent for the surgery. The physician in charge questioned the legality of the verbal consent but proceded after discussion of the situation with the chief of staff. The chief of staff stated that because of the gravity of the situation, intervention was necessary in a timely manner. The parents, fortunately, arrived before the surgery began and signed papers relieving the hospital of any liability.

Surgical intervention was not successful and the physician had the grim task of explaining the situation to Timmy and his parents. The medical explanation was that Timmy had severed his spinal column at the level of his sternum. All of his functions that were controlled from this level and lower were expected to be permanently impaired. In Timmy's case, this meant that he would not be able to walk nor function sexually. It was not evident at this time whether he would have any use of his arms. The next few days would be critical in terms of determining their functioning ability. Because Timmy was so young, his chances of recovery were thought to be quite good. At this point in time, the doctor began to address the issue of a potential head injury. He ordered a CT scan, which showed the appearance of a minor closed head injury which he referred to as a concussion.

The physician tried to explain all of the aforementioned information in as hopeful a manner as possible when talking to Timmy and his parents. Timmy's father became irate and asked for a second opinion and his mother cried and complained about Timmy's lack of a future. Timmy appeared sullen, at first, and then distant and angry. The physician stated that these emotions were to be expected when this kind of news is told to anyone. The staff was briefed about the warning signs of depression and told to remain alert for any indications that Timmy might hurt himself. Timmy was continued on pain and anticonvulsant medications.

Timmy stayed in the hospital for 2 weeks and then was transferred to a rehabilitation unit at a local children's specialty hospital. Although he was 17, he was still considered to be eligible for their services, which focused on recovery of function from various traumatic events. The staff at the specialty hospital included occupational and physical therapists who helped him recover as much of the use of his arms as possible. The determination was made that he would need to be fitted for a wheelchair and that rehabilitation would not help in the use of his legs. Timmy and his parents appeared to be overly optimistic about his potential for recovery and it took many weeks for them to realize that walking again would not happen. The staff also discussed issues related to postconcussion syndrome, which often presents with symptoms of headache, dizziness, concentration difficulties, irritability, and memory difficulties.

Throughout the ordeal the family was supported emotionally by friends and their priest. Timmy spoke mainly with his friends who were present at the accident and his brothers. Neither friends nor family wanted to talk with Timmy about the fact that he would not walk again. The staff tried to discuss Timmy's feelings but he did not want to speak about them and mainly talked about using the wheelchair and other handicap devices.

Near the end of the summer Timmy was released from the rehabilitation unit. Social workers started to plan how he would be able to function in his parents' home. A ramp was requested to make the home wheelchair accessible as was other equipment that would be needed in the bathroom and bedroom. Timmy's brother and father stated that they would be able to handle his personal care and declined any additional help to which they were entitled. Eventually, they would find that lifting and transferring Timmy from wheelchair to bed, bathing him and doing other activities of daily living were too much for them without professional help. Timmy's father, in an attempt to make his son's life more "normal," purchased a handicap-accessible van which he intended Timmy would eventually be able to drive.

The timing for the present referral is related to the fact school would begin for the fall term quite soon and Timmy's ability to attend had to be determined. The neuropsychological evaluation revealed the following information. Timmy did not appear to sustain any major cognitive or memory impairments as evidenced by his performance on the Wechsler Adult Intelligence Scale-IV and the Wechsler Memory Scale-IV. Behavioral observations during testing revealed some attentional and concentration difficulties, particularly when the directions for each subtest were discussed. The scores were compared to his previous school records, which were used as a premorbid level of functioning. Timmy had been a B student throughout his academic career and that was similar to the IQ and memory scores he received, which placed him within the average range of abilities. Lack of significant cognitive and memory deficits is consistent with most cases of concussion; however, less impairing transient deficits are often evident. The remainder of the neuropsychological tests also indicated that Timmy had some difficulty with attention and concentration. Also indicated were difficulties with inhibition of emotions such as anger and frustration. In comparison to his premorbid personality, as described by friends and family, these were new difficulties. These difficulties are not unusual considering that Timmy suffered from a brain injury in addition to the paramount spinal cord difficulty. Results from the neuropsychological evaluation were incorporated into his overall treatment plan. It was suggested that Timmy could return to school but would benefit from counseling for his emotional needs and aids for his concentration and attentional difficulties (i.e., a note taker or permission to tape his classes). A medical evaluation was suggested to address his physical needs. A special note was made in the neuropsychological evaluation that Timmy should be reassessed at 6 months and 1 year to determine any changes *that would lead to changes in the treatment plan. Many things change within the first year post-trauma, both in terms of his cognitive and memory abilities, as well as the attentional, concentration, and emotional issues. One of the difficulties that may occur is that the school and family may focus predominantly on his physical disabilities and neglect the aforementioned difficulties, hence, the stress on further and repeated neuropsychological evaluation.*

Another question addressed was the prognosis for Timmy. The spinal cord injury was permanent and was addressed by the physician. The prognosis for the aforementioned issues that surfaced on neuropsychological tests is generally dependent upon the type and quality of the interventions which he receives. Also noted was the concern first raised by the attending physician regarding depression secondary to the spinal cord injury. It is "normal" in these circumstances for depression to occur and may continue if not dealt with through therapy and/or medication. Social support for Timmy appears to be good and will help him remain involved with his previous activities as much as he is physically able. One negative event, however, was that his girlfriend was not emotionally capable of handling the circumstances and broke-up with him. At the present time, he does not feel that he is capable of meeting and becoming involved with another girl. This event may need to be addressed in counseling in order to preclude deterioration of his self-esteem. Individuals who become incapacitated from various difficulties are often prone to self-esteem difficulties particularly when they compare their current abilities with their functioning prior to a central nervous system difficulty.

This case illustrates many of the duties of the clinical neuropsychologist. The first task is the corroboration of the findings of the medical doctors with tests that reflect behavioral manifestations of various functions. The clinical neuropsychologist also evaluates all of the surrounding circumstances in a patient's life as he or she determines a prediction of prognosis and provides input in treatment planning. As may be seen, the clinical neuropsychologist would comment on the prognosis for Timmy's concussion based on data from the research literature on the topic, as well as Timmy's particular circumstances. The clinical neuropsychologist would include goals in the treatment plan and the means to attain those goals for each of the deficits which became evident through the neuropsychological evaluation. All of the factors that are important in prognosis and treatment planning will be covered in depth in this chapter and will also be illustrated via the case example.

Introduction

The topics for this chapter are prognosis and treatment planning. These are two very extensive areas to cover and involve many complex issues. **Prognosis** implies an estimation of the individual's ability to return to his or her premorbid level of functioning. Some individuals are not capable of returning to this level, therefore, an estimate of relative strengths and weaknesses in various areas is sought. Often, an expected date or amount of time involved in an individual's recovery of function is requested. Professionals are incorporating ideas regarding the prognosis for the patient from the very beginning of any type of rehabilitation. As stated in chapters 3 and 4, each central nervous system disease or difficulty has its own timeline for restoration of various physical and mental functions. Superimposed on this are all of the patient and situational variables that may extend or subtract from the projected date. A **treatment plan** involves all of the services which will be provided for the client (see Figure 11.1). Successful treatment begins with an appropriate evaluation. The assessment tools must answer questions related to the possibilities of

prognosis
the ability to forecast or predict the long-term pattern of recovery following injury or disease

treatment plan
following brain injury or disease, the process by which one or more professionals formulate a specific plan of action or treatment to ensure the most comprehensive or complete pattern of recovery for the patient

---

TREATMENT PLAN

CLIENT NAME: _____
Insured's SS#: _____

Treatment dates completed:
  1. _____
  2. _____
  3. _____

1. DIAGNOSTIC IMPRESSION (*DSM-IV-TR* Code). Please complete *each axis*:

   Axis I _____

   Axis II _____

   Axis III _____

   Axis IV _____

   Axis V   current   _____
            past year _____

2. MENTAL HEALTH STATUS (with specific data to verify the current diagnosis
   as it relates to this client); you may attach intake summary if appropriate:

3. PSYCHIATRIC AND SUBSTANCE ABUSE/DEPENDENCY HISTORY:

4. IMMEDIATE TREATMENT PLAN

   a. Behaviorally specific and measurable treatment goals

   b. Objective criteria for discharge:

   c. Type of treatment (individual, group, etc) _____
      _____

   d. Medications and prescribing physician: _____
      _____

Termination Date: _____

Provider Signature: _____   Provider Name: _____
Clinic/City: _____
Phone: _____   Date: _____

FIGURE 11.1 Example of a treatment plan

success in treatment and returning to one's previous situation, hence, it implies prognosis. The assessment tools may include, as discussed earlier, review of various records, interviews, behavioral observations, and formal psychometric tests. The treatment plan usually includes multiple protocols dependent upon the outcome of the evaluation and the client's strengths and weaknesses in each area. A treatment plan includes goals and strategies to attain these goals for each area with which the client needs assistance. Often a treatment plan is administered by a case manager whose role it is to coordinate services delivered by multiple disciplines. In some circumstances, a clinical neuropsychologist may serve as case manager, however the usual situation involves social workers functioning as case managers. Social workers are familiar with the multitude of services that a patient may need and the types of programs available to finance these various services.

case manager
the professional responsible for bringing together and monitoring services from several areas of specialty to ensure the patient or client has integrated and appropriate care and to ensure that the specific treatments are not working at cross purposes

Premorbid Patient Factors

The following discussion relates to all of the abilities or disabilities that a patient has prior to a central nervous system disease or injury. These abilities, or lack thereof, will either help or detract from the progress that a patient makes toward the desired rehabilitation goals included within his or her treatment plan. As stated earlier, premorbid factors also factor into a prediction of prognosis and an estimation of the patient's strengths and weaknesses.

INTELLECTUAL ABILITIES

Intellectual abilities have been defined by many researchers and these definitions were included in a previous chapter. Suffice it to say that the definition of intelligence employed is related to the type of test designed to measure this ability. With this caveat in mind, the following are general statements regarding the relationship between premorbid measured intelligence and recovery of cognitive and memory functions posttrauma. Premorbid functioning implies the abilities that an individual possessed prior to any type of central nervous system difficulty. A premorbid measure or estimate of intelligence is important in prognosis and treatment planning as this will be the standard or baseline against which the patient's current level of functioning is compared. Premorbid estimates may come from school records including standardized achievement tests or grades (as in the case study), work samples, military records, and various tests designed to be samples of premorbid functioning.

premorbid functioning
the level of functioning of any ability of the individual that was present prior to the injury and that now may have been lost or changed

The clinical and research literature suggests that certain types of intelligence tend to remain intact or decline at a slower rate during aging. Although aging is a normal process, a parallel is often drawn to abilities which usually decline less with accident or illness. These abilities tend to fall within the category which Cattell referred to as "crystallized" as opposed to "fluid" intelligence (Cattell, 1963). Crystallized intelligence represents acquired skills and general information, often thought to be related to activities such as work, hobbies, or talents. Crystallized intelligence has the advantage of being rehearsed and practiced and is related to formal education and life experiences. Using the Wechsler scales, it appears that crystallized intelligence declines very little as an individual ages (Kaufman, Reynolds, & McLean, 1989). Looking at particular Wechsler Adult Intelligence Scale-III (WAIS-III) subtests, those which are measures of overlearned skills, Vocabulary, Information, Comprehension, and Arithmetic show the least decline with age (Wechsler, 1997). Higher levels of crystallized intelligence may be a protective factor or a cognitive resource

crystallized intelligence
refers to acquired skills and the use of the knowledge in activities such as work or hobbies; it has the advantage of practice

fluid intelligence
involves novel reasoning and use of information to deal with unfamiliar problems or to gain new types of knowledge

against dementia. **Fluid intelligence** tends to reflect a decline with aging. It involves novel reasoning and the efficiency in solving new problems or responding to abstract ideas. It is thought to be related more to adaptability than education or experience. Tests of fluid intelligence such as Wechsler's Digit Symbol and Block Design tend to decline across the life span (Salthouse, 1991). All of these subtests except for Digit Symbol have been retained with the WAIS-IV (Wechsler, 2008). They are thought to measure the same constructs (i.e., crystallized or fluid intelligence) but the individual subtests now load on different composite indices. Information and Vocabulary are core subtests on the Verbal Comprehensive Index Scale with Comprehension being a supplemental subtest and Block Design is a core subtest on the Perceptual Reasoning Index Scale.

Another issue, often controversial, is the question regarding brain size and intelligence. Brain size as measured by MRI correlates modestly ($r = .35$ approximately) with summed test scores (Bigler, 1995). Hence, brain size contributes to ability level which is also related to academic achievement. However, this is a modest correlation and not proof that nature is the stronger in the **nature–nurture question** (Huttenlocher, 2002). In other words, brain size does not clearly underlie superior intelligence but interacts with environmental events and the experience of these events (i.e., education, etc.). Brain disease or injury reduces the amount and connectivity of brain tissue and, in this manner, diminishes mental abilities and social skills. Researchers have shown that the level of premorbid mental ability determines, to some extent, the amount of cognitive loss following injury and also the risk for dementia and its course (Bigler; Grafman, Lalonde, Litvan, & Fedio, 1989).

nature–nurture question
a long-standing debate as to whether nature (genetics) or nurture (learning) has the most significant impact on the development of a particular human ability or characteristic

Many researchers have found consistent relationships between estimated or known premorbid ability and level of cognitive impairment with brain injury or disease (Lezak, Howieson, & Loring, 2004). One theory described by Satz (1993) postulates that the amount of "brain reserve capacity" (BRC) represents structural or physiological brain advantages (such as size and/or redundancy of interconnections) or disadvantages. Advantages will be higher educational levels, higher test scores both premorbidly and postmorbidly, and a better level of functioning of the brain after disease or injury.

In a similar vein, the effects of education on neuropsychological functioning are pervasive (Heaton, Ryan, & Mathews, 1996). In other words, those individuals who have attained a more advanced level of education score better on neuropsychological tests even with brain impairment. It has also been found that education was associated with greater control over processing and with greater conceptualization ability, capacities inherent in substantial cognitive reserve (Le Carrett et al., 2003). It is not an unreasonable conclusion to suggest that brighter individuals take advantage and excel more with advanced education.

Illiteracy can affect the development of cognitive abilities, processing strategies, processing pathways, and functional brain organization (Castro-Caldas, Petersson, Reis, Stone-Elander, & Ingvar, 1998). Normative data frequently do not include individuals with low levels of education or who are illiterate. If they are included, they are grouped into a larger subcategory often referred to as those with less than 10 years of education, which may be misleading (Gladsjo, Schuman, & Evans, 1999). Researchers suggest that more work is needed to develop norms for these particular groups.

Suffice it to say that those with higher measured intelligence and/or educational attainment have an advantage in prognosis and treatment planning for rehabilitation after central nervous system accident or injury. Patients with higher measured intelligence and/or educational attainment have a potentially greater cognitive reserve after brain impairment, which translates into the potential to sustain more damage and be able to function well afterward. This, however, does not imply that more intelligent or educated individuals do not need to take precautions against brain injury. Research has shown, however, that individuals with lower premorbid measured intelligence or education tend to place themselves in situations where they are more likely to incur brain impairment (Silver, Hales, & Yudofsky, 2002). Another advantage for individuals with higher premorbid measured intelligence or education is that these individuals are more likely to understand the goals of rehabilitation and have the motivation to achieve these goals. However, as reported by many researchers, more intelligent or better educated individuals tend to complain more about difficulties which they sustain and how those difficulties affect the quality of their lives.

The clinical neuropsychologist working with Timmy may view him as an excellent candidate for rehabilitation. Timmy has an advantage in his prognosis and treatment plan for rehabilitation efforts due to his premorbid intellectual abilities. A B average in school implies that he has been an above-average student, which leads to the supposition of brain reserve capacity and also motivation in order to attain these grades. The aforementioned research would suggest that Timmy should have the ability to understand the goals of his treatment plan and have the motivation to accomplish these goals. One particularly positive event is that he is very close to graduating from high school and he may be motivated to graduate with his class.

PERSONALITY FACTORS

The premorbid personality of an individual may have a great effect on the individual's coping with central nervous system disease or difficulty. These same personality variables affect the quality of adjustment to his or her situation and possible handicaps and also to his or her ability to benefit from any type of rehabilitation efforts. Premorbid personality also has an effect on the level of expectation the individual has regarding his or her ability to return to the previous level of functioning (Newcombe, 1982).

Another way in which premorbid personality factors may affect the individual is not so much a difference in personality but an exaggeration of already existing qualities (Silver et al., 2002). An example would be an individual who was premorbidly short-tempered; upon receiving a traumatic brain injury (TBI) in the frontal area which controls the ability to inhibit behavior, the person may become even more short-tempered and have difficulties with inhibition of behavior when provoked. Anger, impulsivity, and other forms of acting out behavior exhibited by an individual who did not display these characteristics premorbidly may be indicative of frontal lobe damage.

The effects of premorbid adjustment may not become apparent until the patient needs emotional or social support outside of a hospital or rehabilitative setting (Kaplan, 1990). Individuals who have been emotionally stable and mature in how they managed their lives premorbidly are more likely to be offered help from others than those individuals whose premorbid adjustment included antisocial traits or behaviors. Individuals with antisocial traits may not have developed the social support network or the types of friendships which would be helpful when they developed a central nervous system disease or difficulty (Silver et al., 2002).

Based on what is known regarding Timmy's premorbid personality, it appears that he was considered to be an average 17-year-old boy by his friends and family. He had a girlfriend and did not display any unusual or antisocial traits. The difficulties with frustration and anger regarding his situation and the lifelong disabilities that he will be facing are normal responses to a traumatic situation. It should be easier for others to cope with and understand his anger and frustration because they are able to attribute these emotions to the circumstances and not assume that these are traits which Timmy has had most of his life.

SOCIAL SUPPORT NETWORK

Social support is defined as information from others that one is loved and cared for, esteemed and valued, and part of a network of communication and mutual obligation (Taylor, 2007). In order for an individual to make as positive a recovery as possible from a central nervous system difficulty, it is necessary to have support from others. Individuals who make up one's social support network may be parents, siblings, friends, coworkers, church members, pets, or even other individuals who have sustained the same type of difficulty. People with high levels of social support experience less stress when they confront a stressful experience and they cope with it more successfully (Taylor, 2009). However, a caveat to this statement is that the support needs to be of a positive nature. Studies have shown that it is not the number of people but the quality of their support which is critical in recovery (Rook, 1984). One individual who exhibits a truly positive attitude is better than several who are present but negative in their approach to the patient or defeatist in their analysis of the patient's potential to recover. Social support has been shown to reduce physiological and neuroendocrine responses to stress; hence, it would be consistent to state that positive social support would be helpful to those who have incurred central nervous system difficulties. Warm social contact can release oxytocin, which may be linked to lower stress responses (Grewen, Girdler, Amico, & Light, 2005). It has also been shown that believing that social support is available (Uchino & Garvey, 1997) or thinking about the sources of the support can also give beneficial effects (Broadwell & Light, 1999).

In our case study, Timmy appears to have social support from his family, friends, and the clergy. The negative event which could possibly affect his recovery is the termination of the relationship with his girlfriend. Timmy and his parents' difficulty with being realistic regarding the use of his legs could also become a negative factor if they continued to avoid facing the reality of the situation. The most encouraging factor, however, is that there does not appear to be any negativity in any of the individuals who are currently supporting Timmy.

AGE

The discussion of age as it relates to prognosis and treatment planning includes several areas. First, the age at which an accident or illness is sustained is of great importance. Second, there are certain ages in which individuals are more at risk for certain types of central nervous system difficulties and trying to prevent these is crucial. Third, the normal course of aging is explored to compare to factors which may be accident or disease related.

It is often thought that there exist two particularly important age periods for the central nervous system, from birth to age 5 and during the later years arbitrarily beginning with a standard retirement age of approximately 65. Taking into account the fact that children vary one from another much more than adults, it is generally thought that the central nervous system is not adequately developed physically until approximately the age of 5. However, newer research suggests that the central nervous system may be continuing to develop into the 20s (Giedd et al., 1999). Using fMRI brain scans researchers have shown that adolescents' brains undergo many structural changes (Casey, Getz, & Galvan, 2008). One major change is thickening of the corpus callosum which causes improved information processing (Giedd et al., 2006). However, the cerebral cortex does not finish maturing until 18–25 years, whereas the amygdala matures earlier. Researchers suggest that this may be the reason why adolescents experience strong emotions but often appear unable to control them (Nelson, 2003). In addition, there is the influence of the environment as a factor in brain changes, such as a recent study in which the corpus callosum thickened and more brain connections were formed when adolescents resisted peer pressure (Paus et al., 2008).

Hence, nature and nurture always interact with age in brain development. Therefore, a patient who receives a brain insult or suffers from a central nervous system disease at an earlier age may not be able to fully develop all of his central nervous system functions. However, in seeming contradiction, it is also the case that children show less behavioral effects and recover faster from brain difficulties. The plasticity of the brain appears to be the reason that children show less behavioral effects and recover faster from brain injury. Plasticity is the behavioral or neural ability which the brain exhibits to reorganize after brain injury. Literally, healthy brain tissue assumes the role of and functions for the impaired brain tissue. Plasticity explains how the individual in the case study in Chapter 7 was able to survive being crushed by a sliding glass door at the age of 4 in a way that a mature adult may not have.

Another issue related to age has to do with certain behaviors which are particular to different age groups. The 15–24 age group sustains more closed head injuries than any other age group, followed by very young children and the elderly. The 15–24 age group tends to engage in more risky behaviors than any other age group which could put them at risk for numerous types of difficulties. There is also a sense of invulnerability exhibited by individuals in this age group which is not present to such a degree in older individuals. This may also relate to the current research addressing the age when the central nervous system is fully functioning. In addition, individuals in this age group may be experimenting with various legal or illegal substances and, while under the influence of these chemicals, also engaging in behaviors that they may not have at other times. The very young and the elderly are the other groups that sustain closed head injuries at a high rate but the cause is often falls.

The final topic under the section on age is a discussion of normal aging. It is not normal to develop dementia with age. However, more cases of this difficulty arise in the aging population. It is also the case that as time passes, technology allows more and more individuals to live longer than has been the case in past generations. Hence, with more individuals surviving for longer periods of time it becomes difficult to understand the behaviors which are due to aging and those which have a different etiology. The general overriding conclusion is that there tends to be certain levels of decline with aging. Major difficulties tend to indicate the presence of disease or injury.

Similar to the age-related changes that occur in the entire human body, the central nervous system also experiences a certain amount of change as one ages. Abilities tend to be somewhat slower and any task that is timed may show a decrement. Major changes in abilities are not to be expected with normal aging and many serve as warning signs of a more serious difficulty.

Physiologically, the following changes all occur during normal aging: decline in brain volume, cortical atrophy evidenced by wider sulci, narrowed gyri, thinning of the cortical mantle, increasing dilation of the ventricles, and changes in the temporal lobes and in the basilar–subcortical regions. Neuronal loss may account for many of these changes. Cerebral blood flow tends to show a decline particularly in areas already described. While these are merely a list of normal changes due to aging, none of these are evidence for significant behavioral sequelae.

As discussed within the section on intelligence, crystallized abilities tend to remain intact longer than fluid abilities. Also discussed in the same section was the idea of cognitive reserve. Two large-scale studies have added credence to the idea that a protective cognitive reserve may begin early in life. A large-scale study of aging and dementia was conducted with Roman Catholic nuns as subjects. The study compared intelligence, as defined in the study, with evidence of dementia later in life (Snowdon, Greiner, Kemper, Nanayakkara, & Mortimer, 1999). The findings suggest that individuals who scored higher on the measure of intelligence were less likely to develop dementia. A second study

plasticity
the flexibility of the brain which allows the individual to recover from some types of brain injury or insult because other areas of the brain take over the lost function; more widespread in children and more limited in adults

related scores on standardized intelligence tests administered at age 11 to signs of dementia 50 years later (Whalley et al., 2000). Those individuals who had higher intellectual ability had less decline and were less likely to exhibit signs of dementia. An interaction with other factors is indicated by a study which showed that an active lifestyle in a favorable environment helps to preserve cognitive functioning (Schaie, 1994). It is more likely that individuals with higher intellectual ability are more actively engaged than others.

When looking at Timmy's case his age could be considered to be a positive factor in prognosis and treatment planning as he has passed early childhood. It can be assumed that his central nervous system had developed but not reached the age where normal aging is a consideration. Teuber (1975) found that on a number of tests, recovery of soldiers from head injuries is greater in the 17–20 age group, where Timmy's age would fall, than in the 21–25 age group. However, Timmy's accident is possibly an example of individuals who may have felt invulnerable and did not take the necessary precautions before diving. Hence, his age may help him recover physiologically but his lack of insight into the reason the accident happened may work against him. Hence, the clinical neuropsychologist may need to focus on helping Timmy become realistic about his actual abilities and disabilities.

GENDER

The relationship between the brain and gender continues to be a very controversial area. In an extensive search of the literature, Kimura (1999) reports research that indicates gender differences in many brain functions. In the area of motor skills, males are better than females at target throwing and catching (Hall & Kimura, 1995) and females are better at fine motor skills (Nicholson & Kimura, 1996). Within spatial analysis, males excel over females in mental rotation (Collins & Kimura, 1997), spatial navigation (Astur, Tropp, Sava, Constable, & Markus, 2004), and geographical knowledge (Beatty & Troster, 1987), whereas females are better at spatial memory (McBurney, Gaulin, Devineni, & Adams, 1997). In the area of mathematical aptitude, females excel at computation (Hyde, Fennema, & Lamon, 1990) and males excel at mathematical reasoning (Benbow, 1988). Under the topic of perception, females excel at all of the following abilities: sensitivity to sensory stimuli (Velle, 1987), perceptual speed (Majeres, 1983), sensitivity to facial and body expression (Hall, 1984), and visual recognition memory (McGivern et al., 1998). Verbal abilities clearly favored females in the area of fluency (Hyde & Linn, 1988) and verbal memory (McGuinness, Olson, & Chapman, 1990). Kimura was not able to find any environmental reasons for any of these results and hence made inferences that genetics may be the cause.

Physiologically male brains are larger than female brains and differences in body size cannot account for the difference (Ankney, 1992). Male brains have more neurons and body size does not account for this (Pakkenburg & Gundersen, 1997). Males have more gray matter than females and females' gray matter is organized differently than males. Hence, these findings suggest that, proportionally, the size of each gender's brain does not explain the structural differences.

Lateral asymmetry is not as pronounced in women as in men and there is considerable overlap between men and women (Levy & Heller, 1992). **Lateral asymmetry** (left larger than right) in the planum temporale is seen more often in men than in women (Kulynych, Valdar, Jones, & Weinberger, 1994). Male brains have been found to have a larger asymmetry in the Sylvian fissure than female brains (Witelson & Kigar, 1992). Kolb and Whishaw (2009) state that these two findings taken together argue for a sex difference in the organization of language-related functions. Many studies claim that women have more interhemispheric connections in both the corpus callosum and the anterior commissure than do men. The posterior part of the callosum is significantly larger in women than

lateral asymmetry
comparable areas of either brain hemisphere which do not have similar functions or structure

in men (Witelson, 1985). Women have a larger anterior commissure than men probably due to the number of neuronal fibers in the two sexes, a difference thought to be due to the way the two hemispheres interact (Allen & Gorski, 1992). The ridges on fingertips are asymmetrical. This finding is greater in women and the pattern of ridges is correlated with performance on certain cognitive tests (Kimura, 1999).

According to the controversial research on gender, Timmy's prognosis and treatment plan for rehabilitation would benefit more if he were born female. This appears to be due to the supposition that there are more areas of the brain that are able to compensate for other areas in the female brain. The same information has been hypothesized regarding left-handed individuals. Unfortunately, Timmy is a right-handed individual.

Types of Difficulties Expressed by the Patient

Earlier chapters discussed the major central nervous system diseases and difficulties, the etiology of these difficulties, and the current types of treatment available. The present discussion focuses on the course of each difficulty as it pertains to prognosis and treatment planning. The reader should keep in mind that the issues in this section interact with those discussed within the previous section.

NATURE AND EXTENT OF CHANGES

Any type of central nervous system accident or illness implies that some type of change in the functioning of the central nervous system will occur. Also significant is the type and extent of the changes as they impact the patient's recovery.

Beginning with a discussion of brain injury, the concepts of diffuse versus focal damage often come into play. **Diffuse damage** affects many areas of the brain but usually the damage is not equal. Diffuse brain damage usually occurs due to a circumstance that causes widespread difficulties such as an infection, anoxia, degenerative disorders, and closed head injuries. The reader is referred to Chapters 3 and 4 for examples of diffuse damage. Many behavioral sequelae occur due to diffuse damage including difficulty with memory, attention, concentration, higher level and complex reasoning, and response slowing. The individual may also experience **emotional flattening** or **emotional lability**. Emotional flattening means that emotions are not experienced with any degree of excitement, whereas emotional lability, implies that emotions fluctuate quite dramatically. Many of these symptoms occur early on and they may worsen as time goes by.

Focal damage implies that a very circumscribed area is affected. Infections, tumors, lesions, and trauma are all examples of causes of focal damage. The area or site of the damage will give an indication of the types of behaviors that should be expected (Heilman & Valenstein, 2003). However, very few patients have damage which is confined to the area of the focal difficulty. In situations of focal damage, many times symptoms which are thought to accompany diffuse damage occur and cause difficulty in diagnosis.

When one is discussing lesions to the brain, the cause is important in prognosis and treatment planning. A clean wound or a clear pattern of tissue involvement will give the clinical neuropsychologist more concrete information than injury or illness that affects multiple areas. The depth and extent to which a cortical lesion involves subcortical tissue makes the symptom picture much more complex with the addition of possible disrupted pathways, damaged integrative centers (Kumral, 2001), or impairment of verbal skills (Ferro, 2001). **Diaschisis**, first described by Von Monakov (1969), is thought to be a form

diffuse damage
the general or widespread impact of any injury or illness on brain function

emotional flattening
refers to the outward expression of emotions when virtually no stimulus can elicit an emotional response; may also be described as emotional blunting or affective flattening

emotional lability
refers to outward expression of emotions that vary widely; it may encompass a "normal" mood for the individual interspersed with depression or manic-appearing behaviors

focal damage
an area of localized insult to the brain

diaschisis
the suspension of functions that are associated with structures remote to the damaged area; it is assumed these areas have been temporally disconnected

of shock to the nervous system due to disruptions in the neural network connecting the area damaged by the lesion with functionally related areas that may be at a distance away or even in the opposite hemisphere. Diaschisis is often thought to be a nonpermanent phenomenon and one that improves spontaneously. However, other researchers invoke the concept to explain the appearance of permanent changes in functions not directly associated with the lesion site (Gummow, Dustman, & Kearney, 1984). A chronic form of diaschisis may appear similar to a **disconnection syndrome** due to the fact that both appear as a loss of function surrounded by an area of the brain that is intact and at a distance from the lesion. However, researchers have found a difference in causality. Lesions which may or may not extend to white matter cause diaschisis, whereas disconnection syndromes result from damage to white matter that cuts cortical pathways, disconnecting one or another cortical area from the communication network of the brain (Filley, 1995).

disconnection syndrome
behavioral syndrome resulting from the disconnection of two or more brain areas rather than from the damage to a specific brain region

Regardless of the nature of the lesion, its severity is the most important variable in determining the individual's level of impairment. Etiology also plays some role, in that TBI patients tend to recover more arm and leg movements and speech than stroke patients (Kertesz & Gold, 2003). However, this interacts with age as patients with TBI tend to be younger than patients who had stroke.

A degenerative type of difficulty implies a much different type of prognosis and treatment planning as compared to brain injury or insult. **Degeneration** as a term implies that the individual is experiencing a difficulty in which the course has a downhill or negative slope. Dementias of various causes are often the types of difficulty thought of when one uses the term degenerative. Another factor is whether the difficulty causes diseased or dead brain tissue to be left behind in its wake. Dead brain tissue often causes other difficulties or diseases by impinging on tissue or occupying extra space. An example of this is the tau plaques and neurofibrillary tangles of Alzheimer's type dementia. The ability to predict function is less clear in these circumstances.

degeneration
death of neurons or neuronal processes in response to injury in the degenerating neuron or in some cases in the brain

Considering Timmy's case, it would appear that he has sustained focal damage due to his mild closed head injury or concussion. Timmy's spinal cord injury could also be considered a focal injury, however, as it has repercussions on other areas which are innervated by the spinal cord.

COURSE OF ILLNESS OR INJURY

The course of a central nervous system illness or injury relates to whether there is a standard pattern of progression or recovery due to the etiological factors involved or whether the course is more individualistic depending on various patient factors discussed earlier. Some difficulties, such as Alzheimer's type dementia, have a standard pattern of decline in abilities which helps the clinical neuropsychologist predict prognosis and formulate the treatment plan. Even though Alzheimer's type dementia is a progressive illness, the stage in which the individual is functioning may affect the prognosis and help with intervention. Early assessment may allow for a treatment plan which helps the individual remain longer in the earlier stages of Alzheimer's type dementia. A different pattern exists in a relapsing–remitting disorder such as multiple sclerosis. The prognosis and treatment plan is more individual in this type of disorder and includes periods of acceleration of symptoms or decline and periods in which the progress of the illness is slower.

Another variable in the course of the accident or illness is when in the sequence of the difficulty the clinical neuropsychologist first becomes involved. Prognosis and treatment planning will vary significantly depending upon whether it is undertaken soon after the patient is diagnosed or many months or years later. As stated earlier, statements of prognosis and development of treatment plans are based on neuropsychological data gained through assessment. Due to the changes that occur in the central nervous system after an accident or illness, it has become standard to evaluate the patient soon after diagnosis, at 6 months, and at 1-year and 2-year intervals. Accounts indicate that recovery tends to progress in spurts and there are often periods in which there is improvement in performance and also periods when it appears that the same abilities have declined (Kertesz & Gold, 2003). Improvements in cognitive functions also tend to appear most substantially on testing at 6 months and 1 year (Gerschwind, 1985). Using TBI as an example of changes that occur during 6 months and 1 year postincident, significant improvements in cognitive ability which included memory, processing speed, language abilities, and constructional skills, were observed (Novack, Alderson, Bush, Meythaler, & Canupp, 2000). There were also gains in community integration but not in driving ability. In most circumstances, patients make the most rapid gains in the first weeks and months following medical stabilization (Bode & Heinemann, 2002). These time frames relate to the events which often occur soon after diagnosis versus later when the central nervous system has had a chance to recover on its own or with assistance.

Returning to Timmy's condition, we must look at two issues: the spinal cord injury and the mild closed head injury. The course of the spinal cord injury is static; it will not become any better nor will it worsen. The difficulties that will progress are outside of the control of the central nervous system and involve muscle atrophy. The course of his closed head injury, however, will be determined by many of the patient and situational factors already discussed. It is a positive factor that he has sustained a closed rather than open head injury. The CT scan did not indicate that there was any appreciable bleeding or edema. Cognitively, he has had mild symptoms described earlier as **postconcussion syndrome**. Postconcussion syndrome is a new term that will be included in *Diagnostic and Statistical Manual of Mental Disorders, Fifth Edition* (DSM-V) when released. It describes the aftereffects of a medically documented concussion including neuropsychological or cognitive assessment of difficulties with attention or memory. Other symptoms which may exist include easy fatigability, disordered sleep, headache, dizziness, anxiety, depression, changes in personality, and/or lack of spontaneity.

> **postconcussion syndrome** constellation of physical and psychological symptoms that may occur as a result of a medically verifiable concussion

Ways to Enhance Recovery

In general terms, there are four ways in which recovery may happen or be encouraged: spontaneous recovery, recovery of old functional systems, development of new functional systems, and changing the environment. The four areas covered in this section will be a basic introduction not an evaluation of techniques or programs available, such as will be the case in future chapters.

SPONTANEOUS RECOVERY

The central nervous system is no different than any other area of the body in that some recovery of function happens purely on the body's own with the passage of time. Technically, **spontaneous recovery** implies any positive change or movement toward premorbid functioning without intervention. Many of the functions that improve with spontaneous recovery may have only been temporarily impaired and are thus reversible. In these cases, the brain has not been irreparably damaged and is able to resume normal functioning with the passage of time. This type of recovery is often the reason that some patients show very rapid recovery soon after a brain injury. This process does not occur in degenerative difficulties where the lost functions do not recover with the passage of time.

> **spontaneous recovery** the body's ability to recover from illness or injury without outside assistance

edema
an abnormal accumulation of fluid in intercellular spaces of the body or brain

Edema is one of the main reversible events in brain injury. **Edema** is the swelling of the brain that may follow many types of trauma. An example of edema in another part of the body is the swelling that occurs when a particular area is bruised or a bone is broken. With the brain, the swelling occurs within the confines of the skull. Dependent on the extent of the edema there may develop an increase in pressure within the brain which in turn may damage or destroy various cells. Another difficulty could occur if the pressure pushes against a blood vessel causing it to rupture or become blocked.

hemorrhage
in neuropsychology, it refers to cerebral hemorrhage which is defined as massive bleeding into a structure of the brain

Another related effect which may be temporary is the loss of blood flow to brain cells. The actual cause may be an occlusion by emboli within the brain, thrombi from other areas, or blood flow loss caused by **hemorrhage**. Hemorrhage, technically, is the escape of blood from the vessel. Similar to edema, if the loss of blood flow is only partial or lasts a short time, the brain cells may become impaired but not die. In these types of situations improvement may be expected with time.

There are many and varied factors which may temporarily affect the cells of the brain. Trauma may have a lasting effect or may "shock" but not permanently impair the person. In this circumstance diaschisis, as described earlier, may also occur. Drugs, dehydration, metabolic imbalances, and biological deficiencies may also cause nonpermanent damage. In each of these situations, however, there is the potential for more serious difficulties.

RECOVERY OF OLD FUNCTIONAL SYSTEMS

Throughout the text it has been stated that behavior may be regulated by differing areas of the brain. In regard to early developmental periods, a task may have been performed by a specific area within the brain but, as development progressed, other areas of the brain may have replaced the original sites in regulating these functions. When a central nervous system accident or illness occurs, it is natural for the brain to revert to a developmentally earlier system that may be present but has not been used for an extended period of time. If all of the connections within the older systems remain intact, then the earlier system may be substituted for the impaired function or area. In many cases, it is easier for an individual to have an injury that permanently affects a functional system. The organism then naturally attempts to revert to an earlier developmental stage.

Another approach is the current thought that we may be able to either regroup cells from other areas or actually develop new cells to replace the diseased or damaged cells. Research in this area is growing at an astronomical rate. By the time this text becomes available it is almost guaranteed that new information regarding growth of neurons, which has not been included in the discussion, will be available. The reader is cautioned to pay particular attention to research in this area within the next few years, particularly because the issue of stem cell research has recently been addressed at the federal level (i.e., the government has now allowed the use of stem cells within federally funded research which was previously forbidden). Many times the injury or illness will affect the white matter which connects and supports neurons instead of impacting only the neurons themselves. Axons that link cells to one another are able to **sprout**, even after injury, causing additional cell connections.

sprouting
a process within a damaged neuron in which the remaining neurons or parts of a neuron sprout terminals to connect to a previously innervated area

DEVELOPMENT OF NEW FUNCTIONAL SYSTEMS

As described earlier, in cases of central nervous system illness or injury, destruction of any functioning system causes difficulties. Spontaneous recovery and use of old functional systems are the easier ways for the central nervous system to recover from any difficulty.

When the loss is permanent and/or the two aforementioned approaches are not possible, then it is necessary to attempt to form new links which function as a replacement for the injured part of the system or to develop a new system entirely. Creation of a new system may be accomplished through substitution of one area of the brain for another. Some of the more common scenarios involve tasks that involve both hemispheres of the brain and one hemisphere is impaired. For example, both occipital lobes are involved with vision; hence, if one is damaged, the other may be able to compensate. The difficulty which occurs is that at the optic chiasma, the optic nerves decussate so that if one hemisphere is lost, the other cannot completely fill in all of the visual fields. Hence, the new system is clearly a substitute and may not return the individual to his premorbid level of functioning.

A different way to change and add a new functional system is to try to complete a task in a different manner. For example, the literature shows that there are many different learning styles. Each individual has a preferred style. If the preferred style is visual but the visual apparatus is injured, the individual may be able to learn a task using an auditory modality.

Another way to change or enable a task to be completed is to make it easier or more complex. Making a task simpler could involve the use of a letter board to point to when a patient is unable to form words after a stroke. The opposite approach could also help in completing a task. Luria (1963) described a patient who was unable to walk after a central nervous system difficulty. After lines were placed on the floor and he was asked to move his feet from line to line, he was able to complete the task.

CHANGING THE ENVIRONMENT

After a review of spontaneous recovery issues and the use of old functional and new functional systems, some patients are still not able to complete tasks. In these situations, changing the physical environment of the individual may be the best way to ensure adequate quality of life and help to return the person to, as close as possible, his premorbid functioning. The changes that can be made to the environment are many and varied and are only limited by the imagination of the client and those involved with his or her treatment.

In Timmy's case, we can see that each of the four types of recovery are present. A period of spontaneous recovery definitely occurred as he began to cope with his spinal cord injury. Spontaneous recovery was also a factor in recovery from his closed head injury. The use of old functional systems came into play as he began to use his arms to help him propel his wheelchair when his legs were immobile. New functional systems were used as he began to try other means to move, and so forth. Finally, changing the environment was a major function in his case as the family home needed to be fitted for handicap access in various areas. The alteration of a vehicle for handicap driving is also an example of a change in the environment.

Forensic Issues in Prognosis and Treatment Planning

As has been discussed earlier, many difficulties with the central nervous system occur under circumstances where there is a degree of fault or blame attached. Circumstances such as medical malpractice, liability of a manufacturer for a defective product, liability for a defective service, or negligence on the part of a citizen which causes an injury to another unsuspecting individual are all situations which may lead to involvement with the legal system. With the addition of individuals who have been injured at their employment site and are involved with worker compensation and individuals who are filing disability claims, one sees the vastness of areas in which central nervous system difficulties may result in legal proceedings.

Clinical neuropsychologists participate within the legal realm as impartial objective assessors when hired by the court and expert witnesses when hired by either side in a litigation. **Forensic neuropsychology** is the term which is used when the clinical neuropsychologist provides neuropsychological evidence and opinions for court systems on issues involving cognitive status. Forensic activities are becoming a greater part of the professional practice of clinical neuropsychologists (Sweet, Peck, Abrahamowitz, & Etzweiler, 2003). The majority of clinical neuropsychologists are employed in private practice and of these, the number one referral source has become attorneys (Sweet, Moberg, & Suchy, 2000). The increase in the involvement within the forensic arena has developed since the 1980s. Taylor (1999) discussed several reasons for the emergence of neuropsychologists as litigation experts. These reasons include an increasing traumatic brain injured population, development of advocacy organizations, the advent of Neurolaw, an increasing supply of clinical neuropsychologists, and response to the legal system.

forensic neuropsychology
neuropsychological practice in which a clinician neuropsychologist provides evaluation or consultative sessions to an individual involved in a proceeding that is potentially adversarial in nature

LITIGATION ISSUES

There are many issues that exist in forensic clinical neuropsychology particularly within the interface between law and psychology. There exist different philosophies and codes of conduct within law and psychology which the clinical neuropsychologist must understand. The scientist–practitioner model was introduced in the opening chapter and is particularly important in the forensic arena due to the standards for admissibility of evidence. Clinical neuropsychology is grounded in empirical research; however, the validity of assessment tools must be proven for forensic purposes.

For many years, the **Frye standard** (*Frye v. United States*, 1923) was the prevailing standard governing the admissibility of expert testimony. This standard stated that evidence must be "generally accepted" within the field from which it was derived (Laing & Fisher, 1997). Recently, there has been a change in addressing the admissibility of expert evidence referred to as the **Daubert standard** (*Daubert v. Merrell Dow Pharmaceuticals, Inc.*, 1995). This decision has given judges the task of determining if the methodology used by an expert in arriving at an opinion is sound (Dixon & Gill, 2002). Hence, it has become more difficult for some individuals to be accepted as experts in their field. However, clinical neuropsychologists whose judgments are based on sound science tend to applaud this decision.

Frye standard
a standard in legal proceedings based on a ruling in 1923 which stated the information from an expert witness in one's field must use evidence that is "generally accepted" within the field from which it was derived

Daubert standard
a standard in legal proceedings based on a 1993 decision which stated that judges have a right to determine if the information presented by an expert witness has a sound basis and is admissible or not

WORKER COMPENSATION ISSUES

There are many and varied situations in which an individual may be hurt at his or her place of employment. Focusing solely on central nervous system difficulties, however, does not narrow the number of these situations when one looks at the variety of types of work and the circumstances in which an individual may be employed.

Worker compensation, previously known as *workmen's compensation*, dates to 1902; it originated in Maryland and the first federal law went into place in 1906. The initial worker compensation programs were designed to reduce litigation and speed up the delivery of benefits when an individual is injured at his or her place of employment. In order to receive worker compensation, the individual must agree that he or she will not file a lawsuit against his or her employer, usually categorized as a tort of negligence. In this circumstance, worker compensation functions as a form of disability insurance. Worker compensation pays medical bills and hence functions as health insurance. Worker compensation also pays premiums to dependants in case of the death of the worker and in that sense is a form of life insurance.

Worker compensation comes into play when an individual claims that the injury that he or she received not only happened at his or her place of employment but also that there is some implied responsibility of the employer to take care of the employee. Worker compensation is a benefit which a majority of employed individuals are able to partake. Individuals who are self-employed or work for a very small organization also have access to this because it is not a benefit in the strict sense of the word. Hence, even if the individual does not receive health insurance or have social security wages deducted automatically from his paycheck, he or she is eligible for worker compensation. The program varies in its administration by state. There is the supposition that it follows federal guidelines but there are large differences in how the decisions are made regarding employer liability and the amount that must be reimbursed to the employee.

The first step in the process is that the worker reports a central nervous system difficulty to the employer. For instance, an employee fell due to a loose carpet and hit his head sustaining a concussion. An incident report is the first step and next an application is completed. Usually a contracted agency responds and makes a determination of the extent of disability and the negligence on the part of the employer. In many circumstances, when an individual receives worker compensation, he or she receives less salary than he or she normally would. When an employee receives worker compensation, he or she also relinquishes the legal right to sue the employer.

The role of the clinical neuropsychologist in this situation may vary depending on the referral source and whether he or she is asked to evaluate the claimant to deliver expert witness testimony. Evaluation, as described earlier, must be impartial and objective and should rest on the most empirically verifiable tools available. **Expert witness testimony** implies that the court has recognized the clinical neuropsychologist as an expert based on training and experience and will use his or her testimony to render a decision. One of the difficulties the clinical neuropsychologist may face is malingering or secondary gain on the part of the injured party. Tests are available to screen for this particular problem and the professional must be conversant with these tools.

expert witness testimony
a clinical neuropsychologist who is recognized by the court as an expert in his or her field based on education and experience

SOCIAL SECURITY DISABILITY

Social Security payments are another avenue through which an individual may apply for assistance after he or she has incurred a central nervous system accident or illness. The Social Security Administration (SSA) administers two programs that provide benefits based on disability: the Social Security Disability Insurance (SSDI) program (Title II of the Social Security Act) and the Supplemental Security Income (SSI) program (Title XVI) of the act. Title II provides for payment of disability benefits to individuals who are insured under the act by having contributed through Social Security tax on wages as well as some dependents of insured individuals. Title XVI provides for SSI payments to individuals (including children younger than age 18) who are disabled and have limited income and resources.

Most disability claims are processed through a network of local Social Security field offices and state agencies (usually called Disability Determination Services or DDSs). Appeals for claims may be made to these offices. The DDSs are funded by the federal government and the state agencies are responsible for developing medical evidence and rendering the initial determination whether the claimant is disabled or not or blind. The DDS tries to obtain evidence from the claimant's own medical sources first. If that is unavailable or insufficient, the DDS will arrange a consultative examination (CE) in order to obtain more information. The results of the CE are submitted to the DDS office for inclusion in the client's data file. The judgment of disability is made by a two-person team consisting of a medical or psychological consultant and a disability examiner.

The role of the clinical neuropsychologist may be as the treating professional in which case the DDS may request information regarding the claimant and his or her prognosis and treatment plan. A clinical neuropsychologist may be requested to perform, for a fee, examinations and/or tests that are needed or a full neuropsychological evaluation. The final way a clinical neuropsychologist may be involved is to testify at administrative law judge hearings or respond to written interrogatories from the administrative law judge.

Returning to Timmy's case study, it is clear that there is no liability in this case which may be pursued. However, it is also clear that Timmy will need to be cared for by others for the remainder of his life and possibly will not be able to work. Timmy's parents helped him in the process of applying for assistance from the Supplemental Security Insurance (SSI) program. They were able to obtain funds to help with Timmy's care and also pay his family for services that they had chosen to provide for him. Without the program, Timmy's accident could have financially devastated his family for the rest of their lives.

Summary

The chapter began with a rather complex case of a 17-year-old boy who sustained both a spinal cord injury and a mild closed head injury. The case was integrated within each section of the chapter to illustrate the issues related to prognosis and treatment planning. In this case study the prognosis is poor for the spinal cord injury and good for the mild closed head injury. The treatment plan was very involved and covered many of the areas included within this chapter with the addition of needing the services of multiple professionals in addition to the clinical neuropsychologist.

The chapter continued by explaining premorbid patient variables, which include intellectual abilities, personality characteristics, social support networks, age, and gender. Reviewing each of these areas prior to prognosis and treatment planning gives the clinical neuropsychologist a baseline from which to compare the current situation. The nature and extent of changes caused by the central nervous system difficulty as well as the course of the difficulty give the clinical neuropsychologist additional information regarding the difficulties themselves. These are then compared to premorbid factors in the prognosis and treatment planning areas.

Ways to enhance recovery are introduced in this chapter, not as a critique of programs but as a way to look at how different levels of evidence may affect prognosis and treatment planning. The areas discussed are spontaneous recovery, the use of old functional systems, introduction of new functional systems, and/or changing the environment.

The chapter concluded with a brief look at forensic issues and their impact on central nervous system difficulties. Particularly salient are issues of worker compensation and Social Security Disability payments.

Questions for Further Study

1. Why is it crucial to understand the patient's level of premorbid functioning?
2. How does a treatment plan vary based on whether a client has good versus poor premorbid circumstances or issues?
3. What must a clinical neuropsychologist demonstrate in terms of skills to be termed an *expert witness*?

References

Allen, L. S., & Gorski, R. A. (1992). Sexual orientation and the size of the anterior commissure in the human brain. *Proceedings of the National Academy of Sciences of the United States of America, 89*(15), 199–201.

Ankney, C. D. (1992). Sex differences in relative brain size: The mismeasure of woman too? *Intelligence, 16,* 329–336.

Astur, R. S., Tropp, J., Sava, S., Constable, R. T., & Markus, E. J. (2004). Sex differences and correlations in a virtual Morris water task, a virtual radial arm maze, and mental rotation. *Behavioral Brain Research, 151*(1–2), 103–115.

Beatty, W. W., & Tröster, A. I. (1987). Gender differences in geographical knowledge. *Sex Roles, 16,* 565–590.

Benbow, C. P. (1988). Sex differences in mathematical reasoning ability in intellectually talented preadolescents: Their nature, effects, and possible causes. *Behavioral and Brain Sciences, 11,* 169–232.

Bigler, E. D. (1995). Brain morphology and intelligence. *Developmental Neuropsychology, 11,* 377–403.

Bode, R. K., & Heinemann, A. W. (2002). Course of functional improvement after stroke, spinal cord injury and traumatic brain injury. *Archives of Physical Medicine and Rehabilitation, 83,* 100–106.

Broadwell, S. D., & Light, K. C. (1999). Family support and cardiovascular responses in married couples during conflict and other interactions. *International Journal of Behavioral Medicine, 6,* 40–63.

Casey, B. J., Getz, S., & Galvan, A. (2008). The adolescent brain. *Developmental Review, 28,* 62–77.

Castro-Caldas, A., Petersson, K. M., Reis, A., Stone-Elander, S., & Ingvar, M. (1998). The illiterate brain. Learning to read and write during childhood influences the functional organization of the adult brain. *Brain, 121,* 1053–1063.

Cattell, R. B. (1963). Theory of fluid and crystallized intelligence: A critical experiment. *Journal of Educational Psychology, 54,* 1–22.

Collins, D. W., & Kimura, D. (1997). A large sex difference on a two-dimensional mental rotation task. *Behavioral Neuroscience, 111,* 845–849.

Daubert v. Merrell Dow Pharmaceuticals, Inc., 43 F.3d 1311 (9th Cir. 1995)

Dixon, L., & Gill, B. (2002). Changes in the standards for admitting expert evidence in federal civil cases since the Daubert decision. *Psychology, Public Policy and Law, 8*(3), 251–308.

Ferro, J. M. (2001). Neurobehavioral aspects of deep hemispheric stroke. In J. Bogousslavsky & L. Caplan (Eds.), *Stroke syndromes* (2nd ed.). Cambridge, MA: Cambridge University Press.

Filley, C. M. (Ed.). (1995). *Neurobehavioral anatomy.* Niwot, CO: University Press of Colorado.

Frey v. United States 293F.103 DC (1923).

Giedd, J., Blumenthal, J., Jeffries, N., Castellanos, F., Liu, H., Zijdenbos, A., et al. (1999). Brain development during childhood and adolescence: A longitudinal MRI study. *Nature Neuroscience, 2,* 861–863.

Giedd, J. N., Clasen, L. S., Lenroot, R., Greenstein, D. Wallace, G. L., Ordaz, S., et al. (2006). Puberty-related influences on brain development. *Molecular and Cellular Endocrinology, 25,* 254–255.

Gerschwind, N. (1985). Mechanism of change after brain lesions. *Annals of the New York Academy of Sciences, 457,* 1–13.

Gladsjo, J. A., Schuman, C. C., Evans, J. D., Peavy, G. M., Miller, S. W., & Heaton, R. K (1999). Use of oral reading to estimate premorbid intellectual and neuropsychological functioning. *Journal of the International Neuropsychological Society, 5,* 247–254.

Grafman, J., Lalonde, F., Litvan, I., & Fedio, P. (1989). Premorbid effects upon recovery from brain injury in humans: Cognitive and interpersonal indices. In J. Schulkin (Ed.), *Preoperative events: Their effects on behavior following brain damage* (pp. 277–304). New York: Erlbaum.

Grewen, K. M., Girdler, S. S., Amico, J., & Light, K. C. (2005). Effects of partner support in resting oxytocin, cortisol, norepinephrine and blood pressure before and after warm partner contact. *Psychosomatic Medicine, 67,* 531–538.

Gummow, S. J., Dustman, R. E., & Kearney, R. P. (1984). Remote effects of cerebrovascular accidents: Visual evoked potentials and electrophysiological coupling. *Electroencephalography and Clinical Neurophysiology, 58,* 408–417.

Hall, J. (1984). *Nonverbal sex differences.* Baltimore: Johns Hopkins University Press.

Hall, J. A. Y., & Kimura, D. (1995). Sexual orientation and performance on sexually dimorphic motor tasks. *Archives of Sexual Behavior, 24,* 395–407.

Heaton, R. K., Ryan, L., Grant, I. & Mathews, C. G. (1996). Demographic influences on neuropsychological test performance. In I. Grant & K. Adams (Ed.), *Neuropsychological assessment of neuropsychiatric disorders* (2nd ed., pp. 141–163). New York: Oxford University Press.

Heilman, K. M., & Valenstein, E. (Eds.). (2003). *Clinical neuropsychology* (4th ed.). New York: Oxford University Press.

Huttenlocher, P. R. (2002). *Neural plasticity: The effects of environment in the development of the cerebral cortex.* Cambridge, MA: Harvard University Press.

Hyde, J. S., Fennema, E., & Lamon, S. J. (1990). Gender differences in mathematics performance: A meta-analysis. *Psychological Bulletin, 107,* 139–155.

Hyde, J. S., & Linn, M. C. (1988). Gender differences in verbal ability: A meta-analysis. *Psychological Bulletin, 104,* 53–69.

Kaplan, S. P. (1990). Social support, emotional distress and vocational outcomes among persons with brain injuries. *Rehabilitation Counseling Bulletin, 34,* 16–23.

Kaufman, A. S., Reynolds, C. R., & McLean. (1989). Age and WAIS-R intelligence in a sample of adults in the 20–74 year age range: A cross sectional analysis with educational level controlled. *Intelligence, 13,* 235–253.

Kertesz, A., & Gold, B. T. (2003). Recovery of cognition. In K. M. Heilman & E. Valenstein (Eds.), *Clinical neuropsychology* (4th ed., pp. 617–639). New York: Oxford University Press.

Kimura, D. (1999). *Sex and cognition.* Cambridge, MA: MIT Press.

Kolb, B., & Whishaw, I. Q. (2009). *Fundamentals of human neuropsychology* (p. 324). New York: Wadsworth.

Kulynych, J. J., Valdar, K., Jones, D. W., & Weinberger, D. R. (1994). Gender differences in the normal lateralization of the supratemporal cortex: MRI surface rendering morphometry of Heschel's gyrus, and the planum temporale. *Cerebral Cortex, 4,* 107–118.

Kumral, E. (2001). Multiple, multi-level and bihemispheric strokes. In J. Bogousslavsky & L. Caplan (Eds.), *Stroke syndromes* (2nd ed.). Cambridge, MA: Cambridge University Press.

Laing, L. C. (Ed.), & Fisher, J. M. (1997). Neuropsychology in civil proceedings. In R. M. McCaffrey & A. D. William (Eds.), *The practice of forensic neuropsychology: Meeting challenges in the courtroom* (pp. 118–131). New York: Plenum Press.

Le Carrett, N., Lafont, S., Letenneur, L., Dartigues, J., Mayo, W., & Fabrigoule, C. (2003). The effect of education on cognitive performance and its implications for the constitution of the cognitive reserve. *Developmental Neuropsychology, 23*(3), 317–337.

Levy, J., & Heller, W. (1992). Gender differences in human neuropsychological function. In J. Herron (Ed.), *Neuropsychology of left-handedness.* New York: Academic Press.

Lezak, M. D., Howieson, D. B., & Loring, D. W. (2004). *Neuropsychological assessment* (4th ed.). New York: Oxford University Press.

Luria, A. R. (1963). *Restoration of Function After Brain Injury.* New York: Macmillan.

Majeres, R. L. (1983). Sex differences in symbol-digit substitution and speeded matching. *Intelligence, 7,* 313–327.

McBurney, D. H., Gaulin, S. J. C., Devineni, T., & Adams, C. (1997). Superior spatial memory of women: Stronger evidence for the gathering hypothesis. *Evolution and Human Behavior, 18,* 73–87.

McGivern, R. F., Mutter, K. L., Anderson, J., Wideman, G., Bodnar, M., & Huston, P. J. (1998). Gender differences in incidental learning and visual recognition memory: Support for a sex difference in unconscious environmental awareness. *Personality and Individual Differences, 25,* 223–232.

McGuinness, D., Olson, A., & Chapman, J. (1990). Sex differences in incidental recall for words and pictures. *Learning and Individual Differences, 2,* 263–285.

Nelson, C. A. (2003). Neural development and lifelong plasticity. In R. M. Lerner, F. Jacobs, & D. Wertlieb (Eds.), *The Handbook of applied developmental science* (Vol. 1), Thousand Oaks, CA: Sage.

Newcombe, F. (1982). The psychological consequences of closed head injury: Assessment and rehabilitation. *Injury, 14,* 111–136.

Nicholson, K. G., & Kimura, D. (1996). Sex differences for speech and manual skills. *Perceptual and Motor Skills, 82,* 3–13.

Novack, T. A., Alderson, A. L., Bush, B. A., Meythaler, J. M., & Canupp, K. (2000). Cognitive and functional recovery at 6 and 12 months post-TBI. *Brain Injury, 14*(11), 987–996.

Pakkenburg, B., & Gundersen, H. J. (1997). Neocortical neuron number in humans: Effects of sex and age. *Journal of Comparative Neurology, 384,* 312–320.

Paus, T., Toro, R., Lenard, G., Lerner, J. V., Lerner, R. M., Perron, M. et al. (2008). Morphological properties of the action-observation cortical network in adolescents with low and high resistance to peer influence. *Social Neuroscience, 3*(3–4), 303–316.

Rook, K. S. (1984). The negative side of social interaction: Impact on psychological well-being. *Journal of Personality and Social Psychology, 46,* 1097–1108.

Salthouse, T. A. (1991). *Theoretical perspectives on cognitive aging.* Hilsdale, NJ: Lawrence Erlbaum Associates.

Satz, P. (1993). Brain reserve capacity on symptom onset after brain injury: A formulation and review of evidence for threshold theory. *Neuropsychology, 7,* 273–295.

Schaie, K. W. (1994). The course of adult intellectual development. *American Psychologist, 49,* 304–313.

Silver, J. M., Hales, R. M., & Yudofsky, S. C. (2002). Neuropsychiatric aspects of traumatic brain injury. In S. C. Yudofsky & R. E. Hales (Eds.), *Textbook of neuropsychiatry* (3rd ed., pp. 625–672). Washington, DC: American Psychiatric Press.

Snowdon, D. A., Greiner, L. H., Kemper, S. J., Nanayakkara, W., & Mortimer, J. A. (1999). Linguistic ability in early life and longevity: Findings from the Nun Study. In J. M. Robine, B. Forette, C. Franceschi & M. Allard (Eds.), *The paradox of longevity* (pp. 103–114). Berlin: Springer.

Sweet, J., Moberg, P., & Suchy, Y. (2000). Ten year follow-up survey of clinical neuropsychologists: Part II. Private practice and economics. *The Clinical Neuropsychologist, 14,* 479–495.

Sweet, J., Peck, E., Abrahamowitz, C., & Etzweiler, S. (2003). National Academy of Neuropsychology/ Division 40 (American Psychological Association) Practice Survey of Clinical Neuropsychology in the United States, Part II: Reimbursement experiences, practice economics, billing practices, and incomes. *Archives of Clinical Neuropsychology, 18,* 557–582.

Taylor, J. S. (1999). The legal environment pertaining to clinical neuropsychology. In J. Sweet (Ed.), *Forensic neuropsychology: Fundamentals and practice* (pp. 419–442). Lisse, Netherlands: Swets & Zeitlinger.

Taylor, S. E. (2007). Social support. In H. S. Friedman & R. C. Silver (Eds.), *Foundations of health psychology* (pp. 145–171). New York: Oxford Press.

Taylor, S. E. (2009). *Health psychology* (7th ed.). New York: McGraw-Hill.

Teuber, H. L. (1975). Recovery of function after brain injury in man. In R. Porter & D. W. Fitzsimons (Eds.), *Outcome of severe damage to the nervous system: Ciba Foundation Symposium* (Vol. 34, pp. 159–190). Amsterdam: Elsevier North-Holland.

Uchino, B. N., & Garvey, T. S. (1997). The availability of social support reduces cardiovascular reactivity to acute psychological stress. *Journal of Behavioral Medicine, 20,* 15–27.

Velle, W. (1987). Sex differences in sensory functions. *Perspectives in Biology and Medicine, 30,* 490–522.

Von Monakov, C. (1969). Diaschisis. In K. H. Pribram (Ed.), *Brain and behavior. I. Mood states and mind.* Baltimore: Penguin Books.

Wechsler, D. (1997). *Wechsler Adult Intelligence Scale-III.* San Antonio, TX: The Psychological Corporation.

Wechsler, D. (2008). *Wechsler Adult Intelligence Scale-IV.* San Antonio, TX: The Psychological Corporation.

Whalley, L. J., Starr, J. M., Athawes, E. R., Hunter, D., Pattie, A., & Deary, I. J. (2000). Childhood mental ability and dementia. *Neurology, 55*(10), 1455–1459.

Witelson, S. F. (1985). The brain connection: The corpus callosum is larger in left-handers. *Science, 229,* 665–668.

Witelson, S. F., & Kigar, S. L. (1992). Sylvian fissure morphology and asymmetry in men and woman: Bilateral differences in relation to handedness in men. *Journal of Comparative Neurology, 323,* 326–340.

Cognitive and Memory Rehabilitation

12

Learning Objectives

After reading this chapter, the student should be able to understand:

- The components of cognition as well as why taking a multidisciplinary approach and working with a patient's family are important in cognitive rehabilitation
- The concepts of ecological validity and treatment efficacy as they relate to cognitive rehabilitation
- The different types of attention as well as techniques to use in assessing and treating attentional difficulties
- The definition of memory and how it is related to attention as well as assessment and treatment techniques for improving memory
- The types of behaviors exhibited in dysexecutive syndromes and approaches to treating these difficulties
- The problems in assessing a patient's unawareness as well as treatment approaches to facilitate awareness

Topical Outline

- History
- Theories for Working With Cognitive Impairment
- Models of Cognitive Processing
- Measuring Efficacy and Outcome
- Cognitive Rehabilitation Techniques
- Dysexecutive Syndromes
- Unawareness

Mick is now a 20-year-old college student. He was referred for a follow-up neuropsychological evaluation and rehabilitation for any deficits which may have developed subsequent to the removal of a rare brain tumor at age 17. He has had several previous evaluations at the appropriate times after he had brain surgery.

Mick's difficulties began during his junior year in high school. He had always been a B student and was athletic, on the baseball and golf teams. He also worked in his spare time as a referee for elementary school basketball teams and caddied at the local golf course. He had never suffered from any central nervous system illness or injury. Historical information indicated the primary difficulty which ran in his family was depression. During the spring term of his junior year, Mick began to have very severe and disabling headaches, which his primary doctor diagnosed as migraines and prescribed medication. After many months and experiencing no appreciable relief, he was referred to a local medical center. The medical team was unable to determine the cause of his symptoms particularly because he was young, athletic, and appeared to be in excellent physical condition.

Mick and his family became very frustrated with the continuation of his symptoms and the physician's inability to determine the causal factors. The family requested that his case be transferred to a quite well-regarded medical center approximately 6 hours from his home. Mick and his mother drove to the medical center and he was admitted for a 2-week evaluation and treatment program. During this time, his mother, like other family members of patients, stayed in a nearby hotel.

Mick was evaluated by a multidisciplinary team which included a neurologist, a neurosurgeon, and an internal medicine specialist who all ordered multiple medical tests and scans. The team came to the conclusion that Mick had a very rare stellate-shaped brain tumor that was space occupying but noncancerous. The team also felt that the tumor needed to be removed as soon as possible. They began preparations for surgery after they spoke to Mick and his mother. Mick was more comfortable with his mother being present during the explanation of the surgery and possible risk factors. Mick's mother gave consent for the procedure due to the fact that he was not of legal age. These risk factors were similar to those with any surgery and included the unlikely risk of mortality and also with this particular surgery, there were risks of stroke, paralysis, seizures, and loss of or changes in cognitive functioning. The surgery was scheduled for 2 days later, which allowed Mick's father and younger brother to drive there. In addition, the time was scheduled in this manner to allow Mick to further understand not only the possible risks, but also learn about the postsurgery recovery process.

The surgery went well and the neurosurgeon was able to excise the entire tumor. He was very pleased and the case was ultimately submitted for publication because it was a very rare type of tumor. However, in the surgical process it appeared that the motor strip was damaged or that this area had already been damaged by the tumor. Regardless of the cause, Mick was left with some unusual paralysis in his right foot and toes. He was able to stand on his foot for limited amounts of time and was unable to uncurl his toes. As Mick did not develop more serious side effects, the family left the medical center.

Upon returning home and preparing to return for his senior year of high school, several other difficulties began to surface. Mick was very fatigued for a large part of the day. He was told that this was normal but felt it to be excessive. He also did not want to be around his friends or girlfriend and began to isolate himself in his room with his computer. With the family history of depression, his mother became suspicious that this may be occurring. When school began for the fall semester, he was not as able to concentrate as he had previously and his attention began to wander. These difficulties caused him to become angry with himself and he began to unfavorably compare his current performance to his premorbid level.

At his mother's suggestion, Mick went to see his primary doctor who then referred him to a psychiatrist. The psychiatrist prescribed an antidepressant in addition to the medications which Mick was already taking to preclude seizures and to help with the problem with his foot. After trying multiple medications, he was still not feeling like his usual self and was becoming very frustrated. His primary physician suggested that he return to the medical center which had completed the surgery. He was again admitted and completed not only many medical tests but was also administered a complete neuropsychological evaluation. The treatment team stated that they felt Mick should stay long enough for them to regulate his medication for depression. They also stated that the neuropsychological evaluation indicated that his overall IQ and memory scores were lower than would be expected for his academic history. They surmised that this was related to the attention and concentration difficulties which Mick had described but did not rule out any other type of difficulty that may have been a secondary result of surgery. Mick stayed at the hospital for 4 weeks. He tried several medications until the treatment team felt comfortable that his symptoms were lessening. He was also evaluated for cognitive rehabilitation focusing on issues of attention, concentration, and memory.

After his release from the hospital, Mick began his senior year of high school, albeit a few weeks late. He averaged B− to C+ grades, which were slightly below his previous level. He attempted to be involved in sports but was hampered by his toe and foot difficulties. He also felt somewhat awkward socially because other people knew he had had brain surgery. He graduated with his class and enrolled in a private college 2 hours from his home. The rigors of the first semester of college were very stressful and Mick found himself drinking with the "guys in the dorms" to help lessen his stress. He continued to have difficulties throughout the spring semester and was placed on academic probation. He returned to the medical center each year to be evaluated and they suggested that he seek help for his cognitive and emotional issues in the community near the college he attended.

Mick decided to change schools for his 2nd year and enrolled in a large public university near his first college where he was still in contact with the "guys in the dorm." He felt the workload was better suited to his level of functioning. He dropped a class each semester until the school stated he was about to lose his financial aid if he did not carry at least three courses per semester.

During many of the weekends, Mick returned home to alleviate worries about his very stressful situation. On one trip home, he borrowed his mother's car. When the car was returned, his mother looked in the trunk and was surprised to see it full of empty bottles of alcohol. This discovery was the final incident which caused his parents to confront him about his behaviors subsequent to the surgery. His parents felt that they had been quite understanding of the ramifications of surgery but also felt that Mick may have taken advantage of the situation or may be in serious need of professional services. Mick agreed with his mother that seeking help and obtaining an evaluation and remediation of possible difficulties related to the surgery and other surrounding issues were the appropriate course of action. It was approximately 3 years after the surgery when Mick was seen by the clinical neuropsychologist for outpatient evaluation and rehabilitation. Mick had attempted to attend two universities, live in the community, and work during the summers. He had succeeded somewhat but had not partaken of any resources in the community. Mick's manner of coping with stress had been to drink with his friends.

The case of Mick provides the reader with many interesting issues to pursue regarding his postsurgical condition. Mick clearly has some physical and neuropsychological issues which have remained after the removal of the tumor. The cause of these may never be known, but the difficulties must be addressed. In addition, Mick has been suffering from depression possibly as a reaction to his medical issues and has also engaged in heavy drinking. The drinking is perhaps typical for his age and gender in a college situation. Therefore, it needs to be evaluated as to whether it is beyond the norm and a reaction to circumstances. Finally, regardless of the cause, Mick has been warned not to drink while taking his medications and subsequent to a central nervous system difficulty.

Introduction

The topics of cognitive and memory rehabilitation are quite broad. The history of these fields, however, is rather short with the practice of rehabilitative techniques dating from the 1970s. In this chapter, we will first explore the history of these fields. Imbedded within the history are numerous issues which relate not only to the type of remediation but also to service delivery. Salient among these issues is who is the focus of care, the patient or the patient and his or her surrounding others. The question relates to a holistic form of treatment involving significant others versus a focus solely on the patient. Another issue which will surface repeatedly throughout the discussion is efficacy of treatment or the outcome of each treatment modality. The issue of accountability for the effectiveness of treatment is not only related to the effectiveness of the treatment itself but also relates to those who pay for the treatment, such as insurance providers.

History

As alluded to earlier, cognitive (broadly defined) and memory rehabilitation have a relatively short history with most researchers stating that the practice of neuropsychological rehabilitation began in the 1970s. The insights which established the foundations of treatment programs came predominately from the efforts of cognitive psychologists and cognitive neuropsychologists. The subjects on which they based their conclusions varied from laboratory animals to the ever-growing population of individuals who had survived traumatic brain injury and other central nervous system injuries and illnesses.

Even though the practice of cognitive rehabilitation is a relatively recent phenomenon, psychologists have been interested in the reconstruction or repair of neurons and structures within the central nervous system for over 100 years. As early as 1888, John Hughlings Jackson speculated on the mechanisms of recovery from hemiplegia (Prigatano, 1999). In 1938, Karl Lashley stated that he felt that there were multiple structures and functions related to the process of recovery (Prigatano, 1999). During World War I and after, Kurt Goldstein established the first rehabilitation program for brain-injured soldiers in Germany. This program used assessment and vocational rehabilitation techniques. Goldstein (1942) was also the first to describe the impairment of "abstract attitude" as a basis for inappropriate social behavior. Alexander Luria, during World War II, developed an approach to the study of higher cerebral functions, their recovery, and rehabilitation, based on his work with victims of missile wounds. Luria (1963, 1973) described the presence of functional systems which mediated various cognitive functions. These levels of functional systems were then incorporated into the foundation of much of modern clinical neuropsychology and rehabilitation. As can be seen, while there were few early treatment programs, the interest in recovery and rehabilitation was generated quite early.

An additional issue is that service delivery has changed dramatically over time. Managed care and insurance companies have had both good and bad influences on care as discussed in an earlier chapter. The original idea for managed care was developed in order that all people could be guaranteed the same level of basic care by providers. Unfortunately, as time has passed, managed care has come to signify lack of choice for the patient regarding treatment options and providers. At the same time as managed care has become the focus of treatment delivery, there has been a movement within the rehabilitation field for services to be delivered in a more **ecological contextual framework** of service delivery. As stated earlier, ecological validity refers to an assessment device or treatment program which relates to the normal activities in a patient's life. In this manner, the rehabilitation addresses social, emotional, and environmental variables as an integral part of cognitive and memory rehabilitation. The family and significant others are now considered to be an integral part of the treatment program. Finally, developments in computer technology and neuroscience have made for continual advances in treatment programs.

ecological contextual framework
a broad approach to rehabilitation that includes family, friends, and caregivers in the rehabilitation process

As can be seen historically, the treatment of cognitive deficits tended to have evolved through time periods based on theoretical ideas. The practice of rehabilitation and its coordination with the service delivery system appears to have followed. Sohlberg and Mateer (2001) discuss a paper written by Coelho (1997) dividing the history of cognitive rehabilitation into several eras. In the 1980s, the era was described as the era of proliferation for brain injury rehabilitation. The number of brain injury rehabilitation programs in the United States grew from 10 to more than 500. Also during this period, the National Brain Injury Foundation and the Brain Injury Interdisciplinary Special Interest Group within the American Congress of Rehabilitation Medicine were established. In the late 1980s there were also major government research funds available for the first time.

The 1990s were officially designated the "decade of the brain" by George H. W. Bush (1990), then president of the United States. This was part of an effort involving the Library of Congress and the National Institute of Mental Health of the National Institutes of Health to educate the public regarding benefits to be derived from brain research. The Human Genome Project provided an incredible wealth of data regarding the functioning and nonfunctioning of the human brain. Excitement proliferated regarding the continuous discoveries that were happening regarding the brain.

The new millennium or the current state of affairs can be considered an era of consolidation. Even though we now know more than ever before regarding the brain, economic and government priorities have not kept step. Health care reform is spoken of daily but the reality is a downsizing of programs, shorter hospital stays, less outpatient care, and more severely impaired children being integrated into regular classrooms. Many researchers feel that with the recent accumulation of knowledge, the only way for this to be translated into services is for patients and their families and friends to advocate for more services.

In reference to the case study of Mick, he has been able to partake of treatment during both the "decade of the brain" and the new millennium. In terms of service delivery, he has worked with a local hospital and a world-renowned institution. His treatment had been paid through his parents' insurance while he was a minor and then switched to medical assistance once he reached legal age and applied for Social Security Disability Insurance (SSDI). Both private insurance and SSDI required that the professionals working with Mick submit a diagnosis and treatment plan with detailed explanation regarding the length of treatments, modalities used, and how the effects of treatment would be assessed.

Theories for Working With Cognitive Impairment

BASIC ASSUMPTIONS

There exists a set of assumptions which need to be articulated before one pursues the particular procedures to work with individuals with various difficulties. One of the assumptions is that cognition cannot be isolated. Cognition involves all of its component processes such as attention and concentration. In addition, brain injury or illness affects cognitive, social, behavioral, and emotional functioning. Each of these areas interacts with the other. It is inappropriate to consider treating cognitive functioning without attending to the others.

A second assumption is that working with individuals in a rehabilitation capacity requires a multitude of specialties and skills. Treatment for cognitive and memory difficulties relies on information from behavioral, sociological, psychological, and neuropsychological disciplines.

A third assumption is that a clear conceptualization of the difficulties being experienced by the individual is necessary before any form of rehabilitation is initiated. Without a clear-cut diagnosis or understanding of the patient's difficulties, it becomes impossible to treat the individual. The issue of differential diagnosis was discussed in an earlier chapter when it was made clear that without an appropriate diagnosis the clinical neuropsychologist may be focusing on the wrong set of strengths and weaknesses.

A fourth assumption is that the fields of cognitive psychology and the neurosciences are growing rapidly. It is essential to understand the theoretical underpinnings of attention, memory, and executive functions in order to develop effective treatment.

Finally, in the process of rehabilitation, the clinical neuropsychologist needs to work as a partner with the patient and his or her family. The clinical neuropsychologist will teach the new skills and techniques but will require the aid of the external support system to carry out the program in the world outside of rehabilitation. This has become particularly important as the economy has taken a downturn and less and less money is available for rehabilitation, particularly for inpatient services.

Mick's case illustrates all of the basic assumptions in working with brain impairment. In Mick's case, the premise that cognition cannot be isolated is true. He continues to need intervention for attentional and concentration difficulties and behavioral and emotional issues. Mick continues to need the services of various specialists working together on his case. In his case, these specialists include a neurologist, a psychiatrist, a clinical psychologist, and a physical therapist in addition to the clinical neuropsychologist who has become his case manager. Mick's treatment team also needs to have a clear idea of the diagnosis and concomitant issues which Mick faces. Mick's case began with the removal of a rare tumor but remains with cognitive, attention, and concentration difficulties, as well as memory, emotional, and social issues. These difficulties are residual to the tumor removal and the trauma to the motor strip. The process of rehabilitation for Mick includes his parents, friends, and siblings to help Mick transfer the skills which he learned in his various therapies into current real-life circumstances. This is the essences of what is meant by the term *ecological validity* of any treatment program.

Models of Cognitive Processing

cognitive processing model analysis of particular cognitive processes (e.g., attention) in a laboratory setting using normal subjects; this could be contrasted with a clinical model

Sohlberg and Mateer (2001) discuss five models for conceptualizing various cognitive processes that need to be addressed in the treatment plan. **Cognitive processing models** look at the cognitive task under consideration based on the normally functioning population. They then apply the knowledge that has been learned to the disabled individual.

Factor-analytic models use psychometric approaches to understand various cognitive processes. Performance on tests that are designed to measure attention, concentration, and various other components of cognition are factor analyzed to determine constructs. Neuroanatomical models identify particular brain regions that are thought to be related to each of the components of cognition. Clinical models of cognition observe the functioning of the disabled population to understand the functioning of components of cognition. Functional descriptions of cognitive processes include describing how cognitive processes might be used for completing day-to-day tasks.

Also related to Mick's case, each of the five models have been utilized in his treatment plan. The cognitive processing model was used to understand normal cognitive functioning and compare it to his functioning to look for strengths and weaknesses. The factor-analytic model is imbedded in all of the neuropsychological tests which he took. The neuroanatomical model was essential in obtaining ideas as to what functions were governed by the areas impeded by his brain tumor. The clinical model was evident in observing Mick as he functioned. The functional description model involved his ability in carrying out his day-to-day activities.

factor-analytic model
a method to understand a particular cognitive process (e.g., attention) using the statistical tool of factor analysis; information is gathered from the performance of normal subjects on psychometric tests

neuroanatomical model
an attempt to understand various cognitive processes (e.g., attention) by identifying the different brain regions that are responsible for the ability

clinical model
an attempt to understand a particular cognitive process (e.g., attention) by observing individuals with central nervous system disease or damage

functional description
description of how a particular cognitive process might be used for the completion of day-to-day tasks

Measuring Efficacy and Outcome

As has been stated earlier, the field of cognitive rehabilitation is growing very rapidly. As recently as the 1990s and earlier, there was a dearth of research regarding the efficacy of treatment programs (Sohlberg & Mateer, 1989). At present, there is a growing and much needed body of literature on the topic of efficacy of treatment programs. However, outcome or efficacy research is still hindered by the following difficulties: heterogeneity of clients, heterogeneity of treatment approaches and settings, and the fact that rehabilitation is predominantly accomplished within clinical settings which lack research as a focus. Heterogeneity of clients implies that many of the outcome studies are completed on single case studies and/or patients with dissimilar etiology grouped together. In grouped studies, the treatment results for certain deficits and their progress are often evaluated together and this makes the understanding of the effectiveness of various treatment modalities difficult. The same is true with heterogeneity of treatment approaches and settings, which may be combined into a single research report and, thus, distort the findings. In addition, the fact that most clinical rehabilitation facilities lack the personnel and financial backing to complete research with available patients causes the field to lose crucial data regarding efficacy.

Even though the personnel and funds are lacking it is still imperative to document outcomes particularly in the current age of accountability. Treatment efficacy is used to justify the time and resources expended by clients, caregivers, and therapists, to estimate service delivery needs and costs, and to inform the development and delivery of treatment (Sohlberg & Mateer, 2001). Adequate outcome research is necessary, according to Sohlberg and Mateer (2001), in order to:

1. Determine whether and which interventions result in functional gains, reduction of handicap, and achievement of goals;
2. Determine whether gains are maintained over time and, if so, to what degree;
3. Ascertain whether the intervention results in better outcomes than would be expected or observed without provision of rehabilitation and, if so, how; and
4. Obtain the information needed to modify programs to be more effective.

The measurement of treatment effectiveness should be specific to the intervention or treatment modality (see Figure 12.1). As stated earlier, single-case study designs which explain how the individual patient progressed have often been utilized. Even in single-case study methodology, the treatment should be evaluated via a pre-post inventory of skills that were targeted within the rehabilitation program. Other ways to evaluate treatment gains may include measuring progress toward goals or using Goal Attainment Scaling (Malec, 1999). There exist many other scales that evaluate a set of skills which the patient may have have difficulty with prerehabilitation and have mastered posttreatment. These will provide information regarding particular types of treatment gains.

In Mick's case, it is crucial to have outcome data regarding the treatments which are available to him. The choices of treatment modalities and time and effort for all involved are related to the effectiveness of the treatments. In particular, when Mick knew that a treatment approach had worked with other patients, it increased his motivation to participate. Efficacy of treatment also helped engage his family in the transfer of learning to his current life situation. Finally, his insurance providers were more willing to fund treatments which had a proven record of successes than those that did not or had no data available.

FIGURE 12.1
Criteria for empirically validated treatment. *Source:* Adapted with permission from Chambless, D. L., Baker, M. J., Baucom, D. H., Beutler, L. E., et al. (1998). Update on empirically validated therapies II. *The Clinical Psychologist, 51,* p. 4. Copyright 1998 by the American Psychological Association.

CRITERIA FOR EMPIRICALLY VALIDATED TREATMENT

Well-established treatments

I. At least two good between-group design experiments demonstrating efficacy in at least one of the following ways:
    A. Superior (i.e., statistically significant) to pill or psychological placebo or another treatment.
    B. Equivalent to an already established treatment in experiments with adequate sample sizes.

or

II. A large series of single-case design experiments ($n > 9$) demonstrating efficacy that:
    A. Used good experimental designs
    B. Compared the intervention to another treatment (as in I.A)

Further criteria for both I and II:

III. Experiments must be conducted with treatment manuals or detailed descriptions.
IV. Characteristics of the client samples must be clearly specified.
V. Effects must have been demonstrated by at least two different investigators or investigating teams.

Probably efficacious treatments

I. Two experiments showing the treatment is superior (i.e., statistically significant) to a waiting-list control group.

or

II. One or more experiments meeting the Well-Established Treatments criteria I.A or I.B, III, and IV, but not V.

or

III. A small series of single-case design experiments ($n > 3$) otherwise meeting the Well-Established Treatments criteria.

Cognitive Rehabilitation Techniques

ATTENTION

Now that we have discussed the lack of efficacy research, we will begin our examination with what is known regarding effective and proven treatments. As stated earlier, the concept of concentration has several components and one of the oldest in terms of research study is *attention*. Attention implies the ability to focus on a task or set of directions to benefit from some form of instruction or rehabilitation (see Figure 12.2).

Individuals who have sustained brain injury or illness consistently report difficulties associated with decreased reaction time and reduced speed of information (Ponsford & Kinsella, 1992; Stuss et al., 1989). Sohlberg and Mateer (2001) have completed a great deal of research on the concept of attention. These researchers suggest a clinical model of attention consisting of five components, which include focused attention, sustained attention, selective attention including vigilance and working memory, alternating attention, and divided attention. Each or all of these types of attention may be affected by central nervous system difficulty.

Prior to any form of rehabilitation for attention or any other difficulty, the clinical neuropsychologist must have completed some form of assessment or an assessment must have been completed prior to referral. As stated previously, the reason for the assessment

---

PATIENT HANDOUT: ATTENTION STRATEGIES

Useful strategies you can use to try to manage persistent attention problems.

Reduce distractions by:
- Turning off radios, TVs, etc. when concentrating (e.g., trying to read) or when having a conversation.
- Using earplugs.
- Closing curtains so you are not tempted to stare out the window.
- "De-cluttering" your environment.

Avoid crowds:
- Plan your day to shop and/or drive during "off" hours.
- If you must be in a crowded situation, don't require yourself to do something that demands a lot of concentration.

Manage fatigue:
- As soon as you begin to feel overwhelmed, take a short break—the sooner you do this, the faster you will be able to get back to what you were doing and be effective.
- Be persistent and keep coming back to what you were doing.
- Don't push yourself so hard that you get frustrated.
- Get enough sleep—naps are good! Just be sure you can still sleep during the night.

Avoid interruptions:
- Turn off your phone or use an answering machine when you are trying to get something done.
- Hang a "do not disturb" sign on your door if you live in a busy household.

Get sufficient exercise:
- Research shows that a more efficient body means a more efficient brain.
- Regular exercise is good for thinking skills.

Ask for help.

FIGURE 12.2 Patient Handout: Attention Strategies. *Source:* Adapted from Sohlberg & Mateer (1989).

is that it allows the clinical neuropsychologist to specify which particular areas need to be remediated. Therefore, there is no lost time or guessing as to what is or are the particular problems(s) which need to be addressed. In most clinical neuropsychological evaluations, attention abilities are evaluated as part of a larger cognitive assessment. The majority of neuropsychological test batteries contain some components directly related to attention. Kinsella (1998) has written extensively regarding the difficulty with multifactorial neuropsychological tests and favors standardized measures to evaluate discrete components of attention. Having discrete measures of attention may also increase the understanding of how attention operates within the brain (Sohlberg & Mateer, 2001). The Test of Everyday Attention (Robertson, Ward, Ridgeway, & Nimmo-Smith, 1996) addresses some of the issues raised by Kinsella. The test contains eight tasks designed to measure abilities or disabilities with four different attention functions: sustained attention, selective attention, attentional switching, and auditory–verbal working memory. This test has a fair degree of ecological validity but it is suggested that it be combined with observation and interview to obtain a clearer picture of the functioning of the individual outside of the rehabilitative setting. The aforementioned statements are made with the caveat that tests, interviewers, and observations all involve time and money. The clinical neuropsychologist should try to use the most cost-effective approach to determine the needs of the patient.

Addressing the approaches to manage attention problems, the reader is reminded of the discussion earlier in the chapter where basic principles of rehabilitation were discussed. At this juncture, it is important to reiterate that cognition cannot be remediated in isolation and that other functions will also come into play as the clinical neuropsychologist works to restore this ability. In addition, it is necessary to remember that with any type of disability, the difficulty affects not only cognitive functions but also may cause social, behavioral, and emotional issues.

Overall, there are basically four methods in which to alleviate difficulties with attention. The four will be briefly described and then further elaborated. The first is termed *attention process training* (APT) and uses cognitive exercises to improve attentional systems. It is primarily based on neuropsychological theory. The second approach is use of strategies and environmental supports, including both self-managed strategies and modification to the environment. These are based on behavioral and neuropsychological theories. The third approach is the use of external aids to help patients track and organize information. These are also based on behavioral and neuropsychological principles. The final approach involves psychosocial support to address emotional or social factors which are caused by or exacerbate attentional difficulties. Sociological and psychological theories are the root of these techniques.

The majority of APT programs are focused on the assumption that attentional ability may be improved by stimulating a particular aspect of attention. There are many programs which address various components of attention all based on the particular theory of attention employed. Treatment usually consists of a series of repetitive drills or exercises designed to practice tasks with increasing attentional demands. These tasks may be presented to the patient orally or through computer programs. Repeated activation and stimulation of attentional systems are thought to facilitate changes in cognitive capacity (Niemann, Ruff, & Baser, 1990). A very good example of a computer-based program is the APT program, which is widely used with individuals with brain injury (Park, Proulx, & Towers, 1999). While this is thought to be an excellent program, it still resembles laboratory tasks more than the aforementioned activities of daily life. This difficulty is again one of the reasons for the impetus toward making rehabilitation more ecologically valid.

The second approach to attention difficulties is the use of compensatory strategies and/or environmental supports. These strategies may sometimes be used with APT. At other times, these supports may be used later in treatment when the patient is adapting to living at home. Self-management strategies are self-instructional routines that help an individual focus attention on a task, monitor his or her activity, and screen out distractions. Orienting procedures may be developed for any type of task for which the client has difficulty. The goal of these procedures is to encourage clients to monitor their activities consciously, thereby avoiding attentional lapses. Pacing strategies help clients overcome difficulties with fatigue or maintaining attention for a prolonged period. Pacing helps the client to develop realistic expectations of progress as well as keeping the person performing for longer periods.

Environmental supports for attention problems need to be carefully tailored to the client's difficulty. Task management strategies may include things such as determining which locations cause greater distress due to divided attention. It would then be suggested to the client that they avoid such places and substitute situations where divided attention is not needed. Other strategies may include determining which environmental noises (phone ringing, light shining in the room, etc.) may distract the individual from finishing the task at hand. Again, once these are determined, the environment can be altered. Environmental modifications very often are modifications to the physical environment which help the client organize and/or focus. Examples of these include file cabinets and organizing and labeling the contents on the outside of cupboards. External devices are also very helpful for those with attention difficulties. Examples include calendars, day planners, pillboxes, and key finders. As stated previously, it is imperative to tailor these external aids to the specific attention problems of the client.

Psychosocial support is the final area to be utilized for attention problems and its importance cannot be understated. Considerable research has shown a clear connection between emotional state and cognitive functioning (Kay, 1992). Psychosocial support may include listening, brain injury education, relaxation training, psychotherapy, and grief therapy. Kay describes many different emotions which may arise after central nervous system trauma such as a "shaken sense of self," "fear of going crazy," and "conditional anxiety" regarding one's performance post-trauma. All of these issues will also be addressed in the next two chapters on individual and family therapy.

After reviewing the four types of intervention available for attention difficulties, it is time to apply these to Mick's case example. He was evaluated by the clinical neuropsychologist and it was determined that a trial of APT would be appropriate for him. Using the principles which stress tailoring the program to the client's needs, the clinical neuropsychologist used tasks to improve sustained attention such as paragraph listening comprehension exercises and mental math activities. Mick stated that over a period of a few weeks, this helped him to remain on task with his schoolwork and not lose focus. The clinical neuropsychologist also made use of environmental supports and helped Mick determine the best study environment to focus on his schoolwork. It turned out that he had been uncomfortable in the library feeling others were staring at him, but now that he understood the value of a quiet, non-distracting environment, he began to do his studying there. The last part of his treatment for attention focused on his need for psychosocial support. He was very uncomfortable with his perceived differences from his premorbid state and from other students. Group therapy was not available near his college but he did discuss his concerns in individual therapy. He described therapy as helping him feel more normal than he had since his surgery.

MEMORY

As has been reviewed within the section on attention, several concepts must be kept in mind with any form of memory retraining or rehabilitation. The first is that there must be an assessment before any form of rehabilitation in order that the particular memory deficits

needs assessment
the assessment of the types of rehabilitation necessary based on the strengths and weaknesses of the client

are determined. The rehabilitation literature often refers to this as a **needs assessment**, which is often part of a larger cognitive assessment (see Figure 12.3). Research has shown that individuals with memory deficits often have other deficits particularly in the area of attention, as discussed in the previous section. The second concept is that any rehabilitation effort must be individually tailored to the client. The particular needs of the client as well as all of the support services and systems which are available to the person need to be considered when developing the treatment program.

FIGURE 12.3 Needs assessment example. *Source:* Adapted from Sohlberg & Mateer, (1989).

EXTERNAL COGNITIVE AIDS: NEEDS ASSESSMENT (ADULT CLIENT)

Client Name _____ Date _____

Clinician Name _____

I. COGNITIVE PROFILE

Check the areas of concern. For those areas, describe the nature of the impairment.

☐ Episodic memory (ability to remember daily events and personal experiences)

_____

☐ Semantic memory (ability to remember facts and knowledge-based information)

_____

☐ Prospective memory (ability to initiate a planned future action at a specific time)

_____

☐ Procedural memory (ability to learn procedures or steps—may be learning without awareness)

_____

☐ Retrograde amnesia (pattern of memory loss for events prior to injury)

_____

☐ New learning (ability/rate of learning new information)

_____

☐ Decreased attention

_____

☐ Limitations in executive functions (e.g., initiation, planning, organization, etc.)

_____

☐ Reduced reasoning/problem solving

_____

☐ Language problems affecting ability to read or write

_____

1 of 3

(continued)

FIGURE 12.3 (*continued*)

II. PHYSICAL PROFILE

☐ Visual problems affecting ability to read or write

_____

☐ Motoric difficulties affecting ability to write in, manipulate, or carry system

_____

☐ Auditory problems affecting ability to hear alarms or watch beeps

_____

III. PERSONAL FACTORS

A. Current or Past Use of Memory/Organizational Aids (Check all that apply)

☐ No systems used   ☐ Notes to self
☐ Calendar in the home   ☐ Wears a watch
☐ Datebook system   ☐ Elaborate organizational
☐ Spouse/partner keeps track of things   system
☐ Other_____

Comments: _____

_____

B. Level of Acceptance/Awareness of Memory Impairment (Check best description)

☐ Has limited understanding or awareness of impairment due to organic brain
  damage
☐ Exhibits significant psychological denial (difficulty accepting disability)
☐ Can state knowledge of impairment but does not think aids are necessary
☐ Openly discusses memory problem but inconsistent in using compensation
  strategies
☐ Appears willing to learn and use aids

C. Client Preferences for a Memory System

1. Appearance (color, style, size) _____

_____

2. Types of functions (e.g., calendar, to do list, budget planner, etc.)

_____

3. Mode (electronic, written, auditory, pictorial) _____

_____

2 of 3

(continued)

To begin our discussion of memory remediation, many researchers on memory state that there are three strengths exhibited by most persons with severe memory impairment. These strengths are the preservation of immediate memory or attentional abilities, procedural memory, and old learning. It may be assumed that if these are preserved in seriously affected individuals, the same abilities should be preserved in individuals with less severe memory difficulties. These three memory strengths are relied on in most of the rehabilitation efforts which will be discussed. The literature on memory rehabilitation has often divided memory aids into three different types of programs. The first methods are those which restore or improve memory ability across a variety of tasks and contexts. Examples of techniques in this category which will be described further include memory practice drills, mnemonic strategy training, prospective memory training, and meta-memory training. The second set of techniques is termed *domain-specific memory*

FIGURE 12.3 *(continued)*

D. Financial Resources

☐ Insurance (or other third-party payer) willing to pay

☐ Personal funds available

☐ Funds available up to_____dollars

☐ No funds available

E. Available Support

☐ Patient would need to utilize systems independently due to lack of available support

☐ Family/staff/significant others able and willing to be trained but will require structured program

☐ Persons to be involved with patient will vary; will need to provide description of system and procedures for using it

IV. SITUATIONAL FACTORS

Context: Describe goal of external aid

_____

When and where would it be used?

_____

Functions of systems—external aid system needs to provide the following functions:

☐ Autobiographical information (personal history, orientation sheets, photos, fact sheets, etc.)

☐ Daily schedule

☐ Calendar

☐ Things to do

☐ Daily diary/events log

☐ Specific journal (e.g., anger log)

☐ Therapy goals

☐ Other _____

Recommendations: _____

_____

_____

3 of 3

errorless learning
a method of instruction that reduces errors in the acquisition phase; the task is practiced until the client achieves correct answers without experiencing failures

intervention approaches. Examples of strategies in this category include mnemonic strategy training for specific information, expanded rehearsal time, use of preserved priming, and creating a personal history. The third category of memory rehabilitation is the use of external aids. Examples of external aids include things such as pillboxes and key finders (see Figure 12.4).

In each of the aforementioned approaches, one of the main treatment techniques involves the concept of errorless learning. **Errorless learning** is a method of instruction that reduces errors in the acquisition phase (Wilson, Baddeley, Evans, & Shiel, 1994). Wilson et al. compared errorless and errorful learning conditions in five people with

THERAPY PROTOCOL TO TEACH A NAME

1. The client is told that he or she will practice remembering things and that the first item to be practiced is the therapist's name. "My name is _____. What is my name? That's right, I am glad you remembered."

2. There is a brief interval and the clinician says, "Now let's practice again. What is my name?"

3. If the client remembers the name, the clinician proceeds to the next longer interval (Step 4). If the response is incorrect, the clinician repeats the interval again. If the client cannot correctly remember for three consecutive initial intervals, therapy is terminated and the clinician tries again at a later date.

4. The third interval lasts about 10 seconds and is filled by saying, "Good. I will give you more chances to practice this as I'm working with you today. Let's try again. What is my name?"

5. If the correct answer is given, the clinician proceeds to Step 6. If an incorrect response is given, the clinician immediately provides the client with the correct answer and goes back to Step 2.

6. The fourth interval lasts about 20 seconds and is filled by saying, "Good, you are remembering my name very well, and you are remembering after a longer period of time. That's the idea—for you to be able to remember for longer and longer times so you will always remember it. I'll be asking my name every once in a while just to give you practice. What is my name?"

7. If the correct answer is given, the clinician proceeds to Step 8. Each time an incorrect response is given, the clinician says, "Actually, my name is _____. What is my name?" This allows the client to finish a trial with success. Then the clinician asks for the information, using the last time interval where there was successful recall.

8. The clinician continues to ask the client to recall his or her name after increasingly longer intervals (2 minutes, 4 minutes, 8 minutes, 16 minutes, etc.).

FIGURE 12.4 Memory aid for client. *Source:* Adapted from Brush and Camp (1998a). Copyright 1998 by Haworth Press.

different types of memory impairment. In all cases, the errorless learning condition was more effective in accuracy of learning and/or efficacy. Wilson and Moffat (1994) have developed guidelines which have proven to be helpful with any form of memory treatment. The guidelines begin by stating that information should be simplified, making instructions clear and concise. This should help by reducing the amount of information to be remembered. The clinical neuropsychologist should continually check whether the client understands the task and also help the client link new information to current information thereby making associations. The client usually needs help organizing the information to be remembered. Finally, distributed practice works better than massed practice. Several minutes a few times a day is better than an hour at a time, which may lead to fatigue or confusion.

The following four approaches are forms of restorative memory interventions. Memory practice drills are used to improve damaged memory in a manner similar to the approach used to treat a damaged muscle. The drill repeats information over and over with the hope that it will be remembered. There has been no research support for this approach even though these types of drills are abundant in computer programs and workbooks used in clinical practice. With drill work, the only increases have been in isolated components of attention (Sohlberg, McLaughlin, Pavese, Heidrich, & Posner, 2000).

Mnemonic strategy training uses visual imagery, verbal organizational strategies, and semantic elaboration in order to provide a structure for the individual to recall particular information (Sohlberg, Mateer, & Geyer, 1985). The most popular and thoroughly researched mnemonic strategy is the use of visual imagery (Wilson, 1986). In general, studies suggest that mnemonics appear to work in laboratory situations but often have little benefit in real-life contexts (Miller, 1992). Hence, this is another difficulty with ecological validity. Prospective memory training is an approach in which clients are administered repetitive prospective memory tasks. **Prospective memory** is the ability to remember to carry out intentions. An example of this approach is the Prospective Memory Process Training (PROMPT) in which the client is asked to carry out a target task within a matter of minutes (Sohlberg et al., 1985). Many variables including time, type of task, use of distractor, and so forth may be varied in this approach. The PROMPT approach, when compared to memory drills, showed an increase in the ability to remember and carry out assigned tasks (Raskin & Sohlberg, 1996). Meta-memory training is an approach in which clients learn about the nature and effects of their memory deficits. Meta-memory training is a form of awareness training. Through this approach clients learn about their perceived vs. actual memory strengths and weakness.

The techniques which are referred to as domain-specific approaches to treatment of memory difficulties are designed to deal with a particular task or issue. Glisky and Schacter (1989) have described three characteristics of domain-specific training. The goal is to alleviate specific problems rather than resolving memory processes or improving general memory functioning. Information learned has practical value to the client. Finally, the purpose of the acquired knowledge is to teach clients information or procedures they can implement independently. Examples of tasks which could be used with domain-specific training include operating a walker or wheelchair, range-of-motion exercises, names of people or objects, academic procedures, or basic swallowing or other oral motor exercises. Expanded rehearsal is a domain specific approach used with a technique termed *spaced rehearsal*. In this approach, the individual practices successfully recalling information over progressively longer time intervals. Priming is another approach used with individuals who have severe memory impairments. The method of vanishing cues uses the fact that individuals may recall previous information but forget the event in which they learned it (Glisky, Schacter, & Tulving, 1986). A faded cueing technique is used to teach complex behavior. The patient is first given enough information to obtain a correct response and then parts of the information are withdrawn across trials. Creation of a personal history has been useful for individuals who suffer from retrograde amnesia. Retrograde amnesia is the inability to retrieve information prior to brain impairment. These individuals also suffer from the impairment of learning new information. The creation of an autobiography, often with the help of family or friends, and the use of pictures and anecdotal information often help to bring some of the lost memories back to the individual's consciousness.

External aids are used in addition to any or all of the aforementioned strategies. External aids also need to be demonstrated or taught to the individual in order for the individual to use them effectively and independently in his or her own life. As with other treatment modalities, external aids need to be geared to the strengths and weaknesses of the client. Examples

prospective memory
the ability to carry out intended actions

of external aids include written planning systems, electronic planners, computerized systems, auditory or verbal systems, and task-specific aids such as key finders or pillbox reminders.

Returning once again to Mick's case study, it was revealed through careful assessment that he was suffering from some memory difficulty. Mick tried many of the aforementioned restorative techniques but none worked for him. He tried APT and that appeared to alleviate most of his difficulties. In addition, he used some of the external aids to help organize his materials. He purchased and labeled multiple folders for his classes. He labeled all of his computer disks, particularly those related to academic issues. He also, grudgingly, used a pillbox to help him recall which pills to take throughout the day. With the help of his individual therapist, he used his day planner to make sure that all of his appointments were recorded. Further, the therapist suggested that each professional office be asked to call and remind Mick the day before his appointment.

Dysexecutive Syndromes

Dysexecutive syndromes are often among the most devastating problems which occur following frontal lobe damage caused by accident or illness. The frontal lobes are the most highly evolved areas within the human brain housing our executive functioning. The reason that humans are assumed to be more intelligent than other animals is the size of our frontal lobes. The frontal lobes control our higher order cognitive processes and our abilities to think abstractly, reason, and plan, in addition to our abilities to inhibit certain behaviors which may be termed *socially inappropriate*. Hence, dysexecutive syndromes are characterized by changes in the ability to initiate, maintain, and inhibit behavioral responding as well as organize thoughts and behavior, generate ideas, and possess self-awareness (Sohlberg & Mateer, 2001). Patients with dysexecutive syndromes may display a rigid and concrete thinking style and may experience difficulty generating fluent and novel thoughts. Behavioral and personality changes, which will be addressed in the next chapter, are often common with frontal lobe difficulty. Patients with frontal lobe difficulties may experience mood swings, be quick to anger or to become irritable, and are less sensitive to the feelings or perspectives of those around them (Prigatano, 1991). Even minor damage to executive functioning is capable of causing extreme disruption in independent functioning. Executive functions may be considered those abilities that are required to complete goal-dependent activity that is not overlearned, automatic, and routine. One reason that frontal lobe damage is often difficult to detect is that seemingly opposite symptoms are often manifested in the same individual. An example given by Sohlberg and Mateer (2001) is of a patient who was having difficulty with initiative characterized by an inability to start activities independently without external prompting while also displaying impulsivity characterized by inappropriate verbal comments and "acting before thinking."

Mateer (1999) has described a clinical model of several components of dysexecutive syndrome which aid in the remediation of difficulties (see Figure 12.5). Several of the components which are critical for handling nonroutine or novel situations are also described by Norman and Shallice (1986). The six components include initiative and drive which involve the cognitive system that starts behavior. Response inhibition is the ability to inhibit behavior in a multitude of situations. Task persistence is the ability to maintain behavior once it is initiated until a task is completed. Organization is the ability to organize thoughts and actions and allows the individual to respond in an organized manner to relevant stimulation. Generative thinking is the ability to generate solutions to problems and think in a flexible manner. Creativity is a component

FIGURE 12.5 Examples of strategies for remediation of dysexecutive symptoms. *Source:* Adapted from Sohlberg & Mateer (1998).

SELF-INSTRUCTION TO HELP MANAGE IMPULSIVITY, REDUCED PLANNING AND ORGANIZATION, POOR PROBLEM SOLVING, ETC.

Metacognitive strategy: Use an acronym such as WSTC: "What should I be doing?"; "Select a strategy"; "Try the strategy";"Check the strategy"

Self-monitoring: Providing external feedback on errors and successes, with clients recording errors and comparing performance across trials. Can have clients verbalize impressions. May rely on external feedback to recognize errors

Verbal mediation: Verbalizing each step of a multistep task as it is completed (e.g., "First, I'll select a recipe; now I'll get out all the ingredients; now I'll read the recipe all the way through aloud; now I'm putting in the flour . . .")

Problem-solving process: Problem identification and analysis; generating possible hypotheses with supporting evidence; evaluating the solution

Task completion process—goal management training (GMT): Stop!; define the main task; list the steps and learn the steps; execute the task; check

of generative thinking. Awareness is the ability to have insight into one's actions and feelings. It is also the ability to use environmental feedback to modify behavior. Lezak, Howieson, and Loring (2004) state that executive functions can be conceptualized as having four components, which are volition, planning, purposeful action, and effective performance. They state that all of these are necessary for appropriate, socially responsible, and effective self-serving adult conduct. In addition, they state that it is rare to see a patient who has difficulty with only one of these areas. It appears that many of Mateer's separate abilities are grouped together in the Lezak et al. schema and, as can be seen, these different functions are likely interrelated and interconnected. Regardless of the groupings of the symptoms, it is clear that any or all of the aforementioned difficulties may be part of the dysexecutive syndrome.

As with any of the areas covered in this chapter, a thorough assessment needs to be completed prior to any form of rehabilitation. The difficulty with assessing dysexecutive symptoms is that many of the cognitive tasks usually administered by a clinical neuropsychologist provide enough direction and/or structure that the patient is able to perform well and dysexecutive symptoms may not be detected. Observation of the client in a naturalistic setting, if possible, or observing the client completing assigned tasks in the clinic is another approach to gathering information which may detect dysexecutive symptoms otherwise not observed. The Profile of the Executive Content System (PRO-EX) provides seven scales in which to rate important executive abilities (Braswell et al., 1993). Usually the clinical neuropsychologist observes the client completing an assigned task and then rates the person. Another observational task which often helps with the determination of dysexecutive symptoms is route finding. Route finding is a task in which the client determines the easiest and most feasible manner to get to a stated destination. The route may be made by car, bicycle, walking, or whatever the preferred mode of transportation for the client. Route finding involves many executive functions which must be used to successfully complete an assigned route. There are also questionnaires available which assesses dysexecutive symptoms. The main difficulty with questionnaires is that they only include the individual's perception of functioning on the questionnaire items as opposed to their actual functioning.

In addition to difficulties with assessing dysexecutive syndromes, there is also a question regarding the type of approach to rehabilitation often referred to as the *functional versus process continuum*. A functional approach attempts to improve abilities in particular settings. This is often referred to as a *top-down approach* and affects specific targeted behaviors. In contrast, the process approach looks at changing the various cognitive processes contributing to changes in ability. This approach is often referred to as a *bottom-up approach* and is more likely to result in generalization to other behaviors or situations (Levine et al., 2000). Effective treatment of dysexecutive symptoms may involve either functional or process approaches or a combination of the two based on the needs of the client. Due to the nature of dysexecutive symptoms, it is necessary for the clinical neuropsychologist to develop a very good therapeutic relationship with the client, regardless of the type of rehabilitation. The development of a therapeutic relationship based on empathy, respect, and trust will increase the likelihood that a client will cooperate and benefit from rehabilitation (Horvath & Luborsky, 1993). This relationship is particularly important in individuals who have difficulties with frontal lobe pathology. In the literature, the relationship is often referred to as the therapeutic alliance.

> **therapeutic alliance**
> a therapeutic relationship based on empathy, respect, and trust, which increases the likelihood that the client will comply with treatment and/or benefit from services

There tend to be four types of therapeutic approaches for working with dysexecutive symptoms. The first two focus on factors external to the client and use automatic responding. These two approaches are environmental management and teaching task-specific routines. The second two approaches attempt to improve internally generated cognitive–behavioral responses. These approaches are training in the selection and execution of cognitive plans and self-instructional therapies.

Environmental management is a broad category which encompasses many techniques. The goal of each technique is to help the client manage in the external world and prevent problems which could arise due to impairments with initiation and self-regulation. One approach is to organize the physical environment so that it compensates for frontal lobe difficulties. Many of the organizational principles discussed earlier would also work well here such as filing, labeling, calendars, or other means to organize the physical environment. Also included could be cues or prompts, as discussed earlier, for personal care, cooking, socializing, and other activities. As stated earlier, the introduction of these would require a great deal of practice on the part of the client. Physiological factors are often overlooked when working with central nervous system difficulties. When a person is physically uncomfortable or disabled, it is possible that executive function difficulties become worse. Each of the following should be addressed with an individual who suffers from dysexecutive symptoms, nutrition, sleep hygiene, activity level, and medication management.

Teaching task-specific routines is another broad category which aims to teach a client a behavior or set of behaviors that is adaptive for a specific setting. Once the behavior is taught, it should be able to be replicated as an automatic response or habit. The first part of the remediation is to define the task. Next, the task needs to be modified to the level the client is capable of performing. The steps in the task need to be practiced until the client is able to perform the routines. A difficult component is cuing the client to perform the task and working with motivation. Burke, Zencius, Weslowski, and Doubleday (1991) summarized the steps as:

1. Writing a task analysis or steps in the routine;
2. Developing and implementing a checklist to make sure all steps in the routine are clear and explained;
3. Including practice for each step, using errorless learning; and
4. Making sure reinforcement and motivation to succeed are embedded in training.

Examples of routines which may be taught in this manner include dressing, housecleaning, hobbies, and other activities which may be broken into component parts.

The selection and execution of cognitive plans includes training for goal selection, planning/sequencing, initiation, execution, and sense of time. The difference between the skills taught in this section and the previous section is that the current tasks are designed to instill generalization to similar tasks or to cues that could signal the completion of a similar task. There is no sufficient research available to determine whether improvement occurs due to generalization or whether the specific executive functions required to complete the task have improved. Planning activities, errand completion tasks, and time management tasks are all ways in which the client may learn to compensate for dysexecutive symptoms with the hope that the learning will transfer to similar situations. In order for these techniques to be successful, Sohlberg and Mateer (2001) suggest that the clinical neuropsychologist practice all of the following:

- Clearly define the objectives of the activity;
- Make sure the client understands the objectives and has support to complete the activity;
- Measure the performance to determine success or areas that need improvement;
- Include a sufficient number of tasks or hierarchy of tasks; and
- Have a method of measuring generalization of executive skills.

The final approach to treatment of dysexecutive symptoms is self-instructional or meta-cognitive routines. The background of these approaches is from the work of Vygotsky and Luria who suggested that volitional behavior originates not in mental acts but rather is mediated by inner speech. Much of the research was completed watching children transfer their external speech control over their behavior into internal speech (Luria, 1982). Luria also felt that the frontal lobes were crucial in the regulation of internal self-talk and that dysexecutive syndromes were due to frontal lobe difficulties. Self-instructional techniques are also used by behavioral psychologists as they attempt to teach children with impulsivity disorders to regulate their behavior (Meichenbaum & Goodman, 1971). Since the 1970s and 1980s, the ideas presented previously have been used to develop programs in self-regulation of dysexecutive symptoms. Cicerone and Giacino (1992) have developed a treatment program for remediation of planning and error utilization deficits. They make it clear that the goal is not to train a specific task but to guide the internalization of self-regulation processes. Goal management training (GMT) is one of the few task completion procedures which has been evaluated (Levine et al., 2000). The researchers stated that they were able to see improvement and that it was generalizable to other tasks. These researchers suggest that this approach works best with clients who have some degree of self-awareness. Hence, some clients may be too severely disabled to benefit from this type of approach.

Now that we have explored the dysexecutive treatment modalities, it is time to consider whether Mick could benefit from any of these approaches to treatment. Due to the fact that Mick's tumor was removed from the prefrontal area near the motor strip, it is likely that he sustained some dysexecutive symptoms. He appears to have some difficulty with attention and motivating himself to complete his schoolwork. The APT, as discussed previously, worked well for him. In addition, he undertook, with the help of his therapist, practice in self-instructional routines. He stated that it helped him to accomplish tasks when he was able to have an internal dialogue as he progressed through the task.

Unawareness

Unawareness or the lack of awareness of one's own difficulties is a common consequence of focal or diffuse brain injury or disease. In the past, theoreticians have described lack of awareness as a form of psychological denial or inability to cope with physical issues.

Current thinking is that central nervous system unawareness has at least some organic components. The frontal lobes appear to be critically involved in self-awareness as well as the posterior and subcortical structures (Damasio, 1994).

There are several models of unawareness, each of which leads to a specific type of assessment and rehabilitation. A review of the various theories leads to several common components within the concept of unawareness. The most basic level of lack of awareness is the inability to understand that a deficit is present. It is described by various researchers as lack of information, lack of intellectual awareness, or cognitive impairment. Another difficulty is the inability to apply information one has acquired to real-world situations or contexts. The last difficulty often observed is denial. Denial may have many causes—from psychologically not being able to face the difficulty, to the inability to understand the difficulty and therefore deny its existence.

Sohlberg and Mateer (2001) have reviewed the unawareness literature and discuss several important characteristics of awareness disorders. There are various types of unawareness whose causes are often complex. Even with multiple etiological sources, there is often a primary and secondary source which can be identified (Giacino & Cicerone, 1998). Sources of unawareness may be cognitive impairment or the person may have normal intellectual and sensory function. This confusing statement is due to the fact that the frontal lobes are critical to awareness and may be selectively impaired (Stuss, 1991). An individual may have knowledge regarding their awareness difficulty but not be able to apply the information or understand the consequences. Awareness is connected to executive functioning and the two share anatomical structures. It is often helpful to mold the treatment to the source of the awareness problem. Psychological unawareness appears to be more difficult to remediate than any other type.

Now that we have reviewed issues related to unawareness, we will proceed to assessment. As is true with many of the topics within this chapter, measurement of awareness is difficult. Most researchers agree that awareness cannot be measured directly but must be inferred. The three most common approaches to measuring awareness are analyzing the client's verbal description of his or her functioning, comparing a client's reports with another person's report, and comparing the client's prediction of his or her functioning with his or her actual performance. Analyzing the client's report of functioning provides a measure of how the client views him- or herself. It also gives an indication of the mismatch between the client's report and the client's ability. Hence, this is often used to assess the awareness of disability. Comparing a client's report of his or her functioning with that of another person is another measure of the client's awareness. The comparison may be made through observation, interviews, or the use of various questionnaires which have been designed for this specific purpose. Another type of assessment is the comparison between the client's predicted versus actual performance. The most effective manner to use this approach is with discrete tasks that have real-life significance.

As may be inferred, there is a paucity of research-backed techniques for the treatment of awareness difficulties (see Figure 12.6). At present, three approaches are most often used: individual awareness enhancing programs, caregiver training and education, and procedural training and environmental support (PTES). An individual program of awareness training addresses the particular situation of the client. It is most appropriate for clients with psychological or psychological and organic causes of their deficits, who have at least some understanding of their difficulties, and who have the cognitive capacity to integrate information and experience. Educational approaches are often used to provide clients with the basic information about their neurological difficulty. Another approach is to review the client's medical record with the client as a means to understand the difficulty. A third approach is to review others' perceptions of the client and compare them to the client's own view of functioning.

FIGURE 12.6 Sample educational exercises. *Source:* Adapted from Chittum et al. (1996); Zhou et al. (1996).

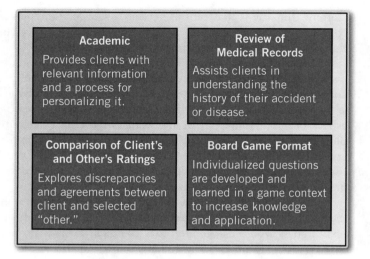

Academic
Provides clients with relevant information and a process for personalizing it.

Review of Medical Records
Assists clients in understanding the history of their accident or disease.

Comparison of Client's and Other's Ratings
Explores discrepancies and agreements between client and selected "other."

Board Game Format
Individualized questions are developed and learned in a game context to increase knowledge and application.

Any educational program needs to minimize defensiveness on the part of the client. The clinical neuropsychologist must also be aware of the emotional reaction the client is having to the information. Experiential exercises are another manner to increase a client's self-awareness. The goal of these exercises is to help client's experience changes in their ability. The second approach is training or educating the family or caregiver. The same approaches previously discussed may also be used with these individuals. PTES is often the final approach for individuals with limited awareness. The goal is to maximize functioning without being concerned whether a client understands or acknowledges his or her limitations.

Returning to Mick, it is clear that he has some understanding of his difficulties. He would then be most likely to benefit from some form of education. With the aid of his individual therapist, he was able to understand how his difficulties were caused by the particular tumor he had and the surgical aftereffects. Family education was also introduced with the aid of the therapist and greatly helped the family comprehend the limits of Mick's ability to understand his own deficits.

Summary

The chapter began with the case of Mick who developed a very rare brain tumor. Removal of the tumor was successful but left him with some difficulties due to the fact that it was situated in the prefrontal area. Mick also sustained some motor difficulties in his foot and toes due to the surgery or the tumor impinging on his motor strip.

Historical information begins the chapter and is followed by a general theoretical discussion of cognitive and memory difficulties. Mick's case, which discusses the various types of cognitive and memory difficulties which may occur due to central nervous system disease or trauma, is traced throughout the chapter.

Each of four different types of difficulties is reviewed in the chapter. These difficulties are problems with attention, memory, executive functioning, and awareness of difficulties. Each of the four is discussed in terms of current knowledge regarding etiological factors. Assessment tools are discussed for each topic as well as specific types of difficulties that may arise in the assessment of each area. Rehabilitation for each area is described with reference to the research literature. Each section is concluded with application to Mick's case.

Questions for Further Study

1. Describe the reason why ecological validity is an important topic within rehabilitation.

2. Why would insurance companies be particularly interested in the efficacy of various rehabilitation strategies?

3. Within the area of interviewing and testing, using a common language is crucial for the patient and clinical neuropsychologist. Is this also the case with rehabilitation?

References

Braswell, D., Hartry, A., Hoornbeek, S., Johansen, A., Johnsen, L., Schultz, J., et al. (1993). *Profile of the executive control system: Instruction manual and assessment.* Wake Forest, NC: Lash and Associates.

Burke, W. H., Zencius, A. H., Weslowski, M. D., & Doubleday, F. (1991). Improving operative function disorders in brain injured clients. *Brain Injury, 5*(3), 241–252.

Bush, G. H. W. (1990). *Decade of the brain* (Presidential Proclamation 6158). Washington, DC: Office of the Federal Registrar.

Cicerone, K. D., & Giacino, J. T. (1992). Remediation of executive function deficits after traumatic brain injury. *Neurorehabilitation, 2*, 73–83.

Coelho, C. (1997, October). *Outcomes, efficacy and effectiveness of rehabilitation for cognitive-communication disorder following traumatic brain injury in adults.* Paper presented at the annual meeting of the Oregon Speech-Language-Hearing Association, Eugene, OR.

Damasio, A. R. (1994). *Descartes' error: Emotion, reason, and the human brain.* New York: Grosset/ Putnam.

Giacino, J. T., & Cicerone, K. D. (1998). Varieties of deficit unawareness after brain injury. *Journal of Head Trauma Rehabilitation, 13*(5), 1–15.

Glisky, E. L., & Schacter, D. L. (1989). Extending the limits of complex learning in organic amnesia: Computer training in a vocational domain. *Neuropsychologia, 27*, 107–120.

Glisky, E. L., Schacter, D. L., & Tulving, E. (1986). Learning and retention of computer-related vocabulary in amnesia patients: Method of vanishing cues. *Journal of Clinical and Experimental Neuropsychology, 8*(3), 292–312.

Goldstein, K. (1942). *Aftereffects of brain injuries in war: Their evaluation and treatment: The applications of psychologic methods in the clinic.* New York: Grune & Stratton.

Horvath, A. O., & Luborsky, L. (1993). The role of the therapeutic alliance in psychotherapy. *Journal of Consulting and Clinical Psychology, 61*, 561–573.

Kay, T. (1992). Neuropsychological diagnosis: Disentangling the multiple determinats and functional disability after mild traumatic brain injury. *Physical Medicine and Rehabilitation State of the Art Reviews, 6*, 109–127.

Kinsella, G. (1998). Assessment of attention following traumatic brain injury: A review. *Neuropsychological Rehabilitation, 8*(3), 351–375.

Levine, B., Robertson, I. H., Clare, L., Carter, G., Hong, J., Wilson, B. A., et al. (2000). Rehabilitation of executive functioning: An experimental-clinical validation of goal management training. *Journal of the International Neuropsychological Society, 6*, 299–312.

Lezak, M. D., Howieson, D. B., & Loring, D. W. (2004). *Neuropsychological assessment* (4th ed.). New York: Oxford University Press.

Luria, A. R. (1963). *Restoration of function after brain injury* (B. Haigh, Trans.). New York: Macmillan/ Pergamon.

Luria, A. R. (1973). *The working brain: An introduction to neuropsychology* (B. Haigh, Trans.). New York: Basic Books.

Luria, A. R. (1982). *Language and cognition.* Washington, DC: Winston & Sons.

Malec, J. F. (1999). Goal Attainment Scaling in rehabilitation. *Neuropsychological Rehabilitation, 9*, 253–275.

Mateer, C. A. (1999). The rehabilitation of executive disorders. In D. T. Stuss, G. Winocur & I. Robertson (Eds.), *Cognitive neurorehabilitation* (pp. 314–332). Cambridge, England: Cambridge University Press.

Meichenbaum, D. H., & Goodman, J. (1971). Training impulsive children to talk to themselves. A means of developing self-control. *Journal of Abnormal Psychology, 77*, 115–126.

Miller, E. (1992). Psychological approaches to the management of memory impairments. *The British Journal of Psychiatry., 160*, 1–6.

Niemann, H., Ruff, R. M., & Baser, C. A. (1990). Computer-assisted attention retraining in head-injured individuals: A controlled efficacy study of an outpatient program. *Journal of Consulting Clinical Psychology, 58*, 811–817.

Norman, D. A., & Shallice, T. (1986). Attention to action: Willed and automatic control of behavior. In R. J. Davidson, G. E. Schwartz & D. Shapiro (Eds.), *Consciousness and self-regulation* (pp. 3–18). New York: Plenum Press.

Park, N., Proulx, G. B., & Towers, W. M. (1999). Evaluation of the Attention Process Training programme. *Neuropsychological Rehabilitation, 9*(2), 135–154.

Ponsford, J. L., & Kinsella, G. (1992). Attention deficits following closed-head injury. *Journal of Clinical and Experimental Neuropsychology, 14*, 822–838.

Prigatano, G. P. (1991). Disturbances of self-awareness of deficit after traumatic brain injury. In G. P., Prigatano & D. L. Schacter (Eds.), *Awareness of deficit after brain injury: Clinical and theoretical perspectives* (pp. 111–126). New York: Oxford University Press.

Prigatano, G. P. (1999). *Principles of neuropsychological rehabilitation.* New York: Oxford University Press.

Raskin, S. A., & Sohlberg, M. M. (1996). The efficacy of Prospective Memory Training in two adults with brain injury. *Journal of Head Trauma Rehabilitation, 11*(3), 32–51.

Robertson, I., Ward, T., Ridgeway, V., & Nimmo-Smith, I. (1996). The structure of normal human attention: The test of everyday attention. *Journal of the International Neuropsychological Society, 2*, 525–534.

Sohlberg, M. M., & Mateer, C. A. (1989). *Introduction to cognitive rehabilitation: Theory and practice.* New York: Guilford Press.

Sohlberg, M. M., & Mateer, C. A. (2001). *Cognitive rehabilitation: An integrative neuropsychological approach.* New York: Guilford Press.

Sohlberg, M. M., Mateer, C. A., & Geyer, S. (1985). *Prospective Memory Process Training (PROMPT).* Wake Forest, NC: Lash and Associates.

Sohlberg, M. M., McLaughlin, K., Pavese, A., Heidrich, A., & Posner, M. (2000). Evaluation of attention process training and brain injury education in persons with acquired brain injury. *Journal of Experimental and Clinical Neuropsychology, 22*, 656–677.

Stuss, D. T. (1991). Disturbances of self-awareness after frontal system damage. In G. P. Prigatano & D. L. Schacter (Eds.), *Awareness of deficit after brain injury: Clinical and theoretical perspectives* (pp. 63–83). New York: Oxford University Press.

Stuss, D. T., Stethem, L. L., Hugenholtz, W., Picton, T., Pivik, J., & Richard, M. T. (1989). Reaction time after head injury: Fatigue, divided and focused attention, and consistency of performance. *Journal of Neurology, Neurosurgery and Psychiatry, 52*, 742–748.

Wilson, B. A. (1986). Rehabilitation of memory. New York: Guilford Press.

Wilson, B. A., & Moffat, N. (Eds.). (1994). *Clinical management of memory problems.* San Diego, CA: Singular Publishing Group.

Wilson, B. A., Baddeley, A., Evans, J. J., & Shiel, A. J. (1994). Errorless learning in the rehabilitation of memory impaired people. *Neuropsychological Rehabilitation, 4*(3), 307–326.

Individual Therapy

13

Key Terms

postconcussion syndrome
confidentiality
vulnerable adult
legal guardian
minor
boundaries
hysteria
Oedipus complex
Electra complex
id
pleasure principle
superego
ego
reality principle
oral stage
anal stage
phallic stage

latency
genital stage
unconscious
defense mechanism
transference
free association
symptom substitution
unconditioned stimulus
unconditioned response
conditioned stimulus
conditioned response
extinction
spontaneous recovery
stimulus generalization
trial-and-error learning
law of effect
operant

reinforcement contingency
reinforcer
positive reinforcement
negative reinforcement
punisher
partial reinforcement
organismic valuing process
self-actualization
conditions of worth
unconditional positive regard
empathy
genuineness
nondirective attitude
inauthentic living
normal anxiety
neurotic anxiety
eclecticism

Learning Objectives

After reading this chapter, the student should be able to understand:

- The ethical issues involved in the therapist–patient relationship
- The psychodynamic school of therapy and Freud's contribution to its development
- The behavioral school of therapy and its foundation in classical and operant conditioning
- The cognitive revolution which led to the development of the cognitive behavioral framework
- The humanistic–existential philosophy of therapy and its emphasis on the client-centered approach
- The types of emotional difficulties which commonly occur with central nervous system damage, their origins, and appropriate therapeutic methods for these difficulties

Case Vignette

G rant was referred by the Academic Advising Office at his university during the fall of his senior year to help with academic issues. Grant had been having difficulties in class particularly with multiple choice exams and spoke with one of his professors regarding his concerns. His professor suggested that he contact the Academic Advising Office on campus to help deal with his difficulties. An astute academic advisor inquired regarding when his difficulties began and any etiological factors he could identify. Due to the events described later, the advisor then suggested that Grant obtain a neuropsychological evaluation and any other help deemed appropriate to improve his classroom performance.

The difficulties which Grant discussed with the advisor and led to him receiving neuropsychological services began the previous spring semester. He was a soccer player and during a game he headed a ball, which resulted in what was thought to be a concussion. His coach had him sit out the rest of the game but then return to play for the next game. Grant had the same experience once again and was very wary afterward of continuing to play. By the end of the season he had received what was later determined to be three concussions. He did not seek any medical treatment nor did his coach inform him that he could more easily have another concussion after receiving the first. No one told him that he also could develop seizures due to the concussions. Upon questioning, he stated that his roommate described to him behaviors that could possibly have been seizures. During the season he did not refrain from the use of alcohol. While it was a team policy to not use substances during the season, this was not well enforced. No one suggested to Grant that it was detrimental to consume alcohol after any type of brain trauma. During the past summer there occurred an incident which eventually led to Grant receiving medical attention. He stated that he was leaving a friend's house early in the morning heading toward his car when he was attacked from behind by an unknown number of assailants and robbed. He was badly beaten and lost consciousness. He awoke to find that the person or persons had stolen his car. He crawled to his friend's house and the police and an ambulance were called. Once the paramedics arrived, they evaluated Grant and determined that he needed hospital treatment.

At the hospital, he was admitted and received a CT scan. The scan revealed that the assault caused a concussion. According to Grant's account, this was probably the last of four concussions. An emergency room physician telephoned his parents who arrived very quickly. Neither of Grant's parents knew of the previous injuries which he had sustained through his sports participation. Both parents were very concerned about his condition and also very angry at the lack of help offered by his coach to their son. When Grant was eventually questioned, he could not describe anything that would help the police and was never able to recover his wallet or his vehicle. These events caused a great deal of stress for him due to the loss of his identification, credit cards, and a car that belonged to his parents.

Grant stayed in the hospital for 2 days while his primary doctor and a neurologist determined the best course of treatment. He was given medication to prevent seizures and cautioned not to drink any alcohol. He was also advised that he should not return to his sport however difficult that may be for him. Grant and his parents received much information regarding the effects of multiple concussions to the brain. They also were informed that if the college he was attending was notified regarding his difficulties, they should provide help for him with course work. Accommodations are guaranteed under provisions of Section 504 of the Civil Rights Act (1973), which ensures that any school which receives federal funding offer a free and appropriate education, including at the college level.

Grant's parents felt a need to contact his school and speak with the coach. The coach was an older individual who felt that his team needed to just "tough it out" when it came to physical adversity. The parents, lacking any satisfaction after talking with the coach, contacted the Director of Student Services. The Director assured the parents that he was very concerned about Grant's condition. He also stated that the coach, although very well respected, did not speak for the entire school or its policies. The Director assured Grant's parents that the school would be changing its team policies regarding sports and injuries. However, it was too late to help Grant who had already received his injuries.

While in the hospital, Grant received a mental status examination from the admitting physician which showed that he was oriented times three (person, place, and situation). He was also given a small battery of neuropsychological tests administered by the hospital clinical neuropsychologist to assess his current cognitive functioning and determine his strengths and weaknesses. The battery of tests was small because Grant was in the hospital and the clinical neuropsychologist did not want to tax him in an already stressful situation. The clinical neuropsychologist felt he could obtain enough information to determine whether Grant was capable of functioning outside of the hospital setting using the Wechsler Adult Intelligence Scale-IV, the Wechsler Memory Scale-IV, the Category Test, and the Minnesota Multiphasic Personality Inventory-2. Further testing could then be completed after Grant left the hospital if it was necessary. The evaluation revealed that he had significant short- and long-term memory difficulties. He exhibited difficulties with concentration and attention and was somewhat unaware of appropriate social behavior. His overall measured intelligence did not appear to be greatly affected. He stated, however, that he felt less competent in his school work. During the intake interview, he stated that he was aware that he had become more short tempered, easily frustrated, and did not have a great deal of tolerance for his own shortcomings.

As noted previously, Grant was released after 2 days in the hospital and recuperated for the remainder of the summer. He began the fall semester of his senior year with a full complement of courses in order to complete the requirements for his major and for graduation. He stated that he became frustrated after receiving his first tests on which he did not perform at his usual level. He also felt somewhat embarrassed when called on in class and was not always prepared to answer the questions. He read the assigned material but somehow could not bring it to mind when he was called on to perform. He also stated that he felt awkward socially. He was not able to drink as he used to without acting foolish. The combination of these factors led him to talk with the professor who sent him to Academic Advising and hence led to the present neuropsychological evaluation.

Grant discussed all of the aforementioned information with the clinical neuropsychologist. At the clinical neuropsychologist's request records were obtained from his previous evaluation at the hospital for the purpose of comparison. The clinical neuropsychologist replicated the previously given tests in order to develop a pattern of strengths and weaknesses. The tests results were quite similar to the original evaluation. They were compared to his high school grades, college grades, and American College Testing (ACT) scores as a measure of premorbid functioning. It was clear that Grant was still experiencing short- and long-term memory difficulties, attention and concentration difficulties, and various symptoms which were evident from interview and the personality test such as diminished frustration tolerance, lack of tolerance for his own difficulties, and a growing problem with both anger management and self-esteem.

Grant was assured that all of the findings were related to the concussions and that no new difficulties had become apparent. As was explained to Grant, many of the cognitive deficits were *a direct result of the head trauma. The emotional symptoms could also be due to the frontal areas which were involved in his concussions from his sports injuries and the assault. The emotional symptoms could additionally be secondary reactions to having brain trauma. Grant was diagnosed with Cognitive Disorder Not Otherwise Specified. Grant was also told by the clinical neuropsychologist that his symptoms are consistent with a diagnosis of postconcussion syndrome, which is not currently included within the diagnostic manual. However, the diagnosis will be included in the forthcoming revision of the* Diagnostic and Statistical Manual of Mental Disorders, Fifth Edition (DSM). *Much research has been accumulated regarding the effects of concussions and multiple concussions, which is the reason for its inclusion within the next DSM. Grant was instructed in what to expect in terms of how the concussions would impact his life. It was suggested to Grant that he begin individual therapy to help with some of the feelings which surfaced due to the types of deficits he was aware he was experiencing. It was also suggested that the family could benefit from family therapy to understand the effects of Grant's central nervous system difficulties on the family as a whole. Grant was highly resistant to any form of "talk" therapy and felt that only "crazy" people went to therapy. After a period of time, when he began to realize his emotional reactions were causing problems in his life, he agreed to begin individual therapy.*

postconcussion syndrome constellation of physical and psychological symptoms that may occur after a medically verifiable concussion

This case presents a quandary for the clinical neuropsychologist. The individual in question would clearly benefit from rehabilitative strategies to help with memory, concentration, and attention difficulties. The chances of him accepting those services are quite good. However, this individual could also benefit greatly from individual therapy in order to deal with the feelings which are attributed to the changes in his abilities. These feelings are normal considering the circumstances and do not suggest the presence of any significant psychological impairment. The client, however, evidences a common negative reaction to obtaining such services, particularly with this age group and gender. The task for the clinical neuropsychologist is to normalize the use of these services and establish for the client how necessary these services are considering his particular circumstances. If this is possible, there is a good chance that the client will use the services offered and develop coping skills to deal with feelings he has not previously felt. Hence, the client must learn not only the skills to cope with feelings but also develop an understanding that it is normal to acknowledge various types of feelings.

The treatment plan which the clinical neuropsychologist developed included rehabilitation for Grant's memory, attention, and concentration difficulties using techniques discussed within this text. The clinical neuropsychologist also began an individual therapy relationship with Grant to help him discuss various emotional issues. Due to the fact that Grant probably would not be in a therapeutic relationship had he not sustained central nervous system trauma, the first few therapy sessions were spent educating Grant regarding the roles of the client and therapist. The next few sessions were spent discussing emotions, how to separate one emotion from another, how to label them, and how emotions are experienced physically and psychologically. The remainder of the therapy sessions were spent discussing how to manage his emotions when he could not predict their occurrence, coping skills for anger and frustration, and skills to alleviate depressive symptoms. At the completion of many sessions, Grant began to verbalize that therapy was beginning to help him and that he was now able to separate emotions and work on strategies to alleviate various emotions. He stated that this helped him not only in school and socially but that it also helped him feel more in control of his life after experiencing more than a year of feeling that his life was out of his control. Grant agreed to consider joining a therapy group with other individuals in his age bracket for mutual support. In addition, after learning a great deal about feelings and their expression, he stated that it would be a good idea to include his family in some form of therapeutic intervention. He now felt that he understood his feelings and circumstances and that his family could benefit from understanding how his difficulties affected the family as a whole.

Introduction

This chapter has two main topics that it will cover. The first topic is an introduction to the field of individual therapy. The reader will be referred at various points in the chapter to research which will review various types of psychotherapy in more depth. The second topic is an examination of the most salient types of difficulties encountered by individuals who have sustained central nervous system disease or damage and how these difficulties are treated therapeutically. Many of the therapeutic techniques used with individuals with central nervous system difficulties will be the same as in standard or traditional therapy. However, due to the particular issues which may surface with this population, there are specific issues that need special consideration. Grant's case is a clear example of issues which surfaced only after he had received multiple concussions.

Individual Therapy

This text is not designed to instruct the reader in all there is to know regarding the therapeutic process. Undergraduate programs begin the task and it is completed once an individual finishes a graduate program and becomes licensed to practice therapy. The task for this chapter is a basic introduction to the field of psychotherapy, particularly the qualities of the therapeutic process which separate it from any other type of relationship.

The topic of individual therapy implies that we are focusing on two individuals interacting in some manner, one being the therapist and the other being the client. The following chapter will cover family and group therapy including all of the issues that surface when there is more than one client.

To begin the discussion we make the assumption that the therapist, or in this situation the clinical neuropsychologist, is trained in the art and science of therapy. In the real world, many professions and people dispense counseling, including physicians, clergy members, attorneys as well as family and friends. In this discussion, we are assuming that the clinical neuropsychologist has been trained in a graduate program and is licensed to practice in a particular state. Another assumption which will set this discussion apart from any other discussion of therapy is that the clinical neuropsychologist is an expert in the functioning of the brain in both healthy and diseased or damaged states. A further assumption is that the clinical neuropsychologist understands how therapy should be delivered to individuals with brain deficits which may be different than therapy with clients who have not sustained central nervous system trauma. Other types of counselors may not take into account the difficulties inherent in this type of therapeutic endeavor.

ETHICS

As was discussed earlier, there exists a code of conduct developed by the American Psychological Association to which licensed psychologists must abide. There also exist sanctions which may be implemented if an ethics violation is detected. In our discussion of individual therapy, there are particular ethical principles which are very important and which may help the reader understand more fully the process of therapy.

confidentiality

the statement that is given at the beginning of psychotherapy that assures the client of privacy of information verbally and in written form; reasons to break the confidential relationship include threats of suicide, homicide, physical or sexual abuse (client as perpetrator or victim), and abuse of a vulnerable adult (client as victim or perpetrator)

Confidentiality is one of the most salient issues which separate therapy from any other type of relationship between two or more people. Confidentiality clearly states that everything that is said to the therapist or within therapy remains in that context except in certain circumstances. The therapist must notify the client of these circumstances at the beginning of therapy before the client begins to discuss any of these issues. The issues include threats of (a) suicide, (b) homicide, (c) child abuse committed by the client or the client is the victim, and (d) abuse of a vulnerable adult or someone who is unable to care for himself or herself committed by the client or the client is the victim. The clinical neuropsychologist, as opposed to other counselors, needs to be aware of the individual's ability to understand when and if the confidential relationship may need to be broken. Some individuals with central nervous system difficulties may be considered to be a **vulnerable adult** in a legal sense or may have a **legal guardian**. In the case of a legal guardian, confidentiality issues would be explained to the legal guardian in addition to the client. It is then necessary to determine whether the guardian remains present during the therapeutic process. This is not an ethically sanctioned issue but more related to whether the client understands or is comfortable with another person present. If a client has a legal guardian or if the client is a **minor** (underage, defined by each state), then the client must be notified that the parent or guardian is allowed to know the topics discussed within the therapy session.

vulnerable adult

an individual who is incapable of taking care of himself or herself or of his or her affairs because of physical or mental difficulties

legal guardian

through a court of law, a legal guardian is a person appointed to guard the person or property of another individual who, for physical or mental reasons, is incapable of taking care of his/her person or affairs

In addition to confidentiality, there are several other issues which separate therapy from any other type of relationship. In therapy, the focus is on the client and his or her difficulties. There is no attempt made to have the relationship be reciprocal in any manner. If it becomes reciprocal, it is an indication that the focus may have shifted from the needs of the client to the needs of the therapist. **Boundaries** are particularly important in a therapeutic setting. Clients must know that the therapist is there to help them, listen to their feelings, discuss problems, and, in the case of central nervous system difficulties, provide advice or suggest rehabilitation strategies. However, the therapist is not the client's friend, does not visit with the client outside of the therapeutic situation, does not accept gifts, and does not provide information about his or her personal life. The reason for establishing clear boundaries is in order for the therapist to remain objective in his or her evaluation of the client's difficulties and his or her choice of treatment strategies. In the case of central nervous system difficulties, it may happen that the patient or his or her spouse, family, or other significant person may become dependent on the clinical neuropsychologist. The risk for dependency is always an issue in therapy but with central nervous system difficulties, the changes in an individual's life may be greater and the need for someone to normalize what feels out of control may also be greater. Hence, the clinical neuropsychologist, while compassionate and caring, must keep a watchful eye on the issue of dependency. It clearly states in the ethics manual that due to the chances of impaired objectivity, therapists are not allowed to work therapeutically with friends or family. Another ethical issue which is extremely important when dealing with potentially vulnerable individuals is the issue of sexual relationships with clients. It is absolutely imperative that no sexual improprieties occur particularly in situations where a client may not understand the clinical implications and become a victim of the therapist.

minor

an individual who is legally younger than the age of majority (defined by state or territory) and hence does not have the same rights as an adult

boundaries

the ability of the clinical neuropsychologist to keep a professional therapeutic relationship intact; implies that the client does not become invested in the therapist's life

In Grant's case, it is clear that he is cognizant of his surroundings and able to understand the particulars of the confidentiality statement. The main ethical issue for the clinical neuropsychologist working with Grant is his hesitation to enter a therapeutic relationship. The clinical neuropsychologist, therefore, must work through his resistance and help Grant trust that he is a safe person who will not invade Grant's personal space but help him sort out and cope with emotional issues.

SETTING

Now that we have discussed important ethical issues, we will continue with a discussion of therapy. The setting for therapy is similar to that of a testing situation. The main concern is the comfort of the client. Additionally, the room should be free of any distracting material as many clients may have attention or concentration difficulties. The goal of therapy is to help the client express emotions, label them if the client has little experience with emotions, and develop techniques through which he or she is able to work with these emotions.

THEORIES OF THERAPY

Before delving into a general outline of psychotherapy, a note on terminology needs to be included. There are therapists who use the word *client* and those who use the word *patient*. In this text the terms have been used interchangeably. Therapists who practice therapy from a more medical model tend to use the term *patient* and those who use the term *client* tend to favor a more humanistic approach which may also imply a more business type of a relationship. Corsini and Wedding (2008) suggest that neither word truly describes accurately the person who is receiving services. However, within clinical neuropsychology, the reader may encounter the term *patient* more often due to issues with central nervous system difficulties. In addition the terms, *counseling* and *psychotherapy* may seem interchangeable to many people. Many practitioners view counseling as a shorter process versus psychotherapy being seen as a longer process possibly continuing for months or years. Counseling is often seen as problem oriented, whereas psychotherapy is seen as person oriented.

There exist many schools or theories of therapy through which therapists deliver their services to clients. While there exist more than 400 named therapies, most have similarity to one of the three major schools of thought (Corsini & Wedding, 2008). As time passes, many innovative approaches come and go as issues surface with older therapies. However, when perusing the extant literature regarding psychotherapies, there appears to be a fit between each therapy and one of the three main philosophical orientations: psychodynamic, cognitive–behavioral, and humanistic–existential. Within the literature, psychodynamic approaches are often referred to as the first force in psychology, cognitive–behavioral approaches as the second force, and humanistic–existential approaches as the third force.

Many texts state that psychodynamic forms of therapy have their origins in the work of Sigmund Freud (1856–1939). Although it may be true that Freud began psychoanalysis, it is also true that there were others who predated Freud in their treatment of patients. Paul Dubois (1848–1918) and Pierre Janet (1859–1947) are known to predate Freud. Freud formulated his original ideas regarding human nature on six case studies. Some theorists go so far as stating that most of the widely practiced forms of psychotherapy are based on some element of psychoanalytic theory or technique. As will be discussed further, there has generally been a lack of scientific proof regarding many of Freud's concepts. When one looks at the research on psychotherapy, it is clear that psychotherapy does work with a high success rate of two thirds to three fourths of patients self-reporting feeling better (Lambert & Bergin, 1994). Hence, even though psychoanalytic concepts may be difficult to research individually when the therapy is included within large outcome studies, it appears to be effective. Large outcome studies suggest that it is not the type of therapy but qualities of the therapeutic relationship which lead to behavioral change (Lambert & Bergin). Even with equivocal research support, more than anyone in the

hysteria
physical manifestations of psychological disorders; a term not currently in use

Oedipus complex
the Freudian concept that a male child has sexual feelings toward his mother and jealousy toward his father

Electra complex
the Freudian concept that a female child has sexual feelings for the parent of the opposite sex and jealousy for the same sex parent

id
the portion of the psyche that developed first; it contains primitive urges toward sex and aggression that demand immediate gratification

pleasure principle
the principle through which the id develops and functions; it pushes for immediate gratification of sexual and aggressive impulses

superego
a Freudian concept similar to what is thought of as one's conscience; it develops through interactions with parents, school, and other situations in life

ego
the portion of the psyche that deals with the constraints of reality; the ego must satisfy the impulses of the id and the constraints of the superego

reality principle
the principle by which the ego develops and functions; it allows the ego to interact with the world at large

oral stage
Freud's first stage of psychosexual development (0–2); the focus is putting everything in one's mouth

anal stage
Freud's second stage of psycho-sexual development (ages 2–3); the focus is on independence and the major issue is toilet training

past 100 years, Freud has had an influence on therapy as well as religion, law, sexuality, sociology, anthropology, history, literature, and most other liberal arts fields (Luborsky, O'Reilly-Landry, & Arlow, 2008).

Freud began his career as a Viennese physician who was trained in neurology. He encountered several patients, all female, whose symptoms did not make logical or anatomical sense. He then attempted to understand the reasons why these individuals exhibited the symptoms which they did. In the process, he developed a system of how the mind works, stages of development, and stages of personality formation (see Figure 13.1). After that endeavor, he proceeded to develop a theory of what caused psychiatric difficulties and how to help these individuals, which ultimately led to his principles of psychoanalysis.

Freud's patients were suffering from what was diagnosed as hysteria, a term not presently included in the current diagnostic nomenclature. It has been replaced by somatoform disorders, which are defined as physical symptoms with a predominantly psychological cause. Other writings state that the patients suffered from hysterical neurosis. *Neurosis* is also an outdated term which has been replaced by anxiety. Freud's female patients stated that they had been victims of incest. When Freud published his findings, he was harshly criticized regarding his views on childhood sexuality. During the time period in which he was writing, the scientific community would not acknowledge the fact that children could be sexually molested during childhood. Freud was ostracized by his medical colleagues due to these statements until he revised his theory and explicitly stated that the cases of incest reported were not true but merely childhood wishes. The denial of incest led to significant changes to his theory. Ultimately, it led to the inclusion of Freud's ideas regarding infantile sexuality and the development of the Oedipus complex and Electra complex. However, in the process of disavowing the claims of his patients, he paved the way for modern day difficulties with sexual abuse and harassment. The reason that conviction rates are very low for sex crimes in the United States can be directly related to Freud's ideas, which have made their way into mainstream society. Blaming the victim of sexual crimes and asking questions in a court setting regarding the authenticity of an assault or the willingness to participate on the part of the victim can be traced directly to Freud's suppression of his discovery of incest within the lives of his patients (Klein & Tribich, 1981; Masson, 1984).

The elaboration of Freud's theory followed his denial of incest in the lives of his patients. He developed a tripartite theory of personality functioning including the id, ego, and superego. The id was the center of basic needs and operated on the pleasure principle. The pleasure principle was described as the unregulated search for gratification of physical, sexual, and erotic pleasures at the immediate moment. The superego was the conscience of the individual. It was the introjection of standards of right and wrong, moral and immoral that the individual developed from interacting with the world and particularly parents. The ego was the mediating part of the personality whose job was to gratify id impulses while satisfying the constraints of the superego. The ego operated on the reality principle, meaning that it functioned within the sanctions of society and put reasonable choices before pleasurable demands.

Freud discussed five stages of personality development. The first stage or oral stage (0–2 years) was when the child operated predominately on id impulses. It was also when most objects were put in one's mouth. Abraham (1924) stated that people whose oral desires were excessively frustrated as children developed into pessimists as adults, whereas those whose oral desires had been gratified as children tended to be more optimistic as adults. The anal stage (2–3 years) was when the child exerted

MAJOR CONCEPTS IN PSYCHODYNAMIC THEORY		
Concept	Description	Summary
Freud's Psychoanalytical Theory		
Levels of consciousness	The mind consists of three levels of consciousness: conscious, preconscious, and unconscious	Only a small part of the mind is fully conscious. The unconscious mind, the largest part of the mind, contains our baser drives and impulses
Structure of personality	Id, ego, and superego	The id, which exists only in the unconscious, represents a repository of instinctual impulses and wishes demanding instant gratification. The ego seeks to satisfy the demands of the id through socially acceptable channels without offending the superego—the moral guardian of the personality
Governing principles	Pleasure and reality principle	The id follows the pleasure principle, i.e., the demand for instant gratification regardless of social necessities. The ego follows the reality principle by which gratification of impulses must be weighed in terms of social acceptability and practicality
Defense mechanisms	The ego uses defense mechanisms to conceal or distort unacceptable impulses, thus preventing them from rising into consciousness	The major defense mechanisms include repression, regression, projection, rationalization, denial, reaction formation, sublimation, and displacement
Stages of psychosexual development	Sexual motivation is expressed through stimulation of different body parts or erogenous zones as the child matures	The five stages of psychosexual development are oral, anal, phallic, latency, and genital. Overgratification or undergratification at any stage can lead to personality features or fixations characteristic of that stage
Other Theories		
Key points	Greater emphasis on the ego and social relationships than Freud, and lesser emphasis on sexual and aggressive motivation	Carl Jung's analytical psychology introduced such concepts as the personal unconscious, archetypes, and the collective unconscious.
		Alfred Adler's individual psychology emphasized self-awareness, goal-striving, and ways in which people compensate for underlying feelings of inadequacy or inferiority.
		Karen Horney focused on ways in which people relate to each other and the importance of parent-child relationships.

FIGURE 13.1 Chart of Freud's major concepts. *Source:* Adapted from *Major concepts in psychodynamic theory*, Cengage Learning.

independence and the task to be learned was toilet training. A child may react to frustrations during this phase by becoming stubborn or disagreeable. Overcompensation may be shown by the individual becoming extremely clean, very punctual, or stingy with one's possessions as an adult. The **phallic stage** (3.5–6 years) was the time of infantile sexuality and the Oedipus or Electra complex. The child was presumed to have sexual feelings for the opposite sex parent and jealousy toward the same sex

phallic stage
the third of Freud's psychosexual stages of development; the stage where the focus is on the functions of the genitals and where the Oedipus and Electra complexes develop

latency
Freud's fourth stage of psycho-sexual development; the focus is on school and development of competence

genital stage
the final stage of Freudian psychosexual development; mature sexual relations are possible if the individual has mastered the Oedipus or Electra complexes

unconscious
a level of awareness where Freud felt unpleasant sexual and aggressive emotions resided in order that they did not cause emotional difficulty for the client on a day-to-day basis

defense mechanism
Freud's concept which states that various mechanisms of the ego function automatically to keep unpleasant information from the individual's conscious awareness

transference
the main task of psycho-analysis; the patient transfers feelings from a significant relationship onto the analyst who then assists the patient to understand the feelings

free association
a therapeutic technique in which the psychoanalyst remains quiet as the patient speaks; the contents are thought to come from the patient's unconscious

symptom substitution
the replacement of one symptom for another; this signals that the underlying issue has not been resolved

parent. Latency occurs during school age (6 years to the onset of puberty) when the child was mastering skills outside of the parental relationship. During the latency stage, there was no mention of sexuality. The genital stage was the final stage of development and occurred in late adolescence into adulthood. The child successfully mastered this stage if he or she identified with the same-sex parent and was hetero-sexual. Freud did not consider homosexuality as successful mastery of this stage.

Freud felt that certain experiences, mainly sexual or aggressive, were often too difficult for a person to encompass consciously, and were automatically relinquished to another level of the psyche termed the unconscious. Defense mechanisms such as repression, and so forth, were used automatically by the psyche to keep these experiences out of awareness. When the defense mechanisms failed, the repressed information manifested itself as anxiety. According to Freud, the presence of anxiety in his patients was a signal that repressed material needed to be uncovered. Freud's method of uncovering the information which produced anxiety was ultimately termed *psychoanalysis*.

Psychoanalysis, as traditionally described, was a long and protracted process. The patient usually met with the analyst 5 days per week for 1 hour. During the time of early analysis, there were no insurance reimbursements; hence, the cost of treatment was borne by the patient. Psychoanalysis was thought to be the treatment of the lei-sure class. Traditional psychoanalysis consisted of four distinct phases: the opening phase, development of transference, working through transference, and termination. The opening phase lasted 3–6 months. During this time, the patient was evaluated to determine if he or she were suitable for psychoanalysis. The patient had to be verbal, of at least average intelligence, not in imminent danger to self or others and not actively psychotic. During the opening phase, the patient and analyst sat facing one another and both participated in the session. Development of the transference was the second stage and began when the client lay recumbent on a couch and the analyst sat out of view behind the patient's line of sight. The goal was for the patient not to react to the expressions on the therapist's face as the client discussed personal information. Transference was the unconscious transfer of feelings from the source of the emo-tion to a safer figure. The information which was the content of the transference came from the unconsciousness of the patient. During this phase, the client spoke freely or free associated while the therapist was quiet and may have taken notes. The development of transference may occur quickly or take several years. **Working through the transference** was the phase when the analyst pointed out themes in the transference material to the patient. Working through implies that whatever issues surfaced may then be dealt with under the assumption that symptom substitution would not occur. Symptom substitution is the occurrence of another symptom after the original symptom which brought the individual to analysis had been uncovered and worked through. Working through also happened quickly or took a prolonged amount of time. Termination was equivalent in length of time to the opening phase. The analyst predicted for the patient that analysis would be coming to an end. The return of symptoms was also predicted and normalized. The return of symptoms often occurs after a close relationship of many years nears an end and fears of facing issues on one's own may surface. Analysis was concluded by allowing the patient the oppor-tunity to return, if necessary, but also supporting the patient with tools to understand life's tasks on his or her own.

Freud's theory, as stated previously, had a large impact on multiple areas of society. Within psychology, Freud has often been referred to as the father of modern psychother-apy. Many of the most famous therapists had their original training with Freud or in his methods. However, many of his followers found fault with various tenets of his theory and developed their own type of therapy. Those individuals who separated from Freud but retained many of his ideas or concepts within their theories and therapies are termed *pseudoanalytic* or more commonly called *psychodynamic*. Alfred Adler (1870–1937) took issue with Freud's intrapsychic focus and developed his own interpersonal theory (Adler, 1931/1958). Adler also felt that all children felt inferior at a young age due to their dependence on others. He stated that the individual develops his or her own personal lifestyle as a way to manage and then overcome these feelings of inferiority (Adler, 1929). Adler also felt that birth order was a significant concept in how the individual functioned within his family. In addition, due to his focus on social systems, particularly the family, Adler is often seen as the father of modern family therapy. Carl Jung (1875–1961) felt Freud's concept of the unconscious was too negative, focusing only on sex and aggression. Jung's theory, in particular, was at variance with Freud's conceptualization of the unconscious. Jung's theory contained multiple concepts within his conceptualization of the unconsciousness, both positive and negative, these elements he felt were always striving for balance (Jung, 1911/1956).

Modern psychoanalysts follow Freud's original ideas but may modify his methods of analysis to fit the constraints of modern society. Modern analysts usually meet their patients once per week for at most 1 or 2 years. The four phases of psychoanalysis are usually condensed to lessen the time involved in analysis. The major component of modern analysis is the development of transference and its working through.

As was stated earlier, there are multiple forms of psychodynamic therapies, each of which originate within the tenets of psychoanalysis. Each form, however, has taken issue with a particular component of the theory and has created an alternative view of the alleviation of the patient's difficulties. The major differences between the various types of psychodynamic forms of therapy are the belief in an unconscious or its contents, that its contents often reflect inner behavior, and that the core of psychotherapy is the development of transference and its resolution. There are many other theorists which followed after Freud and the reader is referred to Corsini and Wedding (2010)[1] for a more thorough review of major theories.

Psychodynamic theories flourished in the period from the 1930s to the 1950s. In the 1950s, there began a feeling of unease within the therapeutic community regarding psychodynamic therapies. Many theorists, already trained, had issues with the tenets of the theory itself. Other researchers expressed dissatisfaction with the fact that psychodynamic therapies did not have sufficient research backing or that it appeared to be impossible to study the tenets of the theory in any type of scientific manner. Still, other critics stated that the theory was too negativistic, time consuming, and did not give clients any clear-cut skills to help them alleviate problems as they occurred in their lives.

Returning to our case study, Grant has many emotional issues which have occurred directly due to structural brain trauma or secondarily due to reactions to the changes within his life. Psychoanalysis, even as practiced in the modern day, does not appear to be the treatment of choice for his issues. Grant is aware of most of the causes of his difficulties, which may make a process of uncovering not appropriate for him. Grant also has expressed a lack of willingness to attend therapy and would probably benefit more from a type of therapy which is of shorter duration and more concrete and directive. Hence, the clinical neuropsychologist did not employ psychodynamic techniques when working with Grant.

---

[1] Corsini, R. J., & Wedding, D. (2010). Current Psychotherapies (10th ed.) Belmont, CA: Thomson-Wadsworth.

Behaviorism, the second force in psychology, originated as a form of learning theory in a laboratory setting and was then translated into methods of therapy. Early behaviorists were very clear that they did not believe in any form of unconscious processes and the only behaviors which could be dealt with in a therapy context were observable, countable activities. John Watson (1919) stated that "States of consciousness, like the so-called phenomenon of spiritualism, are not objectively verifiable and for that reason can never become data for science." At one point further along in time, Watson (1930) stated "Give me a dozen healthy infants, well-formed, and my own specified world to bring them up in and I'll guarantee to take any one at random and train him to become any type of specialist I might select—doctor, lawyer, artist, merchant, chief, and yes, even beggar-man and thief, regardless of his talents, penchants, tendencies, abilities, vocations, and race." The very strong statement made by Watson garnered him much praise but also a good deal of criticism. One of Watson's most ardent critics was British psychologist William McDougall (1871–1938) whose work focused on the instinctual basis of human behavior, a position which Watson denied as valid (Schultz, 1969). Other researchers took issue with Watson's dismissal of thought, emotion, and particularly free will (Schultz, 1969). Therapists, many trained in psychoanalytic methods, felt Watson's behaviorism was too simplistic and would only work when the subjects were animals or those of very low intelligence.

The basic theory and therapy methods of early behaviorism came from classical conditioning developed originally by Ivan Pavlov (1849–1936) and operant conditioning developed by John Watson and elaborated on by B. F. Skinner. The later introduction of cognitive–behavioral approaches came from the works of Albert Ellis (1913–2007) and Aaron Beck (1921 to present) who felt that pure behaviorism did not totally represent the totality of human experience and that thought and emotion were capable of being altered using the laws of learning. As will be seen, similar to the varieties of approaches to psychoanalysis, behavioral and cognitive–behavioral therapies have undergone changes as time has passed and have been marked by a diversity of viewpoints. When applied to therapy, behavioral and cognitive–behavioral therapies have garnered more research backing than most of the other forms of therapy.

In Russia, at the turn of the century, Ivan Pavlov, a Nobel laureate in physiology, established the foundations of classical conditioning. His work was predominately conducted using dogs as subjects. The basic paradigm for classical conditioning included the following: an **unconditioned stimulus** (US) caused an **unconditioned response** (UR) naturally without any learning. An example would be food powder (US) leads to salivation (UR) in a hungry dog without any experimental interference. The **conditioned stimulus** (CS) was then paired (or associated) with the US which over time produced a **conditioned response** (CR) which looked indistinguishable from the UR. An example would be a bell (CS) paired with food powder (US) which over time, with many pairings, produced salivation (CR) similar to the UR. The ability of the CS to elicit the CR diminishes in the absence of pairings. This diminishing connection is termed **extinction**. CRs are, therefore, not a necessarily permanent aspect of an organism's behavioral repertoire. The CR, however, would reappear in a weak form when the CS was presented alone after extinction. This recovery of response after extinction is referred to as **spontaneous recovery**. Once a CR has been conditioned to a CS, similar stimuli may elicit responses or what is called **stimulus generalization**. An example would be a child who was bitten by a large dog who would then be likely to respond with fear even to smaller dogs. The opposite occurs during **stimulus discrimination** when the organism learned to respond differently to stimuli that were distinct from the CS on some dimension. As may be becoming apparent, classical conditioning was a paradigm which easily explained the development of anxiety, particularly

unconditioned stimulus
a response that unconditionally, naturally, and automatically triggers a response

unconditioned response
an unlearned response that occurs naturally in response to a unconditioned stimulus

conditioned stimulus
a neutral stimulus that when paired with the unconditioned stimulus elicits a response indistinguishable from the original

conditioned response
a response that is indistinguishable from the unconditioned response which occurs in the presence of the conditioned stimulus

extinction
the lack of a response; behaviorally, it occurs with the lack of reinforcement or lack of association in classical conditioning

spontaneous recovery
the recovery of a response after extinction

stimulus generalization
after conditioning has been accomplished, similar stimuli may elicit a response

phobias, and then lent itself to treatment using counterconditioning methods such as systematic desensitization. Watson and Rayner (1920) conducted a classic study which could not be replicated now due to ethical issues which clearly showed the development of fear through classical conditioning. They placed a child, Albert, near a laboratory rat and then made a loud noise which caused Albert to cry. After several pairings Albert feared the rat when it was placed near him. His fear also generalized to other furry objects. Watson and Rayner did not make any effort to alleviate Albert's fears after the experiment. Fortunately, Mary Cover Jones, under Watson's direction, was able to recondition the child to not fear the stimulus but it took daily practice of reintroducing the feared animal at closer and closer distances (Marx & Hillix, 1973).

At the same time that Pavlov was working on the tenets of classical conditioning, E. L. Thorndike (1874–1949) was also pioneering research on animal learning in the United States. Thorndike used cats attempting to escape from puzzle boxes as subjects. Thorndike's cats learned an association between a **stimulus** and a **response** or a stimulus–response (S–R) connection. The cats learned that the appropriate response led to the reward of escape from the puzzle boxes. The cats learned through **trial-and-error learning** or through random responding until they happened on the correct response. Thorndike referred to the relationship between behavior and its consequences as the **law of effect** (Thorndike, 1911). This law stated that if a response was followed by satisfying consequences, it becomes more probable, and if a response was followed by dissatisfying consequences, it becomes less probable to occur. Skinner took Thorndike's ideas a step further in order to analyze behavior experimentally. He manipulated the consequences of an organism's behavior in order to see the effect it had on subsequent behaviors. An **operant** was a behavior that was emitted by an organism designed to affect its environment. Operants were not elicited by specific stimuli as were classical conditioning behaviors. A **reinforcement contingency** was a consistent relationship between a response and the changes in the environment it produced. **Reinforcers** were any stimuli which when made contingent on a behavior occurring increased the probability of that behavior recurring. As we translate these principles into therapy, it is very important that the reinforcement be something applicable to the individual, as opposed to other species who tend to respond more universally to food or the cessation of pain. When a behavior is increased and followed by the delivery of an appetitive stimulus, such as food, the event was called **positive reinforcement**. When the behavior is followed by the removal of an aversive stimulus it was termed **negative reinforcement**. The principle of extinction also occurred in operant conditioning when a behavior no longer produced predictable consequences. A **punisher** was any stimulus that when it was made contingent on a response, the probability of that response over time decreases. Punishment was the delivery of an unpleasant outcome following a response. **Positive punishment** occurred when a behavior was followed by the delivery of an aversive stimulus. **Negative punishment** occurred when a behavior was followed by the removal of an appetitive stimulus. Schedules of reinforcement described not only when reinforcement was delivered but also the effect on a behavior, which was often crucial in therapy. **Partial reinforcement** occurred when not every behavior was followed by reinforcement. Schedules of partial reinforcement have major affects on behavior. **Fixed ratio (FR) schedules** deliver reinforcement after a certain number of responses. FR schedules lead to a high rate of responding because there was a direct relationship between responding and reinforcement, an example of this would be a vending machine. **Variable ratio schedules** deliver reinforcement after an average number of behaviors. These schedules generate the highest rate of responding and the greatest resistance to extinction. Gambling is thought to operate on this type of schedule. **Fixed interval schedules** deliver reinforcement after a certain amount of time. Behavior occurs less frequently at the beginning

trial-and-error learning
a type of learning that occurs after an organism has made random attempts at solving a problem

law of effect
behavior that is followed by favorable conditions will recur, behavior that is followed by unpleasant circumstances will not recur

operant
a behavior that has an effect on the environment

reinforcement contingency
a consistent relationship between a response and the changes in the environment it produced

reinforcer
if delivered contingent on a response, it increases the likelihood of the response reoccurring

positive reinforcement
when a behavior is followed by an appetitive stimulus and therefore increases

negative reinforcement
when a behavior is followed by the removal of an aversive stimulus

punisher
any stimulus that when made contingent on a response, decreases the occurrence of that response

partial reinforcement
a situation in which not every behavior is reinforced; it can be based on time or number of behaviors

fixed interval schedule
a reinforcement is delivered after a fixed period

FIGURE 13.2
Chart of major classical and operant
conditioning principles

CLASSICAL VS. OPERANT CONDITIONING

Operant Conditioning (R ← SRF)
- A **voluntary** response (R) is followed by a reinforcing stimulus (SRF).
- The voluntary response is more likely to be emitted by the organism.
- A reinforcer is any stimulus that increases the frequency of a behavior.
- To be a reinforcer, a stimulus must immediately follow the response and must be perceived as contingent upon the response.

Classical Conditioning (S ← R)
- An involuntary response (UCR) is preceded by a stimuli (UCS), or
- A stimulus (UCS) automatically triggers an **involuntary** response (UCR)
- A neutral stimulus (NS) associated with UCS automatically triggers a conditioned response.
- The NS becomes a conditioned stimulus (CS).

---

of the time period and quite frequently near the end. **Variable interval schedules** deliver reinforcement after an average period of time. This schedule generated a moderate but very stable response rate.

The principles of classical and operant conditioning (see Figure 13.2) are the basis for the three early forms of behavior therapy. Applied behavioral analysis was a direct extension of Skinner's (1953) radical behaviorism. It relied on the fundamental assumption of operant conditioning that behavior is a function of its consequences. Treatment procedures were based on altering relationships between behaviors and their consequences. Applied Behavior Analysis used reinforcement, punishment, extinction, stimulus control, and other procedures derived from laboratory research. Cognitive processes, including emotions, were not considered proper subjects for scientific analysis and hence not dealt with in a psychotherapeutic context.

An application of classical conditioning was the Neobehavioralistic Mediational Stimulus–Response (S–R) Model. The S–R model was meditational because it included intervening variables and hypothetical constructs. The S–R theorists had been particularly interested in anxiety, as stated previously, and developed techniques such as systematic desensitization and flooding. Private events, including imagery had been an integral part of this theory. The rationale was that covert processes followed the laws of learning that govern overt behaviors.

Social–Cognitive theory was an approach which rested on the theory that behaviors are based on three separate but interacting regulatory systems (Bandura, 1986). The three systems were external stimulus events, external reinforcement, and cognitive mediational processes. The inclusion of cognitive processes was a significant change from operant or classical conditioning approaches to psychotherapy. Psychological functioning, according to this view, involved a reciprocal interaction among three interacting sets of influences, behavior, cognitive processes, and environmental factors. In social–cognitive therapy, the person was the agent of change. The theory emphasized the human capacity for self-directed behavior change which was a very important concept for therapy.

Two theories, alluded to earlier, borrowed heavily from the social–cognitive approach. Aaron Beck developed a theory of Cognitive–Behavioral Therapy (CBT) which focused predominately on the laws of learning applied to thinking (Beck, Rush, Shaw, & Emery, 1979). He theorized that cognitive errors or cognitive distortions were the key elements which caused individuals to experience psychiatric distress. Beck began his work with depression and subsequently continued to apply his theory to anxiety disorders, personality disorders, and issues related to relationship difficulties. The key issue in the therapeutic process was to stop an escalation of nonproductive thinking which was related to a person's misperception of an event rather than how the event actually occurred. Albert Ellis, the founder of Rational Emotive Behavior Therapy (REBT), also developed a theory and therapy based on thinking as the primary cause of difficulty for the individual (Ellis, 1962). Ellis used the term *irrational thinking* for a style similar to Beck's misperception of events. Ellis's ABCDE approach to treatment involved the client being involved in an activating event (A) that lead to an emotional consequence (C). Ellis, however, taught the client that a belief (B) was really what lead to the event at C. Hence, the task of the therapist was to teach the client to dispute (D) the belief which then leads to a new and healthier emotion (E). The beliefs which Ellis referred to were absolutistic or all-or-none manners of thinking about events which caused a person to be upset when not necessary.

After a review of the various forms of behavioral and cognitive–behavioral theories it may appear that Grant would benefit from one or more of these approaches. The clinical neuropsychologist determined that his overall anxiety regarding changes in his abilities could be helped through the process of systematic desensitization developed from classical conditioning which involves relaxing in the presence of the anxiety producing stimuli. The clinical neuropsychologist also thought that Grant could also benefit from CBT or REBT to help him deal with his thinking style when he becomes upset, frustrated, or angry. Either type of therapy would help him look at the events which he feels are causing his emotions and try to develop cognitive coping skills to not feel as he does. The clinical neuropsychologist did not feel that Grant would benefit from any form of stimulus–response program because his difficulties were less behavioral in origin and more cognitive and emotional.

The third force in psychotherapy encompasses Humanistic and Humanistic–Existential theories. The main theorists which influenced others within this area were Carl Rogers (1902–1987) and Rollo May (1909–1994). The humanistic and existential theories were developed during the same period, roughly the 1950s, as the behavioral theories. The humanistic and existential theories, as a group, were opposed to the basic tenets of the psychoanalytic theories, particularly in terms of the unconscious, stages of development, and the lack of free will. Humanistic and existential theories were not deterministic and viewed the individual as capable of rising above his circumstances. The humanistic and existential theories were at variance with the behaviorists and cognitive behaviorists over their view of determinism which was based on contingencies or associations, their lack of focus on thoughts and feelings (except for the more cognitive theories), and their focus on only observable countable events. Maslow (1968) and Matson (1969) separately articulated six basic premises of humanistic psychology:

1. People's creative power is a crucial force, in addition to heredity and environment.
2. An anthropomorphic model of humankind is superior to a mechanomorphic model.
3. Purpose, rather than cause, is the decisive dynamic.
4. The holistic approach is more adequate than an elementaristic one.
5. It is necessary to take humans' subjectivity, their opinions and viewpoints, and their conscious and unconscious fully into account.
6. Psychotherapy is essentially based on a good human relationship. (Ansbacher, 1977)

Contrary to the beliefs held by many, much research has been accumulated on the humanistic types of therapy particularly the necessary qualities of the therapist perpetuated by Rogers.

organismic valuing process
a Rogerian concept; individual moves toward or away from events based on their effect on the individual's obtaining his or her needs or moving toward self-actualization

self-actualization
Roger's use of Maslow's concept; it refers to becoming the best or most fully functioning person that an individual is capable of becoming

conditions of worth
a Rogerian concept; it describes the rewards and punishments that society applies to an individual's behavior

unconditional positive regard
a Rogerian concept; one of the three qualities necessary for a therapist to provide effective therapy; implies positive feelings toward the client regardless of behaviors

empathy
one of Roger's three necessary conditions for a therapist; it implies that the therapist feels as close as possible to the feelings the client is experiencing

genuineness
one of Roger's three characteristics for a therapist; it implies that the therapist is a real person in the therapeutic situation

nondirective attitude
a Rogerian term; implies the manner in which the therapist acts during therapy that allows the client to explore issues that he or she feels are important

inauthentic living
an existential concept; it implies that an individual has given up his or her identity for the identity of the masses

normal anxiety
an existential concept; a normal reaction to change or risk taking that is synonymous with mental health

The Humanistic theory is best conceptualized by the Client-Centered Therapy approach of Carl Rogers. Rogers thought that each individual worked toward growth and development to become the best and most effective person possible. In Rogerian terms, the client used his or her **organismic valuing process** to move toward events or experiences which helped him or her become better or move toward **self-actualization**. As the individual makes choices, almost always he or she begins to encounter **conditions of worth**. Conditions of worth are the sanctions or rewards and punishments of the larger society with which we all must cope on the way to having our needs met. According to Rogers, a healthy individual was one who was able to continue to move forward toward self-actualization in spite of the conditions of worth. However, an individual who focused predominately on conditions of worth may have lost himself or herself or have forgotten his or her values. This individual was one whom Rogers stated may have developed psychiatric difficulties. According to Rogers, the goal of psychotherapy was to help the individual refocus on what he truly wanted and needed to continue on his journey toward self-actualization. In order to help the client, the therapist exhibited three qualities which Roger's felt were essential to the therapeutic process. The three qualities were **unconditional positive regard**, or the feeling of overall acceptance of the client, **empathy**, the ability to feel as close as one is able to the feelings of another and **genuineness** or **congruence**, the ability to be a real human being in the therapeutic process not a blank slate to be projected upon. Rogers stated that when these conditions were exhibited by the therapist, there would inevitably be therapeutic movement by the client (Rogers, 1951). Each of these components which Rogers stated were necessary has been subjected to extensive research and when the research was completed it was determined that all were necessary for effective therapy (Rogers, 1951). Rogers also described the **nondirective attitude** as reflecting the therapist's beliefs in the client's inherent growth tendency and right to self-determination. Research which looked at multiple forms of therapy also supports Rogers's view that the therapeutic relationship accounts for a significant percentage of the variance in positive outcome in all theoretical orientations toward psychotherapy (Asay & Lambert, 1999).

Existential psychotherapy adopted many of the concepts from humanistic psychotherapy and then added to them. One addition was distinguishing between inauthentic and authentic life. **Inauthentic living** was characterized by "the everyday," "publicness," "idle talk," and a living out of one's life as an "anonymous one" (Heidegger, 1927/1962). The inauthentic mode was typified by the "organizational man" (Whyte, 1956) or the company person who often gave up his or her individual identity in return for the identity of the larger whole. In the authentic mode, one acknowledged responsibility for one's life, in spite of the anxiety involved in so doing. In addition, the individual recognized his or her uniqueness and strove to not be one of the crowd but who he or she really was.

Existential therapists state that an inauthentic life may be at the root of psychiatric difficulties. They also discussed **normal anxiety**, which was experienced when one truly lived out one's life versus **neurotic anxiety** when the individual conformed and often lost oneself. The goal of therapy was to help an individual live a more authentic life and therefore more in tune with his or her wants and desires. In addition, the individual was also encouraged to trade his or her neurotic anxiety for normal anxiety.

Existentialism, whether in philosophy or psychotherapy, was the only area which focused on the fact that the unique quality of a person was his or her ability to contemplate his or her own demise. Rather than causing the individual to become depressed, it allowed the individual the freedom to make choices when he or she realized that his or her life was finite. Yalom (1981) also stated that there are four givens which, even if not addressed by the individual, were the substance of existence: death, freedom, isolation, and meaninglessness.

Existential therapy did not have a standard method of therapy but utilized Rogers's relational aspects (unconditional positive regard, empathy, and genuineness) to structure the therapeutic relationship. The issues discussed earlier were implemented in the therapy process as was seen necessary. After reviewing the major components of existential thought, it becomes clear that there has been little research backing for their concepts because they are more philosophical in nature than most other theories (Walsh & McElwain, 2002).

Returning to Grant, it is apparent that he could benefit from a humanistic type of therapy probably similar to that described by Carl Rogers. In a safe therapeutic environment, he may be able to discuss some of the issues which are currently of concern to him. Grant may work very well with a combination of client-centered and cognitive therapy. In the real world this is termed **eclecticism**, which is the combination of therapeutic techniques in order to fit the needs of the client. A large proportion of therapists use this sort of approach compared to those who consider themselves purists in subscribing to and using only one type of therapy for all patients. As discussed by Garfield and Bergin (1994) "the long dominance of the major theories is over and an eclectic position has taken precedence" (p. 7). In clinical neuropsychology, where the client's difficulties are so varied, most therapy is conducted from an eclectic point of view.

Emotional Difficulties With Central Nervous System Disease or Damage

After reviewing the various theories of psychotherapy, the reader should now have a grasp of the major schools of thought. However, as has been discussed throughout this text, individuals with central nervous system diseases or difficulties often require a nonstandardized or nontraditional approach to the treatment of their problems. This section addresses the most often exhibited emotional difficulties which those individuals with central nervous system problems face. The reader will also develop an understanding of how these particular issues are alleviated using nonstandard therapeutic modalities. Finally, when applicable, the aforementioned theories will be used.

DIFFICULTIES

The diagnostic process which the clinical neuropsychologist uses to diagnose difficulties from which a client is suffering has already been discussed. In review, the diagnosis is used for appropriate treatment planning and rehabilitation/therapy, communication among professionals, research, and insurance reimbursement. Any of the symptom sets with their appropriate labels may occur in individuals who have compromised central nervous systems and hence, individuals may be formally diagnosed with any of the difficulties listed. In addition, individuals who have suffered central nervous system insult or disease often have specific emotional issues which may not completely fit the diagnostic criteria. These emotional issues occur with enough frequency to be considered specific emotions which need to be evaluated carefully by the clinical neuropsychologist in each individual case. More research has been generated regarding emotional sequelae after head trauma, stroke, and various dementing processes than most other central nervous system difficulties. Throughout this section, it will be stressed which emotions tend to surface with or as a reaction to specific etiological factors.

ACQUIRED BRAIN INJURY

The first discussion of emotional reactions comes from the research on head injury also referred to as acquired brain injury. Prigatano (1992) has identified three important groups

neurotic anxiety
an existential concept; involves the anxiety that is felt by the individual who is afraid to take risks or remains in familiar circumstances because it feels safer

eclecticism
the use of many different styles or theories of therapy based on the needs of the client

of factors in the development of behavioral problems following brain injury. The first are organic factors related to the site, source, and, severity of injury and include emotional consequences such as impulsivity, distractibility, and cognitive difficulties. The second are related to the individual's reaction to change and are associated with feelings of loss, grief, and frustration. The third refers to characterological factors with particular attention to the person's premorbid level of behavior control, social interaction style, self-esteem, personal style, and history of motivation and achievement. A similar model was developed by Sbordone (1990) termed the P-I-E-O model. *P* stands for person and reflects important aspects of the person's history and personality style. *I* stands for injury and involves the specific physical, cognitive, and behavioral impairments resulting from the injury. *E* stands for environment in which the person is functioning and includes the social support network and the expectations and demands placed on the person. *O* stands for outcome and involves the history of successes and failures the person has experienced since the injury. Prigatano and Sbordone both state that each individual is different in how he or she responds to brain injury particularly due to the type of injury sustained, premorbid factors, social support, and various personal and situational variables. However, with all of this in mind, several emotions tend to surface due to the difficulty itself which includes impulsivity, lack of attention, concentration, difficulties, distractibility, changes in frustration tolerance, difficulties with socially acceptable behaviors, and lack of motivation. Emotions which the individual may begin to experience as he or she assesses his or her situation and abilities or disabilities and may begin to compare himself or herself to previous functioning include grief and loss, depression, and possible suicidal ideation, anxiety, and anger. These emotions are often referred to as secondary or reactive, as in a reaction to a particular situation. In response to the secondary emotions, the individual may act out with various self-destructive actions and/or chemical use and abuse.

The first set of emotions tends to occur rapidly with brain insult without the individual feeling that he or she has control over their appearance. For example, a person may begin to use rude or vulgar language without realizing the consequences of it or being aware that he or she did not speak in that manner in the past. In a case study in an earlier chapter, the individual began to express offensive sexual language to the staff and her family soon after receiving a traumatic brain injury and while still hospitalized. All of the individuals who were present during her outbursts were appalled by the graphic nature of her language. The client, at that point only a few days post-injury, did not appear to have conscious control of her behavior. Six months later, she had no recollection of any of her other behaviors done impulsively such as obtaining a wheelchair, going to the elevator, and getting lost because she did not know to which floor she needed to return. Another variable to consider is that the individual will behave and exhibit different emotions dependent on where he or she is in the recovery process. Those who recently received an injury are more likely to exhibit less controlled behaviors and emotions than those who received their injuries months ago. The same client exhibited impulsive behavior 6 months later by drinking excessively after being warned of the consequences. The difference, however, is after she experienced the ramifications of the incident, she decided that she could and would control the behavior. The goals of early therapy are to reduce the frequency and severity of impulsive behaviors in order to reduce the likelihood of further injury to self or others, to support basic care and treatment goals, and to not inadvertently reinforce inappropriate behaviors. At this point in the treatment process, the use of the principles of applied behavioral analysis is in order to place contingencies on behaviors. Consistency in relating to the patient by all those involved with care, from medical staff to family members, will help to structure the environment. Structure is important for the patient to make sense of a situation that may appear out-of-control or frightening. Consistency is also a cornerstone of behavioral treatment.

As the client improves and is further from the date of injury, CBT, as discussed earlier, is a good choice. CBT works particularly well with individuals diagnosed with head injury and who have a fair-to-good prognosis. The prognostic factor implies that the client will continue to progress with his or her thinking abilities which will be helpful if he or she is to benefit from any form of cognitive therapy. In summary, during the initial stages of head injury a focus on environmental management and behavioral intervention is appropriate, particularly if the individual had severe trauma. The next goal would be training compensatory and self-regulating strategies. The development of insight and awareness and working toward acceptance of permanent losses or changes in ability is appropriate once the individual has mastered behavioral goals. Another way to conceptualize the change in treatment is from an external locus of control over behavior to an internal locus of control. Hence, the clinical neuropsychologist would employ behavioral principles when in the external locus of control mode, and cognitive–behavioral strategies when in the internal locus of control mode. If the aforementioned circumstances are progressing very well and the client has the appropriate premorbid personality style, he or she may benefit from the use of client-centered or Rogerian style of therapy. Appropriate premorbid personality style implies that the client was a relatively well-adjusted individual pre-trauma or without suffering from a major mental illness.

One of the issues which occurs frequently with head-injured patients and which is often voiced by family is whether the behavior exhibited is deliberate or nondeliberate. This question is often raised when the outcome of the behavior is harmful or hurtful to another person. Very often, it is thought that behaviors exhibited early in the recovery process are not deliberate on the part of the client. As treatment progresses, the clinical neuropsychologist working with the patient may need to look at the person's premorbid way of handling emotions. In addition, Sohlberg and Mateer (2001) suggested several questions which the clinical neuropsychologist may need to explore as he or she works toward determining the deliberateness of the behavior and the most appropriate treatment approach.

- Is the person confused and not understanding what is expected of him or her?
- Is the person easily distracted and/or forgetful?
- Is the person potentially able to perform an expected behavior but sometimes is inadequately trained or supported in doing so?
- Is the person adequately motivated to participate?
- Is the person fearful, angry, or depressed and is this preventing him or her from focusing on the task at hand?
- Is the person avoiding situations that are frustrating, painful, or boring?
- Is the person getting enough sleep? Does the person have ample rest periods?

Grant's case of multiple concussions, as stated earlier, clearly fits within the topic of acquired brain injury. Grant's clinical neuropsychologist already decided to employ an eclectic approach to therapy using the relational atmosphere of Rogerian therapy to make Grant comfortable and feel in control of the session. The clinical neuropsychologist also employed systematic desensitization to help Grant alleviate his anxiety and cognitive techniques to help him cope with feelings of not living up to his premorbid potential. In addition, the clinical neuropsychologist decided to inquire regarding the answers to the aforementioned questions particularly in relationship to Grant's self-perceived schoolwork difficulties. After reviewing each question with Grant, the clinical neuropsychologist was able to make some suggestions to help Grant succeed in school and also gave him some information to pass on to his teachers if he so desired. Grant was rather hesitant to let more people know of his disability but after this discussion, he decided it could greatly help his schoolwork. In terms of answers to the questions, Grant often felt he did not clearly understand what was expected of him. The clinical neuropsychologist suggested that he request a written guide or template to help him with each assignment. Grant stated that he was somewhat distracted and forgetful, which was already being addressed within his rehabilitative treatment plan. Grant stated that he was quite able to perform each activity asked of him. He also stated that he was motivated because he wanted to feel normal within his circumstances. Grant admitted that he was getting depressed and having never experienced the emotion before, did not know how to cope. The clinical neuropsychologist made a referral for Grant to discuss his symptoms with a psychiatrist and complete a medication evaluation. The clinical neuropsychologist also used cognitive–behavioral therapy to help with Grant's depression. Even though situations were not easy for him, Grant stated that he had attended all of his classes regardless if they were boring or not. Finally, Grant admitted that he was having a large problem with sleep and fatigue. He had been told that traumatic brain injury would increase his fatigue level but he had been pushing himself to maintain his premorbid schedule. He also was becoming depressed, which interfered with getting to sleep and staying asleep which led him to admit that he had tried several ways to induce sleep including alcohol, marijuana, and over-the-counter sleeping pills. He had been warned about these substances but once he returned to school, he felt pressured to resort to old ways of coping. The clinical neuropsychologist suggested that Grant discuss his sleep issues with the psychiatrist. In conclusion, the clinical neuropsychologist felt that these questions helped further focus the goals of therapy and also gave Grant information to share with his school.

STROKE AND CARDIOVASCULAR DIFFICULTIES

A somewhat different picture occurs with the emotional ramifications of stroke and other cardiovascular difficulties. To begin the discussion, one of the salient issues is the difference in demographics. As was stated earlier, head injury is most common in the 15–30 year old range and far more common in males. Many times, the reason for the head injury is some form of athletic or possibly impulsive type behavior which is known to occur within an age bracket that tends to feel invulnerable. This implies two issues that are involved in treatment planning. A younger age is good prognostically in terms of cortical recovery but could also be detrimental if the head injury is severe and the individual will remain in that capacity for the rest of his or her life. The second issue relates to the premorbid personality dynamics in a person who may be quite daring. This particular personality style may be a catalyst to return to his or her lifestyle quickly and therefore serve as motivation to participate in rehabilitation. On the other hand, the same personality style may impede rehabilitation and foster development of a defeatist attitude. A different pattern tends to occur with individuals who have suffered a stroke. In terms of demographics, this type of difficulty is more likely to occur in midlife or later life with the majority of strokes occurring in individuals older than the age of 60. The reasons for this tend to relate to diet, exercise, and other lifestyle factors which may cause an accumulation of risk factors which predispose an individual to develop a stroke. As is the case with head injury, more males than females are diagnosed with this difficulty. However, changes in societal demands and life experience have altered the number of stroke cases in females. In the past, as has been the case with heart attacks, females have been treated somewhat differently than males. Currently, physicians are aware that stroke and heart attack affect both genders but that the symptoms may appear quite different in each gender.

In the case of stroke, many victims state that they had little or no warning of the impending event. Other individuals state that there was some initial numbness 1 or 2 days before the stroke to which they had not paid attention. Famed choreographer Agnes DeMille (1905–1993) described her stroke in the following way. She was in the dressing room of the Hunter College Playhouse in New York with a few members of her dance company about to sign the contract of a replacement dancer when, suddenly, she was not able to write. She stated that she felt no pain and was not sure exactly when the stroke occurred. She felt as if a chalk-line had been drawn down her face and body dividing it in two, one side worked fine the other was nonfunctional. She was amazed that it could happen with no warning whatsoever and stated "when your life is altered you'd expect a thunderclap or something . . . but nothing . . . this is deadly . . . very deadly" (The Brain Series, Public Broadcasting System, 1984). Agnes DeMille was able to recover quite well due to her determination and as she described "it was what I had learned as a trained dancer, I did what I had to do no matter how hard it was" (Public Broadcasting System). Not all stroke victims have this level of drive and determination.

When stroke is diagnosed medically, it is most often referred to as a left hemisphere or right hemisphere stroke, with there hardly ever being a combination of the two. Either type of stroke usually causes the individual to experience some form of paralysis on the opposite side of the body. Left hemisphere strokes very often involve language as the most salient symptom and aphasia of various forms often occurs. Right hemisphere strokes often cause difficulties with recognition of objects or other types of nonverbal difficulties.

Early after the onset of the stroke and similar to head-injured patients, individuals may exhibit inappropriate behaviors or verbiage, if able to speak, over which the person appears to have no control over. After a period of time, as the person progresses in treatment, and the difficulties which remain residual to the stroke become evident, the person's emotional reactions may change. Research shows that those individuals with left hemisphere strokes tend to have a more catastrophic reaction to their circumstance than those with right hemisphere strokes. Goldstein (1948) described the catastrophic reaction of the patient as an intense emotional reaction to the realization of the aphasic consequences of their stroke. In contrast, Gianotti (1988) referred to the indifference of right hemisphere patients, particularly those with right posterior lesions who also showed signs of the neglect and **anosognosia**. Anosognosia is an indifference to impairment particularly in the contralateral side to the infarct. He proposed that this indifference to their condition caused an unrealistic appraisal of their situation, resulting in a more positive outlook. Also researched has been the depression exhibited in an almost exaggerated fashion in left hemisphere stroke patients versus right hemisphere patients who tend to deny depressive symptoms. Ross (1981) cites evidence of right hemisphere patients who deny depression at the same time may be exhibiting excessive and unwarranted laughing and crying. These types of reports suggest that with stroke patients, measures of emotions should often be accompanied by reports from significant others.

Davidson and Irwin (1999) suggest an anatomical explanation for the difference in reactions between those with left versus right hemisphere damage. They propose that the anterior regions and the amygdala of the left hemisphere support positive emotions and approach behaviors, while the right hemisphere supports negative emotions and withdrawal behaviors. Arguing that the left hemisphere subserves positive emotions while the right hemisphere subserves negative emotions is often referred to as the **valence hypothesis**. Many studies with stroke patients lend support for the valence hypothesis stating that the majority of left hemisphere stroke patients rated themselves as more depressed than did right hemisphere stroke patients (Gasparrini, Satz, Heilmann, & Coolidge, 1978; Gianotti, 1993; Robinson, Kubos, Starr, Rao, & Price, 1984). The research tends to conclude that the valance hypothesis for stroke studies is not straightforward. Issues of choice of subject and method of assessment when denial of symptoms and lack of insight are present are problematic. However, overall, there are indications that increased anxiety and other types of exaggerated emotional response may be a feature of left hemisphere stroke.

In summary, similar to head-injured patients, those who have sustained any form of stroke tend to have emotional reactions soon after the onset of stroke which appears to be out of their control or outside of their normal range of affect. In these circumstances, principles of applied behavioral analysis to control these inappropriate behaviors appear to be the best possible option. As time passes, differences appear in felt emotions and their behavioral sequelae between those individuals with left versus right hemisphere stroke. Neither type of stroke appears to allow the individual to experience an accurate representation of their true strengths and weakness. At this point in time, cognitive–behavioral therapy may be applicable for the client with the goal being an accurate appraisal of the circumstances of one's life.

It is very clear that Grant did not suffer from a stroke. However, it would be appropriate for the clinical neuropsychologist to reiterate the lifestyle factors which relate to the development of a stroke, particularly as they apply to Grant's life. As an example of how therapy worked well, Agnes DeMille's case used not only her personal determination but also behavioral goals to deal with paralysis and cognitive–behavioral techniques to help her accept realistically the abilities and disabilities which she had.

CORTICAL AND SUBCORTICAL DEMENTIAS

The demographics for the occurrence of dementia are more similar to stroke than to head injury. The majority of individuals are in mid-to-late life with a preponderance of males. However, as one looks at the average life expectancy of the two genders, it becomes evident that in the later years, females outnumber males and therefore in sheer numerical terms, more females develop dementia later in life.

The emotional responses of individuals who suffer from dementia are almost the opposite of what happens to those who suffer from stroke or head injury. Early emotions which occur with the dementing process often relate to the perception of changes in one's functioning and loss of ability. Hence, in the first two stages of the dementing process, the individual has much more insight than is the case later. Depression, therefore, is likely to occur much earlier for those who suffer from dementia. The clinical neuropsychologist could employ cognitive–behavioral techniques to help the individual cope with depression while he is still intellectually more intact.

As time passes and the individual progresses into the later stages of dementia, insight and awareness tend to diminish. Behavioral inhibition of various emotions also tends to dissipate. Hence, the reverse of the use of behavioral principles from head injury or stroke is the case in the situation when the client is suffering from dementia.

As was the case with the discussion of stroke, Grant clearly does not fit the clinical picture of an individual with a dementing process. However, because the role of traumatic brain injury as a risk factor for developing Alzheimer's disease is still controversial, it behooves the clinical neuropsychologist to discuss this with Grant. Many studies have reported a significantly higher incidence of traumatic brain injury history for Alzheimer's patients (Lye & Shores, 2000; Mortimer, French, Hutton, & Schuman, 1985). Risk of developing Alzheimer's disease after a severe traumatic brain injury is greatest for subjects lacking the Apo E4 allele (Guo et al., 2000).

In conclusion to this section regarding emotional reactions in those individuals with central nervous system diseases or difficulty, there appears to be some similarities across problems which then leads to some general advice regarding psychotherapy. In all of the difficulties, there tends to be two types of emotional problems, those which are solely due to biological factors and emotions which have at least a partial psychological origin, particularly when insight and awareness of one's disabilities is evident. At times, an individual will also act out as in the use of substances as he or she becomes aware of his or her deficits.

For the majority of difficulties, the biological factors which cause emotions, particularly outbursts that appear to be out of the individual's control, tend to occur near the beginning of the difficulty (i.e., soon after a head injury or the onset of stroke). As with anything discussed within clinical neuropsychology, there are exceptions to this statement which in this case are the various cortical and subcortical dementias in which the more out-of-control emotions occur later in the disease process. Regardless, when the actual out-of-control emotions occur, the most appropriate type of therapeutic intervention for the clinical neuropsychologist to use are principles of operant conditioning or applied behavioral analysis. In this process, it is important to delineate the specific behaviors in question, the type of contingencies involved and the desired behavioral outcome. As the time has passed, most of the difficulties and the out-of-control behaviors have lessened. Whether this is due to behaviors progressing or actual changes in brain structure and function, it may be time for other forms of psychotherapy. CBT or REBT may be very helpful when working with individuals as they assess their strengths and weaknesses and compare these to their perception of their own premorbid functioning. The goal is to look at what the situation truly is versus the exaggerations which often happens as one's life is altered. Again, this may not be an applicable sequence when cortical or subcortical dementias are considered. However, the same principles of CBT or REBT may be used but it would happen within stages one or two of the illness. Depression, which is often apparent as one sees one's life altered, tends to respond very well to the insights of the aforementioned therapies (Beck et al., 1979). If this issue does not respond or the individual is not receptive to this form of therapy, antidepressant medication has been proven to be very effective.

Once the clinical neuropsychological senses that the patient has developed more behavioral control over out-of-control behaviors and when the patient has managed a more realistic view of his or her situation, it may be appropriate to introduce a more humanistic or existential type of psychotherapy. Many individuals find a discussion of the topics often covered within existential therapy to be helpful particularly if the individual is older and already facing issues of mortality.

In addition to there being many types of emotions which occur and psychotherapies which are more applicable to each type, there are other general issues which the clinical neuropsychologist must keep in mind throughout therapy. The first is that change is always difficult for everyone and with central nervous system difficulties, it is a major factor. Secondly, one's self-esteem, particularly in Western cultures, is often tied to one's abilities. As an individual develops various disabilities, the effects on self-esteem or the patient's sense of self must be kept in mind. Thirdly, similar to an individual suffering with grief, very often, social support occurs early in the process and then begins to dwindle as time passes. The clinical neuropsychologist should encourage clients to be as social as possible. Finally, because each case is different, the clinical neuropsychologist needs to consider all of the issues discussed in earlier chapters which pertain to voice tone, and so forth, to accommodate the particular patient.

Summary

The chapter began with a case study of a college aged male who suffered from multiple concussions. He was aware of his deficits and willing to begin cognitive rehabilitation. However, there were several emotional issues which surfaced as a reaction to his head trauma. He was not amenable to individual therapy without a lot of coaching.

Before any discussion of therapy, the ethical issues which are the cornerstone of therapy were discussed. The ethical issues are particularly salient with individuals who have central nervous system difficulty.

The chapter focuses on the place of individual therapy within clinical neuropsychology. The major schools of therapy, psychodynamic, behavioral, cognitive-behavioral, and humanistic were discussed with variants on each approach. In addition, the major emotional difficulties that tend to occur with central nervous system difficulties were addressed. Each difficulty was addressed using particular therapeutic techniques.

Questions for Further Study

1. If a client is resistant to expressing the emotional sequelae of central nervous system difficulties, how forceful should the clinical neuropsychologist be in suggesting therapy? Explain.
2. Under what type of circumstances is individual therapy appropriate and when should family or group therapy be considered?
3. The ethics of therapy are very important, describe circumstances where the ethical provisions for the client change with central nervous system difficulties.

References

Abraham, K. (1924). The influence of oral erotism on character formation. *Selected papers of Karl Abraham* (Vol. 1, pp. 393–496). London: Hogarth Press.

Adler, A. (1929). *The practice and theory of individual psychology*. New York: Harcourt, Bruce & World.

Adler, A. (1958). *What life should mean to you*. New York: Capricorn Books. (Original work published 1931)

Ansbacher, H. L. (1977). Individual psychotherapy. In R. J. Corsini (Ed.), *Current psychotherapies*. Itasca, IL: F. E. Peacock.

Asay, T. P., & Lambert, M. J. (1999). The empirical case for the common factors in therapy: Quantitative findings. In M. A. Hubble, B. I. Duncan & S. D. Miller (Eds.), *The heart and soul of change: What works in therapy* (pp. 23–55). Washington, DC: American Psychological Association.

Bandura, A. (1986). *Social foundations of thought and action: A social cognitive theory*. Englewood Cliffs, NJ: Prentice-Hall.

Beck, A. T., Rush, A. J., Shaw, B. F., & Emery, G. (1979). *Cognitive therapy of depression*. New York: Guilford Press.

Corsini, R. J., & Wedding, D. (2010). *Current psychotherapies* (9th ed.). Belmont, CA: Thomson-Wadsworth.

Davidson, R. J., & Irwin, W. (1999). The functional neuroanatomy of emotion and affective style. *Trends in Cognitive Sciences, 3*, 11–21.

Ellis, A. (1962). *Reason and emotion in psychotherapy*. Secaucus, NJ: Citadel.

Garfield, S. L., & Bergin, A. E. (Eds.). (1994). The effectiveness of psychotherapy. In *Handbook of psychotherapy and behavior change* (p. 7). New York: Wiley.

Gasparrini, W. G., Satz, P., Heilmann, K. M., & Coolidge, F. (1978). Hemispheric asymmetries of affective processing as determined by the Minnesota Multiphasic Personality Inventory. *Journal of Neuropsychology, Neurosurgery and Psychiatry, 41*, 470–473.

Gianotti, G. (1988). Disorders of emotions and affect in patients with unilateral brain damage. In F. Boller & J. Giratman (Eds.), *Handbook of neuropsychology* (Vol. 3, pp. 345–361). Amsterdam: Elsevier.

Gianotti, G. (1993). Emotional and psychosocial problems after brain injury. *Neuropsychological Rehabilitation, 3*(3), 259–277.

Goldstein, K. (1948). *Language and language disturbances.* New York: Grune and Stratton.

Guo, Z., Cupples, L. A., Kurz, A., Auerbach, S. H., Volicer, L., Chui, H., et al. (2000). Head injury and the risk of AD in the MIRAGE study. *Neurology, 54,* 1316–1323.

Heidegger, M. (1962). *Being and time* (J. Macquarrie & E. Robinson, Trans.). New York: Basic Books. (Original work published 1927)

Jung, C. G. (1956). *The psychology of the unconscious: Revised as symbols of transformation. Collected works* (Vol. 6). Princeton, NJ: Princeton University Press. (Original work published 1911)

Klein, M., & Tribich, D. (1981). Freud's blindness. *Colloquium, 2*(2)–*3*(1), 52–59.

Lambert, M. J. & Bergin, A. E. (Ed.). (1994). The effectiveness of psychotherapy. In S. L. Garfield (Ed.), *Handbook of psychotherapy and behavior change* (pp. 143–149). New York: Wiley.

Luborsky, E. B., O'Reilly-Landry, M., & Arlow, J. A. (2008). Psychoanalysis. In R. J. Corsini & D. Wedding (Eds.), *Current psychotherapies* (pp. 15–60). Belmont, CA.: Thomson-Wadsworth.

Lye, T. C., & Shores, F. A. (2000). Traumatic brain injury as a risk factor for Alzheimer's disease: A review. *Neuropsychology Review, 10,* 115–129.

Marx, M. H., & Hillix, W. A. (1973). *Systems and theories in psychology.* New York: McGraw-Hill.

Maslow, A. H. (1968). *Toward a psychology of being* (2nd ed.). Princeton, NJ: Van Nostrard.

Masson, J. M. (1984). *The assault on truth: Freud's suppression of the seduction theory.* New York: Farrar, Straus & Giroux.

Matson, F. W. (1969). Whatever became of the third force? *American Association of Humanistic Psychology Newsletter, 6*(1), 14–15.

Mortimer, J. A., French, L. R., Hutton, J. T., & Schuman, L. M. (1985). Head injury as a risk factor for Alzheimer's disease. *Neurology, 35,* 264–267.

Prigatano, G. (1992). Personality disturbances associated with traumatic brain injury. *Journal of Consulting and Clinical Psychology, 60,* 360–368.

Public Broadcasting System. (1984). The Brain. *The enlightened machine.* Burlington, VT: PBS.

Rehabilitation Act of 1973. 93rd Congress, H. R. 8070, Pub. L. No. 93–112, (1973).

Robinson, R. G., Kubos, K. L., Starr, L. B., Rao, K., & Price, T. R. (1984). Mood disorders in stroke patients: Importance of location of lesion. *Brain, 107,* 81–93.

Rogers, C. P. (1951). *Client-centered therapy.* Boston: Houghton-Mifflin.

Ross, E. D. (1981). The aprosodias. Functional-anatomic organization of the affective components of language in the right hemisphere. *Archives of Neurology, 38,* 561–569.

Sbordone, R. (1990). Psychotherapeutic treatment of the client with traumatic brain injury: A conceptual model. In J. S. Kreutzer & P. Wehman (Eds.), *Community integration following traumatic brain injury* (pp. 125–138). Baltimore: Paul H. Brookes.

Schultz, D. P. (1969). *A history of modern psychology.* New York: Academic Press.

Skinner, B. F. (1953). *Science and human behavior.* New York: Macmillan.

Sohlberg, M. M., & Mateer, C. A. (2001). *Cognitive rehabilitation: An integrative neuropsychological approach.* New York: Guilford Press.

Thorndike, E. L. (1911). *Animal intelligence: Experimental studies.* New York: Macmillan.

Walsh, R. A., & McElwain, B. (2002). Existential psychotherapies. In D. J. Cain & J. Seeman (Eds.), *Humanistic psychotherapies* (pp. 253–278). Washington, DC: American Psychological Association.

Watson, J. B. (1918). *Behaviorism.* New Brunswick, NJ: Transaction. (Original work published 1924)

Watson, J. B. (1919). *Psychology from the standpoint of a behaviorist.* Philadelphia: J.B. Lippincott Company.

Watson, J. B. (1930). *Behaviorism* (revised edition). Chicago: University of Chicago Press.

Watson, J. B., & Rayner, R. R. (1920). Conditioned emotional reactions. *Journal of Experimental Psychology, 3,* 1–14.

Whyte, W. H. (1956). *The organization man.* Garden City, NY: Doubleday, Anchor Books.

Yalom, I. (1981). *Existential psychotherapy.* New York: Basic Books.

Family and Group Therapy

14

Learning Objectives

After reading this chapter, the student should be able to understand:
- Family dynamics and the ethical considerations involved in family therapy
- The various schools of thought in family therapy including each one's focus and goals
- Psychoeducational versus psychotherapeutic family therapy approaches in relation to treating individuals with central nervous system difficulties
- The ethical considerations of group therapy vs. individual and family therapy
- The various stages and types of group therapy and how and why they are used

Topical Outline

- Family Therapy
- Group Therapy

Renee is a 14-year-old White female. She was having difficulties with other children who had been bullying and making fun of her at school. The school counselor felt that many of her behaviors which led her to being teased were not under her control. Renee came to the attention of a child guidance center through a school referral. She was then referred from the child guidance center psychologist for neuropsychological evaluation and treatment.

The child guidance center psychologist evaluated Renee through an interview and a collateral interview with her mother. The two interviews indicated that Renee had multiple verbal tics and motor mannerisms which she did not appear able to control. Vocal difficulties began as small, almost insignificant sounds while in elementary school for which Renee was teased by the other children. Her parents did not understand the reason for her difficulties with the other students and punished her for her alleged misbehavior. As she began middle school, Renee began to have more serious difficulties and other students began to berate her and call her a "troublemaker." Renee joined a group of friends who also felt as if they were outcasts from the main social group. The school counselor sent a message to her parents that Renee was at a point where she had joined a group of adolescents who were known troublemakers and the counselor was afraid for her safety and her future.

During a parent–teacher conference held when Renee was 13, the homeroom teacher stated that her grades were very poor and she was in danger of suspension. Renee's father was very angry and felt that Renee had gotten into trouble in order to get attention. Renee's mother, who had observed the progression of Renee's vocal mannerisms and motor mannerisms, was more sympathetic and felt that Renee may need more support than punishment. Renee's 16-year-old brother, Brandon, felt embarrassed by his sister. Brandon stated that now that Renee was getting near the age for senior high school, he wished she would attend a different high school than he did.

The child guidance center psychologist referred Renee to the clinical neuropsychologist. Given all of this preliminary information and after reviewing medical and school records, the clinical neuropsychologist decided that he would begin the evaluation by interviewing each family member. He also sent behavioral rating scales to the school to be completed by Renee's teachers. The clinical neuropsychologist began the interviews with Renee. She was somewhat shy in the interview situation and appeared to feel that she was the identified patient. The **identified patient** is a term often used for the individual who is the reason a family is referred for family therapy. She was dressed all in black, including T-shirt, slacks, and tennis shoes, with pierced earrings that were reminiscent of the peace signs of the 1960s and a cross for a necklace. She was clean and well kempt but had very long hair, which was not the current style for her age group. She sat with very good posture and was very attentive to the questions which were asked of her. The clinical neuropsychologist was impressed with the contrast between the clothes she wore and the physical presence she presented. As Renee spoke, she exhibited various tics, twitches, and yawned frequently. When more difficult topics, such as her relationship with her father were discussed, she made guttural vocal sounds, which she tried to mask by coughing. Renee stated that she had a normal early life until she began second grade. At that point, she began to have various twitches and other mannerisms that she was not able to control. She hid these as best she could but occasionally, her mother or brother would notice. Her mother tried to help her decrease them and said they reminded her of Renee's great uncle. Her mother also stated that she should hide them from others, including her father, because people would not understand. Renee's brother Brandon behaved cruelly and made fun of her every chance he could. Renee stated that during elementary school she could control the mannerisms better than at the present time. While in elementary school, she had close friends who did not make fun of her. Middle school was different because there were many more kids and cliques had formed based on looks, family income, drug use, and so forth. Renee indicated that she tried to focus on

identified patient
the family member with the presenting symptom; the person who initially seeks treatment or for whom treatment is sought

her schoolwork but the stress of being bullied caused her tics to worsen. In desperation, she found it easiest to "hang out" with the kids who were considered the "losers." In order to be accepted into this group, Renee had changed her style in clothes. She stated that she had not used any form of drugs nor engaged in sexual behaviors but her father did not believe her. She was also aware that her brother was seen as "perfect" in her father's eyes. Renee said that through all of her difficulties, she secretly felt that her mother was her best friend and took her side against her brother and father.

Renee's mother, Mrs. Summit, gave a very detailed history of Renee's prenatal and postnatal development. Mrs. Summit stated that she had a very normal full-term pregnancy with Renee. Postnatally Renee achieved all of the developmental milestones at the appropriate times. It was not until second grade that she noticed that Renee had any type of vocal or motor tic. These mannerisms were initially small and easy to dismiss except when Renee was nervous or stressed. As time went by, Mrs. Summit had helped Renee cover up for these difficulties by drawing attention to her study behavior or other activities. By the seventh grade it was apparent that there was no longer any way to protect Renee from the bullying of the other kids. Mrs. Summit was very worried about Renee's self-esteem and her safety with her group of friends. She was also very concerned because her husband blamed Renee for the tics, twitches, and vocal mannerisms stating that she was using these behaviors to get attention away from her brother.

The interview with Renee's father was very short and to the point. Mr. Summit believed his daughter was deliberately misbehaving at school, making poor choices in friends, and deliberately trying to embarrass him and his family. He did not want to have social events at their home when their daughter was present because he was embarrassed about her appearance and behavior. Mr. Summit was not comfortable talking with the clinical neuropsychologist and felt this was another attempt by Renee and her mother to disrupt his very busy work schedule.

Renee's brother Brandon was also not interested in speaking with the clinical neuropsychologist. He stated that his sister was "weird," "nuts," and an embarrassment to him and his family. He felt, just as his father, that Renee was trying to obtain some of his attention, which he rightly deserved because he was the smart and competent child in the family.

After gathering all of the interview information, the clinical neuropsychologist decided that a battery of neuropsychological tests would assist in diagnosis. The tests would also help answer the question whether Renee was fabricating her difficulties or whether she had some form of central nervous system difficulty. The clinical neuropsychologist's suspicion was the latter.

Intellectual assessment revealed that Renee had a measured IQ in the Above Average range. Her IQ score was corroboration of her early school grades before she reached middle school. Memory assessment did not reveal any type of deficit. The remainder of selected neuropsychological assessment tools did not reveal any form of difficulty. Personality tests, however, indicated the presence of anxiety, self-esteem issues, and a developing low-grade depression. Throughout all of the testing, Renee appeared to be doing her very best. However, she also exhibited significant motor and vocal tics and twitches. As she tried to contain these mannerisms, they only appeared to get worse.

The clinical neuropsychologist suspected that Renee was suffering from Tourette's disorder. Although more often seen in males than females, the clinical neuropsychologist felt that Renee was not able to control the behaviors in question and that they must be neurological in origin. The clinical neuropsychologist was also aware that Tourette's disorder has a genetic component and Mrs. Summit had made a reference to Renee's behavior being similar to behaviors exhibited by one of her great uncles. In order to be absolutely certain of the diagnosis and to be able to work with Renee's father who was quite skeptical, the clinical neuropsychologist made a referral to a prominent local neurologist for evaluation. As the clinical neuropsychologist had predicted, the neurologist confirmed that it was his best judgment that Renee was suffering from Tourette's disorder and should be treated for this.

Tourette's disorder is a neurological difficulty involving a pattern of involuntary facial and motor tics. Tourette's disorder and other tic-related disorders are transmitted within families and, *although thought to be genetic, the precise mode of transmission is not known. The type of the disorder or its severity may be different from one generation to another and modified by nongenetic factors. Individuals with Tourette's disorder are at greater risk for attention deficit/hyperactivity disorder (ADHD). However, those individuals who do not exhibit tic-related behaviors but who are treated with stimulants may see the appearance of tic symptoms. In Renee's case, the genetic transmission appears evident through her mother's account of her uncle's behaviors. A comorbid diagnosis of ADHD does not fit Renee's symptom pattern nor has she been treated with stimulants. A second difficulty which may also occur with Tourette's disorder is obsessive–compulsive disorder. Again, it did not appear that Renee was exhibiting any symptoms of this difficulty. The treatment for Tourette's disorder contains multiple components. Behavior therapy is often used to help the individual identify triggers and respond with alternative behaviors. Cognitive–behavioral treatment helps to alleviate anxiety, which is often an exacerbating factor. Family therapy is particularly applicable as many individuals have family members who do not understand this type of seemingly uncontrollable difficulty and feel that the patient is producing behaviors to garner attention or to be otherwise problematic. Cognitive rehabilitation is used to help with any deficits which surface during assessment.*

The clinical neuropsychologist felt that a combination of treatment approaches would help Renee and included them in Renee's treatment plan. Individual therapy to help her discuss her anxiety and other concerns was suggested. Behavioral techniques were included within individual therapy to help her to ascertain any trigger events and develop alternative behaviors. A psychiatric referral to assist with mediation management of her symptoms was made. In addition, due to the family dynamics, it was strongly suggested that the family partake of family therapy to help understand Renee's difficulties and stop the shame and blame interactions which had surfaced within the family unit. Cognitive rehabilitation was not suggested given the results of the neuropsychological evaluation which suggested that Renee did not have any significant cognitive or memory deficits.

Introduction

In this chapter family and group therapy are the topics. The goal of the chapter is not to present the reader with enough knowledge to become a practitioner but to allow the reader to have enough basic knowledge to understand the diverse forms of therapy. As was the case with individual therapy, there are specific ethical issues which will be discussed as well as differences in the setting and other factors when there is more than one client. Within family therapy, in particular, there will be a discussion of the various patterns and constellations occurring in a family. Examples of types of families include single- versus two-parent families, heterosexual- versus homosexual-parent families, parents from two divorced families joined together, and parents who have a combination of biological and adopted children. In addition to the form a family may take will be a discussion of what makes a normal family versus a dysfunctional family. Family and group therapy each have various dominant schools of thought which will be covered. In addition, the issues which are most pertinent for central nervous system difficulties will be explored. Somewhat different than the discussion of individual therapy is the format of family and group therapy modalities. Family therapy may be utilized with or without the client having central nervous system difficulties being present. The reason for each circumstance will be explained but generally relates to educational versus therapeutic functions. In group therapy, the client is usually present in the setting and the role of the group is often supportive or confrontive regarding the patient's behaviors. Group therapy is often composed of individuals with similar central nervous system difficulties.

Family Therapy

It has often been stated that all individuals are born into some form of family (even those who are adopted) and that the family often determines how an individual understands or copes with events. Within a family, each person experiencing the very same event may feel that the event has occurred differently. If each family member experiences a situation differently then he or she may relate to each other differently as a situation develops within the family. This difference in perspective within a family group was the impetus for Adler's work with birth order. This example of differences in perspective within a family illustrates one of the major issues which often occur within a family.

Historically, family therapy as a form of psychotherapy, developed later than did individual therapy. The beginning dates are usually in the 1950s. Schools of family therapy developed as therapists saw a basic lack of treatment success with certain patients. These patients would often make initial psychotherapeutic progress only to regress when they returned to their family unit. Hence, the idea of the sick family unit began to develop as a fundamental concept. As these ideas began to circulate and challenge the prevailing point of view, it began to be seen as a paradigm shift or a change in belief system. The previous way of thinking in which the focus of treatment was the individual began to be replaced by the focus being on an identified patient who was viewed as manifesting troubled or troubling behavior maintained by problematic transactions within the family or perhaps between the family and the outside community (Goldenberg & Goldenberg, 2008b). The resulting transition to a new paradigm, according to Kuhn (1970), a theorist in the philosophy of science, is a scientific revolution.

Early work regarding the effects of the family on specific family members came from the study of the etiology of schizophrenia. One of the earliest theories regarding the causal factors for this difficulty was the lack of warmth and caring by the primary caregiver, at that time, usually the mother. The term "refrigerator mother" or "schizophrenogenic mother" was used to explain how the lack of closeness and caring caused the symptoms of schizophrenia (Fromm-Reichman, 1948). While the theory was believable in the 1950s, it has since been disproved in favor of biochemical etiological factors for schizophrenia (Braff, Schork, & Gottesman, 2007). The importance of this research, however, was a focus at that time on other family members in addition to the identified patient. Bateson, Jackson, Haley, & Weakland (1956), who were early theorists and therapists, went a step further and described schizophrenia as resulting from pathological family interactions. In addition, it was stated that mixed communication signals over a long period of time could lead to schizophrenia. An example would be a caregiver who verbally expresses affection but nonverbally pushes the child away. Bateson (1972), who was an anthropologist, was the first to see how a family might operate as a **cybernetic system**. A cybernetic system is a concept first coined by Wiener (1948), a mathematician, to describe regulatory systems that operate by feedback loops. In a cybernetic system, the locus of pathology changes from the identified patient to the social context and the interactions between individuals are analyzed, rather than the troubled person.

After the realization that schizophrenia was not caused by bad parenting, the idea of the inclusion of other family members in therapy was applied to various difficulties, particularly within the child guidance area. During the late 1950s and into the 1960s the perpetuation of the various theories of family therapy began. While many of the theories are termed theories of marital and family therapy, the dynamics of working with two individuals in a marital or couple setting are, however, quite different than working with several people in a family setting.

cybernetic system
a concept to describe regulatory systems operating by feedback loops; term coined by Wiener in 1948

FAMILY DYNAMICS

nuclear family
a family composed of a husband, wife, and their offspring

family
two or more people related by birth, marriage, or adoption residing in the same unit

household
all people who occupy a housing unit regardless of relationships

socioeconomic status
person's position in society as determined by income, wealth, occupation, education, place of residence, and other factors

social class
divided into three categories: upper, middle, and lower class

normal family
average type of family; this term is not synonymous with healthy but lacks significant dysfunctional qualities

dysfunctional family
a family in significant discord; may have issues related to violence, neglect, abuse, chemical dependency, or other serious issues that disrupt adequate family functioning

enmeshed family
a family organization in which boundaries between members are blurred and members are over involved in one another's lives

disengaged family
a family organization with overly rigid boundaries, in which members are isolated and feel unconnected to one another; this type of family has few interactions with one another

As time has passed, the ideas regarding the defining characteristics of a family have changed. At the time when family therapy first began, roughly in the 1950s, the **nuclear family** was considered to be the normal family. The nuclear family was embodied by a family with two parents, one of each gender and two or more children divided equally between genders. The mother was the primary caretaker and usually did not work outside of the home, whereas the father was the primary breadwinner who had a limited role with the children. Changes in the social, economic, and political arenas have changed the composition of the average family in the United States.

According to the U.S. Census Bureau (2010a) a **family** "consists of two or more people related by birth, marriage or adoption residing in the same unit." On the other hand, a **household** "consists of all people who occupy a housing unit regardless of relationship." Current researchers suggest that there is no such thing as a typical or traditional family configuration. According to the U.S. Census Bureau (2010b), of the total number of families accounted for, 23.3% are married couples with children, 28.2% are married couples without children, 16.4% are household groups with children, 26.4% are single-person households, and 5.6% are nonfamily households.

The **socioeconomic status** (SES) of a family is the government's measure of the family's relative economic and social ranking within a community (Kreiger, 2001). Measures of SES typically include the adult's occupation, education level, community/group associations, and income. Other measures typically include location of residence and certain home amenities, such as television, computer, telephone, books, and so forth. **Social class** is divided into three categories: the upper class, the middle class, and the lower class. Upper-class families tend to be the wealthiest in the country. Middle-class families have the largest variability in occupation, education, and wealth from upper-middle class (affluent professionals such as physicians and attorneys), to lower-middle class (such as teachers and clergy). Lower-class family members are often unskilled laborers with little education or recent immigrants or refugees. All of this information is presented for the reader to bear in mind as we look at the changes to the family situation when a member develops a central nervous system illness or injury.

Another issue within family therapy is the definition of normal family. The defining characteristic of *normal* does not have anything to do with the composition of the family but more to do with the roles and rules of the members. The majority of researchers in family therapy state that one of the main issues which make a **normal family** versus a **dysfunctional family** is lack of violence. Anytime violence is present, whether emotional, physical, sexual, or a combination thereof, it is considered a nonhealthy situation. Therefore, a defining feature of a normal family is the absence of violence. A caveat which needs to be addressed is that normal does not necessarily imply healthy. A family may have the absence of violence as a defining feature but not be considered to be healthy for various other reasons. Family therapy researchers, particularly those using the family systems family therapy approach, often use the terms *enmeshed* and *disengaged* to describe the structure and communication pattern of dysfunctional families. **Enmeshed families** are those in which the members suffer from a lack of individuality and privacy. In this type of situation, they may read each other's mail, listen to one another's telephone calls, and be in the bathroom at the same time. The defining feature is the lack of boundaries and the need for personal identity and privacy. On the other extreme is the **disengaged family** in which the members have little contact and little interest in one another's life. In a disengaged family, it is as if several separate individuals are residing within the same home. In order to be termed *normal*, the absence of enmeshed or disengaged qualities is key.

A further concept which is often used in family therapy is the concept of family alliances. These alliances are often related to which individuals are more comfortable talking or communicating with one another. **Dyads** are two-person alliances in which the two are often aligned in a power situation with other members of the family. **Triads** are three-person alliances in which there is often better communication than with the rest of the family. Dyads and triads are examples of different groupings within a family which are often in conflict with one another.

If we focus solely on the demographics of a family, Renee's family fits the norm for a nuclear family, particularly a traditional nuclear family. Renee's parents are married and are the same age and religion. Mr. Summit works as an executive in a computer-related industry, whereas Mrs. Summit volunteers her time at a neonatal nursery in a nearby hospital. Renee and her brother Brandon are heterosexual children of the opposite gender with Brandon receiving more attention than Renee. If we observe the same family with an eye for clues toward mental health, the picture is quite different. There exists emotional violence and, possibly, some physical (but not clearly stated) aggression. The family is quite disengaged except for the alliances consisting of mother and daughter and father and son. Hence, they meet the stereotypic definition of nuclear family but lack major indications of a healthy family.

ETHICAL ISSUES

One of the major ethical issues in a situation with more than one client is confidentiality. For the sake of review, the circumstances in which the confidential relationship may be broken include threats of suicide, threats of homicide, child abuse with the client as victim or perpetrator, and abuse of a vulnerable adult with the client as the victim or perpetrator. In the situation with a family, the confidentiality concept still applies but the explanation of confidentiality becomes more difficult. The explanation must be delivered in a manner that all of the members of the family who will be present for therapy are capable of understanding. The clinical neuropsychologist will first need to decide the youngest age of family members who will be allowed in the therapy session before confidentiality is explained. Once this decision has been made the clinical neuropsychologist must deliver the statement in a manner in which the youngest or most disabled (sometimes the same person) understands. This implies that the language may need to be altered dependent on the particular family circumstances.

In a family therapy session, it is often the case that one individual has received a *Diagnostic and Statistical Manual of Mental Disorders*, *Fourth Edition*, *Text Revision* (*DSM-IV-TR*) diagnosis for family therapy in order to be reimbursed by insurance. The clinical neuropsychologist must be careful that the family does not use the diagnosis within therapy to label one member of the family as the sole individual who is having difficulties. In a similar manner, it is important that the clinical neuropsychologist differentiate the function of record keeping by name versus the actual client for family therapy. Very often, records are kept under the name of the identified patient, which should not imply that this is the only person who is having difficulties. Family therapy produces a situation in which the individuals within the family may not keep all of the therapy information confidential, which is less of an ethical issue and more of a therapeutic issue.

In family therapy, the clinical neuropsychologist, if he or she so desires, may use structured interviews to gain information, behavioral scales to collect observational

dyad
an alliance, temporary or permanent, between two people in a family situation; the communication is often better between the two than in the larger family unit

triad
a three-person alliance or relationship; communication is often better within the triad than within the larger family unit

confidentiality
discussions or information considered privileges and not to be shared

data, and assessment tools to garner information regarding communication. In all of these circumstances, the interviews, scales, tests, and so forth must be the most up-to-date that are available and must be normed on the population for which they will be used. In addition, if individual assessment tools will be used, the ethical issues discussed earlier must also be upheld.

STAGES OF FAMILY THERAPY

Although there are many theories which will be discussed further, there are also general principles of family therapy which apply to each form of therapy. The first step in the beginning of family therapy is the introduction. In individual therapy, introductions are much simpler usually involving the decision to make the situation more or less formal. In family therapy, every issue becomes not necessarily more important but may have greater ramifications as more people are involved. In addition, from the very first contact with the family, the clinical neuropsychologist tries to develop and build on a **working alliance** with the family. A working alliance does not imply that the therapist is looking to befriend the family but that the aim is to create an atmosphere in which each member feels supported and able to voice previously unexpressed or unexplored problems (Goldenberg & Goldenberg, 2008a). Within Renee's family, with such strong personality dynamics, it is very important for the clinical neuropsychologist to determine with whom to introduce himself first. If he introduces himself to Renee first, it allows her to be or feel more special but it could also signify that she is the reason that the family is in family therapy. If the clinical neuropsychologist introduces himself to Mr. Summit, who already is powerful within the family and nonsupportive of therapy, it could give him more power or align the clinical neuropsychologist with him. Further ramifications could occur if the clinical neuropsychologist were to greet Mrs. Summit or Brandon first. One therapeutic strategy to alleviate this difficulty is to address oneself to the family as a whole. In this situation, the introductions would not be made in the waiting room due to reasons of confidentiality and privacy. Hence, in the first meeting within the office, the clinical neuropsychologist could state, "Welcome, members of the Summit family, I am pleased to meet you, I am Dr. Smith, a clinical neuropsychologist who will be working with all of you."

The next issue is the discussion of confidentiality and its limits before any member of the family has a chance to speak regarding issues he or she may not have otherwise discussed. While the required breaking of confidentiality remains identical for individual, family, or group therapy, the therapist can be required to reveal therapeutic material discussed in family and group more easily than material discussed with a single client, because with more individuals more issues which require **mandated reporting** may surface. In addition, the family or group members themselves are not ethically or legally bound to maintain confidentiality amongst themselves.

The discussion in the section on ethics alluded to how different the delivery of the confidentiality statement is in a family circumstance. The difficulties are many and include not only the phrasing of the statement based on developmental or disability factors but also the aforementioned issues of including all of the members of the family in the discussion. Beginning family therapists often find it very difficult to pay equal attention to all of the family members and to neither exclude nor alienate any member. Also within the discussion of confidentiality, the clinical neuropsychologist must help the family determine whether they will keep all of their family therapy discussions confidential. A discussion with the family may be necessary in order to help them to determine if friends or other people may know of their issues discussed in the session. It is important to obtain

working alliance
a relationship between the members of a family and the therapist; the relationship is designed to allow the family to feel safe enough to discuss previously nondiscussed issues or concerns

mandated reporting
information that, by law, must be reported to legal authorities

consensus from members and not have some members discuss therapy with their friends and others not, otherwise a lack of trust may develop regarding the information which is discussed within the family therapy session.

After introductions and confidentiality are discussed, the clinical neuropsychologist must obtain intake information from all participants. Information regarding the identified patient may be available at the start but information from all members is also important. The clinical neuropsychologist must decide if the intake information will be gathered separately from each person or if it will be obtained in front of the other members. The advantage to private interviews is that the clinical neuropsychologist may obtain information on significant issues that otherwise would not be available. The disadvantage is that the clinical neuropsychologist could become the bearer of family secrets. It is always important that the clinical neuropsychologist does not accept or solicit secrets from any family member. The reason secrets are forbidden is that the clinical neuropsychologist must remain objective in order to be effective. Secrets preclude objectivity and may cause the clinical neuropsychologist to view family members differently based on the information contained within the secret. If intake information is garnered with other family members present, the person being interviewed may withhold information that he or she does not want to discuss in front of the rest of the family.

After the intake information is obtained and before therapeutic techniques are put into place, a few sessions are usually spent involving all members of the family in the identified patient's difficulties. Involving all members of the family is termed **spreading the problem** or making each member aware that they contribute to the functioning or nonfunctioning of the family unit. In cases of central nervous system difficulties, it is often the case that the family needs to know their role in the perpetuation of the identified patient's difficulty. There are three general ways to incorporate all of the members into the family therapy process and any or all of these strategies may be used dependent on the particular family circumstances.

spreading the problem
including all members of the family in discussion of the patient's problem

The first way to include all members of the family is an activity in which the clinical neuropsychologist asks each member of the family the reason for his or her presence at the meeting. Any member may begin the discussion or the clinical neuropsychologist may choose someone to begin speaking. Very often, family members express resentment or anger at being in therapy or concern that they not be labeled as a cause of the family difficulty. The expressed emotions are often a good starting point for the clinical neuropsychologist to evaluate which particular strategy to employ with the family. The ultimate aim of the discussion is to encourage all of the members to participate and become interested in the process.

A second strategy is to have an already planned warm-up activity to facilitate family member's participation. Examples which a clinical neuropsychologist could use include, "Imagine you are given $1,000 and must decide how the family would use it for a vacation. Demonstrate to me how that would be discussed." Or, "How does your family communicate? Provide a topic and show me." Although these are often used in typical family therapy situations, other hypothetical questions for discussion may be developed with the central nervous system disease or difficulty as a topic. An example could be, "Now that you are absent one person to complete strenuous household chores, how will you divide the tasks?"

Development of family rules is the third way to involve all family members and is often necessary in large groups. The rules are written out during the session and sent home with the family to enforce with one another. The aim is to force the family members to think how each person affects the behavior of others. The rules should be generated from the family, but the clinical neuropsychologist may need to prompt the family with examples, such as "No finishing sentences" or "No interrupting."

Returning to Renee's family, the early steps in family therapy will now be reviewed. It was already stated that the introductions should be made in the office, not the waiting room, in order that all participants could be addressed at once. There does not need to be any change in the phrasing of the confidentiality statement because all participants are capable of understanding the wording. The clinical neuropsychologist determined that intake information should be gathered from each member of the family in a joint session. This was decided due to the fact that in this particular family, the chances of secret or spiteful information being brought out in private sessions was great. The clinical neuropsychologist also decided that all three ways to engage the family would be utilized because of the resistance and antagonism on the part of some family members. The discussion regarding the need for family therapy led to blame being directed at Renee for her behavior. After much education regarding her diagnosis, the family members began to acknowledge that Renee had a neurological problem not a behavioral problem and that they would participate in the sessions. The second exercise was used to evaluate the communication patterns within the family. The question addressed was how a family vacation would be decided. Mr. Summit took the lead and made his decisions focusing mainly on the enjoyment of himself and his son. The clinical neuropsychologist kept records of the discussion to be used later in the therapy process. Finally, the family members had no difficulty providing rules for the family. The major difficulty was having all of the members agree to abide by the rules and not just hold each other accountable. The Summit family rules include:

- No finishing sentences
- No reading each other's minds
- No calling each other names
- No swearing or verbally abusive terms

The Summits decided that they would tape the rules to their refrigerator in order that all members could remember them. The clinical neuropsychologist made it very clear that any of the vocal mannerisms, which were beyond Renee's control, could not be used against her as a violation of the family rules.

THEORIES OF FAMILY THERAPY

As may be seen, the structure and functioning of family therapy is quite different than individual therapy. As was the case with individual therapy, there exist many types of family therapy. Most of these fall under four major rubrics, which are object-relations family therapy, family systems family therapy, structural family therapy, and strategic family therapy. A review of the main types of family therapy will be presented. The reader is referred to Goldenberg and Goldenberg (2008)[1] for a more in-depth analysis of all of the forms of family therapy.

Object Relations Family Therapy

Object relations family therapy is based upon psychodynamic views and concepts. One of the earliest object relations family therapists was British psychologist Melanie Klein (1882–1960). Many of her followers formed an independent group termed the *British Middle School* in an attempt to avoid splitting the British Psychoanalytic Society into rival factions (Slipp, 1988). These theorists included Michael Balint (1896–1970), Ronald Fairbairn (1889–1964), Harry Guntrip (1901–1975), and Donald Winnicott (1896–1971), all of whom had a slightly different view toward object relations family therapy. Object relations family therapists contend that the need for a satisfying relationship with some object (i.e., another person) is

---

[1] Goldenberg, H., and Goldenberg, Z. (2008). Family Therapy: An Overview. Belmont, CA: Wadsworth-Thomson.

the fundamental motive in life (Scharff & Scharff, 1997). According to the object relations perspective individuals bring memories of loss or unfulfillment from childhood, defined as introjects into current dealings with others, seeking satisfaction but sometimes contaminating family relations in the process. In this theory, contamination implies the spoiling or ruining of a relationship within the family. Object relations family therapists argue that individuals unconsciously relate to one another in the present largely on the basis of expectations formed during childhood. These individual intrapsychic issues and family interpersonal difficulties are examined in the therapy setting. Building upon the idea of transference, object relations family therapists help family members gain insight into how they internalized objects from the past. They also help family members understand how these internalized objects intrude on current family relationships. The goal of object relations family therapy is awareness within the family members of the unresolved introjects from their families of origin. Once awareness is achieved, the next step is a development of understanding of how these issues have caused current familial difficulties. The focus on the past and how it affects partner selection and family dynamics makes it evident that object relations family therapy works with the parents more than with the children during the beginning of therapy. As time passes, the parenting styles are explored based upon the relationship to the aforementioned issues. A focus on past issues and unconscious motivation make object relations family therapy similar to psychodynamic individual therapy. Object relations family therapy tends to encompass the most number of sessions compared to the other forms of family therapy.

introject
an object relations family therapy concept; it implies that the individual brings memories of loss or unsatisfying childhood relations into adult relationships which are likely to cause conflicts

contamination
an object relations family therapy term; it implies spoiling or ruining a family relationship

Family Systems Family Therapy

Family systems family therapy is based on the work of Murray Bowen (1913–1990). Bowen conceptualized the family as an emotional unit, a network of interlocking relationships, best understood when analyzed within a multigenerational or historical framework (Goldenberg & Goldenberg, 2008b). Hence, the family systems approach looks at the various systems or groupings within the family of procreation but also includes the family of origin. It is therefore also referred to as *transgenerational family therapy*. Bowen argued that family members are tied in thinking, feeling, and behavior to the family system and thus that individual emotional problems arise and are maintained by relationship connections with fellow members. Those members with the strongest affective connections (or fusion) with the family are the most vulnerable to personal emotional reactions to family stress (Bowen, 1978). The degree to which an individualized separate sense of self, independent from the family (differentiation of self) occurs is correlated with the ability to resist being overwhelmed by emotional reactivity in the family. The greater the differentiation, the less likely the individual is to experience personal dysfunction. Hence, the goal, particularly for Bowen as a spokesperson for family systems family therapy, is the individuation of the self within the family. Family systems family therapy tends to work well with families which are on the enmeshed end of the enmeshed–disengaged continuum. Family systems family therapy borrows from psychodynamic theory but focuses predominately on the ability of the individual to be both a member of the family and also an individual with a clear sense of identity. The attempt to balance two life forces, family togetherness, and individual autonomy was, for Bowen, the core issue for all humans (Wylie, 1990).

fusion
a family systems concept; implies a strong affective connection to the family that may lead to difficulty with differentiation of self

differentiation of self
a family systems family therapy term; it means the degree to which an individual is able to maintain a separate identity and also be a member of the family

Structural Family Therapy

Structural family therapy focuses on family organization and the rules which govern transactions. The structural approach pays particular attention to family rules, roles, alignments, and coalitions as well as to the boundaries and subsystems that make up the overall family system. Many of these basic constructs are already familiar to the reader and attest to the influence of structural family therapy's leading spokesperson, Salvador Minuchin (1921 to present) and his associates (Minuchin, 1974; Minuchin & Fishman, 1981). Symptoms are viewed as means of diffusing conflict, diverting attention from more basic family conflicts. Symptoms are maintained by a family structure unable to adapt to changing environmental or developmental demands. The role of the therapist is to challenge rigid repetitive transactions within a family, helping to allow family reorganization. Structural family therapists consider they have reached their therapeutic goal when the family has restructured itself and freed its member to relate to one another in nonpathological patterns (Prochaska & Norcross, 1999). Structural family theory focuses less on past or unconscious issues and more on the current patterns within the family.

Strategic Family Therapy

Strategic family therapy is often used synonymously with communication theory. Communication theorists are concerned with how verbal and nonverbal messages are exchanged within a family. They pay attention to what is occurring rather than why it is occurring. In a sense, they observe the process of communication rather than drawing any inferences about each member's inner conflicts. The original ideas for strategic family therapy were developed from 1952–1962 by Jay Haley (1923–2007), Gregory Bateson (1904–1980), Don Jackson (1920–1968), John Weakland (1919–1995), and Paul Watlawicz (1921–2007) at the Mental Research Institute in Palo Alto, CA. Strategic family therapy concepts often involve not only direct communication strategies but also indirect challenges to communication such as paradoxical intention. A paradoxical intention or suggestion is one in which the therapist suggests a behavior to a family which may appear to be opposite of what is desired. The aim is to have the family rebel and to do the opposite of what is suggested. The premise is that these therapists believe families develop unworkable solutions to problems such that the solutions become problems themselves. Consequently, these therapists have developed a set of brief therapy procedures using various forms of paradox aimed at changing undesired family interactive patterns (Watzlawick, Weakland, & Fisch, 1974). These are risky techniques and the family therapist must know and understand the communication patterns of the family before attempting to use a paradoxical technique. An example of a paradoxical suggestion made by the clinical neuropsychologist would be "Discuss the issue we were debating in the session at home and disagree about it if necessary until the next family session." The therapist hopes that the family will do the opposite of his suggestion and function well. Strategic family therapists are not interested in family history or intrapsychic insight but more interested in the present and in changing behaviors.

After reviewing the main forms which family therapy takes, Renee's clinical neuropsychologist decided that a combination of structural and strategic family therapy would work best with the Summit family. The structural approach would address the father–son and mother–daughter coalitions, which tended to surface regularly within the family. The strategic approach would allow the clinical neuropsychologist to assist the family with communication skills. After therapy has progressed, it may be possible to invoke a paradoxical suggestion but only after the clinical neuropsychologist understands the family functioning quite well.

ROLE OF FAMILY THERAPY WITH AN INDIVIDUAL WITH CENTRAL NERVOUS SYSTEM DIFFICULTIES

As was discussed earlier in this chapter, there tend to be two functions of family therapy, regardless of the technique used, when dealing with individuals who have sustained central nervous system illness or injury and their families. The approaches are psychoeducational and psychotherapeutic. Very often, however, the functions blend together as will be seen in the following discussion.

paradoxical intention
a strategic family therapy concept; a technique used to suggest the opposite of the behavior that a therapist would like a family to produce

PSYCHOEDUCATIONAL FUNCTION OF FAMILY THERAPY

The psychoeducational role of family therapy is to present and disseminate information regarding the central nervous system accident or illness sustained by one of the family members. Very often information is given to the patient, family, or to both early in the treatment process. This information may be helpful but quite often the information is overwhelming, inadequate, or delivered at the wrong time. In each of these situations, the information does not become incorporated into the functioning of the family and it becomes a situation in which the family operates without knowledge.

The role of the psychoeducational family therapy session is for the clinical neuropsychologist to assume a didactic or teaching role in relation to any and all of the information needed by the family. The timing for discussing the information is critical. The family should be receptive and as stated, information presented too early in the accident or illness process may be a mistake. In contrast, information delivered too late may have to work its way through resentment and anger. The timing should be left to the clinical neuropsychologist who has hopefully been working with the family for some time, preferably as case manager and is able to gauge when they are receptive.

The information discussed with the family must be phrased in terms which are understandable to the members. It does not need to be extremely technical but should cover how the patient will be able to function and the reasons for the changes. It is often the case that this type of discussion will elicit multiple and diverse emotions on the part of the family members. The clinical neuropsychologist should be aware and cognizant of this as he or she is teaching about central nervous system functioning. Hence, even though this section describes a didactic function of family therapy, there is never a clear demarcation between this function and an emotionally laden discussion.

PSYCHOTHERAPEUTIC FUNCTION OF FAMILY THERAPY

As was stated in the previous section, family members will invariably have diverse emotional reactions to the difficulties experienced by a family member. Often the reactions are empathy for the plight of the family member and his suffering. At other times, the reactions are due to the changing roles within the family and the newly acquired responsibilities which various family members must assume. The type of central nervous system difficulty is not the issue in this form of family therapy. The psychotherapeutic function of this form of family therapy is designed to allow family members an opportunity to voice their feelings in a safe environment.

PRESENCE OR ABSENCE OF THE PATIENT IN FAMILY THERAPY

As may be seen, many of the issues which the clinical neuropsychologist will discuss with the patient's family are related to inabilities or limitations on the part of the patient. The clinical neuropsychologist needs to take this into account when he or she decides whether the patient should be included within a particular family therapy session. If the patient is capable, the clinical neuropsychologist should consult with him or her about whether he or she would prefer to be present in either type of family therapy.

The circumstances which existed within Renee's family necessitated a combination of both psychoeducational and psychotherapeutic family therapy. Even though Renee's difficulties had been evident for a long period, it appears that much information was missing or misunderstood regarding her difficulties. Secondly, as stated earlier, a combination of structural and strategic family therapy approaches would help address some of the other issues within the family. The alliances between father–son and mother–daughter need to become less rigid and the family needs to become more of a functioning whole. In addition, communication needs to become more egalitarian within the family and less top-down authoritarian from the males to the females. With a combination of the two functions of therapy and the resistance on the part of some family members, the clinical neuropsychologist would hope that the family would be able to work for at least 10–12 sessions within the therapeutic context. Success in the family context could be evaluated by means of questionnaires or through asking each member of the family how he or she would evaluate the current functioning of the family compared to his or her functioning prior to family therapy. Ultimately, it is hoped that Renee will feel more supported and less blamed by her family for behaviors which are out of her control. It is also hoped that with additional education, the members will understand better the cause of her behaviors that will lessen the stress level for Renee, which will in turn help alleviate triggers for her symptoms.

Group Therapy

INTRODUCTION

As was described in the introduction to this chapter, there are several types of therapy to be discussed under the heading of group therapy. The discussion will follow a similar format of family therapy. The general principles of group therapy and ethical issues will be reviewed first and will then be followed by the theoretical views on group therapy.

HISTORY

The uses of group therapy have been many and varied. As early as 1905, Pratt used a group approach termed the *home sanatorium treatment* to work with tuberculosis patients. The purpose of the group was to inspire the patients and lift their spirits to aid medical compliance (Trull, 2005). Pratt used a combination of lectures and group discussion and paid particular attention to the depression which was developing in the tubercular patients. As time went on, Pratt became more sophisticated about the psychological aspects of the group interaction. He appreciated the importance of an atmosphere of mutual support created by patients having a "common bond in a common disease" (Spotnitz, 1961, p. 29). In 1918, Lanzell used a lecture approach to medical group therapy which was extended to patients suffering from psychological disorders (Schaffer & Galinski, 1974). Thus, use of group therapy with individuals suffering from a medical difficulty which led to secondary psychological problems foreshadowed the use of group therapy in clinical neuropsychology.

    Another use of group therapy in addition to the mutual support for medical patients was the financial incentive involved with treating large groups of people. After World War II (WWII), a large number of veterans returned with psychiatric difficulties due to the emotional trauma associated with combat. At the present time, we would refer to these difficulties as post-traumatic stress disorder (PTSD). During WWII, it was referred to as *battle fatigue* and individuals did not understand that the difficulty involved brain impairment. The use of the group format was not made as a therapeutic choice but was an effective and efficient manner to economically help large numbers of people. However, the therapeutic value for individuals being in a group together with others with similar difficulties proved to be very successful.

Another form of group therapy which is difficult to evaluate due to its insistence on anonymity is Alcoholics Anonymous (AA). Developed by two recovering alcoholics Bill Wilson and Dr. Bob, AA is a group format designed with the specific purpose of helping people refrain from alcohol use (Alcoholics Anonymous World Services, Inc., 2001). Many other groups have been patterned after this approach, such as Narcotics Anonymous (NA), Overeaters Anonymous (OA), and Gamblers Anonymous (GA). All of these groups are 12-step programs based upon the medical model where the difficulty in question is described as a medical problem over which the individual has no control. The difference between these groups and others already discussed is that they are usually led by paraprofessionals. However, the principles behind the groups may be used by clinical neuropsychologists in their work with individuals with central nervous system difficulties.

At the present time, group therapy is again resurfacing as a cost-effective means to treat individuals with central nervous system difficulties. State and local branches of the Brain Injury Association of America often sponsor these groups, which may or may not be run by professionals.

paraprofessionals
individuals who have been trained to assist professional mental health workers; many of these individuals do not have formal degrees and some, such as in Alcoholics Anonymous, may be recovering from the same difficulty for which they are helping others

PRINCIPLES OF GROUP THERAPY

A group is more than a collection of people. Dependent upon how it is structured, the group members share some core attitudes and values, accept each other, and relate to each other in varying ways. They accept membership in the group to deal with the problems they have in common as well as to satisfy some individual needs.

Members who desire participation in a group agree to conform at least minimally to the group standards. Cartwright and Zander (1968) offer the following statement as characteristics of individuals in groups:

- They engage in frequent interaction.
- They define themselves as group members.
- They are defined by others as belonging to the group.
- They share norms concerning matters of common interest.
- They participate in a system of interlocking roles.
- They find the group to be rewarding.
- They pursue interdependent goals.
- They have a collective perception of their unity.
- They tend to act in a unitary manner toward the environment.

Most groups begin as a collection of individuals who do not start with the previously mentioned characteristics. The more of these characteristics the group members develop, the stronger the group will be. In general, groups progress through a series of stages. The stages through which a group generally progresses are often described as the exploratory stage, the transition stage, the action stage, and the termination stage. Various theorists employ differing terms for the same stages, such as starting the group, early group development, termination, and follow-up (Budman & Gurman, 1988). The exploratory stage is when group members introduce themselves and each describes the goals he or she hopes to achieve. In group therapy with central nervous system difficulties, it is also a time to describe the circumstances which led to one's difficulty. During this stage, the group members may be evaluating one another (Hollander, 1964) or assigning roles to one another and the power and influence of each member becomes apparent (Bonney, 1969). The transition stage begins when one or more members begin to self-disclose at a level deeper than the sharing of diagnostic information. Some members may feel threatened or uncomfortable as this is an uncommon activity in most social circumstances (Carhuff, 1969). The action stage is when the majority of the work of the group is accomplished. The termination stage signals the ending of self-disclosure. Usually, termination work begins two or three sessions before the actual end of therapy. When the group is composed of individuals with central nervous system difficulties, the progression through these stages may be slower or more erratic.

Groups, particularly when they are working with various psychiatric and/or central nervous system difficulties, are termed *open* versus *closed*. **Open groups** are those in which members may join at any time and begin their group experience at the point where the group is functioning. The philosophy of open groups is that all are welcome and that the group will be able to accommodate changes which are inevitable when members come and go. There are no predetermined number of sessions to which each member must attend. AA and other 12-step programs are examples of open groups. **Closed groups** restrict admission to the group to the beginning. All members of the group start at the same point and progress through the educational or therapeutic program together. The closed group meets for a predetermined number of sessions. The philosophy of closed groups is that the coming and going of various members is too disruptive of the group process for it to be allowed. When working with individuals with central nervous system difficulty, closed groups, such as those for stroke victims are more often the norm.

Groups and for that matter, family therapy as a group, often encompass more time than individual therapy. The usual group session runs from 90 minutes to 2 hours. Groups vary in number but a standard group size is 8–10 members. More individuals are difficult to manage when dealing with central nervous system difficulties. However, groups which are run by paraprofessionals often have more group members and include more facilitators. Examples of larger groups would be those sponsored by local branches of the Brain Injury Association of America. Many groups are homogenous having mainly individuals who have been diagnosed with a particular disability. The rationale behind homogeneous groups is that individuals with the same disability or difficulty may share more common concerns than with those who have a different type of disability or difficulty. For example, individuals who have sustained a stroke may have much more in common with one another but very little in common with those who have Alzheimer's disease. Other theorists view a heterogeneous group with various central nervous system difficulties as more helpful to the clients. Further, there are issues regarding single-sex groups versus the inclusion of both males and females, as well as the appropriate age range for group members. The clinical neuropsychologist most often has made decisions regarding all of these variables before group therapy begins. One particular variable that the clinical neuropsychologist must always consider is that there are circumstances in which a patient is not appropriate for group therapy. Most researchers agree that actively suicidal, homicidal, psychotic, or very demented patients would not gain anything from a group experience and may be quite disruptive to the larger group. The final distinction is between groups that are designed to have an educational function versus those where the main goal is psychotherapeutic. As was seen with family therapy, there is often overlap between these two functions. Hence, an educational group leader must know how to manage the feelings of the group member, and a psychotherapeutic group leader must be able to provide didactic information when needed.

In the situation with Renee, her clinical neuropsychologist suggested that at some point subsequent to family therapy she might consider group therapy. The goal which her clinical neuropsychologist had in mind would be a supportive group. In order to be supportive and also bring insight regarding the number of other individuals who suffer with various neurological difficulties, her clinical neuropsychologist suggested a group of adolescents or young adults who have various central nervous system difficulties. In this

open groups
group members may join or leave at any time

closed group
group members have defined participation, all must participate from start to finish

manner, Renee would be able to understand that other individuals her own age also struggle with various difficulties which are beyond their control. She may learn strategies which others have used to help deal with their relationships and circumstances.

ETHICAL ISSUES

The foremost ethical issue, similar to family and individual therapy, is confidentiality. It is a challenge for the clinical neuropsychologist to deliver the confidentiality statement to a larger group and to make sure that all of the members understand the ramifications of the statement. Many clinical neuropsychologists have each group member repeat or paraphrase what he or she has heard in order to ensure his or her understanding. In other circumstances, a written statement is also included with the verbal statement to aid with understanding. The written statement of confidentiality is signed by the group member and kept in his or her file. The members of the group also need to decide whether they will share information regarding the group discussion with others outside of the group. As is the case in family therapy, the clinical neuropsychologist needs to work with the members on developing a consensus regarding this issue. In addition, as was stated with family therapy, the members of the group need to be cognizant that information revealed in group setting does not share the same rights to legal privacy as in individual therapy. For example, if in a group of young adults (18–24 years of age) a member made a comment regarding his or her father's infidelity, if the parents eventually divorced, the member may be called on to repeat the statement in a deposition or court setting.

An issue which may occur in group therapy that is less likely to occur in other forms of therapy is members developing friendships with other members and meeting outside of the session. If the goal is socialization, this may not be a difficulty. If this leads to cliques or rivalries, it may impair the group process. If members of the group become attracted to one another and decide to date or become intimate with one another this could also upset the dynamics of the group. Groups which are designed for individuals who have central nervous system difficulties are more likely to have these issues due to the members' potential difficulties with impulsivity and judgment. A discussion of these issues at the beginning of the group may need to be followed by a further discussion as time goes by and relationships begin to be formed.

THEORIES OF GROUP THERAPY

It is often thought that every school or major theory of individual therapy has its own group counterpart. If this is the case, then the question remains: Why group versus individual therapy? Yalom (1975) answers this question with a list of curative factors which he feels are unique to group therapy, which include (a) imparting information, (b) instilling hope, (c) universality, (d) altruism, (e) interpersonal learning, (f) imitative behavior, (g) corrective recapitulation of the primary family, (h) catharsis, and (i) group cohesion.

A second question which often arises, particularly due to the diversity of group types, regards the effectiveness of group therapy. Reviews of the research literature assessing the efficacy of group psychotherapy consistently conclude that group treatment is more effective than no treatment (Bednar & Kaul, 1994; Burlingame, MacKenzie, & Strauss, 2004; Riva & Smith, 1997). The most recent critique of group therapy suggests that certain models of group therapy for certain diagnostic difficulties may prove to be the most effective (Burlingame et al., 2004).

The following discussion will cover the main frameworks for group therapy which include psychoanalytic, psychodrama, Gestalt, and behavioral group therapy. Early approaches which were significant in the development of the field of group therapy but are not as heavily practiced at present will not be included. These groups include sensitivity groups, T-groups, and encounter groups which have had some ethical issues for which the reader is referred to Trull (2005).

Psychoanalytic Group Therapy

Group analytic psychotherapy is a term applied by Foulkes (1898–1976) to the work he began in 1938 and is contained in four volumes of his writing (1948, 1964, 1975a, & 1975b). He described how he began his work using the principles of psychoanalysis before WWII but he felt the need for the social component. During WWII, he began to use psychoanalytic principles in a group setting which he felt answered the need for the social component. He then began group analytic psychotherapy as an experimental approach at a military hospital in Northfield, Birmingham, England during WWII (Bridger, 1946; Main, 1946). Subsequent to Foulkes' introduction of the social component, the majority of the other forms of psychoanalytic group therapy were basically psychoanalytic therapy carried out in a group setting (Trull, 2005). There were some differences in how issues were handled with more than one client such as seating arrangements and the involvement of the therapist. The core of these approaches, however, includes the basic ideas and tenets of psychoanalysis: the opening phase, the development of transference, working through the transference, and termination. The group becomes a vehicle through which individual group members understand the effects of their unconscious on their current behavior. The focus is clearly on one individual at a time rather than a group process. In this manner, Foulkes' original ideas regarding the social content are not followed. Wolf (1975) believed very strongly that psychodynamic therapy is workable in a group setting and that the therapist is the reason for success or failure. He also stated that in a group setting, an individual should be better able to tolerate anxiety because he or she is able to lean on the group for support. Additional benefits for the individual group members include observing how others in the group communicate with one another, participating in a situation in which the individual is not the sole focus of the therapist's attention, and giving and receiving help from other members. In a general sense, psychoanalytic group therapy employs the four phases of psychoanalysis but also includes the social dimension which various theorists such as Adler (1964) felt was missing from traditional psychoanalysis.

Psychodrama

Psychodrama is a group therapeutic approach designed to evoke the expression of feelings involved in personal problems in spontaneous dramatic role-play (Moreno, 1946, 1959). Psychodrama consists of a therapy group centered around acting out of emotionally significant scenes for the purpose of both catharsis and the acquisition of new behaviors. Group members role-play past, present, or anticipated conflict situations to release feelings and to practice more adaptive behavior. The dramatic method is invoked to allow participants to relive and reformulate their problems in the present. Psychodrama, in general, involves a patient, a stage on which the drama is played, a director or therapist, "auxiliary egos" (other patients, therapist aids, and others), and an audience (Moreno, 1948). The director assigns the patient a role, and the supporting cast is made up of the auxiliary egos. The audience may provide acceptance and understanding or may participate themselves. Moreno felt that acting out a situation, listening to the responses of the auxiliary egos, and the reactions of the audience led to a deeper level or catharsis and self-understanding.

Moreno also felt that psychodrama could be particularly useful for shy individuals or for individuals lacking in social skills. In this particular manner, psychodrama could prove to be quite helpful for individuals with central nervous system difficulties. A recent meta-analysis suggests that psychodrama is an efficacious treatment, although it was based on a small number of studies (Kipper & Ritchie, 2003).

Gestalt Group Therapy

Gestalt is the German word meaning *whole* or *configuration*. Perls (1893–1970), who is considered the creator of Gestalt therapy, was trained as a psychologist and a physician in pre–World War I Germany. After exposure to many soldiers and their difficulties along with the teachings of various neo-Freudians, he began to develop his own theory of personality. Perls felt that personality was multilayered. The outer layer, which he termed the *cliché layer*, was felt by Perls to be very ingenuine. The second layer was the role-playing layer where the learned roles of mother, father, son, daughter, teacher, and so forth resided. Beneath this layer, Perls described the impasse layer. Sometimes this is termed the *death layer* by Russians. Within this layer is a feeling of emptiness. For many people, the subjective experience of being without clichés or role-playing is frightening. The fourth layer is the implosive–explosive layer. At this layer, a person is clearly aware of emotions that are either expressed or imploded. The last layer is the genuine personality stripped of all of the learned or as Perls would say, "phony," ways of being in the world (Simkin, 1979). Perls felt that the personality operated in a hierarchical manner to survive. However, to truly work on any potential problems, the individual needed to achieve a level of awareness. The group setting with various techniques developed by Perls, such as the "hot seat" in which all of the group focused on one individual, should help the individual bring his or her feelings into awareness (Perls, 1947/1969). Awareness, according to Perls, was the key in the restoration of health (Perls). It is very difficult to evaluate the effectiveness of the Gestalt approach due to the lack of research and the level of emotionality this particular approach engenders (Trull, 2005).

Behavioral Therapy Groups

Behavior therapy and subsequently, cognitive–behavioral therapy began with the work of Watson and Pavlov. Behavioral approaches pride themselves on being scientific and technique focused as compared to other forms of therapy which emphasize the therapeutic alliance, past issues, and the release of emotions. The hallmark of behavioral and cognitive–behavioral treatment is assessment of the behaviors or, in the case of cognitive–behavioral, the thoughts which will be changed. In group therapy, all of the members complete behavioral inventories before, during, and after treatment. After the exact behaviors which need to be changed are delineated, behaviorists will assign clients to a homogenous group to work on the particular problem in question. Research has supported the efficacy of behavior and cognitive–behavioral group interventions for the treatment of depression, social skills deficits, pain, agoraphobia, and other conditions (Rose, 1991).

After carefully reviewing Renee's treatment plan and recommendations, her clinical neuropsychologist determined that if she chose to pursue group therapy, a combination of approaches could be helpful. Psychodrama could help Renee understand and cope with reactions of other people to her disability. A behavioral approach would allow her to do work in a group setting on assertiveness skills. As she has experienced taunting and bullying, she has not developed appropriate ways to stop or reduce this behavior on the part of others. The psychodrama approach could fulfill an emotionally focused role for her, whereas behavioral group therapy could be a more didactic approach.

Summary

The chapter begins with a case study of an adolescent female who developed Tourette's disorder. After a valiant attempt at hiding the difficulty, it surfaced and began to cause difficulty within the family. The young woman also began to have difficulties with her school due to bullying.

The topic of this chapter is family therapy. Its goal is to look beyond the identified patient and to include all of the members of the family unit as much as possible in the causes of the problem and possible solutions. The ethical issues and differences in procedures with more than the client are discussed. The major schools of thought in family therapy are reviewed with reference to the case study. In addition, the various uses of family therapy for those who have a family member stricken with a central nervous system difficulty are reviewed.

Group therapy as another venue for treatment of those with central nervous system difficulties is also introduced. The ethical issues and circumstances for conducting a group are reviewed. The main frameworks through which group therapy is delivered are also investigated.

Questions for Further Study

1. Are there circumstances in which a family is too dysfunctional to benefit from any form of family therapy? Explain your answer.
2. Group therapy may be conducted by professionals or paraprofessionals often those who have had a particular difficulty or disorder. Are there any circumstances in which family therapy could be conducted by a paraprofessional or is that always contraindicated?
3. If the goal of group therapy is for all members to participate and to gain from their experience, is there an optimal number of members for a group? Under what circumstances could cotherapists work with a group?

References

Adler, A. (1964). *Social interest: A challenge to mankind.* New York: Capricorn Books.

Alcoholics Anonymous World Services, Inc. (2001). *Alcoholics Anonymous: The story of how many thousands of men and women have recovered from alcoholism.* New York: Author.

Bateson, G. (1972). *Steps to an ecology of mind.* New York: Ballantine Books.

Bateson, G., Jackson, D. D., Haley, J., & Weakland, J. H. (1956). Thoughts on therapy for schizophrenia. *Behavioral Science, 1*, 251–261.

Bednar, R. L., & Kaul, T. J. (1994). Experimental group research: Can the cannon fire? In A. E. Bergin & S. L. Garfield (Eds.), *Handbook of psychotherapy and behavior change* (pp. 631–663). New York: Wiley.

Bonney, W. C. (1969). Group counseling and developmental processes. In G. M. Gazda (Ed.), *Theories and methods of group counseling in the schools.* Springfield, IL: Charles C. Thomas.

Bowen, M. (1978). *Family therapy in clinical practice.* New York: Jason Aronson.

Braff, D., Schork, N. J., & Gottesman, I. I. (2007). Endophenotyping schizophrenia. *American Journal of Psychiatry, 164*(5), 705–707.

Bridger, H. L. (1946). The Northfield experiment. *Bulletin of the Menninger Clinic, 10*(3), 71–76.

Budman, S. H., & Gurman, A. S. (1988). *Theory and practice of brief therapy.* New York: Guilford Press.

Burlingame, G. M., MacKenzie, K. R., & Strauss, B. (2004). Small-group treatment: Evidence for effectiveness and mechanics of change. In M. J. Lambert (Ed.), *Bergin and Garfield's handbook of psychotherapy and behavior change* (5th ed., pp. 647–696). New York: Wiley.

Carhuff, R. R. (1969). *Helping and human relations: A primer for lay and professional helpers. Practice and research* (Vol. 2). New York: Holt, Rinehart and Winston.

Cartwright, D., & Zander, A. (1968). *Group dynamics.* New York: Harper and Row.

Foulkes, S. F. (1948). *Introduction to group analytic therapy.* London: William Heinemann Medical Books Ltd.

Foulkes, S. H. (1964). *Therapeutic group analysis.* London: George Allen and Unwin Ltd.

Foulkes, S. H. (1975a). *Group-analytic psychotherapy. Methods and principles.* London: Gordon and Breach Science Publishers Ltd.

Foulkes, S. H. (1975b). Qualifications as a psychoanalyst as an asset as well as a hindrance of a future group analyst. *Group Analysis, 8*(3), 180–182.

Fromm-Reichman, F. (1948). Notes on the development of treatment of schizophrenics by psycho-analytic psychology. *Psychiatry, 11,* 253–273.

Goldenberg, I., & Goldenberg, H. (2008a). Family therapy. In R. Corsini & D. Wedding (Eds.), *Current psychotherapies* (8th ed., pp. 402–436). Belmont, CA: Thomson-Wadsworth.

Goldenberg, H., & Goldenberg, I. (2008b). *Family therapy: An overview* (7th ed.). Belmont, CA: Thomson-Wadsworth.

Hollander, E. P. (1964). *Leaders, groups, and influence.* New York: Oxford University Press.

Kipper, D. A., & Ritchie, T. D. (2003). The effectiveness of psychodynamic techniques a meta-analysis. *Group Dynamics Theory and Practice, 7,* 13–25.

Kreiger, N. (2001). *Critical perspectus on racial and ethnic differences in health and later life.* National Academic Press.

Kuhn, T. (1970). *The structure of scientific revolutions.* Chicago: University of Chicago Press.

Main, T. F. (1946). The hospital as a therapeutic institution. *The Bulletin of the Menninger Clinic, 10*(3), 66–70.

Minuchin, S. (1974). *Families and family therapy.* Cambridge, MA: Harvard University Press.

Minuchin, S., & Fishman, H. C. (1981). *Family therapy techniques.* Cambridge, MA: Harvard University Press.

Moreno, J. L. (1946). *Psychodrama* (Vol. 1) Beacon, NY: Beacon House.

Moreno, J. L. (1948). *Psychodrama* (2nd ed.). New York: Beacon House.

Moreno, J. L. (1959). Psychodrama. In S. Arieti (Ed.), *American handbook of psychology* (Vol. 2, pp. 1275–1396). New York: Basic Books.

Perls, F. (1969). *Ego, hunger, and aggression.* New York: Random House. (Original work published 1947)

Prochaska, J. O., & Norcross, J. C. (1999). *Systems of psychotherapy: A transtheoretical analysis* (4th ed.). Pacific Grove, CA: Brooks-Cole.

Riva, M. T., & Smith, R. D. (1997). Looking into the future of group research: Where do we go from here? *Journal for Specialists in Group Work, 22,* 266–276.

Rose, S. D. (1991). The development and practice of group treatment. In M. Hersen, A. E. Kazdin, & A. Bellack (Eds.), *The clinical psychology handbook* (2nd ed., pp. 627–642). New York: Pergamon Press.

Schaffer, J. B. P., & Galinski, M. D. (1974). *Models of group therapy and sensitivity training* (p. 12). Englewood Cliffs, NJ: Prentice Hall.

Scharff, J. S., & Scharff, D. F. (1997). Object relations couple therapy. *American Journal of Psychotherapy, 51,* 143–173.

Simkin, J. S. (1979). Gestalt therapy. In R. J. Corsini and contributors (Eds.), *Current psychotherapies* (2nd ed., pp. 328–367). Itasca, IL: F. E. Peacock Publishers.

Slipp, S. (1988). *The technique and practice of object relations family therapy.* Northvale, NJ: Aronson.

Spotnitz, H. (1961). *The couch and the circle.* New York: Knopf.

Trull, T. (2005). *Clinical psychology* (7th ed.). Belmont, CA: Wadworth-Thomson.

U.S. Census Bureau. (2010). Glossary. Washington, DC: Government Printing Office. Retrieved September 30, 2010, from http://factfinder.census.gov/home/en/epss/glossary_f.html

U.S. Census Bureau. *Estimated median age at first marriage. United States Census Bureau Current Population Survey: March and annual social and economic supplements, 2005 and earlier.* Washington, DC: Government Printing Office.

Watzlawick, P., Weakland, J. H., & Fisch, R. (1974). *Change: Principles of problem formation and problem resolution.* New York: Norton.

Wiener, N. (1948). Cybernetics. *Scientific American, 179*(5), 14–18.

Wolf, A. (1975). Psychoanalysis in groups. In G. M. Gazda (Ed.), *Basic approaches to group psychotherapy and group counseling* (2nd ed.). Springfield, IL: Charles C. Thomas.

Wylie, M. S. (1990). Family therapy's neglected prophet. *Family Therapy Networker, 15*(2), 25–37.

Yalom, I. D. (1975). *The theory and practice of group psychotherapy.* New York: Basic Books.

Psychopharmacology

15

Learning Objectives

After reading this chapter, the student should be able to understand:

- The history of psychopharmacology including relevant legislation and protective measures instituted by the U.S. government
- The biochemistry of drug functioning, drug interactions, and adverse drug reactions
- The types, functions, and characteristics of various categories of psychotropic medications including antianxiety medications, antidepressant medications, mood stabilizers, antipsychotic medications, and psychostimulant medications
- The arguments for and against prescription privileges for psychologists

Topical Outline

- Principles of Psychopharmacology
- Principles of Drug Action
- Psychotropic Medications
- Prescription Privileges

Becky is a 47-year-old White female whose original referral to the clinical neuropsychologist was made by one of her friends who had also been treated by the clinical neuropsychologist. Becky's presenting complaint was depression and difficulty with relationships. However, after the initial intake interview it was very clear that she was suffering from post-traumatic stress disorder (PTSD) as well as depression and anxiety.

Historically, Becky is the oldest child of her biological parents. Her mother died when she was 46 and her father is 83 years old and remarried. Becky's parents had a total of 14 children whose current ages are the following: Becky, age 47 (eldest); Ron, age 46; Don, age 45; Ralph, age 43; Simon, age 42; Sue, age 40; Joan, age 38; Laurie, age 37; Margaret, age 36; Jim, age 35; John, age 34; Joe, age 32; Allie, 31; and Bob, age 30. All of Becky's siblings are living and most are married with children. Almost all of Becky's siblings reside within 20 miles of one another in a semi-rural area near a mid-size city. Becky's brother Joe, the only one with whom Becky is friendly, lives in Indiana and has distanced himself from the family. As adults, all of the brothers, except Joe, are alcoholics and some of the sisters have drinking problems.

Becky described her growing up as harsh and punitive. She was aware that her father was physically abused as a child and now understands that the pattern of physical abuse continues from generation to generation unless there is some form of intervention. Her mother had a healthy childhood but with so many children, she began to adopt her husband's punitive behaviors in order to manage all of the children. Becky's father worked outside of the home and had little contact with the children except in the role of disciplinarian. According to Becky, her mother always appeared to be pregnant and overworked. Due to the fact that she was the oldest girl, Becky was called on to take care of the other children very early in her life.

Gender roles were quite evident within her family with both explicit and implicit messages that womens' role in life was to serve men. Hence, Becky's role was to take care of her younger brothers until the next girl was old enough to help with the household and childcare duties. Because Becky's mother was so busy, events transpired which her mother either was not aware of or could not control. The problems which Becky described included being touched, fondled, and sexually penetrated by her four younger brothers next in line after her. Once another sister was born, the focus of the boys attention began to change. Becky believes that all of her sisters were sexually violated by at least one, but possibly, many of her brothers.

As soon as Becky graduated from high school at age 17, she moved out of the family home. She went to live with several girlfriends in a town near her home. The young women worked during the day and partied at night. In an unfortunate situation after the other girls had left with other men, Becky was left alone with a man who had been drinking and she was sexually assaulted. She tried to get away and was left bruised and battered. Subsequent to the assault, the man began to terrorize Becky for many days by waiting for her outside of her home. He finally found an opportunistic time and assaulted her a second time. Lacking a way to cope with the incident, she moved back to her family home. After 2 months, she married a man, Ray, she had met at a dance. Becky was not aware that Ray was an alcoholic because she had focused mainly on wanting to leave her family home.

Soon after the marriage, Becky's husband began to have affairs with other women. Ray stated that the affairs were due to Becky's lack of availability and Becky, due to her previous history, believed what he said. She recounted an incident which was particularly demeaning in which her husband brought home a woman with whom to have sex and expected Becky to cook breakfast for both of them the next morning. During the course of the marriage, Becky had a total of six children, four girls and two boys. She recalled periods of depression and desperation which she did not know how to overcome. She went to a clergy member who told her to be a better wife. She was *hospitalized in her late 30s for what she called a nervous breakdown. After she was released, her aftercare plan included a partial care program and group therapy. Becky felt that all of the interventions were helpful including many of the medications she was prescribed for depression while in the hospital. The only problem Becky had with the medications was that each one left her with a different type of side effect.*

After her hospitalization, Becky attempted to return to her previous life and demanded that her husband stop having affairs and drinking. Ray attended an inpatient chemical dependency program but never stopped seeing other women. Becky was finally able to leave her husband when it was determined that her daughters had been sexually assaulted by Becky's brothers. The continuation of sexual violence into her children's generation shocked her so dramatically that she involved law enforcement. Becky also obtained counseling services for each of her daughters.

At the time that Becky divorced she did not feel mentally competent to take care of her children. She went to court and agreed to allow her ex-husband and his soon-to-be second wife have the primary physical custody of all six children. Becky felt extreme guilt and shame that she was not healthy enough to take care of her children. Even though she had relinquished physical custody, she maintained visitation rights and felt she would be able to work toward having full physical custody. Becky moved into an apartment on her own with the intention of putting her life in order and resuming custody of the children. Becky enrolled and began to take classes at the local vocational college. She felt that her background as a homemaker and occasional daycare provider did not make her competitive within the job market.

Approximately 14 months after she was discharged from the inpatient unit for psychiatric services, she had completed 1 full year of college and had begun the second. Becky had obtained a work–study award and was assigned clerical duties in the administration building. Becky had attended a 6-month partial care program and was now involved in weekly group therapy for sexual assault survivors. She felt that she was ready to resume care of her children who were now 22 (F), 21 (F), 20 (F), 18 (M), 16 (F), and 14 (M). The older children had already established residence on their own and the oldest girl had given birth. Therefore, Becky decided that she would try to obtain custody for the youngest three. Ray was not happy but acquiesced to her wishes mainly because his present wife had brought her four children to live with them when they were married. Three less children appeared to solve a space and financial problem.

Soon after the three children moved in one of Becky's friends and also the group therapy counselor both suggested that she might benefit from individual attention, both, being quite observant, suggested the clinical neuropsychologist described at the beginning of the case study. The main concerns which both Becky's friend and group counselor had were attention and concentration difficulties as well as a tendency to "space out." The group counselor thought Becky might be dissociating and was concerned about her safety, particularly driving a vehicle. Becky's friend described a similar symptom in layperson's terms in which she "wasn't home in her head."

The first appointment with the clinical neuropsychologist was for an initial intake interview and to determine if any testing was necessary. Becky was on time for the appointment, well dressed but very nervous. She related the aforementioned information at times with teary eyes. She agreed that her concentration and attentional abilities were often poor and that she did "space out" returning to the circumstances of her sexual assaults. She also described vivid nightmares which appeared to be unpredictable in their occurrence and would leave her sleep deprived for the next day's activities. She also mentioned that passing the age her mother was when she died had been particularly difficult. The clinical neuropsychologist suggested a battery of neuropsychological tests to confirm these symptoms. He also suggested that Becky schedule a physical to rule out any medical problems which could potentially cause similar symptoms.

After all of the neuropsychological testing and the physical were completed, Becky and the clinical neuropsychologist scheduled an appointment to develop a treatment plan. The report from Becky's physician suggested that she was going through menopause and experiencing fluctuating hormones, which could affect her mood, concentration, attention, sleep, sex drive, appetite, and many other areas. The physician suggested that she discuss these findings with the clinical neuropsychologist because the symptoms in question appeared to predate the onset of menopause. The physician also reported that Becky had a history of low blood pressure and blood clots in her legs. If the symptoms were due to menopause, the physician would recommend hormone replacement therapy (HRT) or a type of antidepressant which often alleviates menopausal symptoms with consideration of how these drugs interact with her other medical difficulties.

The clinical neuropsychologist also found evidence of concentration, attention, and mood difficulties on the battery of tests. There is now a problem because it was not possible to clearly determine the etiology of Becky's symptoms. Becky was experiencing menopause, which causes some difficulties for most women. She also has a history of sexual assault and described many of the symptoms of PTSD. Particularly striking is the dissociation or spacing out episodes which are not symptoms of menopause.

The clinical neuropsychologist reviewed all of the material and determined that a multifaceted treatment plan would be the most effective. He thought that Becky should begin individual therapy to help her work through the multiple sexual assaults she had experienced and to develop skills for determining healthy from nonhealthy relationships. The clinical neuropsychologist also felt that Becky could benefit from ongoing attendance at her group therapy. Finally, he felt that Becky could benefit from medications to alleviate some of the symptoms from which she is suffering. While these medications would not cure the difficulties, they could help her function better in her day-to-day life and gain as much as possible from her therapy. The clinical neuropsychologist referred her to a psychiatrist who prescribed alprazolam (Xanax) 0.5 mg to be taken when she became anxious or felt panicky, trazodone (Desyrl) 50 mg, an antidepressant which is often used to aid in sleep, and sertraline (Zoloft) 50 mg, a selective serotonin reuptake inhibitor (SSRI) for depression. These doses are on the low end due to her low blood pressure. Becky was warned that alcohol use was dangerous while taking these medications and to be very careful while driving until she knew how the medicines would affect her. She was referred to her primary physician for a discussion regarding the use of HRT for menopausal symptoms. This was particularly important because she suffered from blood clots in her legs, which is often a contraindication for hormone treatment.

A s has been the case with many of the individuals discussed in this text, Becky has multiple issues which require a multifaceted treatment approach. She was treated with several forms of psychotherapy but without cognitive or memory remediation. This case, however, is the first time in which the reader encounters the role of medication in the treatment process. In addition to the use of medication, its potential side effects and contraindications and the interface with her overall physical condition, are the issues regarding who should prescribe her drugs. However, the clinical neuropsychologist practices in a state where the law does not allow a psychologist who has received advanced training and completed and passed a national board exam to be able to prescribe psychotropic medications (i.e., antianxiety medications, antidepressants, antipsychotic, and other mental health medications). This is a very controversial issue both within the mental health and the physical medicine communities.

psychotropic medications a category of medications that are used to treat mental health issues; included within this class are antianxiety medications, antidepressants, antipsychotics, lithium, stimulants, such as methylphenidate (Ritalin), and other drugs that may have uses in mental health but were not developed for such purposes such as donepezil (Aricept)

Introduction

The topic for this chapter is the use of psychotropic medications in clinical neuropsychology. *Psychotropic* refers to any form of substance, legal or not, which has an effect on an individual's psychological makeup. The beginning of the chapter will introduce the reader to the basics of psychopharmacology including terminology and the process involved with medication development, including protection for human subjects who are involved with drug trials for the development of medications. The second section of the chapter will cover the various categories of medications used in mental health. Chemicals such as alcohol and illegal drugs which are often used by an individual to self-medicate or treat oneself, will not be included. The chapter will be concluded with the heated controversy regarding prescription privileges. Many issues are involved with this discussion including the availability of prescribers, education necessary for prescription privileges, issues related to overlap of services by professional groups, and the cost of medications and safety for the consumer. In the case of central nervous system difficulties, the consumer is often a vulnerable adult or minor child and hence, their issues are compounded. At present, the professions which are allowed to prescribe psychotropic medications include physicians (primarily **psychiatrists**), **nurse practitioners**, and **physicians' assistants** and in some locales psychologists and **pharmacists**.

Principles of Psychopharmacology

Pharmacology stands at the center of medical services. It relates the mechanisms of drug action to the treatment of disease. Pharmacology interacts with biochemistry, immunology, cell biology, genetics, physiology, and pathology. Psychopharmacology is the study of the behavioral effects of drugs. Very often psychopharmacology is viewed as the study of chemical treatment of various mental disorders. In clinical neuropsychology, psychopharmacology is the study of the effects of psychotropic drugs on central nervous system disease or difficulty.

HISTORY

The study of psychopharmacology begins with the study of drugs and ends with their application and effectiveness. The major differences between pharmacy and psychopharmacology is that the former refers to the prescription of all medications whereas the latter involves medications which treat mental health difficulties. As a starting point for the discussion of medications themselves, drugs often appear to have unusual names to the average consumer. However, there are really only three names for each drug. The chemical name is the scientific name that describes its atomic and molecular structure. The generic name, or **nonproprietary name**, is an abbreviation of the chemical name. The **trade name** (or brand or **proprietary name**) is selected by the pharmaceutical company which sells the product. Trade names are protected by **copyright**, which comes from the Federal Patent and Trademark Office. The symbol ® indicates that a drug is registered and restricted to the drug manufacturer (Olson, 2001). The restriction also extends to the manufacture of the drug with the particular trade name.

In the past, drugs were developed by trial and error. Now there are systematic scientific research programs which the Food and Drug Administration (FDA) carefully monitors. The drugs are first tested using animal subjects. Once they have been evaluated using animals, the FDA may approve an application for an **Investigational New Drug** (IND). All INDs must undergo all four phases of clinical evaluation mandated by the FDA. The exception is in the case of a drug such as for HIV, which may receive **expedited approval**.

The INDs must go through all of the following phases involving use with human subjects, for which there are guidelines to protect them from harm. In Phase I, the drug is tested on healthy volunteers. In Phase II, the drug is used with human subjects who have

self-medication
a term that is often used when an individual tries to alleviate their symptoms by employing any or all of the following without consulting a physician: alcohol, illegal drugs, other individual's prescriptions, and various herbal treatments

prescription privilege
the legal ability to prescribe medications of a particular type

psychiatrist
a medical doctor who has a specialty in the treatment of mental illness predominately through the use of medication

nurse practitioner
a registered nurse who has completed advanced study to practice independently; this individual is not able to complete all of the tasks of a medical doctor but may prescribe certain classes of medication

physicians' assistant
an individual with an advanced degree beyond registered nurse but not to the extent of a medical doctor

pharmacist
distributes prescription drugs to individuals and advises on selection, dosage, interactions and side effects of medications

generic name
the abbreviation for the chemical name of a drug

Investigational New Drug
a drug that has successfully passed testing on animals and an application has been made to begin the four phases of testing with humans

expedited approval
early approval of an IND after Phase III testing has produced satisfactory because of the need for the drug; examples would include drugs for HIV and the H1N1 virus

the disease for which the drug is thought to be effective. Phase III involves larger numbers of patients in medical research centers receiving the drug to garner information regarding infrequent or rare adverse effects. The FDA will approve drugs if Phase III studies are satisfactory. Even though it has been stated that all drugs must go through all four phases, Phase IV is voluntary and involves postmarket evaluation of the drug's effects. The pharmaceutical company receives information from doctors and other health care professionals regarding the therapeutic effects and any possible adverse reactions to the drugs. The average length of time for this process to be completed is 10 years and costs about $800 million (Pharmaceutical Manufacturers Association, 2004).

Drugs or medications are now tightly controlled by regulations and prescriptions are required for the medications which will be discussed in relationship to the treatment of central nervous system difficulties. Controls on drugs are for consumer safety as are the trials for drug approval. It has not always been the case that drugs and drug use were controlled and regulated in the United States or throughout the world. Prior to the early 1900s, any substance could be produced and sold within the United States without any control regarding safety or purity. The publication of Upton Sinclair's (1906) *The Jungle* exposed the horribly unsanitary conditions in the meatpacking industry and shocked the American public and Congress. Several months after the book's publication, with pressure from then President Theodore Roosevelt, the Pure Food and Drug Act was passed. This act prohibited interstate commerce in adulterated or misbranded foods and drugs. The Pure Food and Drugs Act was administered by the Department of Agriculture.

In the early 1900s, Dr. Hamilton Wright thought that the United States could gain favored trading status with China by leading international efforts to aid the Chinese in their efforts to reduce opium importation. An international conference was held in 1912 at the request of the United States to discuss controls on the opium trade. Dr. Wright drafted a bill that was submitted by Senator Harrison of New York, which stated its intent as follows: "An act to provide for the registration of, with collectors of internal revenue, and to impose a special tax upon all persons who produce, import, manufacture, compound, deal in, dispense, or give away opium or coca leaves, their salts, derivatives, or preparations and for other purposes" (Harrison Narcotics Tax Act, 1914). This act was termed the Harrison Act and required physicians and pharmacists to register with the Treasury Department when they prescribed the aforementioned preparations. However, this was not an attempt to control drug purity but to limit expansion and availability of these drugs through taxation.

Despite these acts, there were many instances where manufacturers tried to produce and sell adulterated or misbranded products. During the 1930s, the use of "sulfa" was expanded as an effective antibiotic agent. A chemist who was looking for a liquid form found that sulfanilamide would dissolve in diethylene glycol. The concoction looked and tasted fine but diethylene glycol caused kidney poisoning and 107 people died from Elixir Sulfanilamide. There was no way for the government to intervene using the existing laws and seeing a crisis with no regulation to stop it, the Food, Drug, and Cosmetic Act was passed in 1938 (Young, 1967). The major change with this act was the provision for testing for toxicity before marketing. This led to the provision for a **New Drug Application** (NDA) status. This act also made it clear that directions for taking a drug must be included and also differentiated between over-the-counter and prescription drugs. In 1962, the Kefauver-Harris Amendment added important provisions including the aforementioned testing on humans. This act followed the unfortunate birth defect scandal due to the drug thalidomide being excessively prescribed to pregnant women. During the early 1960s, predominately in West Germany but also in the United States, hundreds of babies had been born with deformed limbs due to thalidomide. In 1966, the FDA began

New Drug Application
a formal proposal by pharmaceutical companies to the FDA to approve a drug for sale and marketing

the process of evaluating the formulations of prescription drugs. In the next 8 years, the FDA removed 6,133 drugs manufactured by 2,732 companies (Ksir, Hart, & Ray, 2008). In addition, from 1994–2003, the FDA approved an average of 32 new drugs per year.

Narcotics to the average person refers to drugs that are manufactured and sold illegally. Pharmacologically, narcotics are drugs which cause certain effects such as analgesic pain-killers. Although the Harrison Act controlled opioids, which are narcotics, and cocaine, which is not a narcotic, enforcement focused mostly on opium, which led Treasury Department agents to be known at that time as narcotics officers. The division within the Treasury Department charged with enforcement officially became the Narcotics Division. In response to prohibition and improprieties within the existing department, in 1938, Congress formed a separate Bureau of Narcotics within the Treasury Department.

The 1960s saw a great change in society regarding social mores and there was increased use of various illegal drugs. In response to this, the 1965 Drug Abuse Control Amendment was instituted and the Bureau of Narcotics became the Bureau of Narcotics and Dangerous Drugs. The Comprehensive Drug Abuse Prevention and Control Act of 1970 replaced and updated all previous drug laws and was often referred to as the Controlled Substances Act. This law stated that the drugs controlled by the act were under federal jurisdiction regardless of international or interstate commerce, but did not eliminate state regulations. The act excludes alcohol and tobacco products from its control, often thought due to the influence of alcohol and tobacco company lobbyists. The act dealt with the prevention and treatment of drug abuse by using federal funds to expand the role of community mental health centers and public hospitals in the treatment of those who misuse drugs. In terms of enforcement of drug use, it moved the focus from the Treasury Department to the Department of Justice.

The Controlled Substances Act led to the following drug schedules (see Figure 15.1). The major distinction between the schedules are that Schedule I drugs have no accepted medical use, whereas Schedules II–V drugs are primarily prescription drugs and further controlled. Schedule I drugs have a high potential for abuse and have no currently acceptable medical use in treatment in the United States. Examples of Schedule I drugs are heroin and marijuana. Schedule II drugs have a high potential for abuse which may lead to severe psychological or physical dependence but have accepted medical use. Examples of Schedule II drugs are morphine and methamphetamine. Schedule III drugs have less potential for abuse which may lead to moderate physical or high psychological dependence and have accepted medical uses. Examples of Schedule III drugs are barbiturates and anabolic steroids. Schedule IV drugs have a lower level of abuse potential which may lead to limited physical or psychological dependence and that have accepted medical use. Examples of Schedule IV drugs are alprazolam (Xanax) and chlorohydrate. Schedule V drugs have a low potential for abuse and limited physical or psychological dependence but have medical use. Examples of Schedule V drugs include drug combinations which include codeine. Due to the changes in society post-1960s and the increases in drug use, many pharmacies declined to carry what were then termed *Class A narcotics*. Class A narcotics are synonymous with drugs that were later termed *Schedule I drugs*.

The Controlled Substances Act separated enforcement of drug use, which was the responsibility of the attorney general, from the decision regarding which drugs are to be controlled that is decided by the secretary of the Department of Health and Human Services (HHS). The Drug Enforcement Agency (DEA) was created in 1975 as the enforcement arm of the Justice Department.

The Omnibus Drug Act of 1988 made additions to the already existing act by including control over registration of airplanes, money laundering, firearms sales to felons, chemicals used to make drugs, and the death penalty for drug-related murders. A 1994

FIGURE 15.1
Summary of controlled substance
schedules

Schedule	Criteria	Examples
Schedule I	a. High potential for abuse b. No currently acceptable medical use in treatment in the United States c. Lack of accepted safety for use under medical supervision.	Heroin Marijuana MDMA (Ecstasy)
Schedule II	a. High potential for abuse b. Currently accepted medical use c. Abuse may lead to severe psychological or physical dependence.	Morphine Cocaine Methamphetamine
Schedule III	a. Potential for abuse less than I and II b. Currently accepted medical use c. Abuse may lead to moderate physical dependence or high psychological dependence.	Anabolic steroids Most barbiturates Dronabinol
Schedule IV	a. Low potential for abuse relative to III b. Currently accepted medical use c. Abuse may lead to limited physical or psychological dependence relative to III.	Alprazolam (Xanax) Barbital Chloral hydrate Fenfluramine
Schedule V	a. Low potential for abuse relative to IV b. Currently accepted medical use c. Abuse may lead to limited physical or psychological dependence relative to IV.	Mixtures having small amounts of codeine or opium

modification of the act extended the death penalty to drug lords and other major drug production and distribution figures. A cabinet level position controls and regulates this act and the individual in that position was given additional power and control in 1998 with the development of the Office of National Drug Control Policy.

Returning to our case study, Becky has been administered several antidepressants and antianxiety medications by prescription. Each of these medications have potential side effects, contraindications, and possible interactions with each other. Becky's antianxiety medications would be Schedule IV drugs and her antidepressants are Schedule V. Her antianxiety medication because of the abuse potential, was given with a 6-month refill prescription, whereas she may be prescribed a year of refills for her antidepressants, which have lower levels for potential abuse.

HUMAN SUBJECTS PROTECTION

As alluded to earlier, human subjects must be used for a drug to be approved for human consumption. Protection for human subjects has a history dating back to post–World War II and many of the provisions came after the deplorable experiments conducted on living humans by the Nazis during World War II. Soon after the end of World War II and during the trials of Nazi war criminals, the Nuremberg Code was developed (Mitscherlich & Mielke, 1949). The initial six principles were used to assist in the prosecution of Nazi war criminals. The Nuremberg tribunal later added four other principles, which then became the Nuremberg Code. The Belmont Report, a document developed by the National Commission for the Protection of Human Subjects of Biomedical and Behavioral Research (1979) at the Department of Health, Education, and Welfare described the code as stating many of what are now assumed the basic principles governing the ethical conduct of research involving human subjects. The first premise is for voluntary consent on the part of the subject. It implies capacity or ability to

Nuremberg Code
a document created and used after World War II to prosecute Nazi war criminals; it states the basic rights of human subjects used in research and has been the prototype for various other codes for protection of human subjects

consent, freedom from coercion, and comprehension of the risks and benefits involved. Other provisions require the minimization of risk and harm, a favorable risk/benefit ratio, qualified investigators using appropriate research designs and freedom for the subject to withdraw from the study at any time. Similar provisions were made by the World Medical Association (1996) in its Declaration of Helsinki: Recommendations Guiding Medical Doctors in Biomedical Research Involving Human Subjects. Many other organizations have taken information from these documents including the Department of Health and Human Services that requires researchers who they fund to provide clear and detailed information regarding human subject protection. The American Psychological Association (APA) in its code of ethics, clearly states similar principles as those already discussed (APA, 2002). Ultimately, the delineation of principles for humane treatment of human subjects in research led to the creation of the Institutional Review Board (IRB) and its procedures (Penslar & Porter, 2009). Any research at any institution which uses humans as subjects of research must submit a proposal delineating the research and the protections for the human subjects before the researcher is allowed to use human subjects. Approval from an IRB must be done before any pharmaceutical company may administer drugs to human subjects. The FDA has made provisions for institutions engaged in human subject research to have their research reviewed by an outside IRB if the institution does not have such a board. In January, 2005, the Office of Management and Budget approved the Federalwide Assurance (FWA) forms and related documents and the IRB or Independent Ethics Committee (IEC) registration forms. This change affected any researcher who received federal funding through the HHS. New forms and procedures were generated to make a clear and uniform approach to the protection of human subjects. These forms and procedures also affect individuals who are employed at other institutions who have IRBs but are working with an individual who is covered by the FWA. The reader is referred to HHS Office for Human Research Protections Web site (http://www.hhs.gov/ohrp/) for a further discussion of these changes. In addition to human subjects' protection, there also exists corresponding review boards for the humane treatment of animals that are used as research subjects. The APA (2002) clearly delineates the appropriate treatment of animals in research programs.

At present, Becky has not been prescribed any medication which has not been approved through drug trials for the symptoms she has exhibited. However, Becky's psychiatrist may determine that an **off-label or unlabeled** use of a medication, technically the use of a medication for an illness or affliction for which it was not approved by the FDA, may be of help to her. Off-label use of medications is a common practice among prescribers once a drug has been shown to be effective for a difficulty for which it was not intended. An example is the antidepressant paroxetine (Paxil), which was designed and tested to treat symptoms of depression but has also been proven to help with the symptoms of obsessive–compulsive disorder (OCD). The discovery was thought to have occurred when an individual who had comorbid depression and OCD benefited from the relief of symptoms of both difficulties when taking paroxetine (Paxil). In a different situation, if Becky was asked to participate in a drug trial of a new medication she would then have her rights as a research subject explained to her. This situation could easily occur, due to the fact that there are many psychotropic drugs that are currently in the review stage and often try to entice participation in a drug study by offering the participant free medication.

> **off-label or unlabeled**
> a prescriber's use of an FDA-approved medication for a difficulty for which it was not approved; often approval of the medication for the new ailment appears later; examples include the use of anticonvulsants and atypical antipsychotics for the treatment of bipolar disorder

Principles of Drug Action

After a discussion of the history of drugs and their regulation including protection of human subjects, this chapter will discuss elementary principles of psychopharmacology.

The reader is referred to Julien (2005) for a more in-depth or extensive discussion regarding these topics.[1] The topics described here will be pharmacokinetics, pharmacodynamics, pharmacotherapeutics, drug interactions, and adverse side effects.

PHARMACOKINETICS

Pharmacokinetics relates to a drug's actions as it moves through the body. The process of progression through the body includes absorption, distribution, metabolism, and elimination. The time it takes for a drug to be absorbed and distributed accounts for the appearance of how long it takes for a drug to begin to have its effects. The time it takes for metabolism and excretion accounts for the time for the termination of the drug's effects after a single dose.

Absorption is the beginning process in which the drug is taken within the body. There are several routes through which the drug may be administered including orally, rectally, through inhalation via the mucus membrane of the mouth or nose, through the skin, through injection in the skin, or injection into the muscle. Each of these routes will cause the drug to enter the system at a different rate. Also related to the speed in which the drug enters the system is the dosage of the drug and the dosage form (liquid, tablet, capsule, injection, patch, spray, or gum). In addition, taking a medication with food or certain beverages often reduces absorption, whereas taking a drug on an empty stomach often enhances the speed of absorption of some drugs. The consumption of more than one drug at a time may affect absorption as the drugs may potentiate one another or compete for receptor sites. Some drugs which are absorbed from the stomach after oral administration are stimulated by grapefruit juice. Grapefruit juice, unlike other citrus juices, inhibits one of the body's intestinal enzyme systems and may result in large increases in serum levels of some prescription drugs (Greenblatt, 2001).

Once absorbed into the bloodstream, a drug is distributed throughout the body by the circulating blood, which is dependent on blood flow, solubility, and protein binding, which is the combining of drug molecules with blood proteins. The drug is quickly distributed to organs with a large supply of blood such as the heart, liver, and kidneys. Distribution to the internal organs, skin, fat, and muscle is slower. The drug may need to cross many cell membranes. The drug is either **water soluble** or **lipid (fat) soluble**. Lipid soluble drugs easily cross cell membranes while water-soluble drugs cannot. Lipid soluble drugs are able to cross the **blood-brain barrier** and enter the brain.

blood-brain barrier group of compacted cells so tightly bound together they keep toxic substances out of the brain

Metabolism is the next stage and refers to the body's ability to change a drug from its dosage form to a water-soluble form, which may be excreted. Drugs may be metabolized in various manners. The most common manner is for a drug to be metabolized into **inactive metabolites**, or products of metabolism, which are then excreted. Some drugs are metabolized as **active metabolites**, which implies that they are capable of having their own effects. Metabolites then undergo further metabolism or may be excreted unchanged. Drugs may be administered as inactive drugs called **prodrugs**, which do not become active until they are metabolized. Most drugs are metabolized in the liver but some may be metabolized in the plasma, kidneys, or membranes of the intestine. The most important drug-metabolizing enzymes found within the liver cells (hepatocytes) are part of the **cytochrome P450 enzyme family**. This gene family has diversified to accomplish the metabolism or detoxification of environmental chemicals, food, toxins, and

---

[1] Julien, R. M. (2005). *A primer of drug action: A comprehensive guide to the action, uses, and side effects of psychoactive drugs* (10th ed.). New York: Worth.

drugs. The function of these enzymes in the hepatocytes will be very important when we discuss the function, distribution, and drug interactions of various psychoactive drugs. In addition, some drugs compete for enzyme metabolism which may cause an accumulation of drugs which may lead to toxicity or other reactions.

Excretion is the final step for the drug when it is eliminated from the body. The majority of drugs are excreted by the kidneys and leave the body via the urine. Drugs may also be excreted by the lungs, skin, intestinal tract, or exocrine glands (sweat, salivary, or mammary glands).

PHARMACODYNAMICS

Pharmacodynamics refers to drug mechanisms that produce physiological and biochemical changes in the body. It is the process in which the average person considers how a drug works. The interaction between a drug and the proteins that constitute the cell membranes, enzymes, or target receptors represents **drug action**. The response resulting from the drug action is the **drug effect**. A drug is usually termed an agonist or an antagonist in its function within the receptor.

An **agonists** are defined as a drug (or hormone or neurotransmitter) that causes a response by interacting with a receptor on (or sometimes in) cells. Agonists have the property of **affinity**, which is the ability to bind to the receptor and stimulate it. Agonists also have the property of **efficacy**, the ability to cause a response through interaction with the receptors.

An **antagonist** drug has the affinity for a receptor but does not stimulate the receptor. The antagonist prevents a response from occurring. Antagonists may be described as **competitive** or **noncompetitive**. A competitive antagonist competes for the receptor site with the agonist. Due to the fact that this type of receptor binds reversibly to the receptor site, administering larger doses of an agonist is able to overcome the antagonist's effects. A noncompetitive antagonist binds to a receptor site and blocks the effects of the agonist. Administering large doses of the agonist does not reverse its action.

Drug potency is the term used to refer to the amount of a drug required to produce a desired response. Drug potency is also used to compare drugs. If a particular drug (Drug A) causes the same response as another drug (Drug B) but at a lower dose, then the first drug is more potent than the second. The **dose–response curve** may be used to explain the dose of drug and its response (see Figure 15.2).

Using the dose–response curve as a graphic, it is easy to see that a low dose usually is related to a low response. When more of the drug is administered, only a small increase in the response is noted. At a certain point, further increase in the dose causes a greater increase in drug response. **Maximum effectiveness** is reached when a further increase in the drug causes little or no increase in response. The relationship between a drug and its desired therapeutic effects and its adverse effects is called its **therapeutic index**. It is also referred to as its **margin of safety**. The therapeutic index measures the difference between an effective dose for 50% of the patients treated and the minimal dose at which adverse reactions occur. Very often, the therapeutic index is cited as the ratio of LD_{50}/ED_{50}. The LD is the lethal dose for 50% of the subjects and the ED_{50} is the effective dose for 50% of the subjects. Prior to the therapeutic index being discerned for a drug for human consumption, it has already been established in preclinical trials with animals. In the process of the animal trials, a relatively good estimate of the therapeutic index has been determined before any drug is administered to humans. Drugs and medications with low therapeutic indices have narrow margins of safety. Lithium, used in the treatment of bipolar disorder, has often been thought to have a low therapeutic index but with continued research, a larger therapeutic index has been achieved for a variant of this medication. As may be

---

drug action
interaction between a drug and proteins in the cell membrane, enzymes, or target receptors

drug effect
response resulting from drug action

agonist
drug that interacts with a receptor in a manner so that the receptor responds as it would with its own neurotransmitter

affinity
ability of an agonist drug to bind to stimulate a receptor

efficacy
ability of an agonist drug to cause a response through interaction with receptors

antagonist
drug that interacts with but does not stimulate a receptor; the antagonist prevents a response

competitive antagonist
drug that competes for a receptor site using an agonist drug

noncompetitive antagonists
drug that binds to a receptor site and blocks the effect of an agonist

drug potency
amount of a drug required to produce a desired effect

dose–response curve
graph comparing the size of response to the amount of drug

maximum effectiveness
level when any further increase in the amount of drug causes little or no response

therapeutic index
ratio of lethal dose to effective dose for half of the subjects in an experiment (LD_{50}/ED_{50})

margin of safety
synonymous with therapeutic index; difference between effective dose for 50% of patients treated and minimal dose at which adverse reactions occur

FIGURE 15.2 Dose-response curves for three stimulants. *Source:* Adapted from Julien (2005).

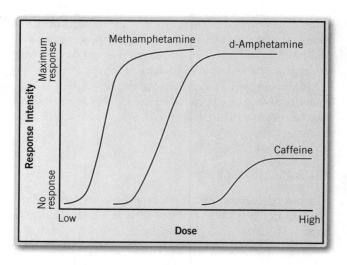

inferred, a drug with a high therapeutic index has a large margin of safety and less risk of toxic effects. Antibiotics are often thought to have high therapeutic indices.

There are several types of receptors on which a drug may have an effect. If a drug has effects on multiple types of receptors, it is termed nonselective and may cause multiple and widespread effects. Receptors are classified by their specific functions. Ionotropic (ion channel–coupled) receptors are those in which the drug or neurotransmitter molecule binds directly to a site or an ion channel and therefore regulates the movement of ions in and out of the postsynaptic cell. Metabotropic (G protein–coupled) receptors are those in which the binding of a drug or neurotransmitter to the receptor begins a series of events within the postsynaptic cell. After a series of events, the drug or neurotransmitter changes the permeability of the cell membrane. Ionotropic receptors are known for rapid response, whereas metabotropic receptors have slower responses due to the intermediary steps. The attachment of the drug to the metabotropic receptor alters the state of a protein in the postsynaptic membrane (G protein), which in turn alters the activity of an enzyme. The two main enzymes involved in this process are adenosine cyclase and phospholipase-C.

PHARMACOTHERAPEUTICS

Pharmacotherapeutics is the use of medications or drugs to treat disease. There are many reasons why a prescriber may choose a particular drug to administer to a particular patient with a particular difficulty.

This text has already discussed various patient variables which have an effect on the rehabilitation strategies chosen. The disease or difficulty from which a person is suffering also has impact on the drug of choice with central nervous system difficulties impacting pharmacokinetic and pharmacodynamics. In addition, the type of care must be considered when making a choice of medication. Variables that need to be considered include the severity of the patient's difficulties, the urgency for treatment, and the prognosis for the patient's future health and condition. **Acute care** is needed if the patient is critically ill and requires immediate assistance. **Empiric care** is based on practical experience rather than scientific data. Very often, information for this type of care comes from how things worked in the past and is then carried forward into the present. **Maintenance care** is treatment for patients with chronic conditions who probably will not completely recover. **Supplemental or replacement care** is treatment to substitute for missing substances within the body. **Supportive care** does not treat the cause of the disease but maintains other threatened body systems. **Palliative care** is treatment for patients who have terminal disease and will not recover.

As stated earlier, the patient's overall health, as well as other personal, medical, and lifestyle factors, must be considered when selecting a drug or medication. Several personal variables are reiterated as they are extremely important at this juncture in the choice of drug treatment, which include age, gender, diet, disease state, drug interactions, gastrointestinal functioning, liver functioning, renal functioning, and cardiovascular functioning.

In the choice of medications, it is also important to consider that there exist multiple medications to treat a particular ailment and that some medications may be more likely to lead to drug tolerance or **drug dependence**. Drug tolerance often occurs when a patient has a decreased response to a drug over time. The patient then needs more of the drug to produce the same response. A current example of this is the concern regarding the overuse of a number of pain medications. Drug dependence occurs when an individual exhibits physical or psychological need for the drug.

drug tolerance
the state of progressively decreasing response to a drug

DRUG INTERACTIONS

Drugs may have interactions with other drugs or with foods. Certain drugs interfere with laboratory tests. Drug interactions predominately include additive effects, potentiation, antagonistic effects, decreased or increased absorption, or decreased and increased metabolism, distribution, and excretion.

An additive effect occurs when two drugs with similar actions are administered to the patient. The drug effects are the sum of the effects of either drug administered alone in higher doses. Prescribers may give two drugs together to avoid higher doses of certain drugs or to decrease the probability of adverse reactions to a particular drug. Potentiation happens when two drugs which produce the same effect are given together and one drug enhances or has a synergistic effect on the other. The effect in this case is that the combination produces greater drug effects than each drug taken alone. Antagonistic drug effects happen when the response to the drugs administered together is less than the response of either drug alone.

The absorption of one drug may be altered by the effects of another drug. Drugs may change the acidity of the stomach and affect the ability of other drugs from being absorbed. Some drugs are able to interact with other drugs and form a compound that is not able to be absorbed. When two drugs are administered together, they may compete for protein-binding sites during distribution, which may lead to an increase in the effects of one drug. Toxic levels may also occur when one drug inhibits another drug from being excreted from the body.

ADVERSE DRUG REACTIONS

An adverse reaction is a side effect that is often harmful. Adverse reactions may be mild and remit after medication discontinuation or may be permanent. Adverse reactions may also be life-threatening or cause a severe disease or chronic difficulty. Adverse reactions may be dose related or patient-sensitivity related. Most adverse reactions are related to the chemical effects of a drug and are often predicted and explained to the patient at the time the prescription is written. Dose-related reactions include secondary effects, hypersusceptiblity, overdose, and iatrogenic effects (see Figure 15.3).

FIGURE 15.3 Common
adverse drug interactions
and drug side effects
for representative psychotropic medications.

Category I: Psychostimulants	
Stimulant Medications Used to Treat ADHD	
Expected benefits of medication: increased ability to focus; decreased distractibility; decreased impulsivity; decreased hyperactivity	
Name of Drug	Most Common Side Effects
Ritalan Psychostimulants	Stomach upset, nausea, vomiting, loss of appetite, changes in growth pattern; dizziness; anxiety; irritability; headache; increased blood pressure and pulse
Category II: Antidepressants	
SSRI Prozac	Common to all SSRIs: Nausea; decreased appetite; weight loss or gain; excessive sweating; insomnia; jitteriness, dizziness; increased appetite; dry mouth
NDRIs Wellbutrin Buproprion	Agitation; insomnia; weight loss; constipation; tremors; seizures
MAOI Nardil Phenelzine	Drowsiness; constipation; nausea, diarrhea; stomach upset; fatigue; dry mouth
Tricyclics Anafranil Clomipramine	Headache; fatigue; dry mouth; drowsiness; shakiness
Category III: Anti-anxiety	
Anti-anxiety medications are used to treat treatment of sleep terror syndrome and anxiety disorders. May also be indicated in treating panic disorder, bi-polar disorder in adolescents, aggressive dyscontrol and tic disorders.	
Expected benefits of medication: Decrease in anxiety; decrease/elimination of sleep terror syndrome; increase in ability to control aggressive behavior; increased control of tic disorder	
Name of Drug	Most Common Side Effects
Buspar Buspirone	Drowsiness; dizziness, lightheadedness; fatigue weakness; blurred vision
Neurotin Gabapentin	Drowsiness; dizziness, fatigue; vision changes; weight gain
Category IV: Mood Stabilizers	
Mood stabilizers are used in the treatment of bi-polar disorder (manic-depressive), excessive mood swings, aggressive behavior, impulse control disorders, and severe mood symptoms in schizoaffective disorders and schizophrenia.	
Expected benefits of medication: Stabilization of mood swings; decrease in aggressive behavior; decrease in impulsivity	
Name of Drug	Most Common Side Effects
Carbolith, Duralith, Eskalith, Lithobid, Lithane, Lithium carbonate, Cibalith-S, Lithium critrate	Drowsiness; increased thirst; tremors; weight gain
Depakote Divalproex sodium	Abdominal pain with cramps; hair loss; anorexia; diarrhea; nausea, vomiting; tremors,
Category V: Anti-psychotics	
Anti-psychotic medications are used in the treatment of schizophrenia and can be helpful in controlling psychotic symptoms (delusions, hallucinations) or disorganized thinking. Anti-psychotics may also be indicated in the treatment of explosive aggression in conduct disorder, disruptive behaviors and agitation in children with developmental delays (mental retardation, autism, or pervasive developmental delays), tic disorders and Tourettes's syndrome, adolescent onset bi-polar disorders, early onset psychotic depression, disruptive behaviors and agitation in children with traumatic brain injuries.	
Expected benefits of medication: Stabilization of psychotic symptoms (decrease or eliminate hallucinations/delusions); decrease in aggressive behavior; decrease anxiety; decrease agitation; decrease disruptive behaviors; increase control of Tic or Tourette's symptoms	
Risperdal Respiridone	Extrapyramidal effects (EPS); agitation, anxiety; headache; weight gain, high blood glucose; sleepiness; low blood pressure when standing up; headache; tremor; constipation, diarrhea, nausea/vomiting

A medication produces not only the effect that it was intended to have but also other untoward effects referred to as secondary effects. Many antidepressants, for example, have a primary effect of relief of depressive symptoms. Secondary effects, dependent on the particular antidepressant, are symptoms such as dry mouth and constipation. An individual may be hypersusceptible to the actions of a drug when given the usual prescribed dosage. A hypersusceptible individual may experience excessive drug effects or side effects. Hypersusceptiblity usually results from difficulties with pharmacokinetics, which cause a higher than expected blood level of the medication. A toxic drug reaction may occur when a drug in the system causes death. **Iatrogenic effects** mimic or appear as pathological disorders. Aspirin is a typical example of a substance which has the potential to lead to gastrointestinal distress and potential bleeding and is easily avoided if the directions are followed carefully. A drug allergy occurs in a situation when a patient's immune system responds to the drug or medication as if it were a dangerous substance. A drug allergy may vary from a rash to the most severe **anaphylactic reaction**, which is swelling of the larynx and bronchioles that impedes breathing and may cause death.

Becky had been prescribed many different antidepressants while she was an inpatient in the hospital and by her primary care physician before working with her psychiatrist. Each of the medications she tried had various side effects. These included an off-label trial of risperidone (an atypical antipsychotic often prescribed as a mood stabilizer), which did not alleviate her depressive symptoms and also caused her to gain 60 lbs, which were difficult for her to shed. At the time the psychiatrist discussed with her the medications he thought were most appropriate, she was very concerned regarding side effects. The psychiatrist discussed the pharmacokinetics with Becky including use with food to avoid a large concentration of drug in her system and possible stomach irritation and to refrain from grapefruit juice. In terms of the pharmacodynamics, the drugs which were prescribed have a good margin of safety. Talking with Becky, the psychiatrist felt she was a responsible person and would take her medication as prescribed and he was not overly concerned regarding her potential for overdose. The type of care Becky is receiving would most likely be termed *maintenance* because she has a long history of PTSD and depression, which may never completely abate. Drug interactions will need to be considered and the psychiatrist requested that Becky discuss the medications be prescribed with her primary care physician before he prescribes any further medications, such as HRT. Side effects to the medications prescribed by the psychiatrist are generally minimal and often become less as the individual's system becomes accustomed to the medications. The most common side effects are dizziness, drowsiness, dry mouth, and constipation. Becky stated she has felt comfortable with the medications chosen by the psychiatrist.

iatrogenic effects
difficulties introduced in a patient by a physician's care; the example in the chapter shows how aspirin to treat one difficulty may cause gastrointestinal ailments

anaphylactic reaction
a serious drug allergy; swelling of the larynx and bronchioles that impedes breathing and may cause death; if caught early it may be treatable

Psychotropic Medications

The term *psychotropic medications* is often used synonymously with psychoactive medications and refers to drugs which have an effect on the brain, or, in the case of clinical neuropsychology, the brain and spinal cord or the central nervous system. This section of the chapter covers the traditional mental health medications which are often used with central nervous system difficulties. The categories which will be explored include antianxiety medications (anxiolytics), antidpressants, mood stabilizers, antipsychotics (typical and atypical), and stimulants such as methylphenidate (Ritalin). Medications which are designed for the particular symptoms of various central nervous system difficulties, such as drugs for Parkinson's disease, cardiovascular functioning, and so forth, are beyond the scope of this chapter and the reader is referred to *Clinical Pharmacology Made Ridiculously Simple*.[2]

---

[2] (2001). *Clinical pharmacology made ridiculously simple*. Springhouse, PA: Springhouse.

Psychotropic medications have their effects on the neurotransmitters which are released from a presynaptic neuron into a synapse to be absorbed by a postsynaptic receptor, muscle, or gland. A majority of the psychotropic medications have effects on the neurotransmitters serotonin, norepinephrine, dopamine, or acetylcholine. Different types of drugs may increase the amount or decrease the amount of various neurotransmitters or combinations of neurotransmitters. Different areas of the central nervous system are affected by each type of medication. These are general statements which do not pertain to all of the medications. Medications and their particular effects will be explained within the applicable sections.

ANTIANXIETY MEDICATIONS

Anxiety, to a certain degree, is a part of most individual's lives. When anxiety causes difficulties with the individual's functioning, whether at work or home, or is secondary to the effects of central nervous system disease or difficulty, it may be time for the individual to consult a prescriber for antianxiety medications.

Antianxiety medications are categorized as barbiturates, benzodiazepines, and buspirone. The barbiturates are older drugs with a low margin of safety and, hence, are not frequently prescribed. The benzodiazepines are of two types, the older drugs such as diazepam (Valium) and chlordiazepoxide (Librium), which have high-abuse potential, and the second-generation drugs which are safer and currently marketed as sleep preparations. The reader may be interested to note that during the 1970s (1972–1978) diazepam (Valium) was the most commonly prescribed medication by physicians, predominately to women. A current medication, buspirone, has a different chemical structure than the other drugs and causes fewer side effects. Due to the fact that all antianxiety medications have some abuse and dependence potential, prescribers often limit the use of these drugs to 6–8 weeks. The rational for this amount of time is that it allows the patient to achieve enough control over the anxiety he or she is experiencing that he or she may benefit from individual therapy or cognitive or memory rehabilitation.

Prior to the development of the anxiolytics, alcohol had been used for hundreds of years to reduce anxiety and induce sleep. Later, opium began to be used in a similar fashion. Bromide and chloral hydrate became available during the latter half of the 19th century and appeared safer and more reliable. In 1912, phenobarbital became the first barbiturate introduced as a form of sedative. Barbiturates were the drug of choice for anxiety and insomnia from 1912 to the 1960s. They were responsible for thousands of suicides, deaths from accidental overdose, dependency, and abuse. Barbiturates are typically grouped based on their duration of activity. The barbiturates are one of the classes of drugs that stimulate the activity of the CYP450 enzymes of the liver. As is the case with benzodiazepines, the barbiturates bind to the receptor site for the inhibitory neurotransmitter gamma-aminobutyric acid (GABA) in the brain stem (Tomlin, Jenkins, Lieb, & Franks, 1999). While barbiturates bind to the $GABA_A$ receptors and facilitate GABA binding, they are also capable of opening the chloride channel in the absence of GABA. This additional action is the cause of the increase in toxicity in comparison to benzodiazepines (Julien, 2005). The tolerance which develops to these drugs is the result of an increased rate of deactivation. Physical and psychological dependencies are also possible with barbiturates. Despite all the adverse difficulties with the barbiturates, they are used occasionally as anticonvulsants, as intravenous anesthetics, to provide for the lowering of intracranial pressure after brain trauma, and to sedate for an amytal interview (Roberts, 2000). An amytal interview is when an individual is administered amobarbital to induce a state of disinhibition to supposedly uncover otherwise guarded information (Kavirajan, 1999).

Antiepileptic drugs are used to treat seizures and have wide use in clinical neuropsychology particularly after head trauma. Epilepsy is the central nervous system disorder in which chronically recurring seizures are the main symptom. The original antiepileptic drugs belong to the two chemically similar classes, barbiturates or hydantoins. Newer drugs either resemble GABA or act on GABA receptors to potentiate neurotransmission. The newer drugs such as carbamazepine and valproic acid became available in the 1980s. Phenobarbital was the first of the barbiturates for seizure control, replacing bromide used in the 19th century. Mephobarbital was also used for epilepsy. Due to the aforementioned side effects and margin of safety, they are infrequently used. All benzodiazepines have antiepileptic properties and a few are used for that purpose such as clonazepam and clorazepate. When benzodiazepines are used for epilepsy in children, there may be untoward side effects.

Benzodiazepines have been the drugs of choice for more than 50 years for short-term treatment of anxiety. With the introduction of benzodiazepines came the introduction of the word *anxiolytic* to replace antianxiety medications. The two words refer to the same types of medications but current research tends to employ the term *anxiolytics*. These drugs are easy to take, have a relatively quick onset, usually within 1 hour, and also have low toxicity. Benzodiazepines produce a psychologically tranquil state, hence the term *tranquilizer*, and induce muscle relation which relieves the muscle tension common in anxiety states. Adverse effects are dependent on the drug and are often related to cognitive impairment. It is often suggested that a therapeutic trial should last no longer than 3–4 weeks and only for patients in whom short-term therapy is beneficial (Holbrook, Crowther, Lotter, Cheng, & King, 2000). For longer term treatment of anxiety, recent research suggests that an antidepressant may be preferred. An individual who is partaking of cognitive therapy, for which a benzodiazepine may interfere may be a good candidate for an antidepressant (Westra, Stewart, & Conrad, 2008).

The pharmacological effects of the benzodiazepine occurs as a result of facilitation of GABA-induced neuronal inhibition at the various locations of $GABA_A$ receptors throughout the central nervous system. Actions of benzodiazepines that completely facilitate GABA binding are termed **complete agonists**. Low doses of these drugs moderate anxiety, agitation, and fear through actions on receptors in the amygdala, orbitofrontal cortex, and insula. Any mental confusion or amnesia is related to GABA receptors in the cerebral cortex and the hippocampus. Mild muscular relaxation is due to the effects on GABA receptors in the spinal cord, cerebellum, and brain stem. Antiepileptic actions are caused by the effects on GABA receptors in the cerebellum and hippocampus. The behavioral rewarding effects and the potential for abuse are probably the result of actions on GABA receptors that modulate the discharge of neurons in the ventral tegmentum and the nucleus accumbens (Julien, 2005).

Given the pros and cons of the use of the benzodiazepines, most researchers suggest that the second-generation anxiolytics should replace the use of the benzodiazepines in the future. The most widely accepted use for the benzodiazepines, at this time, is the production of anterograde amnesia in hospital surgical procedures. The second-generation anxiolytics have predominately been marketed as sleep preparations such as zolpidem whose trade name is Ambien. The second generation anxiolytics are **partial agonists** of GABA receptors. The hope with these newer drugs is to develop medications with the positive effects of the benzodiazepines without the side effects or the potential for abuse and dependency.

Buspirone is the third chemically distinct drug for the treatment of anxiety. Buspirone has its effects on the serotonin 5-HT receptors found in high concentration in the hippocampus, the septum, parts of the amygdala, and the dorsal raphe neuclus. The difference between this drug and other anxiolytics is lack of significant sedation or hypnotic actions, amnesia, mental confusion, or psychomotor impairment. While it does not have these difficulties, it also does not have many of the positive effects of the benzodiazepines such as

complete agonists
a drug that completely facilitates binding on the receptor

partial agonists
a drug that only partially facilitates binding at the receptor site

almost immediate onset, promoting sleep or assisting with alcohol withdrawal. Buspirone is suggested for patients who do not seek immediate relief of symptoms of anxiety and are able to tolerate a slow buildup of the drug in their system or those who have a combination of anxiety–depression symptoms. It has also been suggested that buspirone may be most beneficial when used to augment other medications (Harvey & Balon, 1995).

Becky is taking a benzodiazepine on an as needed basis or PRN. She has not had many of the side effects listed for alprazolam (Xanax). She is pleased that it works quickly when she feels she is in a situation which makes her nervous and uncomfortable. The situations which she is most likely to feel anxiety are those which involve men she does not know and particularly men drinking alcohol. These situations make her symptoms of PTSD intensify and she may have flashbacks. Knowing that PTSD has effects on the central nervous system, her psychiatrist took this into consideration when prescribing her medication dosage. The psychiatrist also reminded Becky that driving a vehicle could be dangerous if she was experiencing PTSD symptoms and/or needed to take alprazolam (Xanax).

ANTIDEPRESSANT MEDICATIONS

In the recent past, depression has been the most often cited emotional symptom for a visit to a mental health or physical medicine professional. Currently, anxiety and depression are tied as primary reasons. In the past, depression was thought to be due to a lack of particular neurotransmitters. Currently, depression is seen as a reversible disease of the brain with distinct neuronal pathology that includes structural and neurochemical changes in specific regions of the brain, particularly the hippocampus (Benninghoff, Schmitt, Mossner, & Lesch, 2002; Glitz, Manji, & Moore, 2002) and frontal cortex (Bremner et al., 2003). Depression is not just a synaptic transmission defect but an intracellular illness that involves differences in certain tropic hormones (proteins) that act normally to maintain cell survival and health (Manji & Duman, 2001).

Antidepressant medications are classified into five major categories based on the biochemical functioning of the medications (see Figure 15.4). These categories include from oldest to newest monoamine oxidase inhibitors (MAOIs), tricyclics, selective serotonergic reuptake inhibitors, atypical antidepressants, and selective norepinephrine reuptake inhibitors (SNRIs).

MAOIs were thought to be the first type of antidepressant medicine dating from the 1950s. One of the first MAOIs, iproniazid, was originally developed for tuberculosis but was then withdrawn due to toxicity. Before being withdrawn, there were records of tubercular patients who felt mood improvement through use of the medication. MAOIs are infrequently used because of the often potentially fatal interactions with foods and medicines. Monoamine oxidase (MAO) is one of the enzymes which breaks down normal neurotransmitters in the body. There are two types of this enzyme, MAO-A and MAO-B. The suppression of the MAO-A enzyme causes the alleviation of depressive symptoms and the side effects are caused by inhibition of MAO-B. In 2003, a nonselective MAOI became available as a transdermal patch which allows slow continuous absorption (Amsterdam, 2003). Little research is yet available regarding the efficacy of the patch. However, if this is an effective medication, it could be used for patients who do not respond to the other types of antidepressants.

The tricyclics were originally used as antipsychotics (Kuhn, 1958). They had little effect on psychotic symptoms but did appear to improve depressed patients' mood. Once it was determined that their effectiveness was not to relieve psychotic symptoms but to alleviate depression, they became the most often used antidepressants from the 1960s until the 1990s (Fava, 2003). Tricyclic antidepressants are named after their chemical structure

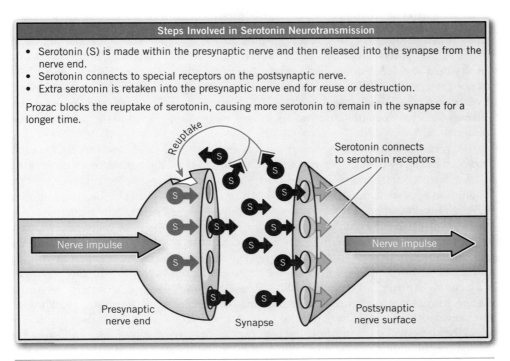

Steps Involved in Serotonin Neurotransmission

- Serotonin (S) is made within the presynaptic nerve and then released into the synapse from the nerve end.
- Serotonin connects to special receptors on the postsynaptic nerve.
- Extra serotonin is retaken into the presynaptic nerve end for reuse or destruction.

Prozac blocks the reuptake of serotonin, causing more serotonin to remain in the synapse for a longer time.

Reuptake

Serotonin connects to serotonin receptors

Nerve impulse

Nerve impulse

Presynaptic nerve end

Synapse

Postsynaptic nerve surface

FIGURE 15.4 Diagram depicting the functioning of one types of antidepressant (SSRI).

and have their effect by increasing the level of norepinephrine and serotonin in the brain. In addition to alleviating symptoms of depression, these drugs have significant anxiolytic and analgesic effects. Compared to other antidepressants, tricyclics have less drug and dietary restrictions than the MAOIs. Tricyclics work as fast as the newer SSRIs and SNRIs even though the newer drugs are marketed as fast acting. In depressed individuals, tricyclics increase mood and physical activity, improve appetite and sleep patterns, and reduce suicidal ideation or preoccupation, even in the elderly (Gasto et al., 2003). Approximately one third of individuals whose symptoms do not abate with other antidepressants respond favorably to tricyclics (Nierenberg et al., 2003). Side effects include sedation, memory impairment, attention difficulties, motor speed problems, and difficulties with dexterity. A serious side effect which is dose specific is cardiac depression and cardiac arrhythmias.

The SSRIs are often the antidepressant of choice at present (Nemeroff, 2003). The initial development of these drugs began in the 1970s and into the 1980s as researchers began to look for faster acting antidepressants with fewer side effects, particularly toxic side effects. There are several SSRIs, each with their own side effects and each with their own potential usefulness. Each SSRI has as its primary pharmacological action the blocking of the reuptake of serotonin into the presynaptic neuron. Fluoxetine, trade name Prozac, was introduced in 1987 and came to the attention of the media in the early 1990s as a drug which induced suicide. Research showed clearly that it did not increase the risk of suicide but that the symptoms of depression were alleviated more quickly than expected, well before the patient's life circumstances changed and, hence, mental health professionals were ill prepared for individuals who began to feel better only to find their lives in shambles. After the initial Prozac scandal, various other SSRIs were developed and the fears regarding these medications have disappeared. At present time, the SSRIs are the most often prescribed type of antidepressant for adults.

The SSRIs were thought to be quicker acting with fewer side effects. The main side effect which tended to occur and become problematic related to sexual functioning. Each of the various SSRIs have marketed themselves to consumers as having fewer sexual side effects than the other drugs in this class. Currently, there are directions to prescribers to not prescribe the SSRIs to children or adolescents younger than the age of 18 years. Even though the Prozac scare has abated, there remains concerns regarding unusual side effects which have occurred in these age groups, particularly related to the issue of suicide (Gunnell & Ashby, 2004).

Atypical and dual-action antidepressants are a group of varied antidepressants each of which has its own particular effect. Bupropion, a dual-action antidepressant marketed as Wellbutrin, affects dopamine and norepinephrine at the synapse (Feighner, 1999). Bupropion appears to suppress the firing of the locus coeruleus (Davidson & Connor, 1998). This drug appears to be very well tolerated with few side effects particularly the absence of sexual difficulty. This medication has also been used for nicotine addiction and attention deficit/hyperactivity disorder (ADHD) in children. Reports indicate very positive effects from the former and poor response from the latter. Mirtazapine, marketed as Remeron, has a unique effect in that it blocks alpha-2 receptors in the presynaptic neuron (Anttila & Leinonen, 2001). These receptors serve as a negative feedback system in that norepinephrine from the synapse binds to these receptors, signaling to the presynaptic neuron to stop releasing additional norepinephrine into the synapse. By blocking these receptors, mirtazapine disrupts the negative feedback loop, allowing for more norephinephrine to be released into the synapse. Norephinephrine then interacts with α_1 receptors on serotonin-containing neurons to increase the firing rate of these cells (Nicholas, Ford, Esposito, Ekstrom, & Golden, 2003). In addition to the blockade of alpha-receptors, mirtazapine also blocks postsynaptic serotonin-2 receptors (Anttila & Leinonen). The net effect is that the overall transmission of serotonin is increased but decreased at this particular subtype of serotonin receptor. Desyrel, marketed as Trazodone, and nefazodone, marketed as Serzone, are unique drugs in their effects as antidepressants. Similar to the previous drugs, these drugs increase the overall neurotransmission of serotonin while blocking the serotonin-2 receptors (Schatzberg, 2000). Trazodone has been used predominately as a sleep aid and is recommended for people with depression complicated by insomnia (Thase, 1999). SNRIs are specific blockers of the neurotransmitter norepinephrine into the presynaptic neuron.

The first SNRIs, atomoxetine, marketed as Strattera, and reboxetine, marketed as Vestra, are now approved by the FDA. Atomoxetine became available in 2003 for the treatment of ADHD in all age groups (Michelson, 2003). Studies have shown it to be as effective as methylphenidate (Ritalin) probably without abuse potential (Heil, 2002). Reboxetine was designed specifically for depression. Due to the fact that it has no effect on serotonin or dopamine neurotransmitters, as well as acetylcholine or histamine, it is thought to have few side effects.

Returning to Becky's medications, she has been prescribed relatively low doses of two different types of antidepressants, sertraline (Zoloft), which is an SSRI, and trazodone, which is a dual-action or atypical antidepressant The rationale for the use of sertraline (Zoloft) is that it has been proven in multiple studies to be effective not only for depression but also for PTSD (Davidson et al., 2001). Trazodone has been effective for sleep and is considered an antidepressant sleeping pill. The psychiatrist felt that this combination would help Becky not only with her depressive symptoms but also with her PTSD symptoms which, under stress, may be quite severe. Becky reports that this combination of medications has worked well for her with minimal side effects.

MOOD STABILIZERS

Mood stabilizers are used solely for the treatment of bipolar disorder. Bipolar disorder, by definition, includes episodes of both major depression and mania. There are two forms: Bipolar I is diagnosed if the manic episodes are severe and Bipolar II is diagnosed if the manic episodes are less severe with these episodes being termed *hypomanic*. Cyclothymic disorder is a difficulty in which the episodes of depressive symptoms and hypomanic symptoms alternate with periods of normal mood for the individual for at least 2 years.

Historically, lithium was the first treatment for symptoms of bipolar disorder and reduced relapse rates. Lithium has effectively treated the symptoms of bipolar disorder but has had little effect on relapse rates. Lithium is an alkali metal and naturally occurs within the body. Lithium was used in the 1920s as a sedative–hypnotic compound and as an anticonvulsant. During the 1940s, lithium chloride was used as a salt substitute for patients with heart disease; however, it led to many deaths. In 1949, Cade used lithium to treat mania in humans after success with animals. However, there were serious side effects. It has become apparent that lithium has a very narrow margin of safety or in other words, it may be quite toxic. Those individuals who are prescribed lithium must have periodic blood tests to ensure that their lithium level does not reach into the toxic range. Other side effects of lithium include weight gain, memory and thinking difficulties, and motivation and concentration problems (Möller & Nasrallah, 2003). The difficulty with lithium treatment is patient compliance. Lithium's side effects often cause patients to discontinue use. In addition, individuals with bipolar disorder often dislike the effects of mood stabilizers because they have relied on the manic phase of the illness to provide them energy and motivation.

The process by which lithium works is not completely understood. However, a recent study (Beaulieu et al., 2008) has shown that lithium may alleviate bipolar behaviors by interrupting the signaling of a dopamine receptor in the brain. Dopamine binds to specific receptors on the cell membrane until this signal induces another signal to be sent causing glycogen synthase kinase 3 (GSK-3) to become increasingly active. GSK-3 is important in the cell's response to many signaling molecules and any affect on the GSK-3 enzyme will have an effect on distribution of signals within the cell. Lithium decreases the ability of D2 receptors (dopamine) to engage the GSK-3 signaling pathway. The D2 receptor and certain enzymes form a package which is held together by a protein called beta-arrestin 2. Together this package can engage the GSK-3 signaling pathway. The researchers found that lithium destabilizes the D2 receptor package by acting on the beta-arrestin 2 protein. The researchers found that this action occurs at the same concentration as the clinically effective doses used in treatment.

Due to the toxicity factor and various side effects, lithium is often not the primary drug of choice for bipolar disorder. Very often it is used in combination with other medications such as anticonvulsants, antidepressants, or atypical antipsychotics. First-generation anticonvulsants are drugs such as phenobarbitol and the barbiturates. These drugs do not work well with bipolar disorder nor do the second-generation anticonvulsants such as valproic acid. Third-generation neuromodulators are now prescribed and shown to be effective (Yatham et al., 2002). Gabapentin, marketed as Neurontin; lamotrigine, marketed as Lamictal; and topiramate, marketed as Topamax, are used alone or more often in conjunction with other mood-stabilizing antidepressants.

Lamotrigine (Lamictal) has gained great acclaim as a treatment for bipolar disorder and the prevention of recurrent episodes. It is not effective for treating acute manic episodes. Lamotrigine inhibits the release of the excitatory neurotransmitter glutamate in the cortex and hippocampus, which causes its actions (Arguelles, Torres-Lopez, & Granados-Soto, 2002). Due to its glutamate-inhibiting action, it may be effective in people who have sustained a traumatic brain injury (Pachet, Friesen, Winkelaar, & Gray, 2003). Side effects include dizziness, tremor, sleep-walking, headache, nausea, and rash. The rash may be serious or even fatal; therefore, the drug is prescribed at a low dose and then titrated upward as is appropriate. Adolescents are thought to be more at risk for the rash; hence, lamotrigine is not indicated for adolescents younger than 16 years old. Gabapentin has been found to be effective in reducing bipolar features when added to other mood stabilizers (Kahn & Chaplan, 2002). Gabapentin's mechanism of effect is unknown. It was originally thought to mimic GABA although that is unclear. Gabapentin does affect some calcium channels and neurotransmitter release (Maneuf et al., 2003). Topiramate has effects similar to valproate in that it inhibits sodium channels (Keck & McElray, 2002) and also increases GABA effects. Topiramate may also antagonize glutamate action at alpha-amino-3-hydroxy-5-methyl-4-isoxazolepropionic acid/kainate receptors (Van Amerigen, Marcini, Pipe, Campbell, & Oakman, 2002). It has some potentially serious side effects such as cognitive difficulties, paresthesias, diminished sweating, and elevated body temperature, particularly in children (Ortho-McNeil, 2003).

As a standard practice, traditional antipsychotics have been used for acute mania. The use of antipsychotics has even predated lithium. Traditional antipsychotics have little effect on depressive symptoms or in preventing relapse. The atypical antipsychotics have been proven effective against acute mania and to prevent relapse in the absence of extrapyramidal side effects (Frye et al., 1998). Clozapine appeared to be more antimanic whereas, risperidone, marketed as Risperdal, appeared more antidepressant potentially aggravating mania. Clozapine is effective but has the potential for serious blood cell reactions such as agranulocytosis (low white blood cell count). Olanzapine marketed as Zyprexa was approved in the mid-2000s by the FDA for the short-term treatment of acute mania.

Becky was evaluated by many different professionals throughout her years of treatment. One psychiatrist thought she had bipolar disorder not depression and PTSD. Due to the fact that the psychiatrist felt she had this difficulty, he removed all of her antidepressant and antianxiety medications and prescribed risperidone (Risperdal). Becky was not happy with the situation, her depressive symptoms returned and she began to have serious difficulties with PTSD. In addition, one of the side effects of risperidone (Risperdal) is weight gain and she gained 80 lbs. The excess weight added to the depression until she became suicidal. Talking with a friend one day, she made up her mind to go against the psychiatrist's advice and ask for another opinion. For many individuals, it is difficult to question the directions given by professionals but she felt her situation was intolerable. She consulted her primary care physician who slowly weaned her off the risperidone (Risperdal) and represcribed her previous medications. After this experience, it becomes very clear why she has been hesitant with the prescriptions she received from the psychiatrist she was referred to by her clinical neuropsychologist. However, the clinical neuropsychologist agreed with her that she was not suffering from bipolar disorder but depression, anxiety, and PTSD.

ANTIPSYCHOTIC MEDICATIONS

Antipsychotic medications are used for the treatment of various psychotic disorders, such as schizophrenia, brief psychotic episode, schizoaffective disorder, and other difficulties with psychotic symptomatology. The antipsychotics treat both the positive and negative symptoms of psychotic disorders. Positive symptoms are those which most nonpsychotic individuals do not experience such as **delusions** or **hallucinations**. Negative symptoms are the absence of normal variations in a number of areas such as mood and motivation. Individuals who suffer from schizophrenia usually have a symptomless childhood and early adolescence and then develop a **prodromal phase** when symptoms begin to develop, usually in late teens or early 20s. The illness occurs when the symptoms are apparent and may wax and wane depending on the severity and type. Researchers debate the typology but current *Diagnostic and Statistical Manual of Mental Disorders, Fourth Edition, Text Revision* (*DSM-IV-TR*) nomenclature describes schizophrenia as undifferentiated, paranoid, catatonic, disorganized, or residual type (American Psychiatric Association, 2000).

Prior to the 1950s, there were no medications available for psychotic disorders. The first antipsychotics were discovered, by accident, as a French researcher Laborit in 1952 was looking for a drug to deepen anesthesia before surgery. Due to the fact that individuals with schizophrenia are often difficult to manage behaviorally and emotionally, the advent of the first antipsychotics were readily accepted and prescribed. It was not until later that it was apparent that the early drugs had serious side effects which were both dose dependent and permanent. After much research, medications became available for the side effects and these were administered at the same time as the antipsychotics. Also the doses were begun at much lower levels and were titrated upward as needed.

The mechanism through which antipsychotics work relates to the particular theory of the etiology of schizophrenia. The earliest theory of schizophrenia was that the individual had an excess of dopamine at the synapse. The earliest antipsychotics or phenothiazines were evaluated based on their ability to block dopamine; in a sense, the more dopamine blocked the better the antipsychotic. The blocking of dopamine diminished the positive symptoms but did little to alleviate the negative symptoms of schizophrenia. In addition to blocking the dopamine-2 receptors, the phenothiazines also block acetylcholine, histamine, and norepinephrine receptors. These secondary effects of early antipsychotics caused various mild-to-severe side effects. The side effects can be grouped based on the cause. Anticholinergic effects such as dry mouth, constipation, urinary hesitation, and blurred vision are due to the typical antipsychotics blocking acetylcholine receptors (Meltzer et al., 1998). Extrapyramidal effects are caused by the antagonizing of dopamine receptors in the nigrostriatal system leading to an excess of acetylcholine transmission (Glazer, 2000; Maguire, 2002). Extrapyramidal effects include akathisia or the inability to sit or stand still, which may lead to medication cessation. Dystonia, which is muscle spasms in the neck (torticollis) or muscles that control eye movements (oculogyric crisis), can occur with typical antipsychotics. Tardive dyskinesia, which is abnormal and involuntary movements of the tongue, limbs, and trunk, is thought to occur in up to 24% of individuals taking typical antipsychotics (Kulkarni & Naidu, 2003). The exact mechanism which causes tardive dyskinesia is unknown but there are several thoughts including hypersensitivity in the dopamine system, an altered balance between the dopamine and acetylcholine systems, free radicals produced from atypical neuroleptics, and altered glutamate functioning (Kulkarni & Naidu, 2003). An additional side effect is neuroleptic malignant syndrome, which is a potentially lethal condition characterized by muscle rigidity, high fever, elevated heart rate and blood pressure, and profuse sweating (Lappa et al., 2002). Death may occur if left untreated.

There are several drugs which have been developed to protect against side effects of the antipsychotics which are benztropine, marketed as Cogentin; trihexiphenidyl, marketed as Artane; procyclidine, marketed as Kemadrin; and biperiden, marketed as Akineton. All of these drugs work by blocking the muscarinic subtype of acetylcholine receptors (Larson, Pfenning, & Richelson, 1991).

Typical antipsychotics have shown to be effective with the positive symptoms of schizophrenia but also lead to numerous side effects. In the 1990s the development of the atypical or second-generation antipsychotics began. These newer medications were designed to alleviate both the positive and negative symptoms of schizophrenia as well as to decrease the number and severity of side effects. Beginning with clozapine in 1990, the following other atypical antipsychotics have been developed: risperidone (1994), olanzapine (1996), sertindole (1997), quetiapine (1999), ziprasidone (2000), and aripiprazole (2003). Each of these drugs has an effect on the ability to antagonize dopamine type 2 receptors (Breier, 2001). Each of these drugs also has an additional effect which causes the differences between the various atypical antipsychotics. At this point in time, it is difficult to tell which antipsychotic will become the mainstay of treatment. Recently, a third generation of antipsychotics has been under development and exhibit a more complicated pattern of receptor interactions than their predecessors. In 2004, the American Psychiatric Association published, renewed, and updated guidelines for the treatment of patients with schizophrenia (American Psychiatric Association, 2004). This statement discusses the use of the second-generation antipsychotics but has not been updated since that time.

Becky, as stated previously, was prescribed an atypical antipsychotic risperidone (Risperdal) for an off-label use for what was thought to be bipolar disorder. The medication was not effective for her due to the fact that she was not suffering from bipolar disorder. She also has not experienced any schizophrenic symptoms for which the medication is intended. Hence, her experience with this class of drugs was poor. However, she probably should not have been prescribed this class of medication.

PSYCHOSTIMULANT MEDICATIONS

Psychostimulants are drugs which elevate mood, increase motor activity, increase alertness, decrease the need for sleep, and increase the brain's metabolic activity. Amphetamines are the group of stimulants which have prescribed uses, particularly for ADHD in children and adults and with narcolepsy.

The amphetamines have a long history. First synthesized in 1887 (Murray, 1998), the amphetamines have been used for many different psychological difficulties since that time. Dextroamphetamine marketed as Adderall is used in the treatment of ADHD and is a combination of several different amphetamines (Spencer et al., 2001). Other nonamphetamines which are regarded as stimulants are also used for ADHD and include methylphenidate marketed as Ritalin, and pemoline marketed as Cylert. Modafinil marketed as ProVigil is used in the treatment of narcolepsy. Methylphenidate blocks the reuptake of dopamine and norepinephrine from the synapse. The mechanism of action for pemoline is unknown but it is thought to affect the presynaptic release of dopamine as well as inhibit its reuptake (Markowitz & Patrick, 2001).

As is the case with the illegal stimulants, there exists the potential for abuse and dependence with all of the stimulants. There also exists an illegal market for these medications and it is not unheard of for individuals to sell their medications when in need.

Returning to Becky, she has not had any experience with psychostimulants. She has not experienced any of the symptoms of ADHD in childhood or as an adult. Further, she has not viewed any of the symptoms of either disorder in her children or other family members. However, Becky has had periods of anxiety and states that caffeine whether in coffee, chocolate, or cola has the potential to make her more anxious. Research corroborates this and it is suggested that those individuals who suffer from anxiety, PTSD, or any other central nervous system difficulty limit their use of caffeine and nicotine.

Prescription Privileges

Now that the functioning of various medications and their effectiveness has been reviewed, a very controversial issue will be discussed. As was stated earlier, many of the medications discussed have been discovered by accident, while others have been specifically created for specific disorders. Many medications were used without prescription before controls on medications and quality standards were developed. The discussion of prescription privileges focus only on the psychotropic medications discussed within this chapter.

Traditionally, the prescription of medications has been the province of medical doctors. Medical doctors receive extensive education throughout their medical training regarding the functioning of various body systems and the effects of various medications on these body systems. Psychiatry is the branch of medicine which focuses on mental illness and its treatment. Originally, psychiatrists primarily used talk therapy to treat patients before the advent of various medications. After the psychotropic medications became available, the role of the psychiatrist changed from a therapist to more of a medication manager. Psychiatrists' appointments were altered from 1 hour to 10–15 minutes and, with the advent of managed care, there was pressure to see more and more patients. Also, after the deinstitutionalization of mental patients, there were more and more patients who needed to be treated. In response to this need, some physician assistants and nurse practitioners began advanced training to prescribe psychotropic medications under the supervision of a medical doctor. In some states, these individuals are able to prescribe medications without the supervision of a medical doctor.

Within the past several years, psychologists have lobbied for the ability to prescribe medications to their clinical patients. The right to prescribe medications is ultimately controlled by the state legislatures in each particular state. At the time of this writing, New Mexico, Louisiana, Guam, and the U.S. military allow psychologists with appropriate advanced training and who have passed a national certification exam to prescribe psychotropic medications. Many other states have bills before their legislatures requesting prescription privileges for psychologists. However, this remains a controversial issue within psychology.

The two sides to this issue are not solely medicine versus psychology but within each discipline itself, there are factions. In the medical community, there are groups which state that the body and medication are the province of medicine; therefore, psychiatrists have been particularly vocal regarding the need to remain the specialty which prescribes psychotropic medications. Psychiatrists have vehemently stated that no other profession has the knowledge base to understand both the total functioning of the human body and the effects of medications, their side effects, and interactions. In summary, this side of the argument is based on the medical training of the psychiatrist and the perceived lack of training of psychologists. There also exists, particularly as the economy worsens, an implicit controversy regarding which discipline will profit from the prescription of medications.

The other side of the argument is also represented by certain medical specialties. General practitioners, family medicine specialists, and gynecologists who often prescribe psychotropic medications when a psychiatric appointment for their client is not available, argue for more trained prescribers. Many of these physicians are aware of the need for more prescribers and often feel not appropriately trained or up-to-date to prescribe psychotropic medications. These same physicians are also aware of the division within the medical community. However, for the best patient care, many argue that appropriately trained and certified psychologists who are already working with a particular client may fill the void. In summary, the argument here focuses on the perceived lack of resources for patients and a somewhat uncomfortable role for physicians to practice outside of their declared specialty area.

Psychology groups have been equally vocal on both sides of this issue. Experimental and behavioral psychologists are quick to state that the definition of psychology is the study of the mind and human behavior, or the study of the brain and the control of human behavior. These psychologists are adamant that the field of psychology must be separated from the fields of biology and medicine and remain defined as a behavioral science. Others express concern that the discipline of psychology will abdicate the effects of the environment on the prediction and control of human behavior in favor of the current trend toward neuroscience. There are still others who feel that the push toward prescription privileges will cause all clinical and counseling psychologists to study an extensive body of knowledge which many do not have the interest nor time to complete.

Overall, the psychologists arguing against prescription privileges state that the definition of the field of psychology must remain behavioral not biological. The nature–nurture argument is voiced regarding the environment and its effects in the study of these behaviors. The potential impact of extra study on what is now a long and arduous journey to a PhD or PsyD, licensure, and, potentially, American Board of Professional Psychology (ABPP) status must be considered and many psychologists fear this will cause potential psychologists to pursue other fields of study.

Psychologists holding opposing or opposite opinions begin with the aforementioned need for more mental health practitioners who are able to prescribe medications. There is a definite lack of psychiatric services within the United States, particularly in the rural areas. It is not an unprecedented situation for a patient to wait months to be seen for medication by a psychiatrist. In some circumstances, patients are referred to other mental health specialties, as stated earlier, to obtain the medications they desperately need. Within clinical neuropsychology, the other specialty areas are often neurology, neurosurgery, or physiatry, specialties which are very familiar with the central nervous system but also very busy. The Veterans Administration, which has been well-known for the training of psychologists and treatment of veterans of Iraq and Afghanistan, also has a long waiting list.

The second area of disagreement is the increasing knowledge regarding the biochemical and physiological underpinnings of various mental illnesses. As time passes, research points to various etiological factors which are based on central nervous system functioning. This added information brings with it a clearer understanding that certain difficulties require medication as part of the treatment regimen. This is not to say that psychology will stop being defined as a behavioral science but that it must incorporate this new knowledge into its paradigm.

Another salient point is that the clinical neuropsychologist or clinical psychologist has more access to a patient than does the psychiatrist and thus is able to observe the effects of medication on the client on a weekly or biweekly basis, whereas a psychiatrist may not see his or her patient for 3–6 months. Within this argument is also the continuity of the care as discussed earlier. The clinical neuropsychologist may be the case manager for the client, and therefore will be very familiar with all of the treatments in which the client is involved.

The next point is that not all psychologists want to or should be educated to prescribe medication. The ability to prescribe medication, when it is available, is only for those who decide to complete advanced education, a preceptorship, and a national examination. Due to the fact that clinical neuropsychologists work predominately with individuals with central nervous system difficulties, it is a very important issue for this group of professionals.

The education which is necessary for a psychologist to prescribe begins with a PhD or PsyD from an APA-accredited program in clinical psychology or related areas of psychology (neuropsychology, counseling, child clinical) plus an APA-accredited internship. The psychologist is required to complete a standardized series of courses which include laboratory components within many of the courses. The Academy of Medical Psychology's *Tenets for Psychopharmacology Training for Psychologists* is the backbone for the training available at various institutions and universities across the United States (Academy of Medical Psychology, 2002). The APA has taken a stand in favor of prescription privileges for psychologists and has endorsed the aforementioned model for the training (Fox & Sammons, 1998). The general format of the education is roughly 30 courses covering biology, biochemistry, physiology, ethics, diverse populations, and medication usage. Several additional components complete the training. The first is an in-depth evaluation of a case study presented to the faculty members of the institution, including an APA style literature review, discussing the role of medication for the client's difficulties. Secondly, the psychologist must complete a preceptorship in which the psychologist co-prescribes with a physician psychotropic medications for 100 clients seen for at least four visits. Finally, the psychologist must satisfactorily complete a national exam. The amount of time it takes to complete these studies will depend on the particular school through which the psychologist is studying and the ability of a practicing psychologist to arrange his schedule to fit course demands. The course work itself may take years plus the time to complete the preceptorship; however, there is no average time for the completion of this education.

Returning to Becky, she is working with a clinical neuropsychologist who has completed the aforementioned education and preceptorship and has passed the national exam. However, the clinical neuropsychologist practices in one of the states in which psychologists do not have prescription privileges. Becky has a history of multiple medications which have been prescribed by psychiatrists and her general practitioner. She has had both good and bad experiences. She feels that it has become difficult to obtain a psychiatric appointment in her area and therefore had relied on her primary physician. Once she began working with the clinical neuropsychologist, she was unpleasantly surprised to learn that he was not able to prescribe her medications. She stated that she would feel much better knowing that the person she sees most frequently could oversee her medications. She also stated that she feels that the clinical neuropsychologist is as well trained as anyone with whom she has worked.

Summary

The chapter begins with the first case study to evaluate the use of psychotropic medications. The client had been prescribed many medications by various providers and had a plethora of side effects from each. Her experiences were used to illustrate various points within the chapter.

The basics of drug development and the protections for those who are subjects in these studies are reviewed. In addition, the biochemistry of drug functioning including pharmacokinetics and pharmacodynamics are discussed.

The major categories of medications which are utilized with mental health issues whether primary or secondary to central nervous system difficulties were reviewed. These categories include antianxiety medications, antidepressants, mood stabilizers, antipsychotics, and psychostimulants. The various types of medications, both the older and newer forms were evaluated particularly in terms of efficacy and safety.

The chapter concluded with a discussion which had begun in a previous chapter regarding prescription privileges. The lack of prescribers of psychotropic mediations has led other fields such as clinical neuropsychology to attempt to gain prescription privileges for those with advanced education and training. The issues on either side of the debate were presented.

Questions for Further Study

1. It is very important that individuals with central nervous system difficulties not consume alcohol or illegal drugs. It is also the case with those prescribed psychotropic medications. How does a clinical neuropsychologist prevent a client from choosing such a behavior?

2. The standard dosage level for most medications is based on a 160-lb male. Should this be altered for an individual with central nervous system difficulties? Explain.

3. What are the pros and cons for individuals with central nervous system difficulties if more clinical neuropsychologists are allowed to prescribe medications?

References

Academy of Medical Psychology. (2002). *Tenents for psychopharmacology training for psychologists.* Lincoln, NE: Author.

American Psychiatric Association. (2000). *Diagnostic and statistical manual of mental disorders* (text revision). Washington, DC: Author.

American Psychiatric Association. (2004). *Practice guidelines for treatment of patients with schizophrenia* (2nd ed.). Arlington, VA: Author.

American Psychological Association. (2002). *Ethical principles for psychologists and code of conduct.* Washington, DC: Author.

Amsterdam, J. D. (2003). A double-blind, placebo-controlled trial of the safety and efficacy of Seleqiline transdermal system without dietary restrictions in patients with major depressive disorder. *Journal of Clinical Psychiatry, 64,* 208–214.

Anttila, S. A., & Leinonen, E. V. (2001). A review of the pharmacological and clinical profile of mirtazapine. *CNS Drug Review, 7,* 249–264.

Arguelles, C. F., Torres-Lopez, J. E., & Granados-Soto, V. (2002). Peripheral antinociceptive action of morphine and the synergistic interaction with lamotrigine. *Anesthesiology, 96,* 921–925.

Beaulieu, J., Marion, S., Rodriguiz, R. M., Medvedev, I. O., Sotnikova, T. D., Ghisi, V., et al. (2008). A β-arrestin 2 signaling complex mediates lithium action on behavior. *Cell, 132*(1), 125–136.

Benninghoff, J., Schmitt, A., Mossner, R., & Lesch, K. P. (2002). When cells become depressed: Focus on neural stem cells in novel treatment strategies against depression. *Journal of Neural Transmission, 109,* 947–962.

Breier, A. (2001). A new era in the pharmacology of psychotic disorders. *Journal of Clinical Psychiatry, 62*(S2), 3–5.

Bremner, J. D., Vythilingam, M., Ng, C. K., Vermetten, E., Nazeer, A., Oren, D. A., et al. (2003). Regional brain metabolic correlates of alpha-methylparatyrosine-induced depressive symptoms: Implications for the neural circuitry of depression. *Journal of the American Medical Association, 289,* 3125–3134.

Cade, J. (1949). Lithium salts in the treatment of psychotic excitement. *Medical Journal of Australia, 2,* 349–352.

Davidson, J. R., & Connor, K. M. (1998). Buprion sustained release: A therapeutic overview. *Journal of Clinical Psychiatry, 59*(4), 25–31.

Davidson, J. R., Pearlstein, T., Londborg, P., Brady, K. T., Rothbaum, B., Bell, J., et al. (2001). Efficacy of sertraline in preventing relapse in post-traumatic stress disorder: Results of a 28-week double-blind, placebo-controlled study. *American Journal of Psychiatry, 158,* 1974–1981.

Fava, M. (2003). Depression with physical symptoms: Treating to remission. *Journal of Clinical Psychiatry, 64*(Suppl. 7), 24–28.

Feighner, J. P. (1999). Mechanics of action of antidepressant medications. *Journal of Clinical Psychiatry, 60*(4), 4–11.

Fox, R. E., & Sammons, M. T. (1998). A history of prescription privileges. *APA Monitor Online, 29*(9).

Frye, M. A., Ketter, T. A., Altshuler, L. L., Denicoff, K., Dunn, R. T., Kimbrell, T. A., et al. (1998). Clozapine in bipolar disorder: Treatment implications for other atypical antipsychotics. *Journal of Affective Disorders, 48*(2–3), 91–104.

Gasto, C., Navarro, V., Marcos, T., Portella, M. J., Torra, M., & Rodamilans, M. (2003). Single-blind comparison of venlafaxine and nortriptyline in elderly major depression. *Journal of Clinical Psychopharmacology, 23*(1), 21–26.

Glazer, W. M. (2000). Extrapyramidal side effects, tardive dyskinesia, and the concepts of atypicability. *Journal of Clinical Psychiatry, 61*(S3), 16–21.

Glitz, D. A., Manji, H. K., & Moore, G. J. (2002). Mood disorders: Treatment-induced changes in brain neurochemistry and structure. *Seminars in Clinical Neuropsychiatry, 7*(4), 269–280.

Greenblatt, D. J., Patki, K. C., von Moltke, L., Shader, R. I. (2001). Drug interactions with grapefruit juice: An update. *Journal of Clinical Psychopharmacology, 21*, 357–357.

Gunnell, D., & Ashby, D. (2004). Antidepressants and suicide: What is the balance of benefit and harm? *British Medical Journal, 329*, 34–38.

Harrison Narcotics Tax Act of 1914, 1, 38 Stat 785 (1914).

Harvey, K. V., & Balon, R. (1995). Augmentation with buspirone: A review. *Annals of Clinical Psychiatry, 7*, 143–147.

Heil, S. H., Holmes, H. W., Bickel, W. K., Higgins, S. T., Badger, G. J., Laws, H. F., et al. (2002). Comparison of the subjective, physiological, and psychomotor effects of atomoxetine and methyphenidate in light drug users. *Drug and Alcohol Dependence, 67*, 149–156.

Holbrook, A. M., Crowther, R., Lotter, A., Cheng, C., & King, D. (2000). Meta-analysis of benzodiazepine use in the treatment of insomnia. *Canadian Medical Association Journal, 162*, 225–233.

Julien, R. M. (2005). *A primer of drug action: A comprehensive guide to the action, uses, and side effects of psychoactive drugs* (10th ed.). New York: Worth.

Kahn, D., & Chaplan, R. (2002). The "good enough" mood stabilizer: A review of the clinical evidence. *CNS Spectrum, 7*, 227–237.

Kavirajan, H. (1999). The amobarbitol interview revisited: A review of the literature since 1966. *Harvard Review of Psychiatry, 7*, 153–156.

Keck, P. E., & McElray, S. L. (2002). Clinical pharmacodynamics and pharmacokinetics of antimanic and mood-stabilizing medications. *Journal of Clinical Psychiatry, 63*(S4), 3–11.

Ksir, C., Hart, C. L., & Ray, O. (2008). *Drugs, society, and human behavior* (12th ed.). New York: McGraw-Hill.

Kuhn, R. (1958). The treatment of depressive state with G-22355 (imipramine hydrochloride). *American Journal of Psychiatry, 115*, 459–464.

Kulkarni, S. K., & Naidu, P. S. (2003). Pathophysiology and drug therapy of tardive dyskinesia: Current concepts and future perspectives. *Drugs of Today, 39*, 19–49.

Lappa, A., Podesta, M., Capelli, O., Castagna, A., DiPlacido, G., Alampi, D., et al. (2002). Successful treatment of a complicated case of neuroleptic malignant syndrome. *Intensive Care Medicine, 28*, 976–977.

Larson, E. W., Pfenning, M. A., & Richelson, E. (1991). Selectivity of antimuscarinic compounds for muscarin receptors of human brain and heart. *Psychopharmacology, 103*, 162–165.

Maguire, G. A. (2002). Prolactin elevation with antipsychotic medications: Mechanisms of active and clinical consequence. *Journal of Clinical Psychiatry, 63*(Suppl. 4), 56–62.

Maneuf, Y. P., Gonzalez, M. I., Sutton, K. S., Chung, F. Z., Pinnock, R. D., & Lee, K. (2003). Cellular and molecular action of the putative GABA-mimetic, gabapentin. *Cellular and Molecular Life Sciences, 60*, 742–750.

Manji, H. K., & Duman, R. S. (2001). Impairment of neuroplasticity and cellular resilience in several mood disorders: Implications for the development of novel therapies. *35*, 5–49.

Markowitz, J. S., & Patrick, K. S. (2001). Pharmacokinetic and pharmacodynamic drug interaction in the treatment of attention-deficit hyperactivity disorder. *Clinical Pharmacokinetics, 40*, 753–772.

Meltzer, H. Y., Casey, D. E., Garver, D. L., Lasagna, L., Marder, S. R., Masand, P. S., et al. (1998). Adverse effects of the atypical antipsychotics. (Collaborative working group in clinical trials evaluations). *Journal of Clinical Psychiatry, 59*(12), 17–22.

Michelson, D., Adler, L., Spencer, T., Reimherr, F. W., West, S. A., Allen, A. J., et al. (2003). Atomoxetine in adults with ADHD: Two Randomized placebo-controlled studies. *Society of Biological Psychiatry, 50,* 112–120.

Mitscherlich, A., & Mielke, F. (1949). The Nuremberg Code (1947). *Doctors of infamy: the story of the Nazi medical crimes.* New York: Schuman.

Möller, H. J., & Nasrallah, H. A. (2003). Treatment of bipolar disorder. *The Journal of Clinical Psychiatry, 64*(6), 9–17.

Murray, J. B. (1998). Psychophysiological aspects of amphetamine-methamphetamine abuse. *Journal of Psychology, 132,* 227–237.

National Commission for the Protection of Human Subjects of Biomedical and Behavioral Research. (1979). *The Belmont report: Ethical principles and guidelines for the protection of human subjects of research.* Washington, DC: Superintendent of Documents, U.S. Government Printing Office.

Nemeroff, C. B. (2003). Advancing the treatment of mood and anxiety disorder: The first 10 years experience with paroxetine. *Psychopharmacology Bulletin, 37*(1), 6–7.

Nicholas, L. M., Ford, A. L., Esposito, S. M., Ekstrom, D., & Golden, R. N. (2003). The effects of mirtazapine on plasma lipid profiles in healthy subjects. *Journal of Clinical Psychiatry, 64*(8), 883–889.

Nierenberg, A. A., Papakostas, G. I., Pertersen, T., Kelley, K. E., Iacoviello, B. M., Worthington, J. J., et al. (2003). Nortriptyline for treatment resistant depression. *Journal of Clinical Psychiatry, 64(1),* 35–39.

Ortho-McNeil. (2003). Letter to Healthcare Professionals.

Pachet, A., Friesen, S., Winkelaar, D., & Gray, S. (2003). Beneficial behavioral effects of lamotrigine in traumatic brain injury. *Brain Injury, 17*(8), 715–722.

Penslar, R. L., & Porter, J. P. (2009). *IRB guidebook.* Washington, DC: Office of Human Research Protections.

Pharmaceutical Manufacturers Association. (2004). *Industry profile.* Washington, DC: Author.

Roberts, I. (2000). *Barbiturates for acute traumatic brain injury* [Data File]. *Cochrane Database of Systematic Reviews,* (2), CD00033. DOI: 10.1002/14651858.CD000033

Olson, J. (1998). *Clinical pharmacology made ridiculously simple.* Miami, FL: Medmaster, Inc.

Schatzberg, A. F. (2000). New indicators for antidepressants. *Journal of Clinical Psychiatry, 61*(4), 9–17.

Sinclair, U. (1906). *The jungle.* New York: Doubleday, Jabber & Company.

Spencer, T., Biederman, J., Wilens, T., Faraone, S., Prince, J., Gerad, K., et al. (2001). Efficacy of a mixed amphetamine salts compound in adults with attention-deficit/hyperactivity disorder. *Archives of General Psychiatry, 58,* 775–782.

Thase, M. F. (1999). Antidepressant treatment of the depressed patient with insomnia. *Journal of Clinical Psychiatry, 60*(S17), 28–34.

Tomlin, S. L., Jenkins, A., Lieb, W. R., & Franks, N. P. (1999). Preparation of barbiturate optical isomers and their effects on GABA (A) receptors. *Anesthesiology, 90,* 1714–1722.

Van Amerigen, M., Marcini, C., Pipe, B., Campbell, M., & Oakman, J. (2002). Topiramate treatment for SSRI-induced weight gain in anxiety disorders. *Journal of Clinical Psychiatry, 63,* 981–984.

Westra, H. A., Stewart, S. H., & Conrad, B. E. (2002). Naturalistic manner of benzodiazepine use and cognitive behavioral therapy outcome in panic disorder with agoraphobia. *Journal of Anxiety Disorders, 16,* 233–246.

World Medical Organization. (1996). Declaration of Helsinki. *British Medical Journal, 313*(7070), 1448–1449.

Yatham, L. N., Kusumakar, V., Calabrese, J. R., Rao, R., Scarrow, G., & Kroeker, G. (2002). Third generation anticonvulsants in bipolar disorder: A review of efficacy and summary of clinical recommendations. *Journal of Clinical Psychiatry, 63,* 275–283.

Young, J. H. (1967). *The medical messiahs: A social history of health quality in twentieth century America.* Princeton, NJ: Princeton University Press.

Pediatric Neuropsychology

16

Learning Objectives

After reading this chapter, the student should be able to understand:

- The components of child development including physical, cognitive, moral, emotional, and social development
- The types and characteristics of acquired central nervous system difficulties in children including traumatic brain injury, pediatric brain tumors, and child abuse
- The characteristics and causes of intellectual deficiency
- The types and characteristics of other neurodevelopmental disorders including learning disabilities, pervasive developmental disorders, and attention deficit/hyperactivity disorder

Topical Outline

Jenny is an 11-year-old White female. She was referred for a multifaceted evaluation including a neuropsychological evaluation, occupational therapy evaluation, audiology evaluation, and speech pathology evaluation. She had been having difficulties in school and was evaluated through the school district by a school psychologist. The results from the school evaluation led to the current referral. Jenny's evaluation from the school psychologist suggested that she suffers from Mild Mental Retardation (intellectual disability) and speech and language impairments. These issues first became apparent when she began to attend school at age 5. She has been receiving special education services through the school and continues to have an Individual Education Plan (IEP) but is generally considered to be mainstreamed. She was diagnosed with Attention Deficit/Hyperactivity Disorder (ADHD) through an external psychological consultation. In response to the diagnosis, her family physician prescribed methylphenidate (Ritalin). Methylphenidate did not appear to work well and led to a 20-pound weight loss. Imipramine was added to the methylphenidate and subsequently she was given a combination of imipramine, pemoline (Cylert), and paroxetine (Paxil), which together led to violent behavior. Currently she takes imipramine 25 mg at a.m., 25 mg at p.m., and 50 mg at bedtime. According to parental report, this has had good effects on her behavior.

Jenny's background includes being one of seven children residing in her family. She has four biological siblings and two stepsiblings in a blended family. Within the biological family, Jenny has three older sisters ages 16, 14, and 13 and a younger brother age 10. The oldest sister suffers from depression, the second oldest sister and her brother both have diagnosed ADHD. Each of these siblings is in individual therapy and also receives medication. Jenny's biological parents divorced due to alleged sexual abuse on the part of the father. Jenny was the victim of the abuse but it was also thought that her sisters were abused due to observed behavioral changes. Jenny's father was prosecuted and is serving a sentence for second degree criminal sexual conduct in a medium security prison. Jenny's mother, ReAnn, remarried a divorced man, Bill, who had custody of his son, age 15, who has diagnosed ADHD and daughter age 14. Bill's son is also in individual therapy and takes medication. ReAnn and Bill are currently maritally separated due to alleged sexual abuse on Bill's part. Jenny was the victim of the stepfather's abuse and, again, there are suspicions that he may have molested other children, both his own biological children and stepchildren. Bill is currently serving a sentence for second degree criminal sexual conduct in a medium security prison. ReAnn has custody of Bill's two children and was able to obtain the custody by not divorcing Bill. ReAnn feels that she needs to keep the family together for the sake of the children. She is aware that the children from each marriage have bad feelings toward one another due to Bill's incarceration but feels that the issues can be worked on through therapy.

Historically, Jenny's medical history is unremarkable. There were no prenatal or postnatal difficulties or any teratogen exposure. She had the usual childhood illnesses such as German measles at 2 years old and chicken pox at 3. ReAnn described potential genetic influences which may have caused Jenny's developmental disability, stating that her (ReAnn's) brother was slow and probably had a learning disability. She also related that her father was also slow and had great difficulty managing money. ReAnn also described behaviors in several cousins which are similar to the symptoms of ADHD that were diagnosed in her biological and stepchildren.

Even if the etiological factors are not discovered, it is clear that Jenny has multiple difficulties, some of which are already diagnosed and some for which she was referred. The fact that she is 11 was an impetus for the clinical neuropsychologist to employ a multidisciplinary team of professionals which is often the case in working with children. Due to the fact that the referral specifically stated a need for neuropsychological, occupational therapy, audiology and speech pathology input, it was then somewhat easier to gather these professionals together. In addition, the clinical neuropsychologist felt a child psychiatrist's medication evaluation would be helpful as would a systems review from a neurologist.

Each of the aforementioned professionals completed their particular assessment and their reports were sent to the clinical neuropsychologist who served as case manager. The clinical neuropsychologist compiled an overall assessment package and then scheduled a meeting with as many professionals as were able to attend, ReAnn, Jenny's special education teacher, and the school psychologist who made the neuropsychological referral. The purpose of the meeting was to share information among the professionals as well as to make plans for implementation of the information gathered. In addition, it is a standard procedure to present information regarding a minor child to the parent. In this particular situation when there are so many needs present, it is important to gather the professionals together, if possible, to answer questions from the parent.

The clinical neuropsychologist began the meeting by introducing all of the participants present and their role in the meeting. The clinical neuropsychologist began the discussion with his assessment results. At the beginning of his discussion, he stated that the tests administered to Jenny were age appropriate and designed to ascertain both strengths and weaknesses. Jenny received scores on the Wechsler Intelligence Scale for Children-IV, which placed her abilities within the very low range of mental abilities. Intelligence assessment results corroborated other academic testing which had been completed throughout her academic career. Her strength was mathematics, which was also a stated strength by her classroom teachers. School records indicate she is able to understand third-grade mathematics. Her weakness is in her verbal skills; she has difficulty expressing herself using words and also understanding information presented verbally. Neuropsychological testing indicated that Jenny has difficulty with attention, concentration, and memory. However, it may be that her memory deficits are due to the former difficulties. The clinical neuropsychologist also assessed Jenny's ability to understand social situations and mores. She was clearly deficit in the understanding of various social situations. The clinical neuropsychologist summarized his findings as a pattern of lowered intelligence with concentration, attention, and memory deficits superimposed on a pronounced lack of understanding of social situations and performance of appropriate behaviors. The clinical neuropsychologist's recommendations included a program of age-appropriate cognitive rehabilitation specifically targeting attention and concentration difficulties. The recommendations also stated that it would be most beneficial for her to partake of the program while receiving medication.

The results from the occupational therapy evaluation were presented by the occupational therapist who revealed that Jenny has difficulty with many sensorimotor issues, which include coordination, balance, and body and spatial awareness. The occupational therapist felt that Jenny could benefit from a program which would focus on fine and gross motor abilities. The occupational therapist was aware that time and transportation to appointments is difficult in such a large family but stressed that a few, possibly three or four appointments, could teach Jenny exercises which she could practice at home. After working on these exercises at home for a few months, she could return for a session to evaluate improvement.

The audiology examination did not reveal any significant difficulties. This finding was very helpful in ruling out the etiology of various behaviors. Due to the fact that there were no major apparent issues, the audiologist did not attend the meeting.

The speech–language evaluation was presented by the speech pathologist who stated that Jenny had multiple deficits. While her strength is in mathematics, her weaknesses are clearly in language comprehension and production. Using formal assessment tools, Jenny tested at the first-grade level. She was particularly deficit in the understanding and production of socially appropriate verbal and nonverbal material. The speech pathologist suggested that Jenny would benefit from continuous speech therapy to develop the aforementioned skills. The inclusion of group therapy to understand, learn, and practice the verbal and nonverbal aspects of social situations was suggested. Again, the therapist was aware of the family situation but stressed the need for these services was paramount. The therapist also stressed that without knowledge of appropriate social behaviors, Jenny could easily become a victim again.

The consultations with the child psychiatrist and neurologist were read by the clinical neuropsychologist. The child psychiatrist stated that the medications which Jenny has been prescribed are appropriate for her age, height, and weight. The concern of the child psychiatrist was the family situation and the confusion which occurs in the home. He made a strong recommendation that Jenny's medications be administered daily and appropriately. He also stated that although the family was of limited means, he felt that appropriate nutrition was essential. He made a recommendation that Jenny be referred to a dietician who would explain, in terms she could understand, the value of a healthy diet and how to make healthy food choices. The child psychiatrist also stated that he was concerned that the habits she formed now would carry through to adulthood. The neurologist's report stated that there were no gross neurological deficits apparent in his systems review. However, he described "soft" neurological signs which in the past may have been interpreted as indicators of minimal brain dysfunction. Although this term is no longer used, it did explain the findings that Jenny had many deficits which together did not clearly fit the pattern of a particular disease or disability. The neurologist felt that the services of occupational therapy and speech pathology were essential. He also suggested that Jenny return yearly for a neurological exam.

After each specialist either presented his or her results or the clinical neuropsychologist read them, there was time for question and answer. ReAnn's main concerns were how to provide help for her daughter, what were the most important issues, and, as a single parent, how she could do all the things which her daughter needed. Each of the specialists present sympathized with her and the lack of time and resources available to her. After some brainstorming, the professionals felt that the family needed the services of a county social worker to help coordinate the needs of all of the family members and also work with financial and transportation issues.

The summary which was developed from the meeting is as follows. It is clear that Jenny has some mental deficits in addition to social deficits which by the American Association of Intellectual and Developmental Disabilities standards, would be described as intellectual deficiency (Schalock et al., 2006) and, by the Diagnostic and Statistical Manual of Mental Disorders, Fourth Edition, Text Revision (DSM-IV-TR), as Mental Retardation (American Psychiatric Association [APA], 2000). The stigma of the term and other words to use were discussed, but the ultimate issue is that she has difficulties. Her strength is mathematics and with this in mind, her right hemisphere should be an area of strength. Her deficits are clearly receptive and expressive language. These results are particularly difficult because modern society tends to function in a more left than right hemisphere manner. Further, Jenny has very apparent social skills deficits. Her hearing and vision are good but her body sense or proprioception is very poor. All professionals and her mother agreed that Jenny is a vulnerable person and one who could easily be led into various unpleasant or dangerous situations. A list of recommendations was drawn up to be given to ReAnn and integrated within her daughter's IEP. It was discussed with ReAnn that she begin to work toward protecting her daughter through various services available. A particular concern is that Jenny is beginning to enter puberty and may easily be perceived as much older than she cognitively is capable of functioning. As was stated by the school psychologist, "she has the appearance of a 13-year-old and the understanding of an 8-year old, which makes her an easy victim."

Superimposed on all of the results from the case meeting is Jenny's history of sexual abuse and a diagnosis of posttraumatic stress disorder (PTSD) from that experience. The participants at the meeting did not address this issue due to the fact that it was being explored through individual therapy. However, it has been shown through research that severe sexual abuse may alter brain functioning. While not the specific focus of the meeting, the clinical neuropsychologist suggested that an MRI be completed to determine any structural or functional difficulties due to the sexual abuse.

After the meeting, the clinical neuropsychologist arranged another meeting with Jenny and ReAnn. He spoke first with ReAnn to again reiterate the consensus of the various professionals. He also stressed that a social worker would be particularly helpful and may be able to find financial resources for some of the suggested interventions. He also stressed the continual need to work with Jenny's victimology and to protect her from further abuse. The clinical neuropsychologist explained to ReAnn the vulnerability issues related to Jenny's appearance versus her understanding of social situations and how that places her in a potentially dangerous position. In addition, the clinical neuropsychologist discussed respite care and other avenues to help ReAnn obtain assistance to coordinate and care for the multiple needs of her family. Finally, the clinical neuropsychologist suggested that ReAnn may benefit from her own individual therapy which she categorically refused. She stated that she understands what is wrong with her children and will take steps to correct things but "not in a million years will I spill my guts to some shrink."

After the meeting with ReAnn, the clinical neuropsychologist spoke alone with Jenny. She appeared distracted and it was difficult for him to obtain her attention. She stated that she was tired of talking to adults and wanted to go back to school and play. She was very concerned that spending so much time at the office may have made her miss recess. She did not comment when asked about the various evaluations nor did she agree or disagree with any of the findings. She appeared very preoccupied with her school day. When asked directly about the school day, she began a discussion of tangential topics. She is aware that she understands math but not to her grade level. She does not understand her difficulties with language because, as she stated, "I am able to read." She was completely unaware of the social issues which the professionals discussed. When asked directly about her relationships with boys and girls at school, she stated "I'll play with anybody who will play with me." Jenny agreed to attend a social skills group through her school but it was not clear whether she understood that this was not a play group. The explanation of the function of the group will be left to the school professional. The clinical neuropsychologist will continue to work with Jenny on issues of abuse, cognitive rehabilitation strategies, and also as the case manager. When a social worker is brought into the situation, the case management services will be transferred to that individual. The transfer is due to the varying needs of Jenny and her family which include financial services, transportation, and other services which are outside of the expertise of the clinical neuropsychologist.

This case study is formatted differently than any other case study thus far discussed. The reason for the multidisciplinary evaluation and treatment planning session is that in most circumstances, this type of multidisciplinary involvement is necessary with children. Even if there were fewer specialists involved, any time children are patients, the family and the school are usually involved. In some cases with children, such as for Jenny's 10-year-old brother, there may already be involvement of law enforcement.

Introduction

This chapter and the next are unique in that they address populations which are outside of the norm within clinical neuropsychology. The majority of assessment tools have been designed, tested on, and used for individuals 18–65 years of age, and the major cognitive and memory rehabilitation strategies and individual therapy and family therapy techniques have also been utilized with clients 18–65 years of age. The next two chapters reflect the norm in terms of numbers of individuals. The ages from birth to 18 years of age and from age 65 to the end of life encompass 80 million and 35 million people, respectively. The issues which each age group faces may be more stressful and varied than those of individuals ages 18–65. Wicks-Nelson and Israel (2009) describe many accounts of individuals' early years as extremes of emotions, behaviors, and encounters. In this chapter, the focus will be pediatric neuropsychology which encompasses children younger than the age of 18 with central nervous system difficulties. Chapter 17 will focus on individuals in the rapidly growing population of individuals ages 65 and older with central nervous system difficulties.

Children

It has often been stated that children experience more changes on a day-to-day basis than most adults with differences in cognition, behaviors, and emotions (Lenroot & Giedd, 2006). This statement does not imply that all children live in a stressful environment, but that each day, a child changes physically, cognitively, morally, emotionally, and socially. The central nervous system was once thought to be somewhat or even almost completely developed by the age of 5 with the brain approximately 90% of adult size (Dekaban & Sadowsky, 1978). However, current research suggests that there continue to be changes into the teens and 20s, which was not known until recent MRI studies (Lenroot & Giedd, 2006). The number of neurons which was once thought to be static from birth is now in the midst of a controversy regarding the ability of neurons to regenerate. These new findings lead researchers to be less sure regarding the average cognitive abilities of each age or stage. As may be seen by looking at any group of children and adolescents, there is a wide variety in height, weight, strength, and the onset of puberty. There is much more variability in what is considered to be normal between children than in adults. However, the variability may lead to various other emotional and social issues.

This chapter is not designed to cover all of child and adolescent psychology. For a more in-depth review the reader is referred to Bergen (2009).[1] This chapter will cover the major views of physical, cognitive, moral, emotional, and psychosocial development as a starting point. It is often easier to understand how the central nervous system is not working after the average working central nervous system has been discussed. Before any treatment issues are covered, ethical issues which pertain to this age group will be described. After a discussion of ethics, the chapter will review assessment, diagnosis, and treatment of central nervous system difficulties as they pertain to this specific age group.

PHYSICAL DEVELOPMENT

cephalo-caudal
the principle of central nervous system development which states that the brain and spinal cord develop first, followed by areas further from the central core

proximo-distal
the principle of central nervous system development which states that structures close to the center of the body develop before the peripheral structures; examples include the heart, lungs, and kidneys

The general principles of growth for a human organism are cephalo-caudal and proximo-distal (see Figure 16.1). **Cephalo-caudal** refers to the growth and development of the central nervous system (brain and spinal cord) before the extremities (arms, legs, etc.). The reason for this is survival—every function within the human being is controlled by the central nervous system—hence, its early and continual development is crucial. **Proximo-distal** refers to the development of the internal structures before body parts farther from

[1] Bergen, K. S. (2009). *The developing person through childhood and adolescence* (8th ed.). New York: Worth.

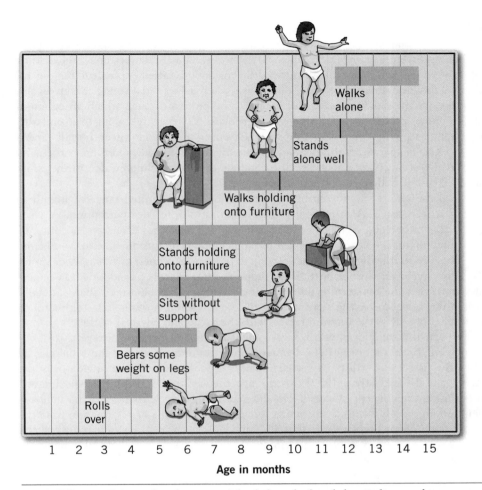

FIGURE 16.1 Motor development. The left end of each bar indicates the age at which 25% of infants tested were able to perform a particular behavior; the vertical line within the bar indicates the age when 50% of the babies tested performed the behavior. The right end of each bar indicates the age at which 90% could do so. *Source:* Adapted from Frankenberg & Dodds (1967).

the center of the body. Again, this is a survival issue, the internal organs, such as the heart, lungs, and kidneys, are necessary in order for the organism to function. After the development of these organs, the organism's energy may be focused on less crucial areas. These principles explain the common phenomena expressed by the layperson that children often have large heads for the size of their bodies. The apparently large head encases the absolutely essential cerebral cortex.

Physical development outside of the central nervous system proceeds along a prescribed course. Height and weight tend to vary together, and as a child becomes taller, he or she also becomes heavier. A child progresses in motor skills through a sequence of steps: rolling from side to side, pulling him-/herself up to a sitting position, creeping, cruising (walking while holding on to a support), and then walking. Each of these has a prescribed range which is considered to be normal. However, even though a child may not attain a

developmental milestone
researchers have developed
certain ranges which are
considered to be normal for the
appearance of various abilities
within children; examples
include talking and walking

developmental milestone at the usual time it does not necessarily imply that there is a deficit. Many variables must be considered before any type of label or diagnosis is assigned to a child. Intervening variables which could delay developmental milestones include time in utero, prenatal, and postnatal difficulties, learning opportunities, exposure to teratogens, and socioeconomic status. Applying a diagnosis is often delayed in a young child to evaluate changes as the child matures. Maturation is the process through which an organism naturally grows and changes. The nature–nurture question is quickly coming to an end with research indicating that genetics and experience work together. However, not all experiences are equal; experiences children have during the brain's growth spurts are particularly important (Walsh, 2006). Labels are also carefully applied to children due to the issues related to teasing, bullying, and stigmatization.

All of the senses function at birth, but each one has a limited range of stimuli to which it is responsive. As a general principle, sensation precedes perception. A sense organ is able to detect a stimulus before the perceptual apparatus deciphers its contents. Very young infants are keenly interested in social stimuli. Infants are able to hear before birth. They are startled by sounds and respond to the sounds of their own language. Vision is the least developed sense at birth, which appears contradictory considering how important vision is for the functioning adult. As the visual apparatus matures, shapes, details, and anything novel causes the infant to scan the area. The senses of smell, taste, and touch also develop rapidly as the infant interacts with the social and physical world.

Through the study of physical development came the concept of stage theories of development. Stage theories of development affect not only physical abilities but also all of the other areas that will be discussed. Although not necessarily the originator of the term, Sigmund Freud (1856–1939) was the first theorist to discuss psychological development using the concept of stages. The concept behind these theories is that abilities develop in an orderly fashion, one ability building on the skills or information from the previous stage. Many theories state that all individuals go through stages in sequence and do not skip a stage. Stress and/or other circumstances may cause an individual to regress to a previous stage in development.

stage theories of development
theories of development in
which one ability is thought to
develop before the next ability
and where the stages build on
one another; stage theories
are thought to apply to all
individuals

With our case study in mind, it is clear that Jenny had a normal prenatal and postnatal development. She was able to meet all of the developmental milestones for height, weight, head circumference, and the functioning of her senses. The issues that brought her to the clinical neuropsychologist do not appear to relate to very early physical development. However, early child abuse, as will be discussed further, may have contributed to delays in various developmental areas that occurred later such as with balance, body sense, and proprioception.

COGNITIVE DEVELOPMENT

Cognitive and/or intellectual development is related to the growth of the nervous system, the genetic inheritance of the individual, and environmental circumstances. For decades, the nature–nurture question has been paramount within the discussion of intelligence. Also paramount in this issue is the question of racial/ethnic differences in these abilities. The discussion within this chapter relates to the most widely accepted theory of cognitive development advanced by Swiss psychologist Jean Piaget (1896–1980). Piaget observed his own three children before he developed his stage theory of cognitive abilities. By today's standards, this was a very small sample from which to draw conclusions. However, when one considers that Piaget was a contemporary of Freud who made his conclusions based on six case studies, it gives an historical perspective. Piaget's theory consists of four levels of cognitive functioning. He also stated that not all individuals, particularly those with developmental delays, may attain the most advanced level of cognitive abilities. The first stage is the **sensorimotor stage** (birth to 2 years) in which infants use their senses and motor abilities to understand the world. The major task of this period is **object permanence** or the understanding that an object exists when out of view. The second stage is the **pre-operational stage** (2–6 years) during which the child thinks magically and uses language to understand the world. The child is **egocentric** in his or her ability to understand the world and feels that he or she is the central focus of most activities in which he or she is involved. The **concrete operational stage** is the third stage (6–11 years). At this time the child is able to begin to think rationally and logically. Using his or her logical abilities, a child is able to understand **conservation** of number, classification, and basic scientific information. The final stage is the **formal operational stage** (12 years to adulthood) and the stage Piaget believed many people did not reach. Thinking within this stage is abstract and hypothetical. The child is able to ponder possibility in addition to actuality, and philosophical and ethical questions are often raised. Piaget has received criticism in the past for underestimating the ages at which children attain various cognitive skills. Various researchers explain advances in the thinking of children since Piaget's writing are due to changes in society and the introduction of the electronic era and not a problem with the theory. The researchers suggest that the ages not the stages of Piaget's theory need changing. For example, Baillargeon (2000) listed 30 studies which reached the conclusion that object permanence occurred before 6 months and a further article by Hespos and Baillargeon (2008) reveals evidence for violation of expected findings.

Two other theories explain cognitive development from somewhat different perspectives. Sociocultural theory states that human development, in this case, cognitive development, results from the dynamic interactions between the individual and his or her society and culture. Hence, sociocultural theory attempts to account for racial or ethnic variations in learning styles. The pioneer in sociocultural theory was Russian psychologist Lev Vygotsky (1896–1934). In Vygotsky's view, each individual learns from a more skilled member of his or her social group through guided participation. Social interaction is of paramount importance in sociocultural theory (Wertsch & Tulviste, 2005). In a sense, Vygotsky foreshadowed the modern concept of mentorship.

Epigenetic theory is a combination of biology, genetics, and neuroscience. Epigenetic theory states that genes interact with the environment to allow, in this case, cognitive development (Gottlieb, 2003). As development progresses, each person proceeds along the course set by earlier genetic–environment interactions which allow a range of possible outcomes termed the *reaction range* (Bergen, 2009).

Jenny, according to Piaget's theory, would be functioning in the preoperational stage. This stage is lower than would be expected for her age. If one reviewed her sociocultural environment, one would see that she has had no adequate role model to help learn appropriate social behavior. Using an epigenetic approach, it may be that she has intellectual deficits due to a combination of defective genes and a deficient social environment. In addition, it is possible that the aforementioned sexual abuse may have altered her brain's ability to attain developmental stages at the appropriate ages.

MORAL DEVELOPMENT

Theories of moral development were developed after Piaget's description of cognitive development. Kohlberg (1963) developed a stage theory of moral development through the use of a moral dilemma problem. Many problems were posed to males of various ages. The most thoroughly utilized moral dilemma was of a poor man named Heinz whose wife was dying. The local druggist was the only person who had the cure and was selling it for

sensorimotor stage
Piaget's first level of cognitive development; the infant uses his or her senses to understand and explore the world; the major task to learn is object permanence

object permanence
the ability to understand that objects and people continue to exist even when they are out of the observer's sight

preoperational stage
Piaget's second stage of cognitive development; it emphasizes language and symbolic thought

egocentric
Piaget's term for a child's tending to think about how the world works entirely from his or her own perspective

concrete operational stage
Piaget's third stage of cognitive development; it includes the abilities to reason logically about direct experiences and perceptions

conservation
the ability to logically determine that a certain quantity will remain the same despite adjustment of the container, shape, or apparent size

formal operational stage
the fourth stage of Piaget's theory of cognitive development characterized by logical and systematic thought; it also includes the ability to manipulate abstract concepts. Piaget did not believe that all individuals attain this level of thinking

10 times the cost to make. The question for the children was how they would explain the situation in which Heinz stole the drug from the pharmacist. The reasoning the children employed to solve the moral dilemma was the basis by which Kohlberg placed children within his various levels of moral thought.

Kohlberg's theory consisted of six levels of moral reasoning divided into three stages. The first stage was **preconventional moral reasoning**, which emphasized rewards and punishments in making moral decisions or explaining moral dilemmas. It is similar to Piaget's preoperational level of thought in terms of egocentric reasoning. The second stage is conventional moral reasoning. Individuals in this stage make decisions based on social roles. In this stage, children are very concerned about rules and being a good boy or girl versus a bad boy or girl. This stage is similar to Piaget's concrete operation stage of thinking. The third stage is postconventional moral reasoning, which emphasizes moral principles in moral decision making. The last stage is similar to Piaget's formal operational thought and uses logic and abstraction. Similar to Piaget's final stage, it is also probable that not all individuals function at this level morally.

According to Kohlberg (1963), cognitive maturity and environmental influence are involved in the moral thinking process. Kohlberg, however, has recently been criticized for not taking cultural and gender issues into account with his theory (Turiel, 2006). He has also been criticized for using only males as subjects. Gilligan (1982, 1993), using female subjects, found differences in how the moral dilemma was solved and attributed this not to lower or poorer moral reasoning in females but clear gender differences. Gilligan (1982) stated that the highest level of moral reasoning for females may not be the impersonal concept of justice found by Kohlberg. She suggested that women at the highest level of moral reasoning focus on a need to protect enduring relationships and fulfill human needs.

In our case study, Jenny would be functioning within the preconventional stage of moral reasoning. This stage is theoretically matching her level of cognitive functioning; however, both are lower than would be expected for her chronological age.

EMOTIONAL DEVELOPMENT

Within the broad term of emotional development is the formation of the bonds of attachment. Attachment develops through a mutual interaction between an infant and caregiver. It develops gradually and is usually evident by the time a child is 7–9 months old. Bowlby (1969), a major child development theorist, viewed attachment as a continuous interaction between the two and that the behaviors on the part of the parent to facilitate attachment appeared to be biologically "wired" into the species for the survival of the young. Bowlby also felt that the type of attachment the child developed helped to shape adaptive or less adaptive pathways to further development. Attachment was thought to lead to expectations regarding the trustworthiness of caregivers to fulfill the child's needs and also influence the child's ability to regulate emotions, cope with stress, and develop a sense of self-confidence and self-worth. Ainsworth and Salter (1973), using a procedure termed the *Strange Situation*, studied infant-caregiver attachment. In the Strange Situation, the caregiver, a stranger, and the infant interact in a comfortable room. The caregiver leaves the room where the infant is playing and returns several times. The manner in which the infant reacts to the caregiver after being in a stressful situation with a stranger is the basis for the attachment style label. Securely attached infants use the caregiver as a basis for exploration. Insecurely attached infants fail to see the caregiver as a resource to cope with stress. The infants either emit fewer signals of distress and ignore the caregiver (avoidant type) or display distress and demonstrate ineffective attempts to seek or seek to avoid contact with the caregiver (resistant type). Recent research has investigated the **disorganized/disoriented attached infant**, which reflects a lack of the ability to organize behaviors under stressful situations (Lyons-Ruth, Zeanah, &

---

preconventional moral reasoning
Kohlberg's first stage of moral reasoning which emphasizes rewards or punishments in solving moral dilemmas

conventional moral reasoning
Kohlberg's second level of moral reasoning which emphasizes social roles and conventions

postconventional moral reasoning
Kohlberg's third level of moral reasoning which emphasizes moral and ethical principles

securely attached infant
infant who has developed a positive relationship with a caregiver which allows the infant to feel safe and explore the environment; this relationship leads to positive relationships in the future

insecurely attached infant
an infant unable to feel emotionally connected to the caregiver and unable to predict that the caregiver will meet his or her needs; therefore, the infant is not able to use the caregiver as a resource in a stressful situation and often has issues with attachment in later life

disorganized/disoriented attached infant
an attachment style characterized by the inability to organize behaviors under stressful situations

Benofi, 2003). The relationship of early attachment to later behavior has been thoroughly researched. Secure attachment is related to adaptive behaviors in childhood (Kobak, Cassidy, Lyons-Ruth, & Ziv, 2006), whereas insecure attachment is linked to maladaptive behavior. Attachment research must be interpreted with caution, however, due to the fact that attachment styles may change based on family circumstances (Thompson, 2000).

Temperament is another variable which is included within the category of emotional development. Temperament most often refers to basic disposition or makeup often evidenced from birth. Chess and Thomas (1972, 1977) were the first to categorize children on the basis of nine dimensions of behavioral style which included reactivity to stimuli, regulation of bodily functions, mood, and adaptability to change. They identified three basic temperamental styles—easy, slow-to-warm, and difficult—and related these to later adjustment in life. However, the researchers felt that the temperamental style of the child interacted with parental reactions and made it a more malleable construct. Current research supports the early work of Chess and Thomas with the addition of aspects of approach and avoidance behaviors, positive and negative emotions, activity level, sociability, attention, and self-regulation (Rothbath & Posner, 2006).

> **temperament**
> basic disposition or emotional makeup of a child often evident from birth

Emotional regulation and reactivity are part of temperament but not identical. Three elements of emotion usually discussed are private feelings, autonomic nervous system arousal, and behavioral expression. The regulation of the expression of emotions is the main task of ages 2–6 (Eisenberg et al., 2004). Children who are capable of appropriate emotional experience are more able to function in every area of their lives (Denham et al., 2003). The effective control of emotions is not possible in toddlers and the continual prodding or chastising by caregivers often makes a bad situation worse. Emotional regulation is dependent upon the development of the limbic system and its connections to the prefrontal cortex. As has been discussed earlier, the prefrontal cortex is one of the later areas within the cortex to develop.

As we look at Jenny's attachment style, it could be classified as insecurely attached. She did not appear to have a solid base on which to feel safe when she dealt with the world and its stressors. Her temperament, possibly due to her intellectual difficulties, may be considered to be difficult. Jenny is 11 but does not appear to have very well-developed emotional control. In her situation, it appears to be related to social–familial factors as opposed to central nervous system structural difficulties. In addition, the aforementioned sexual abuse may play a large component in some of her deficits. However, there is no absolute etiological cause that has been determined and the neurologist stated that she expressed some "soft" signs. Hence, it is clear that Jenny has socioemotional deficits from mixed etiological factors.

SOCIAL DEVELOPMENT

The paramount theorist within the area of psychosocial development was Erik Erikson (1902–1994). He created a developmental theory based on social interaction and the effects which others have on one's behavior (Erikson, 1963). Erikson proposed that during each stage, a more positive or a more negative outcome to a crisis or developmental issue occurred, which helped or harmed the child as he or she matured. Each stage of the eight-stage theory built on the previous stages (see Figure 16.2). The first stage, trust versus mistrust (birth to 1 year), occurred as the infant attempted to have his or her basic needs met. If the needs for food, clothing, and shelter were met in a consistent manner, the child developed a sense of basic trust in the world around him. If these needs were not met or met in an inconsistent fashion, the child may have developed a basic lack of trust in the world and those around him. The second stage, autonomy versus shame and doubt (1–3 years), occurred as children experiment with self-sufficiency. If a child was able to feel comfortable and confident in eating, toileting, exploring, and talking, he or she would develop a sense of autonomy. If the

ERIKSON'S EIGHT STAGES OF PSYCHOSOCIAL DEVELOPMENT			
Stage	**Basic Conflict**	**Important Events**	**Outcome**
Infancy (Birth to 18 months)	Trust vs. Mistrust	Feeding	Children develop a sense of trust when caregivers provide reliability, care, and affection. A lack of this will lead to mistrust.
Early Childhood (2 to 3 years)	Autonomy vs. Shame and Doubt	Toilet Training	Children need to develop a sense of personal control over physical skills and a sense of independence. Success results in feelings of autonomy; failure, feelings of shame and doubt.
Preschool (3 to 5 years)	Initiative vs. Guilt	Exploration	Children need to begin asserting control and power over their environment. Success leads to a sense of purpose. Children who try to exert too much power experience disapproval, which results in a sense of guilt.
School Age (6 to 11 years)	Industry vs. Inferiority	School	Children need to cope with new social and academic demands. Success leads to a sense of competence; failure results in feelings of inferiority.
Adolescence (12 to 18 years)	Identity vs. Role Confusion	Social Relationships	Teens needs to develop a sense of self and personal identity. Success leads to an ability to stay true to oneself; failure leads to role confusion and weak sense of self.
Young Adulthood (19 to 40 years)	Intimacy vs. Isolation	Relationships	Young adults need to form intimate, loving relationships with other people. Success leads to strong relationships; failure results in loneliness and isolation.
Middle Adulthood (40 to 65 years)	Generativity vs. Stagnation	Work and Parenthood	Adults need to create or nurture things that will outlast them, often by having children or creating a positive change that benefits other people. Success leads to feelings of usefulness and accomplishment; failure results in shallow involvement in the world.
Maturity (65 to death)	Ego Integrity vs. Despair	Reflection on Life	Older adults need to look back on life and feel a sense of fulfillment. Success at this stage affords to feelings of wisdom; failure results in regret, bitterness, and despair.

FIGURE 16.2 Erikson's stages of development.

child had difficulty with these tasks and/or was shamed, he or she developed an inner sense of shame and self-doubt. The third stage, initiative versus guilt (3–6 years), encompassed the age when most children began school. During this stage, children either attempted adultlike activities such as family chores or resisted and maintained dependency on the caregiver. At this stage, they began to feel either adventurous or guilty. The fourth stage, industry versus inferiority (6–11 years), encompasses the elementary school years. The child either learned to master skills or felt unable to perform as well as he or she would like. The fifth stage, identity versus role confusion (adolescence), was the stage about which Erikson was most interested and researched and wrote extensively (Erikson, 1968). It was during this stage that the adolescent began to become an adult. Questioning of all aspects of one's life, religion, politics, sexuality, and so forth was common during this stage. Individuals who develop a strong sense of who they were can be considered to have found their own identity; those who remain confused, vacillated, or followed others left the stage confused regarding who they were in relationship to the larger society. The final three stages encompassed different phases of adulthood. Intimacy versus isolation (young adulthood) involved the ability to give him-/herself in any form of loving relationship. When this was not possible, the individual became emotionally isolated often due to fears of rejection or abandonment. The seventh stage, generativity versus stagnation (middle age), addressed the relationship between the individual and the next generation. A sense of generativity was felt when one gave, taught, or encouraged others whereas lack of multigenerational contact or concern lead to a feeling of stagnation or even depression. The final stage (old age) was integrity versus despair. At the end of life, an individual was able to look back at a life well lived and felt a sense of integrity. The opposite situation was when an individual looked back on life and saw only failure or things never tried or accomplished.

Using Erikson's framework, Jenny could be seen as straddling two stages: initiative versus guilt and industry versus inferiority. Her complete lack of appropriate social skills makes it difficult for her to be on track for the appropriate age-related stage. Taking her past into consideration, it is clear that many of the stages were not accomplished in a positive direction. With this in mind, it becomes clear how she has suffered from the lack of trust in her world, felt doubt, and guilt, and is currently encountering inferiority as she has difficulties with her schooling. As described by Erikson, each stage builds on the other, and in Jenny's case, each stage mastered in the negative direction caused more and more difficulties.

Developmental Difficulties

Following this discussion of the various stage theories of development, the chapter will now continue with a discussion of difficulties with development and/or diagnosable problems. However, even though we are focusing on a few specific difficulties, all disorders within the *DSM-IV-TR* may also be diagnosed in children under certain circumstances (American Psychiatric Association [APA], 2000).

Ethical Issues With Children

Prior to any discussion regarding the assessment, diagnosis, and treatment of children, ethical issues as described by the American Psychological Association (APA, 2002) need to be considered. All children younger than the age of 18, by virtue of their age, have different ethical and legal rights than do adults. Children, in most circumstances, do not self-refer for treatment or rehabilitation. In the unusual situation in which a child does self-refer, the parent or legal guardian must be notified and consent to treatment. The stipulations regarding the confidential relationship guaranteed by clinical neuropsychologists are different when working with children. The standard statement, as discussed elsewhere in this text, states that everything remains confidential except in certain circumstances which include threats of suicide, threats of homicide, child abuse where the patient is the victim or perpetrator, and abuse of vulnerable adults where the patient is the victim or perpetrator. In the case of children, the client must also be notified that if the parent asks the content of the therapy session, it must be shared. This stipulation raises questions regarding who is the therapy client and whether a child would trust a therapist to discuss important and/or difficult information. In situations where the child or adolescent has central nervous system difficulties, it may be helpful to have a parent or guardian available to help reiterate the therapist's advice between sessions. As has been stated elsewhere, attention, concentration, and memory are often salient deficits which preclude therapeutic movement. The availability of a third party to recall the information from the therapy session could be invaluable. Conversely, the presence of a third party could be seen as a threat to privacy. Confidentiality issues with children and adolescents are more difficult than with adults and even more problematic when central nervous system issues are apparent.

In addition to confidentiality is the ethics of consent for treatment. All therapy clients must consent before any therapy or rehabilitation is begun. In the case of minors, the parent or guardian is the locus of consent. Sometimes there is resistance on the part of the child or adolescent if pressured to attend therapy. These emotions are compounded in the situation with central nervous system difficulties.

Other ethical issues which are salient with children include assessment tools which must include the most up-to-date, standardized, and age-appropriate available. Also important are the stipulations regarding prevention of any sexual or gender harassment or discrimination. Finally, research using children as subjects must have the consent of the legal guardian for the child to participate. This is also true regarding the records of the child if they are to be used in any form of data analysis. In addition, the Society for Research in Child Development (2009) has a specific set of ethical standards for research with children. Finally, not truly an ethical issue but a ramification of the use of diagnostic labels, is stigmatization. At this juncture, the issue becomes salient due to the fact that children and adolescents often have more individuals involved in their care and therefore there is a greater chance that noninvolved parties may learn of the diagnostic label. The most common scenario is when a school teacher or nurse somehow allows the child's diagnostic label to become public. Children are often unkind to one another and will use anything against one another. Stigmatization due to diagnostic labels and the consequences of these, such as taking medications during the school day, special education classes, or appointments with school counselors during the school day, often become public. It is essential that the effects on the child be paramount when discussing issues related to a particular child.

As was stated previously, any diagnosis discussed in the diagnostic manual may be applicable to children and adolescents. However, there are some central nervous system difficulties which occur more often in this age group than any other and will be reviewed. Until the past 10 years, the role of gender in childhood disorders was virtually ignored. Current research addressing this issue has consistently found gender differences in the overall rates of many difficulties, with males being affected more than females (Rutter & Sroufe, 2000). Overall, males are more vulnerable to neurodevelopmental disorders early in life and females to emotional difficulties later in life (Rutter, Caspi, & Moffit, 2003).

Acquired Central Nervous System Difficulties in Children

TRAUMATIC BRAIN INJURY

Traumatic brain injury (TBI) in adults has previously been reviewed in this text. In the case of children, the etiology of TBI is most often falls, child abuse, moving vehicle accidents, and sports injuries. Within the group of etiological factors, the most preventable are sports-related injuries through the use of helmets or protective gear. The estimated incidence rate is 180 per 100,000 children per year (Kraus, 1995). The site of injury for TBI in children is similar to that in adults with difficulties involving the frontal and temporal lobes and often including diffuse axonal injury. In the past, it was often thought that children recovered more quickly and thoroughly than adults due to the plasticity of their brains. The often referred to Kennard principle stated "if you were to have brain damage have it early" (Kennard, 1942). Recent research suggests that this is not the case and that children and adolescents may appear to recover only to have deficits surface in adolescence as the developmental process proceeds. Damage to an immature brain may interfere with future brain development and deficits may become apparent over time (Limond & Leeke, 2005). This is particularly due to the fact that the frontal lobes are the last regions to develop and are very often the first areas to be damaged in TBI. As stated by Mateer, Kerns, and Eso (1997), the long-term effects of cognitive deficits superimposed on the developmental process produce a different recovery pattern in children. The interaction of development and brain injury can produce a phenomenon often referred to as "growing into deficit" (Mateer et al., 1997).

Treatment for children and adolescents with TBI may be much different than for adults. The younger the child at the time of the traumatic event, the more the child will view the world through a distorted lens and also see him- or herself as different. Children who sustain a TBI later may spend time comparing themselves to their own previous level of functioning. In either scenario, the risk of various emotional sequelae is great. Children and adolescents with TBI, as they mature and their functioning is compared with that of their peers, are at high risk for anxiety, depression (and suicide), chemical dependency, and other behavioral difficulties such as school failure. With this in mind, it is essential that the mental health needs of a child or adolescent be taken into consideration in the treatment plan. Modulation of emotions, discussed with adult patients, is also a difficulty for children who have sustained TBI. This is a very difficult problem for young children who are just beginning to differentiate various emotions and develop control over them. For a child with TBI, anger, rage, envy, and other strong emotions may feel uncontrollable and appear to develop without any clear cause. Again, the treatment plan must focus on ways to predict and control these strong emotions appropriately both for the good of the individual and for his or her family, friends, and the school who must interact with the child or adolescent.

Attention, concentration, memory, and cognition are all potential areas of concern for children and adolescents with TBI (Anderson, Fenwick, Manly, & Robertson, 1998). Prior to any treatment, a thorough neuropsychological evaluation, using appropriate assessment tools particular to the child's age group must be accomplished. Once a pattern of strengths and weaknesses has been determined, it will then become possible to choose the most appropriate rehabilitation strategies from those which are designed for children. The computerized rehabilitation programs evaluated for adults are not appropriate for children. The age of the child, time of injury, and type of deficit must be considered along with where in the developmental process the child functions when choosing a particular rehabilitation program.

A complete treatment plan for a child or adolescent with TBI should include the following. A complete neuropsychological evaluation to determine the client's strengths and weaknesses is the starting point. Particularly in children, a distinction must be made between a deficit or persistent impairment and a delay or lag in development which presupposes the ability to recover the function. Once the strengths and weaknesses are determined, then rehabilitation may be tailored to fit the client's specific needs. A pediatric psychiatric consultation to evaluate the use of medication for any of the aforementioned issues is always suggested. Dependent upon the etiological factors and other co-occurring difficulties, the services of speech pathology, occupational therapy, and physical therapy may be necessary. Individual therapy to address depression or other negative behaviors and control of any externalizing emotions may be accomplished by the clinical neuropsychologist. The school must be involved to provide the best services for the disabilities apparent. In the treatment of adults with TBI, the main focus for rehabilitation is the workplace, whereas with children, the main focus must be the school. In order to function well in the school setting, a child must have social, academic, and behavioral skills, all of which may be impaired due to a TBI. It is necessary that each of these be addressed within the school setting or the child will be at risk for feelings of frustration and lowered self-esteem. In most situations, an IEP will be developed as discussed in the case study. A social worker or social services may be involved in case management as well as providing other information regarding the financial costs of treatment, and so forth. In many situations, the clinical neuropsychologist has the role of case manager but consults with social services for additional information. The involvement of family and friends is crucial for the continued functioning of the individual in as normal of a situation as possible. Family and friends may need further information regarding TBI and what to expect in terms of the recovery of the client. The final component of the treatment plan is the neuropsychological reevaluation at various intervals, usually yearly, to determine any changes which have occurred and to help evaluate the effectiveness of the treatment plan.

Looking back at our case study, it appears that Jenny has not sustained a TBI. However, as will be discussed further, abuse (in her case sexual abuse) has been known to affect the functioning of the cerebral cortex and may be a contributing factor to some of the difficulties which she has exhibited. If it is determined that this is the case, then additional goals would be added to her existing IEP.

PEDIATRIC BRAIN TUMORS

Tumors of the brain are the second most common form of childhood tumor and also the second most common malignancy, exceeded only by the leukemias (Blaney et al., 2006). Recent estimates indicate between 2.5 and 3.5 new cases per 100,000 are diagnosed each year in the United States (Packer, MacDonald, Rood, Forbes, & Keating, 2005). Differences in incidence figures for tumors exist by age with the highest rates between birth and 4 years, followed by ages 4–7, with a significant decline in incidence between ages 10 and 14 (Packer et al., 2005). There has been a significant increase in the number of diagnosed tumors since the 1990s, most often attributed to better and more advanced diagnostic procedures (Smith, Freidlin, Reis, & Simon, 1998). There exist several differences by age in the site of the tumor with younger children having more brain stem and cerebellar tumors (**infratentorial**) and adolescents exhibiting tumors to all other areas within the brain (**supratentorial**). Even with early or better detection, cranial brain tumors remain the second leading cause of death in children and adolescents.

There are several different types of brain tumors which are listed in descending order based on the number of cases in the age range 0–14 years: embryonal tumors, pineal tumors, glioneuronal/neuronal tumors, choroid plexus tumors, ependymomas, oligodendrogliomas, and astrocytomas. Diagnosis of brain tumors in childhood is based upon nonspecific signs such as developmental delays, regression from an earlier level of functioning, and signs of intracranial pressure such as nausea, vomiting, and headache. Localizing symptoms for infratentorial tumors include headache, nausea and vomiting, balance and gait problems, and signs of cranial nerve dysfunction. Signs of supratentorial tumors include unilateral or migraine headaches, endocrine abnormalities, various forms of seizures, and visual field difficulties (Duffner, Jackson, & Cohen, 1996). Signs and symptoms may occur early on, later, or during the diagnostic process depending upon the particular type of tumor (Maria & Menkes, 2006).

There are usually three choices for treatment of brain tumors in children: surgical resection, chemotherapy, and/or radiation or a combination of these. The treatment decision is made based on the age of the child, features of the tumor such as its location and grade, and its accessibility to surgical intervention. Evaluation of success of treatment based on neuropsychological test results including global measures of intelligence and school success has been severely criticized due to lack of specificity (Ris & Noll, 1994). However, current outcome research has included more specific data regarding the client's strengths and weaknesses in the following domains: specific intellectual abilities, academic achievement, memory and attention, speech and language, and quality of life (Dennis, Spiegler, Riva, & MacGregor, 2004).

After the physiological treatment has been completed and an appropriate neuropsychological evaluation has detailed the client's strengths and weaknesses, a treatment plan may be developed. Effects of the physical treatment will need to be addressed including any iatrogenic effects. Cognitive dysfunctions which surface after treatment or later, as in the case with TBI, may be addressed with a program of cognitive rehabilitation. Emotional difficulties as a result of the physical treatment or secondary to the restrictions or changes in life due to the tumor will need to be addressed in individual therapy by the clinical neuropsychologist. In addition, family therapy may be necessary to help members adjust to changes in cognition, personality, or behavior caused by the tumor, its treatment, or as a reaction to the tumor.

When discussing Jenny's case, it is clear that she has not experienced any form of central nervous tumor. However, it can be seen that her treatment plan is very similar to that developed for a child who has experienced a cranial tumor.

CHILD ABUSE

While it is true that child abuse has been evident throughout civilization, research on the incidence and treatment of the phenomenon dates from the 1960s (Cicchetti & Olsen, 1990). The term the **battered child syndrome** was first used by pediatricians C. Henry Kempe and associates (Kempe, Silverman, Steele, Droegemueller, & Silver, 1962). These physicians became alarmed at the number of nonaccidental injuries which they saw in children. The term *child abuse* is usually viewed as an umbrella term for physical, sexual, and emotional abuse, neglect, and sexual harassment. The perpetrators are often caregivers but also include others in power relationships to a child such as clergy, educators, law enforcement personnel, parents' friends, neighbors, and siblings. By 1970, each of the states within the United States had mandated the reporting of child abuse. In 1974, Congress passed the Child Abuse Prevention and Treatment Act (1974) to focus national attention on the problem and to prescribe actions that the states should take (Wicks-Nelson & Israel, 2009). The various categories within the broader term *child abuse* are all thought to be underreported phenomena. A recent report by the United States Department of Health and Human Services Administration on Children, Youth and Family (2007) stated that there were approximately 12 victims per 1,000 children in 2005. Within the overall total in this study, 63% of victims experienced neglect, 17% experienced physical abuse, 9% were sexually abused, and 7% suffered emotional abuse. Many cases are often difficult to classify due to the fact that several types of abuse may be evident. It is often easier to detect physical abuse than any of the other forms which effects not only the reporting but also the feeling on the part of victims that if they were not physically abused, it is not a serious problem. The treatment literature indicates that one in four females and one in six to eight males are sexually abused before the age of 18 (Briere & Elliott, 2003).

battered child syndrome a term which describes physical, sexual, and/or emotional abuse of a child; the term was first used by physicians in the 1960s

The understanding of the cause of abuse is difficult. When the perpetrator of the abuse is a caregiver, research indicates that the person tends to be of a younger age, often not conversant in appropriate parenting skills (Connelly & Strauss, 1992). Other characteristics of perpetrators include low stress tolerance, difficulty inhibiting impulsive behavior, mood changes, and physical difficulties. There also exists a higher incidence of substance abuse and partner violence in those who abuse their children (Wekerle, Wall, Leung, & Trocmé, 2007). However, most abused children do not go on to abuse their own children.

Certain characteristics of children put them more at risk for abuse due to the fact that they may demand extra attention or appear different. Children and adolescents who are at highest risk for abuse are those who have disabilities or those whose behaviors or mannerisms may cause them to adversely interact with the caregiver (Wolfe, 2006). The social context in which a child lives may also contribute to the potential for abuse. Many factors interact but the child who lives in a violent situation within the culture of poverty or where there is heavy chemical usage is more often the victim of abuse (English, 1998).

Difficulties for children who are abused are many and varied, beginning with the basic lack of developmental milestone attainment to the extreme of PTSD and brain impairment. It has also been noted that early abuse may disrupt the functioning of the stress-regulating system (the limbic-pituitary-adrenocortical system), alter neurotransmitter systems, and possibly alter brain structures and functions.

As was evident to early pediatricians, signs and symptoms of physical abuse are often marks or bruises, broken bones, and so forth, in places on the body which may be visible or may be hidden under clothing. Some perpetrators dress their children in a manner in order to hide the physical evidence. Sexual abuse may not be evident on a general physical exam but become evident due to genital irritation, injury, or frequent urinary tract or bladder infections. Children who are sexually abused may exhibit behavioral symptoms that resemble anxiety, depression, or PTSD. Emotional abuse is difficult to uncover and is often evident through behavioral signs of low self-esteem and self-confidence or possibly behaviors on the opposite end of the continuum such as aggression. Research indicates that most children who have been physically abused have also been emotionally abused. Many sexually abused children have also been emotionally abused but many have been coerced into thinking they were in a special relationship with the perpetrator. Neglect often surfaces through symptoms such as failure to thrive, not making development milestones for height and weight, inappropriate dress for the weather, or poor hygiene. Sexual harassment and bullying often surface as the child begins to feel bad about himself or herself and tries to avoid the situation in which the event occurred.

While the emotional and neuropsychological scars are not the same for each type of abuse or for each child, there are several general components to treatment which must be addressed. The outcome of child maltreatment is affected by many factors including the type and severity of abuse, developmental timing, characteristics of the child's family, peer relationships, and neighborhood (Finkelhor, Ormrod, & Turner, 2007). The child or adolescent must understand that he or she is not at fault for the incidents that have happened to him or her. Perpetrators have been known to go to great lengths to involve victims in their abuse to the point of instilling what is referred to as the *Stockholm syndrome*, or the feeling of attachment to one's persecutor (De Fabrique, Romano, Vecchi, & Van Hasselt, 2007). The child or adolescent must learn that the events which happened to him or her are not normal human relationships. The child or adolescent may need further guidance in avoiding abusive types of relationships in the future. A thorough neuropsychological evaluation is necessary to determine whether any deficits have occurred due to the particular form of abuse. As was stated earlier, it is not true that children will recover easier and quicker due to their age and any deficits need complete remediation whether they are cognitive, attentional, concentration, or memory. Anxiety, depression, and PTSD must be dealt with and can be treated at the same time as any other deficits including any physical injuries from any form of abuse.

Neurodevelopmental Disorders

As a group of difficulties, neurodevelopmental disorders are those which result from insult or abnormality within the developing central nervous system. The difficulty may occur during the prenatal, perinatal, or postnatal periods and results in neuropsychological dysfunction. Most definitions of neurodevelopmental disorders imply that the difficulty occurs prior to birth or within the first 3 years after birth (Capute & Accardo, 1996). The difficulties are quite dissimilar from acquired brain impairment in that the child may have never experienced a time period of normal central nervous system functioning.

MENTAL RETARDATION (INTELLECTUAL DEFICIENCY)

One of the most prevalent neurodevelopmental disorders is mental retardation with a rate of approximately 1% of school-aged children (Yeargin-Allsopp & Boyle, 2002). As discussed within the case study, the American Association on Intellectual and Developmental Disability has officially changed the terminology from *mental retardation* to *intellectual deficiency*. In fact the organization's title has changed due to society's change in how it perceives disability. The organization was called the American Association on Mental Retardation until 2006. With these changes came changes in the criteria for mental deficiency which may encompass more individuals. It is crucial to have a complete neuropsychological evaluation due to the fact that provisions of service are often based upon the results of the evaluation. The definition of intellectual deficiency used in *DSM-IV-TR* (which employs the term mental retardation) encompasses three components, which include significantly subaverage intellectual functioning and deficits in adaptive skills, both of which occur within the developmental period prior to the age of 18 (APA, 2000). The *DSM-IV-TR* uses the following scores on tests of measured IQ as part of the determination of the level of mental retardation: mild mental retardation, IQ 50–70 (85% of the population with mental retardation), moderate mental retardation, IQ 34–55 (10% of the population with mental retardation), severe mental retardation, IQ 20–40 (3–4% of the population with mental retardation), and profound mental retardation, IQ lower than 20 (1–2% of the population with mental retardation. With this tripartite definition, it is possible for an individual to have significantly subaverage intellectual skills but good adaptive skills and therefore not be diagnosed as suffering from mental deficiency. In this particular situation, it would be difficult for the individual to obtain support services without a diagnosis. Obtaining an appropriate measure of intellectual functioning is crucial using a current test designed for the appropriate age group. The most often utilized intelligence tests for this type of assessment are the Wechsler Intelligence Scale for Children-IV (Wechsler, 2009) and the Stanford-Binet-V (Roid, 2003). Adaptive functioning which must be assessed using a reliable and valid scale for the appropriate age group is most often assessed through the Vineland Adaptive Behavior Scales, Second Edition (Vineland-II; Sparrow, Balla, & Cicchetti, 2005).

Treatment for mental deficiency is dependent upon the strengths and weaknesses which become apparent through the assessment. Each individual is very different and his or her strengths and weaknesses may vary widely. Intellectual deficiency raises questions for professionals and family alike regarding independent living, education, employment, relationships, and sexuality to which there are no straightforward clear-cut answers. In addition, individuals may have many comorbid difficulties with a rate of three to four times in general population, which may also need treatment (APA, 2000). The etiological factors which lead to intellectual deficiencies are organic, multigenetic (multiple genes), and/or psychosocial. Treatments that are specific to a particular etiology will be addressed in that section.

FETAL ALCOHOL SYNDROME

As discussed in a previous chapter, various teratogens may affect the child in utero and lead to many neurological difficulties. Fetal alcohol syndrome (FAS) is a set of symptoms which are completely preventable and nonremovable once they have occurred. The incidence of FAS is 3 in 100 live births (Sampson, Streissguth, Brookstein, & Barr, 2000) and it is the leading single known cause of mental retardation in the United States (Pulsifer, 1996). Alcohol is not the only substance which may potentially cause neurological difficulties. Environmental agents such as radiation, lead, mercury, polychlorinated biphenyls (PCB), and diseases such as syphilis, AIDS, and rubella may cause low birth weight, malformation, and/or behavioral impairments (Taylor & Rogers, 2005). However, alcohol is completely legal and preventable. Illegal drugs such as cocaine and heroin may also cause serious difficulties, but research is equivocal regarding cognitive difficulties due to the effects of confounding variables (Frank, Augustyn, Knight, Pell, & Zuckerman, 2001).

FAS is considered to be due to the effects of alcohol consumption by the mother, which leads to abnormal brain development and a myriad of neurodevelopment disorders and/or birth defects. Some of the difficulties cause a distinct facial appearance such as a flat upper lip and narrowed eye openings. Other difficulties are related to impaired growth and various neurological signs. Learning disorders and cognitive difficulties, similar to those seen with TBI, are often present (Fryer, McGee, Matt, Riley, & Mattson, 2007). There is no way to predict how many and what type of symptoms the child may have and these symptoms may also continue into adulthood. The range of difficulties which may occur due to exposure to alcohol is vast. The term fetal alcohol-related neurological development disorders (ARND) has been used to describe mild-to-severe disturbances of physical, behavioral, emotional, and/or social funding following in utero alcohol exposure (Mahone & Slomine, 2008).

It is difficult to describe the treatment for intellectual deficiency due to FAS due to the diversity of the symptoms. As with any central nervous system difficulty, a complete neuropsychological evaluation is needed to determine the strengths and weaknesses of the client and to provide data for treatment planning. Once the strengths and weaknesses have been determined, a treatment plan similar to that discussed in the section on TBI would apply depending upon the types of deficits which appeared. A child with intellectual deficiency would be guaranteed to receive services from the school based on Public Law No. 94-142 which was discussed in an earlier chapter. The child would also have an IEP with various goals and work with a team of specialists depending upon the necessary needs. If the child has apparent physical needs which could benefit from the skills of speech pathology, occupational therapy, or physical therapy, then appropriate referral would be made.

DOWN SYNDROME

Down syndrome is the most common genetic cause of mental retardation (intellectual deficiency). It was first described by John Langdon Down in 1866. Down termed a set of symptoms which he observed as "mongoloid idiocy," a reversion to an earlier stage of evolutionary development, and saw it as evidence for a racial division of intelligence (Down, 1866). The incidence of Down syndrome is estimated at 1 in 800 to 1,000 live births (Capone, 2000). In 1959, it was discovered that the cause of the syndrome was a trisomy on chromosome 21. It appears to occur almost randomly, is not inherited, and is most often related to maternal age; however, paternal age has also been implicated (Fisch et al., 2003). The brain pathology apparent with Down syndrome is virtually identical to the abnormal plaques and tangles found in Alzheimer's disease; however, it occurs at ages 35–40 and by age 70, three-quarters of individuals with Down syndrome exhibit symptoms. Other serious health risks exist such as heart defects and shortened life span which has increased recently (Patja, Ivanainen, Vesala, Oksanen, & Ruoppila, 2000).

The intellectual disability is a significant difficulty and measured intelligence often ranges from moderate to severe deficits (Moldavsky, Lev, & Lerman-Sagie, 2001). With severe deficits, it is often difficult to mainstream a child for education even though by law, an education is guaranteed. There are also serious deficits in social abilities, both of which appear to worsen with age often and thought to be related to the onset of dementia (Hawkins, Eklund, James, & Foose, 2003).

Rehabilitation must include a complete, often abbreviated, neuropsychological evaluation to determine the client's strengths and weaknesses. Once this is accomplished, various services or treatments may be implemented. Most children acquire speech but it is often delayed and may be very difficult to understand. Individuals with Down syndrome very often require the services of multiple professionals and often are incapable of living on their own or outside of a treatment setting. Employment or attendance at a sheltered workshop is dependent upon the strengths and weaknesses of the particular individual.

CULTURAL FAMILIAL INTELLECTUAL DEFICIENCY

The term *cultural familial mental retardation* or *intellectual deficiency* is often used for these individuals who do not have a specific biological cause for their intellectual deficiencies. *Garden variety* and *undifferentiated* are other terms which reflect the large number of cases which are not readily distinguished from one another (Crnic, 1988). Very often, these individuals have mild forms of mental retardation which does not become apparent until they enter the school system.

It has been observed for many decades that mild mental retardation tends to occur disproportionately in the lower socioeconomic classes and within some racial or ethnic groups. Many variables may cause the difficulties such as low parental education, parental attitudes, lack of social support, lack of learning opportunities, and stressful life events (Sameroff, 1990). Due to the fact that these individuals have a milder form of intellectual deficiency, it is possible for many to attain up to a sixth-grade education, become employed, and live on their own. Many comorbid difficulties exist which need to be addressed through neuropsychological evaluation. The evaluation would determine the individual's strengths and weaknesses which would then lead to an appropriate treatment plan for any services required.

As may be seen in the case study, Jenny is suffering from mild intellectual deficiency from unknown etiology. She currently receives services through the school and has an IEP which addresses all of the various intellectual deficits which the school is able to remediate.

It is unclear whether the intellectual deficiency is related to childhood sexual abuse but she is currently in counseling to work on issues related to the abuse. She is also attending social skills group therapy, which should help her understand appropriate versus inappropriate social behaviors both on her part and on the part of others who interact with her.

LEARNING DISABILITIES

The study of learning disabilities has historically been driven by two major scientific questions. The first question is to understand individuals who display specific deficits that appear discrepant with their intelligence and other abilities. The second question is how to provide services for children who exhibit these deficits. Early on, it was suggested that these children had minimal brain dysfunction, a term that is no longer used. Learning disabilities and learning disorders refer to specific difficulties with reading, writing, and arithmetic, which are often termed dyslexia, dysgraphia, and dyscalculia, respectively. Many children have more than one learning disability and often have other coexisting language difficulties and other behavioral issues (Wicks-Nelson & Israel, 2009).

Reading disorder involves a difficulty in the ability to readily identify words in running text in order to discern the meaning of the text (Vellutino, Fletcher, Snowling, & Scanlon, 2004). The prevalence of reading disorder varies based upon sampling differences and issues with a consistent definition. On the conservative side, 4–10% of the U.S. school-aged population has a reading disorder (Tannock, 2005b) and on the more liberal definition side, the estimates are 10–15% of the school-aged population (Lyon, Fletcher, Fuchs, & Chlabra, 2006). Boys are diagnosed at a 3:1 ratio to girls with genetics as the main explanation (Lipka & Siegel, 2006). Reading disorder tends to continue through the elementary and secondary years and often into adulthood (Snowling, Muter, & Carroll, 2007).

The current understanding of the etiology of reading disorders involves a relationship to language impairment (Vellutino et al., 2004). A very important concept is **phonological processing**, which involves using the sound structure of language to process written words. Snowling, Bishop, and Stothard (2000), however, state that in addition to phonological processes, the child must understand syntax and semantic components and that these change over time.

Disabilities of written expression involve difficulty with both transcription and text generation. **Transcription** includes putting ideas into written form (Berninger & Amtmann, 2003). **Text generation** involves the creation of meaning in written form (Wicks-Nelson & Israel, 2009). The prevalence of writing disorders is approximately 6–10% of school-aged children (Tannock, 2005a).

Mathematics disorder refers to the area of arithmetic difficulty. The main difficulties involve the understanding of number and the learning, representation, and retrieval of basic arithmetic facts (Cirino, Fletcher, Ewing-Cobbs, Barnes, & Fuchs, 2007). Few studies exist evaluating the prevalence of mathematics disabilities and those which are available tend to vary in how they measure deficit. With these issues in mind, it appears that 5–8% of school-aged children have some form of mathematics disability (Geary, 2004).

The etiology of learning disorders involves many specific brain areas. Current research suggests that possibly underlying many of the disorders is a difficulty with language. A major area of interest is therefore the left hemisphere, which is specifically involved with language. Many studies have utilized brain scans of the various structures as an individual performs various tasks related to reading, writing, and arithmetic with results implicating Broca's and Wernicke's areas. Genetic influences have also been investigated. Parents of children with reading disabilities have a high incidence of similar difficulties (Carroll &

Snowling, 2004). Chromosomes 6 and 15 have been identified as markers as well as chromosome 18 and 2 through linkage studies (Plomin & McGuffin, 2003). Spelling difficulties tend to occur frequently in families with an indication of difficulty with chromosome 15 (Schulte-Korne et al., 1998). It also appears that mathematics difficulty has a familial component with higher rates in more closely related individuals. Kovas et al. (2007) suggest that mathematics and reading disability may have a shared genetic vulnerability.

After a complete neuropsychological evaluation to determine the individual's strengths and weaknesses, a treatment plan focusing on the apparent needs may be prepared. Several programs have been evaluated to address various underlying factors. The psycho-educational approach targets various perceptual and cognitive processes underlying disabilities and involves eye–hand coordination, spatial relationships, and language (Hammill, 1993). However, current neuropsychological research suggests three approaches for effective treatment: task-analytic methods, cognitive, and cognitive–behavioral. Task-analytic methods involve direct instruction in acquiring the needed skills. Gettinger and Koscik (2001) suggest that the program outline specific goals and objectives, present information in small steps with specific directions, and incorporate practice and feedback. The cognitive approach has as its goal the awareness in the student of the demands of the learning task. Organization and strategy use have been applied to reading, mathematics, memory skills, and study skills (Wong, Harris, Graham, & Butler, 2003). The cognitive–behavioral approach helps students direct their own learning. A combination of organization skills, self-monitoring, and self-instruction has been utilized for writing skills deficits (Graham & Harris, 2003).

Returning to the case study, Jenny suffers from speech and language impairments. She may be helped by one of the three aforementioned programs. At the present time, she receives services from a speech pathologist who specializes in these types of deficits. In the future, the clinical neuropsychologist may incorporate one of the aforementioned techniques within his therapy with Jenny.

PERVASIVE DEVELOPMENTAL DISORDERS

The term pervasive developmental disorder (PDD) encompasses five different disorders: autism, Asperger's disorder, Rett's disorder, childhood disintegrative disorders, and PDD Not Otherwise Specified (NOS; APA, 2000). All of these disorders are considered to be a variation of a similar core set of symptoms which include delays in communication and socialization and difficulties attaining developmental milestones. There is a high incidence of various degrees of mental retardation within this group but it is not synonymous with the terms.

Autism is the best known of the pervasive developmental disorders and is often the term to which the symptoms of the other four disorders is compared. Kanner (1943) was the first to describe the particular symptoms which comprise autism. The same three symptoms comprise what is currently termed the autism triad: difficulties with social interaction, disturbed communication, and restricted, repetitive, stereotypical behavior and interests (APA, 2000). It is interesting to note that even though the child with autism has such serious difficulty, a meta-analysis showed that at least half of the autistic children demonstrated secure attachment in the Strange Situation (Van Ijzendoorn et al., 2007). Other difficulties which occur in conjunction with autism include sensory and perceptual difficulties, some being oversensitive, while others being undersensitive, and some developing a difficulty with overselectivity and fixating on a particular stimulus. While subaverage intelligence is not a diagnostic feature of autism, 70–75% of individuals exhibit mental retardation often in the severe or profound range (Joseph, Tager-Flusberg, & Lord, 2002).

The prevalence of autism is difficult to obtain and the mass media has made it appear to the average person that there is an epidemic of autism. Research published between

1966 and 1991 reported a rate of 4.4 cases per 10,000 and between 1992 and 2001, the rate was 12.7 (Wicks-Nelson & Israel, 2009). However, other studies have shown much higher rates. The Centers for Disease Control and Prevention (CDC) reported a rate of 67 per 10,000 8-year-olds with autistic disorder, Asperger's disorder, or PDD-NOS (CDC Press Release, 2007). The report came with the caveat that there was uncertainty whether the increase reflected actual cases or better studies. With all of the changes in number of cases, the gender differential has remained constant with boys displaying autism at a rate of 3.5–4.00 to 1 girl (Volkmar, Klin, & Schultz, 2005).

Many neurobiological variables have been implicated as causal factors in autism. The structures most consistently implicated are the temporal lobe, limbic system, the frontal lobes, and the cerebellum (Schultz & Klin, 2002). Another finding is atypically large brain size in toddlers which is not evident at birth but occurs in a growth spurt soon after (Newsom & Hovanitz, 2006). Etiological factors include medical conditions such as meningitis, hearing impairment, and some genetic disorders (Bailey, Hatton, Mesibov, Ament, & Skinner, 2000). Fragile X syndrome and tuberous sclerosis are two genetic conditions specifically associated with autism (Volkmar, Lord, Bailey, Schultz, & Klin, 2004). The relationship between vaccines and autism has also been investigated after it appeared as a sensationalistic story in the popular press. The main issue has been the use of thimerosal, a mercury-containing preservative which may have placed children at risk for PDD. The bulk of the research studies fail to support the connection (Costello, Foley, & Angold, 2006) but the debate appears to be continuing.

Asperger's disorder was first written about in 1944 but was not included within the *DSM* until the early 1990s. Symptoms of Asperger's disorder include qualitative differences in social interaction and restrictive, repetitive, and stereotypical interests and behaviors. It resembles autism but lacks any significant delay in language, cognitive development, and adaptive behavior (with the absence of social interaction). Individuals with Asperger's disorder appear to have interest in others but lack appropriate understanding of social cues and relationships.

The prevalence is difficult to determine but appears much less than autism. Boys are diagnosed more than girls and both at a later age (Dawson & Toth, 2006). It is thought that many individuals with this difficulty will be able to function quite well in society, living independently, working, and raising a family once they master social skills.

Rett's disorder has a poorer outcome than other PDDs. This disorder occurs most often in girls who begin life with normal development and then regress and deteriorate. Head circumference, head measurements, walking, and social abilities all decline. The prevalence is not known, though it has been estimated at 1 in 15,000–22,000 females (Volkmar & Klin, 2000). Childhood disintegration disorder was first described in 1908 by Theodore Heller. Development is normal for at least 2 years and symptoms develop before age 10 when many skills begin to be lost including two of the following: language, social skills, bowel and bladder control, play, and motor skills. In addition, two of the criteria for autism must be present and the disorder is usually associated with severe mental retardation. There exists evidence for neurological disturbances with this disorder including abnormal electroencephalogram (EEG) results and seizures. The prevalence is estimated at 1 child in 100,000 and is greater in male than female children.

PDD-NOS is a category used when symptoms of autism and other PDDs are present but no clear-cut syndrome occurs. With the vagueness of the defining criteria, it is possible for children with various severities of difficulties to be categorized here.

The assessment for PDD involves a complete, if often abbreviated, neuropsychological evolution. It also requires the input from parents to garner a clear picture of the child and to establish a history of prenatal, birth, developmental, familial, and medical factors. Early intervention is often the best treatment for PDD and is also the best prognostic indicator. The treatment, whether in early intervention or later, begins with the assessment of strengths and weakness. Following the assessment, the treatment approaches are predominately behavioral and educational. Medications may be utilized to target specific behaviors such as aggression or self-injury. Behavioral treatments using the principles of operant conditioning may target specific skill deficits such as language, social skills, or maladaptive behavior such as self-injury. Behavioral techniques have also been combined into comprehensive treatment programs over long periods of time to work on primary and secondary difficulties.

PDDs are covered by the Individuals With Disabilities Education Act (IDEA). Individuals who have PDD may benefit from special education classes or from full inclusion with the classroom. There exist a variety of opinions regarding the risks and benefits for students within the educational system (Burack, Root, & Zigler, 1997).

ATTENTION DEFICIT/HYPERACTIVITY DISORDER

ADHD has been referred to by various terms throughout the past century reflecting the focus on either the behavioral hyperactivity component or the lack of attention component. Currently, the *DSM-IV-TR* recognizes three subtypes of ADHD: predominantly inattentive type (ADHD-I), predominantly hyperactive–impulsive type (ADHD-HI), and combined type (ADHD-C). The diagnosis is made before age 7 and the symptoms must not reflect developmental level. In addition to these deficits necessary for diagnosis, children with ADHD often have difficulty with motor coordination (Barkley, 2006a), perform poorer on measures of intelligence and academic achievement (Barkley, 2006a), and have difficulty with goal-directed behavior (Clark, Prior, & Kinsella, 2002) and with adaptive behavior. Children with ADHD tend to have other comorbid mental disorders at a higher rate than the general population. Learning disabilities, externalizing disorders, anxiety, and mood disorders tend to be the most often occurring.

The prevalence of ADHD has been estimated at 3–7% of U.S. school-aged children (APA, 2000). However, there is a continual debate whether the figure is actually higher or lower than reported. The gender ratio is approximately 3.4 boys to 1 girl and may be higher in clinic samples (Barkley, 2006b).

There have been various theories which attempted to explain ADHD. Arousal level, sensitivity to reward, aversion to delay, and deficits in executive function appear related to inattention, whereas delay aversion relates to hyperactivity–impulsivity (Martell, Nikolas, & Nigg, 2007). Numerous brain structures are implicated in ADHD including the frontal lobe and underlying regions, parietal lobe, temporal lobe, corpus callosum, and cerebellum. Several neurotransmitters have also been implicated particularly deficiencies in dopamine and norepinephrine, which are also related to frontal lobe functioning (Smith, Barkley, & Shapiro, 2006). Numerous studies indicate the families of children with ADHD have higher rates of psychopathology including ADHD.

Treatment, as with all of the disorders discussed thus far, begins with a thorough neuropsychological evaluation and also includes rating scales completed by teachers and parents and particular tests designed to assess ADHD. Pharmacological treatments, behaviorally based interventions, and a combination of the two are the most widely employed and evidence-based (APA Working Group on Psychoactive Medications for Children and Adolescents, 2006). Within the area of medications, stimulants are the drugs of choice. Behaviorally oriented treatments include parent training, classroom management, and individual and group therapy with behavioral goals.

As was stated earlier, Jenny has a diagnosed difficulty with ADHD. She is receiving appropriate medication. She also is addressing psychosocial issues in individual therapy with the clinical neuropsychologist and group therapy through the school system.

Summary

The chapter began with a case study of a preteen female with multiple central nervous system difficulties and psychological difficulties. The case was used to illustrate the differences which occur when one has a child or adolescent as a client. Ethical issues in particular are different for a client who is younger than the age of majority.

The various forms of development are reviewed to compare normal functioning from a disorder. The topical areas are physical, cognitive, moral, and social development with the most well-known theories as examples. Central nervous system disorders or dysfunctions which are the most common in children and adolescents are reviewed. Included within the discussion are etiological factors, assessment issues, and treatment modalities.

Questions for Further Study

1. It has been stated many times in this text that children vary more one from another within the umbrella of normality. Why is this the case?
2. Children, compared to adults, have additional individuals involved in their lives such as parents and school personnel. How do these others impact the neuropsychological assessment and/or rehabilitation?
3. Clinical neuropsychologists, when working with children, often work in a treatment team. What are the advantages/disadvantages to this approach?

References

Ainsworth, M. D., & Salter, D. (1973). The development of infant-mother attachment. In M. Bettye, H. Caldwell, & N. Ricciuti (Eds.), *Review of child development research* (Vol. 3, pp. 1–94). Chicago: University of Chicago Press.

American Psychiatric Association. (2000). *Diagnostic and statistical manual of mental disorders* (text rev.). Washington, DC: Author.

American Psychological Association. (2002). *Ethical principles for psychologists and code of conduct.* Washington, DC: Author.

Anderson, V., Fenwick, T., Manly, T., & Robertson, I. (1998). Attentional skills following traumatic brain injury in childhood: A componential analysis. *Brain Injury, 12*(11), 937–949.

APA Working Group on Psychotropic Medications for Children and Adolescents. (2006). *Report of the Working Group on Psychotropic Medications for Children and Adolescents: Psychopharmacological, psychosocial, and combined interventions for childhood disorders: Evidence base, contextual factors, and future directions.* Washington, DC: American Psychological Association. Retrieved September 14, 2009, from http://www.apa.org/pi/families/resources/child-medications.pdf

Bailey, D. B., Hatton, D. D., Mesibov, G., Ament, N., & Skinner, M. (2000). Early development, temperament, and functional impairment in autism and fragile X syndrome. *Journal of Autism and Developmental Disorders, 30,* 49–59.

Baillargeon, R. (2000). How do infants learn about the physical world? In D. Muir & A. Slater (Eds.), *Infant development: The essential readings* (pp. 195–212). Malden, MA: Blackwell.

Barkley, R. A. (Ed.). (2006a). Associated cognitive, developmental, and health problems. In *Attention-deficit hyperactivity disorder: A handbook for diagnosis and treatment.* New York: The Guilford Press.

Barkley, R. A. (Ed.). (2006b). Primary symptoms, diagnostic criteria, prevalence, and gender differences. In *Attention-deficit hyperactivity disorder: A handbook for diagnosis and treatment.* New York: The Guilford Press.

Bergen, K. S. (2009). *The developing person through childhood and adolescence* (8th ed.). New York: Worth.

Berninger, V. N., & Amtmann, D. (2003). Preventing written expression disabilities through early and continuing assessment and intervention for handwriting and/or spelling problems: Research into practice. In H. L. Swanson, K. R. Harris & S. Graham (Eds.), *Handbook of learning disabilities* (pp. 345–363). New York: The Guilford Press.

Blaney, S. M., Kun, E., Hunter, J., Rourke-Adams, L. B., Lau, C., Strother, D., et al. (2006). Tumors of the central nervous system. In P. A. Pizzo & D. G. Poplack (Eds.), *Principles and practice of pediatric oncology* (5th ed.). Philadelphia: Lippincott Williams & Wilkins. (electronic version)

Bowlby, J. (1969). *Attachment and loss: Vol 1 Attachment*. New York: Basic Books.

Briere, J., & Elliott, D. M. (2003). Prevalence and psychological sequelae of self-reported childhood physical and sexual abuse in a general population sample of men and women. *Child Abuse and Neglect, 27*, 1205–1222.

Burack, J. A., Root, R., & Zigler, E. (1997). Inclusive education for students with autism: Reviewing ideological empirical, and community considerations. In D. J. Cohen & F. R. Volkmar (Eds.), *Handbook of autism and pervasive developmental disorders* (pp. 796–807). New York: John Wiley.

Capone, G. T. (2000). Down syndrome: Advances in molecular biology and the neurosciences. *Developmental and behavioral pediatrics, 44*, 591–599.

Capute, A. J., & Accardo, P. J. (Eds.). (1996). The spectrum of motor dysfunction. In *Developmental disabilities in infancy and childhood* (Vol. II, 2nd ed.). Baltimore: Brookes Publishing Co.

Carroll, J. M., & Snowling, M. J. (2004). Language and phonological skills in children at high risk of reading difficulties. *Journal of Child Psychology and Psychiatry, 45*, 631–640.

CDC Press Release. (2007). *CDC releases new data on autism spectrum disorders (ASDs) from multiple communities in the United States*. Retrieved September 14, 2009, from http://www.medical-newstoday.com/articles/62625.php

Chess, S., & Thomas, A. (1972). Differences in outcome in early intervention in children with behavior disorders. In M. Roff, L. Robins & M. Pollack (Eds.), *Life history research in psychopathology* (Vol. 2, pp. 35–46). Minneapolis: University of Minnesota Press.

Chess, S., & Thomas, A. (1977). Temperamental individuality from childhood to adolescence. *Journal of the American Academy of Child Psychiatry, 16*, 218–226.

Child Abuse Prevention and Treatment Act, Pub. L. No. 93-247, § 1191 (1974).

Cicchetti, D., & Olsen, K. (1990). The developmental psychopathology of child maltreatment. In M. Lewis & S. M. Miller (Eds.), *Handbook of developmental psychology* (pp. 261–279). New York: Plenum Press.

Cirino, P. T., Fletcher, J. M., Ewing-Cobbs, L., Barnes, M. A., & Fuchs, L. S. (2007). Cognitive arithmetic differences in learning difficulty groups and the role of behavioral inattention. *Learning Disabilities Research and Practice, 22*, 25–35.

Clark, C., Prior, M., & Kinsella, G. (2002). The relationship between executive function abilities, adaptive behavior, and academic achievement in children with externalizing behaviour problems. *Journal of Child Psychology and Psychiatry, 43*, 785–796.

Connelly, C. D., & Strauss, M. A. (1992). Mother's age and risk for physical abuse. *Child Abuse and Neglect, 16*, 709–718.

Costello, E. J., Foley, D. L., & Angold, A. (2006). 10-year research update review: The epidemiology of child and adolescent psychiatric disorders II. Developmental epidemiology. *Journal of the American Academy of Child and Adolescence Psychiatry, 45*, 8–25.

Crnic, K. A. (1988). Mental retardation. In E. J. Mash & L. G. Terdal (Eds.), *Behavioral assessment of childhood disorders: Selected case problems* (pp. 317–354). New York: Guilford Press.

Dawson, G., & Toth, K. (2006). Autism spectrum disorders. In D. Cicchetti & D. J. Cohen (Eds.), *Developmental psychopathology* (2nd ed., pp. 317–357). Hoboken, NJ: John Wiley and Sons.

De Fabrique, N., Romano, S. J., Vecchi, G. M., & Van Hasselt, V. B. (2007). Understanding Stockholm syndrome. *FBI Law Enforcement Bulletin, 76*(7), 10–15.

Dekaban, A. S., & Sadowsky, D. (1978). Changes in brain weight during the span of human life: Relation of brain weights to body heights and body weights. *Annals of Neurology, 4*, 345–356.

Denham, S. A., Blair, K. A., DeMulder, E., Levitas, J., Sawyer, K., Auerbach-Major, S., et al. (2003). Preschool emotional competence: Pathway to social competence. *Child Development, 74*, 238–256.

Dennis, M., Spiegler, B. J., Riva, D., & MacGregor, D. L. (2004). Neuropsychological outcome. In D. A. Walker, G. Perilongo, J. A. G. Punt & K. E. Taylor (Eds.), *Brain and spinal tumors in childhood* (pp. 213–227). London: Arnold.

Down, J. L. (1866). Observations on an ethnic classification of idiots. *London Hospital, Clinical Lectures Report, 3,* 259–262.

Duffner, P. K., Jackson, L. A., & Cohen, M. E. (1996). Neurobehavioral abnormalities resulting from brain tumors and their therapy. In Y. Frank (Ed.), *Pediatric behavioral neurology* (pp. 289–307) Boca Raton, FL: CRC Press.

Eisenberg, N., Spinard, T. L., Fabes, R. A., Reiser, M., Cumberland, A., Shepard, S. A., et al. (2004). The relations of effortful control and impulsivity to children's resiliency and adjustment. *Child Development, 75,* 25–46.

English, D. J. (1998). The extent and consequences of child maltreatment. *The Future of Children, 8*(1), 39–53.

Erikson, E. (1963). *Childhood and society* (2nd ed.). New York: Norton.

Erikson, E. (1968). *Identity: Youth and crisis.* New York: Norton.

Finkelhor, D., Ormrod, R. K., & Turner, H. A. (2007). Re-victimization patterns in a national longitudinal sample of children and youth. *Child Abuse and Neglect, 31,* 479–502.

Fisch, H., Hyun, G., Golden, R., Hensle, T. W., Olsson, C. A., & Liberson, G. L. (2003). The influence of paternal age on Down Syndrome. *The Journal of Urology, 169,* 2275–2278.

Frank, DA., Augustyn, M., Knight, W., Pell, T., & Zuckerman, B. (2001). Growth, development, and behavior in early childhood following prenatal cocaine exposure: A systematic review. *Journal of the American Medical Association, 285,* 1613–1625.

Fryer, S. L., McGee, C. L., Matt, G. E., Riley, E. P., & Mattson, S. N. (2007). Evaluation of psychopathological conditions in children with heavy prenatal alcohol exposure. *Pediatrics, 119,* e733–e741.

Geary, D. C. (2004). Mathematics and learning disabilities. *Journal of Learning Disabilities, 37,* 4–15.

Gettinger, M., & Koscik, R. (2001). Psychological services for children with learning disabilities. In J. N. Huges, J. M. L. Greca & C. Cooley (Eds.), *Handbook of psychological services for children and adolescents* (pp. 421–438). New York: Oxford University Press.

Gilligan, C. (1982). *In a different voice: Psychological theory and women's development.* Cambridge, MA: Harvard University Press.

Gilligan, C. (1993). Adolescent development reconsidered. In A. Garrod (Ed.), *Approaches to moral development: New research and emerging themes* (pp. 103–132). New York: Teacher College Press.

Gottlieb, G. (2003). Probabilistic epigeneses of development. In J. Valsiner & K. J. Connolly (Eds.), *Handbook of developmental psychology* (pp. 3–17). Thousand Oaks, CA: Sage.

Graham, S., & Harris, K. R. (2003). Students with learning disabilities and the process of writing: A meta-analysis of SRSD studies. In H. L. Swanson, K. R. Harris, & S. Graham (Eds.), *Handbook of learning disabilities* (pp. 323–344). New York: The Guilford Press.

Hammill, D. D. (1993). A brief look at the learning disabilities movement in the United States. *Journal of Learning Disabilities, 26*(5), 295–310.

Hawkins, B. A., Eklund, S. J., James, D. R., & Foose, A. K. (2003). Adaptic behavior and cognitive functions of adults with Down syndrome: Modeling change with age. *Mental Retardation, 41,* 7–28.

Hespos, S., & Baillargeon, R. (2008) Young infants' actions reveal their developing knowledge of support variables: Converging evidence for violation-of-expectation findings. *Cognition, 107*(1), 304–316.

Joseph, R. M., Tager-Flusberg, H., & Lord, C. (2002). Cognitive profiles and social-communicative functioning in children with autism spectrum disorder. *Journal of Child Psychology and Psychiatry, 43*(6), 807–821.

Kanner, L. (1943). Autistic disturbances of affective contact. *Nervous Child, 2,* 217–250.

Kempe, C. H., Silverman, F. N., Steele, B. B., Droegemueller, W., & Silver, H. K. (1962). The battered child syndrome. *Journal of the American Medical Association, 181,* 17–24.

Kennard, M. A. (1942). Cortical reorganization of motor function. *Archives of Neurology and Psychiatry, 48,* 227–240.

Kobak, R., Cassidy, J., Lyons-Ruth, K., & Ziv, Y. (2006). Attachment, stress, and psychopathology: A developmental pathways model. In D. Cicchetti & D. J. Cohen (Eds.), *Developmental psychopathology. Volume 1: Theory and method* (2nd ed., pp. 333–369). Hoboken, NJ: John Wiley and Sons.

Kohlberg, L. (1963). The development of children's orientations toward a moral order: I. Sequence in the development of moral thought. *Vita Humana*, 6, 11–33.

Kovas, Y., Haworth, C. M. A., Harlaar, S. A., Petrill, S. A., Dale, P. S., & Plomin, R. (2007). Overlap and specificity of genetic and environmental influence on mathematics and reading disability in 10 year-old twins. *Journal of Child Psychology and Psychiatry*, 48, 914–922.

Kraus, J. F. (1995). Epidemiological features of brain injury in children: Occurrence, children at risk, causes, manner of injury, severity and outcomes. In S. H. Broman & M. E. Michael (Eds.), *Traumatic head injury in children* (pp. 22–39). New York: Oxford University Press.

Lenroot, R. K., & Giedd, J. N. (2006). Brain development in children and adolescents: Insights from anatomical magnetic resonance imaging. *Neuroscience and Biobehavioral Reviews*, 30, 718–729.

Limond, J., & Leeke, R. (2005). Practitioner review: Cognitive rehabilitation for children with acquired brain injury. *Journal of Child Psychology and Psychiatry*, 46, 339–352.

Lipka, O., & Siegel, L. S. (2006). Learning disabilities. In D. A. Wolfe & E. J. Mash (Eds.), *Behavioral and emotional disorders in adolescents: Nature, assessment, and treatment* (pp. 410–443). New York: The Guilford Press.

Lyon, G. R., Fletcher, J. M., Fuchs, L. S., & Chlabra, V. (2006). Learning disorders. In E. J. Mosh & R. A. Bakley (Eds.), *Treatment of childhood disorders* (pp. 512–594). New York: The Guilford Press.

Lyons-Ruth, K., Zeanah, C. H., & Benofi, D. (2003). Disorder and risk for disorder during infancy and toddlerhood. In E. J. Mash & K. A. Barkley (Eds.), *Child psychopathology* (2nd ed., 589–631). New York: Guilford Press.

Mahone, E. M., & Slomine, B. S. (2008). Neurodevelopmental disorders. In J. E. Morgan and J. H. Ricker (Eds.), *Textbook of clinical neuropsychology* (pp. 105–127). New York: Taylor and Francis.

Maria, B. L., & Menkes, J. H. (2006). Tumors of the nervous system. In J. H. Menkes & H. Sarnat (Eds.), *Child neurology* (7th ed., pp. 739–802). Philadelphia: Lippincott Williams & Wilkins.

Martell, M., Nikolas, M., & Nigg, J. T. (2007). Executive function in adolescents with ADHD. *Journal of the American Academy of Child and Adolescent Psychiatry*, 46, 1437–1444.

Mateer, C. A., Kerns, K. A., & Eso, K. L. (1997). Management of attention and memory disorders following traumatic brain injury. In F. D. Bigler, E. Clarke & J. E. Farmer (Eds.), *Childhood traumatic brain injury: Diagnosis, assessment, and intervention* (pp. 153–175). Austin, TX: Pro-Ed.

Moldavsky, M., Lev, D., & Lerman-Sagie, T. (2001). Behavioral phenotypes of genetic syndrome: A reference guide for psychiatrists. *Journal of the American Academy of Child and Adolescent Psychiatry*, 40, 749–760.

Newsom, C., & Hovanitz, C. A. (2006). Autistic spectrum disorders. In E. J. Mash & R. A. Barkley (Eds.), *Treatment of childhood disorders* (3rd.ed., pp. 455–511). New York: The Guilford Press.

Packer, R. J., MacDonald, J. J., Rood, T. J., Forbes, K., & Keating, R. (2005). Neoplastic diseases. In R. B. Davis (Ed.), *Child and adolescent neurology* (2nd ed.). Malden, MA: Blackwell.

Patja, K., Ivanainen, M., Vesala, H., Oksanen, H., & Ruoppila, J. (2000). Life expectancy of people with intellectual disorder: A 35-year follow-up study. *Journal of Intellectual Disability Research*, 44, 591–599.

Plomin, R., & McGuffin, P. (2003). Psychopathology in the postgenomic era. *Annual Review of Psychology*, 54, 205–225.

Pulsifer, M. B. (1996). The neuropsychology of mental retardation. *Journal of the International Neuropsychological Society*, 2, 159–176.

Ris, M. D., & Noll, R. B. (1994). Long-term neurobehavioral outcome in pediatric brain-tumor patients: review and methodological critique. *Journal Clinical and Experimental Neuropsychology*, 16, 21–42

Roid, G. H. (2003). *Stanford-Binet Intelligence Scales: Fifth Edition*. Itasca, IL: Riverside.

Rothbath, M. K., & Posner, M. J. (2006). Temperament, attention, and developmental psychopathology. In D. Cicchetti & D. S. Cohen (Eds.), *Developmental psychopathology. Volume 2: Developmental neuroscience* (2nd ed., pp. 465–501) Hoboken, NJ: John Wiley and Sons.

Rutter, M., Caspi, A., & Moffit, T. E. (2003). Using sex differences in psychopathology to study causal mechanisms: Unifying issues and research strategies. *Journal of Child Psychology and Psychiatry, 44*, 1092–1113.

Rutter, M., & Sroufe, L. A. (2000). Developmental Psychopathology: Concepts and challenges. *Development and Psychopathology, 12*, 265–296.

Sameroff, A. J. (1990). Neo-environmental perspectives in developmental theory. In R. M. Hodapp, J. A. Burack, & E. Zigler (Eds.), *Issues in the developmental approach to mental retardation* (pp. 93–113). New York: Cambridge University Press.

Sampson, P. D., Streissguth, A. R., Brookstein, F. L., & Barr, H. M. (2000). Environmental health perspectives: On categorization in analysis of alcohol teratogenesis. *Environmental Health Perspectives, 108*(3), 421–428.

Schalock, R. L., Buntinx, W., Brothwick-Duffy, S., Luckasson, R., Snell, M., Tasse, M., et al. (2006). *User's guide: Mental retardation definition, classification, and systems of supports* (10th ed.). Washington, DC: American Association on Intellectual and Developmental Disabilities.

Schulte-Korne, G., Grimm, T., Nothen, M. M., Muller-Myhosk, B., Cichon, S., Vogt, I. R., et al. (1998). Evidence for linkage of spelling disability to chromosome 15. *American Journal of Human Genetics, 63*, 279–282.

Schultz, R., & Klin, A. (2002). Genetics of childhood disorders: XLIII Autism, Part 2: Neuronal foundations. *Journal of the American Academy of Child and Adolescent Psychiatry, 41*, 1259–1262.

Smith, B. H., Barkley, R. A., & Shapiro, C. J. (2006). Attention deficit/hyperactivity disorder. In E. J. Mash, & R. A. Barkley (Eds.), *Treatment of childhood disorders* (3rd ed. pp. 65–136). New York: The Guilford Press.

Smith, M. A., Freidlin, B., Reis, L. A., & Simon, R. (1998). Trends in reported incidence of primary malignant brain tumors in children in the United States. *Journal of the National Cancer Institute, 90*, 1269–1277.

Snowling, M. J., Bishop, D. V., & Stothard, S. E. (2000). Is preschool language impairment a risk factor of dyslexia in adolescence? *Journal of Child Psychology and Psychiatry, 41*, 587–600.

Snowling, M. J., Muter, V., & Carroll, J. (2007). Children at family risk of dyslexia: A follow-up in early adolescence. *Journal of Child Psychology and Psychiatry, 48*, 609–618.

Society for Research in Child Development. (2009). Ethical standards for research with children. Retrieved September 13, 2009 from http://www.srcd.org/ethicalstandards.html

Sparrow, S. S., Balla, D. A., & Cicchetti, D. (2005). *Vineland Adaptive Behavior Scales, second edition (Vineland-II)*. San Antonio, TX: Pearson.

Tannock, R. (2005a). Disorders of written experience and learning disorders not otherwise specified. In B. J. Sadock & V. A. Sadock (Eds.), *Comprehensive textbook of psychiatry* (pp. 3123–3129). Philadelphia: Lippincott Williams & Wilkins.

Tannock, R. (2005b). Reading disorders. In B. J. Sadock & V. A. Sadock (Eds.), *Kaplan & Sadock's comprehensive textbook of psychiatry* (8th ed., pp. 3107–3115). Philadelphia: Lippincott Williams & Wilkins.

Taylor, E., & Rogers, J. W. (2005). Practicioner review: Early adversity and developmental disorders. *Journal of Child Psychology and Psychiatry, 46*, 451–467.

Thompson, R. A. (2000). The legacy of early attachments. *Child Development, 71*, 145–152.

Turiel, E. (2006). The development of morality. In W. Damon, M. Lerner, (Series Eds.) & N. Eisenberg (Vol. Ed.), *Handbook of child psychology, volume, 3, social, emotional and personality development* (6th ed., pp. 789–857). Hoboken, NJ: Wiley.

United States Department of Health and Human Services Administration on Children, Youth and Family. (2007). *Child maltreatment 2005*. Washington, DC: Government Printing Office.

Van Ijzendoorn, M. H., Rutgers, A. H., Bakersman-Kraneburg, M. J., Van Daalen, E., Dietz, C., Buitelaar, J. K., et al. (2007). Parental sensitivity and attachment in children with autism spectrum disorder: Comparison with children with mental retardation, with language delays, and with typical development. *Child Development, 78*, 597–605.

Vellutino, F. R., Fletcher, J. M., Snowling, M. J., & Scanlon, D. M. (2004). Specific reading disability (dyslexia): What we have learned in the past four decades? *Journal of Child Psychology and Psychiatry, 45*, 2–40.

Volkmar, F. R., & Klin, A. (2000). Pervasive devlopmental disorders. In B. J. Sadock & V. A. Sadock (Eds.), *Kaplan & Sadock's comprehensive textbook of psychiatry* (Vol. 2, 7th ed., pp. 2659–2678). Philadelphia: Lippincott Williams & Wilkins.

Volkmar, F. R., Klin, A., & Schultz, R. T. (2005). Pervasive developmental disorders. In B. J. Sadock & V. A. Sadock (Eds.), *Kaplan & Sadock's comprehensive textbook of psychiatry* (8th ed., pp. 3164–3182). Philadelphia: Lippincott Williams & Wilkins.

Volkmar, F. R., Lord, C., Bailey, A., Schultz, R. T., & Klin, A. (2004). Autism and pervasive developmental disorders. *Journal of Child Psychology and Psychiatry, 45,* 135–170.

Walsh, D. (2006). Betwixt and between: A new view of the adolescent brain. *Minnesota Medicine,* 89(3), 36–43.

Wechsler, D. (2003) *The Wechsler Intelligence Scale for Children-IV.* San Antonio, TX: The Psychological Corporation.

Wekerle, C., Wall, A. M., Leung, E., & Trocmé, N. (2007). Cumulative stress and substantiated maltreatment: The importance of caregiver vulnerability and adult partner violence. *Child Abuse, 31,* 1427–1447.

Wertsch, J., & Tulviste, P. (2005). *L. S. Vygotsky and contemporary developmental psychology.* New York: Routledge.

Wicks-Nelson, R., & Israel, A. (2009). *Abnormal child and adolescent psychology* (p. 1). Upper Sadle River, NJ: Pearson.

Wolfe, V. V. (2006). Child sexual abuse. In E. J. Mash & R. A. Barkley (Eds.), *Treatment of childhood disorders* (3rd ed., pp. 647–727). New York: Guilford Press.

Wong, B. Y. L., Harris, K. R., Graham, S., & Butler, D. I. (2003). Cognitive strategies instruction research in learning disabilities. In H. L. Swanson, K. R. Harris, & S. Graham (Eds.), *Handbook of learning disabilities* (pp. 383–402). New York: The Guilford Press.

Yeargin-Allsopp, K. O., & Boyle, C. (2002). Overview: The epidemiology of neurodevelopmental disorders. *Mental rehabilitation and development disorder research reviews,* 8(3), 113–116.

Geriatric Neuropsychology

17

Learning Objectives

After reading this chapter, the student should be able to understand:

- The normal aging process and the changes that take place in the brain, immune system, physical appearance and movement, senses, circulatory system, sexuality, and cognitive ability
- The ethical issues that need to be considered in working with older adults
- The theories of aging including cellular clock theory, free-radical theory, mitochondrial theory, and hormonal stress theory
- The characteristics of depression in older adults
- Various other central nervous system difficulties which often occur in the older population including dementia, elder abuse, substance abuse and dependence, polypharmacy, and late-onset schizophrenia

Topical Outline

- Normal Aging
- Theories of Aging
- Ethical Issues
- Difficulties That Occur With Aging

*D*r. Solomon Jr. was self-referred for a neuropsychological evaluation based on issues which he had been observing in his own behavior. He was concerned that he had been more tired than he should, that he often forgot questions which colleagues asked of him, had occasional trouble hearing, and had a diminished sex drive. He was aware that some of the difficulties which he had been experiencing were common in those older than age 65 years but he was unsure to what extent. He had contemplated retirement but felt that his heart was in his surgical practice. He had also thought working fewer hours might help. He was quite aware of the mind–body relationship and had recently received a complete physical. His blood work was normal except for slightly elevated cholesterol. He had taken steps toward remediation by altering his diet and adding to his exercise regime. He does not find taking medication to be the answer. After a thorough discussion, he admitted that some of the physical changes had left him feeling somewhat depressed.

Dr. Solomon Jr. was born in a rural area to a nonfarming family. His father was the local country physician and his mother was the organist for their church. He had two older sisters, one who is 75 years old, and the eldest who is deceased. The elder sister died of a heart-related ailment in her late 60s. She left behind a husband and two grown sons. Dr. Solomon Jr.'s parents lived into their 80s with no official record of cause of death. However, considering his difficulty with cholesterol and his sister's heart difficulties, he suspected that heart disease was a contributing factor for the deaths. He described his father as a very organized and articulate gentleman until his late 70s when he began to have difficulty with his memory. During that period of time, it was expected that older individuals would have some memory trouble and it was difficult for the family to convince Dr. Solomon Sr. to retire. Mrs. Solomon did not appear to have the difficulty with memory which her husband experienced, but she was not under as much public scrutiny. Therefore, Dr. Solomon Jr. was not able to state with precision if his mother had any memory deficits. His mother's eyesight became poor as she entered her 70s and she played the majority of her organ hymns from memory, an advantage which kept her in the position of organist until shortly before she died.

Personal medical history indicated that Dr. Solomon Jr.'s prenatal, birth, and postnatal health was normal. He suffered from chicken pox, scarlet fever, and measles, as was common for most children during that time period. He was a very good student in the elementary grades and very interested in science and athletics. During secondary school, he was captain of the football team and learned German to fulfill a language requirement. It was also during his senior year of high school that he met the woman whom he would eventually marry. Dr. Solomon Jr. was on the honor roll at graduation. He immediately applied to and was accepted into a liberal arts college where he studied biology and was premed, though at that time his college had no official program. His fiancée began a 4-year nursing program at the same college. Both individuals were excellent students and completed college magna cum laude and Phi Beta Kappa. After college, Dr. Solomon Jr. attended medical school at one of the most prestigious schools on the East Coast while his wife began to work in pediatrics at a large local hospital. Before they left for the East Coast, the couple were wed. As difficult as it was to move away from the smaller, more rural atmosphere and leave behind family and friends, both parties were very busy and loneliness did not immediately become a problem. Three years into Dr. Solomon Jr.'s medical schooling, his wife decided it was time to begin a family and within the next 4 years, they had a daughter and then a son. By the time Dr. Solomon Jr. had completed his medical education including his residency, he and his wife felt it was time to return to their rural roots.

Dr. Solomon Jr. spoke with his father regarding the transition which would ultimately lead to taking over his father's practice. The transitional circumstances worked for several years but the younger Solomon began to feel that the senior Solomon's practice was too general. Dr. Solomon Sr.

noticed the discontent in his son and suggested that his son follow his interests and stated that he would advertise for a physician who specialized in family practice to continue his practice. Hence, Dr. Solomon Jr. and family moved to the closest metropolitan area where he could focus his attention on a practice in surgery but was also within driving distance of family. The family appeared to be comfortable with the move and each person began to follow his or her own path to fulfill his or her needs and desires. For many years, things went well and Dr. Solomon Jr. added partners to his practice. Due to the fact that he began the practice, he became the managing partner. Over time, the stresses of handling personnel issues as well as difficult and complicated surgical procedures caused Dr. Solomon Jr. to lose sleep. He also felt that it began to interfere with his life outside of the office. After many conversations with his wife, Dr. Solomon Jr. attempted to delegate some of the office responsibilities; however, he felt that was even more stressful. With little sleep some days, he felt that he was not at his best during his surgical procedures. Not realizing that the cognitive effects of lack of sleep had impacted him, he took his memory difficulties as early signs of dementia. Worrying that it might be apparent to others, he began to avoid any unnecessary social obligations and had a dictionary at work lest he could not remember a particular word. All of these events, added together, caused him to feel depressed, which further added to his developing negative self-image.

The clinical neuropsychologist completed an intake interview to gather the aforementioned information. The clinical neuropsychologist then determined that a complete neuropsychological evaluation would elucidate any symptoms present. The clinical neuropsychologist also felt that a complete evaluation would assist Dr. Solomon Jr. in understanding whether he was experiencing significant difficulties or suffering from stress and lack of sleep.

The results of the neuropsychological evaluation indicated that Dr. Solomon Jr. scored two standard deviations above average on the intellectual component. The intelligence test results were reflective of his grades in high school, college, medical school, and his profession. It was significant that his subtest scores were not impaired by age-related motor speed slowness, which often happens as one ages. Memory evaluation indicated that Dr. Solomon Jr. exhibited some short-term deficits but not enough to place his scores in the impaired range or interfere with the results of other tests. Further evaluation indicated that he did not suffer from any significant attention, concentration, or higher order cognitive deficits. The results of the evaluation were compiled and presented in a feedback session to Dr. Solomon Jr. His reaction was a combination of relief and confusion. He was extremely relieved to not be suffering from any form of apparent dementia and that his intelligence had remained intact. However, he understood that neuropsychological tests reflected behavioral sequelae of brain impairment and were not capable of the same degree of certainty as an MRI or other form of brain scan. He was confused regarding the symptoms which he had been experiencing and the test results. A discussion ensued in which the clinical neuropsychologist reviewed the pattern of normal aging within the brain, the senses, and the body. The clinical neuropsychologist also reiterated that lack of sleep, stress, and the combination of the two may easily diminish performance and with concerns regarding aging, may lead an individual to misinterpret symptoms. The discussion frustrated Dr. Solomon Jr. because he knew and understood the concepts that the clinical neuropsychologist discussed but had not applied them to his own circumstances and felt somewhat foolish.

The treatment plan that the clinical neuropsychologist developed with Dr. Solomon Jr. focused less on his initial concerns and more on what was gleaned from the interview regarding his current life circumstances and coping skills. The clinical neuropsychologist suggested that the two spend several individual therapy sessions addressing his stressors. Through discussion, it was determined that Dr. Solomon Jr.'s major stressors were work related. Fears that his current performance was not comparable to the internal standard he had set for himself when he was a much younger surgeon appeared to exacerbate the intensity of his stress. Cognitive–behavioral techniques were utilized to help Dr. Solomon Jr. realistically appraise his situation regarding what was expected of him as the head of the practice and as a surgeon. Dr. Solomon Jr. began to realize that holding himself to the performance standards he had self-imposed 30 or more years ago was unrealistic and had created intense pressure leading to anxiety and fear. He was able to evaluate what was a reasonable surgical practice for a man close to 70 years old without being defensive. He decided to reduce his surgical practice by one-half and involve his partners to a greater extent. In a similar manner, he was able to begin to delegate management of the practice to others in the organization relieving him of the sole leadership role. A few sessions after he had made these changes, he informed the clinical neuropsychologist that he had begun to sleep better and was feeling less overwhelmed and depressed. He also felt that his need for a dictionary had lessened but was not ready to remove it from his office. Through additional sessions, the clinical neuropsychologist began to explore with Dr. Solomon Jr. when he would consider retirement and how he would spend his time and energy. The topic of retirement immediately escalated his anxiety, as it was clear that Dr. Solomon Jr. equated retirement with the end of life. The clinical neuropsychologist discussed the fact that for many professional people, the thought of retirement was extremely anxiety ridden due to the fact that their identity is tied to their role as a professional. Slowly, over a period of several more sessions, Dr. Solomon Jr. began to understand that he could experience good years physically and mentally after retirement and that retirement was not a punishment for poor performance or a reflection on an impending dementing process.

Introduction

As discussed in the previous chapter, this chapter covers the second age group which is frequently not included within the diagnostic, assessment, and treatment literature. The population of individuals who are 65 years and older within the United States has been growing rapidly. The growth in the population is related to medical advances which have increased the average life expectancy, nutrition, exercise, lifestyle changes, and technology utilized to treat various difficulties. At the present time, the average **life expectancy** for individuals who are 65 years old in the United States is 18 more years, 20 for females, 16 for males (National Center for Health Statistics, 2006). The average life expectancy for individuals born in 2009 in the United States is 78.1 years (National Center for Health Statistics, 2008). Life expectancy varies by gender, by ethnic group, and by a combination of the two factors together. It is projected that the population will consist of 54,804,000 adults who are 65 years and older by the year 2020 (United States Census Bureau, 2008).

life expectancy
the number of years that will likely be lived by the average person born in a particular year

The presence of such a large number of older adults has put stress on various areas within society. One area which has been particularly strained is the health care system. Even though many more people have been living for a much longer period of time, it remains the case that individuals who are 65 years and older use the health care system to a larger extent than any other group with the exception of children (Aday & Andersen, 1974; Rice & Fineman, 2004). Approximately one-third of the total health care costs in the United States are incurred by adults 65 years and older. Older individuals have many issues in addition to health care which relate more to social concerns and include retirement planning, financial issues, housing issues, social support, and family and marital issues.

This chapter will address the issues in aging which are particularly related to clinical neuropsychology. Normal aging versus its counterpart in disease process will be the first section covered. The next topics investigated will be the most pervasive central nervous system difficulties which are evident within this age group. As was the case with Chapter 16, ethical issues and concerns which are salient for this age group will be addressed prior to any discussion of rehabilitation.

Normal Aging

The following section will discuss the current research regarding what is known concerning the brain, the immune system, the senses, physical stature, the cardiovascular and respiratory systems, and sexuality in an average individual who is not experiencing any central nervous system difficulties. The information will be used as a comparison to help the reader understand the difference between the changes expected with aging and symptoms which may be indications of a difficulty or disease process. A definitional distinction has been made by many researchers regarding the grouping of all individuals 65 years and older into one large cohort. Many researchers have divided the older population into two groups, termed the young old (ages 65–74) and the old-old (ages 75 years and older). Dividing the groups in such a manner often helps to draw conclusions from studies to population groups which may not apply to all of the individuals 65 and older years of age.

THE BRAIN

As with all abilities discussed in this text, it is important to remember that each individual will differ in rate of change with aging and, as stated in the introduction, various personal variables will affect the process of normal aging. Therefore, the statements made in this chapter are intended to reflect average functioning. The brain loses an average of 5–10% of its weight between the age of 20 and 90. Brain volume also decreases (Bondare, 2007). Researchers speculate regarding the etiology of the normal changes but have not reached firm conclusions. Speculations include a decrease in dendrites, damage to the myelin sheath which covers the axons, and/or death of brain cells.

The prefrontal cortex of normal individuals shrinks more with aging than other areas which is related to a decline in working memory and other cognitive activities (Pardo et al., 2007). General slowing of the overall functioning of the brain and spinal cord occurs and leads to poorer coordination and impairment on timed intelligence test tasks (Birren, Woods, & Williams, 1980). Using neuroimaging it has been shown that older adults were more likely to exhibit slower processing on a cognitive task than were younger adults (Rypma, Eldreth, & Rebbechi, 2007).

Normal aging has been implicated in the reduction of neurotransmitters, including acetylcholine, dopamine, and gamma-amino butyric acid (GABA; Dickstein et al., 2007). Normal reduction in dopamine may cause difficulties with planning and execution of motor actions (Erixon-Lindroth et al., 2005). Reductions in acetylcholine may be the cause of small declines in memory.

A very controversial issue discussed at various points within the text is the topic of neuronal regeneration. It has now been accepted that neurogenesis can occur in humans (Libert, Cohen, & Guarente, 2008). However, it has only been demonstrated within the hippocampus, which controls memory, and the olfactory bulb related to the sense of smell (Gould, 2007; Verret, Trouche, Zerwas, & Rampon, 2007). The researchers do not know the precise function of new cell generation and their survival is a matter of speculation at this time (Kolb & Wishaw, 2009).

Dendritic growth is possible in humans and has been documented in adults as old as 70 (Eliasieh, Liets, & Chalupa, 2007). Researchers following adults as they age suggest that from the 40s to the 70s, dendrites increased; however, this did not occur into the 90s (Coleman, 1986). It is possible that this may compensate for the loss of neurons through the 70s but not into the 90s. How this is possible has not been determined, and whether it could occur further into old age if there were adequate environmental stimulation is an open question.

neurogenesis
the development of new neurons

Adaptation is the ability of the brain to change and an example has been shown in the ability of the aging brain to change lateralization. Researchers have been able to show that lateralization of function in the prefrontal cortex is less in older than in younger adults when engaging in cognitive tasks (Rossi et al., 2004). The ability to change lateralization is another example of the concept discussed earlier termed plasticity in brain function. When an area of the brain functions less than adequately, the brain is able to redistribute tasks to accommodate aging. Hence, the brain may sustain many insults and illnesses and still be able to function.

THE IMMUNE SYSTEM

Many studies have documented an overall decline in functioning of the immune system with aging (Larbi et al., 2008). When and if an individual is under stress has an effect by diminishing the functioning of the immune system and accelerating aging (Colonna-Romano et al., 2008). Malnutrition or lack of appropriate nutrients may lead to a decreased level of protein within the body. Decreased protein may cause a lowered level of T cells whose job it is to destroy infected cells. Proper or adequate nutrition and appropriate exercise have been shown to improve immune system functioning (Pedersen, Ostrowski, Rohde, & Bruunsgaard, 1998). A connection has been made between depression and immunity. A lowered immune profile is more strongly apparent in older than younger individuals (Herbert & Cohen, 1993). The campaign by the health care system to vaccinate older adults against the flu and pneumonia is related to the normal decline in the functioning of the immune system (Kumar & Burns, 2008). An older adult who develops the flu is more likely to not recover or to develop a secondary infection, often pneumonia, than a younger person.

PHYSICAL APPEARANCE AND MOVEMENT

Changes in physical appearance and movement begin in middle age (40–65 years old) and become more apparent with older age. Wrinkles and age spots tend to be the most noticeable of normal changes. Height declines for both genders. The amount of loss is at most 2 inches but usually is approximately 1–2 inches, and is related to bone loss in the vertebrae. Weight also tends to decline after age 60 years due to the fact that muscle is often replaced by fat, which weighs less. Older adults tend to move more slowly than younger adults across a variety of activities of various levels of difficulty (Rossit & Harvey, 2008). Regular exercise, particularly walking, has been shown to be very helpful in maintaining mobility and decreasing the onset of physical disability.

THE SENSES

The majority of research in the area of sensation has been completed on vision. There are many changes which occur in normal visual aging, including changes in visual acuity, color vision, and depth perception. Visual acuity tends to decline for most adults beginning in middle age and becoming more apparent with advanced age. Driving in the dark becomes a difficult task for many individuals due to an increased intolerance for glare (Stutts, 2007). Dark adaptation or the ability to recover when going from a well-lit environment to a darker environment tends to diminish. The overall surface area of the visual field is diminished and thus objects which are farther from the center of the visual field may be more difficult to detect (Stutts, 2007). The yellowing of the lens of the eye may result in decline in color vision (Scialfa & Kline, 2007).

Normal aging changes in hearing are much greater in the old-old than in the young-old. The oldest individuals may have been exposed to the highest levels of environmental stimuli without protection for their ears, whereas the younger the person, the more likely ear protection had been used. Another variable to consider is that the Occupational Safety and Health Administration (OSHA) guidelines began in 1970, which affected those who worked in industrial settings (Flemming, 2001). Hearing difficulties may naturally occur due to degeneration of the cochlea, the receptor for hearing within the inner ear (Frisina & Walton, 2006). Structural damage to the hearing apparatus related to accident or illness is not normal aging. Various attitudes exist among older adults in relation to hearing loss. Many older adults do not recognize that they have a hearing problem; some individuals actively deny that they have a hearing difficulty, and some accept hearing loss as a natural effect of aging. Women are more likely than men to seek help or treatment for any hearing difficulty.

A majority of older adults lose some of their sense of smell, taste, or a combination of the two (Roberts & Rosenberg, 2006). Healthy older adults lose less of these abilities than nonhealthy older adults. In general, researchers have found greater decline in the sense of smell than in the sense of taste (Schiffman, 2007). The different pattern that may ensue with normal loss in taste and smell is due to a reduced sense of enjoyment when eating. When foods lose their appeal or do not taste as they had previously, it may lead an individual to consume less and risk losing nutrients or even become malnourished. A different pattern which may develop to compensate for lack of taste is the consumption of saltier, sweeter, and spicier junk foods (Hoyer & Roodin, 2003). Changing to a less healthy diet to compensate for lack of taste may again lead to a decrease in nutrients or malnutrition.

Changes in touch and pain are also part of the normal aging process. The loss of sensitivity may cause an individual to become injured without knowing and thus risk infection. Another difficulty is that a higher pain threshold may cause an individual to not recognize an injured muscle, joint, and/or tendon, and therefore more invasive treatments must be utilized when the person seeks treatment.

CIRCULATORY SYSTEM

The heart and lungs lose a percentage of their normal capacity to function with normal aging. The heart must beat harder and faster to circulate blood throughout the body. The lungs lose 40% of their capacity between ages 20 and 70 (Lynn-Davies, 1977). The lungs also lose elasticity, the chest shrinks, and the diaphragm weakens. Exercise, however, has been shown to improve both heart and lung functioning in older adults.

SEXUALITY

The majority of research studies suggest that, in the absence of disease or the belief that sexuality should not be an activity engaged in by older adults, sexuality may be a lifelong activity. One of the major determinants of sexual functioning is the presence of a partner. Women are more affected by this due to the fact that they live longer than men. Men tend to remarry a younger woman if their spouse dies. Normal aging does produce some changes in physical functioning involved with sexuality. Orgasms are less frequent for males as they age. Added stimulation is needed to produce and maintain an erection in the majority of healthy older males. Healthy older females lubricate less than when younger and may need a gel or cream to assist with intercourse in order to avoid pain. Menopause has most likely been completed in older females and many report a relief from the fear of pregnancy.

In our case study, Dr. Solomon Jr., a physician by profession, has failed to apply all of his knowledge regarding normal aging to himself. He therefore has fears that appear to be related to how his body is functioning. In general, his physical exam revealed a very healthy individual for his age. His elevated cholesterol should be lowered by a healthy diet and exercise regime which he has already begun. Most of the bodily systems discussed in this section appear to be intact for him. His concerns regarding memory and word finding are not substantiated by test results. However, his report of lack of sleep certainly could cause these difficulties. His diminished sex drive, though not unusual, may be the result of his fears regarding his overall performance and worry regarding developing a dementing process. Sexual desire and functioning is often diminished when an individual has concerns and worries and is further diminished when the concerns are related to one's sexual performance.

COGNITIVE ABILITIES

The previous section discussed structural and functional changes in the brain and body. The present section discusses the effects of these changes on the abilities which we often group together under the umbrella of cognitive functioning. These abilities include attention, speed of processing, memory, and higher order cognitive functioning.

selective attention
the ability to focus on a specific part of an experience while ignoring other parts

Changes in attention are considered to be part of normal aging and are evident in selective, divided, and sustained attention. Selective attention is the ability to focus on an aspect of an experience and filter out irrelevant stimuli. In general, older adults perform poorer at this than younger adults (Brown, McKenzie, & Doan, 2005). Divided attention is the ability to concentrate on more than one activity at the same time. When two or more tasks are relatively simple to complete, the age groups tended to perform equally well. However, when the multiple tasks became more complex, the older adults displayed more difficulty with this type of task (Maciocas & Crognale, 2004). Sustained attention is the ability to detect and respond to small changes in the environment which occur at random times. This ability has also been referred to as *vigilance*. Similar to the discussions on divided attention, when the tasks were simple all age groups performed in a similar manner, whereas when the tasks became more complex, the older adults performed poorer particularly when the tasks involved decision making (Isella et al., 2008).

divided attention
the ability to concentrate on more than one activity at the same time

sustained attention
the ability to respond to random events in the environment that draw one's attention

The speed at which information is processed, often termed *reaction time*, declines with age. There is a substantial amount of variability in this function between individuals. The decline is related to the decline in the functioning of the brain and central nervous system. Health and exercise also relate to rate of decline in this ability, with healthy older adults who exercise more declining less in measured reaction time.

Stereotypically, it is often thought that there is a large memory deficit with aging. Studies suggest that memory changes with aging but not all memory changes in the same way (Smith, 2007). The types of memory which have been shown to decline with aging includes episodic memory, semantic memory, working memory, perceptual speed, explicit memory, implicit memory, source memory, and prospective memory. Episodic memory is the structure of one's own life as revealed in memory, the personal events, and when they occurred. Advancing age is linked to increased difficulty in retrieving information about one's life accurately (Siedlecki, 2007). Semantic memory is defined as knowledge of how the world works. Older adults tend to be better able to recall semantic than episodic memory. A difficulty, however, is often referred to as the "tip-of-the-tongue" phenomenon where individuals feel as if they should be able to remember familiar information but are not able (Buscur & Madden, 2007). Older adults are more prone to this type of difficulty than younger adults and some even jokingly refer to this as a "senior moment."

Working memory has often been used interchangeably with short-term memory, but recently researchers have referred to it as memory actively used to solve problems or make decisions (Baddeley, 2007). Working memory tends to decline with aging. Perceptual speed, which is related to working memory, also declines with age (Bopp & Verhaeghen, 2007). Explicit memory is defined as memory of facts and experiences that an individual can consciously state. This memory is also referred to as *declarative memory* and shows a decline with aging. Implicit memory is memory for skills and procedures, which an individual may not be able to consciously describe. This type of memory is less likely to be affected by aging (Kessels, Bockhorst, & Postma, 2005). Source memory is memory for when information was learned and difficulties with it increase with aging. Prospective memory is memory to complete an act in the future. Declines in this ability are age related but also related to content. Older adults are better able to remember to do an action when there is more meaning attached to the action. Higher order cognitive processes are also affected by aging. Baltes (2003) described the differences between those abilities which declined and those which remained stable or improved using the terms *cognitive mechanics* and *cognitive pragmatics*. Cognitive mechanics consists of the speed and accuracy of the processes involved in sensory input, attention, visual and motor memory, discrimination, comparison, and categorization. Many researchers suggest that decline in these abilities begins in middle age (Li et al., 2004). Cognitive pragmatics includes reading and writing skills, language comprehension, educational qualifications, professional skills, and knowledge about the self and how to cope with life. Cognitive pragmatics may decline with age but there is also the possibility that it may improve. Cognitive mechanics and pragmatics have been compared to the distinction between fluid and crystallized intelligence. The similarity has become so strong that many researchers now refer to fluid mechanics and crystallized pragmatics (Lovden & Linderberger, 2007).

perceptual speed
how fast a task may be completed

source memory
the ability to remember where something was learned

cognitive mechanics
the "hardware" of the mind that reflects the neurophysiological architecture of the brain developed through evolution

cognitive pragmatics
the culture-based "software programs" of the mind

Theories of Aging

There are four major biological theories which attempt to explain the causes of aging: cellular clock theory, free-radical theory, mitochondrial theory, and hormonal stress theory. Hayflick's (1977) cellular clock theory states that cells are able to divide approximately 75–80 times and that, as we age, our cells become less able to divide. Hayflick did not know why cells die. However, based on cell death, he placed an upper limit on life span at 120–125 years. Recent researchers have been able to understand that cells die due to telomeres. Telomeres are DNA sequences that cap chromosomes (Shay & Wright, 2007). Each time a cell divides, the telomeres shorten and after 75–80 replications they may no longer reproduce and the cell dies.

telomeres
structures at the end of a chromosome consisting of repetitive DNA and serving to stabilize the chromosome

Free radical theory states that individuals age due to the fact that when cells metabolize energy, the by-products include unstable oxygen molecules termed free radicals. The free radicals maneuver throughout the cell and damage DNA and other cellular structures (Laurent et al., 2008).

free radicals
unstable oxygen molecules often implicated in aging

Mitochondrial theory states that aging is due to decay of mitochondria. The decay appears due to oxidative damage and loss of micronutrients supplied by the cell (Druzhyna, Wilson, & LeDoux, 2008). The damage is thought to occur due to free radicals, which are by-products of mitochondrial energy production. The damage from free radical initiates a cycle in which oxidative damage impairs mitochondrial function which results in generation of more free radicals. The result is that the affected mitochondria become so inefficient that they cannot generate enough energy to meet cell needs (Lee & Wei, 2007).

Hormonal stress theory states that aging in the hormonal system may lower resistance to stress and increase the likelihood of disease (Finch & Seeman, 1999). Under stress, the body responds by releasing certain hormones. It is thought that as people age, the hormones stimulated by stress remain at elevated levels longer, and that the elevated levels are related to increased risk for many diseases (Magri et al., 2006).

Applying the various theories of aging to the case study would be difficult not because of the theories but due to the fact that Dr. Solomon Jr.'s difficulties appear to be more related to worry about impairments than actual impairments. Therefore, hormonal stress theory would not likely fit with his situation. He has been worried about his lack of abilities and possibly caused himself more stress and possibly decreased the function of his immune system by the worry.

Ethical Issues

Before looking into any form of difficulty which may occur more frequently in older adults, issues which may more often occur with this population must be discussed.

One of the major issues related to older adults receiving any form of treatment or rehabilitation is access to services and the ability to afford services. While this is not an issue related to the *Ethical Principles of Psychologists and Code of Conduct* (American Psychological Association [APA], 2002), it is an ethical issue due to the fact that it impacts the ability of individuals to obtain services when needed. Older adults are more likely than younger adults to not be able to access services when needed. Various reasons exist for this, including stigmatization when using services and, therefore, not partaking of services, lack of transportation to services, and services being or located in areas which may be inaccessible to an older adult. Other difficulties are related to the insurance program that the individual is on or, in some cases, lack of insurance. Many insurance programs require that an individual obtain a referral from his or her primary provider to obtain specialized services. A visit to the primary provider may not be difficult or there may be a waiting list, difficulty getting to the appointment, or a major national health issue which inundates the health care system such as the H1N1 virus at the time of the writing of this text. Other programs, such as medical assistance for those who are receiving services from the welfare system and Medicare and/or Medicaid for those who are retired or disabled, may not reimburse providers to the extent of private insurance carriers. Therefore, providers may have a quota of individuals which they will service with these forms of insurance. All of these issues may make it more difficult for older individuals to obtain services.

Healthy older adults have some changes in bodily and sensory functioning and nonhealthy older adults may have more difficulties in these areas. In terms of receiving services from providers for treatment and rehabilitation, not all providers are aware of the normal changes with aging. It would behoove all clinical neuropsychologists to become competent in these issues in order to make sure that they are clear regarding effects of disease or difficulty versus normal aging. Another issue is that individuals need accommodations such as potentially louder and clearer speech on the part of the provider. Cohort effects may make it difficult for those who are now aged to be treated by someone who is much younger. It is necessary to afford all people the respect that they deserve and also be cognizant of an age group which is more comfortable being addressed by surname such as Mr. or Mrs. rather than by their first name. Another cohort effect may relate to the rehabilitation process and that is the use of technology. Many older adults are becoming conversant with e-mail and computer usage in general. Other older adults have experienced resentment toward the lack of personal connection the computer has caused. When giving information, the clinical neuropsychologist must be aware of these types of cohort effects.

An ethical issue which the clinical neuropsychologist should be very aware of is elder abuse. When interviewing, testing, or conducting therapy, any form of abuse—physical, sexual, or financial—must be reported and investigated. As a person ages, he or she becomes more of a target for unscrupulous individuals and sometimes these individuals are within the client's own family.

Guardianship and/or conservatorship is an ethical and legal issue which would need to be considered when and if an individual is unable to care for himself or herself, make his or her own decisions, or handle his or her own finances.

Dr. Solomon Jr.'s difficulties, which fall within the ethical continuum, include cohort effects and personal identity issues. Dr. Solomon Jr. is from a cohort which does not easily ask for help or easily partake of it. Dr. Solomon Jr. also has the major portion of his identity involved with his professional role as physician and surgeon. To engage Dr. Solomon Jr. in any form of therapy or rehabilitation, the clinical neuropsychologist must keep these issues in mind and discuss issues in language which implies that Dr. Solomon Jr. understands the issues that face him. Due to the fact that he has some feelings of unease at not applying his knowledge to himself, it is imperative that the clinical neuropsychologist normalizes that experience by stating that very often, professionals make the worst clients or some type of similar statement. In Dr. Solomon Jr.'s situation in particular, as with all clients in general, maintaining dignity is very important.

Difficulties That Occur With Aging

This section of the chapter focuses on difficulties which tend to occur more frequently or for different reasons in older adults. It is not intended to be a reiteration of the chapter on differential diagnosis but a closer look at the etiology and treatments for particular difficulties.

DEPRESSION

The feeling of depression is a common difficulty throughout the life span. Depression is an overriding dysphoric mood accompanied by various physical and psychological symptoms which vary by individual. Physical symptoms may involve eating too little or too much, sleeping too little or too much, an inability to sit still, or a feeling one must always be moving. Psychological symptoms include difficulties concentrating, making decisions, enjoying activities which were previously enjoyable, and possible thoughts of suicide. Depression may occur at any time in the life cycle but tends to occur with greater frequency when an individual is under stress and/or is experiencing many changes, particularly negative, in his or her life.

Older adults, as has been discussed throughout this chapter, face many and varied changes which other age groups do not. Normal aging changes and disease process difficulties both may affect an individual. Many older adults have witnessed great changes in technology and society as a whole and feel left out or left behind. Those individuals who have spent their lives in the workforce may find it difficult to face retirement. Those who have been working at home may find it difficult to have a spouse present all of the time when they are accustomed to managing the house and their time on their own. Retirement has been shown to be a stressful change for those working both in and out of the home. If the relationship between partners was good prior to retirement, it may be strained by too much time together. If the relationship was strained before retirement it clearly will not improve on its own with more time together. Other stressors which may lead to depression include any number of changes such as change in residence, change in friendships, loss of friends and/or family due to death, and often a loss of sense of self in relationship to the previous roles one has had in the community. In Western societies, particularly the United States, there is an extraordinary focus on youth. As one's body and mind age and one's concomitant roles change, it can lead an individual to feel disheartened.

Within the cohort who is currently aged, there is a gender difference in level of reported depression with women having higher levels than men. This may reflect the fact that women in the cohort tend to live much longer than men. Research indicates that older adults who engage in regular exercise are less likely to be depressed, whereas those who are in poor health and/or experiencing pain are more likely to be depressed (Kostka & Praczko, 2007). It has been anticipated by researchers that the number of older adults with depression will increase as the large cohort of baby boomers (those born between 1946 and 1964) moves into late adulthood (Parmalec, 2007). It has also been hypothesized that there will be less of a gender difference in reported depression.

Treatment for older adults with depression begins with a neuropsychological evaluation in order to assist in the differential diagnosis of depression from any other physical or mental ailment. If the individual has not had a complete physical recently, it is also suggested that it be obtained to assist in the diagnostic process due to the fact that many medical conditions may have symptoms which overlap with many mental conditions.

dexamethasone suppression test
a medical test used to determine the presence of various forms of depression; whether it can distinguish the different disorders is still under debate

The **dexamethasone suppression test** (DST) has been used by the medical community as a blood test to detect various forms of depression (Rush et al., 1996). The hypothalamic-pituitary-adrenal (HPA) axis is frequently activated during periods of stress and depression and results in the release of cortisol from the adrenal cortex. A synthetic steroid, dexamethasone (DEX), will often signal this axis not to release cortisol. Depressed patients demonstrate a significantly higher nonsuppression rate than controls even though the rate is low in many studies (Arana, Baldessarini, & Ornsteen, 1985). Patients with severe or psychotic depression demonstrate relatively high rates of nonsuppression or high postdexamethasone cortisol levels (Schatzberg, Rothschild, & Stahl, 1983).

Treatment of depression is dependent on whether it is a stress-related (endogenous) or related to biochemical factors (exogenous). For either type of depression, medications may be helpful but for biochemical (neurotransmitter) imbalances, it is essential to treat the depression with medication. The essential issue to consider with medication is that metabolism changes as one ages and the dosage of antidepressant medication must be adjusted to fit the age and health of the individual. It is also essential to discuss other

polypharmacy
administering many different medicines concurrently for the treatment of the same disease

medications which the individual is taking to avoid drug interactions or polypharmacy. Another factor which is often overlooked when treating older adults is alcohol or other mood-altering drug consumption. Similar to the issues which may occur with other medications would be interactions or difficulty with antidepressants and other drugs of abuse.

Individual therapy is the other type of treatment for depression which may be helpful to individuals with either form of depression. Cognitive–behavioral therapy has been proven to be a short-term effective approach which does not delve into the past history of the individual. Cognitive–behavioral therapy may be a good fit for an older adult who does not want to reveal personal information but it is more interested in learning a skill to overcome depression.

It is essential for the clinical neuropsychologist to keep in mind when evaluating older adults for other difficulties that depression is an extremely common comorbid symptom or diagnosis. It is even more important to be aware that in cases of depression, there is always the potential for suicide risk. Older adults have an increased risk of suicide due to the aforementioned stresses and changes in their lives. Approximately 25% of individuals who commit suicide in the United States are 65 years of age or older (Church, Siegel, & Fowler, 1988). The older adult most likely to commit suicide is a male who lives alone, has lost his spouse, and is experiencing poor health (Ruckenhauser, Yazdani, & Ravaglia, 2007).

DEMENTIA

Dementia was discussed in an earlier chapter. It is included within the discussion of aging due to the fact that it affects older adults more often than those who are younger. It also is often misdiagnosed as depression and vice versa. Hence, the cardinal symptoms of dementia will be revisited and the role of aging will be expanded upon.

Dementia is the broad term which encompasses any neurological condition in which the primary symptom is deterioration in cognitive functioning. Included within the term are dementias due to Alzheimer's disease, frontotemporal dementia, vascular dementia, and any other form of dementia from an unspecified etiology. It has been estimated that 20% of individuals older than the age of 80 have a form of dementia. Many other individuals, younger and older, may have what has been termed a predementia condition.

Using Alzheimer's disease as an example, researchers have been able to understand that the disease involves a deficiency of acetylcholine, which plays an important role in memory (Amenta & Tayebati, 2008). The brain begins to deteriorate and shrink and healthy tissue is replaced by amyloid plaques and neurofibrillary tangles. Researchers are seeking ways to interrupt the destruction which occurs. Although researchers are not certain regarding the etiology of Alzheimer's disease, two factors are clearly related: genes and age (Bird, 2008; Vasudevaraju, Bharathi, Garruto, Sambamurti, & Rao, 2008). The number of individuals older than 65 with Alzheimer's disease doubles every 5 years. The apolipoprotein E (ApoE) gene, which is a genetic component, is indicative of the likelihood of Alzheimer's disease. The presence of the ApoE gene lowers the age for onset of Alzheimer's disease (Sando et al., 2008). Researchers have recently related lifestyle factors to the risk for Alzheimer's disease. Lifestyle factors such as those which increase the risk of cardiac difficulties have been implicated such as obesity, smoking, atherosclerosis, and high cholesterol (Almeida et al., 2008; Gazdinsky, Kornak, Weiner, & Meyerhoff, 2008; Luchsinger, 2008). Researchers have found that older adults with Alzheimer's disease are more likely to have cardiovascular disease than those who do not have Alzheimer's disease (Cole & Vassar, 2009). Similar to many other problems with aging, exercise has been shown to decrease the risks of Alzheimer's disease (Middleton, Kirkland, Maxwel, Hogan, & Rockwood, 2007).

Dementia has many forms of treatment that may be more preventive or more rehabilitative. Due to the lifestyle factors enumerated earlier, it would be helpful in the prevention of dementia for an older adult to eat a healthy diet, engage in appropriate exercise, refrain from smoking, and avoid excess alcohol usage. These are all suggestions that have been repeated throughout the chapter but also pertain to preventing cognitive deficits.

Early detection is another factor in the process of treating dementia. Mild cognitive impairment (MCI) is a transitional state between the cognitive changes of normal aging and the early symptoms of Alzheimer's disease and other dementias (Peterson & Negash, 2008). While MCI is not included within the current diagnostic manual, it will be included within *Diagnostic and Statistical Manual of Mental Disorders-V* (*DSM-V*) when released and is used extensively within the research literature (Jeste, 2009).

Early detection may often surface in a neuropsychological evaluation and in functional magnetic resonance imaging (fMRI) brain scans. Once detected, early treatment, particularly for Alzheimer's type dementia, may be begun. Cholinesterase-inhibiting drugs have been

predementia condition
a condition that occurs before dementia is formally diagnosed which resembles the cognitive and/or memory deficits of dementia

mild cognitive impairment
a transition stage between the cognitive decline of normal aging and the more serious problems caused by Alzheimer's disease

approved by the Food and Drug Administration (FDA) for use with Alzheimer's disease such as donepezil (Aricept), rivastigmine (Exelon), and galantamine (Razadyne). These drugs are used to slow the progression of dementia but are not able to stop or cure the difficulty.

Individuals who have dementia may benefit from individual therapy from the clinical neuropsychologist in order to work on coexisting depression or other conditions. The individual may also have fears and/or a grief reaction to knowledge of having dementia.

Family members may also benefit from individual, family, or group therapy to deal with the issues of caring for an individual who has a dementing illness. Family is a necessary support, if available, for the individual with dementia. However, caring for someone who has dementia can be a very draining process. Depression is common in caregivers of patients with Alzheimer's disease. In a meta-analysis, Pinquart and Sorensen (2006) found that female caregivers reported providing more caregiving, having higher levels of burden and depression and lower levels of well-being and physical health, than male caregivers.

ELDER ABUSE

As was discussed in the section on ethics, abuse of older adults is becoming a more serious problem as more individuals live for a longer period of time. This statement is not meant to discount any abuse which may have occurred earlier in one's history but to add credence to the list of serious difficulties which continue to grow as the population ages.

Similar to the definition of child abuse, elder abuse may involve neglect and emotional, physical, and/or sexual abuse. The most likely perpetrator is a spouse or family member. Elder abuse is grossly underreported due to fears of retaliation and concerns regarding dependency on the individual who is the abuser. In a recent research review, 6% of older couples stated that they had experienced physical violence in their relationship within the last month (Cooper, Selwood, & Livingston, 2007). If abuse is severe or prolonged, it may lead to posttraumatic stress disorder (PTSD). As has been discussed earlier, PTSD may lead to brain impairment, particularly in the area of the hippocampus related to memory.

The treatment for elder abuse is multifaceted and dependent upon whether it is possible to help the older adult remove himself or herself from the situation. Various reasons exist which would cause an individual to remain in an abusive situation (the reader is referred to Walker, 2009).[1] In the older years, fear of retaliation may be significant as well as feelings of inability to live outside of the home for various financial and social reasons.

Once an individual is away from an abusive situation, a neuropsychological evaluation may be needed to determine if any deficits have developed due to the abuse. Dependent upon the strengths and weaknesses of the client, as shown by the assessment profile, appropriate cognitive and/or memory remediation may be begun. Individual therapy conducted by the clinical neuropsychologist or group therapy with other individuals who have suffered from abuse may be beneficial to address feelings of shame, blame, anger, lack of trust, and possible depression and/or anxiety. It must always be kept in mind, however, that cohort effects may lead an individual to deny or discount abuse even when it is clearly evident to external observers. Therefore, therapy may take longer to address the abuse than with younger clients.

SUBSTANCE ABUSE AND DEPENDENCE AND POLYPHARMACY

As one ages, the likelihood of various ailments developing is increased and with an increase in ailments may come medications. Each medication has the potential for side effects.

---

[1] Walker, L. E. A. (2009). *The battered woman syndrome* (3rd ed.). New York: Springer Publishing Company.

In addition, as one ages, metabolism slows and the level of any medication must be evaluated and possibly decreased. As one ages, there is the possibility for increased levels of pain from various ailments, such as arthritis, broken bones, and cancer. Pain medications have many strong side effects and a strong addiction potential. The older adult may already be taking medications and adding painkillers may cause interactions as well as the possibility of an individual becoming addicted.

Another situation exists for older adults that does not exist for any other age group and that is changes in roles and status as one ages and enters retirement. As described earlier, in a society that values youth, losing one's roles or status may cause feelings of depression and anxiety to surface. It is not uncommon for older adults who have not had a chemical use or abuse problem earlier in life to develop one once they become older and/ or retired. In addition, chemical abuse may be exacerbated by the combination of medications which may be used and lowered metabolism. As one's roles in society diminish, one may not be in the public eye as in the past. It is much easier for an older adult to conceal a chemical dependency problem than it is for an individual who must report to work each day or take care of a family and its various needs.

If and when it is determined that an individual has a chemical use or misuse difficulty, a neuropsychological evaluation may be able to delineate the nature and affects of any deficits which have arisen. The first issue to address after evaluation is which drug(s) and/ or medication(s) need to be curtailed and which medications need to be continued for various medical conditions. If alcohol abuse or dependency is not apparent and the individual decides that social drinking is a positive activity, then education regarding the amount of alcohol and its effects should be discussed. In the situation in which there appears to be a serious medication or substance abuse difficulty, the clinical neuropsychologist may need to refer the client to a specific program for detoxification and continued treatment. Once the client is not dependent on a substance, any cognitive deficits which have surfaced may then be addressed in cognitive or memory rehabilitation. Individual or group therapy conducted by the clinical neuropsychologist may also assist to determine the underlying issues which led to the chemical misuse. The clinical neuropsychologist may also help the individual develop healthy coping skills and enlarge his or her social support network.

LATE-ONSET SCHIZOPHRENIA

Research has confirmed that schizophrenia is a neurodevelopmental disorder with abnormalities found in frontal, temporolimbic, dopaminergic, and glutaminergic systems (Keshavan, Kennedy, & Murray, 2004). Neurocognitive deficits are a core stable trait of the schizophrenic illness that account for much of the observed impairment (Green, 1996; Green, Kern, Braff, & Mintz, 2000). Research into schizophrenia suggests deficits exist in sustained and selective attention, learning and memory, executive functioning, and self-awareness.

Late-onset schizophrenia has been a debatable concept within the literature with the traditional age of onset thought to be in the later teens to early 20s. Researchers have found that in most late-onset schizophrenia patients, they had a prodrome or a phase in which symptoms began in middle age (40s–60s). The typical age of onset individuals with schizophrenia and older individuals with schizophrenia are similar in reported family history of schizophrenia, early childhood maladjustment, severity of positive symptoms, presence of gross structural abnormalities on cerebral MRI, overall pattern of neuropsychological deficits, and qualitative responses to neuroleptic medication (Jeste et al., 1997). The differences, which did stand out, were that in late-onset schizophrenia there appears to be more females, less severe negative symptoms, and better neuropsychological performance (Jeste et al., 1995). The schizophrenic symptoms were managed with lower doses of antipsychotic medications, which is extremely helpful due to the changes in metabolism with age. Researchers have speculated that the greater number of females in the late-onset schizophrenia group may be due to the effects of menopause. Particularly, it has been thought that estrogen may work as a protective factor against thought disorders. Researchers have gone so far as suggesting that estrogen replacement therapy be a supplement to antipsychotic medication for postmenopausal women. Even with all of the aforementioned research, there still exists a controversy regarding the occurrence of schizophrenia after age 60.

If late-onset schizophrenia is suspected, a thorough neuropsychological evaluation would determine the strengths and weaknesses which the individual possesses and help in treatment planning. Treatment for late-onset schizophrenia would be similar to early onset beginning with antipsychotic medications. Cognitive and/or memory remediation could follow. Individual and/or group therapy performed by the clinical neuropsychologist could be beneficial to deal with both the positive and negative symptoms of schizophrenia. It is also proven helpful to continue support to help an individual remain on a medication regime. Additionally, family therapy may be beneficial to help the family members understand the actions of the individual with schizophrenia and also help that individual with the aforementioned medication regime.

Returning to the case study of Dr. Solomon Jr., he appears to have been suffering from a mild form of depression. Education and stress management techniques appear to have been very helpful in his treatment. He thought that he may have had an early dementing process but test results have proven otherwise. He has not been a victim of elder abuse or exhibited any of the symptoms of late-onset schizophrenia.

Summary

This chapter begins with a case study of an individual who has passed the normal age for retirement. Being a professional person, he has continued to work but has been noticing some deficits in himself, mainly memory, which he fears may be related to some form of dementing process.

The starting point for the chapter is a discussion regarding normal aging versus disease process. Many individuals often mistake difficulties for what is expected with age. Physical, cognitive, emotional, and social change are all discussed in comparison to disease process.

The ethical and cohort issues which need to be addressed with older adults are discussed in detail. The remainder of the chapter discusses the most common difficulties which occur with the population who are older than the age of 65.

Questions for Further Study

1. Why is it very important to distinguish normal aging from disease process?
2. Individuals who are older now may have different cohort effects than individuals in the baby boomer generation or Generation X or Generation Y. Why is it important in clinical neuropsychology to understand not only cohort effects but also world events which individuals have experienced?
3. It has been said that the changes with retirement may be so great that they trigger latent central nervous system difficulties. How is this possible?

References

Aday, L. A., & Andersen, R. (1974). A framework for the study of access to medical care. *Health Seminars Research, 9*(3), 208–220.

Almeida, O. P., Garrido, G. J., Lautenschlager, N.T., Hulse, G. K., Jamrozik, K. G., & Flicker, L. (2008). Smoking is associated with reduced cortical gray matter density in brain regions associated with incipient Alzheimer disease. *American Journal of Geriatric Psychiatry, 16*, 92–98.

Amenta, F., & Tayebati, S. K. (2008). Pathways of acetylcholine synthesis, transport, and release as targets for treatment of adult-onset cognitive dysfunction. *Current Medicinal Chemistry, 15*(5), 488–498.

American Psychological Association. (2002). *Ethical principles of psychologists and code of conduct.* Washington, DC: Author.

Arana, G. W., Baldessarini, R. J., & Ornsteen, M. (1985). The dexamethasone suppression test for diagnosis and treatment in psychiatry. *Archives of General Psychiatry, 42*, 1193–1204.

Baddeley, A. D. (2007). *Working memory: Thought and actions.* New York: Oxford University Press.

Baltes, P. B. (2003). On the incomplete architecture of human ontogeny: Selection, optimization, and compensation as foundation for development theory. In U. M. Staudinger & U. Lindenberger (Eds.), *Understanding human development* (pp. 17–44). Boston: Kluwer.

Bird, T. D. (2008). Genetic aspects of Alzheimer's disease. *Genetics in Medicine, 10*, 231–239.

Birren, J. E., Woods, A. M., & Williams, M. V. (1980). Behavioral slowing with age: Causes, organization and consequences. In L. W. Poon (Ed.), *Aging in the 1980's: Psychological issues.* Washington, DC: American Psychological Association.

Bondare, W. (2007). Brain and central nervous system. In J. E. Birren (Ed.), *Encyclopedia of gerontology* (2nd ed.). San Diego, CA: Academic Press.

Bopp, K. L., & Verhaeghen, P. (2007). Age-related differences in control processes in verbal and visuospatial working memory: Storage, transformation, supervision and coordination. *The Journal of Gerontology B: Physiological Sciences and Social Sciences, 62*(5), 239–246.

Brown, L. A., McKenzie, N. C., & Doan, J. B. (2005). Age-dependent differences in the attentional demands of obstacle negotiation. *Journal of Gerontology A: Biological Sciences and Medical Sciences, 60*(7), 924–927.

Buscur, B., & Madden, D. J. (2007). Information processing/cognition. In J. E. Birren (Ed.), *Encyclopedia of gerontology* (2nd ed.). San Diego, CA: Academic Press.

Church, D. K., Siegel, M. A., & Fowler, C. A. (1988). *Growing old in America.* Wylie, TX: Information Aids.

Cole, S. L., & Vassar, R. (2009). Linking vascular disorders and Alzheimer's disease: Potential involvement of BACE1. *Neurobiology and Aging, 30*(10), 1535–1544.

Coleman, P. D. (1986). *Regulation of dendritic extent: Human aging brain and Alzheimer's disease.* Paper presented at the meeting of the American Psychological Association, Washington, DC.

Colonna-Romano, G., Bulati, M., Aquino, A., Vitello, S., Lio, D., Candore, G., et al. (2008). B cell immunosenescence in the elderly and in centenarians. *Rejuvenation Research, 11*(2), 433–439.

Cooper, C., Selwood, A., & Livingston, G. (2007). The prevalence of elder abuse and neglect: A systematic review. *Age and Aging, 37*(2), 151–160.

Dickstein, D. L., Kabaso, D., Rocher, A. B., Luebke, J. I., Wearne, S. L., & Hof, P. R. (2007). Changes in the structural complexity of the aged brain. *Aging Cell, 6*(3), 275–284.

Druzhyna, N. M., Wilson, G. L., & LeDoux, S. P. (2008). Mitochondrial DNA repair in aging and disease. *Mechanisms of Aging and Development, 129*(7–8), 383–390.

Eliasieh, K., Liets, L. C., & Chalupa, L. M. (2007). Cellular reorganization in the human retina during normal aging. *Investigative Ophthalmology and Visual Science, 48*(6), 2824–2830.

Erixon-Lindroth, N., Farde, L., Wahlin, T. B., Sovago, J., Hollidin, C., & Backman, L. (2005). The role of the striatal dopamine transporter in cognitive aging. *Psychiatry Researcher, 138*, 1–12.

Finch, C. E., & Seeman, T. E. (1999). Stress theory of aging. In V. L. Bengtson & K. W. Schaie (Eds.), *Handbook of theories of aging.* New York: Springer.

Flemming, S. H. (2001). OSHA at 30: Three decades of progress in occupational safety and health. *Job Safety and Health Quarterly, 12*(3), 23–33.

Frisina, R. D., & Walton, J. P. (2006). Age-related structural and functional changes in the cochlear nucleus. *Hearing Research, 217*, 216–223.

Gazdinsky, S., Kornak, J., Weiner, M. W., & Meyerhoff, D. J. (2008). Body mass index and magnetic resonance markers of brain integrity in adults. *Annals of Neurology, 63*(5), 652–657.

Green, M. F. (1996). What are the functional consequences of neurocognitive deficits in schizophrenia? *American Journal of Psychiatry, 153*, 321–330.

Green, M. F., Kern, R. S., Braff, D. L. & Mintz, J. (2000). Neurocognitive deficits and functional outcome in schizophrenia: Are we measuring the "right stuff"? *Schizophrenia Bulletin, 26*, 119–136.

Gould, E. (2007). How widespread is neurogenesis in mammals? *Nature Reviews: Neuroscience, 8*, 481–488.

Hayflick, L. (1977). The cellular basis for biological aging. In C. E. Finch & L. Hayflick (Eds.), *Handbook of the biology of aging*. New York: Van Nostrand.

Herbert, T.B., & Cohen, S. (1993). Stress and immunity in humans: A metaanalytic review. *Psychosomatic Medicine, 5*, 364–379.

Hoyer, W. J., & Roodin, P. A. (2003). *Adult development and aging* (5th ed.). New York: McGraw-Hill.

Isella, V., Mapelli, C., Morielli, N., Pelati, O., Franceschi, M., & Appollonio, I. M. (2008). Age-related qualitative and quantitative changes in decision-making ability. *Behavioral Neurology, 19*, 59–63.

Jeste, D. (2009). *Report of the DSM-V neurocognitive disorders work group*. Retrieved October 18, 2009, from American Psychiatric Association Web site: http://www.psych.org/MainMenu/Research/DSMIV/DSMV/DSMRevisionActivities/DSM-V-Work-Group-Reports/Neurocognitive-Disorders-Work-Group-Report.aspx

Jeste, D. V., Harris, M. J., Krull, A., Kuck, J., McAdams, L. A., & Heaton, P. (1995). Clinical and nonpsychological characteristics of patients with late-onset schizophrenia. *American Journal of Psychiatry, 152*, 722–730.

Jeste, D. V., Symonds, L. L., Harris, J., Paulsen, J. S., Palmer, B. W., & Heaton, R. K. (1997). Nondementia non praecox dementia praecox? Late-onset schizophrenia. *American Journal of Geriatric Psychiatry, 5*, 302–330.

Keshavan, M., Kennedy, J., & Murray, R. (2004). *Neurodevelopment and schizophrenia*. Cambridge: Cambridge University Press

Kessels, R. P., Bockhorst, S. T., & Postma, A. (2005). The contribution of implicit and explicit memory to the effects of errorless learning: A comparison between younger and older adults. *Journal of the International Neuropsychological Society, 11*, 144–151.

Kolb, B., & Wishaw, I. (2009). *Fundamentals of human neuropsychology* (6th ed.). New York: Worth.

Kostka, T., & Praczko, K. (2007). Interrelationship between physical activity, symptomology of upper respiratory tract infections, and depression in elderly people. *Gerontology, 53*, 1876–193.

Kumar, R., & Burns, E. A. (2008). Age-related changes in immunity: Implications for vaccine responsiveness. *Expert Review of Vaccines, 7*, 467–479.

Larbi, A., Franceschi, C., Mazzatti, D., Solana, R., Wikby, A., & Pawelec, G. (2008). Aging of the immune system as a prognostic factor for human longevity. *Physiology, 23*, 64–74.

Laurent, G., Solari, F., Mateescu, B., Karaca, M., Castel, J., Bourachot, B., et al. (2008). Oxidative stress contributes to aging by enhancing pancreatic angiogenesis and insulin signaling. *Cell Metabolism, 7*(2), 113–124.

Lee, H. C., & Wei, Y. H. (2007). Oxidative stress, mitochondrial DNA mutation, and apoptosis in aging. *Experimental Biology and Medicine, 232*, 592–606.

Li, S. C., Lindenberger, U., Hommel, B., Aschersleboen, G., Prinz, W., & Baltes, P. B. (2004). Transformations in the couplings among intellectual abilities and constructed cognitive processes across the lifespan. *Psychological Sciences, 15*, 155–163.

Libert, S., Cohen, D., & Guarente, L. (2008). Neurogenesis directed by Sirt 1. *Nature: Cell Biology, 10*, 373–374.

Lovden, M., & Linderberger, U. (2007). Intelligence. In J. E. Birren (Ed.), *Encyclopedia of gerontology* (2nd ed.). San Diego, CA: Academic Press.

Luchsinger, J. A. (2008). Adiposty, hyperinsulinemia, diabetes and Alzheimer's disease: An epidemiological perspective. *European Journal of Pharmacology, 585*(1), 119–129.

Lynn-Davies, P. (1977). Influence of age on respiratory system. *Geriatrics, 32*, 57–60.

Maciocas, J. B., & Crognale, M. A. (2004). Cognitive and attentional changes with age: Evidence from attentional blink deficits. *Experimental Aging Research, 29*, 137–153.

Magri, F., Cravello, L., Sarra, S., Cinchetti, W., Salmoiraghi, F., Micale, G., et al. (2006). Stress and dementia.: The role of the hypothalmic-pituitary-adrenal axis. *Aging: Clinical and experimental research, 18*, 167–170.

Middleton, I. E., Kirkland, S. A., Maxwel, C. J., Hogan, D. B., & Rockwood, K. (2007). Exercise: A potential contributing factor to the relationship between folate and dementia. *Journal of the American Geriatric Society, 55*, 1095–1098.

National Center for Health Statistics. (2006). *United States health.* Atlanta: Centers for Disease Control and Prevention.

National Center for Health Statistics. (2008). *U.S. mortality rate drops sharply in 2006, latest data shows.* Atlanta: Centers for Disease Control and Prevention.

Pardo, J. R., Pardo, J. V., Lee, J. T., Sheikh, S. A., Surerus-Johnson, C., Shah, H., Munch, K. R., et al. (2007). When the brain grows old: Decline in anterior cingulate and medial prefrontal function with normal aging. *Neuroimage, 35*, 1231–1237.

Parmalec, P. A. (2007). Depression. In J. F. Birren (Ed.), *Encyclopedia of gerontology.* San Diego, CA: Academic Press.

Pedersen, B. K., Ostrowski, T. K., Rohde, T., & Bruunsgaard, H. (1998). Nutrition, exercise and the immune system. *Proceedings of the Nutrition Society, 57*, 43–47.

Peterson, R. C., & Negash, S. (2008). Mild cognitive impairment: An overview. *CNS Spectrum, 13*, 14–23.

Pinquart, M., & Sorensen, S. (2006). Gender differences in caregiver stressors, social-resources, and health: An updated meta-analysis. *Journals of Gerontology B: Psychological Sciences and Social Sciences, 61*, 33–45.

Rice, D. P., & Fineman, N. (2004). Economic implications of increased longevity in the United States. *Annual Review of Public Health, 25*, 457–473.

Roberts, J. B., & Rosenberg, I. (2006). Nutrition and aging: Changes in the regulation of energy metabolism with aging. *Physiology Reveiw, 86*, 651–667.

Rossi, S., Miniussi, C., Pasqualetti, P., Babilioni, C., Rossini, P. M., & Capppa, S. F. (2004). Age-related functional changes of prefrontal cortex in long term memory: A repetitive transcranial magnetic stimulation study. *Journal of Neuroscience, 24*, 7939–7944.

Rossit, S., & Harvey, M. (2008). Age related differences in corrected and inhibited pointing movements. *Experimental Brain Research, 185*, 1–10.

Ruckenhauser, G., Yazdani, F., & Ravaglia, G. (2007). Suicide in old age: Illness or autonomous decision of the will? *Archives of Gerontology and Geriatrics, 44*, 5355–5358.

Rush, A. S., Giles, D. E., Schlesser, M. A., Orsulak, P. J., Parker, C. R., Jr., Weissenburger, J. E., et al. (1996). The dexamethasone suppression test in patients with mood disorders. *Journal of Clinical Psychiatry, 57*(10), 470–484.

Rypma, B., Eldreth, D. H., & Rebbechi, A. (2007). Age-related differences in activation-performance relations in delayed-response tasks: A multiple component analysis. *Cortex, 43*, 65–76.

Sando, S. B., Melquist, S., Cannon, A., Hutton, M. L., Sletvold, O., Saltvedt, I., et al. (2008). APOE epsilon4 lowers age at onset and is a high risk factor for Alzheimer's disease; a case-control study from central Norway. *BMC Neurology, 8*, 9.

Schatzberg, A. F., Rothschild, A. J., & Stahl, J. B. (1983). The dexamethasone suppression test: Identification of subtypes of depression. *American Journal of Psychiatry, 140*, 88–91.

Schiffman, S. S. (2007). Smell and taste. In J. E. Birren (Ed.), *Encyclopedia of gerontology* (2nd ed.). San Diego, CA: Academic Press.

Scialfa, C. T., & Kline, D. W. (2007). Vision. In J. E. Birren (Ed.), *Encyclopedia of gerontology* (2nd ed.). San Diego, CA: Academic Press.

Shay, J. W., & Wright, W. E. (2007). Hallmarks of telomers in aging research. *Journal of pathology, 211*, 114–123.

Siedlecki, K. L. (2007). Investigating the structure and age invariance of episodic memory across the adult life span. *Psychology and Aging, 22*, 251–268.

Smith, B. (2007). Memory. In J. E. Birren (Ed.), *Encyclopedia of gerontology.* San Diego, CA: Academic Press.

Stutts, J. C. (2007). Driving behavior. In J. E. Birren (Ed.), *Encyclopedia of gerontology* (2nd ed.). San Diego, CA: Academic Press.

United States Census Bureau. (2008). Projections of the population by selected age groups and sex for the United States: 2010 to 2050 (U.S. Population Projections). *National population projections released 2008 (based on census 2000).* Retrieved September 27, 2009, from http://www. census.gov/population/www/projections/summarytables.html

Vasudevaraju, P., Bharathi, S., Garruto, R. M., Sambamurti, K., & Rao, K. S. (2008). Role of DNA dynamics in Alzheimer's disease. *Brain Research Reviews, 58*(1), 136–148.

Verret, L., Trouche, S., Zerwas, M., & Rampon, C. (2007). Hippocampal neurogenesis during normal and pathological aging. *Psychoneuroimunology, 32,* 526–530.

Walker, L. E. A. (2009). *The battered woman syndrome* (3rd ed.). New York: Springer Publishing Company.

The Future of Clinical Neuropsychology

18

Learning Objectives

After reading this chapter, the student should be able to understand:
- The issues that relate to the future of education and training in clinical neuropsychology
- The upcoming changes to the health care system and access to health care as they relate to neuropsychology
- How the changing demographics of the population affect health care
- How our knowledge of the functioning of the central nervous system continues to change
- The field of neuropsychology and how it is affected by the debate regarding prescription privileges, forensics, and multicultural neuropsychology

Case Vignette

Zoe is a 20-year-old ex-college student and current guardian to her five younger siblings. She was referred to the clinical neuropsychologist for two purposes. The first was an evaluation of her own strengths and weaknesses after being diagnosed with posttraumatic stress disorder (PTSD) by their family physician. He was very concerned that she may have suffered some permanent structural brain deficits due to the severe stress she is currently under. The family physician was very aware of the neuropsychological ramifications of PTSD due to the fact that he has been treating numerous veterans who have served in Iraq and Afghanistan. The second reason for the referral to the clinical neuropsychologist was for information regarding treatment options for her younger sister who sustained a closed head injury.

Historically, Zoe is the oldest child of her biological parents. She has five younger siblings: Sharon (19), David (18), Emily (15), Rose (13), and Dawn (8). The family is Caucasian and of upper-middle class background residing in a rural community, 80 miles from the closest metropolitan area. Zoe's father worked as the vice president of an insurance company and her mother worked part-time as a registered nurse. The family was very close even though many of the children had gone through minor adolescent issues of rebellion. Zoe, being the oldest, was the child who was often used as an example by her parents for the others to emulate. Being the comparison standard often made Zoe feel somewhat pressured to set a good example and she tried to pave the way through elementary school, secondary school, and college. Following in Zoe's footsteps, Sharon and David are both attending private colleges.

Zoe's interests in college had been shaped by the feelings she had that she should be the role model for the other children. Therefore, she had chosen a management major, similar to her father, with a Spanish minor for the added bonus of employability. She stated that she had not ever given a thought as to what her own interests were because she felt the need to appear competent and a good role model.

Clearly not following in her sister's footsteps, Sharon decided that she would major in theater arts. Their parents voiced their concerns regarding eventual employment but Sharon decided not to take their advice. David has also chosen his own path and enrolled in a nursing program. He felt that the work his mother had done was very influential on him and wanted to emulate her. The main concern that the parents had was that nursing, until recently, had been a predominately female profession. The younger children have not voiced concern about future issues and are more involved with age-appropriate activities. Emily is very interested in spending time with her boyfriend and Rose spends a fair amount of time at the mall with her girlfriends watching boys. Dawn, being the youngest, does not have many interests in common with her siblings and is currently very interested in her second grade class's project on dinosaurs.

The incident which caused the stress on Zoe and head injury for Dawn happened 8 months ago. Zoe was in the fall semester of her junior year in college. Her family had decided to take a trip to Disney World during the fall break. Zoe did not attend nor did Sharon or Dave due to college commitments. Each of the three younger children was allowed one friend to take with them. The family decided that driving would save money and allow them to see the countryside. The parents took turns driving and Emily even drove for a short period of time with her learner's permit. They began the trip early in the morning and planned to stop only for meals and exciting attractions. After midnight on the first day of the trip, Zoe's mother was driving the van and, according to other individuals interviewed by a highway patrol officer, appeared to be weaving. Before the officer could stop her and analyze the situation, the van bolted into the oncoming traffic. As far as the officer can remember, the van hit a truck head on as other vehicles swerved to avoid further mishaps. Zoe's parents were killed instantly as was Rose's friend and the driver of the truck. The others survived with broken bones, lacerations, and Dawn received a closed head injury.

Zoe clearly remembers the call she received early in the morning from her uncle describing what had happened and that he was on his way to get her. She remembers him saying something about an adult family member having to sign papers and identify the bodies. Zoe remembers that she felt a complete sense of unreality as she quickly packed her clothes and waited for her uncle. On the trip to the town where the accident occurred, she learned more regarding the circumstances. She was also notified that her aunt had gone to retrieve Sharon and David from their respective schools.

At the morgue Zoe made the grim identifications and signed the necessary papers. Her uncle had already arranged to have the bodies transported home for funeral preparations. The parents of the child who was killed were also there and extremely distraught. Zoe stated that it appeared as if they blamed her for the circumstances.

Once the funerals were completed, the weight of the changes to their lives became clear to Zoe. As the oldest, she became the person her siblings turned to for guidance and comfort. Sharon and David returned to their respective colleges to escape the situation. However, financial issues were paramount and Zoe did not know what to do or say to her siblings. With the aid of her aunt and uncle, she was able to understand her parents financial circumstances. There was enough money currently to pay the mortgage, monthly bills and support Sharon and David in college. Zoe, however, decided that the way to keep the family intact was for her to drop out of college. She found herself suddenly being the parent of five children, two in college, two in adolescence, and one with a head injury.

Zoe did the best she could for the first several months trying to help everyone grieve through the tragedy and at the same time go on with their lives. She also did not feel that she could let down her guard and grieve or express the anger and resentment she was beginning to feel regarding the incredible changes in her life.

The way that Zoe appeared to be handling everything was to not express emotions, which then surfaced as physical symptoms. After the most recent visit to the family physician, she scheduled the appointment with the clinical neuropsychologist. The aforementioned information was gathered through the intake interview which caused her to express a myriad of emotions. Neuropsychological testing of Zoe revealed a young woman with higher than average intellectual abilities. Testing also revealed significant short-term memory deficits, concentration, and attention issues with additional personality testing showing the beginnings of difficulties with anxiety and depression.

The clinical neuropsychologist discussed these findings with Zoe and suggested the following treatment plan. The change from college student to full-time parent may be too overwhelming and the assistance of other family members would be helpful. Knowing that her aunt and uncle were overwhelmed with their own family, the clinical psychologists suggested family therapy including all of the siblings. The goal of family therapy would be for all to voice their issues and concerns and to divide some of the responsibilities within the family. Individual therapy was suggested to allow Zoe to express her resentments and other feelings in a safe place, which could help alleviate her stress level. A trial of memory retraining was suggested to help alleviate some of the day-to-day difficulties she has been experiencing. A psychiatric referral was also suggested to determine whether medication would be appropriate for her anxiety and depressive symptoms. The clinical neuropsychologist also suggested that Zoe begin taking college classes so that she have some semblance to her previous life. Zoe responded positively to all of the suggestions made by the clinical neuropsychologist. The clinical neuropsychologist also discussed the difficulties to expect with her younger sister and how she could help or intervene and the services she could obtain for her sister.

This case was included in the last chapter as a means to begin discussion of many topics which affect the future of the field of clinical neuropsychology. The client was thrust into a very stressful situation, which previously was thought to be uncommon for her age. However, as time passes, more and more college-age individuals are experiencing stressful situations, such as warfare and natural disasters, which cause their lives to change dramatically. Zoe also had little information regarding how to deal with the situation and few resources. The case study relates to all of the topics covered thus far in the text and to areas for further study, which will be discussed next.

Introduction

A concluding chapter is designed to draw together what has been covered in a text thus far and to point toward future issues. Thus far, the text has covered an historical framework of brain science, an overview of central nervous system structures and functioning, and the etiology and symptomology of acquired versus degenerative disorders. When the author teaches a course in applied clinical neuropsychology, the aforementioned topics become the first unit of material. The next set of chapters focuses on ethical and practice issues, interviewing, the basics of psychometrics, and the various forms of testing and evaluation including intellectual assessment, memory assessment, and neuropsychological test batteries. These topics become the second unit of material. The next section of the text and the third section of the course include diagnosis, treatment planning, and all of the various forms of treatment available for central nervous system difficulties: cognitive and memory rehabilitation, individual therapy, family therapy, and medication. The final unit addresses patient populations which are outside of the normal 18–65 years of age on which most tests have been normed. Children and elders also have a plethora of issues which other age groups do not encounter. The concluding chapter addresses current issues and future directions and completes the four units of course material. The discussion of how the material is related to course construction and application is a suggestion and not a crucial way to use the material in the text.

Relating back to the case study, Zoe has difficulties with her central nervous system which could be described as acquired. She has been diagnosed with PTSD and provisionally with anxiety and depression. She and the clinical neuropsychologist developed a treatment plan to work toward alleviating these difficulties with a combination of individual and family therapy, memory retraining, and pharmacological therapy. Educational information was given to her regarding services for her sibling and available financial resources.

The Future of Education and Training in Clinical Neuropsychology

As had been stressed throughout the text, the number of individuals across the life span who suffer from central nervous system disorders and difficulties continues to increase. Medical technology continues to expand and allow many individuals to live and live well, whereas in the past they may not have survived. Advanced diagnostic techniques have also made it possible for difficulties to be diagnosed earlier and therefore treatment to begin sooner. In addition, the general populace has become more educated regarding central nervous system difficulties and willing to seek treatment. The general populace has also assumed more of an advocacy role when a family member, friend, or loved one develops a difficulty. Finally, the sheer number of individuals with particular ailments appears to have increased. However, figures are not always accurate regarding each particular ailment due to the fact that many studies group patients with various diagnoses together. Examples of this are studies which include individuals with head injury or individuals with dementia as subjects without further explaining the type or severity of head trauma or dementia.

With this in mind, it is clear that there is a need for clinical neuropsychologists who have been adequately trained and certified or licensed to practice with patients with various central nervous system difficulties. As was discussed earlier in the text, the majority of clinical neuropsychologists received their graduate education within APA accredited clinical psychology programs. These programs had specialty tracks or subprograms in clinical neuropsychology. At the present time, it is still quite likely that professionals will complete their training in this manner. It is also likely that most individual's predoctoral internships will include clinical neuropsychology and that a large number of individuals will complete a postdoctoral program or residency in clinical neuropsychology. As was discussed earlier in the text, due to the variability in education between clinical neuropsychologists, APA Division 40, the National Academy of Neuropsychology, the Board of Clinical Neuropsychology, and the Association of Postdoctoral Programs in Clinical Neuropsychology sponsored a meeting in 1997, termed the Houston Conference, to recommend a model for training for the independent practice of clinical neuropsychology (Boake, 2008). The model which was accepted at this conference includes course work and practical experience at the doctoral and postdoctoral levels. The first stage of training was development of competence in general professional psychology at the doctoral and internship level. The second stage of training was in brain–behavior knowledge and clinical neuropsychology skills to be developed at the doctoral, internship, and postdoctoral levels. A 2-year postdoctoral residency or fellowship was included which was designed to be similar to residency training in medicine. Continuing education units (CEUs) in the area of clinical neuropsychology were included due to the continual changes within the field (Hannay et al., 1988). Many states require completion of a certain number of CEUs when clinical neuropsychologists renew their licenses to practice. As of 2009, seven states and most Canadian provinces lack mandated CEUs (Neimeyer, Taylor, & Wear, 2009). Subsequent to this training, many individuals, after working as a clinical neuropsychologist and demonstrating their skills and abilities, apply for and are granted the status of American Board of Professional Psychology (ABPP) certification in clinical neuropsychology. To be granted ABPP status, one must demonstrate appropriate credentials, present a work sample representative of one's competency, and pass an oral examination. The American Board of Clinical Neuropsychology (ABCN) offers ABCN certification after passing a written examination, peer review of a work sample, and an oral examination.

Another manner in which individuals may complete their graduate education is through graduate programs in neuropsychology. Many of these programs are housed within departments of psychology and contain course work in both the experimental component and the clinical component of neuropsychology. Often, however, these programs are geared more to research than to clinical practice in neuropsychology.

A growing area of graduate education is within the domain of neuroscience. Neuroscience is often defined as the multidisciplinary study of the brain and hence, neuroscience programs are not always housed within psychology departments. Many of the programs are within biology or physiology programs or medical schools. Programs in neuroscience are often those which train researchers in various areas of brain functioning. The reader is referred to Association of Neuroscience Departments and Programs Web site (http://www.andp.org/indexnew2b.asp) for a list of current programs.

In the recent past, the economy of the United States and the world at large, has taken a downturn. As a result of a declining economy, there has been less funding available for undergraduate and graduate programs. While it can generally be said that graduate education may be less expensive than undergraduate education due to the fact that the majority of programs are at public universities, an individual's education must be financed in some manner. As in any time of financial crisis, individuals may need to be creative in finding financial resources for their education.

A program which pays for undergraduate education in return for a specified number of years service to one's country is the U.S. Armed Forces Reserve Officer Training Corps (ROTC). The same ROTC program will continue to fund an individual's graduate education for a further time commitment. The time commitment varies dependent upon whether the individual has an active duty assignment or is in various other capacities. If the reader is interested in this program, it is suggested that he or she visit with a local armed forces recruiter or the Military Health System Web site (http://www.health.mil/Education_And_Training/Graduate_and_Continuing_Education.aspx).

A specific government program is designed to place professionals in underserved rural areas. The goal of the program is to place individuals from various professions such as physicians, clinical neuropsychologists, and social workers in underserved rural areas which often have difficulties recruiting such professionals. With the same commitment to a number of years of service in a rural area, the National Health Service Corps (NHSC) Loan Repayment Program will finance an individual's graduate education (http://nhsc.hrsa.gov/loanrepayment/).

Managed care organizations, particularly those which include hospitals, often finance advanced education for employees in specialty areas. However, it is unlikely that an entire graduate education could be financed in this manner and more likely that the aforementioned CEUs would be financed.

Another source of finances for advanced graduate education is similar to financial aid at the undergraduate level. Some graduate programs provide financial aid similar to undergraduate schools whereas others may not, and the reader is advised to carefully evaluate the information he or she receives from each school. Many states have grants or merit scholarships available. Finally, loans through government programs or financial institutions are available.

Finally, on March 23, 2010, President Obama signed into law the Patient Protection and Affordable Care Act (PPACA) or Public Law No. 111–148, often referred to as the Health Care Reform Act. On March 30, 2010, he signed the Health Care and Education Reconciliation Act of 2010, Public Law No. 111–152. The aim of Public Law No. 111–152 is twofold. The first component is the designation of $10 million dollars set aside for doctoral, postdoctoral, and internships in professional psychology. The second component is the establishment of a loan repayment program for psychologists in pediatric care, expansion of eligibility to the program to psychologists, psychology programs, and psychology schools for geriatric education and training programs (APA, 2010). It has not been made clear how these provisions will be put into place at this time. However, they are very favorable for the education of clinical neuropsychologists in furthering their education, particularly with the underserved populations of children and elderly.

Returning to our case study, it is clear that Zoe and her family need the services of a competent clinical neuropsychologist. It is also an issue for her that in her community, this may be difficult. Eighty miles is not an extremely long drive for services but considering the family circumstances and stress level of Zoe, it would be better to have services available in her community. Due to the lack of services in rural areas, many metropolitan hospitals require professionals to spend 1 day per week in rural satellite clinics. At the time of this writing, Zoe's clinical neuropsychologist had been serving her and her siblings through their primary care doctor's clinic. The clinical neuropsychologist was able to schedule appointments at the satellite clinic twice per month. The change in locale became very helpful for Zoe and her family; however, all appointments must match the scheduled time when the professional was in their community which also became difficult at times.

Changes in the Health Care System and Access to Health Care

The health care system within the United States, similar to other countries, is often driven by politics. Most individuals who have responded to large-scale media surveys state that the health care system is in need of a thorough overhaul but vary as to the manner in which this should be accomplished. In a 2007 online poll, the 14th Commonwealth Fund's *Modern Healthcare* survey argued for the need for change. The survey conducted by Harris Interactive on behalf of the Commonwealth Fund (2007) sampled 211 opinion leaders in health policy and innovations in health care delivery. A large majority of health care opinion leaders stated that strengthening primary care, encouraging care coordination and the management of care transitions, and promoting care management of complex patients were important or very important.

In general, politicians from both the conservative and liberal positions have proposed strategies for changing the system. Issues range from a reform of the health insurance system to a reform of the delivery of services to reform of how one obtains insurance to obtain services. Lobbyists from various interests such as insurance companies, pharmaceutical companies, and various other constituencies have also been vocal at the federal level.

Another issue which falls within the area of health care reform is the debate regarding tort reform. Proposed changes in this area may make it more difficult for an individual to file a claim for medical malpractice. In addition, changes in laws may cap the amount of money which may be paid in damages from medical malpractice. Weiss (2009), quoting an analysis by the Congressional Budget Office (CBO; 2008), reports that states that have imposed caps on noneconomic damages have had lower malpractice premiums, greater access to high-risk specialty care for patients, and cost savings due to decreased "defensive medicine." As outlined in the 2008 CBO report, the reforms which are usually sought in the tort system usually are one of two types. The first area is a cap on the amount of money awarded for noneconomic damages, and the figure used in many states where this already exists is $250,000. The second reform is aimed at changing the principle of joint-and-several liability to a "fair-share" rule which would limit the liability of each individual defendant to his or her percentage share of responsibility for the injury. The American Medical Association (2010) and many Republican lawmakers suggest that malpractice reform should be a major component of any health care legislation (Grassley, 2009). The counter argument made by Democrats and many trial lawyers is that malpractice reform is a scapegoat and a way to ignore the more serious issues which plague the health care and health care delivery system (American Association for Justice on Medical Negligence, 2009). However, it is an open question whether the money saved from malpractice insurance is passed on to the consumer.

At the time of this writing, President Obama had recently signed into law the Health Care Reform Bill. The actual bill is more than 2,000 pages and includes many stipulations. In essence, 32 million Americans who were previously uninsured will now be able to have insurance. It is a multifaceted law with some components becoming effective immediately and some not until 2014. Not included within the bill was tort reform. For purposes of this text, the current and future general changes will be summarized as well as issues particular to clinical neuropsychology.

Six months from the day the bill was signed into law (September 23, 2010), insurers will no longer be able to exclude children with preexisting conditions from being covered by their family insurance policy. Also, adults who have preexisting conditions and have been uninsured for 6 months will be eligible for insurance from a pool, and subsidies will be available to help them afford the premiums. Another area which will come into effect immediately is for senior citizens relying on Medicare and have already spent $2,700 on drugs. Coverage stops until that person has spent $6,154 on drugs; however, individuals will receive $250 from the government to help with the "doughnut hole" or time and financial interval when their medications are not subsidized.

Children and individuals up to age 26 will be able to remain on their parents insurance as of the signing of the bill. Six months after the bill goes into effect "qualified health plans" must provide, at no additional cost, immunizations, and all other preventive health services for infants, children, and adolescents.

The longer term goal of the Health Care Reform Bill is to provide health insurance to 32 million uninsured people. For those individuals who already have health insurance through their employer, the military or via veterans benefits, there should be few changes. For uninsured individuals, an exchange program that will allow individuals to shop for the least expensive insurance similar to the way in which a larger company may insure a group of workers. None of these changes will go into effect until 2014 but when they do, individuals who are not insured will receive a tax penalty. The gap in the time from signing until 2014 is to allow the insurance and health care industries to ready themselves for the inevitable influx of new patients. The gains will be in a greater number of clients who will purchase insurance and avail themselves of the health care system. The detriments for the insurance industry will be the necessity to cover individuals with potentially serious difficulties and their extensive use of the health care facilities.

Charges which impact psychology and particularly clinical neuropsychology have already been alluded to in that the 32 million uninsured individuals will now be able to be insured. Among these individuals are invariably those who have preexisting central nervous system difficulties and find it difficult to be insured. Changes in the Medicare program will also benefit patients with central nervous system difficulties.

The overall change in philosophical focus from treatment to prevention is crucial for central nervous system difficulties. Many of the disorders or difficulties discussed within this text could have been identified and treated earlier if screening measures had been in place. This statement relates again to the philosophical change from treatment to prevention or early intervention.

One of the major changes with health care reform for professionals is that psychological services are now at parity with medical/surgical services. This statement implies that insurance providers, if they include mental health and/or chemical dependency treatment, must provide reimbursement rates comparable to coverage for medical problems. As has been discussed throughout the text, central nervous system difficulties often coexist with other psychiatric and/or chemical dependency issues. Psychological and/or chemical dependency issues may have been premorbid conditions or they may have occurred in response to central nervous system difficulty as a reaction to the difficulty or changes the difficulty causes in one's life. Chemical use or misuse may be a result of use as a coping mechanism, stress reliever, or for self-medication in the absence of psychiatric medication.

Another area that is particularly helpful for clinical neuropsychologists working with individuals with central nervous system difficulties is the creation of an infrastructure to support comparative effectiveness research to enhance treatment decisions. This implies that competitive grants for funding to evaluate treatments for various disorders should come to fruition. This is particularly salient in a declining economy where institutions have had little funding for this type of research in the past few years.

Returning to our case study, the changes in the health care system will be very helpful for Zoe and her siblings. Both Zoe and her youngest sibling have preexisting conditions and the changes will ensure that they will receive health care. Also important for them is the focus on prevention and the provision for immunizations for all of the children. If their parents had lived, it would have been very advantageous to have all of the children remain on their health plan until the age of 26. However, because Zoe has become the legal guardian of her siblings, it may be possible for them all to remain on the plan originally purchased by her parents. At the time of the writing, that option had not been determined.

The Changing Demographics of the Population

As was discussed earlier, the number of individuals with various central nervous system difficulties or disorders continues to increase. This is due to not only to actual increases in the number of individuals with the aforementioned difficulties but also earlier detection through general education and advanced technology. Added to the increases in the number of central nervous system survivors is a growing number of individuals who have sustained head trauma due to warfare in Iraq and Afghanistan. It has been estimated that 10–20% of the troops have sustained some form of traumatic brain injury (TBI) due to the type of munitions utilized, particularly improvised explosive devices (IEDs), literally homemade bombs. In addition, the military vehicles in which soldiers have been transported have not adequately protected the troops from the supersonic shockwaves produced by the IED explosions.

Another growing group of individuals have received a diagnosis of PTSD due to various forms of natural disasters. At the time of this writing, it is 4 years subsequent to Hurricane Katrina's devastation on the southern coast of the United States. Many residents were left without any belongings, food, or shelter, and often were separated from family members and their pets. Many survivors claim to have been treated poorly by the government in terms of rescue and relief efforts.

The international crisis at the time of this writing has been the January 12, 2010 earthquake in the very poor country of Haiti. Following this has been an international outpouring of relief which has been delayed getting to the populace. Also of concern has been the issue of the spread of disease through unsafe water and close contact within communities. In addition is the issue regarding whether children have been removed from the area for their safety or have been taken against their will for potentially illegal adoption. Following the devastation in Haiti, a massive 8.8 earthquake hit the coastal area of southern Chile on February 28, 2010. Survivors are also without supplies even though international efforts also have been extensive. Additionally, a 7.1 earthquake hit China on April 14, 2010. At the time of this writing, the death toll has been estimated at 1,700 individuals with rescue crew still attempting to find survivors. Finally, at the time of this writing it has been over 100 days since the explosion of the British Petroleum oil rig in the Gulf of Mexico leaving several dead and devastation in its wake. It may be assumed that PTSD will be diagnosed heavily in this aftermath.

In each of these incidents, as has been discussed earlier, PTSD may lead to permanent structural brain impairment. Lack of food and water may also lead to serious and possibly permanent difficulties. The spread of various diseases may also impact central nervous system functioning.

In addition to the increase in the number of individuals with various central nervous system difficulties, there has been an overall increase in the population at the two extremes of the age spectrum who use the bulk of medical services. The rate of births which has remained steady for the past 45 years is now increasing due to an increase in birth rate among many ethnic groups within the United States. The Hispanic population has grown at the rate of 4%, which is greater than any other racial group on the census form (U.S. Census Bureau, 2005). In addition, individuals who are recent immigrants to the United States have evidenced a population increase (Day, 2008).

On the opposite end of the age spectrum, and discussed earlier, is the increase in the number of elderly individuals within both the young–old and old–old categories. In 2006, 37 million Americans or approximately 12% of the population were 65 years and older and 5.5 million were 85 years and older (Administration on Aging, 2008). As the baby boomers begin to turn 65 in 2011, it is predicted that the number of older people in the United States is likely to be twice as large in 2030 than in 2000 (U.S. Census Bureau, 2005). Various medical and lifestyle issues have contributed to this increase. A large increase in this population is projected as the baby boomer generation, those born between 1946 and 1964, begin to enter retirement years. It is projected that the baby boomer generation will tax heavily the health care system due to sheer numbers. However, the baby boomers have been known for engaging in preventive health care throughout life and therefore, may utilize the health care system at a later age than those individuals who are presently elderly. However, an added difficulty is that at the time of the increase in older adults, there is also a projected increase in retirement of health care providers (U.S. Department of Health and Human Services, 2003). In addition, there appears to be a decline in the number of 18–30 year olds who may be recruited into health care fields (U.S. Department of Health and Human Services, 2003).

Another change in demographics affects the potential caregivers for older adults who throughout time have been women (Pinquart & Sorenson, 2006). On average, men die 7–8 years before women (Kinsella & Velkoff, 2001). Therefore, as an aging issue, women may be caring for adult children and for frail mothers (Grundy & Henretta, 2006).

Across the world, the population is aging even faster than within the United States with Europe encompassing the 30 countries who have the oldest populations (United Nations Department of Economic and Social Affairs, Population Division, 2007). Japan has the oldest population with 27.9% of its citizens older than 60 years of age.

The individuals within our case study fall within the younger age of the population with the youngest within one of the age groups utilizing the majority of health care services. Zoe and possibly her siblings are also part of the growing number of survivors of traumatic events. These individuals will also stretch an already overloaded health care system. In addition, Zoe and her siblings are very young but her primary doctor and the clinical neuropsychologist are baby boomers and may retire before they can be replaced or the family no longer requires services.

Changes in Our Knowledge of the Functioning of the Central Nervous System

Discussed throughout this text has been the speed at which our knowledge is increasing regarding the central nervous system. Although the knowledge base has increased rapidly, there are still many issues or questions which have not been answered. Paramount among these issues is the extent to which the brain and particularly the neurons are able to regenerate. It has been shown that cells within the peripheral nervous system are able to be replaced but the same has not been shown with neurons within the central nervous system. It was always thought that loss of neurons was irreversible in the adult human brain because dying neurons could not be replaced. Generation of new neurons was thought to occur during a specific developmental period. However, the question is open and researchers, particularly those experimenting with neurons in other animals, are beginning to see the possibility of regeneration.

Eriksson et al. (1998) began their work investigating neurogenesis in the adult human hippocampus. Many, if not all studies, subsequent to that time refer back to this research as a comparison. The reason for this is that Eriksson and colleagues had the unique opportunity to study patients who received bromodeoxyuridine (BrdU) for tumor staging purposes within a treatment study and some patients also consented to have their brains examined after their death. This study gave Erikkson's group the opportunity to study and demonstrate adult neurogenesis in postmortem tissue samples from the hippocampus and subventricular zone of the caudate nucleus. Since the time of the Eriksson et al. study, many other studies have demonstrated neurogenesis in animals and extrapolated it to humans. Knoth et al. (2010) mapped features associated with adult neurogenesis in the hippocampal area in rodents throughout the life span. Again, while not being able to say conclusively that this occurs in humans, it has provided information regarding the presence of markers, which eventually may be translated into knowledge regarding the adult human brain.

Research focusing on both animals and humans has shown the presence of neurogenesis in the hippocampus and dentate gyrus. Further research has begun to show the development of neurogenesis when an individual experiences stroke, epilepsy, or Alzheimer's disease (Jin et al., 2004, 2006). These studies demonstrate that new neurons from the subgranular zone of the dentate gyrus and the subventricular zone of the lateral ventricle migrate to the site of central nervous system injury to replace cells which have died (Mulchandani, 2010). The aim of the research is not only to discover if and under what type of circumstances the brain engages in neurogenesis but also to then begin to use the findings in order to work toward more advanced rehabilitation techniques or treatments.

Another area which is changing dramatically is the neuroimaging of TBI and PTSD (Van Boven et al., 2009). The changes in technology have been funded by government grants in order to better treat survivors of warfare in Iraq and Afghanistan. However, the technology may be utilized in other circumstances for biomarkers of brain structure, function, and metabolism.

Symmetry of brain structures is another area where research has recently focused. The issue here is whether an ability once thought to be predominantly localized within one hemisphere could be replaced by functioning of the opposite hemisphere.

Advances in the understanding of brain structures and functioning relate to both Zoe's difficulties with PTSD and her younger sister's TBI. New imaging techniques which show the actual structural changes are extremely helpful. They are then able to be followed by neuropsychological testing which will delineate behavioral strengths and weaknesses. In addition, the ability of the brain to engage in neurogenesis in the human is a fantastic concept and stem cell use to replace damaged neurons for both Zoe and her sister may be exceptionally helpful.

Future of Prescription Privileges and the Use of Medications With Central Nervous System Difficulties

As was discussed earlier within the text, there remains a shortage of prescribers of psychotropic medications. The APA in 1995 took a stand that with advanced training, clinical psychologists should be allowed to prescribe these particular types of medications. This includes clinical neuropsychologists who are working with patients who have central nervous system difficulties. The most recent state to take prescription privileges to its legislature is Oregon in which it passed. However, at the time of this writing, the governor of Oregon vetoed the bill. New Mexico, Louisiana, the U.S. military, and Guam allow prescription privileges for psychologists at the time of this writing.

A controversy has developed in Louisiana regarding which licensing board should have jurisdiction over prescribing psychologists—the Board of Psychology or the Medical Board. At the time of this writing, medical psychologists are required to obtain a license from the Louisiana State Board of Medical Examiners (LSBME). This is a very contentious issue which has caused a great deal of unease within the membership of the Louisiana Psychological Association. Some psychologists voice concern regarding the possibility of control over psychological practices by the medical profession. This issue has obviously not been settled and may lead to animosity between individuals licensed by the Board of Psychology and those licensed by the Board of Medical Examiners.

One of the issues which is salient, regardless who is the prescriber, is that most medications and their doses are based on an average 160-lb male. However, in the case of central nervous system difficulty or disorder, the body's ability to metabolize and utilize medications may be significantly altered. Therefore, the dosage and even the type of medication may need to be evaluated. Psychotropic medications in the case of central nervous system difficulties may be used for preventing difficulties or they may be used to control depression, anxiety, and so forth, which may arise secondary to the central nervous system issue.

Returning to our case study, Zoe was referred to a psychiatrist for medication evaluation for treatment of depression and anxiety. It would have been more convenient for her to receive this service from her clinical neuropsychologist, however, that individual does not practice in a state which allows psychologists prescription privileges. Zoe's sister may need a psychiatric referral for emotional difficulties due to her TBI. Again, it would be more convenient for her if she could work with the clinical neuropsychologist. She particularly requires a prescriber who understands brain functioning and age differences when prescribing medication.

Forensic Issues Reprised

As has been discussed earlier in this text, involvement in forensic activities has become a common part of the professional practice for clinical neuropsychologists (Sweet, Peck, Abramowitz, & Etzweiler, 2003). Clinical neuropsychology journals and professional meetings are replete with articles and information regarding forensic activities. As time passes, it can be surmised that more time in the clinical neuropsychologist's schedule will be devoted to forensic activities.

At a time when the health care system within the United States is changing drastically, it appears that the practice of forensic clinical neuropsychology will remain static if not continue to grow. This statement is based less on changes in the health care system and more on the sheer need related to the number of individuals with central nervous system difficulties. As stated earlier, the numbers continue to grow and many of the causes of these difficulties involve litigation whether for malpractice or civil litigation cases involving TBI or neurotoxin exposure, disability evaluation for children under the Individuals With Disabilities Education Act, evaluations for civil commitment, and competency evaluations. A separate and growing area of evaluation within clinical neuropsychology is the assessment of incomplete effort and malingering.

Described in an earlier section of the text was a distinction between clinical neuropsychological evaluations and forensic clinical neuropsychological evaluations. The major difference, which is at issue currently, is the admissibility of neuropsychological methodology. The change in admissibility from the Frye to Daubert standard for the level of scientific background for evidence has left clinical neuropsychologists in a quandary. In a sense, attorneys have interpreted the Daubert standard to imply that only a "fixed battery" approach due to its inherent psychometrics is admissible for a clinical neuropsychologist to base his or her opinion upon. The major difficulty which this causes is that the Halstead-Reitan Test Battery (HRTB) is the only neuropsychological test battery which appears to meet the criteria. Many clinical neuropsychologists argue that this clearly restricts their ability to function in a court setting. In a recent survey, only 15% of clinical neuropsychologists use a strict fixed battery approach and most agree that the HRTB's normative data are quite dated (Sweet, Nelson, & Moberg, 2006). At the time of this writing, much debate is ensuing regarding the use of other forms or types of neuropsychological tests in forensic settings. Also at issue is the use of interview and observational data.

Looking at our case study, it would appear to be a scenario in which litigation could arise. Both Zoe and her sister were evaluated using the HRTB, which could be admissible in court. However, due to the extreme emotions involved and the fact that the accident could be considered due to her mother's negligence, no litigation ensued. In the future, Zoe's sister may file for disability if her TBI impairs her ability to adequately function.

Multicultural Neuropsychology: Neuropsychology Around the World

The world in which we live changes at a speed that few individuals are able to comprehend. The vast technology which is available today allows individuals to communicate with one another almost instantaneously from different parts of the globe. In a sense, we truly live as world citizens. How these statements translate into the practice of clinical neuropsychology is multifaceted.

One of the major tasks of clinical neuropsychology remains assessment or the measurement of strengths and abilities after central nervous system illness or injury. As was discussed earlier, assessment must be tailored to the language, culture, race, and ethnicity of the individual and the competence of the clinical neuropsychologist. Issues related to the use of interpreters and the ability of current tests to be adequately translated was discussed earlier. Also important is the fact that many concepts or constructs may not be translatable culture to culture. Some researchers have even suggested that each culture is so unique as to invalidate the possibility of meaningful cross-cultural assessment of neuropsychological functioning. This line of thought has been supportive of indigenous neuropsychological and cognitive assessment instruments, particularly in Asian settings (Chan, Shum, & Cheung, 2003). Therefore, one of the major tasks for clinical neuropsychologists worldwide is the development of a manner in which to assess and communicate regarding central nervous system issues culture to culture or within a culture such as in the United States.

Clinical neuropsychologists are focusing on the cultural gap similar to the gender gap discussed earlier. Whereas the majority of students entering clinical psychology programs are female, the bulk of clinical neuropsychology practitioners are male. In a similar vein, as many ethnic and racial groups increase beyond the birthrate of Caucasians in the United States and also abroad, the number of non-Caucasian clinical neuropsychological professionals does not keep pace. One of the aims of the changes in the health care system in the United States is to include individuals from various ethnic backgrounds in education. An aim of the International Neuropsychological Society is to include clinical neuropsychologists in a worldwide discussion of assessment and treatment of central nervous system difficulties. However, there still often remains the gap between the ethnicity of the patient and the ethnicity of the provider.

Returning to our case study, it is apparent that multicultural assessment is of limited applicability. However, there is a similar manner, Zoe and her sister were at first uncomfortable with a male provider until they began to know the particular individual.

Summary

The final concluding chapter of this text begins with a sad case study of a young college student thrust into the role of guardian for her siblings, one of which has TBI. While this may appear to be an unusual scenario, more and more younger individuals are faced with circumstances for which they are unprepared.

The case study is interwoven into each of the concluding sections which address various salient issues within clinical neuropsychology. For many of the topics the information is so new that definitive conclusions regarding the effects of the information are impossible to explain.

Embedded within this last chapter is the change in the health care system within the United States, which came into effect after the signing of the Health Care Reform Bill by President Obama. At the time of this writing, the effects of the legislation are unclear and it is suggested that the reader remain cognizant of the issue throughout the next few years.

Questions for Further Study

1. How do you foresee the changes in the health care system affecting the practice of clinical neuropsychology?
2. Why must a competent clinical neuropsychologist be aware of multicultural issues?
3. The issue of prescription privileges crosses the boundaries of many disciplines. Make a detailed argument for or against this privilege from the perspective of clinical neuropsychology.

References

Administration on Aging. (2008). *A profile of older Americans: 2008.* U.S. Department of Health and Human Services. Washington, DC: U.S. Government Printing Office.

American Association for Justice on Medical Negligence. (2009). Five myths about medical negligence. Washington, DC: American Association for Justice.

American Medical Association. (2010). Medical liability reform. Retrieved April 15, 2010, from http://www.ama-assn.org/ama/pub/advocacy/current-topics-advocacy/practice-management/medical-liability-reform.shtml

American Psychological Association. (2010). Health-care reform. Retrieved April 15, 2010, from http://www.apa.org/health-reform

Boake, C. (2008). Clinical neuropsychology. *Professional Psychology: Research and Practice, 39*(2), 234–239.

Chan, A. S., Shum, D., & Cheung, R. W. Y. (2003). Recent development of cognitive and neuropsychological assessment in Asian countries. *Psychological Assessment, 15,* 242–247.

Commonwealth Fund. (2007). *The Commonwealth Fund/"Modern Healthcare" Health care opinion leaders survey: Transparency of health care quality and price information in the United States.* Retrieved April 15, 2010, from http://www.commonwealthfund.org/Content/Surveys/2007/The-Commonwealth-Fund—Modern-Healthcare—Health-Care-Opinion-Leaders-Survey—Transparency-of-Health.aspx

Commonwealth Fund. (2008). *Fundamental change needed to improve health care in the U.S.; Delivery system requires major fix, say health care leaders.* Retrieved June 23, 2010, from http://www.commonwealthfund.org/Content/News/News-Releases/2008/Apr/Fundamental-Change-Needed-to-Improve-Health-Care-in-the-U-S–Delivery-System-Requires-Major-Fix—Sa.aspx

Congressional Budget Office. (2008). *Key issues in analyzing major health insurance proposals.* Retrieved June 23, 2010, from http://www.cbo.gov/ftpdocs/99xx/doc9924/12-18-KeyIssues.pdf

Day, J. (2008). *Population profile of the United States.* Retrieved April 15, 2010, from U.S. Census Bureau Web site: http://www.census.gov/population/www/pop-profile/natproj.html

Eriksson, P. S., Perfilieva, E, Björk-Eriksson, T., Alborn, A. M., Nordborg, C., Peterson, D. A., et al. (1998). Neurogenesis in the adult human hippocampus. *Nature Medicine, 4,* 1313–1317.

Grassley, C. (2009). Health Care Reform—A Republican View. *The New England Journal of Medicine, 361*(25), 2397–2399.

Grundy, E., & Henretta, J. (2006). Between elderly parents and adult children: A new look at the intergenerational care provided by the "sandwich generation." *Aging and Society, 26,* 707–722.

Hannay, H. J., Bieliauskas, L. A., Crosson, B. A., Hammeke, T. A., Hamsher, K. deS., & Koffler, S. P. (1998). The Houston Conference on specialty education and training in Clinical Neuropsychology. *Archives of Clinical Neuropsychology, 13*(2).

Jin, K., Peel, A. L., Mao, X. O., Xie, L., Cottrell, B. A., Henshall, D. C., et al. (2004). Increased hippocampal neurogenesis in Alzheimer's disease. *Proceedings of the National Academy of Science, 101,* 343–347.

Jin, K., Wang, X., Xie, L., Mao, X. O., Zhu, W., Wang, Y., et al. (2006). Evidence for stroke-induced neurogenesis in the human brain. *Proceedings of the National Academy of Science, 103,* 13198–13202.

Kinsella, K., & Velkoff, V. A. (2001). *U.S. Census Bureau series P95/01-1: An aging world: 2001.* Washington, DC: US Government Printing Office.

Knoth, R., Singec, I., Ditter, M., Pantazis, G., Capetian, P., Meyer, R., et al. (2010). Murine features of neurogenesis in the human Hippocampus across the lifespan from 0 to 100 years. *PLos ONE, 5*(1), e8809.

Mulchandani, H. (2010). Recent advances in neural stem cell research: How stem cells in the brain are altered by a changing environment. *Student Pulse Online Academic Student Journal.* Retrieved April 15, 2010, from http://www.studentpulse.com/articles/193/recent-advances-in-neural-stem-cell-research-how-stem-cells-in-the-brain-are-altered-by-a-changing-environment

Neimeyer, G. J., Taylor, J. M., and Wear, D. M. (2009). Continuing education in psychology: Outcomes, evaluations and mandates. *Professional Psychology: Research and Practice, 40*(6), 617–624.

Pinquart, M., & Sorenson, M. (2006). Gender differences in caregivers experiences: An updated meta-analysis. *Journal of Gerontology: Psychological Sciences, 6/B,* 33–45.

Sweet, J. J., Nelson, W. W., & Moberg, P. J. (2006). The TCN/CAN 2005 "salary survey": Preferred practices, beliefs, and incomes of U.S. neuropsychologists. *Clinical Neuropsychologist, 20,* 325–364.

Sweet, J. J., Peck, E., Abramowitz, C., & Etzweiler, S. (2003). National Academy of Neuropsychology/ Division 40 of the American Psychological Association Practice survey of clinical neuropsychology in the United States. Part II: Reimbursement experiences, practice economics, billing practices, and incomes. *Archives of Clinical Neuropsychology, 18*(6), 557–582.

United Nations Department of Economic and Social Affairs, Population Division. (2007). *World population ageing 2007* (Summary Tables). Retrieved June 23, 2010, from United Nations Population Division Web site: http://www.un.org/esa/population/publications/WPA2007/SummaryTables_new.pdf

U.S. Census Bureau. (2005). Hispanic population passes 40 Million, Census Bureau Reports. *U.S. Census Bureau News.* Washington, DC: U.S. Department of Commerce.

U.S. Department of Health and Human Services. (2003). *Changing demographics: Implications for physicians, nurses, and other health workers.* Washington, DC: Author.

Weiss, N. (2009). No hasty health care reform. Retrieved March 6, 2010, from www.forbes.com/2009/12/14/health-care-reform-politics-opinions-contributors-nirit-weiss.html

Van Boven, R. W., Harrington, G. S., Hackney, D. B., Ebel, A., Gauger, G., Bremmner, J. D., et al. (2009). Advances in neuroimaging of traumatic brain injury and posttraumatic stress disorder. *Journal of Rehabilitation Research and Development, 46*(6), 717–756.

Glossary

ablation an experiment developed by Flourens, which involved removing parts of the brains of animals (usually birds); the removal of a part of the brain led to generalized, not localized, disorders of behavior

acquired disorders disorders caused by an accident, insult, or disease process coming from a source outside of the cortex

action potential the massive momentary reversal of the membrane potential from 270 to 150 mV; it is synonymous with the firing of the neuron

active metabolites metabolites that have drug actions of their own

active zones areas of protein accumulation at the end of the axon that allow neurotransmitters to be expelled into the synapse

activities of daily learning activities that any individual does on a daily basis such as personal hygiene, cooking and meal planning, going to work or school, and leisure activities

acute care care in an emergency situation or one in which the patient is critically ill

adenosine triphosphate (ATP) the energy source for neurons and other cells; ATP consists of adenosine bound to ribose and three phosphate groups

affective flattening absence or near absence of any signs of emotional expression either positive or negative

afferent nerves nerves that carry information to the central nervous system from the senses

affinity ability of an agonist drug to bind to stimulate a receptor

aftercare plan a treatment plan for individuals who are residing in the community to ensure they have all of their needs provided

agnosia the loss of the ability to interpret sensory stimuli, such as sounds or images

agonist drug that interacts with a receptor in a manner so that the receptor responds as it would with its own neurotransmitter

agoraphobia fear of situations in which escape is often not possible; very often occurs after an individual experiences a panic attack

alcoholic dementia dementia due to alcohol consumption

allele any one of a number of viable DNA codings that occupy a given position on a chromosome

alogia impoverishment in thinking; very concrete answers to questions and lack of spontaneous speech; a term used in relation to schizophrenia

alternate-form reliability the same people are tested with one form of a test on one occasion and with another, equivalent form on a second occasion; the correlation between the scores represents the reliability coefficient

Alzheimer's type dementia dementia characterized by neurofibrillary tangles and amyloid plaques; a diagnosis cannot be made until autopsy but is termed Alzheimer's type based on behavioral symptoms

American Educational Research Association organization founded in 1916 as a professional organization representing educational researchers in the United States and around the world

American Psychological Association (APA) APA was founded at Clark University in 1892 for the advancement of psychology as a science; it is the major organization representing psychology in the world

amnesia total or partial loss of memory that can be associated with brain damage, a dissociative disorder, or hypnosis

amnion a bag or container that encloses a clear fluid in which the embryo floats

amyloid plaques deposits of aluminum silicate and amyloid peptides believed to cause loss of neurons and vascular damage

anal stage Freud's second stage of psychosexual development (ages 2–3); the focus is on independence and the major issue is toilet training

anaphylactic reaction a serious drug allergy; swelling of the larynx and bronchioles that impedes breathing and may cause death; if caught early it may be treatable

angiography the use of radiopaque substances to allow visualization of blood vessels; it is considered a form of X-ray

anosognosia man indifference to impairments, particularly those on the contralateral side; often a reaction to a right hemisphere stroke

anoxemia the blood supply lacking oxygen

anoxia complete absence of available oxygen to the brain

antagonist drug that interacts with but does not stimulate a receptor; the antagonist prevents a response

anterograde amnesia memory difficulty occurring after some type of trauma where the person loses the ability to learn new material

aphasia an impairment of the ability to use or comprehend language, usually acquired as a result of a stroke or other brain injury; it may involve difficulties with spoken, written, or gestured language; loss of expressive or receptive language

Apo E (Apolipoprotein E) a normally occurring protein that is involved with phospholipids and cholesterol processing within the body

ApoE4 allele the normally occurring protein where the E4 gene is linked to Alzheimer's disease

apraxia inability to perform purposeful movements

Army Alpha during World War I, this intelligence test was created and emphasized verbal abilities in determining a level of intelligence; this test was given to all recruits

Army Beta a test developed in conjunction with the Army Alpha test, which used nonverbal abilities to determine an intelligence level; this test was given to those recruits who did poorly on the Army Alpha test and were considered to be illiterate

assessment process refers to the methods of assessment or data gathering and related procedures used by the clinical neuropsychologist to reach a clinical diagnosis

Association of State and Provincial Psychology Board (ASPPB) the association of all of the licensing boards in the United States and Canada

astrocytes one of the large neuroglial cells composed of nervous tissue

astrocytomas tumors caused by growth of astrocytes; they tend to not grow very quickly and are rarely malignant

asylum an early institution specializing in the care of the mentally ill

attention deficit/hyperactivity disorder a mental disorder characterized by difficulties with attention and concentration and may also be accompanied by hyperactivity

aura a sensation, as of a cold breeze or a bright light, that precedes the onset of certain disorders, such as an epileptic seizure or migraine headache

automatism material learned early in life and used throughout life without effort to access it

autonomic nervous system this division regulates the body's internal environment; it is part of the peripheral nervous system

autoreceptors receptors that reside at the end of the axon and regulate the amount of neurotransmitter in the synapse

avolition the inability to initiate and persist in goal-directed activity

axis in the *DSM* diagnostic schema, an axis is where information is recorded regarding a specific diagnosis or the medical and social information regarding the overall functioning of the individual

axon hillock the structure on the body of the axon that determines whether an impulse is strong enough to cause an action potential

axon the structure that sends information from the cell body of the neuron to the synapse

basal ganglia the set of structures involved with voluntary motor behavior; the structures are the amygdala, caudate, putamen, and globus pallidus

battered child syndrome a term which describes physical, sexual, and/or emotional abuse of a child; the term was first used by physicians in the 1960s

battle fatigue the World War II term for what is known today as PTSD

binge drinking the drinking of an excessive amount of alcohol within a short period often with the intent of becoming quickly intoxicated

Binswanger's disease caused by multiple infarcts in the periventricular area and cerebral white matter with demyelization; the disease causes symptoms of dementia

blastocyst the cells that develop into the embryo

blind analysis the process in which the clinical neuropsychologist evaluates a client's test data without interview information, records, or behavioral observation

blood-brain barrier group of compacted cells so tightly bound together they keep toxic substances out of the brain

board of psychology a state organization composed of psychologists and public members who determine whether a psychologist is eligible for a license to practice and who enforce the ethics code; it does not have the force of law but can sanction individuals

Boulder model a psychology meeting held in Boulder, CO, which led to the development of a model of graduate training (PhD), which included courses in both the science and practice of psychology

boundaries the ability of the clinical neuropsychologist to keep a professional therapeutic relationship intact; implies that the client does not become invested in the therapist's life

brain electrical activity mapping the use of a computer to map the recordings of an EEG to evaluate the brain's activity

brain hypothesis the hypothesis that the brain is the source of human thought and behavior

brain–behavior relationship a relationship that exists between certain functions of the brain and overt behaviors

cardiac hypothesis the hypothesis that the heart is the center of rational thought

case manager the professional responsible for bringing together and monitoring services from several areas of specialty to ensure the patient or client has integrated and appropriate care and to ensure that the specific treatments are not working at cross purposes

case study a detailed analysis of an individual focusing on his or her history and current life situation; it is often a way to study individuals with central nervous system illness or injury

cataplexy rigid maintenance of a body position over an extended period

catatonia motor abnormalities including involuntary or excessive motor activity with no goal or direction; the term is used in relation to schizophrenia

cell doctrine a term synonymous with the ventricular localization hypothesis, i.e., that the ventricles were the location of higher order mental and spatial processes

Center for Mental Health Services the federal agency within the United States SAMHSA that leads national efforts to improve prevention and mental health treatment services for all Americans; CMHS pursues its mission by helping states improve and increase the quality and range of treatment, rehabilitation, and support services for people with mental health problems, their families, and communities

central alveolar hypoventilation syndrome abnormal blood oxygen and carbon dioxide levels

central canal traverses the length of the spinal column and contains cerebrospinal fluid

cephalo-caudal the principle of central nervous system development which states that the brain and spinal cord develop first, followed by areas further from the central core

cerebellum the structure at the back of the brain involved with movement, coordination and posture; it is often referred to as the "little brain"

cerebral cortex the convoluted surface layer of gray matter of the cerebrum that controls the coordination of sensory and motor information

cerebral ischemia the restricted blood flow to the cerebral area of the brain

cerebral ventricles a system of four communicating cavities within the brain that are contiguous with the central canal of the spine; they contain cerebrospinal fluid

cerebrospinal fluid a clear fluid that functions as a cushion for the brain within the skull and is made in the choroid plexuses; it flows through the ventricles and the subarachnoid space

channel proteins a protein found either attached or inserted into a cell membrane that allows hormones or other molecules to pass across the membrane

choroid plexuses a group of capillaries that produce cerebrospinal fluid

chromosomes the human has 23 pairs of chromosomes; they contain strands of genes that contain DNA

clean wound brain damage along the path of the object affecting the brain

Client's Bill of Rights the statement which must be visibly present in a psychologist's office which describes the client's rights including the right to file a complaint and the process for filing such complaint

clinical model an attempt to understand a particular cognitive process (e.g., attention) by observing individuals with central nervous system disease or damage

clinical neuropsychology a division of psychology that specializes in the clinical assessment and treatment of patients with brain injury or neurocognitive deficits

clinical psychology a branch of psychology devoted to the assessment, diagnosis, and treatment of mental and behavioral disorders

closed group group members have defined participation, all must participate from start to finish

closed head injury impact from an accident or injury causes brain damage but does not penetrate the skull

coding application of a diagnostic category along with a code number; this is often completed for medical records purposes or insurance reimbursement

cognitive mechanics the "hardware" of the mind that reflects the neurophysiological architecture of the brain developed through evolution

cognitive pragmatics the culture-based "software programs" of the mind

cognitive processing model analysis of particular cognitive processes (e.g., attention) in a laboratory setting using normal subjects; this could be contrasted with a clinical model

collateral interviews interviews conducted with persons familiar with the client to ensure a correct understanding of the client by the clinical neuropsychologist

comorbidity two or more diagnostic categories that tend to occur at the same time within the individual

competitive antagonist drug that competes for a receptor site using an agonist drug

complete agonists a drug that completely facilitates binding on the receptor

complex partial seizure an epileptic seizure that occurs in one cerebral hemisphere and causes impairment of awareness and/or responsiveness

compulsions behavioral patterns such as washing or counting used to suppress aberrant thoughts such as washing, checking, or counting

computed tomography (CT) scan a computer-assisted imaging process based on multiple X-ray images of the brain; it provides a three-dimensional perspective of the brain with clear differentiation of brain structures

concrete operational stage Piaget's third stage of cognitive development; it includes the abilities to reason logically about direct experiences and perceptions

conditioned response a response that is indistinguishable from the unconditioned response which occurs in the presence of the conditioned stimulus

conditioned stimulus a neutral stimulus that when paired with the unconditioned stimulus elicits a response indistinguishable from the original

conditions of worth a Rogerian concept; it describes the rewards and punishments that society applies to an individual's behavior

conduction aphasia a type of aphasia characterized by abnormal comprehension and inability to repeat words correctly; also called associative aphasia and commissural aphasia

confidentiality discussions or information considered privileges and not to be shared; the statement that is given at the beginning of psychotherapy that assures the client of privacy of information verbally and in written form; reasons to break the confidential relationship include threats of suicide, homicide, physical or sexual abuse (client as perpetrator or victim), and abuse of a vulnerable adult (client as victim or perpetrator)

congenital physical problems present at birth which develop later in life and which can be attributed to genetic causes

congruence one of Roger's three necessary qualities of a therapist; it implies that the therapist is a real person with the client

conservation the ability to logically determine that a certain quantity will remain the same despite adjustment of the container, shape, or apparent size

consolidation the process through which information is stored in long-term memory

construct validity refers to whether a scale measures the unobservable social construct (such as "fluid intelligence") that it purports to measure; it is related to the theoretical ideas behind the trait under consideration

contamination an object relations family therapy term; it implies spoiling or ruining a family relationship

content validity the extent to which the items of a test or procedure are in fact a representative sample of that which is to be measured

continuing education credits (CEU) advanced study postlicensing that is required by most states to renew a psychologist's license to practice

contralateral control the premise that one side of the brain controls the motor and sensory functions of the opposite side of the body

contrecoup secondary impact in a traumatic brain injury as the brain ricochets back and forth or side to side within the skull

conventional moral reasoning Kohlberg's second level of moral reasoning which emphasizes social roles and conventions

convergent validation a test must demonstrate that the test correlates highly with other variables with which it theoretically should

copyright the right granted by law to author, publisher, and so forth to exclusive rights for publication, sale or distribution of a work; in the United States, this extends for a period of 28 years with the privilege of renewal for another 28 years

corpus callosum a large mass of myelinated axons connecting the right and left hemispheres; it functions to allow communication between the two hemispheres

corpus striatum a mass of gray matter beneath the cortex and in front of the thalamus in each cerebral hemisphere; it includes two major substructures, the caudate and the lentricular nuclei

correlation coefficient a number between −1 and +1, which measures the degree to which two variables are linearly related

cortical atherosclerotic dementia multiple infarcts of the large blood vessels which supply blood to the brain; this leads to symptoms of dementia

cortical dementia damage within the cerebral cortex, which leads to symptoms of dementia

coup the initial impact in a traumatic brain injury as an object or event impinges on the skull covering the brain

criterion validity the effectiveness of the test in predicting behavioral criteria on which psychologists agree

crystallized intelligence refers to acquired skills and knowledge and the use of knowledge in activities such as work or hobbies; it has the advantage of practice

culture bound recurrent, locality-specific patterns of aberrant behaviors and troubling experiences that may or may not be linked to a particular *DSM-IV-TR* diagnostic category

Current Procedural Terminology (CPT) code numbers that were developed by the *ICD* and used in the *DSM* to signify a particular diagnosis. Using the same CPT codes allows for ease in medical records and insurance reimbursement

cybernetic system a concept to describe regulatory systems operating by feedback loops; term coined by Wiener in 1948

cytochrome P450 enzyme family a system of enzymes primarily in the liver but may be in the kidneys that are involved in the metabolism of numerous drugs; many drugs inhibit these enzymes, potentially causing drug–drug interactions

cytoplasm the internal fluid that holds organelles in place within the cell

Daubert standard a standard in legal proceedings based on a 1993 decision which stated that judges have a right to determine if the information presented by an expert witness has a sound basis and is admissible or not

declarative or explicit memory the aspect of human memory that deals with factual material that is conscious and can be discussed or declared

decussate the term is used to refer to the point where the optic nerves converge and half of the axons cross to the other side of the brain

defense mechanism Freud's concept which states that various mechanisms of the ego function automatically to keep unpleasant information from the individual's conscious awareness

deferred as it relates to diagnosis, the term implies that a diagnosis is not being made at this time; deferring a diagnosis may be caused by a lack of information or an inability to determine which difficulty exists between two that share similar symptoms

degeneration death of neurons or neuronal processes in response to injury in the degenerating neuron or in some cases in the brain

degenerative disorders destruction of neurons and/or various structures within the brain

degradation the process by which neurotransmitters are chemically broken apart by enzymes within the synapse

dendrites the structures that receive information and send it to the body of the neuron

deoxyribonucleic acid (DNA) the genetic code of the human being

Department of Health and Human Services the U.S. government's principal agency for protecting the health of all Americans and for providing essential human services, especially for those who are least able to help themselves

depolarization the loss of the difference in charge between the inside and outside of the plasma membrane of a muscle or nerve cell caused by a change in permeability and migration of sodium ions to the interior

developmental milestone researchers have developed certain ranges which are considered to be normal for the appearance of various abilities within children; examples include talking and walking

dexamethasone suppression test a medical test used to determine the presence of various forms of depression; whether it can distinguish the different disorders is still under debate

diabetes mellitus *type 1 diabetes*: A severe, chronic form of diabetes caused by insufficient production of insulin and resulting in abnormal metabolism of carbohydrates, fats, and proteins; *type 2 diabetes*: A mild form of diabetes that typically appears first in adulthood and is exacerbated by obesity and inactive lifestyle.

***Diagnostic and Statistical Manual of Mental Disorders,* text revision (*DSM-IV-TR*)** the diagnostic manual published by the APA; it is used by all mental health professionals and many physicians to diagnose mental disorders

diagnostic classification system a system for classifying medical and psychiatric disorders; it lists symptoms of a particular disorder and various other important facts for diagnosis; in psychology, it usually refers to the *DSM-IV-TR* published by the American Psychiatric Association

diaschisis the suspension of functions that are associated with structures remote to the damaged area; it is assumed these areas have been temporally disconnected

diencephalon the region of the brain that includes the thalamus and hypothalamus

differentiation of self a family systems family therapy term; it means the degree to which an individual is able to maintain a separate identity and also be a member of the family

diffuse damage the general or widespread impact of any injury or illness on brain function

disconnection syndrome behavioral syndrome resulting from the disconnection of two or more brain areas rather than from the damage to a specific brain region

discriminant validation a test should not correlate with variables with which it should differ

disengaged family a family organization with overly rigid boundaries, in which members are isolated and feel unconnected to one another; this type of family has few interactions with one another

disorganized/disoriented attached infant an attachment style characterized by the inability to organize behaviors under stressful situations

dissociation a disruption in the usually integrated functioning of identity or perception of an event

dissociative amnesia amnesia that has no known physical or structural cause but may be related to emotional trauma such as PTSD

divided attention the ability to concentrate on more than one activity at the same time

Division 40 (Clinical Neuropsychology) a division of the APA, which works to further the development of neuropsychology

domain a type of behavior that the researcher desires to sample

dose–response curve graph comparing the size of response to the amount of drug

double dissociation technique a research technique in which lesions have opposite or dissimilar effects on two distinct cognitive functions; it was developed to help determine when cognitive functions are independent

Down syndrome the disorder, which leads to mild mental retardation caused by a trisomy on chromosome 21

Drug Abuse Resistance Education (DARE) a program developed to assist children and adolescents to respond against peer pressure to consume alcohol or other drugs

drug action interaction between a drug and proteins in the cell membrane, enzymes, or target receptors

drug effect response resulting from drug action

drug potency amount of a drug required to produce a desired effect

drug tolerance or drug dependence the state of progressively decreasing response to a drug

dual relationships the situation in which a psychologist is in a professional role with an individual and at the same time in a different type of relationship with the same individual; examples include therapist and teacher or friend and therapist

dualism the view that within each person resides two entities, a mind with mental properties and a body with physical properties

dyad an alliance, temporary or permanent, between two people in a family situation; the communication is often better between the two than in the larger family unit

dysfunctional family a family in significant discord; may have issues related to violence, neglect, abuse, chemical dependency, or other serious issues that disrupt adequate family functioning

echoic memory the auditory aspect of sensory memory where there is a brief echo or sound in memory after the original stimulus has ceased; the duration is up to 3 or 4 seconds

echolalia senseless repetition of a word or phrase spoken by another person

echopraxia repetition by imitation of the movements of another person

eclecticism the use of many different styles or theories of therapy based on the needs of the client

ecological contextual framework a broad approach to rehabilitation that includes family, friends, and caregivers in the rehabilitation process

ecological validity the functional and predictive relationship between a patient's performance on a particular test or battery and his or her behavior at home, work, school or in the community

edema an abnormal accumulation of fluid in intercellular spaces of the body or brain

Edwin Smith Surgical Papyrus early Egyptian manuscript which described the techniques used to treat various forms of difficulties including brain trauma

effect size a measure of the strength of the relationship between two variables; in scientific experiments, it is often useful to know not only whether an experiment has a statistically significant effect but also the size of any observed effects

efferent nerves nerves that carry motor signals away from the central nervous system

efferent neurons neurons that carry information from the central nervous system to the periphery

efficacy ability of an agonist drug to cause a response through interaction with receptors

ego the portion of the psyche that deals with the constraints of reality; the ego must satisfy the impulses of the id and the constraints of the superego

egocentric Piaget's term for a child's tending to think about how the world works entirely from his or her own perspective

ego-dystonic a Freudian term that implies that the ego or the part of the personality that relates to reality and external circumstances is not comfortable with a particular action or event

Electra complex the Freudian concept that a female child has sexual feelings for the parent of the opposite sex and jealousy for the same sex parent

electrochemical process as the action potential travels down the axon, it is electrical, whereas, the release of neurotransmitters at the synapse is chemical

electroencephalography (EEG) a record of brain wave patterns as an individual completes a task

embolus similar in structure to a thrombus but develops outside of the brain and then travel to the cortex

embryo an organism in the early stages of development, before it has reached a distinctly recognizable form; in humans, the time between fertilization and the eighth week of development

embryonic period The period of prenatal growth from the time of implantation to the end of the first trimester

emergence reactions behaviors exhibited when a drug used for anesthesia is decreasing in the system; common behaviors are dreamlike state, confusion, excitement, and irrational behavior

emotional flattening refers to the outward expression of emotions when virtually no stimulus can elicit an emotional response; may also be described as emotional blunting or affective flattening

emotional lability refers to outward expression of emotions that vary widely; it may encompass a "normal" mood for the individual interspersed with depression or manic-appearing behaviors

empathy one of Roger's three necessary conditions for a therapist; it implies that the therapist feels as close as possible to the feelings the client is experiencing

empiric care care that is based on practical experience more than scientific study; often the care is based on "clinical lore" or what worked in the past

endogenous term originally used to describe mental illness that was curable; currently it refers to the etiology of mental illness as biochemical

endoplasmic reticulum (ER) a network of tubules within a cell that transports synthesized lipids and membrane proteins to other locales

endorphins naturally occurring brain hormones which help alleviate pain or lead to a feeling of euphoria

enhanced CT a CT scan with the use of a control dye to provide better visualization of brain structures

enmeshed family a family organization in which boundaries between members are blurred and members are over involved in one another's lives

epilepsy any of various neurological disorders characterized by sudden and recurring attacks of motor, sensory, or psychic malfunction with or without loss of consciousness or convulsive seizures

episodic buffer the fourth component to Baddeley's working memory system; a temporary and limited storage system to hold and integrate information from various modalities

episodic memory memory for specific experiences that can be defined in terms of time and space

equipotentiality the idea that mental abilities depend upon the entire brain functioning as a whole

error variance any condition that is irrelevant to the purpose of the test is error variance; uniform testing conditions try to prevent error variance

errorless learning a method of instruction that reduces errors in the acquisition phase; the task is practiced until the client achieves correct answers without experiencing failures

Ethical Principles of Psychologists and Code of Conduct the ethics code developed by APA in 2002 that strives to reflect both the aspirations and practical aspects of ethical decisions made by members of the psychology profession

etiological causal factor(s) of a disease or disability if it is known

evoked potential the ability to record changes in EEG activity in response to sensory stimuli; the response is termed an evoked potential or event-related potential

exocytosis neurotransmitter release from synaptic boutons into the synapse

exogenous term originally used to denote mental illness that was incurable; currently, it relates to the etiology of mental illness as environmental or stress related

expedited approval early approval of an IND after Phase III testing has produced satisfactory because of the need for the drug; examples would include drugs for HIV and the H1N1 virus

experimental neuropsychology the field of psychology that focuses on brain–behavior relationships usually using animals as subjects

expert witness testimony a clinical neuropsychologist who is recognized by the court as an expert in his or her field based on education and experience

extinction the lack of a response; behaviorally, it occurs with the lack of reinforcement or lack of association in classical conditioning

extrapyramidal the system that modulates movement and motion, muscle tone, and posture

face validity the extent to which the items of a test or procedure appear superficially to sample that which is to be measured

factor analysis a statistical procedure in which all of the scores are correlated with one another to determine those variables or factors which account for the most variance in the data

factor-analytic model a method to understand a particular cognitive process (e.g., attention) using the statistical tool of factor analysis; information is gathered from the performance of normal subjects on psychometric tests

family two or more people related by birth, marriage, or adoption residing in the same unit

fixed battery when the same tests are given to all subjects in a study eliminating variable circumstances

fixed interval schedule a reinforcement is delivered after a fixed period

fixed ratio schedule a schedule of reinforcement in which a reinforcer is delivered after a set number of responses

flashbacks the recurrence of a memory, feeling, or a perceptual experience from the past

flexible battery a series of tests that are altered based on the individual being tested

fluid intelligence involves novel reasoning and use of information to deal with unfamiliar problems or to gain new types of knowledge

focal damage an area of localized insult to the brain

forensic neuropsychology neuropsychological practice in which a clinician neuropsychologist provides evaluation or consultative sessions to an individual involved in a proceeding that is potentially adversarial in nature

forensic within the context of clinical neuropsychology, it relates to use of neuropsychological tests by the examiner to produce objective evaluation within criminal and civil matters

formal operational stage the fourth stage of Piaget's theory of cognitive development characterized by logical and systematic thought; it also includes the ability to manipulate abstract concepts. Piaget did not believe that all individuals attain this level of thinking

free association a therapeutic technique in which the psychoanalyst remains quiet as the patient speaks; the contents are thought to come from the patient's unconscious

free radicals unstable oxygen molecules often implicated in aging

free-floating anxiety usually refers to anxiety with the lack of a specific situation or object that causes the anxiety; the feeling is that the anxiety is always there

frontal lobes the lobes in the front of the brain; they are responsible for higher order cognitive abilities such as thinking, reasoning, and planning

Frye standard a standard in legal proceedings based on a ruling in 1923; which stated the information from an expert witness in one's field must use evidence that is "generally accepted" within the field from which it was derived

functional description description of how a particular cognitive process might be used for the completion of day-to-day tasks

functional magnetic resonance imaging (fMRI) measures changes in neuronal activity that accompany changes in cerebral blood flow and blood oxygenation; based on these the researcher is able to infer the activity levels of various brain regions

fusion a family systems concept; implies a strong affective connection to the family that may lead to difficulty with differentiation of self

G proteins any of a class of cell membrane proteins that function as intermediaries between hormone receptors and effector enzymes and enable the cell to regulate its metabolism in response to hormonal changes

gamma-aminobutyric acid (GABA) the most common inhibitory neurotransmitter in the central nervous system

general intellectual factor or **g** a construct used in the field of psychology to quantify what is common to the scores of all intelligence tests

generalized seizure a seizure which affects both hemispheres of the brain

generic name the abbreviation for the chemical name of a drug

genital stage the final stage of Freudian psychosexual development; mature sexual relations are possible if the individual has mastered the Oedipus or Electra complexes

genuineness one of Roger's three characteristics for a therapist; it implies that the therapist is a real person in the therapeutic situation

germinal period the period from conception to the implantation of the zygote in the uterus

glioblastoma multiform one of the most common and most aggressive types of brain tumors in humans

glioblastomas tumors of the brain that are a form of gliomas; they grow quickly and are highly malignant

gliomas tumors that develop from glial cells within the brain

Golgi complex a system of membranes that package molecules into vesicles

group intelligence tests tests that are administered to individuals in large groups and do not require one-to-one administration; group tests are often used to test large groups of people such as in the military and to save time and manpower through the use of fewer administrators

hallucination a misperception of reality or a misrepresentation of the information gained through one's senses; often a positive symptom of schizophrenia; hallucinations may be auditory (hearing voices), visual (seeing things that are not there), tactile (misperception of touch), or olfactory (misperception of smell)

Health Insurance Portability and Accountability Act (HIPAA) a federal law implemented in 2003 to protect the privacy of individuals' medical and psychological records; it requires various provisions by any provider who uses any electronic medium to send information regarding a patient

hemorrhage in neuropsychology, it refers to cerebral hemorrhage which is defined as massive bleeding into a structure of the brain

hippocampus the structure responsible for memory functions

Hippocratic Oath an agreement that Hippocrates demanded of physicians ensuring that they would do no harm in their quest to appropriately treat their patients

hit rate successful result

holistic medicine a type of medical practice that treats the entire patient; it involves physical, psychological, and spiritual aspects of healing

household all people who occupy a housing unit regardless of relationships

humors the belief that a balance of bodily fluids including blood, mucus, and yellow and black bile were responsible for the functioning of the body and the brain

hyperpolarization to produce an increase in potential difference across a biological membrane

hypothalamopituitary portal a vascular network that carries hormones from the hypothalamus to the anterior pituitary

hypothalamus the organ that regulates the release of hormones by the pituitary gland

hypoxia reduced amount of available oxygen to the brain

hysteria physical manifestations of psychological disorders; a term not currently in use

iatrogenic effects difficulties introduced in a patient by a physician's care; the example in the chapter shows how aspirin to treat one difficulty may cause gastrointestinal ailments

iconic memory the initial aspect of sensory memory lasting a very brief period, approximately 250 milliseconds after exposure

id the portion of the psyche that developed first; it contains primitive urges toward sex and aggression that demand immediate gratification

identified patient the family member with the presenting symptom; the person who initially seeks treatment or for whom treatment is sought

idiopathic in seizures, the situation when the cause of the seizure is unknown

immediate memory a term synonymous with short-term memory

impaired judgment inability to perform the role of a psychologist due to a psychological or physical disability; hence one's judgment is not unbiased

inactive metabolites metabolites that are excreted and have no drug action of their own

inauthentic living an existential concept; it implies that an individual has given up his or her identity for the identity of the masses

incidental memory a form of informal learning resulting from other activities and which is generally more important for most of the skills and knowledge we learn during the majority of our lives

Individual Educational Plan (IEP) a plan to address each of the stated needs of the student with specific, concrete, goal-oriented programs

individual intelligence tests intelligence tests administered using one examiner and one examinee

infarct localized necrosis resulting from obstruction of a blood vessel

inferior colliculi the principal midbrain nucleus of the auditory pathway that receives input from several more peripheral brain stem nuclei in the auditory pathway as well as inputs from the auditory cortex

infratentorial tumors that occur in younger children usually within the brain stem and cerebellum; tumors occur in these areas because of the development of various brain structures

insecurely attached infant an infant unable to feel emotionally connected to the caregiver and unable to predict that the caregiver will meet his or her needs; therefore, the infant is not able to use the caregiver as a resource in a stressful situation and often has issues with attachment in later life

interitem consistency reliability that includes a single administration of a test; it is a measure of the consistency of responses to items on the test to other items

internal consistency a measure based on the correlations between different items on the same test (or the same subscale on a larger test); it measures whether several items that propose to measure the same general construct produce similar scores

International Classification of Diseases (ICD-10) a classification system of diseases, health conditions, and procedures developed by the World Health Organization (WHO); it represents the international standard for the labeling and numeric coding of diseases and health-related problems

International Neuropsychological Society (INS) founded in 1967, it is an organization that works to further the development of neuropsychology

International Testing Committee association of national psychological associations, test commissions, publishers, and other organizations committed to promoting effective testing and assessment policies and to the proper development, evaluation, and uses of educational and psychological instruments

intersex condition in which an individual shows intermingling, in various degrees, of the characteristics of each sex, including physical form, reproduction organs, and sexual behavior

intracranial brain stimulation stimulation of brain tissue used in treatment of various central nervous system diseases, such as Parkinson's disease

introject an object relations family therapy concept; it implies that the individual brings memories of loss or unsatisfying childhood relations into adult relationships which are likely to cause conflicts

Investigational New Drug a drug that has successfully passed testing on animals and an application has been made to begin the four phases of testing with humans

item-specific implicit memory unconscious memory from specific events

Korsakoff's syndrome memory and cognitive difficulties due to alcohol consumption and the absence of the vitamin thiamine

Krebs cycle a series of chemical reactions that produce ATP

lacunar strokes small infarcts in the basal ganglia, internal capsule, and pons, which lead to sensory and motor symptoms

latency Freud's fourth stage of psychosexual development; the focus is on school and development of competence

lateral asymmetry comparable areas of either brain hemisphere which do not have similar functions or structure

lateralization the idea that certain abilities reside in one side of the brain or the other; for the majority of individuals, verbal abilities reside in the left hemisphere and spatial abilities reside in the right hemisphere

law of effect behavior that is followed by favorable conditions will recur, behavior that is followed by unpleasant circumstances will not recur

legal guardian through a court of law, a legal guardian is a person appointed to guard the person or property of another individual who, for physical or mental reasons, is incapable of taking care of his/her person or affairs

lesion approach the lesioning of animals and sometimes humans to study the effects of the lesion on various brain functions

licensing boards boards which are composed of professional and lay persons who grant licenses to practice to various professions (e. g., psychology, nursing, etc.); boards are also able to impose sanctions on those with licenses

life expectancy the number of years that will likely be lived by the average person born in a particular year

limbic system set of structures related to emotional behavior; the structures are the mammillary bodies, the amygdala, the fornix, the cingulate cortex, and the septum in addition to the hippocampus

lipid (fat) soluble tendency of a chemical to dissolve in fat, as opposed to water

lipid bilayer a membrane that covers the neuron and is made of two layers of fat; it allows selective permeability to certain substances

localization theory the theory that certain abilities are localized to certain areas of the brain

long-term disability (LTD) insurance an insurance program to replace lost income when an employee is disabled for a long period

lysosome a cellular organelle that contains digestive enzymes and provides the neuron help in recycling and reusing materials

magnetic resonance imaging (MRI) a brain imaging technique requiring the use of magnetic fields; gives a clearer image than CT scan and is less dangerous because it does not use radiation

mainstream the practice of bringing students out of the isolation of special schools and into the "mainstream" of student life; students in special education classes are integrated into the general classroom

maintenance care treatment for patients whose lives may be improved but their difficulty or disease will never completely remit

mandated reporters professionals, because of their interaction with the public, who must report any physical or sexual abuse of children or vulnerable adults

mandated reporting information that, by law, must be reported to legal authorities

margin of safety synonymous with therapeutic index; difference between effective dose for 50% of patients treated and minimal dose at which adverse reactions occur

maximum effectiveness level when any further increase in the amount of drug causes little or no response

mean the arithmetic mean of a list of numbers is the sum of all the members of the list divided by the number of items in the list

medulla a part of the hindbrain that regulates respiration and cardiovascular functioning

melancholia a type of major depressive episode; specific symptoms include loss of pleasure and vegetative symptoms such as early morning awakening, weight loss or gain, and excessive guilt

meningiomas the type of tumor that develops from cells that cover the meninges; most meningiomas are benign

mental hygiene movement the movement to treat psychiatric patients with kindness and dignity; it instigated the release of mental patients from prison and the building of mental hospitals

mesencephalon the middle of three vesicles that arise from the neural tube and is considered part of the brain stem

meta-analysis the evaluation of multiple studies using factor analytic methodology

metabotropic receptors receptor limited to G proteins and are more prevalent than ionotropic receptors; effects are slower, longer lasting, more diffuse, and more varied

metastatic intracranial neoplasm cancerous tumor originating in different parts of the body and then transported to the central nervous system

metencephalon composed of the pons and the cerebellum and contains part of the fourth ventricle

microtubules the tubules that quickly transport materials within the neuron

mild cognitive impairment a transition stage between the cognitive decline of normal aging and the more serious problems caused by Alzheimer's disease

mind–body question philosophical question regarding the relationship between the physical body and the spiritual mind

minor an individual who is legally younger than the age of majority (defined by state or territory) and hence does not have the same rights as an adult

mitochondria the organelle that is the site of energy production for cells

monism the view that there is only one basic and fundamental reality, that all existence is this one reality; hence, the mind and body operate according to the same principles

mood reactivity the capacity to be cheered up when presented with positive events

moral therapy therapy created for mental patients based on the ideas of the mental hygiene movement; kindness and respect were the main components

multiaxial system this term refers particularly to the *DSM* and its use in diagnosis; multiaxial implies that information is recorded regarding multiple issues that relate ultimately to treatment of the individual

multitrait–multimethod matrix an approach to examining construct validity developed by Cambell and Fiske; there are six major considerations when examining a construct validity through the MTMM matrix, which are as follows: (a) evaluation of convergent validity, (b) evaluation of discriminant validity, (c) trait-method unit, (d) multimethod/trait, (e) truly different methodology, and (f) trait characteristics

myelencephalon the posterior portion of a developing vertebrate hindbrain or the part of the adult brain composed of the medulla oblongata which connects to the spinal cord

myelin sheath the fatty substance that covers the axon and speeds conduction

National Council on Measurement in Education an organization that is incorporated exclusively for scientific, educational, literary, and charitable purposes

nature–nurture question a long-standing debate as to whether nature (genetics) or nurture (learning) has the most significant impact on the development of a particular human ability or characteristic

needs assessment the assessment of the types of rehabilitation necessary based on the strengths and weaknesses of the client

negative punishment when a behavior is followed by the removal of an appetitive stimulus

negative reinforcement when a behavior is followed by the removal of an aversive stimulus

negative symptoms diminution or loss of normal functions; examples include restriction of emotion or motivation in schizophrenia

neuroanatomical model an attempt to understand various cognitive processes (e.g., attention) by identifying the different brain regions that are responsible for the ability

neurodegenerative disorders disorders that involve progressive loss of function or destruction of neurons or various structures of the brain

neurofibrillary tangles composed of tau protein; tangles of dead tissue in the brain symptomatic of Alzheimer's disease

neurogenesis the development of new neurons

neurogenic theory of migraine headache a theory that states that migraine headache is caused by the serotonergic and adrenergic pain-modulating systems

neurolaw a synthesis of medicine, neuropsychology, rehabilitation, and law that is designed to help individuals with central nervous system difficulties and their interactions with the legal system

neuroplasticity the brain's natural ability to form new connections to compensate for injury or changes in one's environment

neurotic anxiety an existential concept; involves the anxiety that is felt by the individual who is afraid to take risks or remains in familiar circumstances because it feels safer

neurotoxin a substance considered to be a poison within the central nervous system

neurotransmitters a chemical that is released at the terminal ends of the axon; their function is to excite or inhibit the postsynaptic cell

New Drug Application a formal proposal by pharmaceutical companies to the FDA to approve a drug for sale and marketing

nodes of Ranvier the gaps in the myelin sheath that speed axonal conduction

nomenclature the name and labels that make up a categorization symptom such as the *DSM* or *ICD*

nonbizarre delusion a delusion is a false belief or set of false beliefs, often seen in psychotic disorders; nonbizarre implies the content is not peculiar or unique

noncompetitive antagonists drug that binds to a receptor site and blocks the effect of an agonist

nondeclarative or implicit memory memory that tends to be nonconscious or lacks awareness

nondirective attitude a Rogerian term; implies the manner in which the therapist acts during therapy that allows the client to explore issues that he or she feels are important

nonproprietary drug name similar to the generic drug name

normal anxiety an existential concept; a normal reaction to change or risk taking that is synonymous with mental health

normal curve the normal distribution with a mean of 100 and a standard deviation of 15

normal family average type of family; this term is not synonymous with healthy but lacks significant dysfunctional qualities

norms conversion of the raw scores of the sample group into percentiles in order to construct a normal distribution to allow ranking future test takers

nosology a classification system such as the *DSM* or *ICD*

nuclear family a family composed of a husband, wife, and their offspring

nucleus the center of the neuron containing DNA

Nuremberg Code a document created and used after World War II to prosecute Nazi war criminals; it states the basic rights of human subjects used in research and has been the prototype for various other codes for protection of human subjects

nurse practitioner a registered nurse who has completed advanced study to practice independently; this individual is not able to complete all of the tasks of a medical doctor but may prescribe certain classes of medication

object permanence the ability to understand that objects and people continue to exist even when they are out of the observer's sight

obsessions intrusive and often nonsensical thoughts, images, or urges that the individual tries to suppress or resist

occipital lobe the center for vision, located in the back of the brain

Oedipus complex the Freudian concept that a male child has sexual feelings toward his mother and jealousy toward his father

off-label or unlabeled a prescriber's use of an FDA approved medication for a difficulty for which it was not approved; often approval of the medication for the new ailment appears later; examples include the use of anticonvulsants and atypical antipsychotics for the treatment of bipolar disorder

oligodendrocytes teuroglia consisting of cells similar to but smaller than astrocytes, found in the central nervous system and associated with the formation of myelin

oligodendrogliomas a glioma which is thought to originate from oligodendrocytes of the brain

open groups group members may join or leave at any time

open head injury a brain injury which occurs when an object penetrates the skull and exposes the brain to the elements

operant a behavior that has an effect on the environment

oral stage Freud's first stage of psychosexual development (0–2); the focus is putting everything in one's mouth

organismic valuing process a Rogerian concept; individual moves toward or away from events based on their effect on the individual's obtaining his or her needs or moving toward self-actualization

palliative care the treatment for those individuals who have terminal illnesses very often this involves the use of hospice care

paradoxical intention a strategic family therapy concept; a technique used to suggest the opposite of the behavior that a therapist would like a family to produce

paraprofessionals individuals who have been trained to assist professional mental health workers; many of these individuals do not have formal degrees and some, such as in Alcoholics Anonymous, may be recovering from the same difficulty for which they are helping others

parasympathetic nervous system one of two systems within the autonomic nervous system; its role is calming and the opposite of the sympathetic nervous system

parathesis numbness or tingling in an extremity, often a symptom of panic attacks

parietal lobe the association cortex that integrates information from the senses

partial agonists a drug that only partially facilitates binding at the receptor site

partial care a program, often administered by a county mental health center, that is used as a transitional program for individuals who are going from hospitalization to independent or semi-independent living

partial reinforcement a situation in which not every behavior is reinforced; it can be based on time or number of behaviors

partial seizures in partial seizures, the electrical disturbance is limited to a specific area of one cerebral hemisphere (side of the brain)

peptide any of various natural or synthetic compounds that build two or more amino acids on hydrolosis; peptides form the constituent parts of proteins

perceptual speed how fast a task may be completed

phallic stage the third of Freud's psychosexual stages of development; the stage where the focus is on the functions of the genitals and where the Oedipus and Electra complexes develop

pharmacist distributes prescription drugs to individuals and advises on selection, dosage, interactions and side effects of medications

phenomenology the branch of a science dealing with the description and classification of phenomena

phonological loop from Baddeley and Hitch's model of working memory; deals with sound and consists of two parts: short-term phonological storage with auditory memory traces and an articulatory rehearsal component that can review the memory traces

phonological processing the use of the sound structure of a language to process written words; a concept that is thought to be deficient in reading disorders

phrenology inaccurate theory developed by Gall which stated that bumps on the head related to certain abilities residing within the brain; the theory led to belief in reading the bumps and increasing abilities by rubbing the corresponding bumps

physical abuse episodes of abusive behavior which result in physical injury to a person

physicians' assistant an individual with an advanced degree beyond registered nurse but not to the extent of a medical doctor

Pick bodies composed of tau protein and shaped differently than neurofibrillary tangles; they are symptomatic of Pick's disease

pineal gland a small, cone-shaped endocrine organ in the posterior forebrain

pituitary gland a gland that releases hormones that stimulate other parts of the body

placenta a system of tissues in which small blood vessels from the mother and embryo entwine; it brings nutrients to the embryo and removes waste products from it

plasticity the flexibility of the brain which allows the individual to recover from some types of brain injury or insult because other areas of the brain take over the lost function; more widespread in children and more limited in adults

pleasure principle the principle through which the id develops and functions; it pushes for immediate gratification of sexual and aggressive impulses

pneumoencephalography a painful and now obsolete medical procedure in which cerebrospinal fluid is replaced with air to allow the structure of the brain to show up more clearly on an X-ray picture

polydrug the use of multiple substances at the same time; also may refer to individuals who use more than one substance but do not combine them or use them at the same time but may be abusing or dependent upon one or all of the substances

polypharmacy administering many different medicines concurrently for the treatment of the same disease

pons the structure that relays information from the cerebellum to the cerebral cortex

positive punishment when a behavior is followed by the delivery of an aversive stimulus and therefore decreases

positive reinforcement when a behavior is followed by an appetitive stimulus and therefore increases

positive symptoms an excess or distortion of normal function; examples include the delusions or hallucinations of schizophrenia

positron emission tomography (PET) a technique used to visualize brain activity based on cerebral blood flow; it tracks the metabolism of glucose, oxygen, and/or neurotransmitters

postconcussion syndrome constellation of physical and psychological symptoms that may occur after a medically verifiable concussion

postconventional moral reasoning Kohlberg's third level of moral reasoning which emphasizes moral and ethical principles

postpartum an episode of major depressive episode that occurs within 4 weeks of giving birth

posttraumatic stress disorder (PTSD) a mental disorder occurring after a traumatic event outside the range of usual human experience and characterized by symptoms such as reliving the event, reduced involvement with others, and exaggerated startle response; earlier terms for PTSD include shell shock and battle fatigue

preconventional moral reasoning Kohlberg's first stage of moral reasoning which emphasizes rewards or punishments in solving moral dilemmas

predementia condition a condition that occurs before dementia is formally diagnosed which resembles the cognitive and/or memory deficits of dementia

premorbid conditions or premorbid functioning any difficulties that occur before a central nervous system accident or illness; the level of functioning of any ability of the individual that was present prior to the injury and that now may have been lost or changed

prenatal development the steps in the formation of structures of the central nervous system

preoperational stage Piaget's second stage of cognitive development; it emphasizes language and symbolic thought

prescription privilege the legal ability to prescribe medications of a particular type

presenting complaint the statement which the client makes as the reason for seeking services from a health care provider

principle of mass action Lashley's idea that the extent of brain impairment is directly proportional to the amount of tissue damage

privileged communication a communication between a patient and client or certain providers of services that may be withheld from a court of law

procedural memory long-term memory of skills and procedures or how-to-do-it knowledge; a form of implicit memory

process approach testing based on understanding the qualitative nature behind clinical psychometric instruments

prodrome an early or premonitory sign or symptom of a disorder; a prodrome occurs for most individuals who experience schizophrenia

prodrugs drugs that are inactive until acted upon by enzymes in the body

prognosis the ability to forecast or predict the long-term pattern of recovery following injury or disease

proprietary drug name synonymous with trade name; the name that a pharmaceutical company has chosen for its drug; the trade name is copyrighted

prospective memory the ability to carry out intended actions

provisional a diagnostic qualifier added to the diagnosis when there is presently not enough information to state clearly that the diagnosis exists; assumption is that information will be gathered over time to remove the term from the diagnosis

proximo-distal the principle of central nervous system development which states that structures close to the center of the body develop before the peripheral structures; examples include the heart, lungs, and kidneys

psychiatrist a medical doctor who has a specialty in the treatment of mental illness predominately through the use of medication

psychotropic medications a category of medications that are used to treat mental health issues; included within this class are antianxiety medications, antidepressants, antipsychotics, lithium, stimulants, such as methylphenidate (Ritalin), and other drugs that may have uses in mental health but were not developed for such purposes such as donepezil (Aricept)

Public Law 94-142, or the Education for All Handicapped Children Act of 1975 a law that states that all children in the United States are entitled to a free and public education in the least restrictive environment

punisher any stimulus that when made contingent on a response, decreases the occurrence of that response

pyramidal neurons pyramid-shaped neurons; they send information from one region of the cortex to another brain area

qualitative form of neuropsychological assessment a battery of tests that is not fixed and is altered based on the needs of the client

raw scores refers to the number of points that the examinee scored on a particular test or subtest; most tests transfer raw scores to another scale for user convenience

reality principle the principle by which the ego develops and functions; it allows the ego to interact with the world at large

recall retrieval of information from long-term memory without any cues

recognition the presentation of cues to help an individual remember

referral source the person or agency initially referring the client for service such as a physician or school; the client may also self-refer

rehearsal involves repetition of information which allows it to remain in working memory long enough to be transferred to long-term memory

reinforcement contingency a consistent relationship between a response and the changes in the environment it produced

reinforcer if delivered contingent on a response, it increases the likelihood of the response reoccurring

relative refractory period the period during which the neuron is able to fire again with greater than normal amount of stimulation

release of information a form signed by an individual to give permission to a professional to view information from other sources; only competent individuals and adults may sign these forms, parents or legal guardians must sign for minors or those not capable of understanding

reliability the extent to which a test is repeatable and yields consistent scores

response a behavior emitted by an organism

restriction of practice a sanction by the Board of Psychology that restricts the psychologist from practicing within a specific area or with individuals who have specific difficulties

reticular activating system a set of structures that are related to arousal and alertness

retrograde amnesia disorder of memory characterized by an inability to retain old, long-term memories, generally for a specific period extending back from the onset of the disorder

reuptake the return of excess neurotransmitter into the presynaptic axon

reverberating neural circuits described by Hebb as self-contained networks which sustain a neural impulse in order for it to remain in immediate memory

ribosome a structure within the rough endoplasmic reticulum that synthesizes proteins

scaled score a scaled score is a conversion of a participant's raw score on a test or a version of the test to a common scale that allows for a numerical comparison among participants

Schwann cells the cells that produce myelin in the peripheral nervous system; the only cells capable of helping with axonal regeneration

scientific method a method of research in which a problem is identified, a hypothesis is formulated, and relevant data are gathered; from these data, cause–effect relationships can be stated

scientist–practitioner model guidelines that state that to be accredited by the APA, a clinical or counseling doctoral program must contain a prescribed number of classes or credits in the scientific bases of behavior and a certain number of classes or credits in the practice of psychology

securely attached infant infant who has developed a positive relationship with a caregiver which allows the infant to feel safe and explore the environment; this relationship leads to positive relationships in the future

selective attention the ability to focus on a specific part of an experience while ignoring other parts

self-actualization Roger's use of Maslow's concept; it refers to becoming the best or most fully functioning person that an individual is capable of becoming

self-medication a term that is often used when an individual tries to alleviate their symptoms by employing any or all of the following without consulting a physician: alcohol, illegal drugs, other individual's prescriptions, and various herbal treatments

semantic memory memory for meaning without reference to the time and place of learning

sensorimotor stage Piaget's first level of cognitive development; the infant uses his or her senses to understand and explore the world; the major task to learn is object permanence

sensory memory or **registration** the ability to retain impressions of sensory-based information after the original stimulus has ceased

shell shock World War I term for what is currently referred to as PTSD

short-term disability (STD) insurance an insurance program to replace lost wages when an employee is disabled for a short period

short-term memory see working memory

signal proteins proteins that transfer a signal to the inside of the neuron when particular molecules bind to them on the outside of the membrane

single photon emission tomography (SPECT) a technique that measures the emission of single photons of a given energy from radioactive probes; these emissions are used to construct images of the probes located within the body, thereby detailing the flow of blood in a given area

sleep apnea a sleep disorder in which an individual abruptly awakens because they stop breathing

social class a ranking of the family within society; usually referred to as upper class, middle class, or lower class; very often determined by SES factors

Social Security Administration an agency of the U.S. government that operates through money obtained from individuals' taxes; it is designed to provide income and insurance upon retirement and also oversees the SSI and SSDI programs

Social Security Disability Insurance (SSDI) one of the three basic protections provided by Social Security; when a worker's earnings are stopped or reduced for a year or more because of a severe impairment, the worker and eligible family members can receive monthly cash benefits from SSDI; benefits continue until the individual dies or is able to work again

socioeconomic status person's position in society as determined by income, wealth, occupation, education, place of residence, and other factors

sodium–potassium pump functions to maintain the cell potential; it pumps sodium ions out of the cell and potassium ions into the cell by active transport

somatic nervous system consists of peripheral nerves that send sensory information to the central nervous system and motor nerves that project to skeletal muscle

source memory the ability to remember where something was learned

specifiers used to define a more homogeneous subgrouping of individuals with a disorder who share certain common features

split-brain studies studies conducted on humans with severed corpus callosums to determine the extent of communication between the two hemispheres

split-half reliability a measure of the reliability of a test based on the correlation between scores on two halves of the test, often the odd- and even-numbered test items

spontaneous recovery the body's ability to recover from illness or injury without outside assistance

spreading the problem including all members of the family in discussion of the patient's problem

sprouting a process within a damaged neuron in which the remaining neurons or parts of a neuron sprout terminals to connect to a previously innervated area

stage theories of development theories of development in which one ability is thought to develop before the next ability and where the stages build on one another; stage theories are thought to apply to all individuals

standard deviation the square root of the variance; it is usually employed to compare the variability of different groups

standard score any score expressed in units of standard deviations of the distribution of scores in the population, with the mean set at zero

standardization uniformity of procedure in administering and scoring a test

standardized administration a consistent test format that allows the test to be administered to any subject and results compared to other subjects who have taken the test

statistical significance statistical evidence that there is a difference in the data from a study and is unlikely to have occurred by chance

stellate neurons star-shaped neurons that are small with short axons or no axons

stimulus discrimination when an organism learns to respond differently to the stimuli that are distinct from the conditioned stimuli on some dimension

stimulus generalization after conditioning has been accomplished, similar stimuli may elicit a response

subcortical atherosclerotic dementia multiple infarcts of the smaller blood vessels lead to difficulties in blood supply to subcortical areas; these infarcts then lead to symptoms of dementia

Substance Abuse and Mental Health Services Administration (SAMHSA) a subdivision of the U.S. Department of Health and Human Services; the SAMHSA has as its mission to build resilience and facilitate recovery for people with or at risk for mental or substance use disorders

subtypes used to define mutually exclusive and exhaustive subgroupings within a diagnosis

sundowning in patients with dementia, the worsening of symptoms as the day progresses

superego a Freudian concept similar to what is thought of as one's conscience; it develops through interactions with parents, school, and other situations in life

superior colliculus nucleus of the tectum in the midbrain that receives visual properties and controls whole-body reflexes to visual stimuli

supplemental or replacement care treatment of a patient for the missing substances that may have been destroyed by other treatments; often this may be thought of as restoring a patient's physical status to endure further treatment such as in chemotherapy

Supplemental Security Income (SSI) a government program that provides economic assistance to persons faced with unemployment, disability, or agedness, financed by assessment of employers and employees

supportive care treatment does not cure a disease but focuses on other body system

supratentorial a brain tumor that occurs in older children in the more advanced areas of the cortex

sustained attention the ability to respond to random events in the environment that draw one's attention

sympathetic nerves the part of the autonomic nervous system that arouses the organism in the situation of "fight or flight"; has an effect opposite of the parasympathetic nerves or nervous system

symptom substitution the replacement of one symptom for another; this signals that the underlying issue has not been resolved

symptomatic in seizures, the situation when the cause of the seizure is known

synapse the junction across which a nerve impulse passes from an axon terminal to a neuron, muscle cell, or gland cell

synaptic vesicles structures that store neurotransmitters; the vesicles release the neurotransmitters into the synaptic cleft when a nerve impulse reaches the synaptic cleft

syndrome a group of symptoms that tend to occur together and therefore receive a diagnostic label

tau proteins that researchers believe result from abnormal phosphorylation

telencephalon area that includes the cortex, basal ganglia, limbic system, and olfactory bulbs

telomeres structures at the end of a chromosome consisting of repetitive DNA and serving to stabilize the chromosome

temperament basic disposition or emotional makeup of a child often evident from birth

temporal lobe the lobe responsible for processing information through learning; the left temporal lobe is related to speech and the right to music or tone patterns

Test of Variables of Attention (TOVA) a computerized test designed to detect symptoms of attention deficit/hyperactivity disorder

test batteries groupings of tests brought together to serve a specific purpose

testing the limits a manner of neuropsychological testing that forgoes timing in favor of evaluating the ability of the client; the results generated are not comparable to available norms; often used with clients who have motor disabilities which makes timing a disadvantage in overall score

test–retest reliability involves administering the test to the same group of people at least twice; the first set of scores is then correlated with the second set of scores

text generation the creation of meaning in written form

thalamus the major relay center for the brain; all senses except for smell send information through the thalamus and pass it on to the cortex

therapeutic alliance a therapeutic relationship based on empathy, respect, and trust, which increases the likelihood that the client will comply with treatment and/or benefit from services

therapeutic index ratio of lethal dose to effective dose for half of the subjects in an experiment (LD_{50}/ED_{50})

thrombus fibrinous clot formed in a blood vessel

tolerance usually associated with alcohol consumption but can relate to other drugs; the need for more and more of a substance to achieve the same level of intoxication or "high"

totipotent capable of becoming any cell in the body

tracer the process of replacing a stable atom of a compound with a radioisotope of the same element to enable its path through a biological system to be traced by the radiation it emits

trade name the same as the proprietary name

transcranial magnetic stimulation procedure in which the brain is stimulated through the skull

transcription the ability to compose ideas and translate them into written form

transference the main task of psychoanalysis; the patient transfers feelings from a significant relationship onto the analyst who then assists the patient to understand the feelings

transient global amnesia an anxiety producing temporary loss of short-term memory during which the individual will not be able to remember events for the past few hours and will not be able to retain new information for more than a few moments; differentiated from the memory difficulties associated with stroke and subarachnoid hemorrhage

treatment plan following brain injury or disease, the process by which one or more professionals formulate a specific plan of action or treatment to ensure the most comprehensive or complete pattern of recovery for the patient

trephination the oldest known surgical technique in which a small piece of bone is removed from the skull leaving a hole in the skull; the procedure has been done for medical and religious reasons

triad a three-person alliance or relationship; communication is often better within the triad than within the larger family unit

trial-and-error learning a type of learning that occurs after an organism has made random attempts at solving a problem

trophoblast the cells in the blastocyst that will develop into the germinal period and provide nutrition and support for the embryo

tropic hormones anterior pituitary secreted hormones that regulate the activity of other endocrine glands

umbilical cord two arteries and one vein that connect the baby to the placenta

unconditional positive regard a Rogerian concept; one of the three qualities necessary for a therapist to provide effective therapy; implies positive feelings toward the client regardless of behaviors

unconditioned response an unlearned response that occurs naturally in response to an unconditioned stimulus

unconditioned stimulus a response that unconditionally, naturally, and automatically triggers a response

unconscious a level of awareness where Freud felt unpleasant sexual and aggressive emotions resided in order that they did not cause emotional difficulty for the client on a day-to-day basis

unemployment insurance a program that an employer must provide to workers in which money is taken out of the worker's salary to use in the event that he or she is unable to work

valence hypothesis theory that discusses the relative contribution of right versus left hemispheric functioning

variable interval schedule the delivery of reinforcement after a variable amount of time

variable ratio schedule the delivery of reinforcement after a variable number of responses

variance in statistics, in a population of samples, the mean of the square of the differences between the respective samples and their mean

vascular theory of migraine headache theory that the aura is associated with intracranial vasoconstriction and the headache with an inflammatory reaction around the walls of dilated cephalic vessels

ventricular localization hypothesis the hypothesis that mental and spiritual processes reside within the ventricular canals

Veterans Administration (VA) a U.S. government agency created to service the physical and mental health needs of those who had served in the armed forces

visual field cuts denotes the loss of vision caused by a stroke or brain damage; for example, if the right occipital lobe is damaged by a stroke, the person may have difficulty processing the left half of the visual field

visuospatial sketch pad a portion of working memory assumed to hold information about what we see and to be the mechanism for the temporary storage and manipulation of spatial and visual information such as shapes, colors, or location of items in space

vivisection a surgical procedure on a living animal or human for physiological investigation

vulnerable adult an individual who, because of physical or mental difficulties or both, is determined to not be able to care for him- or herself and his or her affairs in the community

vulnerable adult an individual who is incapable of taking care of himself or herself or of his or her affairs because of physical or mental difficulties

waiver programs programs designed to allow individuals that normally would not meet the criteria of a program to enter the program if they meet a set of criteria

water soluble tendency of a chemical to dissolve in water

Wechsler Intelligence Scale for Children-IV (WISC-IV) the most current form of the Wechsler scales designed for use with children; it yields a Full Scale IQ and composite scores measuring Verbal Comprehension, Perceptual Reasoning, Working Memory, and Processing Speed

withdrawal symptoms that occur after the cessation of use of a substance; each drug has its own symptoms of withdrawal

workers' compensation a program that must be available to employees; if a worker is injured or develops an illness on the job, the employer must provide some compensation

working alliance a relationship between the members of a family and the therapist; the relationship is designed to allow the family to feel safe enough to discuss previously nondiscussed issues or concerns

working memory once referred to as short-term memory, this is the second stage of memory in which several bits of information can be stored for a brief period; it is thought to be more active than passive short-term memory

working through the transference the third phase of psychoanalysis in which the psychologist discussed themes that surfaced in the transference material and applied then to the client's life

X-ray an imaging method in which radiation effects the density of different parts of the brain to various degrees, which then appear on the X-ray film

zero-order kinetics metabolism at a steady state regardless of quantity of substance consumed

zygote a single cell that is the result of fertilization

Index

Note: An *f* or *t* following the page number indicates a figure or table.